WESTERN CIVILIZATION

An Urban Perspective

D. C. HEATH AND COMPANY
Lexington, Massachusetts Toronto London

WESTERN CIVILIZATION

An Urban Perspective

VOLUME II
From the 17th Century to the Contemporary Age

F. ROY WILLIS
University of California, Davis

INTRODUCTION: CIVILIZATION AND THE PAST

Cities have been a major driving force in the development of Western civilization. The highest achievements of man, Sophocles proclaimed in his play *Antigone*, are "language, and wind-swift thought, and city-dwelling habits." The city, from the time of its earliest appearance some five thousand years ago, has focused and magnified man's energies in the task of mastering his environment, enriched his understanding by providing a multiplicity of human contacts, and provided the stimulus to the highest creativity in all forms of science and art. It has at the same time been responsible for many of the darkest features of Western civilization—the spoliation of the environment; the coercion of vast numbers of individuals by government, armies, and economic exploiters; the exclusion of vast segments of the population from intellectual and social advancement; and perhaps even the glorification of war. The city has always been at the extreme of the Western experience.

In recent years, the process of urbanization has been explored with considerable success by a large range of social scientists, including the urban geographer, the political scientist, the sociologist, the social anthropologist, the economist, and the historian. Their findings have thrown great light on such basic concerns as the impact of population growth, the spatial pattern of city development, the occupational structure of cities at varying stages of development, class relationships, family structure and mores, functioning of political systems, and relationship to environment. All of this is enormously helpful to the historian of civilization. But the historian must always remember the one task that distinguishes him from the other social scientists. He must respect the uniqueness of each period of civilization.

This book seeks to meet that challenge by focusing on the achievements of the great cities of Western civilization. Over half of the book is devoted to studies of ten great cities at the height of their creativity. The narrative halts, and we probe into problems of economic and social structure, religion, government and political theory, scientific inquiry, and concepts of beauty and attempts to realize them. In this way, we attempt to combine the findings of the social scientist with the preoccupation of the humanist. The focus on a great city at the moment when it has won a dominating role in a particular period of civilization gives us the opportunity to linger long enough to familiarize ourselves with the city's physical layout, its buildings and its government, its ways of work and of leisure, the thoughts of some of its citizens, and the creation of its artists and writers. For this reason, quotations and photographs are a very important part of the book. Prose quotations are used not only to introduce great writers or statesmen, but to allow the inhabitants of the city to give their own views on the city and its way of life. There is a great deal of poetry too, which is chosen for its historical as well as its literary interest. Reading it, one might bear in mind the whimsical advice of the American poet Marianne Moore:

I, too, dislike it.
Reading it, however, with a perfect contempt for it, one discovers in it, after all,
a place for the genuine.[1]

In the same way the photographs, contemporary paintings, etchings, and city plans are intended to build one's familiarity with the contemporary character of the city. Perhaps in a small way they can help the reader feel that kinship with a period in the past that drove Edward Gibbon to write his monumental *Decline and Fall of the Roman Empire*. "It was at Rome," he related in his *Autobiography*, "on the 15th of October, 1764, as I sat musing amidst the ruins of the Capitol, while the barefoot friars were singing vespers in the Temple of Jupiter, that the idea of writing the decline and fall of the city first started to my mind."

Several questions have been asked about each city. The first and most basic is, *How did the city produce its wealth?* The city was a provider of services—religious, governmental, legal, military and commercial; a manufacturer of goods itself, by artisans in the pre-industrial age and by factory production after the industrial revolution of the eighteenth century; and often an exploiter, using military force to acquire economic wealth. Secondly we ask, *What social relationships developed inside this economic system?* We shall be interested in the distribution of wealth, the status accorded to birth or profession, the relationship between classes, the extent of mobility within the social structure, and the distinctive ways of life developed within each stratum of society. Thirdly, we turn to the political superstructure to ask, *How did the citizens conceive the relationship of the individual to the state in theory and carry it out in practice?* Underlying all political systems is a theory or theories of government, though these assumptions are not always explicitly formulated. In times of dissatisfaction with an established political system, theorists construct new formulas based on their own conception of man and the ideal form of state; and as we shall see, these theories are occasionally put into practice, usually as the result of revolution. Political theory will therefore accompany the analysis of the distribution of power within the city and, since most of these cities are also capitals, within the state.

[1] Reprinted with permission of The Macmillan Company from *Collected Poems* by Marianne Moore. Copyright 1935 by Marianne Moore, renewed 1963 by Marianne Moore and T. S. Eliot.

Fourthly, we consider, *How did the city spend its wealth?* The consumption habits of different social classes have been subject to a vast amount of detailed research, and it is increasingly possible to re-create the way of life of the less privileged classes as well as that of the elite. Public expenditure as well as private must be assessed, especially that which is used for the beautification of the city or the improvement of its amenities; but we must also consider the waste of a city's resources, from military adventuring to the ravaging of the natural surroundings. Fifthly, we examine the city's intellectual life, asking, *To what goals was the intellectual activity of its citizens directed?* In cities as multifaceted as these, we must emphasize the most salient features of each city's contribution to the intellectual advance of Western civilization—the contribution of Athens to philosophy and drama, of Rome to law, or of Vienna to music, for example. But in each case the contribution of the environment of the city must be explained: why Paris was a magnet for Europe's theologians in the thirteenth century and for its artists and writers in the late nineteenth century; why tiny Lisbon could attract the continent's cartographers and maritime technologists; why Berlin could be transformed in months from the center of military science to an incubator of avant-garde artistic talent and then in an even shorter time back to its military preoccupations.

Finally, we ask, *How did the achievements of the city, in architecture, art, literature and science, reflect the citizens' conception of man, of God, and of beauty?* This question explains the poetry, sculpture, and buildings abundantly represented in these pages. Much of this creation was the exclusive possession of an elite, but that is hardly a reason for excluding it from a history of civilization. On the contrary, it is one of the brightest features of our century that the creativity of past ages is no longer the preserve of a few. Hence, with no further apology, we shall consider what the Parthenon tells us of the Greek concept of man, how a Botticelli Venus reveals the Florentine conception of the divine, how Newton's laws of motion justify the concept of a naturally ordered universe.

City and countryside, however, cannot be isolated from each other, and should not. As late as 1800, only three percent of the world's population lived in cities of more than 5,000 people; and even in 1950, only thirty percent did so. Throughout the development of Western civilization, most people have lived on the land; the city depends on outside supplies for food. We are therefore concerned throughout the book with the life of the rural population as well as the urban, with agrarian technology and the nature of bulk transportation of agricultural products, with the social structure of the countryside and its impact upon the city, and with the needs, the values, and the aspirations of the inhabitants of the countryside. We must thus consider the farms of the Roman campagna as well as Rome, the decaying aristocratic estates as well as prerevolutionary Paris, the turnips and clover of the agricultural revolution as well as Manchester.

The book is undisguisedly enthusiastic about cities, with a few notable exceptions that will be evident to the reader. I only wish that one could show the same admiration for all man's urban creations that Wordsworth did about London, one bright morning at the beginning of the last century:

Earth has not anything to show more fair:
Dull would he be of soul who could pass by
A sight so touching in its majesty:
This city now doth, like a garment, wear
The beauty of the morning; silent, bare,
Ships, towers, domes, theatres, and temples lie
Open unto the fields, and to the sky;
All bright and glittering in the smokeless air.
Never did sun more beautifully steep
In his first splendor, valley, rock, or hill;
Ne'er saw I, never felt, a calm so deep!
The river glideth at his own sweet will:
Dear God! the very houses seem asleep;
And all that mighty heart is lying still! [2]

---

[2] "Composed upon Westminster Bridge, September 3, 1802."

CONTENTS

MAPS

15

THE BAROQUE CITY AND ITS RULERS

As in every period when civilization has achieved a kind of homogeneity, the baroque city of the seventeenth and early eighteenth century was the physical expression of the social and political realities of the age, or more bluntly expressed, the taste of its ruling classes. The baroque city was created by remodeling and expanding existing cities, especially capital cities, on an enormous scale, or by creating totally new cities in equally magnificent proportions. Pope Sixtus V (1585–1590) completed the dome of Saint Peter's, the centerpiece of his city, and cut, through the medieval and Renaissance fabric of Rome, long avenues linking in shimmering vistas great piazzas dominated by ancient Egyptian obelisks. At the Square of the Four Fountains, where the pope's architect ingeniously constructed a church the exact size of one of the piers of Saint Peter's, two long avenues crossed. One linked the monumental entrance gate to the city, which had been designed by Michelangelo, with the papal palace of the Quirinale; the other, the ancient basilica of Santa Maria Maggiore with Santa Trinità dei Monti, from which the view extended over the whole of ancient Rome. The popes had become stage designers, and Rome was their theater. In Paris, the Bourbon kings, masters of a bureaucrat-designed absolutism, brought the shape of the city under the same discipline they were enforcing on society at large. The river front became a display of grandiose facades raised by royal decree, especially where the squat courtyard of the Louvre palace was expanded in long pedimented galleries to link it with the tall pavilions of the Tuileries palace and the controlled vistas of the regimented gardens beyond. Great squares with inner gardens were built to provide apartments for the nobles—at first playful and jovial in red brick with yellow plastered motifs, as suited the taste of the popular King Henry IV,

The Ducal Palace, Karlsruhe. Karlsruhe, constructed in 1715 as a huge star radiating from the ducal palace, was one of the most ambitious of baroque urban planning. (German Tourist Information Office photo.)

St. Peter's, Rome.   After the completion of Michelangelo's dome in 1590, the nave was lengthened, and in 1656 Bernini began the colonnades around the entrance square. (TWA photo.)

later grey and somber in massive limestone, reflecting the growing self-esteem of Louis XIII and Louis XIV.   Where the river Neva emptied into the rain-drenched marshes of the Gulf of Finland, the autocrat of Russia, Tsar Peter I (reigned 1689–1725), laid the foundation stone for the new imperial capital of Saint Petersburg, which soon became a pastel panorama of palaces, schools, ministries, triumphal arches, monumental avenues, and geometric gardens.   Even in London, amid the congeries of a medieval city rebuilt in all its confusion after the great fire of 1666, Christopher Wren raised the vast dome of Saint Paul's Cathedral.   Frustrated in his desire to slap an orderly plan onto the city as a whole, he transferred to the more amenable task of building suburban palaces the baroque ideals of orderly vistas and splendid facades.

The baroque city was the direct expression of the will of powerful monarchs or of privileged upper classes.   It was to be the setting they sought for their social life, and at times it turned into their plaything. This urbanism, this new design of city and building, combined a wild emotional exuberance with a disciplined order, and particularly with a mathematical regulation of space.   It was the product of a fusion—of the desire for order and the desire for freedom, of the unrestricted imagination of the artist and the orderly experimental mind of the scientist, of the sensuous religiosity of the South with the puritanical abnegation of the

North. It is tempting in analyzing this age to present it as a series of contrasts—of the absolutism of France and the parliamentarism of England, of the Catholic Reformation and Puritanism, of Roman baroque and French classicism. But this is misleading. All the differences are differences of degree and not differences of kind. France was not completely enslaved, and England was not completely free. We are about to explore variations within a surprisingly unified culture, not unrelated societies.

**FUNCTIONS
OF THE
BAROQUE CITY**

The Renaissance had merely modified the medieval city, changing the character of a few streets or squares and adding a few great palaces or churches to quarters that remained essentially medieval in character. Great new cities were conceived on paper, like those of Filarete, but were never completely built. But in the seventeenth and early eighteenth centuries, old cities were transformed and vast new cities completed. The surprise of this period of city building was that the function of the new city and the style in which it was built were in perfect harmony.

Functions of the Baroque City:
Paris

The Palace. The most important function of the new city was to be the residence of the ruler and that small group of the upper classes who formed his court. It therefore required a palace or palaces and a large number of palatial houses in fairly close proximity. The palace served a kind of psychological function, impressing on the mass of the subjects their inferiority by the contrast of their own homes with that of the sovereign and emphasizing by physical separation their remoteness from political decision making. The most obvious separation occurred when the kings moved just outside their capital cities to palaces built as towns in themselves, as the French king Louis XIV did at Versailles or the Austrian empress Maria Theresa at Schönbrunn. In these cases there was a ten- or twenty-mile walk for the common people of the city to glimpse even the outside of their sovereign's residence. But even where the palace was built as the central building of a city, as was more often the case, the architect used every trick he possessed to emphasize the separation from the rest of the city; the east facade of the Louvre palace in Paris, added by Louis XIV, has a ground floor so plain and forbidding that few would be attracted to approach closer. Were one tempted to go nearer, especially at the smaller palaces of the tiny German states or the houselike palace of the Danish kings, a permanent military detachment acted as a discouragement; or long rows of serrated grillwork provided a physical barrier. Louis XIV's chief minister, Colbert, summed up the purpose of palace building neatly: "In the absence of impressive acts of war, nothing marks the greatness of mind of princes better than the buildings that compel the people to look on them with awe, and all posterity judges them by the superb palaces they have built during their lifetime." [1]

[1] E. A. Gutkind, *Urban Development in Western Europe,* Vol. 5, *France and Belgium* (New York: Free Press, 1970), p. 115.

The Louvre Palace, Paris. The long facade facing the river Seine was constructed in the sixteenth century by Catherine de Médicis and Henry IV, to link the old courtyard of the Louvre palace with a new Tuileries palace that was destroyed in 1871. (French Embassy and Press Information Division photo.)

The palace itself served a large number of purposes. It was the setting in which an extremely complicated ceremonial was acted out. Every aspect of the ruler's day was exploited to provide time-consuming tasks for the court nobility, who were in many cases almost entirely excluded from the real exercise of political power. Louis XIV provided the model that was copied by almost every monarch of Europe. At his levée, or getting-up, for example, he expected all the courtiers to assemble outside his bedroom. The most privileged were admitted first to see him presented with holy water and to ask him favors. Then all were brought in to see him put on his clothes, and to note who was specially favored with the task of handing him his shirt. They stayed long enough to see him shaved, take a glass of wine and water, and say prayers. Finally they trailed after him to daily mass. Such meaningless ceremonies enabled the king to exploit the vanity and ambition of his nobility, keep them in sight and thus unable to plot sedition, and sap their finances in conspicuous consumption. This artificial court life existed in the smallest courts, like that of Nassau, which controlled a principality of only a few thousand inhabitants; and it was enforced on even the most recalcitrant nobility. Peter compelled his nobles to look like Frenchmen by shaving them himself! The ceremonial, however, took place amid a display of the finest products of each country's handicraft and industry, and it served to exhibit to possible purchasers, native or foreign, the country's glassware, tapestry, silver and metal work, textiles, and armor. The Gobelins tapestry factory, for example, could easily be visited after its products had been admired in Versailles.

The Bureaucracy. The palace also accommodated the bureaucrats who actually exercised the power of government; or where the palace was insufficiently large for the growing horde of middle-class administrators required by the centralizing monarchs, special government ministries were erected nearby. The worldwide affairs of the Catholic Church were run from the Vatican palace, which expanded to include more than a thousand rooms, twenty courtyards, and eighty staircases. Government ministries in Versailles were concentrated around the entrance to the palace courtyard, where three vast avenues met in an arrowhead; here, in carefully proportioned buildings, were the mansions for Messieurs des Bâtiments (Buildings); Messieurs des Receveurs Généraux (Tax collectors); and so on. Peter the Great decided to copy the bureaucratic pattern of Stockholm; and in the original design for Saint Petersburg, he assigned a frontage of the central Basil Island to twelve identical government ministries. The idea of a governmental section of town, devoted to office buildings, was born with the baroque city; and only too frequently monotony was the architect's inspiration as well as the character of the bureaucrat's life.

Staircase, Schloss Augustus-burg, Brühl, Germany.
Baroque architects like Balthasar Neumann (1687–1753) achieved the height of theatricality in their treatment of monumental staircases, in which complex geometrical patterns are combined with colorful stucco designs and ceiling paintings. (German Tourist Information Office photo.)

Town Houses of the Aristocracy. The presence of the court required large numbers of houses for the aristocracy, built on a splendid enough scale for them to entertain each other. Peter insisted that every Russian noble build himself a house in Saint Petersburg, and forbade the use of stone for building anywhere else in Russia until his city was completed. French nobles demanded a town house separated from its neighbors by high walls, with an inner court surrounded by stables and offices, and frequently a broad garden behind the house. One of the most sumptuous examples of real-estate speculation occurred in Paris when a group of engineers, in return for building a bridge, were given the right to drain the two little islands upstream from the Ile de la Cité and to sell off the resultant building lots. In a short time, the Ile Saint Louis became the favored quarter for nobles and lawyers, whose mansions rimmed the island and provided ever changing views of the river and its traffic. In London, where aristocratic life was considerably less formal, most of the well-to-do lived in terrace houses; but from the seventeenth century on, they were built in squares. Not only did the square have the advantage of creating open space, which was turned eventually into a park. of lawns and trees, but it established the class homogeneity of those who lived on the square by making the houses roughly the same in price, a triumphant distinction not even achieved on the Amsterdam canals.

The Army's Demands on the City. The army accompanied the monarch into the city, and was indeed the insurance of his power. "The name citadel is given to a particular part of a town, fortified on both the town

and the country sides, and it is principally intended for the quartering
of soldiers to keep the inhabitants of the town loyal in their duty," wrote
one French theorist. The army required a fortified building or area to which
it could withdraw in time of rebellion, and from which it could retake the
city, a place that would symbolize to the citizens the power of the monarch.
The slender spire of the Peter and Paul Cathedral marked for Saint Petersburg the fortress island where Russia's tsars held their political prisoners;
in 1917 the taking of the fortress was one of the primary tasks of the Bolshevik revolutionaries. In London and Paris, medieval fortresses, the Tower
and the Bastille, remained the principal royal garrisons; but vast numbers
of barracks buildings were put up. This was even truer in Berlin where
almost a quarter of the population were soldiers. The soldiers required
parade grounds, which were created in the center of the town. The Champ
de Mars, where the Eiffel Tower stands now, was the main parade ground
in Paris. The English horse guards drilled on the wide sandy grounds behind Whitehall. Even in a city like Boston, Massachusetts, one of the principal uses of the common was for the drilling of the militia. To see the soldiers
on parade was one of the most popular free entertainments for city crowds;
and when James Joyce, at the end of *Ulysses*, has Molly Bloom meditate
on the regiments she has known, he is appealing to emotions that have
been three centuries in the making:

*I love to see a regiment pass in review the first time I saw the Spanish cavalry
at La Roque it was lovely after looking across the bay from Algeciras all the lights
of the rock like fireflies or those sham battles on the 15 acres the Black Watch
with their kilts in time at the march past the 10th hussars the prince of Wales own
or the Lancers O the lancers theyre grand or the Dublins that won Tugela.* [2]

Molly felt something of the fascination of the French aristocrat Saint-
Simon when he watched the mock battle rehearsed for Louis XIV on the
plain outside Compiègne: "A wonderful sight—the vast army, cavalry,
and infantry deployed, and the game of attacking and defending the city.
But what struck me most, and remains as clear in my mind today after
forty years, was the King on that rampart in supreme command over the
whole army and that vast mass of myrmidons around him crowded on the
rampart and spread out across the plain." [3] The army too wanted triumphant avenues, long broad streets up which it could march in victory or
simply in routine celebrations; and these streets also served the purpose
of breaking up the rebellious lower-class quarters of the city into isolated
islands that could be subdued individually, while the intersections of the
new avenues, marked by a circle, or *rond point*, was an ideal point for the

[2] James Joyce, *Ulysses* (New York: Random House, 1966), p. 749.
[3] Duc de Saint-Simon, *Louis XIV at Versailles*, trans. Desmond Flower (London: Cassell,
1954), p. 50.

placing artillery in time of insurrection. The army was also a great consumer of urban land for its barracks and its arsenals, as well as a major employer for such industries as uniform making or gun founding.

New Fortifications. The wider and more effective range of cannons constricted the city enormously because new fortifications of a more complex and land-consuming size had to be constructed. The medieval wall was almost useless by the beginning of the seventeenth century, and military engineers were creating ever more ingenious patterns of masonry and earthworks to blunt the bombardment of artillery. But the new walls were so large that once constructed they could hardly ever be moved outward to accommodate increased populations. Space had to be found inside the city by giving up the gardens and orchards that had sweetened most medieval cities, by building upward to an average six stories and sometimes to ten, and especially by crushing the poor into ever more constricted quarters. Fortunately for Paris, Louis XIV decided that France was to be defended at its frontiers, where his engineer Vauban was constructing the most impregnable fortress cities in Europe. He allowed Paris to become an open city, turning the ramparts into boulevards and the city gates into triumphal arches; and when a wall was constructed at the end of the eighteenth century around a Paris that had doubled in area, its purpose was to enforce the collection of city import taxes, not defense. London, too, managed without a new city wall; but most capitals did not. Berlin, Copenhagen, Amsterdam, Vienna, Munich, Rome, were all restricted by their walls, the one advantage for the future being the easy conversion of the ramparts and their line of fire, or esplanade, into a green belt around the old city. The famous Ring of boulevards in Vienna is the product of such a conversion.

Needs of Business. The economic function of the city, even of those primarily administrative capitals, remained important. The need for a central machinery for handling the business transactions of the commercial revolution was met by the stock exchange and the banks. Wren made a new Royal Exchange, not Saint Paul's Cathedral, the focal point of his plan for the rebuilding of London. Peter gave the tip of Basil Island to the Bourse, which was rebuilt several times to give it the dominant role in the city's river facade. The location of the stock exchange, the great banks, and the overseas trading companies led to the specialization of one area of the city in large-scale commercial transactions. In London, it was the "City," the area that lay between Saint Paul's Cathedral and the Tower of London, that developed the extraordinary mixture of specialized stores, stock traders, bankers, artisans, guildsmen, news reporters, shipping companies, artisans, and lawyers, that delighted such observers of humanity as Dr. Johnson and Charles Dickens. Immediately below the City

lay the docks, the other requirement of all the great commercial centers.
Here again there was a great similarity in Europe's great cities. The same
forest of masts could be seen in the Pool of London, in the Sea of Straw of
Lisbon, or at the Elbe docks in Hamburg. Even the inland cities were
dependent on water transport, and crowded docks were to be found on the
Seine in Paris, the Moscva in Moscow, the Danube in Vienna and Budapest, and the Po in Milan. For all the large cities, one primary function of
this shipping was to supply food and raw materials for its artisan classes,
supplies usually brought from distant areas. The social peace of the city was
dependent on the regular maintenance of this supply. When the Seine
froze in 1788, preventing the arrival of food barges, it added directly to the
misery of the lower classes that erupted in revolution the next year.

Church Building in the City. Finally, the requirements of religion had to
be met, although churches rarely were the most important buildings constructed. At one extreme, there were churches that were deliberately
conceived as the physical expression of great religious movements. The
church of the Gesú in Rome was the triumphant assertion by the Jesuit order
of the ambition of the Catholic Reformation; the four churches named after
the points of the compass in Amsterdam represented a Calvinism that had
won independence from Spain's repression; Saint Paul's in London is the
most urbane expression of the ecumenical character of the Anglican
Church. But frequently the churches served the other purposes of the city.
The splendid domed church of the Invalides in Paris is, as its name suggests,

Hôtel des Invalides, Paris.
This military hospital was
founded by Louis XIV to
house 7,000 disabled soldiers.
The Emperor Napoleon was
buried beneath the great
dome. (Interphototèque.)

Library, Wiblingen Monastery, Germany. This colorful room illustrates the baroque use of simulated marble columns, writhing statues, and ceiling paintings that seem to open the room to the sky. (German Tourist Information Office photo.)

attached to a military hospital, while the great Austrian and South German monasteries in which baroque architecture achieved its most fanciful forms seem more calculated to provide a wide range of aesthetic and worldly pleasures to the monks than to satisfy the code of Saint Benedict.

Thus, the urban planners had to provide for the requirements of a royal court and aristocracy, for a well-to-do commercial bourgeoisie, for a large military class, and to a minor degree for the churches. They presupposed the existence of a large laboring class, but rarely made provision for it.

THE STYLE OF THE BAROQUE CITY

Meaning of Baroque. The style of the baroque city builder exactly suited the functions of the baroque city; and many of those who disapprove of the style are in reality disapproving of the function, the most obvious example being nineteenth-century Protestants, who disapproved of the sensual appeal of Rome's Catholic Reformation churches. We must begin by removing the confusion of nomenclature. The word *baroque* originally meant odd-shaped, but it came to be applied to the architecture of Italy from the mid–sixteenth century on because that architecture too was characterized by unusual, extravagant shapes. This style was predominant in Italy through the seventeenth and much of the eighteenth century, and passed from there to conquer Spain and Portugal and the Catholic states of Germany and Austria. The main characteristics of the style in architecture were movement and tension, attained by the use of undulating curves, sculptured

Saint Jerome, in Saint John Nepomuk Church, Munich. In a tiny chapel they built next to their own home in Munich, the Asam brothers, Cosmas and Egid, combined painting, sculpture, and architecture in a wildly dramatic composition celebrating the Trinity. (German Tourist Information Office photo.)

figures, and vast wildly colorful paintings; theatricality, created by constant employment of optical illusions, by a combination of richly colored marbles, precious stones, stucco, and shining metals with statuary of unrestrained voluptuousness; and a deep emotionalism, which made churches the demonstration of the spiritual significance of relics, the sufferings of the saints, or the kindliness of the Virgin. Baroque thus came to mean a series of specific tricks in architecture, sculpture, and painting: facades composed of two convex and a concave curve; altars like theatrical stages; statues that swarmed over the wall and ceiling instead of sitting in well-defined niches; ground plans composed of ovals rather than squares of circles; ceiling paintings that gave the illusion of opening to the sky.

It is often said that the North of Europe rejected the baroque because its artists and patrons were repelled by these features of its style. Inigo Jones, the English king's architect at the beginning of the seventeenth century, wrote scornfully of the style of Rome: "Ye outward ornaments oft to be sollid, proporsionable according to the rulles, masculine and unaffected. . . . All thes composed ornaments the which Proceed out of ye aboundance of dessigners and wear brought in by Michill Angelo and his followers in my oppignon do not well in solid Architecture."[4] The answer of these North-

[4] Cited in Nikolaus Pevsner, *An Outline of European Architecture* (Harmondsworth, England: Penguin, 1964), p. 309.

Royal Naval College, Greenwich. Designed by Christopher Wren (1632–1723) as a home for pensioned sailors, the college combines strict adherence to classical detail in the decoration of the buildings with a baroque freedom in the treatment of the twin towers. (British Tourist Authority photo.)

erners, in England, France, and the Netherlands in particular, was to revert to what they considered pure classicism, by which they meant continuance of the style of the High Renaissance. This implied correct use of the orders of capitals, solid balance rather than movement in facades, simplicity and sobriety of interior decoration, and restraint in the use of color. What is important, however, is that the artists and architects of the North never achieved this classical ideal because they never entirely rejected characteristics of baroque style and because they shared the intellectual ideals of the baroque age. For this reason it is justifiable to speak of the baroque city in both southern and northern Europe. Whether the motifs were those of Roman baroque or French classicism, the cities were baroque creations. Let us look more closely at what they had in common.

Principal Features of the Baroque Style. One should first note that the baroque artists and architects of Italy were admirers of geometry and mathematics, a taste that they inherited from the Renaissance and that was greatly magnified by the scientific progress of the century. The city planners were fascinated by geometrical patterns, and they loved to work out abstractly all the variations possible in the planning of the city. In the simplest form, they worshipped the straight line, the search for the infinite, and from this they hit on the notion of the endless vista down a street of identical houses. They loved the intersections of straight lines, which could be opened out into traffic circles embellished with fountains or statues, or where vistas could be dramatically terminated with some impressive building. They elaborated squares, oblongs, ovals, and stars, which were all eventually tried in actual city building. This mathematical basis for the city was just as appealing in the North as in the South because the functions it served were the same. Everywhere the pedestrian was displaced along with the curved medieval streets, and the well-to-do in their carriages enjoyed the long avenues that on foot were both tiresome and tiring. The London squares, the half-star of the new city of Karlsruhe, even the canals of Amsterdam, carried on this baroque absorption with the geometrical ordering of space. The three avenues that converge at the entrance to the château of Versailles and those that meet in the Piazza del Popolo in Rome are virtually identical.

The desire for the infinite showed itself in many other ways, in South and North. Mirrors became a favorite interior decoration, the most grandiose use of them being in the Hall of Mirrors in Versailles, the most important room in the whole kingdom of France. The ceiling painting was adopted in the North with almost no change of style, as when Louis XIV masquerading as Apollo floated over the heads of his courtiers, in the acres of canvases painted for Versailles by the court painter Le Brun. The vast formal gardens sought the merging of the man-made and the natural, preferably at some point on the infinite horizon. The great palaces, whether at Munich, Hampton Court, or Versailles, made use of artificial canals to lead the eye out through receding forest to the far skyline.

Above all, it was in espousing baroque emotionalism that the artists and architects satisfied the desires of their patrons. Sheer size was emotionally

Adoration of the Lamb, by Bacciccio (1639–1709). In this sketch for a ceiling fresco in the Jesuits' church in Rome, Bacciccio used foreshortening of his figures to create the illusion of swirling movement in the heavens. (Courtesy the De Young Museum, San Francisco.)

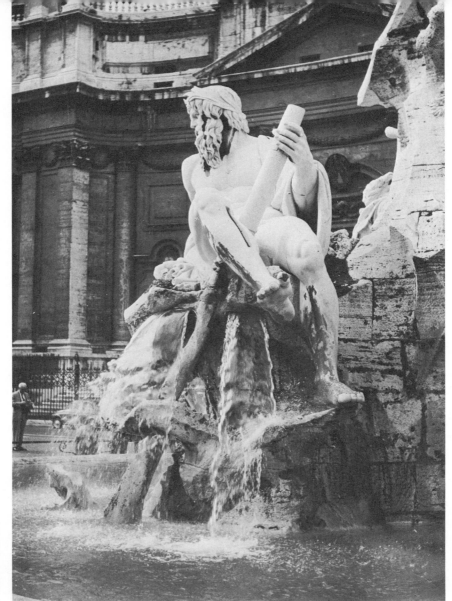

Fountain of the Rivers, Rome.
Gianlorenzo Bernini (1598–1680) modelled his statues after ancient Roman river gods, in creating a centerpiece for Rome's oval Piazza Navona. (Italian Government Travel Office photo.)

impressive. The garden front of Versailles is six hundred yards long; it took the brass roof from the Pantheon to construct the huge twisted columns of Bernini's shrine over the high altar of Saint Peter's. The exuberance of Italy reached the North in such devices as the use of fountains and the decoration of parks or streets with writhing or soaring statues of pagan gods, and especially in the planning of interior space. The key was the use of the oval for the floor plans, ceiling paintings, and even for niches in facades. The result of the use of ovals instead of squares or circles was a charming, vibrant eloquence that the seventeenth and eighteenth century courtiers thought ideally suited to their way of life. These patterns produced what is often called spatial polyphony, a weaving into an intricate pattern of several important lines of architectural emphasis. Christopher Wren was the great master of this art in England; and he used it fully, when after the Great Fire he was given the task of drawing up new plans for fifty-one city churches. His ingenuity reached its greatest height in the towers he gave to the churches, an amazing variety within a simple form achieved by playing with geometric patterns. And this same quality can be felt in all the baroque cities, even when the most determined attempt has been made to use pure classical forms. The Paris and Versailles of Louis XIV, the London of Wren, the Saint Petersburg of Peter the Great, the Washington of the French city planner Pierre Charles L'Enfant, the Rome of Bernini, all are unmistakably the products of the same age.

Plan for Washington, D.C., by Charles L'Enfant (1754–1825). L'Enfant's plan of 1791 for a grid-iron pattern of streets broken by diagonal avenues radiating from the White House and the Capitol was not fully implemented until 1901. (French Embassy Press and Information Division photo.)

AUTOCRACY IN RUSSIA

Politics in all European states in the seventeenth century was concerned with a dialogue between monarchy and the upper classes, with both the landed nobility and the wealthiest bourgeoisie; and this was a dialogue from which the majority of Europe's inhabitants were excluded. As a result of this dialogue—which ran the whole gamut of confrontation from a genuine debate over principles to civil war—absolute monarchy became the normal form of government in most European states, but the monarchy continued to govern largely for the benefit of the upper classes it had tamed.

In England and Holland, the upper classes gained political predominance against would-be absolute monarchs, and also governed largely for their own benefit. Their form of government was dictated by forces common to almost all the European states. The belief in the principles of mercantilism led directly to state intervention in the economy at home as, for example, in the abolition of internal trade barriers, and to cutthroat competition abroad for a larger share in a supposedly limited quantity of world trade. The frequent recourse to war among the European states for religious, economic, and territorial gains led to organization of disciplined, costly standing armies and navies, while the many insurrections of the poorer classes in both town and countryside assured employment for the armies at home in time of peace. The burden of the military establishment, the vast inflation due to the influx of American gold and silver, and the increased economic activities of the state required higher revenues, which could only be collected by a more effective bureaucracy. The bureaucracy in its turn recognized that its duty was to further the economic prosperity of the state by reducing the role of such restrictive medieval organizations as the guild. In short, all the functions of the seventeenth- and early-eighteenth-century state were closely interrelated, and it was in the capital city that they found physical expression.

Origins of the Russian State.   The most extreme example of the swing to absolute monarchy occurred in Russia. The first Russian state, governed from Kiev from the ninth until the mid–thirteenth century, had been at least as advanced as contemporary states in western Europe. It had given the Russians a common language written in the Cyrillic alphabet and a common religion, the Greek Orthodox faith it had accepted from Byzantium. While a powerful noble class of boyars clustered around the prince, the majority of the peasantry were probably free, while flourishing trade with Byzantium and to a lesser degree with the West supported a numerous merchant class in such cities as Pskov and Novgorod. This promising evolution was interrupted by the invasion of the Mongol tribes of Tatars led by Genghis Khan and his nephew Batu Khan who, after conquering most of Asia, swept into southern Russia and destroyed Kiev in 1240. The Tatars exercised overlordship over Russia for the next two hundred years, effectively cutting off Russia from its contacts with the West and destroying its commercial ties except those through Novgorod. After the savagery of the initial conquest, the Tatars were satisfied to exact tribute in money and military recruits; but they left behind a tradition of autocratic government that was inherited by the native rulers whom they used as their intermediaries, especially the princes of Moscow. The city of Moscow was a relatively new creation, begun on the frontiers of settlement in the twelfth century; but by the fifteenth century its rulers had annexed so many surrounding territories that they possessed the most important principality under the Tatar ruler. By 1480, they were able to deny the Tatars their tribute and to confine them to three Khanates in the extreme south of Russia. The prince of Moscow, Ivan III (reigned 1462–1505), took the Byzantine emperor's title of *autocrat* after the fall of Constantinople, married the niece of the last East Roman Emperor, and supported the claim that Moscow had inherited the religious preeminence of Constantinople and was thus the Third Rome. At the same time he declared that Moscow had inherited the lands of the former Kievan state, which had extended to Lithuania and Poland; and in a series of wars, he seized from the Lithuanian prince huge territories extending westwards as far as Smolensk.

Moscow under Ivan III.   Ivan III was the true founder of Russian absolutism. He acted, like the Tatars, as though he were unimpeded in his exercise of power by the control of law. He controlled a state church that recognized him as its supreme authority. And he conceived of the landed nobles as a service aristocracy, who were to receive their privileges only to the extent

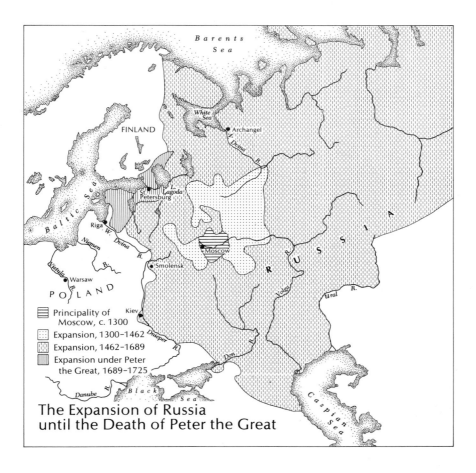

Principality of Moscow, c. 1300

Expansion, 1300–1462

Expansion, 1462–1689

Expansion under Peter the Great, 1689–1725

The Expansion of Russia
until the Death of Peter the Great

The Kremlin, Moscow. The cathedrals of Ivan the Great blend harmoniously today with the elaborate facades of the nineteenth-century palaces and the spare columns of the Soviet palace of congresses. (From M. Ilyin, *Moscow: Architecture and Monuments* [Moscow: Progress Pub., 1968.] p. 15.)

that they served the state. To achieve this goal, he founded a class called *pomietchiks,* who were given lands for their lifetime in return for service to the tsar and in particular for their support against the hereditary aristocracy. He also began the custom, to be greatly expanded later, of tying the peasant to the land, so that he could not avoid working for the landlord or paying taxes to the state. The symbol of this new monarchy in the East of Europe, an area considered by most West Europeans as the extreme of barbarism, was the magnificent Kremlin, built for Ivan by architects brought in from Italy. The original fortress of Moscow had been built in the twelfth century on the junction of two rivers, in the triangular form favored for most Russian cities, and it had been extended a few times, usually in wood. But in 1485–1495, Ivan's Italian architects constructed the huge Kremlin walls that still exist, one and a half miles in length, sixty feet high, and fifteen feet thick, using a deep red brick and breaking the regular crenelation of the wall with riotously decorated watch and gate towers. They created inside, contrasting with the horizontal lines and rich color of the walls, a fantasy of cathedrals, not one vast church but six, brilliantly white and topped with a breathtaking array of onion-shaped domes whose gold leaf could be seen shining from miles away. And next to the cathedrals they built a palace for the metropolitan of Moscow, the head of the Russian church, and a splendid palace for the tsar. In a period of twenty years they created one of the most beautiful complexes of buildings in the world, comparable in its harmony to the Periclean temples on the Acropolis.

The grandeur of this creation of Ivan III belied the real strength of Russian absolutism, however. The immense size of Russia, constantly being increased by conquest and by colonization eastward, challenged any efforts at strict control, while encouraging the constant movement of peasants in search of better lands. The landed aristocracy resisted the tsar's attempts to control them so vigorously that Tsar Ivan IV the Terrible (reigned 1534–1584) determined to use violence to break them. He resettled many Moscow aristocrats on the frontiers and gave their lands to the new service nobility. Thousands of the old boyars were executed, while a regime of terror, called the *oprichnina,* or separate kingdom, was loosed against the nobles. The oprichniks were the first grim secret police of Russia, black-clad sadists on black horses with a dog's head on their saddle who struck indiscriminately throughout central Russia. The reaction came during the reign of Ivan's idiot son, Russia's "Time of Troubles," when the nobles attempted to run the country as an oligarchy, the peasantry rose in agonized rebellion, and the Poles struck as far as Moscow itself. The compromise settlement in 1613, by which an undistinguished nobleman called Michael Romanov became tsar, did not restore in practice an absolutism that had never been challenged in theory. The legal enserfment of the peasantry in 1649 strengthened the control of the nobles. The patriarch of Moscow even claimed theoretical supremacy over the tsar. Taxation of the peasantry brought an inadequate revenue for maintenance of an efficient military force, yet drove them into constant rebellions. Finally, a reaction against foreigners following the Polish invasion led to the isolation of foreign merchants and technicians in ghettos in the big Russian cities, so that the pernicious modernizing influences of the West could not destroy the old ways of Muscovy.

Aims of Peter the Great.   The reign of Peter the Great (1689–1725) is a watershed in Russian history because he achieved efficient autocracy by linking it to the enforced modernization of the political, economic, and social structure of Russia. Peter grew up in the foreign quarter of Moscow, exiled from the Kremlin by the regent, and learned there a fascination with the technical achievements of the West, contempt for the determined resistance to progress of the Muscovite aristocracy, a distaste for the ambitions of the Orthodox clergy, and distrust of the intrigues of the palace guard,

Moscow in the Sixteenth Century. The inner fortress of the Kremlin is dominated by the Belltower of Ivan the Great. Just outside the wall rise the bulbous domes of St. Basil's cathedral.

or *streltsi.* His admiration for Western technology was confirmed during his first visit to western Europe in 1697–1698. The many early defeats in the Great Northern War with Sweden convinced him of the superiority of the Swedish army and navy and also of the Swedish civil service. Traditional Moscow became for him the great obstacle to a modernized Russia. At first he attempted to change the ways of Moscow, compelling the nobles to wear Western dress, to shave their long beards, and to work in the government ministries. But in 1703 he captured the mouth of the Neva River, which enters the Gulf of Finland, a window on the West where he at once began to construct the new capital of Saint Petersburg. To build his city he reopened the dialogue with the Russian nobility. The peasantry was to be more firmly tied to the land; and the landowners were to discover a new way of life in the service of the state. They were to be educated in Western knowledge, in the Guards regiments, the Naval Academy, the artillery, and the engineering schools. They were to be given a chance to rise through a Table of Ranks, by their service to the state in the military or civil service. And in Saint Petersburg, under the watchful eye of the tsar himself, they were to enjoy the amenities of European social life, whose economic requirements would be met by the forcible transfer of the merchant colony of Archangel.

The Creation of Saint Petersburg. Everything in Saint Petersburg, however, indicated the autocratic character of its founder. The site was sloppy marshland, where dysentery killed ten thousand of his first conscripted city builders. The nobility had to be compelled to leave the cold but salubrious climate of Moscow for the eternal drizzle of the Baltic coast; they were ordered to build homes whose size was assigned them by the police, after an inspection of their homes in Moscow. Tradesmen were moved into segregated streets, such as the Street of the Cannonmakers, the Street of the Armorers, and so on. The government ministries were grouped in identical pavilions on the central island, which Peter had hoped to turn into a new Amsterdam. The navy was given the island of Kronstadt, out in the river; the army had its barracks on the island of Saint Peter and Saint Paul, and later its parade grounds, as in Paris, on the Champ de Mars. During the next hundred years, Peter's successors shifted their model of urbanism from Amsterdam to Rome and Paris. On the south bank of the

The Admiralty, St. Petersburg, by G. A. Kochalov. In the development of the South bank of the Neva river in the late eighteenth century, the empress Catherine's vast Winter Palace was erected next to the shipyards and naval headquarters of the Admiralty.

river, great baroque perspectives were opened up: the three avenues converging on the new Winter Palace, now the Hermitage Museum; the long facades of the imperial and aristocratic palaces along the river front, which remind the present-day viewer of Paris; gigantic squares and gardens; and everywhere the unifying force of color in the light yellow stucco that decorated all the buildings. Saint Petersburg was an artificial creation, the will of one man. It forced Russia headlong into the technology of the West, especially the military technology. But it split Russia between the autocracy and the part of the upper classes and bourgeoisie who had accepted West European ways and the vast majority of the population who remained untouched by them, except to provide the human and financial resources to pay for the modernization. Yet, because the modernization was the act of

Francis I, by Joos van Cleve the Elder (c. 1485–1540). (John G. Johnson Collection, Philadelphia.)

an autocrat, it was not the product of the drive of individuals working within a system that encouraged initiative, the secret of the West's dynamism.

ABSOLUTISM IN FRANCE

Foundation of French Absolutism. The absolutism of Louis XIV in France, which was the model for the majority of European states in the seventeenth and early eighteenth centuries, was tainted by this same defect, but to a lesser degree. To start with, Louis did not have to work at such breakneck speed as Peter, because the foundations of French absolutism had been securely laid during the previous two centuries. At the end of the fifteenth century, Louis XI had left the monarchy a standing army, a large income from regular taxation, the undisputed right to legislate and to judge, the power of making war or peace, and the right of nominating bishops and abbots. Louis's successors for the next half-century, in spite of their wasteful wars in Italy, ran France as a supreme example of the "new monarchy." This evolution was interrupted, although temporarily, by the Wars of Religion (1562–1598). The wars were only partly an attempt by the more fanatical of France's fourteen million Catholics to wipe out Calvinism, which was the religion professed by about one million of the country's most enterprising commercial and professional classes. The French kings attacked the Calvinists because they regarded their fortified cities and their superbly organized network of congregations as a threat to the absolute powers of the monarchy, especially in the outlying provinces. Three great factions of the nobility fought each other, and incidentally laid much of France waste, to gain control of the throne. The Queen Mother, Catherine de Médicis, controlled the policy of her three ineffective sons, Francis II, Charles IX, and Henry III, who reigned successively during the wars (1559–1589); she considered the measures to which she sank, including the murder of three thousand Calvinists in Paris on Saint Bartholomew's Day in 1572, as necessary for the protection of her family. The surprising result of the wars was, however, to strengthen the monarchy.

Henry IV, the Vert Galant. The victor in the wars, the Bourbon faction's leader Henry of Navarre, who became king on the assassination of Henry III in 1589, was a cynical, tough, and charming character, whose qualities were precisely what the monarchy required to end the chaos of the wars. He displayed his cynicism by twice converting from Calvinism to Catholicism; then, as a Catholic, he granted religious toleration to the Calvinists by the Edict of Nantes, turning them in one stroke of the pen into the most loyal and productive segment of his population. He used force for ten years after his accession to crush the extreme Catholics and bring an end to Spanish intervention in France. And finally, by sheer charm—or rather by being himself the ideal Renaissance courtier, a combination of scholar, soldier, and lover—he made himself the most popular king France has ever had. Everywhere he was known affectionately as the *vert galant,* the green gallant.

The wars, moreover, had strengthened the monarchy in relation to any opposition. The nobility had killed off each other. The chaos had severely weakened the middle classes, forcing many Calvinists to emigrate and hampering the development of industry and commerce. The commercial classes in France, unlike those in England and Holland, were not in a position to make a claim for a share in political power, but rather sought the king as their sole guarantor against a return of feudal confusion. This attitude was expressed in a new political philosophy by a group called the *Politiques,* who held that royal sovereignty was the only guarantee of peace and internal order. Their great writer, Jean Bodin, in his influential *Six Books on the Republic,* argued that a true state only exists when it has a sovereign who exercises "supreme power over citizens and subjects, unrestrained by law"; that a king governs by the will of God, and is responsible only to God; and that the king is the sole maker of law, including, if he wishes, laws giving toleration to Calvinists. The wars, in short, had given the French monarchy a well-reasoned justification of its own pretensions to absolute power.

Henry IV and Renovation of Paris. Perhaps most important of all, Henry made Paris a true capital city once more. Under Catherine de Médicis, Paris had been in a state of more or less open rebellion against the monarchy, a city divided into isolated social groups alien to each other, tormented by disease and starvation, and ignored by an extravagant court. It had finally welcomed Henry in 1594, after he had become a Catholic for the second time. (He supposedly remarked, "Paris is worth a mass"!) Henry in turn repaid Paris by beginning the process of making it a city worthy of the monarchy's new pretensions. First came work of restoration, the clearing of the garbage-piled streets, repair of ruined buildings, restoration of the water supply, rebuilding of the bridges. Then came the revival of commerce, aided by the policies of Henry's able financial minister, Sully, whose frugality restored the reliability of government bonds and whose mercantilism encouraged the foundation of new industries in Paris. Last came the shaping of the city according to royal standards of taste, a practice that was to continue for almost three centuries and was to be responsible for the present-day appearance of Paris. "I would be very pleased," the king wrote Sully about a street being built on the left bank, "if you would see to it that those who are beginning to build in the aforesaid street make the facades of their houses all of the same [architectural] order, for it would be a fine ornament to see this street with a uniform facade from the end of the bridge. Farewell, my friend, Henry." The tip of the Ile de la Cité set the standards for new urban groupings—a charming combination of grey stone bridge, uniform red brick houses with yellow stone facing, and tall slate roofs. In its triangular form and bold play of perspective, that led the eye to a strategically placed statue of Henry on horseback, it was already heralding the baroque city. Delighted with this first effort at urban planning, Henry created the first residential square, the Place des Vosges at the eastern, aristocratic edge of Paris; and he indicated the precise social character of the individual houses by selling off one side himself to chosen families who had been ennobled for legal and bureaucratic service.

Rule of the Cardinals.   Henry's assassination in 1610 flung France back into chaos, as his wife struggled unsuccessfully to prevent the nobility from ignoring the nine-year-old King Louis XIII. The state treasury was shared out among them, and the provinces became virtually independent of the crown. To end this state of administrative anarchy, Cardinal Richelieu, the brilliant, secular-minded churchman who ran the government on Louis's behalf from 1624 to 1642, made use of the one class of bureaucrats he felt to be completely trustworthy, the traveling commissioners. These officials, renamed *intendants,* were given greatly expanded duties in running the taxation, law courts, and police in the provinces; and they remained the primary instrument of royal absolutism until the revolution of 1789. Under Richelieu, royal government was centralized round the person of the chief minister, who worked through his own appointees on the royal council and in the main government ministries in Paris and through the provincial intendants. Even the buildings of Paris showed this new emphasis, because just to the north of the Louvre, Richelieu constructed for himself the Palais Cardinal (now the Palais Royal), a large palace with a long rectangular and completely private garden. Around the Richelieu Quarter, all his top bureaucrats sought to build themselves homes in the same formal style as their patron's, the solid, luxurious buildings themselves a proof of the wealth that could come to the middle classes who served the crown faithfully. Richelieu's successor as chief minister, Cardinal Mazarin, was a clever persuasive Italian who made himself the lover, and perhaps the husband, of Anne of Austria, the widow of Louis XIII. He attempted to run France on behalf of Louis's five-year-old son Louis XIV by relying entirely on the system created by Richelieu. He was challenged, however, by the Paris uprising known as the Fronde (1648–1652), which almost upset all the progress toward absolutism that the monarchy had made in the previous half-century.

The Fronde, so-called after the mud-throwing of Paris children, was an unplanned explosion of anger by all the classes in France who felt they had grievances against the monarchy. It began when a decade of poor harvests drove the peasantry into violent attacks on the tax collectors and the wealthy Parisians who were trying to buy up their lands cheap.

**Louis XIII by Peter Paul Rubens
(1577–1648).** Rubens, the greatest
baroque painter of Flanders, used
sumptuous costumes and elegant
backgrounds to create an aura of
opulence around his royal sitters. (The
Norton Simon Foundation.)

It reached Paris when the Parlement, which represented the rich lawyers
and claimed the right to register all royal edicts before they became law,
demanded reform of the corruption caused by sale of government offices
and a reduction in the powers of the intendants. When the monarchy
granted the Parlement's demands, the great nobles in turn took over.
Paris was occupied by noble armies, while in the rest of France private
forces of aristocrats plundered and burned. Mazarin fled the country.
The Paris mob terrified the king, who was then thirteen, pouring into his
bedroom in the palace and forcing him to flee—perhaps the formative
experience of his life, since it left him with such distrust for Parisians that
only a complete move of the government to Versailles could assuage it.
Royal armies eventually defeated the remaining noble armies, and both
Louis XIV and Mazarin were able to return to Paris.

Anne of Austria, by Peter Paul Rubens.
(The Norton Simon Foundation.)

Opportunities Open to French Absolutism.   The real results of the Fronde were not evident until the death of Mazarin in 1661 left Louis free to run France his own way by becoming his own first minister. Absolute monarchy had survived its most serious test; it remained to be seen what use a conscientious despot would make of his powers. The situation had never been more favorable for an ostentatious display of the monarchy's powers. All France's rivals were in decline or disorder. England had just emerged from civil wars. The Dutch were severely weakened by naval wars with England and land wars with Spain. Spain itself could no longer raise the great armies and navies whose cost had brought Philip II into bankruptcy. The Thirty Years' War had left Germany an economic shambles, while the Hohenzollern family were just beginning to turn the state of Prussia into a major military force. Poland was in the hands of an anarchist nobility. Austria was distracted by a new attack of the Turks, who in 1683 were to besiege Vienna itself. France, by contrast, was the strongest and wealthiest state in Europe. It had a large population, eighteen million as compared with England's five million. Its agriculture was the most varied and prosperous in Europe, even though France had occasional times of famine. Richelieu had given it a strong navy and a renovated infantry that scored a landmark victory by defeating the Spanish at Rocroi in 1643. Above all, in spite of its continual social conflicts, France had a genuine national patriotism that expressed itself in veneration of the monarchy.

Louis believed sincerely that it was his duty to France and to God to profit from these advantages. Like the majority of Europeans of his day, he held that only through an absolute monarchy could order be guaranteed

Louis XIV's Passage of the Rhine, The Palace of Versailles, by Antoine Coysevox (1640–1720). Louis's triumphs in his early wars provided subject-matter of a suitably sycophantic nature for the fifty sculptors and painters who decorated the ceremonial rooms of Versailles. (Alinari photo.)

and the energies of the nation harnessed for the common benefit. In the memoirs he wrote for his son, he described the misery of peoples governed by popular assemblies and limited monarchies:

The more you grant it [the popular assembly], the more it demands; the more you caress it, the more it scorns you; and what it once has in its possession is retained by so many hands that it cannot be torn away without extreme violence. Out of so many persons who compose these great bodies, it is always the least sensible who assume the greatest license. Once you defer to them they claim the right forever to control your plans according to their fancy, and the continual necessity of defending yourself against their assaults alone produces many more cares for you than all the other interests of your crown, so that a prince who wants to bequeath lasting tranquility to his people and his dignity completely intact to his successors cannot be too careful to suppress this tumultuous temerity.

But I am dwelling too long on a reflection that seems useless for you, or that can at most serve you only to recognize the misery of our neighbors, since it is patent that you will reign in a state where you will find no authority that is not honored to derive its origin and its status from you, no body that dares to depart from expressions of respect, no corporation that does not see its principal greatness in the good of your service and its sole security in its humble submission.[5]

He proposed to set the example of hard work and conscientious attention to all duties, no matter how trival. As a child he had been taught to hate the do-nothing kings of the Merovingian period, especially Louis the Idle; and his own characteristic sobriety, backed by a splendid physique, enabled him to combine the long hours of administration with a punctilious observance of the even more fatiguing round of court ritual. He was the only person at Versailles who was never bored; and he accepted discomfort as a matter of principle. Told that some of the fireplaces at Versailles would stop smoking if the chimneys were made taller, he replied that the smoke did not matter because the chimneys must remain invisible from the gardens. Food was brought several hundred yards and was cold when he ate it; wine froze in the glass. The king remained stoically indifferent. The essential factor was to maintain the majesty of kingship at whatever personal cost. In this work, Louis believed he was answerable to God, who had appointed him, and only to God. This theory, the divine right of kings, sustained him with a sense of self-righteousness, when it became evident even to his leading general that his wars were leading France into ruin. To the courtier Saint-Simon, Louis's conception of government seemed at the end to be the product of his personal failings, "his blindness, his pride in doing everything himself, his jealousy of experienced ministers and generals, his vanity in choosing only such leaders as could not be expected to earn credit for successes."

[5] Louis XIV, *Mémoires for the Instruction of the Dauphin,* trans. Paul Sonnino (New York: Fress Press, 1970), pp. 130–31.

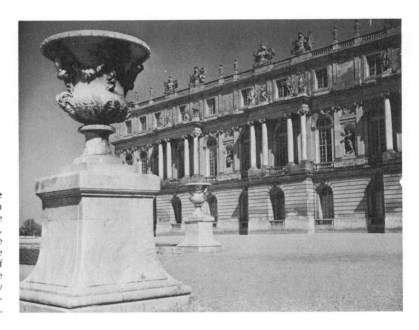

The Garden Facade, The Palace of Versailles. From the Hall of Mirrors in the second story of this facade, the king's control over nature itself could be seen in the geometrical patterning of woods and gardens around the palace. (French Embassy Press and Information Division photo.

Military Agression and Glory. Throughout his reign, Louis's main pre-occupation was to achieve *la gloire,* military glory for France and the monarchy. The ceilings of Versailles are filled with florid portrayals of Louis's victories in his early wars; but in each case there is a material justification, such as the capture of a strategic fortress or the surrender of a rich city. In his first war, the War of Devolution (1667–1668) Louis sought glory by straightening the southward bulge in his border with the Spanish Netherlands, from which, he was told, an invader could reach Paris in four days. His second war, with the Dutch (1672–1678), was partly inspired by the mercantilist desire to destroy the commercial supremacy of the Netherlands, partly by the religious determination to wipe out one of the strongholds of Calvinism, and partly by continuing territorial ambitions on the Spanish possessions on his eastern frontier. For two years his armies were totally successful; but in 1674 the Dutch pierced the dikes to create a flooded barrier between the Rhine and Zuider Zee, and used the time they had gained to put together a coalition of European powers fearful of France's ruthless use of force in support of its growing ambition. To stop Louis's attempt at European hegemony in its early stages, the Dutch were joined by the English, the Spanish, and the Austrians, and several German states; the French were held to a stalemate; and peace was finally bought at the expense of the Spanish, by giving Louis a little more territory from the Spanish Netherlands and the valuable French-speaking province of Franche-Comté, which blocked the invasion route through the Belfort Gap.

Once peace was restored, legal chicanery was used to give France a pretext for seizing important cities in Alsace, including the important bridge town of Strasbourg. Luxembourg was occupied a little later. And in 1688 his forces crossed the Rhine to subjugate the little German state of the Palatine, where they destroyed the elector's palace of Heidelberg. This action precipitated Europe into almost three decades of continuous

war, in which France made no further territorial gains. In his third war, the War of the League of Augsburg (1689–1698), Louis faced again the powers that had foiled his attack on the Netherlands, and again was brought to a standstill. In 1700, he played for the greatest prize of his reign. He would risk war with the rest of Europe to enable his second grandson to inherit the whole Spanish empire that the dying Spanish king had bequeathed to him rather than to the other claimant, the second grandson of the Austrian emperor. In the War of the Spanish Succession (1702–1713) that resulted, the French armies were defeated again and again, in Italy by the forces of Savoy and Austria and in Germany and the Spanish Netherlands by the English under the duke of Marlborough. With a national debt of three billion livres, the peasantry starving, and Paris on the verge of revolt, Louis agreed to the Treaty of Utrecht of 1713, by which Austria was to take most of the European possessions of Spain, including Milan and the Spanish Netherlands. Britain was to take Gibraltar and the island of Minorca and have a monopoly on the supply of slaves to the Spanish empire. Louis's grandson was to retain Spain and its overseas empire, but the thrones of Spain and France were never to be united. The establishment of the younger Bourbon line on the Spanish throne proved of almost no value to France during the next hundred years. The one worthwhile result of twenty-eight years of war was to establish a defensible frontier from the Channel to Switzerland.

Strengths and Weaknesses of the French Economy. In economic policy as in foreign policy, Louis's absolutism produced beneficial results only through the end of the Dutch war. Under the direction of his parsimonious finance minister, Colbert, tax collection was made more efficient and more just; internal barriers to trade were reduced; roads and canals were constructed, including the Languedoc Canal that linked the Mediterranean and the Bay of Biscay; new industries, such as silk and glassmaking, were established; overseas trading companies were founded. But mercantilism led Colbert into some drastic errors, such as a high tariff on Dutch trade and the even worse mistake of forbidding the export of wheat from France; and it led him to accept war as a necessary adjunct to commercial expansion. The wars, however, led to Colbert's own eclipse in the king's favor and to the rise of Louvois, the war minister, who though efficient as an army organizer only encouraged the king's provocation to the anti-French coalition. Colbert also could do nothing to make the king realize the economic contribution that the French Huguenots were making. During Colbert's lifetime, Louis attempted to convert Huguenots by billeting troops with them; and the year after his death, Louis revoked the Edict of Nantes. To gain religious uniformity, which he felt essential to royal absolutism, he drove out of France one hundred thousand Protestants, who included many of France's finest craftsmen and businessmen, nine thousand sailors, six hundred army officers and twelve thousand soldiers. In Europe, the persecution of the Huguenots aroused enormous indignation. In France itself, many thought it a shameful error. According to Saint-Simon:

The revocation of the Edict of Nantes, decided upon without the least excuse or any need, and the many proscriptions as well as declarations that followed it constituted a terrible plot which depopulated one-quarter of the kingdom, destroyed its commerce, enfeebled all parties, caused widespread pillage and condoned the dragonnades, allowed tortures and torments in which many innocent persons of both sexes died by thousands, ruined a numerous people, tore families to pieces, set relatives against one another in a fight for food and property, caused our manufacturers to move abroad, where they flourished and brought wealth to other States at our expense and enabled new and flourishing towns to be built, and gave them the spectacle of so remarkable a people being proscribed, stripped of their possessions, exiled, made to wander over the face of the earth without being guilty of any crime, seeking shelter from their own country.[6]

The Centralization of Culture.   Only in the arts did Louis's centralization of all French life around himself produce an almost unblemished success; and it is the achievements of the writers, sculptors, painters, architects, and musicians of his reign that won it the lasting reputation of being France's golden age.   Colbert himself had begun the process of retaining all patron-

[6] Cited in Maurice Ashley, *Louis XIV and the Greatness of France* (London: Hodder and Stoughton, 1964), p. 93.

Self-Portrait, by Antoine Coysevox. Coysevox, one of the most prolific baroque sculptors in France, has contrasted the firm serenity of his features with the motion of his swirling wig and the diagonal lines of his clothing. (Courtesy De Young Museum, San Francisco.)

age, and of laying down artistic standards, within the court. All painters were brought into an Academy of Painting and scientists into an Academy of Sciences. Intellectual life was dominated by the French Academy that had been founded by Richelieu. Colbert's admiration for Rome and his desire to make Paris a new Rome were evident everywhere—in the Louvre facade, in the antique subjects favored by the painters, in the triumphal arches at the city gates. But when Louis XIV began the expansion of the chateau of Versailles, both the focus and the style changed. Versailles itself became the training ground for the new architects, interior designers, sculptors, and painters. The new generation of artists was to be trained under the three great masters who were creating Versailles: Le Vau in architecture, Le Brun in painting, and Le Nôtre in landscape gardening. From Versailles, too, came the patronage of France's greatest comic playwright, Molière, and tragic playwright, Racine. Molière was an incisive but humane satirist, who made the court rock with laughter at the foibles of the excessively religious, in *Tartuffe;* of the social climber, in *Le Bourgeois Gentilhomme;* of learned women, in *Les Femmes Savantes.* And he could achieve the point at which the greatest comedy probes so deeply that it becomes tragedy, as in the scene from *L'Avare (The Miser)* in which the old miser goes almost demented at the loss of his money:

Thief! Thief! Murderer! Killer! Justice, just heaven! I am lost, I am killed! Some one has cut my throat, some one has stolen my money! Who can it be? What has happened to him? Where is he hiding? What can I do to find him? Where shall I run? Where shall I not run? . . . My mind is troubled, and I don't know where I am, who I am, and what I am doing. Alas! my poor money, my poor money, my dear friend, they have taken you away from me! And, since you have been taken away, I have lost my support, my consolation, my job; everything is finished for me, and I have nothing more to do in the world! Without you it is impossible to live. It is over, I am finished, I am dying, I am dead, I am buried. Is there no one who wants to bring me back to life by giving me back my money?[7]

Racine, by contrast, was a superb poet who was able to build the classical Alexandrine verse, with its strictly prescribed rhythms, into an almost musical form of evocation of deep psychological insights. In *Phaedra,* for example, Phaedra, the wife of Theseus, who is almost mad for the love of her stepson, Hippolytus, attempts to reveal her passion to him:

> *Ah, yes. For Theseus*
> *I languish and I long, not as the Shades*
> *Have seen him, of a thousand different forms*
> *The fickle lover, and of Pluto's bride*
> *The would-be ravishers, but faithful, proud*
> *E'en to a slight disdain, with youthful charms*

[7] Author's translation.

Attracting every heart, as gods are painted,
Or like yourself. He had your mien, your eyes,
Spoke and could blush like you, when to the isle
Of Crete, my childhood's home, he cross'd the waves,
Worthy to win the love of Minos' daughters.
What were you doing then? Why did he gather
The flower of Greece and leave Hippolytus? [8]

It was writers such as Racine who made it possible for a mediocre man like Louis XIV to appear as a Sun King.

A third type of monarchical rule, limited monarchy, was created in England in the seventeenth century. Building upon the powers and the wealth they had achieved under the Tudors, the English propertied classes, both the landed gentry of the countryside and the merchant class of the cities, rejected the attempts of the Stuart kings to form an absolute monarchy on the French pattern. In its place they created a partnership, not of king and people but of king and well-to-do.

OLIGARCHY IN ENGLAND

Rise of the Tudor Gentry. The classes who succeeded in limiting the monarchy had, almost without exception, grown wealthy under the Tudors. By the reign of Henry VIII, the old feudal nobility had almost disappeared, and been replaced by new lords named by the Tudors from the rising class of gentry. The confiscation of the lands of the monasteries and the sale of crown lands had enabled many city merchants, government officials, and lawyers to become landed gentlemen; and they farmed their newly acquired lands with an eye to profit as well as social status. Some great families, intimately trusted by the Tudors, acquired huge portions of the land of the monasteries, and thereby laid the basis for their later demand for political power. Money was also being made in what some writers have called the first industrial revolution. Rapid advances were made in coal mining and in the use of coal as an industrial fuel; in metalworking, especially of brass, iron, and lead; in production of unfinished cloth; and in glassmaking. But the really dramatic rise to fortune was made by merchants in overseas commerce. Under Elizabeth, great trading companies were founded to open up trade with countries like Russia or with the East Indies. English ships were sent to find a northwest passage to China and ended by exploring the northeast coast of the North American continent. Other sailors plundered the Spanish possessions and treasure fleets in the Americas, and supplied African slaves to the Spanish colonies. Other companies like the Virginia company, founded in 1606, saw the settlement of Englishmen in overseas plantations as a source of profitable investment;

---

[8] Racine, *Phaedra,* trans. R. Boswell (New York: Colonial, 1900).

Henry VIII

and the establishment of export crops, like tobacco in Virginia and sugar cane in the West Indian islands, helped the companies turn a belated but large profit for their stockholders. Thus, by the end of the sixteenth century there were a substantial number of landholders, industrialists, and merchants who felt economically independent of the crown, and who were prepared to demand greater influence in government when the policies of the crown were unsatisfactory to them.

The Age of Elizabeth.   As long as the threat from Spain remained, Elizabeth had little opposition from Parliament, to which she turned for money for defense and administration.   Indeed, the national struggle that culminated in the defeat of the armada, combined with a widespread sense of economic prosperity and power, produced a great feeling of national solidarity that, by some inexplicable alchemy, encouraged the genius of William Shakespeare.   The culture of the Elizabethan age was just what a sturdy, exuberant, self-confident, and democratic people wanted—madrigals to sing, love poems to recite, gory tragedies to shudder at, bawdy comedies to rollick over, picturesque manors to be comfortable in. Without Shakespeare, it would have been little more than a charming and somewhat adolescent creation.   But in Shakespeare, with his mastery of psychology, his superb sense of the stage, and above all his unparalleled poetry, drama reached its highest achievement.   The language of Shakespeare (and the contemporary translation of the Bible into English, the King James version) bestowed on English speech a rhythm and subtlety and an emotional significance that have never been lost.   This language, taught to successive generations of schoolboys in England while students on the other side of the Channel were acquiring the sharp clarity of the logic of Descartes, played its role in the dangerous mutual incomprehension of

Eiizabeth I

the English and French peoples that underlay their willingness to fight each other throughout most of the seventeenth and eighteenth centuries. What could be more provocative of national pride than the beautiful lines Shakespeare put in the mouth of John of Gaunt, in his play *Richard the Second:*

This royal throne of kings, this sceptered isle,
This earth of majesty, this seat of Mars,
This other Eden, demi-paradise,
This fortress built by nature for herself
Against infection and the hand of war,
This happy breed of men, this little world,
This precious stone set in the silver sea,
Which serves it in the office of a wall,
Or as a moat defensive to a house
Against the envy of less happier lands—
This blessed plot, this earth, this realm, this England.[9]

At the very time that Shakespeare was writing these lines, Elizabeth had been compelled to appear personally in Parliament to overawe them into granting her revenues she asked, because the sense of national urgency aroused by the armada had subsided. Elizabeth could only appeal to the memory of great deeds done together and to their common pride in England: "I know that I have the body of a weak and feeble woman," she told the prostrate parliamentarians, "but I have the heart of a king, and of a king of England too." Thus, by sheer force of personality she kept the absolutism of her father in being until her death.

[9] William Shakespeare, *Richard the Second*, act 2, sc. 1.

Constitutional Struggle under the Early Stuarts. Her successor, King James I (reigned 1603–1625), was incapable of understanding the secret of Tudor absolutism, that it was a partnership for mutual convenience of king and well-to-do classes. He believed in divine right of kings, wrote a book explaining the theory, and lectured on it frequently to Parliament. "That which concerns the mystery of the King's power," he said, "is not lawful to be disputed; for that is to wade into the weakness of Princes, and to take away the mystical reverence that belongs unto them that sit in the throne of God." Unlike the French kings, however, the English monarchs did not possess a standing army, the right to tax, or a docile bureaucracy. They required parliamentary consent to raise troops and money other than their traditional revenues from customs and their own lands; and they were dependent on the gentry to carry out the administration in the local districts. Both James I and his son Charles I attempted to remedy this weakness, which was particularly apparent as the inflation of the price revolution ate into their traditional revenues. Between 1603 and 1640, almost all the possessing classes of England united against James I and Charles I because their methods of increasing revenue were regarded as constitutional innovations. This is the clearest theme in the English constitutional struggles of the seventeenth century. James I and Charles I attempted to raise revenues that would be independent of parliamentary control, by reviving feudal dues, taking forced loans, and levying payments that were taxes in all but name. They attempted to circumvent the regular administration by founding new bureaucratic councils that would be the instruments of their absolutism. In 1640–1642, both the House of Lords and the House of Commons joined to sweep away these pretensions to royal absolutism. The king's chief minister was executed; and laws were passed to ensure that Parliament should meet at least every three years and should control any extraordinary expenditures.

The Puritan Opposition. The constitutional issue was, however, deeply involved with the problem of Puritanism. The English Calvinists, or Puritans, had made many converts among the landed gentry of the East of England, in the University of Cambridge, and in the merchant class of London. The Stuart kings, like Louis XIV, sought religious uniformity, and not only refused the Puritan demands for change in the Church of England but actively persecuted them. Some fled to find toleration in Holland and in the settlement of Massachusetts; but most stayed behind to oppose the king in England. During the eleven years when Charles I governed without Parliament (1629–1640), he permitted his archbishop of Canterbury to restore extreme ceremonial within the Church and to enforce the use of the Anglican prayer book on the Calvinist Church in Scotland. The Scots reacted by going to war with England in 1638–1639, and their invasion forced Charles I to call Parliament to ask it for money.

But the Puritans in Parliament, once they had helped destroy the king's attempt to create a constitutional absolutism, demanded in 1641 that the position of bishop be abolished and the Church of England remodeled on Calvinist lines. As a result of this controversy, the king found supporters among those who had opposed his absolutist pretensions but could not tolerate the radical religious changes proposed. In 1642, the king attempted to arrest the radical leaders in Parliament, and failing to find them, was forced to leave London to gather his supporters near the loyal city of Oxford. By August, both the king and Parliament were gathering armies for a trial of strength.

The English Civil Wars. Historians are divided as to the motives that drove men to choose between king and Parliament. They agree on the geographical division; the South and East supported Parliament. Socially, this implied that the great landowners and their laborers in the North and

West supported the king, in opposition to the yeomen and lesser gentry of the East and the majority of the merchant class of the big cities. The majority of convinced Calvinists supported Parliament, loyal Anglicans, the king. And here again was a class basis to the decision, since the Calvinist support was among the lesser gentry and the merchants. But was the civil war a class war? There is no doubt that among extreme Puritans it was. The Diggers were a small group who believed in communal ownership of property; the Levellers demanded universal manhood suffrage, and were willing to resort to violence to destroy either royalist or parliamentary despotism. But it is difficult to prove that among the majority of the supporters of both king and Parliament, economic determinism, that is, class sympathy or materialistic motives, dictated the choice of loyalty. Men chose which side to fight for primarily in terms of religious or political loyalty. Many who approved of greater powers for Parliament simply could not bring themselves to fight against the anointed king; many who disapproved of Parliament's pretensions followed their Puritan faith in opposing the king. Brothers joined different sides, a fact that proves to many historians the inadequacy of an economic analysis of the struggle.

In the first phase of the civil wars (1642–1646), the Parliamentarians, or Roundheads, succeeded in defeating the undisciplined armies of the king. In the Puritan country squire, Oliver Cromwell, they found a great general, whose New Model Army, composed mostly of Puritan farmers, was a tough, fanatical force that destroyed the king's main forces at the battle of Naseby (1645) and soon after captured the king himself. Success, however, brought about the dissolution of the parliamentary side, and for the next fourteen years, they tried in vain to produce a viable alternative to royal government. In 1646–1648, Calvinist extremism in Parliament won Charles many supporters from among the parliamentary side; and Cromwell had to go to war again to defeat the new coalition of Scots, Anglicans, and disillusioned parliamentarians that Charles had succeeded in putting together. "We will cut off his head with the crown upon it," Cromwell announced; and in 1649, he did. England became a Puritan republic, or commonwealth. Cromwell purged the Parliament to make it representative of the extreme Presbyterians, but finding them impractical fanatics, he felt compelled in 1653 to take over the state himself. "There was nothing in the minds of these men but overturn," he commented. But Cromwell himself as Lord Protector was even less able to put together a viable government, having as his only support the power of his own army. He could not solve the dilemma of combining rule of the godly, as Calvin proposed, and rule of the whole people, which he sincerely sought. He fought the Dutch at sea, at enormous expense to his own middle-class supporters, and he faced the continual burden of financing his fifty-thousand-man army. His financial exactions destroyed much of his support; the requirements of the godly, which involved as great a proscription of pleasure as in Calvin's Geneva, became increasingly irksome; and after Cromwell's death moderate leaders in the army itself decided to restore the monarchy as the only way to avoid chaos. Charles II, son of the executed king, was called back, on the explicit condition that the powers of the monarchy would be those defined in the constitutional settlement of 1640–1641.

The Restoration.   The Restoration period (Charles II, reigned 1660–1685; James II, reigned 1685–1688) was the height of England's baroque age. In reaction against the drabness of the Puritan revolution, the revived aristocracy led by the pleasure-loving king engaged in all the sensual and emotional excesses, in life and in art. The theater was filled with convoluted tales of amorous intrigue, many of which were being acted out in reality in the court circles. All the foppery of Louis XIV's Versailles was introduced to aristocratic living, the wigs, the ribbons, the high-heeled shoes, the powder and lorgnettes and formalized politeness. But for all the artificiality, there were real achievements in Restoration culture. It produced England's finest composer, Purcell, whose opera *Dido and Aeneas* ranks with the best of the Italian operas of the period; England's greatest architect, Christopher Wren; and some passable poets, including Andrew Marvell. In 1667, the great Puritan poet John Milton published the finest of all baroque poems, alien in spirit to the court of Charles II but with a real affinity for the style of the Catholic Reformation in Rome with its swirling heavens filled

West Facade, St. Paul's Cathedral, London.   The classic columns and triumphal arch of the lower stories of Christopher Wren's cathedral combine harmoniously with the baroque curves and niches of the side towers. (British Tourist Authority photo.)

with saints and angels, fallen or otherwise. In Milton are joined the color and drama of Bernini and the deep diapasons and complex harmonies of Bach, the perfect mingling of the arts that is so typical of the baroque ideal. Here is a baroque painting in words, the fall of Satan from the opening of *Paradise Lost:*

> *. . . Him the Almighty Power*
> *Hurled headlong flaming from th' ethereal sky*
> *With hideous ruin and combustion down*
> *To bottomless perdition, there to dwell*
> *In adamantine chains and penal fire*
> *Who durst defy th' Omnipotent to arms.*

James II, the rather stupid and excessively conscientious brother of Charles II, was unable to live within the framework of government set up in 1660, and he succeeded in uniting both Anglican and Puritan against him by attempting to restore Catholicism, by keeping a standing army, and by accepting French subsidies in place of taxes granted by Parliament. In 1688, the leading aristocrats in England invited the stadholder of Holland, William of Orange, who had married James's Protestant daughter Mary, to invade England, and hold the throne jointly with his wife. In a bloodless revolution, James was sent into exile—he was allowed to escape after he had been captured, to avoid any bloodshed—and Parliament restored once again the constitutional situation of 1641. But this time the circumstances were different, since they were putting on the throne a man who had no right by birth. They were taking for themselves the role of nominating the king of England, ending by that act any pretense that future kings might have to govern by divine right.

Wren's Plan for the Reconstruction of London

Physical Evolution of London.   This constitutional development has its urban counterpart in the physical development of London, whose contrast with Paris is itself graphic evidence of the divergence between the two monarchies.   In 1619, the classicist architect Inigo Jones began the creation of a vast palace complex in Whitehall, that would eventually have run along the Thames north of Parliament, as the Louvre ran along the Seine. Work was interrupted by Charles's quarrel with Parliament over funds; it was taken up again at the end of the first fighting in the civil war, and broken off with the execution of Charles I in front of the barely begun palace.   A new start was attempted again for a brief while until Charles II

sought to avoid reliance on Parliament for his funds.   The land intended for the palace was bought for private homes by members of the nobility.   London, too, was to be denied the baroque town plan that Wren drew up for it after the fire of 1666 had destroyed most of the western part of the city.   An absolute monarch might have enforced the plan, giving London its river terraces, its boulevards, and its monumental vistas.   Private owners refused to pool their property, however, and rebuilt on the plots whose shape

Garden Facade, Hampton Court Palace, by Christopher Wren.   (British Tourist Authority photo.)

Royal Crescent, Bath. The superb terraces of the eighteenth-century spa town of Bath, a summer resort for the nobility of London, mark the high point of English city-planning. (British Tourist Authority photo.)

had been laid out in the Middle Ages. No power existed to subordinate private capitalism to public planning. Yet there was a compromise with the demands of the baroque city planner. The king was not reduced to a position of primus inter pares, like the stadholder of the Netherlands, whose palaces were only glorified town houses. His importance could be asserted on the edge of the city by rebuilding palaces like Hampton Court in the style of Versailles, and even in the parkland he owned in the center of town where avenues, as in Saint James's Park, could be laid out in geometrical patterns like Le Nôtre's. But the well-to-do dominated most of the city, and their baroque was the domesticity of the city square, created not by royalty but by real estate speculators. The only requirement of the city government was that the new buildings should be in brick; and thus, in a century when the population of London grew from two hundred thousand to five hundred thousand, the predominant character of the city was that of the street or square, lined with three-to-four-story houses of undeniable comfort, which had cosily compromised with the demands of the baroque just as their inhabitants had equally satisfactorily compromised with the absolute demands of their monarchy.

SUGGESTED READING

Perhaps the best way to understand the baroque city is to begin with the study of one specific city that was thoroughly remodeled according to baroque principles. Paris is a good example, seen through Orest Ranum, *Paris in the Age of Absolutism* (1968) or Leon Bernard, *The Emerging City* (1970). But one must turn again to Pierre Lavedan's *Histoire de l'urbanisme* (1941), volume 2, or to Lewis Mumford's *The City in History* (1966), for a general survey of the principles underlying city building throughout Europe and its colonies.

The baroque style is described in Victor L. Tapie, *The Age of Grandeur: Baroque Art and Architecture* (1960), while the achievements of individual countries can be admired in H. Gerson and E. H. Huile, *Art and Architecture in Belgium, 1600 to 1800* (1960); Rudolf Wittkover, *Art and Architecture in Italy, 1600–1750* (1958); and Anthony Blunt, *Art and Architecture in France, 1500–1700* (1953). For music, see Manfred F. Bufkozer, *Music in the Baroque Era* (1947).

There are several good surveys of the politics of the baroque age, among them Carl J. Friedrich, *The Age of the Baroque, 1610–1660* (1952); Frederick L. Nussbaum, *The Triumph of Science and Reason, 1660–1685* (1953); John B. Wolf, *The Emergence of the Great Powers, 1685–1715* (1951); and Carl J. Friedrich and C. Blitzer, *The Age of Power* (1957). For the social background, on which much important research has been carried out recently, one might begin with the pioneering work of Pierre Goubert, *Beauvais et le Beauvaisis de 1600 à 1730* (1958) or of J. LeRoy-Ladurie, *Paysans du Languedoc* (1967). In addition, Marc Bloch's study *French Rural History* (1966), originally published in 1931, remains valuable.

The character of Moscow during the long struggles of the tsars to reaffirm their power after the defeat of the Tatars emerges in the biographies of the great tsars, such as Harold Lamb, *The March of Muscovy* (1948) and J. L. I. Fennell, *Ivan the Great of Moscow* (1962). The battles for the throne are best covered in one of the general surveys, of which Nicholas A. Riasanovsky, *History of Russia* (1963) is among the best. C. Bickford O'Brien, *Russia under Two Tsars, 1682–1689* (1952) prepares us for Peter, whose move to Saint Petersburg is explained in B. H. Sumner, *Peter the Great and the Emergence of Russia* (1951) and Harold Lamb, *The City and the Tsar: Peter the Great and the Move to the West, 1648–1762* (1948). The condition of the peasantry is the key to the understanding of Russian social history in Jerome Blum, *Lord and Peasant in Russia* (1961). James H. Billington, *The Icon and the Axe* (1966) is a stimulating interpretation of the whole of Russian cultural history.

The day-to-day absolutism of Louis XIV, with its minute regulation of noble life in Versailles, is described by Saint Simon, *Louis XIV at Versailles* (1963), translated by Desmond Flower, which is a good selection from his diaries. The whole life of France comes alive in W. H. Lewis, *The Splendid Century* (1953). For the Grand Monarque himself, good biographies include John B. Wolf, *Louis XIV* (1968) and the brief Maurice Ashley, *Louis XIV and the Greatness of France* (1946). Pierre Goubert's *Louis XIV et vingt millions de Français* (1966) is very suggestive. On the palace of Versailles, see P. de Nolhac, *Versailles et la Cour de France: L'Art de Versailles* (1930). For the literature of the age, it would be best to read Corneille, *Le Cid;* Molière, *The Miser;* and Racine, *Phaedra,* and then see the relationship of literature to society worked out in J. Lough, *An Introduction to Seventeenth-Century France* (1954).

Tudor English history abounds in fine biographies, perhaps because the people themselves were so excitingly expressive. J. J. Scarisbrick, *Henry VIII* (1968), and J. E. Neale, *Queen Elizabeth I* (1952) are superb. G. R. Elton explains the constitutional development under the Tudors in *England under the Tudors* (1960), and A. L. Rowse makes *The Elizabethan Age* (1950–1955) one of the more colorful moments of history.

For the social background to the English constitutional struggles of the seventeenth century, one should turn to Lawrence Stone, *The Crisis of the Aristocracy, 1558–1641* (1965) and H. R. Trevor-Roper, *The Gentry, 1540–1640* (1953). Christopher Hill, *The Century of Revolution, 1603–1714* (1961) is a reliable survey. After C. V. Wedgwood's biography *Oliver Cromwell* (1956) and her excellent studies of the revolutionary years, *The King's Peace, 1637–1641* (1955) and *The King's War, 1641–1647* (1959), one should consult Michael L. Walzer, *The Revolution of the Saints* (1965) for an explanation of the social origins of Puritan politics.

16
THE PARIS OF THE PHILOSOPHES

Paris was the cultural center of eighteenth-century Europe. It exercised a unifying influence on the society and the intellect of the continent that was felt from Lisbon to Saint Petersburg and from Edinburgh to Palermo. Its taste and ideas were spread by a million admirers who came to love Paris as much as or more than their native lands. Called back to Naples, Abbot Galiani lamented: "Yes, Paris is my homeland. . . . They are exiling me in vain, I shall be back. . . . Ah! my dear Paris! Ah! how I miss you!" To the English actor David Garrick, "London is good for the English, but Paris is good for everyone." And the Russian aristocrat Karamsin, visiting Paris on the eve of the Revolution, expressed the fulfilled enthusiasm of a literate admirer:

So here it is, here is this city which during the course of so many centuries was the model of all Europe, the source of taste, of manners, whose name is pronounced with respect by the learned and the ignorant, by philosophers and artisans, by artists and peasants, in Europe and in Asia, in America and in Africa, whose name has been known to me as long as my own, about which I have read so many things in novels, have learned so many things from travellers, have dreamed and thought so many things. . . . Here it is! I am going to see it! I am going to live there! Ah! my friends, this moment has been one of the most charming of my journey! I have never approached any town with feelings so lively, with such curiosity, with such impatience![1]

But Paris was also the capital of France, in a far more practical sense; it had begun, in Montesquieu's words, "to swallow the provinces." All French life—intellectual, artistic, economic, bureaucratic, judicial, social—

[1] Pierre Gaxotte, *Paris au XVIIIe Siècle* (Grenoble: B. Arthaud, 1968), p. 9. Author's translation.

The Place de Louis XV (now Place de la Concorde). The twin classical pavilions were erected by Ange-Jacques Gabriel (1698–1782) in the mid–eighteenth century as a monumental backdrop to one of the largest squares in Europe. (FPG/ Mathey.)

531

was centralized in Paris. Paris, which at the time of Saint Louis had served a largely beneficial function in unifying the disparate provinces, in providing order and law, and in stimulating the artistic genius of France, was beginning to sap the vitality of the rest of the French state. The great antithesis, Paris–France, that was to run through the rest of French history was already apparent. The English agricultural expert, Arthur Young, was told by the townsfolk of Nancy on the day after the Bastille had been stormed: "We are a provincial town, we must wait to see what is done at Paris; but everything is to be feared from the people [there] because bread is so dear, they are half starved, and are consequently ready for commotion."[2] Thus, the excessive centralization ensured that violent change in Paris would produce vast repercussions throughout the country, to a far greater extent than would have been true in any other country of Europe. In delineating the role of Paris in the eighteenth century, we shall therefore consider three of its many roles: its position as the cultural arbiter of Europe, its function in the centralized society of France, and its character as the incubator of revolution.

THE CULTURAL CENTER OF EUROPE

Subordinate Relationship of Versailles to Paris. In the reign of Louis XIV, Versailles rather than Paris had been the center of French culture, and thus to a large extent, of European culture. But with the unlamented death of the Sun King in 1715, *La Cour* and *La Ville*, as Versailles and Paris were called, changed in relative importance. Louis-Sébastien Mercier, the author of *Tableau of Paris*, which is one of the most revealing commentaries on Parisian society in the eighteenth century, noted the end of Versailles' dominance:

> The word "Court" no longer deceives us as it did in the days of Louis XIV. We do not accept the dominant opinion of the Court, which can no longer make or unmake reputations of any kind, nor do we murmur with ridiculous humility as of yore, "The Court has decided" this or that. The verdict of the Court is merely quashed, and we just say: "They don't know anything about it at Versailles; they have no ideas on the subject; they could not have any; they have, in short, no conception about the matter at all." The Court itself, as all can see, dare not pronounce any favorable verdict on a book, a play, or some other new masterpiece, nor on any event of remarkable or extraordinary nature without first awaiting the sentence of the capital.[3]

The importance of Paris had first been reasserted by the regent, Philip of Orléans, when he moved the five-year-old king, Louis XV, into the Tuileries palace and himself took over Richelieu's old home across the street in the Palais Royal. The court never recovered from the attack on its empty ceremonial led by the debauched but able regent; and when

[2] Arthur Young, *Travels in France during the years 1787, 1788, and 1789* (Garden City, N.Y.: Doubleday Anchor, 1969), p. 148

[3] Louis Ducros, *French Society in the Eighteenth Century*, trans. W. de Geijer (London: G. Bell, 1926), pp. 97–98.

The Palais Royal, Paris. The
gardens of Richelieu's palace,
illustrated in this engraving
of 1679, became a rallying
point for political agitators
during the Revolution.
(French Embassy Press and
Information Division photo.)

in 1722 Louis XV returned to Versailles he was not accompanied by all
the great nobility and high administrators. Even the foreign ambassadors
lived in Paris, and paid only occasional visits to Versailles. The old Cape-
tian palace on the Ile de la Cité remained the seat of the most important
law courts, including the Chambre des Comptes and the military and
naval courts, as well as the meeting place for the Parlement of Paris. Among
government ministries, only those for foreign affairs, war, and the navy
were in Versailles; the rest were scattered in Paris, mostly across the Right
Bank. All the great state cultural and scientific organizations were in Paris,
from the Observatory to the School of Mines. To Louis XV, this neglect
of Versailles was immaterial, since he was seeking a privacy that had never
appealed to his great-grandfather. To Marie Antoinette, the Austrian wife of
Louis XVI, Paris was appealing in its frivolity, and she escaped there when
she could to revel in its masked balls or its evenings of opera. Louis XVI
himself preferred the distraction of his hobby as an amateur locksmith to
the tedium of court life. Without a Sun King, Versailles could not hope to
rival the attractive power of Paris.

Paris as Patron of the Intellect. The presence in Paris of most of the ministries, law courts, and cultural and scientific institutions, and the greatest
university of France was not what attracted foreigners or made it Europe's
cultural capital, however. They were a necessary foundation, but they did
not account for the uniqueness of Paris. What distinguished Paris was a
form of society in which the well-to-do, whether noble or bourgeois, met
on terms of relative equality, and interacted with the leaders of intellectual

and artistic life. The centralization of French life in Paris had led to a concentration there of most of the country's talent and to some degree, that of the continent. Of all the great writers of the century, scarcely one was a native Parisian. Montesquieu was from Bordeaux, Diderot from Champagne, Rousseau from Geneva. The very names of the artists betray their non-Parisian origins. The painter Watteau was Flemish, the furniture-maker Oppenord was from a Dutch family, Meissonier, the master of rococo decoration, from Provence, though born in Italy. Yet Paris attracted them all because in the first place it offered the patronage that was lacking in Versailles and the provinces. Louis XV and Louis XVI were far from being the extravagant patrons of architecture and art that the Sun King had been. Louis XV did little more at Versailles than erect the delightful cube of the Petit Trianon palace. Marie Antoinette's principal effort at building was the erection of the Little Hamlet, a make-believe farm with little cottages and dairy stalls where she and her courtiers could retire to an unspoiled, and carefully cleaned nature. But there was little here to employ the artists of France, who found their patrons among the financiers, the tax farmers, the industrialists, and occasionally the nobility of the capital. Typical among this new class of patrons was Antoine Crozat, who made a fortune as the banker for the Paris clergy and from the monopoly of the Louisiana trade. Crozat built a fine country mansion near Paris and a splendid town house in Paris, where Watteau lodged while he was painting the four panels of *The Seasons*. Here in Paris, too, could be found the wider patronage of the general public, the organized market for art that was beginning to enable the artist to dispense with the favors of an individual patron.

Drawing Room from the Hotel St. James, Place Vendôme, Paris (1776). The unity of style of this room of the Louis XVI period is achieved by a return from rococo to a more classical use of straight lines, rectangles, and Roman floral motifs. (Courtesy the De Young Museum, San Francisco.)

Paris thus became the chief art market in Europe in the eighteenth century, with highly institutionalized methods of sale. Members of the Academy displayed their paintings for sale every two years on August 25 in the Louvre. Artists who were not members of the Academy displayed their paintings in the open air on the Place Dauphine, where Chardin first came to public attention in 1728 with his picture *Le Buffet*. Lavishly illustrated catalogs were sent all over Europe, so that foreign patrons could send their orders or auction bids to their representatives in Paris. In this way, Paris filled the palaces and mansions of Europe with not only its paintings but that cornucopia of lesser arts that was the finest creation of the rococo style—the inlaid furniture of Boulle, the tapestry wall panels of Huet, the clocks of Meissonier, the hand-painted porcelain from Sèvres, and snuffboxes, silver spoons, chandeliers, and candlesticks by the thousand. So great was the market in Paris in the latter part of the century that foreign artists began to flock in to share in it, and thereby contribute to its fame. Even foreign playwrights found it worthwhile to come to Paris to present their works, as the Italian comedy writer Goldoni testified in his *Memoirs*. "I did not look upon my journey to France in the light of a journey of mere pleasure, but . . . I was prompted to accept it from the necessity of securing to myself an establishment." He found in Paris, not only a modest fortune, but a city that fascinated and nearly overwhelmed him:

Paris is a world of itself: everything there is on a large scale, the good and bad both in abundance. Whether you go to theaters, promenades, or places of pleasure, you find every corner full. Even the churches are crowded. In a town of eight hundred thousands souls there must necessarily be more of both good and bad people than anywhere else; and it rests with ourselves to make our choice. . . . Every day I felt myself more and more confused in the ranks, the classes, the manners of living, and the different modes of thinking. I no longer knew what I was, what I wished for, or what I was becoming. I was quite absorbed in the vortex.[4]

What Goldoni had found, however, was a common experience among the sensitive who gave themselves up to the challenge of Paris; the city acted as a hothouse for the intellect, stimulating the growth of one's abilities and rewarding one's achievement. Even the most cynical were compelled to recognize this characteristic. Jean-Jacques Rousseau, who spent much of his career denouncing the evil effects on natural man of the artificial restraints of society, declared that "the spirit which pervades society in Paris develops clear thinking and broadens the mind as much as possible. If you have even a spark of genius, go and spend a year in Paris. Soon you will be all that you can ever be, or else you will never be anything at all." Mercier, after wandering through the teeming crowds in the colonnades of the Palais Royal, where talk rattled as vibrantly as in the stoa of Athens, was struck by the difference from his native province:

[4] Carlo Goldoni, *Memoirs*, trans. John Black (Boston: Osgood, 1877), pp. 352–353.

I am not so absurdly prejudiced as to suppose that there is no good talk outside the capital; or that the clear sun of the arts shines only on Parisians, while the provinces are illumined only by occasional wandering stars. . . . All the same, the mind of man, pressed like a grape by the teeming interests of the city all about him, gives here a more abundant yield. Ideas come more easily to birth, and are themselves more fruitful here; they must be strong enough to withstand the buffetings of criticism, and remain firm in contact with the thousand different and changing individualities which crowd the townsman's life; characters in Paris are more sharply distinct than in the provinces, and some more eccentric. There is a kind of peaceful quality in the life of the smaller towns, where day follows day smoothly as a river flows; but the capital is a storm-tossed sea, eternally troubled by contrary winds.[5]

The Parisian Salons. Paris had succeeded, moreover, in developing an institution, the *salon*, that focused all the city's intellectual stimulation. A salon was a gathering on regular days of the week in the home of one of the dominant ladies of Parisian society, at which dinner was usually served,

[5] Louis-Sébastien Mercier, *The Waiting City: Paris, 1782–88,* trans. Helen Simpson (London: Harrap, 1933), p. 275.

"L'Art de plaire dans la conversation."
Making a favorable impression in society was so vital to an eighteenth-century nobleman that manuals like this instructed him in "the art of pleasing through conversation." (Interphototèque.)

cards occasionally played, but conversation led by the hostess predominated. The character of the guests and the conversation was dictated by the hostess; and by some inexplicable process of selection, certain salons came to be recognized as conferring on their habitués membership in the highest rank of the social and intellectual elite of the capital. In these salons was the ideal mixture of leading intellectuals, open-minded nobles, and clever but elegant women. During the Regency, the serious-minded Marquise de Lambert brought together in her drawing-room in part of Mazarin's old palace such authors as Montesquieu, Marivaux, and Fontenelle; works ready for publication were read aloud and criticized; and for a time acceptance in her salon was almost a prerequisite for acceptance into the Académie Française. On her death, her place was taken by a far livelier and more entertaining woman, Alexandrine de Tencin, an unfrocked nun, the unmarried mother of the great philosopher d'Alembert, a financial speculator, and a well-paid spy. It was at Tencin's salon that some of the ablest foreign visitors to Paris, such as Lord Bolingbroke and Lord Chesterfield from England, were introduced to France's writers, like the Abbot Prévost, author of *Manon Lescaut,* or Tencin's favorite, Montesquieu, whose best book, *The Spirit of the Laws,* she rescued from oblivion by giving away at her expense most of the first edition. But by far the most important was that of Madame Geoffrin, who gathered around her (on Mondays) the finest painters, including Boucher and Chardin, and also (on Wednesdays) the leaders of the French Enlightenment, Diderot, d'Alembert, and Marmontel, at the very time when they were preparing the most important statement of their opinions, the *Encyclopédie;* and she contributed almost half the cost of that twenty-eight-volume work.

Distinguished foreigners gained easy access to the Paris salons. "I well remember seeing all Europe standing three deep around her chair," wrote one of Mme Geoffrin's admirers. Back home, they sought constant news of the intellectual excitement of Paris, exchanging long letters with their hostesses, buying up the books that the Paris presses were pouring out, and begging France's intellectuals and artists to join them in their exile from Paris. Frederick the Great of Prussia, who despised the German language and spoke French almost exclusively, admired Voltaire inordinately, exchanged letters with him for forty-two years, and even brought him to Potsdam for a tormented three-year stay. Catherine the Great of Russia offered to publish the *Encyclopédie* in Russia to avoid the French censors, bought Diderot's library and paid him a salary to keep it for her, and finally brought him to Saint Petersburg for a five-month stay that merely convinced her of the impracticality of his ideas. The leading French intellectuals found themselves in similar demand in Stockholm, Warsaw, Leipzig, or Florence; and even England, the one country that contested the dominance of the French language as the principal vehicle for the intercourse of human minds, fêted Voltaire and Rousseau on their prolonged visits.

Thus, with very few exceptions, Europe recognized the cultural pre-eminence of Paris, and admired the extraordinary instrument for the sharpening of the human mind that had been created by the society of that city. But what precisely was the content of this culture that had been brought to such an exciting peak? And perhaps more important, what were the effects inside and outside France of the admiration of this culture?

THE AGE OF ROCOCO

The Rococo Style in Paris.   For the first time since Paris had become one of the principal shapers of European civilization in the thirteenth century, its cultural impact was not primarily visual. Paris remained a center of the visual arts and itself a superb embodiment of them; but in comparison with its earlier achievements in both Gothic and baroque, its artistic contribution was charming but minor. The city itself expanded greatly with the erection of whole new districts for the aristocracy and wealthier middle classes on the western edge of the city; and here French architects created ever more elegant variations on the basic ground plan of the aristocratic town house. In particular, they recognized the greater intimacy of social life and especially the function of the living-room, or *salon,* by developing a style of sparkling, graceful interior decoration known as *rococo.*

The rococo style was invented during the Regency, itself an age of wild sensual invention. It was an outgrowth of the baroque style, accepting the emotional fantasies of baroque but rejecting the fascination with geometric patterns and magniloquent forms. Its main characteristics were the forms of decoration called *rocaille* (rock) and *coquille* (shell), which were elaborated in infinite variations for almost every type of artistic creation, whether gun barrels, wall panels, doorknobs, or saltshakers. There was thus a unity to an eighteenth-century room that was missing in any earlier period; and the artists recognized their task of producing that unity by mastering every form of decorative art themselves. Meissonier designed houses, tapestry, cutlery,

French Console Table, c. 1740.   The mirror frame carries on the rococo motifs elaborated in the table, combining scrolls, shells, foaming waves, and festoons of flowers. (Courtesy De Young Museum, San Francisco.)

Winter, from The Four Seasons, by François Boucher (1703–1770). In the four panels painted for Louis XV's mistress, Madame de Pompadour, Boucher depicted scenes of noble pastimes in an idealized countryside. (Copyright The Frick Collection, New York.)

plates, funerals, and chairs with equal skill. The French painter who epitomized this achievement was Antoine Watteau (1684–1721), a tubercular genius whose brief career laid down the goals of French painting for the next century. Watteau specialized in movement, the meeting of delicate curves; but he broke with the baroque of painters like Rubens by suffusing his paintings with a soft, delicate languor and an atmosphere of hazy sensuality. His work was exquisitely feminine, with its masterly presentation of the play of light on silks or taffeta, on bouffant hair, or twirling fans. He perfected the *fête galante,* the picture of a group of courtiers idling away the late afternoon in a shadowy glade of some indeterminate forest, pictures of gentle and emotional recollection of the passing of moments of perfect, and undistinguished, contentment. His most famous painting, *The Embarkation for Cythera,* of 1717, displaying a group of nobles preparing to leave the mythical island of love where Venus emerged from the sea, became the model for France's favorite painters until the Revolution. Under the spell of Watteau came such paintings as *The Swing* of Fragonard (1732–1806) and the many portraits of Louis XV's mistress Madame de Pompadour by François Boucher (1703–1770), paintings as charming and as deliberately devoid of emotional stress as a Louis XV wall panel.

On the outer face of Paris, these rococo fripperies left little impression. The architects of the major monuments returned to a sound, if less grandiose resumption of seventeenth-century taste. To this return, Paris owed the marvelous dome of the Church of Sainte Geneviève, designed by Soufflot in 1755, and turned during the Revolution into a Pantheon "for the ashes of the great men of the period of French liberty," and one of the finest squares in the world, the Place de la Concorde, begun by Gabriel the same year.

**The Pilgrimage Church of Vierzehn-
heiligen, near Bamberg.** The spatial
complexity of Balthasar Neumann's
Church of the Fourteen Saints is
achieved by a ground plan of linked
ovals and circles which replace the
rectangular nave and aisles of the customary basilican church. (German
Tourist Information Office photo.)

The Rococo Style in Austria and South Germany.   Outside Paris, however,
the rococo style was adopted with great enthusiasm and skill in Austria
and South Germany, where it produced buildings as subtle in their use of
spatial counterpoint as the great fugues that Johann Sebastian Bach was
writing contemporaneously in musical counterpoint. The patrons who built
these vast new churches, monasteries and palaces were the rulers of the
independent German states, like the elector of Saxony or the bishop of
Würzburg, the abbots of the wealthy monasteries, and the Austrian royal
family and nobility. Their architects were native-born Germans and Austrians who had, however, grasped the best that Italian baroque and French
rococo had to offer, and were prepared to develop their own unique variation of style. They accepted the value of complex spatial planning and the
use of the oval in the ground plan, the interplay of convex and concave
curves in outer facades and inner galleries, and the writhing columns like
Bernini's at Saint Peter's. But they subdued the emotional thrust of the
style's theatricality, muting the colors to pastel shades of pink and blue,
mingling whites and gold in all the complexity of rocaille decoration.

Entering the stairwell of the episcopal palace of Würzburg, glancing up
at the undulating facade and bulbous towers of the monastery of Melk
above the Danube, and especially on entering the sparkling interior of the
pilgrimage church of Vierzehnheiligen near Bamberg, one realizes at once
that the great success of such German rococo architects as Balthasar Neumann (1687–1753) had been to achieve in the molding of space what the

The Chinese Room, Schönbrunn Palace, Vienna. The Empress Maria Theresa followed the prevailing passion for "chinoiserie," that is, genuine or simulated articles in Chinese style, in the tearoom of her summer palace. (Bildarchiv d. Ost. Nationalbibliothek.)

French artists had succeeded in doing only in decoration. Here rococo had become a great architectural style. It is impossible even to list the main achievements of this style, without which central Europe would have been infinitely more barren. Of the multitude of buildings that drained off the wealth of the countryside of Germany and Austria, one must at least mention Frederick's palace of Sans Souci at Potsdam, where he entertained Voltaire; the exuberant pavilions of the Zwinger palace in Dresden, whose startling succession of curving facades served little more purpose than an art gallery and an orangery; the splendid monasteries that lined the Danube, from Melk to Klosterneuburg on the edge of Vienna; and the vast palaces that the Habsburgs built in the capitals of their separate possessions, such as Schönbrunn outside Vienna and the remodeled Hradčany palace on the hill above Prague. Here were the real masterpieces of a style that originated in France but found the weight of tradition too great at home for it to pass from decorative and minor arts into architecture.

It was in "philosophy" rather than art that eighteenth-century Paris dominated Europe, philosophy conceived in the sense of the broadest possible intellectual activity—in political theory, economics, natural science, philosophy, jurisprudence, even technology. France's thinkers, the *philosophes*, believed that they had made their century the "siècle des lumières," the century of enlightenment; and until the unhappy shock of the Revolution they found few to disagree with them.

THE FRENCH ENLIGHTENMENT

The intellectual achievements of the French Enlightenment came rapidly in the sixty years between the death of Louis XIV and the beginning of the American Revolution. In the first place, France's intellectuals had thoroughly absorbed both the substance and the significance of the scientific advances represented by the work of Isaac Newton and the psychological and political theories of John Locke. They had accepted the implication common to both thinkers that the universe was governed by natural laws that could be ascertained by the use of the human reason, especially when that reason was applied to the acquisition of factual knowledge through controlled experiment. The *philosophes* accepted the scientific, rational attitude of mind as the foundation for future progress. That they did so unquestioningly was due to the great advances that science had made following the Renaissance, in what has been justly called the scientific revolution.

The Alchemist, by David Teniers the Younger (1610–1690). The experimental methods of modern chemistry were founded in part on the attempts of alchemists to turn base metals into gold. (John G. Johnson Collection, Philadelphia.)

The Scientific Revolution and the Enlightenment. Science had made little progress during the Middle Ages because the experimental method was not employed to challenge the truth of the established authorities, mostly the scientists of antiquity, whom the Christian Church had integrated into its world view. In addition, ordinary observation seemed to show the truth in most of these authorities. For example, in astronomy, it seemed clear, as Aristotle had said, that bodies fall to the center of the earth; that stars move, as Ptolemy had explained, in crystalline spheres; and that heaven, as the Church taught, lay outside the outermost sphere, the *primum mobile,* that kept the whole system turning. Even the explanation of chemistry that all matter was composed of earth, air, fire and water seemed as reasonable as any other explanation before the apparatus for chemical experimentation had been invented. Simultaneous advances in several spheres, however, made it possible for scientists in the sixteenth and seventeenth centuries first to challenge and then to overthrow most of the established authorities. First, the scientist and technician joined hands, inventing several important tools by which observation and experiment could be carried out. Of these the most important was the telescope, invented in Holland in the seventeenth century, and used with great effect by the Italian astronomer Galileo (1564–1642). From the same skill in lensmaking came the microscope, which was seized on by biologists. The barometer, the pressure gauge for measurement of air and gas pressure, the thermometer, the air pump, all were invented when the need of accurate measurement and tools for experiment was felt. Secondly, scientists realized that further explanation of the natural world was dependent on advances in mathematics. The language of the universe, wrote Galileo, "is written in the mathematical language, and its characters are triangles, circles, and other geometrical figures, without the aid of which it is impossible to understand a word of it, without which one wanders vainly through a dark labyrinth." [6] Arabic numerals had already been adopted in place of Roman numerals in the late Middle Ages. At the end of the sixteenth century, the decimal system was invented to deal with the problem of fractions. Shortly afterwards, an Englishman developed the system of logarithmic tables, cutting by half the time scientists spent in calculation. In 1637, Descartes made public his analytical geometry, a totally new branch of mathematics by which geometrical relationships could be expressed in algebraic equations, and vice versa. At the end of the seventeenth century, the German philosopher Leibniz and the English scientist Isaac Newton independently invented differential calculus. Without these mathematical tools, the scientific revolution would have been impossible. Third, these new tools were used effectively because scientists developed the experimental method, whose principal popularizers were Francis Bacon in England and Descartes in France. "Neither the hand without instruments nor the unassisted understanding can do much," wrote Bacon. "We have good ground of hope, from the close and strict union of the experimental and rational faculty, which have not hitherto been united." [7]

Medicine was the first sphere to show the results that could be obtained from careful observation and experiment; and by the middle of the seven-

[6] Cited in F. Sherwood Taylor, *A Short History of Science and Scientific Thought* (New York: Norton, 1963), p. 138.
[7] Ibid., p. 104.

teenth century, many of the teachings of the Greek writer Galen had been thrown out, notably as a result of the anatomical treatises of Vesalius and the experiments of William Harvey (1578–1657), who in 1628 proved the circulation of the blood. But the most startling advances were made in astronomy because progress in the explanation of planetary motion involved an understanding of the nature of all motion and the relationship of all matter; and it was here that the established authority of Aristotle and Ptolemy was most firmly supported by the repressive instruments of the Catholic Church. Change came relatively slowly. In 1542, a Polish clergyman, Nicolaus Copernicus (1473–1543), in the search for a more perfect explanation of the universe that would agree with his conception of a perfect God, proposed that the earth moved around the sun. To his contemporaries, Copernicus seemed merely to have simplified astronomical explanation without producing any proof for the abandonment of the belief in a heliocentric universe. The Dane Tycho Brahe, whose very accurate observations of the movements of the planets made possible the next advances in mathematical explanation of the heavens, was not convinced of the accuracy of Copernicus's view; and it was only in the early seventeenth century that Johannes Kepler (1571–1630), an erratic genius seeking the accurate description of the harmonies of the music of the spheres, made sense of Tycho's observations. In his three laws of planetary motion, Kepler not only proved that Copernicus was right but produced laws whose accuracy is still accepted. He showed, first, that planets travel around the sun in ellipses rather than circles and that the sun is one of the focuses of the ellipse. His second law states that planets do not travel at uniform speed, but that the motion can be described mathematically: A line drawn from the planet to the sun sweeps over equal areas in equal times. Finally, according to his third law, the time taken by all planets to complete their orbits can be described by a single mathematical formula: The squares of the period of the orbit are proportional to the cubes of their mean distances from the sun. The Italian physicist and astronomer Galileo took the attack upon the authority of Aristotle much further, by attacking his central concept of motion, namely that all bodies would remain at rest unless moved by some external force. Galileo showed that through "inertia" bodies would continue moving forever at the same speed as the planets were doing, unless stopped by some external force. But Galileo was determined to show that all aspects of the Aristotelian system were wrong; that the universe was heliocentric; that the cylindrical spheres were nonexistent; and that the old dynamics was disproved by observation. He was so outspoken in his *Dialogue Concerning the Two World Systems—Ptolemaic and Copernican* that he was condemned by the Inquisition and ordered to recant.

When Galileo died in 1642, many suspected his soul had migrated to the body of Isaac Newton, born in England the same year. Newton was the genius who brought together all the findings in astronomy and physics of the previous two centuries, and described them mathematically. By the time he was twenty-three, he was entirely the master of his age's scientific knowledge, and had already hit upon most of his own contributions to scientific progress.

In the beginning of the year 1665 I found the method for approximating series and the rule for reducing any dignity [power] of any binomial to such a series [i.e. the binomial theorem]. The same year in May I found the method of tangents of Gregory and Slusius, and in November had [discovered] the direct method of Fluxions [the elements of the differential calculus], the next year in January had the Theory of Colors, and in May following I had entrance into the inverse method of Fluxions [integral calculus], and in the same year I began to think of gravity extending to the orb of the Moon . . . and having thereby compared the force requisite to keep the Moon in her orb with the force of gravity at the surface of the earth, and found them to answer pretty nearly. All this was in the two years of 1665 and 1666, for in those years I was in the prime of my age for invention, and minded mathematics and Philosophy more than at any time since.[8]

In 1687, in the most influential book of the seventeenth and eighteenth centuries, *The Mathematical Principles of Natural Philosophy*, he explained in three laws of motion not only the movement of the planets but the relationship of all matter. He showed that all bodies attracted each other, and that the force of attraction is directly proportional to the product of their two masses and inversely proportional to the square of their distance apart. Here was a completely mechanical universe, explicable in simple, elegant mathematical laws. The effect of Newton's book was stunning. In Alexander Pope's famous lines,

Nature and Nature's Laws lay hid in night,
God said, Let Newton be! and all was light.[9]

And it was precisely with this feeling that the Frenchmen of the Enlightenment saw in the scientific revolution the proof of their optimism in the future achievements of the human understanding when working on the physical and the human universe.

Up to this point, only one Frenchman, Descartes, could be numbered with the geniuses of the scientific revolution. But in the latter years of the reign of Louis XIV, science became enormously popular in France. Colbert had founded the Académie des Sciences in 1666, as a meeting place for scientists and amateurs who dabbled in science. Many middle-class scientists found social success in their public lectures on medicine or astronomy. Foreigners poured in to take the courses of prominent chemists. Even court ladies crowded the benches of the more popular lectures. Thus there was a receptive audience in France for the popularization of the great discoveries

---

[8] Ibid., p. 125.
[9] Alexander Pope, "Intended for Sir Isaac Newton," *Epigrams*.

that culminated in the work of Newton. Most influential of the popularizers of science was Fontenelle (1657–1757), secretary of the Académie des Sciences for forty-two years, habitué at all the major salons, and author of the very popular *Plurality of Worlds,* which set out to make clear for any intelligent person the content and meaning of the new sciences. To the intelligentsia of Paris, the scientific revolution, and especially the work of Newton, promised the possibility of the complete comprehension by man of the working of the universe, including the psychology of man and the problem of his political relationships. Thus, the main contribution of the French in the eighteenth century was to apply the lessons of the scientific revolution to other spheres, even though Frenchmen did make direct contributions to science. Buffon, for example, director of the famous Jardin des Plantes, attempted a huge synthesis of all biological knowledge; Lavoisier founded modern chemistry, with his delimitation of basic chemical elements such as oxygen and hydrogen. But it was the belief in science rather than the involvement in the making of science that produced the most important results.

Reform Program of the French Enlightenment. A good part of the work of the philosophes, like that of the early scientists, had to be destructive. They had to begin by clearing away the false knowledge and the erroneous authorities accumulated, as they thought, by centuries of error. The most persistent of the vehicles of error in their eyes was the Christian Church, in all its various forms antipathetic to the progress of reason. The criticism of the Church's persecution and the demand for universal religious toleration was forcibly expressed by Pierre Bayle in his *Historical and Critical Dictionary,* one of the books most influential on the thinking of the Enlightenment. But it was taken up in its most dramatic form by Voltaire, who used reason, ridicule, and pathos in his demand that the infamous thing be crushed: *Ecrasez l'infâme!* And when a Huguenot merchant, Jean Calas, was publicly killed with unspeakable tortures on the ludicrous grounds that he alone had strangled his eldest son to prevent his conversion to Catholicism, Voltaire made all Europe rage against the organization that was permitted to carry out such barbarism in an enlightened age. Even when the philosophes claimed to be defending the existence of God (and most philosophes felt that a Creator was necessary for so perfectly conceived a world), they weakened the position of the established churches by arguing in favor of deism. God, they assumed, had stepped out of this universe once he had created it, and merely left to man the power to know Him by using reason for understanding the laws underlying the universe. Moreover, rather than see morality as a law laid down and interpreted by the churches, the philosophes assumed that man possessed in his own nature the capacity for moral judgment. To follow one's moral judgment, which was dependent on an understanding of the laws of nature, was thus a religious duty for the deists. "All that we do know is that the eternal Lord

Voltaire, by Jean-Antoine Houdon (1741–1828). Houdon, the leading French sculptor in the late-eighteenth century, portrayed Voltaire from a sketch made two days before his death. (Courtesy De Young Museum, San Francisco.)

of nature," wrote Voltaire to Frederick the Great, "has given us the power of thinking, and of distinguishing virtue. . . . In the midst of all the doubts which we have discussed for four thousand years in four thousand ways, the safest course is still to do nothing against one's conscience." [10]

This search for a new morality found a second target in the judicial system. Here the philosophes made a lasting contribution to human betterment. They excoriated the use of torture as a regular part of the judicial process, both for its cruelty and its ineffectiveness as a means of finding truth. "An ancient writer has also said quite sententiously," the *Encyclopédie* article on Torture concluded, "that those who can stand the question [torture] and those who do not have enough strength to stand it lie in an equal way." Punishment, they wrote again and again, should be made to fit the crime, an extraordinary idea at a time when the death penalty was dealt out for minor theft, and imprisonment was regarded as too expensive for the state. This view of punishment was merely one ramification of a new approach to human psychology, whose origin lay in John Locke's

[10] Cited in Crane Brinton, ed., *The Portable Age of Reason Reader* (New York: Viking, 1956), p. 366.

Essay Concerning Human Understanding, which had wide circulation in France. Locke had argued that all human knowledge is the product of sense impressions received by the mind and organized by reason into a coherent view of the outer world. At the basis of much French thinking was his famous paragraph describing the mind as a *tabula rasa*. French writers on psychology, especially Condillac and Helvétius, whose *On the Mind* appeared in 1758, felt that the character of a human being was entirely dependent on the environment in which he received his early sense experiences. Helvétius even argued what became the basis of the doctrine called utilitarianism that morality consisted in increasing human pleasure and decreasing human pain. A society in which this was the goal would be perfectly harmonious, he argued, because it would be in accord with the natural law that underlies human relationships and that had been ignored by previous societies. It therefore followed that the perfect society would be created not only through ecclesiastical and judicial reforms but through reform of education, economics, and government in accordance with a better understanding of the nature of man.

Jean Jacques Rousseau, by Allan Ramsay (1713–1784). Rousseau's demand for a return to the natural life of the countryside is evident even in his choice of clothing. (Swiss National Tourist Office photo.)

"Education can change everything," once it had been dragged out of the hands of the Church, wrote Helvétius; and the expulsion of the Jesuits from France in 1762 seemed a good beginning. True education would permit a child to achieve the natural goodness and the power of reason with which he was born. By the middle of the century a host of books had explained how it should be done, books with titles like *New Maxims for the Education of Children, Treatise on the Education of Children,* and *General Principles for Use in the Education of Children.* But by far the most influential was a rambling novel, *Emile,* by Jean Jacques Rousseau (1712–1778). A child, Rousseau felt, should be entrusted for twenty years to the care of a tutor, sent out into the unsullied countryside where he could grow naturally into an understanding of himself and his relationship to nature, and brought through kindness to nurture the social instincts with which he was born. It was an impossible ideal, as Rousseau admitted, yet it had a message that could be accepted in part at least: that the child's emotions should be educated before his intellect; that kindness rather than discipline was the best tutor; that the life of the countryside was a better training in goodness than the life of the cities; and that the goal of education should be to achieve the child's own potential rather than impose on him social homogeneity. Rousseau held that the realization of the individual began with childhood. Only under such circumstances could he achieve the goal that Rousseau stated so proudly at the beginning of his *Confessions:* "Myself alone . . . I am not made like any one of those who exist. If I am not better, at least I am different."

The Physiocrats. In economics, too, the philosophes held that man should be allowed to follow his natural inclinations in order that the economic system should function in the most productive manner possible. The physiocrats, as these economists came to be called (that is, those who believed in "government by nature"), held that the state should leave things along (*Laissez faire; laissez passer*), avoiding the falsification of trade patterns that comes from tariffs, tolls, export bans, and unfair taxation. Trade should be free to follow its natural pattern, that is, the pattern created when each individual attempts to maximize his own profit from the production and sale of goods. But the physiocrats, and especially their acknowledged leader Quesnay, were unable to appreciate the importance of industry and commerce in the creation of wealth as it was expounded in England by Adam Smith, the true founder of capitalist economics. They were swept away by an emotional belief in the sanctity of the land. To Quesnay, agriculture was the source of the only true wealth, and the only genuine producers were the farmers. At the base of their theories was thus an ideological preference deriving from the "return to nature" rather than an economic rationale; but at least they publicized the harsh fact that the French economic system was vitiated by the tax burdens laid on the peasantry and by the ineffective systems of landholding and farm management. Moreover, in an age of inefficient government, they called for scientific administration; and thus provided one plank of the platform that was to bring the middle classes to accept the need for revolution.

Political Theories of the Enlightenment. Finally, in political theory, the philosophes took as their starting point the axioms that Locke had expressed in his *Two Treatises on Civil Government*, and that Jefferson was to define more succinctly in the American Declaration of Independence. All men were born with inalienable rights to life, liberty, and property; they enter into a contract with their government to preserve these rights in an organized society. The English too seemed to have achieved this system in practice, as the philosophes attested who visited England in the early part of the eighteenth century. In Voltaire's *Philosophical Letters* of 1733, written during his stay in England, he painted an England that never existed, in which all natural rights were enjoyed by everyone, perfect religious tolerance existed, and harmony between the classes had been achieved. But Voltaire was setting an ideal for France, regardless of its applicability to England. So too was Montesquieu, in his widely read *The Spirit of the Laws*, although he was unaware of how he had failed to understand the compromises and corruption that made the English government work. Writing on a vast sociological scale, Montesquieu attempted to find all the laws that control the forms of government men adopt. He was particularly impressed by the effects of climate. Cold countries produce moral people with a capacity for democracy; hot countries produce passionate and somewhat untrustworthy types, with a penchant for despotism, he felt. But his most important proposal, which he believed had been achieved in England, was that limited government should be organized by separation of powers, that is, by the mutual balancing of legislature, executive, and judiciary. He did, however, continue to think of the state as a growing organism, and not as a piece of machinery, as Locke would have it, and for that reason he admired the ancient institutions of France, particularly the law courts or parlements. (He was president of the Parlement of Bordeaux.) His method of defending individual freedom was thus to emphasize the "intermediate bodies," like the parlements, or the representative bodies, called "estates," as means of diluting the power of centralized government. Montesquieu was worshipped for a generation as the man who had shown, as the subtitle of his book said, "the relations which must exist between the laws and the constitution of each government, the manners, climate, religion, commerce, etc."

In 1762, however, in *The Social Contract*, Rousseau, whose uncomfortable passion for excessive honesty had led him to treat as enemies the majority of his friends, turned his scalpel to the question of freedom. To those who read the book inattentively, it appeared to move the doctrines of the philosophes from reform to revolution. "Man is born free, and everywhere he is in chains," Rousseau began. Men had natural rights that had

Denis Diderot, by Jean–Antoine Houdon. (French Embassy Press and Information Division photo.)

been taken away by organized society; private property was the source of social oppression. Then, however, with a realism that escaped many and infuriated more, Rousseau asked how man could be free, given the necessary constraints of living in close contact with others. Here he parted company entirely with the Enlightenment. Man, he said, had a double sense of what is right for himself, his individual will, which is a feeling for what is good for himself regardless of other people, and his awareness of the "general will," the sense that all men living together in a community share of what is best for them as a community. A man is free when he harmonizes his individual will with the general will. The purpose of government is to interpret the general will. While it is doing so, each individual is directly represented by that government, and true democracy has been achieved. Where an individual fails to realize that the general will is being implemented, his government has the right to compel him to follow the general will. In short, in Rousseau's most famous paradox, the government has the right to force man to be free. Thus, two separate messages could be read into the *Social Contract*, a call to revolution and a justification of the right of a small group of leaders to take totalitarian power in order to do what is best for society. The question Rousseau had posed was more important than his solution. He had recognized the inherent problem of democracy, that rule by the majority can imply suppression of the minority. He had asked, How can a minority be as free as a majority in a representative state?

"Printing," from the Encyclo-pédie. The technical articles in the Encyclopédie were illustrated by detailed and extremely accurate engravings, such as this depiction of the preparation of type for printing. (French Embassy Press and Information Division photo.)

The Encyclopédie. The most effective instrument for the spread of the ideas of the philosophes was the *Encyclopédie*, whose twenty-eight volumes appeared between 1751 and 1772. The *Encyclopédie* was the most ambitious of a series of volumes attempting to illustrate all human knowledge that appeared in the middle of the century. Largely the work of Denis Diderot (1713–1784) and Jean d'Alembert (1717–1783), it made an appeal to this technical-minded age by dealing at length and with fine illustrations with both the advances of science and industrial technology. It reproduced engravings, for example, on how to make Auvergne cheese, beat gold, prepare wigs, and manufacture glass. It even explained how to make gunpowder. But most of all it was a vehicle for the ideas of the philosophes in all the areas in which they saw the need for reform; and all the contributors wrote with a personal didactic passion that has distinguished few other encyclopedias. The article on government, for example, stated, "the

greatest good of the people is in liberty. Liberty is to the body of the state
what health is to each individual." Under Press, it noted "the disadvantages
of this liberty [of the press] are so inconsiderable compared to its advantages
that this ought to be the common right of the universe, and it is certainly
advisable to authorize its practice in all governments." Under Political
Economy, Rousseau stated his theory of the general will. Under Political
Authority, Diderot laid down that "the prince owes to his very subjects the
authority that he has over them; and this *authority* is limited by the laws of
nature and the state." [11] Attacked in France by the Church and censored
by the state, the *Encyclopédie* found a surprising welcome in the courts of
Catherine the Great of Russia and Frederick the Great of Prussia; and it was
here, among the "enlightened" despots, that the philosophes hoped to see
many of their ideas put into practice.

Despotic Disciples of the Parisian Enlightenment. The great attraction
of the philosophes to many rulers of the late eighteenth century was
their demand that government be scientific, as well as their belief that
they had hit upon those scientific principles that should be applied for
effective government. Throughout Europe, monarchs pored over the writings of the philosophes, sought their advice by letter, and begged or
bribed them to come in person. A similar attitude was displayed not only
by the rulers of the powerful states like Russia, Prussia, and Austria, but
also by rulers in Spain, Portugal, Sweden, Tuscany, and many lesser German princely states.

The less complicated reforms proposed by the philosophes, such as legal and judicial reforms, were applied at once without too much difficulty. Almost all the enlightened despots, for example, abandoned or
restricted the use of torture, and began a thorough reworking of the body
of law in their countries. Many of them sought to follow the teachings of
the physiocrats. They abolished internal tolls that hampered the movement of goods, cut down on external tariffs, and even occasionally tried
a policy of free trade. A few, of whom Joseph II of Austria (reigned 1780–
1790) was the most important, tried to put an end to serfdom, and restore
the productivity of agriculture. All set out to restrict the power of the
churches in their states, especially the influence of the Jesuits; but again,
none went as far as Joseph, who proclaimed total religious freedom and
equality, set up a secular system of education, and confiscated the vast
wealth of many of the monasteries. Life undoubtedly became more tolerable for the subjects of the enlightened despots, in their relations with the
law, the bureaucracy, the Church, and the landlord. But it is also clear that
the majority of the enlightened despots did not seek far-reaching change,
and that those who did failed to achieve it. Frederick the Great (reigned

[11] Denis Diderot, *The Encyclopedia: Selections,* ed. Stephen J. Gendzier (New York: Harper
Torchbook, 1967), pp. 125, 199, 186.

1740–1786), for example, retained most of the mercantilist controls over Prussia's economy, using all the instruments available to him, such as tariffs, subsidies, and heavy taxation, to direct economic planning from above. Catherine paid little attention to the representative assemblies she called, ignored the proposed legal reforms, strengthened the nobility's hold over Russia's serfs, and told Diderot that the philosophes had no understanding of the practical problems of government: "You work only upon paper which endures all things . . . but I, poor Empress as I am, work on the human skin which is irritable and ticklish to a different degree." As for Joseph, the best-intentioned and most impatient of all the reforming monarchs, he was compelled to drop his plans for freeing the serfs against the opposition of his nobility, abandon his tax reforms, and moderate his plans for integrating the peoples of his empire. He composed his own epitaph: "Here lies Joseph, who had the misfortune to see all his plans fail."

In foreign policy, even Joseph could not break with the cold calculation of national self-interest that gave the lie to the professions of Enlightenment of the despots, nor avoid the disastrous economic effects of the willingness to embark on almost constant war for territorial aggrandizement. Frederick the Great seized Silesia from Austria in 1740, when it became possible to contest the right of a woman, Maria Theresa, to inherit the Austrian throne. He thus plunged Prussia into two devastating wars (the War of Austrian Succession, 1740–1748, and the Seven Years' War, 1756–1763), in which the Russian armies occupied his capital Berlin and he came close to losing his own throne. The most cynical actions of the enlightened despots were, however, the three partitions of 1772, 1793, and 1795, by which they removed Poland from the map as an independent state. Poland was admittedly one of the worst governed states in eighteenth-century Europe, dominated by a hereditary nobility who elected their own monarch in elections that recurrently invited the intervention of the major states of Europe. The country was economically stagnant and politically chaotic. Thus, when Frederick and Catherine agreed to help themselves to large portions of Poland and coerced the Austrians into participating for fear of upsetting the balance of power in eastern Europe, the Poles found no support either among the other states of Europe or among the philosophes themselves. Curiously enough, it was the First Partition that drove the Poles to study the writings of the philosophes, and in the brief intermission before the Second Partition the king, Stanislas Poniatowski, and some of the more wide-awake nobility attempted to found a new constitution, carry out legal reforms, renovate education, and even win over the peasantry. It was too late, however. In 1793, Russia and Prussia alone, and in 1795 the original three partitioners, divided the remainder of Poland between them.

The enlightened despots thus took from Paris only what suited them, creating a new style of monarchy but ignoring the message of liberty and equality that lay at the heart of the French Enlightenment. It is often thought that by alleviating the condition of their subjects they inoculated them against the contagion of the political message of the philosophes. But what of France itself? To what extent was the message of the philosophes heard in their own country?

The Partitions of Poland:
1772, 1793, and 1795

The physiocrats had emphasized agriculture as the principal source of wealth; but they had done so with a definite awareness that the ruling elite in Paris–Versailles was impoverishing the rest of the country by its policy toward the agricultural population. If the role of Paris in eighteenth-century Europe was of a beneficent donor of cultural largesse, its role in France was largely that of an exploiter. We must now examine what forms this exploitation took; what reaction it eventually provoked; and since only a small proportion of the Paris population belonged to the exploiting classes, what forms of social tension existed within the capital city itself. In short, we must combine an analysis of the relationship of the urban to the rural population of France with an inquiry into the country's social structure.

**ESTRANGEMENT
BETWEEN PARIS
AND FRANCE**

Old Peasant and Peasant Woman, by Georges de la Tour (1593–1652). De la Tour sought to illustrate the simple dignity of peasant life, which he often used as the background for biblical scenes. (Courtesy De Young Museum.)

Condition of the French Peasantry. A few statistics will point out the dual nature of the problem. The population of France at the beginning of the eighteenth century was about sixteen million, and it rose to perhaps twenty-two million by midcentury and twenty-six million by 1789. At that time, the peasantry or agricultural population numbered twenty-two million. The urban population may have reached two and a half million, with Paris by far the largest city (with somewhere between five hundred thousand and seven hundred thousand). The nonagricultural, rural population of lesser nobles, clergy, and artisans numbered about one and a half million. One important relationship, therefore, was of the peasant to the urban population, whom they outnumbered at least nine to one.

A second relationship of perhaps greater importance was of the peasant to the landowning classes. The hereditary aristocracy, including the old "nobles of the sword," who had been ennobled by serving the king in battle, and the "nobles of the robe," who were bourgeois ennobled through royal service or purchase of office, owned about twenty percent of the cultivated land. The clergy held about fifteen percent of the land. The middle classes owned about thirty percent of the land, mostly in estates they had bought near the towns where they lived. The peasantry were left the remaining thirty-five percent of the land.

In the mind of the peasant, for very good reason, resentment at these two unequal relationships, country-city and laborer-landowner, tended to merge. Paris and Versailles represented in the first place the insatiable eaters of state taxes that were squeezed in unjust proportion from the peasantry. The most important source of direct taxation was the *taille*, a land tax levied almost exclusively on the peasantry because most towns, including Paris, were exempt and most of the nobles and clergy paid only on land they let out to the peasants. Each parish was assigned a lump sum to collect; the collectors were fellow-villagers, elected to the unpopular job and responsible themselves for failure to come up with the required amount. The collectors, wrote an eyewitness, "form a kind of army which wastes a whole year lounging about the place and collecting little but a thousand curses and insults, and all because as soon as the assessment has been made, it is the interest of those who have been taxed, and who can rely on no protection, to conceal all signs of wealth, and this involves a complete cessation of trade and all commercial transactions." [12] Other direct taxes were a *capitalian,* or head tax, and a *dixième,* or tenth, which were not too effective. The indirect taxes, however, which were collected with terrible efficiency by the forty farmers general, most of whom lived in Paris on the right bank in splendid new mansions, were just as great a nightmare. The *gabelle,* or salt tax, was collected by thousands of *gabelous,* and eluded by thousands of *faux-saulniers,* or salt-smugglers. To buy for their families' needs, many risked imprisonment or the galleys. Excise taxes were collected on individual items, like wine, tobacco, and leather, so that a system of universal spying was adopted by the tax collectors to watch a peasant's consumption. Rousseau said he was once given a fine meal in secrecy by a peasant who told him "he had to hide his wine on account of the excise taxes, and his bread on account of the *taille,* and that he would be a lost man if any one began to doubt that he was not dying of hunger." Finally, the state imposed other burdens, such as the *corvée,* or duty to work on the roads without payment, and the duty to do military service if chosen by lot.

In return for these taxes, the state provided very few services to the peasantry. There were very occasional efforts to alleviate famines, which occurred frequently until the 1740s, but there was no general effort at agricultural improvement of the type demanded by the physiocrats. The greater part of government expenditure, perhaps as much as three-quarters (as became clear when Necker published the government budget for the first time in 1781), went into support of the army and in payment on the public

[12] Ducros, *French Society,* p. 272.

debt accumulated mostly in past wars. Most of the rest went for administrative expenses and for the court and nobles' pensions. The majority of the peasants had little or no knowledge of the wars that were responsible for these taxes, but they could see evidence of the expenditures lavished not only on the nobility but on the clergy and bourgeoisie too. Here the peasant's resentment at royal taxation merged with his hatred of the dues enforced on him by the local lord or seigneur. Even when a peasant owned land, he owed dues to a lord that went back to the medieval system of landholding, namely that every piece of land was held by a lord (*nulle terre sans seigneur*); and these dues were very burdensome. They included the right of the lord to hunt over the peasant's land and to graze his animals on parts of it; the duty of the peasant to use the lord's mill, oven, winepress and market; and the payment by the peasant of various monetary fees, such as the *lods et ventes*, when he sold land, or the *cens*, which was a kind of rent. The rights of the seigneurs were held by the bourgeois who had bought land as well as by the nobles, and the peasant made little distinction in his dislike. One may say that he had a vague and unfocused dislike of the state machinery that imposed the direct and indirect taxes; but a clear, well-directed hatred of the local lord and of the local city. The local lord could be an absentee, living in Versailles or Paris. In that case, the peasant envied his ill-tended lands. "The quantity of waste land is surprising," wrote Arthur Young. "Much of these wastes belonged to the Prince de Soubise, who would not sell any part of them. Thus it is whenever you stumble on a Grand Seigneur, even one that was worth millions, you are sure to find his property desert."[13] The lord, however, was often present in the local château, where he became increasingly the target of peasant dislike, especially with the growth of rural overpopulation that occurred in the second half of the eighteenth century. But the peasant hated the towns too. In one of the complaints presented to the Estates General in 1789, the peasants were described as "bent over the earth which they water with their sweat, from the rising almost to the setting of the sun, and from which they bring forth by the labor of their hands that produce, that abundance, which is enjoyed by the citizens of the towns."[14]

It is true that the hierarchical division of the peasantry ran the whole gamut from *laboureurs*, wealthy rural capitalists with farms of up to several hundred acres, through the *manouvriers*, who held little or no land and had to work on the large estates or in rural textile industry. But all peasants shared the desire for certain specific changes. They wanted a reduction in the burden of state taxation and abolition of seigneurial dues; and they wanted more land. The disaffection of the peasantry increased during the second half of the eighteenth century in spite of France's growing pros-

[13] Young, *Travels*, p. 59.
[14] Cited in E. N. Williams, *The Ancien Régime in Europe: Government and Society in the Major States, 1648–1789* (New York: Harper & Row, 1970), p. 199.

perity, or because they failed to share in it. The majority of the peasantry scraped a bare subsistence from the land, especially when rural population grew by two million in the fifty years before the Revolution, and they therefore had no surplus agricultural produce to sell. Moreover they were the primary sufferers from the cyclical crises that invariably began with a poor harvest but precipitated other forms of rural unemployment, as among the textile spinners. The peasantry was ripe for a social revolution that would be directed both against the landlord and against the cities.

Dangerous Isolation of the Upper Aristocracy. The peasantry, however, were not the only group in the French provinces that felt disenchanted with the French ruling class. Both the nobility and the clergy were divided into those who were the beneficiaries of France's social structure and those who felt exploited by it, and in a very real sense the division was again between those who enjoyed the amenities of Paris and Versailles and those who resented them. Of the four hundred thousand members of the nobility, only a few hundred constituted *Les Grands*, the real aristocrats for whom the court life of Versailles and the social whirl of Paris were formed. Their way of life was inordinately expensive, and many ran through fortunes trying to keep up with the requirements of society. Clothes and jewels, extravagant meals for hundreds of guests, carriages and servants, gambling and hunting, absorbed ever increasing sums as prices rose inexorably throughout the second half of the century. But presence in this social sphere was necessary to maintain one's wealth also, to receive the pensions and fees payable by the treasury, the governorships of wealthy provinces, or appointments to benefices in the Church. The wealthy stayed together by necessity as well as by inclination. From about 1750 on, however, a vitally important change took place in the character of Les Grands. Both the nobility of the sword and the nobility of the robe, who had spurned each other for generations for the differences in origin of their wealth and social prestige, were prepared to draw together in common defense of their position. The upper nobility, which had always been open at the bottom to new blood as a result of newly acquired wealth or royal service, now sought to exclude new recruits, to maintain for those who had already been admitted to the happy circle of Les Grands a monopoly on all the major offices in the government, the army, the church, and the law. Typical of this trend was the demand of the parlements that holders of their higher offices be able to show they had been noble for four generations. In this effort to block the means of advancement into the upper ranks of society to the lesser nobility and to the middle classes, for whom acquisition of wealth would previously have made possible purchase of entrée into aristocratic society, they were largely successful; and their success encouraged them to undertake not merely a holding action but a conservative revolution, the attempt to replace royal absolutism as created in the seventeenth century by a more decentralized administration that they thought they could dominate.

This exclusiveness of *Les Grands* created a gulf between its members and the majority of the provincial nobility and those bourgeois who, though wealthy or talented enough to acquire the lesser titles of nobility, had not broken into the upper ranks before the middle of the century. Often the barrier was accepted with polite resignation. "I should like to pay you a visit," a provincial noble wrote his sister at court, "but to live in Paris I would have to be your valet. We have 10 to 12,000 livres revenue. With that one cuts a poor figure if one is a count or a baron. However, if you visit me, we will be high and powerful seigneurs." [15] But more frequently it caused bitter resentment. The country noble, barely squeezing a livelihood from an unwilling peasantry and an inefficient agriculture, often lived frugally in a broken-down château, unable to afford a carriage and avoiding visits even to the neighboring town. His only hope of economic survival was to press more strongly for his seigneurial rights and to avoid unnecessary expenditure. The outrage of the recently ennobled bourgeois—in this

The Little Hamlet, Versailles. In this dairy farm, Queen Marie-Antoinette and her courtiers created a make-believe world in which they played at being peasants. (French Embassy and Press Information photo.)

[15] Williams, *Ancien Régime, p. 177.*

case a watch- and harpmaker turned financier and government spy—was expressed in the two masterpieces of satire *The Barber of Seville* and *The Marriage of Figaro*, of Beaumarchais (1732–1799). "Fancy following a woman to Seville when Madrid and the Court offer such a variety of easily won pleasures!" Count Almaviva remarks at the beginning of *The Barber*. "That's just what I'm trying to get away from. I'm weary of the conquests that self-interest or habit or vanity present us in endless succession!" But, once married, Almaviva rouses the anger of his valet Figaro, that epitome of social awareness, by pursuing his bride-to-be. In the monologue that caused Louis XVI to forbid the play's presentation, Figaro breaks out against all the abuses of aristocratic society:

No, my Lord Count, you shan't have her, you shall not have her! Because you are a great nobleman you think you are a great genius. . . . Nobility, fortune, rank, position! How proud they make a man feel! What have you done to deserve such advantages? Put yourself to the trouble of being born—nothing more! For the rest—a very ordinary man! Whereas I, lost among the obscure crowd, have had to deploy more knowledge, more calculation and skill merely to survive than has sufficed to rule all the provinces of Spain for a century! Yet you would measure yourself against me.

And he glances back at the ironies of his life.

I study Chemistry, Pharmacy, Surgery, and all the prestige of a great nobleman can barely secure me the handling of a horse-doctor's probe. . . . I fudge up a play about the manner of the Seraglio. . . . Immediately, some envoy from goodness-knows-where complains that some of my lines offend the Sublime Porte, Persia, some part or other of the East Indies, the whole of Egypt, and the Kingdoms of Cyrenaica, Tripoli, Tunis, Algiers, and Morocco. . . . I was on the point of giving up in despair when it occurred to someone to offer me a job. Unfortunately I had some qualification for it—it needed a knowledge of figures—but it was a dancer who got it! Nothing was left to me but stealing, so I set up as a banker at. . . . Now notice what happens! I dine out in style, and so-called fashionable people throw open their houses to me—keeping three-quarters of the profits for them-selves. . . . But since everybody was involved in some sort of swindle and at the same time demanding honesty from me, I inevitably went under again.[16]

The Split within the Clergy. The clergy of the Catholic Church were equally split, the barrier again being the nobility's determination to monopo-lize the higher offices. In 1789, only one French bishop was not noble. A majority of the archbishops and bishops and of the abbots of the mon-asteries were absentees, drawing over half of the revenues of their office to support their life either in their country homes or, in the case of sons of the higher nobility, in Versailles and Paris. Certain archbishoprics passed

[16] Pierre-Augustin Caron de Beaumarchais, *The Barber of Seville; The Marriage of Figaro*, trans. John Wood (Harmondsworth, England: Penguin, 1964), pp. 199–202.

regularly to the younger sons of a noble family; Strasbourg, for example, was virtually the property of the de Rohan family, and always brought with it a cardinal's hat. Frequently, a nobleman would make up his revenues by becoming abbot of three or four monasteries at once; and the leaders of the Church, meeting regularly in Paris in a General Assembly, frustrated every effort of the government to tax them and paid instead a "free gift" of about two percent of their income. Lacking any kind of religious vocation, many though by no means all of the upper clergy led a comfortable social life in Paris. To be sent to one's diocese by order of the king was known as "being exiled." The Cardinal de Polignac was bishop of Auch for fifteen years, and never once went there. Talleyrand, the versatile servant of royal, revolutionary, and imperial governments, visited his bishopric of Autun only once, to be elected to the Estates General. The real work of caring for the rural multitudes was done by the village priest, or curé, who had the ungrateful task of collecting the Church's tithe, usually an amount between one-twelfth and one-twentieth of the value of a peasant's produce, in order to send more than half of it to some absentee superior. The annoyance of the local priests was probably less great than the resentment of the aspiring clergy in the middle ranks, the bright young men of peasant or bourgeois background who had taken positions in monasteries or cathedrals or as professors in seminaries, and who found that the highest ranks of the Church were closed to them. This change in the character of a Church that had for centuries offered the main avenue of social mobility to a poor boy of talent had again infected one of the relatively healthy parts of the ancien régime.

The function of Paris and Versailles as the center of government and of privileged society—and thus as the source of taxes, seigneurial dues, and tithes—was therefore regarded with resentment by the majority of the peasantry, by the lower groups of the nobility, and by lower and middle ranks of the clergy. It was, however, the bourgeoisie who were to turn that resentment into support for revolution; and they, as an urban class that had come unwillingly to share the opposition of the non-urban French population to the royal government and the closed aristocracy, had to make a big propaganda effort to win over the disaffected groups of the French countryside.

THE RELUCTANT DISAFFECTION OF THE BOURGEOISIE

The French bourgeoisie, that variegated class engaged in finance, business, commerce, and the professions that lay between the nobility on the one hand and the manual workers on the other, was by far the most economically progressive class in French society. It was also, until the late eighteenth century, socially conservative. From the 1770s on, however, the bourgeoisie became annoyed at the combination of ineffective royal government and of the newly imposed barriers to upward social mobility. They then reluctantly concluded that the teachings of the philosophes on efficient administration could only be applied after political revolution. In this process the evolution of attitude of the bourgeoisie of all France's cities was similar, even though as always it was Paris that gave the lead.

Character of the French Bourgeoisie. The bourgeoisie was not large in number. In Paris at the middle of the century, it has been calculated to number only forty thousand out of a total population of almost half a million. (At the time, there were about ten thousand clergy and five thousand nobles, the rest of the population being shopkeepers, artisans, laborers, and unemployed.) There were also marked differences of wealth and occupation within the bourgeoisie that had great influence on political attitudes of its members. The main division was between those engaged in the professions, such as law, medicine, administration, teaching, and writing, and those in business, whether financial, commercial, or industrial. There was however a constant movement between the business and professional groupings of the bourgeoisie, most notably because of the low social prestige attached to engaging in business. French economic development was hampered throughout the century by the distaste that many middle-class people felt for making money in trade or industry. Many who had prospered sent their sons into law or the Church or the army rather than into the family business; and instead of plowing their profits back into their companies, they preferred to invest in socially remunerative purchases of country châteaux, land, government bonds, or noble marriages for their children. In other words, the middle classes were vitally interested in the social mobility that wealth could buy. In his play *Le Droit du Seigneur,* Voltaire summarized the social plans of a wealthy bourgeois:

I want everything to happen at my pleasure and in accordance with my wishes, for I am rich. So, father-in-law, listen: To dignify myself in my marriage, I am turning myself into a gentleman, and I am buying from the bailiff the flourishing office of royal receiver in the salt granaries: that's not bad. My son will be a counselor, and my daughter will raise herself to some noble family. My grandsons will be presidents: And the descendants of my lord will one day pay court to mine.[17]

Sources of the Bourgeoisie's Wealth. Throughout most of the eighteenth century, and especially in the years 1730 to 1770, the middle classes became increasingly prosperous. Many grew wealthy as a direct result of governmental inefficiency. The government's inability to collect its own taxes, and especially its need for an advance payment of taxes, enriched the farmers general and the thousands of tax collectors they employed. Other financiers supplied provisions for the army, sold the government the bullion it needed for the coinage, and provided the ships and capital for overseas

[17] Cited in Elinor Barber, *The Bourgeoisie in Eighteenth Century France* (Princeton, N.J.: Princeton University Press, 1970), p. 58.

colonization. These extremely wealthy men, with fortunes as great as any in the nobility and town houses and country châteaux to match their fortunes, were able, even in the period of noble exclusivity in the later part of the century, to retain their place in the ranks of Les Grands. The Paris brothers who had made their fortunes in war contracts became the greatest financial power in Paris, and were able to sponsor the entry into Versailles society of Madame de Pompadour, who became mistress of Louis XV.

But the widespread prosperity of the bourgeois class was due to the increasing productivity of the French economy. To some extent, governmental measures helped. The currency was stabilized in 1726; roads and canals were improved; loans and state subsidies were given to private companies considered of national importance, including not only such luxury manufacture as silks or velvet but iron foundries and coal mines too. Perhaps most important, the overseas empire, which the French had been acquiring piecemeal during the seventeenth century but had been unable to turn to profit during the wars of Louis XIV, became extremely lucrative. A few ships traded with Canada and Louisiana; but the real profits were made in the sale of slaves from the French colonies of Senegal and Gorée in West Africa, from the sugar and tropical products of the West Indian islands of Martinique and Guadeloupe, and from the fisheries off Newfoundland and Cape Breton Island. French merchants also opened up trade with the Ottoman empire in the Eastern Mediterranean and with the Mogul empire in India through their trading posts of Pondicherry and Chandernagore. During the century, France's foreign trade quadrupled, and all its port cities showed evidence of the wealth their merchants had accumulated. France's provincial cities enjoyed a building boom unparalleled before the twentieth century. Nantes, which sent one hundred fifty ships and as many as thirty thousand slaves to the Caribbean each year, was almost completely rebuilt in the classical style. Bordeaux, the center of the new trade with India and a participant in the African trade, also maintained its old commerce in wine with northern Europe. Its commerce expanded sixfold, and its merchants not only built themselves fine houses but called in Gabriel, the architect of the Place de la Concorde, to build a monumental square opening onto the river Garonne. Industry, however, lagged behind commerce, although a few large fortunes were made in textiles and iron manufacture. Most manufacturing was on a very small scale, tightly controlled by the guilds, and subject to the most restrictive controls.

The Bourgeoisie Becomes Revolutionary. Until about 1770, the French middle classes were therefore quite content with their economic condition and with the social advancement that their wealth could obtain for them. From that point on, however, they became increasingly outraged at the damaging effects to their economic status of governmental inefficiency and at the barriers to their upward social climb imposed by the nobility. The most immediate effect of governmental inefficiency was the loss of most of the colonial empire in the wars with England. French colonial administrators, like Dupleix in India and Duquesne in Canada, had laid ambitious plans for restricting English colonial expansion, and for annexing a good part of England's overseas possessions. In the War of the Austrian Succession (1740–1748) and the Seven Years' War (1756–1763), the French government tried to wage both a large-scale land war in Europe and a naval and colonial war in North America, the West Indies, Africa, and India. These undertakings proved completely beyond France's ability and resources. In the final campaigns of 1759–1763, the British took possession of almost all France's overseas settlements in Canada, West Africa, and the Caribbean, and its Indian trading stations. Although the British returned a few of the possessions in the West Indies, Africa, and India, French activity was henceforth greatly restricted; and during the war and after, many merchants who were engaged in shipping and overseas commerce went bankrupt. But the effect of the wars upon French governmental finances was in the long run even more disastrous. As early as 1761, the French government had informed its continental allies that it was on the edge of bankruptcy. The root cause was France's inefficient and unjust system of taxation, as a result of which the wealth of the nobility and clergy was largely untapped. Again and again, in the continuing financial crisis that ran from the defeats in the Seven Years' War until the Revolution, finance ministers sought a new system of taxation that would ensure that all Frenchmen would pay taxes in

"Equality Before Taxation." The cartoon represents the three "estates" of nobility, clergy, and all other French citizens carrying an equal share of the burden of the national debt through a national territorial tax. (French Embassy Press and Information Division photo.)

proportion to their wealth. In each case the privileged classes fought back until the king was persuaded to dismiss the reforming minister. French support of the American colonists in their revolt against England, financed exclusively by increased borrowing at interest rates of eight to ten percent, had the disastrous effect of bringing interest on the national debt to half the state's total revenues. Bankruptcy again threatened. The middle classes, who had made the greater part of the loans to the government by purchase of government bonds, thereupon felt themselves threatened by the financial calamity of the state. If one simple solution were followed—repudiation of the national debt—they would be the principal sufferers. If nothing were done, the state would go bankrupt, and the result would be worse: not only would government bonds become worthless but the whole economic structure of France would be endangered.

This threat to the bourgeois's wealth coincided with their discovery that they could no longer buy their way upward in society. The upper ranks of the nobility and the Church had been closed to all except a few of the wealthiest bourgeois families. And this exclusion was being applied successfully in almost all parts of society. It had become almost impossible for lawyers to break into the nobility of the robe by gaining appointments in the Parlement de Paris. The upper levels of the bureaucracy were closed, as were the principal commands in the army and navy. At this point, most of the bourgeois were converted into followers of the philosophes, particularly in the demand for a more egalitarian society. The bourgeois salons in Paris turned first to the demands of the physiocrats for a more efficient administration of the country's economy; but slowly, especially under the influence of the revolution in America, they began to demand institutional change. They were prepared in fact for their role in the Revolution, which was to make France—briefly—a constitutional monarchy.

**THE PARIS
PROLETARIAT
ON THE EVE
OF REVOLUTION**

Nine years before Parisian rioters stormed the state prison of the Bastille, Louis-Sébastien Mercier confidently asserted:

Dangerous rioting has become a moral impossibility in Paris. The eternally watchful police, two regiments of Guards, Swiss and French, in barracks near at hand, the King's bodyguard, the fortresses which ring the capital round, together with countless individuals whose interest links them to Versailles; all these factors make the chance of any serious rising seem altogether remote. . . . We are not practised rioters, we Parisians, and possibly for that very reason an outbreak (if such a thing were ever to occur) would assume alarming proportions. Still, if it should happen, and were met at the outset with prudence and moderation, above all if bloodshed could be avoided, I maintain that the people's ill-humor would evaporate of itself.[18]

[18] Mercier, *The Waiting City*, pp. 108–9.

The Disaffection of the Parisian Worker. Mercier was however closing his eyes to the evidence of popular discontent continually ready to erupt into violence. In 1725, there had been serious uprisings that forced the dismissal of the minister responsible for Paris's food supply. In 1740, the chief minister had been mobbed. In 1752, the mob demonstrated against the archbishop of Paris and rioted for lower bread prices. In 1775, the central markets and granaries were ransacked by hungry crowds, who had to be put down by the troops. But for twelve years after 1775 there was no uprising in the capital, and it appeared to many observers like Mercier that the fifteen-hundred-man Paris guard and the five to six thousand reinforcements stationed in barracks in the city itself were sufficient for any future emergency.

What was universally accepted, however, was the dangerous dissatisfaction of large sections of the Paris population. To many contemporary observers, the conditions of life in lower-class Paris were a sufficient explanation for the sense of grievance. Arthur Young visited it in 1787:

This great city appears to be in many respects the most ineligible and inconvenient for the residence of a person of small fortune of any that I have been; and by far inferior to London. The streets are very narrow, and many of them crowded, nine-tenths dirty, and all without foot-pavements. Walking, which in London is so pleasant and so clear, that ladies do it every day, is here a toil and fatigue to a man, and an impossibility to a well-dressed woman. . . . There is an infinity of one-horse cabriolets, which are driven by young men of fashion and their imitators, like fools, with such rapidity as to be real nuisances, and render the streets exceedingly dangerous, without an incessant caution. [As a result] all persons of small or moderate fortune are forced to dress in black, with black stockings; the dusky hue of this in company is not so disagreeable a circumstance as being too great a distinction; too clear a line drawn in company between a man that has a good fortune, and another that has not.[19]

Condition of the Sans-Culottes. To other observers, and to many twentieth-century historians, it seemed that the discontent reached its height among the day-laborers, or journeymen, who were forbidden to organize into unions and who expressed their bitterness against the low wages paid by their employers by sporadic and ill-led strikes. The most notable of these were in the textile industry, which was the only type of manufacture in Paris to have anything resembling a modern factory organization. On the northern edge of the city there were a few companies that employed several hundred workers, though the average textile workshop still employed only a few workers. But the strikes occurred in most of the oc-

---

[19] Young, *Travels*, pp. 77–78.

cupations where the lag of wages behind prices and the difficulty of getting advancement from journeyman to master provoked resentment. So there were strikes not only by stocking-frame weavers, journeymen hatters, and ribbon weavers, but also by bookbinders, carpenters, and dyers, and especially the large numbers in the building trade. But these strikes were short in length and easily broken, and they were more symptomatic of a generalized disquiet than proof that a distinctive class conflict existed between wage-laborer and capitalist employer.

If Paris did not provide factory employment for large numbers of wage-laborers, and did not do so until 1830–1848, it did provide jobs at just above the subsistence level for semiskilled or manual workers, and at a slightly higher level for independent craftsmen and masters of small workshops, and charity and menial jobs at a level that frequently fell below subsistence for a floating population of the displaced and unfortunate. All these groups composed the *sans-culottes*, the working classes, who by the definition applied during the Revolution did not wear knee breeches and thus did not belong to the well-to-do classes. Some of them lived in localities devoted to specialized trades. The famous fishwives, or *poissardes*, lived around the central markets on the Right Bank, or in the malodorous Place Maubert, where many riots began. Many artisans engaged in furniture making and other handicrafts lived on the eastern edge of the city beyond the Bastille, in the Faubourg Saint Antoine, which had a reputation for unruliness. The tenements of the Ile de la Cité and the neighboring quays lodged the workers from the river docks, the porters, and many of the masons employed by the cathedral. But in general the working-class population was spread throughout the city, although it was more concentrated in the eastern and northern districts than in the newer faubourgs in which the nobility and bourgeoisie had been constructing their new town houses. Masters, craftsmen, and journeymen usually lived not only in the same street, but frequently in the same building; and, of considerable significance for the rapid spread of political propaganda and for the start of demonstrations, they patronized the same wineshops and markets. In spite of the strikes, there is little evidence of antagonism between the smaller master and his workers and not much more of prolonged or organized opposition to large-scale employers. The working classes of Paris were united by one fear, of hunger caused by their inability to buy bread.

Working-Class Grievances. All the working-class agitation of the eighteenth century has been shown to be directly related to rises in the price of bread. In normal times, the Parisian worker spent one-half his income on bread. The riots of 1775, which spread throughout France, were known as the "flour war," because the rioters took over the sale of bread in the markets and reduced the price of a loaf from thirteen and a half sous to eight. The governments of Louis XV and Louis XVI were accused of "famine pacts," of buying up the grain to sell it at exorbitant profits when famine had been precipitated, although for fear of riots they did take elaborate if not always effective measures to ensure the bread supply of the cities through requisitioning, food convoys, and grain storage. In times of harvest failure, such as occurred in 1787 and 1788, these measures broke down completely. The price of bread in Paris doubled, at a time when a general economic depression had thrown up to half of the wage-earning population out of work and reduced the income of the rest.

The Paris working classes therefore had a political platform prescribed for them by their economic situation: they wanted a reliable bread supply at a reasonable price and regular work at reasonable wages. When they became politically active, and at times violent, during the Revolution, these goals remained predominant. But it was not the poorest and most depressed sections of the working classes that were most prepared to demonstrate for a change in their conditions; it was rather the more skilled and better educated among them, such as the shopkeepers, the artisans, and the masters. There is little evidence that these people were directly influenced by the philosophes or by the political writings that were agitating bourgeois Paris, except for a few slogans that seeped down to them. But they did have a strong dislike and distrust for the well-to-do, whom they came during the Revolution to group together as "aristocrats"; a feeling of their right to equality with all other Frenchmen, or more specifically with all other Parisians; and among a substantial minority, a sense of political awareness that was expressed directly by their involvement in the affairs of their own quarter of Paris. When Paris was divided into forty-eight "sections" in 1790, with assemblies and committees for each neighborhood, these working-class leaders would find the political instrument that corresponded to their almost instinctive belief in direct democracy in preference to representative democracy.

There were few Parisians, therefore, who would have agreed with Talleyrand that one had to have lived before 1789 to know how sweet life can be (*la douceur de vivre*). As early as 1753, Lord Chesterfield had predicted to his son:

The affairs of France . . . grow serious, and, in my opinion, will grow more and more so every day. The King is despised, and I do not wonder at it; but he has brought it about to be hated at the same time, which seldom happens to the same man. His Ministers are known to be as disunited as incapable. . . . The people are poor, consequently discontented; those who have religion are divided in their notions of it; which is saying that they hate one another. . . . The French nation reasons freely, which they never did before, upon matters of religion and government, and begins to be spregiudicati; *the officers do so too; in short, all the symptoms which I have ever met with in history, previous to great changes and revolutions in Government, now exist, and daily increase in France. I am glad of it; the rest of Europe will be the quieter, and have time to recover.*[20]

[20] Lord Chesterfield, *Letters to his Son* (London: Dent, 1929), pp. 274–75.

SUGGESTED READING

There is no equivalent for eighteenth-century Paris of Orest Ranum's fine essay, *Paris in the Age of Absolutism* (1968), although much of Ranum's material is relevant to the later years of the ancien régime. Pierre Gaxotte, *Paris au XVIIIe Siècle* (1968) is anecdotal, though based on many contemporary memoirs. Henry Bidou, *Paris* (1939) is a pleasant though superficial account (pp. 184–265). Two older books cover the state of Paris at the outbreak of the Revolution very thoroughly: A. Babeau, *Paris en 1789* (1889) and H. Monin, *L'Etat de Paris en 1789* (1889). Much the most interesting way to approach the study of the city is to read some of the fine memoirs by travellers, especially Arthur Young, *Travels in France during the years 1787, 1788 and 1789* (1969); Carlo Goldoni, *Memoirs* (1877); Jacques Casanova, *Memoirs* (1922); Tobias Smollett, *Travels Through France and Italy* (1919); Horace Walpole, *Letters*, vol. 6; *The Diary of David Garrick Being a Record of His Memorable Trip to Paris in 1751* (1928); and Constantia E. Maxwell, *The English Traveller in France, 1698–1815* (1932). Louis-Sébastien Mercier's huge *Le Tableau de Paris* (1783–88) is abridged in *The Waiting City: Paris 1782–88* (1933).

On the social structure of eighteenth-century France, that is, of the ancien régime, see the modern synthesis by Alfred Cobban, *A History of Modern France,* vol. 1, *Old Regime and Revolution 1715–1799* (1961); C. B. A. Behrens, *The Ancien Régime* (1968), a very suggestive and ambitious survey; Alexis de Tocqueville, *The Ancien Régime and the Revolution,* first published in 1856, for the brilliance of its insights. Modern research has contributed many new findings. Franklin L. Ford, *Robe and Sword: The Regrouping of the French Aristocracy after Louis XIV* (1953) concluded that "the French aristocracy, if it did not have the strength to suppress revolution, had at least recovered enough strength to make revolution inevitable." Robert Forster, *The Nobility of Toulouse in the Eighteenth Century* (1960) provides a local case study. Elinor G. Barber, *The Bourgeoisie in 18th Century France* (1970) found the "revolutionary" attitudes of the middle classes dependent on their attitude toward social mobility. For the sans-culottes, one has to look ahead to the penetrating studies of the revolutionary period: George Rudé's *The Crowd in the French Revolution* (1959) and especially Albert Soboul's *The Parisian Sans-Culottes and the French Revolution, 1793–94* (1964). On the peasantry, the most important research in the provinces was done by Georges Lefebvre, and is summarized in his *The Coming of the French Revolution* (1957) and *The French Revolution from its Origins to 1793* (1962).

Many historians have attempted to seek the similarities that existed among all European society in the eighteenth century. Useful international surveys include M. S. Anderson, *Europe in the Eighteenth Century, 1713–1783* (1961); Albert Goodwin, ed., *The European Nobility in the Eighteenth Century* (1967); Robert Forster and Elborg Forster, *European Society in the Eighteenth Century* (1969). Among the most useful national studies for comparative purposes are Hans Rosenberg, *Bureaucracy, Aristocracy and Autocracy* (1966); Lewis B. Namier, *The Structure of Politics at the Accession of George III* (1957) and *England in the Age of the American Revolution* (1961); and Jerome Blum, *Lord and Peasant in Russia* (1961).

The Enlightenment has been a source of considerable controversy among historians recently. Carl Becker, *The Heavenly City of the Eighteenth Century Philosophers* (1969) argued that the philosophes were not as rational as they thought;

Robert R. Palmer, *Catholics and Unbelievers in Eighteenth Century France* (1961) concluded that "the philosophers, to meet their own needs, reached a conception of nature which was in part that of science . . . and in part that of theology." For more straightforward and also admiring views, see Kingsley Martin, *French Liberal Thought in the Eighteenth Century* (1954) and George R. Havens, *The Age of Ideas* (1955). An ambitious new synthesis is given by Peter Gay, *The Enlightenment: An Interpretation* (1966–69). A difficult, schematic approach is followed by Ernst Cassirer in *The Philosophy of the Enlightenment* (1951), a much freer and more evocative approach by Paul Hazard in his book on the "crisis of the European consciousness," which he placed in the years 1680–1715, *The European Mind* (1963) and in his bubbly survey *European Thought in the Eighteenth Century* (1963). On individual thinkers, consult the authoritative biography by Arthur Wilson, *Diderot: The Testing Years, 1713–1759* (1957); Peter Gay, *Voltaire's Politics* (1965); J. Salwyn Schapiro, *Condorcet and the Rise of Liberalism* (1963). And of course the best introduction to the philosophes is to read their own writings. Good selections from the *Encyclopédie* are chosen in Denis Diderot, *The Encyclopedia: Selections* (1967); Voltaire, *Candide* (1966) is a spicy modern translation by Joan Spencer, and Beaumarchais still sparkles in the new translation by John Wood, *The Barber of Seville* and *The Marriage of Figaro* (1964). Crane Brinton's *The Portable Age of Reason Reader* (1956) contains a wide variety of readings from most European countries. For Jean-Jacques Rousseau, one should read *The Social Contract* and, for his views on education, *Emile;* for Montesquieu, *The Spirit of the Laws* and *The Persian Letters.*

The enlightened despots are surveyed by John G. Gagliardo, *Enlightened Despotism* (1967) and E. N. Williams, *The Ancien Régime in Europe: Government and Society in the Major States 1648–1789* (1970). Useful works on individual rulers include Saul K. Padover, *The Revolutionary Emperor, Joseph the Second, 1741–1790* (1934); George P. Gooch, *Frederick the Great: The Ruler, the Writer, the Man* (1947); Gerhard Ritter, *Frederick the Great* (1968), with Peter Paret's introduction; G. S. Thomson, *Catherine the Great and the Expansion of Russia* (1962).

For the art and architecture of France, see Stéphanie Faniel, *French Art of the Eighteenth Century* (1957); the previously cited Lavedan, *Histoire de l'urbanisme,* vol. 2; Anthony Blunt, *Art and Architecture in France, 1500–1700* (1953); F. Kimball, *The Creation of the Rococo* (1943); and L. Hautecoeur, *Histoire de l'architecture classique en France* (1943–1945), vols. 3 and 4. On French cultural influence, the standard work is Louis Réau, *L'Europe française au siècle des lumières* (1933). Finally, after reading L. D. Ettlinger's article, "Taste and Patronage: The Role of the Artist in Society," in Alfred Cobban (ed.), *The Eighteenth Century: Europe in the Age of Enlightenment* (1969), pp. 217–58, one could spend a few happy hours on the isle of Cythera by idly glancing at the book's sumptuous illustrations.

17
CITIES IN REVOLUTION

In the late eighteenth and early nineteenth centuries, Western society was shaken, and eventually transformed, by forces so far-reaching in their effects that we are justified in calling them revolutionary. These forces—liberalism, nationalism, and industrialism—struck the predominantly rural, hierarchic, and slow-moving society of the ancien régime like a cyclone, totally changing the customary relationships of city to country, of citizen to government, and of individual to individual. Much of the history of Western civilization since the end of the eighteenth century can be interpreted as the working out of the effects of these three forces. As with so many drives within the West, these revolutionary movements were directly related to urban changes, for the cities provided much of their strength and suffered (or enjoyed) their most powerful consequences. The liberal revolution received its most succinct and perhaps most elegant expression in Philadelphia on July 4, 1776, when the Continental Congress declared that it held "these truths to be self-evident, that all men are created equal, that they are endowed by their Creator with certain unalienable rights, that among these are Life, Liberty, and the Pursuit of Happiness." The American Revolution appeared to be direct proof that the Enlightenment's conception of political equality could be realized in practice. Liberalism, however, took on new meaning, or rather a new series of meanings, when revolutionary Paris explored the varieties of political system that could be created within the broad goals of a society based on liberty, equality, and fraternity. The spread of the revolutionary ideals of Paris to the other states of Europe by force of arms, while at first welcomed by many would-be liberals, soon provoked disillusionment; and the conquest of the Revolution itself and then of most of Europe by Napoleon stimulated the forces of nationalism in all the states under French rule. In this chapter we shall consider the origins and development of liberalism and nationalism

The Taking of the Bastille. On July 14, 1789, a mob from the nearby working-class districts of Paris stormed the state prison of the Bastille, which they then tore down stone by stone. (French Embassy Press and Information Division photo.)

573

in cities in which their distinctive features can be most clearly appreciated: Philadelphia, for the first successful revolution for political equality; Paris, for the full anatomy of liberal revolution in a hierarchic society; and Berlin and Naples, for the origins of the nationalist revolt in Germany and Italy. In Chapter 19, we shall observe the birth of the industrial revolution in Manchester, the spread of industrialism to the continent, and the development, in reaction to the blight of the new industrial city, of the theory of socialism.

PHILADELPHIA AND THE ATLANTIC REVOLUTION

The American Revolution was the first successful assertion of the right of colonies to independence from their "mother country." But it was far more than a war for independence because its goal was to safeguard internal democracy, which Americans believed they largely possessed before the Revolution, and considered to be threatened by the British crown. It is because the American Revolution had this character of a drive to secure political equality that some recent historians have regarded it as the beginning of a "democratic revolution," common to Europe and the American colonies, which was intended to assert "the principle that public power must arise from those over whom it is exercised."[1] In this sense, it is justifiable to speak of the American Revolution as the first phase of "the Atlantic Revolution," as the French historian Jacques Godechot does, in spite of the big differences, which we shall explore, between the American and the French revolutions. The Declaration of the Rights of Man was issued in Paris only thirteen years after the Continental Congress subscribed to the Declaration of Independence in Philadelphia; and there was a direct connection between the two. From the vantage point of these two cities, it is possible to survey the whole sweep of the Atlantic Revolution.

The English Colonies in North America. Up to the Revolution—and indeed until the city itself also succumbed to the impact of industrialization in the 1830s—Philadelphia symbolized for many Europeans the most attractive features of the American colonial environment, in its possession of the individual charm of a well-planned city and harmonious community. When William Penn founded Philadelphia in 1682, the pattern of settlement in the British colonies was already well established. In the North, the Puritan colonies of New England, founded primarily as refuges in which the saintly could create their own religious communities, had recognized the economic potential and restrictions of their rockbound territory. Farming was carried out by individual families, assigned land through their township. Production beyond mere subsistence was in wheat, cattle, and corn for sale to newcomers or for the West Indian islands. Along the coast, the towns concentrated on fishing, especially for cod, on ship-

[1] Robert R. Palmer, *The Age of the Democratic Revolution: A Political History of Europe and America, 1760–1800. The Challenge* (Princeton, N. J.: Princeton University Press, 1969), I, 185.

"America," by Giovanni Battista Tiepolo (1696–1770). In this fresco in the palace of the Bishop of Würzburg, Tiepolo reflects the popular European notion of the American Indian as a "noble savage." (German Tourist Information Office photo.)

building, and on the commerce with the West Indies, to which they supplied foodstuffs, rum, English products, and West African slaves. Through their assemblies and especially in the township meetings, New Englanders had developed the habit of administering themselves; and they fought vigorously as early as 1684 the first important royal attempt to restrict their self-government. In the South, from Maryland to the Carolinas, the impetus to settlement had been mercenary rather than religious. Virginia had been founded by a trading company out to make money from gold and trade with the natives; after it became a royal colony in 1624, large estates were granted to anyone who would bring out settlers—fifty acres for himself as "headright" for each person he brought in. Concentration on tobacco, which could only be grown profitably on large estates, further encouraged the growth of plantations worked by slaves; and by the 1680s, Virginia was in the control of a planter aristocracy that already included such families as the Byrds, the Randolphs, and the Washingtons. A similar social and economic pattern existed in the "proprietary colonies," that is, colonies granted by the crown to a proprietor, such as Maryland to Lord Baltimore or the Carolinas to Lord Ashley and others, because the proprietor usually distributed his lands in vast grants to friends and collaborators. Where agriculture favored large-scale farming, as in Maryland, for tobacco, or in South Carolina, for rice, the plantation remained the normal form of farm-

William Penn, after an Original Painting, by Henry Inman (1801–1846). (Loan Collection, Free Library of Philadelphia.)

ing and the basis of social prestige and political power. The individual farmer working his own land, although there were many of his kind in large parts of the South such as the Piedmont or the Shenandoah valley of Virginia, was never able, with the one exception of North Carolina, to take political power from the entrenched planter aristocracy. In the so-called middle settlements, from New York to Delaware, there was a greater range of economic activity and of social class. Large estates, such as those along the Hudson River, alternated with family farms. Religious faith and national origins were widely mixed, from Jew to Catholic, from Negro slave to Dutch aristocrat. Commerce, through the port of New York, encouraged the farmers of New Jersey to produce for the West Indian trade, and other entrepreneurs to go further afield in search of furs and whale oil. To this already variegated colonial scene, the foundation of Pennsylvania added new diversity.

The Foundation of Pennsylvania. William Penn (1644–1718) was a proprietor, like the duke of Baltimore, who was granted his huge province because of his admiral father's favor with the court. But he was also a Quaker, converted to that small offshoot of Puritanism in spite of his father's opposition and totally committed to the Society of Friends' belief that clergy and sacraments were an unnecessary impediment to the "inner light." In America, he saw the opportunity to provide a refuge for the thousands of Quakers from throughout Europe, and indeed from the other American colonies, who were being persecuted for their beliefs. In a pamphlet called *Some Account of the Province of Pennsylvania*, which was translated into several European languages, Penn invited settlement of his colony, and promised the two benefits that remained the lure of Pennsylvania throughout the eighteenth century: complete religious freedom and land on easy terms. Among the many natural advantages of the area, he noted that "the place lies six hundred miles nearer the sun than England, further south, that is, no mean lure to northern Europeans who, not having much of the sun, cherish it more than most." [2] The colonists he wanted, "industrious husbandmen and day laborers . . . laborious handicrafts, especially carpenters, masons, smiths, weavers, taylors, tanners, shoemakers, shipwrights, etc. . . . ingenious spirits," could rent a two-hundred-acre farm for a penny an acre, or buy a large estate for only a hundred pounds. And as the main port and the capital of the province, Penn ordered his commissioners in 1681 to lay out the City of Brotherly Love, Philadelphia:

Let the rivers and creeks be sounded in order to settle a great towne. Be sure to make your choice where it is most navigable, high, dry and healthy. Let every house be pitched in the middle of its plot so that there may be ground on each side for gardens or orchards or fields, that it may be a green country towne that will never be burnt and always be wholesome. [3]

Early Philadelphia.   When Penn arrived to be his own governor in 1682, the little city had already been surveyed and an ambitious grid pattern of streets along the Delaware river front laid out. A year later, he wrote back to London: "This I will say for the good Providence of God, that of all the many places I have seen in the world, I remember not one better seated, so that it seems to me to have been appointed for a towne, whether we regard the rivers or the conveniency of the coves, docks, springs, the loftiness and soundness of the land and the air held by the people of these parts to be very good." [4]

Philadelphia and Pennsylvania prospered together. The colony by 1750 had a population of a quarter of a million people, composed largely of religious groups seeking freedom from the oppression of many parts of Europe: Quakers from England and Wales, Mennonites from Germany, Huguenots from France, Presbyterians from Northern Ireland, and many others. Their diversity was evident in the churches of Philadelphia, which an English clergyman described in 1759 as "eight or ten places of religious worship, viz. two churches [Anglican], three Quaker meeting-houses, two Presbyterian ditto, one Lutheran church, one Dutch Calvinist ditto, one Swedish ditto, one Romish chapel, one Anabaptist meeting-house, one Moravian ditto." [5] The economy was rich and varied, and through the

[2] Cited in Bart Struthers, *Philadelphia: Holy Experiment* (New York: Doubleday, 1945), pp. 1–2.
[3] Ibid., p. 37.
[4] Ibid., p. 38.
[5] Andrew Burnaby, *Travels Through the Middle Settlements of North America* (New York: A. Wessels, 1904), p. 90.

Street Plan of Philadelphia, 1684

0   ½ Mile

(Logan Circle)

(Franklin Square)

VINE — ST.

(City Hall)

Market

CHESTNUT — ST.

Site of State House

(Independence Hall)

WALNUT — ST.

(Rittenhouse Square)

SPRUCE — ST.

(Washington Square)

PINE — ST.

BROAD — ST.

7TH — ST.   6TH — ST.   5TH — ST.   4TH — ST.   3RD — ST.   2ND — ST.   FIRST — ST.

Schuylkill River

Delaware River

Note: Current names are in parentheses.

After the Map by G. Drogenham, published by Jacob Claus (Amsterdam, 1684)

port of Philadelphia the farmers shipped grain and flour, horses and cattle, tobacco, wool, lumber and staves, and bought English manufactured goods like hardware and clothing as well as West Indian products like sugar. The rural hinterland, constantly expanding in area of settlement as the immigrants poured in to take up the rich, inexpensive lands, provided a great stimulus to Philadelphia's growth. By 1760, Philadelphia had out-distanced Boston both in size and in influence in the colonies; and in the urban world of the eighteenth century it had come to be recognized as the equal of most great European cities. "Its fine appearance," wrote a Swedish naturalist, "good regulations, agreeable situation, natural advantages, trade, riches and power, are by no means inferior to those of any, even of the most ancient towns in Europe."

Obstacles to Revolution. Many British observers felt that in this diverse American colonial society a revolution for political equality with Britain would be both unpopular and impossible, although internal struggles for control of political power between the different groups of the American population were inevitable. Because of the vast differences in the character of the economy and the social structure of the different colonies, it was felt that no common grievance could unite the colonists against Britain; and that even if such a grievance existed, the difficulty of organizing a revolt of people of so many different languages and backgrounds spread along 1,200 miles of coast and scattered inland as far as the rough Appalachian range would be insuperable. "America is formed for happiness, but not for empire," wrote Andrew Burnaby.

The colonies, therefore, separately considered, are internally weak. . . . It appears to me a very doubtful point, even supposing all the colonies of America to be united under one head, whether it would be possible to keep in due order and government so wide and extended an empire, the difficulties of communication, of intercourse, of correspondence, and all other circumstances considered. . . . Fire and water are not more heterogeneous than the different colonies in North America. Nothing can exceed the jealousy and emulation which they possess in regard to each other. . . . In short, such is the difference of character, of manners, of religion, of interest, of the different colonies, that I think, if I am not wholly ignorant of the human mind, were they left to themselves, there would soon be a civil war from one end of the continent to the other; while the Indians and negroes would, with better reason, impatiently watch the opportunity of exterminating them all together.[6]

Internal divisions in each colony promised a further source of weakness. Penn himself had constant difficulties in getting the colonists to accept his constitutional plans, and he was forced to change his frame of government several times. The Penn family found itself challenged by a Quaker elite in Philadelphia; the Germans and Scotch-Irish were kept out of membership in the assembly; the Eastern counties were more heavily represented than the Western; and most laborers, servants, farmers, and frontiersmen were discouraged from political participation. Discontent boiled over occasionally only to be diverted in time; in 1764, for example, a band of Scotch-Irish frontiersmen called Paxton's Boys massacred some Christian Indians, marched on Philadelphia, whose government they accused of weakness toward the Indians, and were persuaded to disperse at the last

[6] Burnaby, *Travels*, pp. 152–53.

Philadelphia in 1702.
Twenty years after its foundation, Philadelphia was a prosperous little town clustered around the quays on the Delaware river. (Philadelphia Collection, Free Library of Philadelphia.)

moment by Benjamin Franklin and some other influential leaders. Although the planter aristocracy in some of the Southern colonies maintained a more stable hold over political power, all the colonies felt the turbulence of internal conflict—of the coastal regions and the hinterland, of people of different national and religious origins, of the socially established and the upward aspirants, of factions within the legislatures themselves. But those who concentrated on the divisions within the colonies were misleading themselves, and ended, like Burnaby, in finding it astonishing that the American colonists should wish to revolt against Britain, and be able to sink their differences sufficiently to do so.

Causes of Revolution in America. The American Revolution was made possible, in the long run, because of the positive features Americans felt they enjoyed in the new continent. Most obviously, whatever differences existed in wealth, almost no one was poor, with the exception of the tightly controlled slaves and a very few paupers in the cities. No society in the eighteenth century enjoyed such economic independence, whose basis was the exploitation of a fertile new continent through farming and through trade. Secondly, no other society enjoyed such widespread political participation. The colonists had succeeded in whittling down the powers of royal intervention through the governors and of the colonial elites through the councils, which were usually twelve-man upper houses chosen by the governor; power was largely exercised by the broadly representative lower house, which provided an organ within which ambitious new men of whatever class, or national or religious background, could rise. The acquisition of wealth and the access to political power thus presented ways of upward mobility that were closed in eighteenth-century France. Moreover, until the 1760s, the British government had adopted, almost unconsciously, a policy of "salutary neglect" toward its American colonies, trying only rarely to curb the growth of the political power of the colonial governments and permitting the colonies to evade the restrictive effects of the mercantilist laws officially governing the economic relations of the colonies and the mother country. The American colonists were largely satisfied with the structure of colonial life. Where dissatisfaction existed, they believed machinery existed for remedy, without recourse to internal revolution or external revolt. The Revolution occurred because a sufficiently large number of colonists, though far from a majority, came to feel, in the thirteen years after the defeat of their French rivals in North America in 1763, that the British government was attempting to destroy their satisfactory status within the empire.

The changes introduced by the British government in 1763–1776 affected all sections of American colonial society, and for that reason the Revolution cannot be ascribed to any one group exclusively, either the cities or farms, the radicals or the planters, the merchants or frontiersmen. When the British attempted to solve the Indian problem by banning white settlement west of the Appalachian Mountains, they annoyed not only the frontiersmen but many who had hoped to move west in search of new land. The effort to aid the sugar planters of the British West Indies by enforcing prohibitive duties against sugar from the French islands infuriated the molasses manufacturers and rum merchants. The Stamp Act, intended to raise revenue for support of the British army stationed in the colonies for their defense, by sale of stamps on all types of legal documents, newspapers, and even playing cards, was a heavy direct tax affecting everyone, and it was met both by direct violence against the sellers of the stamps and by the more important complaint that it was taxation without representation. The imposition of import taxes collected at the colonial ports on items such as tea annoyed all the city merchants as well as their customers, while the tightening of the Trade and Navigation Acts infuriated shipbuilders, shipowners, colonial manufacturers, and farmers alike, all of whom objected to the assumption that the colonies represented merely a source of raw materials and a market for the mother country. Finally, when resistance in Boston provoked the Coercive Acts, including the closing of the port and the moving of the capital to Salem, all the colonists assumed this to be the final act of a gigantic conspiracy plotted by the British government to deprive them of their liberty. Historians have uncovered many other motives as well as the desire to be rid of these new encroachments of British power. It has been suggested, for example, that Southern planters saw revolution as a means of canceling their debts to English merchants, and that the smugglers

Philadelphia in 1761.
(Philadelphia Collection,
Free Library of Philadelphia.)

of the seaports were outraged at the curtailment of their activities. But the overwhelming feeling was of repugnance for the political controls exercised by a corrupt and oppressive Britain. Philadelphia's leading citizen summed up the feeling in 1775:

When I consider the extreme corruption prevalent among all orders of men in this old rotten state, and the glorious public virtue so predominant in our rising country, I cannot but apprehend more mischief than benefit from a closer union. I fear they will drag us after them in all the plundering wars which their desperate circumstances, injustice, and rapacity may prompt them to undertake; and their wide-wasting prodigality and profusion is a gulf that will swallow up every aid we may distress ourselves to afford them. Here numberless and needless places, enormous salaries, pensions, perquisites, bribes, groundless quarrels, foolish expeditions, false accounts or no accounts, contracts, and jobs, devour all revenue and produce continual necessity in the midst of natural plenty, I apprehend, therefore, that to unite us intimately will only be to corrupt and poison us also.[7]

The Cities and the Revolution.   The role of the cities was to convert this far-reaching dissatisfaction with Britain expressed by Benjamin Franklin into a movement for independence. The grievances with the mercantilist system of empire were felt strongly in the colonial cities, especially when in the early eighteenth century they had advanced in size and complexity of economic activity beyond the stage of mere transshipment centers. Philadelphia reached this point in the 1740s, when many of its merchants turned to smuggling rather than accept the restriction of the geographical area open to their trade. Its harbor, according to the governor, was soon swarming "with shallops unloading these illegal cargoes, brought at their return, and cheating the King of his dutys, besides carrying provisions and ready money to the Enemy." Moreover, the opening of the inland regions provided a ready market for manufactured goods that the cities, in view of their increasing ability to do so, preferred to supply themselves rather than act as agents for British goods. Surplus capital from the cities also moved westward for land speculation, until blocked by the ban on settlement beyond the Appalachians. The cities too were accustomed to dominating the legislature of their colonies; and so the political elite of Philadelphia, of Newport, and of Boston enjoyed powers that were far more widely distributed geographically, if not socially, than in such rural states as Virginia, New Jersey, or Vermont. It was in the cities that the first counterattack against British policy, through trade boycott, could be most easily planned.

While directly aggrieved, the cities had prepared the theoretical basis for a break with Britain. The ideas of the Enlightenment, both in its English origins and its French development, entered America through the cities.

---

[7] Cited in Bernard Bailyn, *The Ideological Origins of the American Revolution* (Cambridge, Mass.: Harvard University Press, 1967), p. 136.

**The Bank of Pennsylvania,
Philadelphia, by W. Birch.**
The City Tavern, where the
revolutionary committee of
merchants met, stands to the
left of the Ionic portico of
the bank. (Philadelphia
Collection, Free Library of
Philadelphia.)

The club provided a substitute for the salon. Before the Revolution, Philadelphia had more than fifty; and they provided the organization for many of
the militia groups formed when conflict began. Merchants met regularly
in coffee houses and taverns, where local politics was frequently settled;
and it was here that the early revolutionary committees were formed. In
1774, Paul Revere informed the merchants at Philadelphia's fashionable
City Tavern of the closing of the port of Boston! Here, and in such voluntary municipal activities as the fire companies or police protection and
often the establishment of schools, habits of coordination were established
and ideas exchanged easily. Through books published by Philadelphia's
forty-two printers and its seven newspapers, and importation of books,
all the leading works of Enlightenment thought found their way into the
colony; lending libraries dispersed them widely; and the meetings of the
legislature in the State House on Walnut Street (soon to become Independence Hall) were enlivened with references to Locke, to Montesquieu,
and to Voltaire. The ease with which men like Franklin could circulate in
the salons of Paris provided proof of their acceptance into the inner circles
of the Enlightenment.

The cities helped to provide not only the ideas of political equality but
the organization and the men that could seek it. The coastwise shipping
carried the messages among the committees of correspondence that exchanged news among the colonies of acts of the British government and of
measures to combat them. The Sons of Liberty, groups of middle-class

Carpenters' Hall, Philadelphia. The First Continental Congress met in this hall in 1774 to discuss united action of the thirteen colonies against British rule. (Convention and Tourist Bureau, Philadelphia.)

citizens determined to use rabble-rousing techniques to block British measures like the Stamp Act and to create a spirit of insurgency, were predominantly a creation of the coastal cities; and in general, the most radical leaders of the independence movement came from the cities. And it was in the cities that the most far-reaching constitutional changes were carried out. The first Continental Congress, to which Philadelphia acted as host in 1774, was a revolutionary assembly, chosen illegally by revolutionary conventions or by committees of the legislatures, and it evolved during the next two years into a federal government. But some colonies went even further in remodeling their own constitutions. A mass meeting of four thousand people in Philadelphia in May 1776 demanded a constitutional convention; it was called by irregular means; and dominated by democrats from the West and radicals from the city, it set up a constitution that gave all male taxpayers over twenty-one the right to vote and to be elected, and imposed strict controls of the legislature over the other branches of government. The radicals too ensured that Philadelphia would remain faithful to the Revolution by seizing control of the city. The Tory supporters of the British were ostracized, and three thousand fled. The Quaker patriciate, who had tried to remain neutral, were excluded from power. The radical Whigs, representing the newer money made in shopkeeping, craft workshops, and commerce, were able to take the lead from the moderate Whigs, who had first opposed British policy but in 1776 had drawn back from the violence of an independence struggle. In all the colonies, new constitutions were written, although all were not as radical as those of Pennsylvania and Massachusetts. Nevertheless, this "internal revolution" formed a significant part of the message of political equality that Europeans were learning from the American war of independence. Moreover, the principle that all power derives from the people (and not from the colonies which had become states) was reaffirmed in the Constitutional Convention, which met in Philadelphia in 1787; and although the final Constitution compromised with the powers of the states, it provided further stimulus to the growing impatience in Europe for greater political equality in place of the ancien régime.

The State House, Philadelphia, in 1778, by Charles Willson Peale (1741–1827). (Philadelphia Collection, Free Library of Philadelphia.)

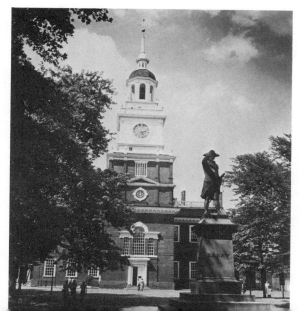

Independence Hall, Philadelphia, Today. In the state house, normally the meeting place of the Pennsylvania legislature, the Second Continental Congress approved the Declaration of Independence on July 4, 1776, and the Constitutional Convention drew up the constitution of the United States in 1787. (Convention and Tourist Bureau, Philadelphia.)

The popularization of the American Revolution in Europe was due to the drama of the war, enhanced by the constitutional changes of the immediate postwar years. But the American colonists were correct in thinking that they were fighting to safeguard an American political heritage that was already in existence by 1763, and was due to the transformation of institutions of British origin by a new people of multinational origins struggling with a completely new environment. Or, in John Adams' famous phrase, "the revolution was complete, in the minds of the people, and the Union of the colonies, before the war commenced in the skirmishes of Concord and Lexington on the 19th of April, 1775." But to Europeans, the Revolution had a universal message. As one German poet wrote:

And man was now again man; many noble beings
Planted eagerly the seed of truth.
Far on Philadelphia's shores there glowed
A sweeter dawn.[8]

PARIS AND THE EGALITARIAN REVOLUTION

Influence of the American Revolution in France. It was in Paris that the impact of the American Revolution was felt most deeply. To the philosophes of the Paris salons, it was an attempt to follow their own theories in an environment that was already favorable; for had not a Frenchman, Hector St. John de Crèvecoeur, in his widely admired *Letters of an American Farmer*, shown that in America man experienced "a sort of resurrection. . . . He now feels himself a man, because he is treated as such." This agreeable notion was fostered widely during the war of independence by no less a propagandist than Benjamin Franklin, who was appointed by the Continental Congress as their representative in Paris. Idolized by the salon society as the Enlightenment's ideal of intellectual sophistication and natural simplicity, Franklin skillfully passed on to Voltaire, Condorcet, Turgot, Helvétius and his other salon acquaintances a somewhat distorted version of events in America; and it became fashionable in the highest society to show one's reverence for his cause by displaying his homely features on hats, watches, snuffboxes, and even handkerchiefs. Turgot wrote the famous epithet, "He stole thunder from the heavens and the scepter from tyrants," a reputation Franklin's successor in Paris, Thomas Jefferson, was unable to match. The dream of American liberty penetrated all groups of French society. The future revolutionary, Brissot, founded a Gallo-American Society in 1787, with Crèvecoeur a founding member. Officers like the Marquis de Lafayette, returning from service in the French expeditionary force in America, spread the praises of the Revolution. Even the artists became involved. The great sculptor Houdon carved Franklin when he was in Paris, and then accompanied him to Mount Vernon to make his uncompromising bust of Washington. Jacques Louis David (1748–1825), the protagonist of the classical revival, displayed his *Oath of the*

[8] Cited in Palmer, *Age of the Atlantic Revolution*, I, 507. Translation modified.

Benjamin Franklin Drawing Electricity from the Sky, by Benjamin West (1738–1820). In his famous experiment of flying a kite in a thunderstorm, Franklin showed that lightning and electricity were identical. (Philadelphia Museum of Art Collection.)

Horatii in 1785, which many interpreted as a study in self-sacrifice à *l'américaine*. It has even been suggested that the peasant soldiers who served in America were responsible for making their own villages insurrectionary in 1789.

Financial Collapse. Yet it was in less ethereal ways, that the American Revolution pushed France into revolution. Helping the Americans win independence brought the French treasury to the edge of bankruptcy. Such help was reputed to have cost two and a half times the normal annual revenue. What was certain was that the borrowing by which the war was financed increased the interest on the national debt from 93 million livres in 1774 to 300 million in 1789, and that this sum was payable largely to the wealthier members of the bourgeoisie and the nobility of the robe. One controller general followed another, every scheme for a reform of the system of taxation being blocked either by the nobility and the parlements or by the tax collectors themselves. Finally, in 1786, the charming, self-confident bureaucrat Calonne proposed to the king that he call an Assembly of Notables composed of nobility, clergy, and administrators who, he felt, could be persuaded to grant the king the right to tax them. The Notables met in February 1787, demanded a dispersion of governmental powers among provincial assemblies dominated by themselves, and refused otherwise the tax proposals. This meeting is often regarded as a backward-looking revolution of the aristocracy for restoration of the power they enjoyed before the time of Richelieu and Louis XIV. It compelled the king to try a second expedient, to decree a new land tax applicable to all classes and to force the Parlement of Paris to register the edict by appearing personally to hold a *lit de justice*, a session in which traditionally the Parlement accepted

The Opening of the Estates General. This medallion was issued to commemorate Louis XVI's ceremonial opening of the sessions of the Estates General on May 5, 1789. (French Embassy Press and Information Center photo.)

the king's wishes. The Parlement, the principal mouthpiece of the nobility of the robe, won a brief popular fame by refusing the edict. Instead they demanded that the king respect the principle of no taxation without representation and summon the one representative body in the nation that enjoyed the customary right of granting taxes, the Estates General, which had not met since 1614. Thus the nobility, both in the Assembly of Notables and the Parlement, called for a broader-based assembly, partly to postpone the day when they would be taxed but largely to provide a constitutional body, dominated by them, that would be a substitute for royal absolutism. They thereby opened the way for the middle classes to carry through their own constitutional reforms.

The Calling of the Estates General. In August 1788, the king ordered the
Estates General to be convoked for May 1, 1789. Election procedures for
election of the three houses—the First Estate of the Clergy, the Second
Estate of the Nobility, and the Third Estate representing everyone else—
were worked out haphazardly, according to jumbled notions of what had
happened in 1614. But the pressure of self-seeking and liberal nobility and
of middle-class reformers called patriots compelled an important concession, that the Third Estate should be twice the size of each of the other
estates. Encouraged by this victory, the reformers flooded the country with
pamphlets and with model grievance petitions (*cahiers de doléances*), which
the electors could send with their representatives to the meeting of the
Estates. When the members straggled into Versailles in April 1789, it became evident at once that the reformers enjoyed unexpected advantages.
The First Estate, far from solidly supporting the upper hierarchy of the
Church, included a majority of parish priests; the Second Estate did not
represent the court, but rather the poorer nobles of the countryside and
the nobility of the robe; and sympathetic nobles and clergymen actually
stood for election to the Third Estate. They included the Estate's finest
propagandist, Abbé Sieyès, whose pamphlet, *What is the Third Estate?* had
wide circulation. To Sieyès, the problem was simple:

1st. What is the third estate? Everything.

2nd. What has it been up to now in the political order? Nothing.

3rd. What does it demand? To become something therein.

The Third Estate itself was not composed of peasants or city workers, who
in fact composed the majority of the population, but of lawyers, bureaucrats, and intellectuals. They were well educated, with a knowledge of the
law and the teachings of the Enlightenment. Royal errors during the first
weeks of the Estates' meetings helped them overcome their regional differences in a common opposition to demeaning treatment. They were
ordered to wear the same clothes as the Third Estate of 1614: hats without
decoration, simple coats, muslin shirts, white stockings, knee breeches.
The nobility were to be resplendent in lace, feathers, gold braid; the clergy
wore their finest robes. They were constantly kept waiting for hours, herded
around by soldiers, and ignored by the king. The king's opening speech
warned of "an exaggerated desire for change," and he refused to compel
the other Estates to unite with the Third Estate in one assembly with common
voting. The Third Estate replied by refusing to do any official business,
although they met every day. On June 13, two parish priests from the First
Estate slipped over to join them, and six more came the following day. On
June 17, the Third Estate declared itself to be the National Assembly, and
invited the other Estates to join it. A majority of the clergy voted to do so;
and on June 20, the self-styled National Assembly, finding its meeting hall
locked—for redecoration, according to the king; as intimidation, according

to the deputies—moved to the nearby tennis court and swore an oath never to disband "until the constitution of the kingdom is established and consolidated upon firm foundations." A few days later, the king capitulated, ordered the nobility to take part in the National Assembly, and promised a long series of reforms. The king's change of mind was probably due to rumors circulating in Versailles that forty thousand armed brigands from Paris were preparing to march on Versailles, and perhaps too to the growing number of riots in the countryside of peasants against the landlords and the Church. What was being glimpsed at Versailles, though far too mistily, was that the revolution for a constitutional monarchy that was being successfully carried through by the Third Estate, which had been made possible by the aristocratic revolution of 1777–1778, had itself provoked, or at least encouraged, two further revolutionary movements, in Paris and in the provinces. It was slowly to become clear that the master of Paris would be the eventual master of all the revolutionary movements.

Character of the Revolutionary Movement. It is however misleading to think of the "Revolutions" going through a series of easily compartmentalized phases, especially if one considers each phase dominated by a particular class. The turnover of leaders and programs has made it possible to speak of the phase of Constitutional Monarchy, in 1789–1792, dominated by the bourgeoisie, of provincial rule through the Girondin party in 1792–1793, of control by the lower bourgeoisie and working class of Paris in the Reign of Terror in 1793–1794, and of the restoration of bourgeois rule in 1794–1799. It is broadly true that the aristocracy sought to return to their former political privileges; that the bourgeoisie wanted governmental efficiency, social mobility, and increased political power; that the peasantry wanted an end to feudal dues, reduction in the burden of taxation, and a larger share of the land; and that the working class of the cities wanted secure work and cheaper food. But class interest is only one of several influences in the Revolution. For one has to recognize that no social class was homogeneous in composition or aims; that no period of government was dominated by a single class; that revolutionary agitation was continuous until 1794 and intermittent afterwards, and that this form of agitation seemed to produce its own momentum. Programs for change interacted; bargains were concluded; personal rivalries intervened; psychological factors, like war-weariness, dislike or love of violence, or national pride, counteracted solely material goals. Purely political conceptions, especially the division between those who loved liberty at the expense of state power and those who sought equality through the action of a powerful state, influenced other conflicts. Miscalculation and pure chance further complicated the conflict of interests. But there is one skein that runs through the whole tangled web of events, the predominant role of Paris, or rather of the group controlling Paris, in determining the course of the Revolution.

The Taking of the Bastille. When Arthur Young noted in his diary on June 27th, "The whole business now seems over, and the revolution complete," he was misreading what he himself had seen of the Paris crowds the previous day. "Every hour that passes seems to give the people fresh spirit," he wrote. "The meetings at the Palais Royal are more numerous, more violent, and more assured; and in the assembly of electors, at Paris, for sending a deputation to the National Assembly, the language that was talked, by all ranks of people, was nothing less than a revolution in the government, and the establishment of a free constitution: what they mean by a free constitution, is easily understood—a *republic*." [9] Paris was in fact equipping itself with the organization of insurrection. The king's cousin Philippe, Duke of Orléans, had openly sided with the Third Estate, and had earlier opened to the people the grounds of his Palais Royal, where almost complete freedom of speech was permitted, seditious pamphlets circulated with impunity in the hundreds, and a large crowd was always available to stone a police spy or encourage a rebellious speaker. According to Camille Desmoulins, who led the attack on the Bastille on July 14th, "It's simpler to go to the Palais Royal [than to the National Assembly]. . . . One proposes one's own motion. If it is supported, the audience gets the speaker to climb onto a chair; if he is applauded he calls the crowd to order; if they whistle in disapproval he leaves; the Romans ran their Forum this way." The duke of Orléans was probably trying to subvert the Guards regiments in Paris who were the mainstay of royal authority; and even a visiting American, Gouverneur Morris, begged an aristocratic friend to tell the king "of his Danger which is infinitely greater than he imagines. That his Army will not fight against the Nation." [10] The electors of Paris, who had chosen the Paris members of the Third Estate, had constituted themselves the new municipal government of Paris, and provided themselves with a volunteer, middle-class force, called later the National Guard. Paris, like the other cities of the nation, had thus spontaneously taken over its own government; and moreover, each of the electoral districts of the capital was continuing to run its own affairs through a district assembly. These districts were reorganized in 1790 into forty-eight sections, with assemblies and administrative committees; and the sections became henceforth the instrument of the adherents of direct democracy. In the early days of July, the Parisian masses began to arm themselves, seizing knives from ironmongers and guns from gunsmiths and all the weapons and powder in the city hall and in the military hospital of the Invalides. Both economic and political events combined to make them use their power. The food supply, depressed by two years of bad harvests and vicious winters, reached the low point that always preceded the bringing-in of the new harvest. The

[9] Arthur Young, *Travels in France during the years 1787, 1788, and 1789* (Garden City, N.Y.: Doubleday Anchor, 1969), p. 130.
[10] John Fisher, *Six Summers in Paris* (New York: Harper & Row, 1966), p. 56.

cyclical crisis in the economy, which had begun with the signature of a partial free-trade treaty with England in 1786, was provoking unemployment among the textile workers and most of the laborers in the warehouses and docks. Perhaps half the workers were unemployed. At this crucial point, the king began to gather troops, mostly foreign, near Paris, and dismissed the undeservedly popular finance minister, Necker. In Paris, Desmoulins yelled to the crowd the news of Necker's dismissal. "To arms," he shouted. "Tonight the Swiss and German battalions are going to massacre the people of Paris." Part of the crowds who had been swarming over Paris for the last three days then extended their search for arms to the royal fortress of the Bastille itself and, after exchanging shots with its few defenders, were allowed inside, where they liberated its seven prisoners and murdered most of the guards. The rest were paraded in the gardens of the Palais Royal, and once they had declared their wish "to join the town and the Nation," were treated as welcome allies.[11] Paris quickly turned into a fortress. Spiked barricades crossed the streets; trenches were dug; the Civil Guard manned every crossing, and constantly checked identification. After a couple of days of hesitation during which his closest relatives set off into exile, the king decided to accept the advice of the National Assembly, and win Paris over with a personal display of good will. On July 17, he drove into the city where he was met by Bailly, the acting mayor of Paris. "Sire, I bring to your Majesty the keys of his good town of Paris," Bailly said. "They are the very keys that were presented to Henri IV. He had reconquered his people, and today the people have reconquered their king."

Reforms of August 1789.   Up to this point, Paris had gained very little from its skirmishings. The customs houses in the wall of the farmers' general had been broken down, and some prices were lowered as a result. But the great shortage of bread was not alleviated. The officials in charge of the food supply were massacred by a mob in late July. It was, however, disorder in the provinces that provoked the first deep-reaching changes in the structure of French society. The peasants, nearly as hungry as the Paris crowds, had for weeks been burning down châteaux, destroying feudal records, seizing grain supplies. During the so-called Great Terror, rumors that the nobility were employing brigands to attack the peasants produced even greater rioting, which was reported to the National Assembly by one of its committees. On August 4, in a dramatic all-night session, the Assembly made an emotional gesture of appeasement. Led by a few liberal nobles, the Assembly voted to end serfdom without compensation, to abolish all other feudal rights in return for a cash payment, and to abolish hunting and similar rights. The clergy was to receive no further tithes. All citizens were to pay taxes. Legal offices could not be sold. And promotion to officer rank in the

---

[11] Georges Pernoud and Sabine Flaissier, eds., *The French Revolution* (Greenwich, Conn: Fawcett, n.d.), p. 29.

army and navy was to be open to all. Thus, the first grievance of the
peasantry was dealt with through the abolition of feudal rights; but the
peasant possessed no more land than before. Many were, however, to
increase their holdings by buying up land confiscated from the Church and
from émigré nobles during the next four years; and it is probably true that
by 1793–1794 the peasantry sought only to conserve their gains and opposed any further revolutionary changes. The Assembly returned to the
more congenial task of turning France into a constitutional monarchy. On
August 27, it issued the Declaration of the Rights of Man and of the Citizen,
which marked the high point of the libertarian, as opposed to the egalitarian, trend of the Revolution. It emphasized the freedom of the individual
from arbitrary arrest, freedom of speech, press, and assembly, and freedom
to enjoy possession of one's property as a "sacred and inviolable right."
Thus, the privileges of birth and the arbitrary use of governmental power
were swept away; and the liberty of the individual to move upward in
society by the amassing of wealth was sanctified.

March of the Fishwives. While these changes were far from a bourgeois
monopoly, as some left-wing writers have presented them, Paris remained
restive. On a nasty, wet October dawn, a crowd of women, mostly from the
central markets, trudged the three or four blocks to the city hall to demand
cheaper bread. During the morning the crowd swelled; church bells were
rung in the tocsin, to call out the citizens to insurrection; the district
assemblies debated; and in the afternoon a crowd of several thousand set
off to Versailles to wring the beloved king away from his evil counselors, by
bringing him bodily back to Paris. The crowd spent an uncomfortable night
on the wet cobblestones and draughty passageways of Versailles, watched
by the National Guard who had followed them from Paris; and the next
morning, in a sour mood, the crowd broke into the palace, killed a few
guards, and demanded that the king return to Paris with them. With the
huge courtyard before the palace filled with a furious crowd chanting "We
want the King in Paris—the King in Paris," Louis XVI gave in to their wishes.
That afternoon a vast procession of National Guards, disarmed bodyguards,
wagons of grain, guns with marketwomen riding on their barrels, the royal
coach, and a hundred members of the National Assembly, made a slow
journey into Paris, where the king was deposited in the Tuileries palace.
Thus, the Paris crowd in one act of physical power impaired the royal
despotism that Louis XIV had seen could only function effectively out of
reach of Paris. But who was master of Paris?

Rule of the National Assembly, 1789–1791. For two years, Paris permitted itself to be governed by the National Assembly, which with some
misgivings had transferred its meetings to the riding salon of the Tuileries
palace two weeks later. There was a marked improvement in the food
supply and an increase in employment as the economy picked up; and

those who favored the work of the Assembly set the tone of the city. The work of the Assembly's constitutional lawyers was slow, but by 1791 they had written a new constitution based on the separation of powers they saw in Montesquieu; but the political control of the middle classes was assured by requiring high property qualifications for voters and deputies, who were ingenuously labeled "active citizens" as compared with the poorer "passive citizens." A series of other important reforms followed; France's hopelessly antiquated administrative system was reworked. The country was divided into eighty-three departments of roughly equal size, with elected officials at every level of government. Equality of rights was given to Protestants and later to Jews. Torture was forbidden, and new legal procedures drawn up. Barriers to free movement of goods inside the country were abolished. To solve the pressing financial problem the lands of the Church were confiscated, and the proceeds from their sale used to back a new paper currency. By the Civil Constitution of the Clergy, the Catholic hierarchy was to be elected, by all active citizens and not merely Catholics; the clergy was to be paid state salaries; and all clergy had to swear to accept the Civil Constitution. The Pope denounced the Civil Constitution, and suspended all clergy who accepted it. The attack on the Church, so consonant with the teachings of the Enlightenment, was one of the worst errors of the Assembly. It weakened the national finances when the paper currency became drastically inflated; it made sincere Catholics enemies of the revolution; and by satisfying the demand for land of many bourgeois and well-to-do peasants, it turned them into conservatives who felt no further need for the revolution. This great surge of reforming activity was heady medicine for many Frenchmen, and for foreigners too. The sense of a glorious new day dawning was captured most vividly in Wordsworth's famous lines:

Bliss was it in that dawn to be alive,
But to be young was very Heaven! O times,
In which the meagre, stale, forbidding ways
Of custom, law and statute, took at once
The attraction of a country in romance!
When Reason seemed the most to assert her rights
When most intent on making of herself
A prime enchantress to assist the work,
Which then was going forward in her name!
Not favored spots alone, but the whole earth,
The beauty wore of promise.[12]

Rise of the Jacobins. Meanwhile, however, less starry-eyed revolutionaries were preparing to profit from the anarchy that the impracticality of the new government was encouraging. The Assembly's grant of total freedom

---

[12] William Wordsworth, *The Prelude*, xi, lines 108–18.

of the press and of political meetings saw the formation of political clubs, of which the most important was the Jacobin Club, founded by left-wing members of the Assembly. Through help with food and money and by throwing its debates open to the public, it won a large popular following in Paris; and through correspondence, the Paris Jacobins created a close-knit network of Jacobin clubs throughout the country, perhaps as many as two thousand in number, which were very close to a conspiratorial underground. With a membership of moderately prosperous middle-class people, it sought ideological rather than class goals—the creation of an egalitarian society through their political activity as an elite who, in Rousseau's sense, could understand the general will and must eventually be entrusted with the task of implementing it. In the early years, however, the meetings of the clubs and of the Assembly itself were chaotic. A noisy audience interjected its comments, shouted down unpopular speakers, and occasionally joined in the voting. The resultant chaos in government was compounded when the king, who still enjoyed important executive functions, and whose collaboration was essential to the success of the constitution being written, fled from Paris in June 1791. He and his family were caught near the Luxembourg border at Varennes, and brought back through leering crowds to undisguised imprisonment in the Tuileries. The soldiers lining the streets reversed their arms, as though they were at a funeral!

Marie Antoinette, by Elisabeth Vigée-Lebrun (1755–1842). Vigée-Lebrun's flattering portraits were highly prized by the leading aristocrats of all the European courts. (Alinari photo.)

The Conflict of Girondins and Jacobins.   The following year, the constitutional monarchy collapsed. The constitution was adopted in September, and a new Legislative Assembly elected shortly afterwards. This Assembly was completely inexperienced, since the members of the National Assembly had disqualified themselves from membership. Only about a third of its members were moderates who wanted to make the constitutional monarchy work; and a struggle for power ensued between the followers of the intriguing propagandist from Chartres, Jacques Brissot, and the more extreme members of the Jacobin Club. The Brissotins, or Girondins, as they came to be called since many of their leaders came from the Gironde department near Bordeaux, were ideological hotheads. They demanded a war to sweep the ideals of the Revolution into the tyrannical states on France's borders and beyond; and they expected popular uprisings in those countries to welcome the French armies of liberation. They sought strict enforcement of the Civil Constitution of the Clergy, and repressive measures against the emigrant nobility. Although many Girondins were originally members of the Jacobin Club, and like the more extreme Jacobin leaders belonged to the relatively affluent middle classes, they differed from them in finding their support in the provinces, especially among the lower professional classes and the craftsmen, artisans, shopkeepers, and more prosperous peasants. They wanted subordination of Paris to the provinces, and reduction of governmental interference in the economy which, given the continuing pressure of the Paris crowds, would inevitably redistribute the wealth of the country in favor of the Parisian working classes. The Jacobins became the party of the Paris radicals, possessing in the section assemblies and committees the means of organizing instant insurrection and in the Jacobin clubs of the smaller cities the means of spreading their orders throughout France. The Jacobin leaders, Robespierre, Danton, Marat, Saint Just, Couthon, believed in effective, interfering government, manipulated by a ruthless elite prepared at any time to sacrifice liberty to the needs of equality. Again, in the battles between the factions, it was the ability to manipulate the Paris mob that ensured victory.

The Assembly and the municipal government of Paris had won a brief ascendancy over the Paris agitators by firing into a demonstrating crowd on the Champ de Mars in July 1791, killing fifty people; and they had even arrested a few extremist leaders and suppressed some newspapers. In the resulting internal calm that followed, and aided by improving food supplies, the Assembly responded to the activities of Austria and Prussia, who had welcomed many emigré nobles, and who were halfheartedly threatening invasion. War fever was whipped up by the Girondins, who demanded a "war of peoples against kings"; and in the spring of 1792 the Girondins were able to force the appointment of a government pledged to a revolutionary crusade beyond the eastern borders. Louis XVI, convinced his own plight would be helped by the defeat of France, supported the new government's declaration of war on his brother-in-law, the emperor of Austria.

The raw French armies, lacking their officers, arms, and training, were easily defeated, and took flight. Defeats on the frontiers, the fear of foreign invasion, the worsening inflation and a new food crisis, and the urging of professional agitators brought Paris again to the boil. The final provocation was the publication of a manifesto of the duke of Brunswick, who commanded the Austrian and Prussian armies invading France, which threatened "if the Palace of the Tuileries is entered by force or attacked, if the least violence, the least outrage be done Their Majesties, the King, the Queen, and the Royal Family, if their security, preservation, and liberty be not provided for immediately, they will exact an exemplary and ever-memorable vengeance thereon by delivering the city of Paris to military punishment and total destruction." Paris moreover was armed, with pikes distributed by the Legislative Assembly and fifty thousand arms given out by the new mayor of Paris. On August 9, the old municipal government was replaced by a revolutionary one called together by craftsmen from the agitated Faubourg Saint Antoine, and the new government threw the city hall doors open to the crowd throughout the sultry night. The tocsin was sounded from the churches, and in the morning radical leaders led the mob against the Tuileries palace. When fighting broke out between his Guards and the crowd, the king and the royal family took refuge in the Assembly chamber. Six hundred Guards and four hundred attackers lost their lives, however, and when the new Paris government demanded that the Assembly depose the king, it suspended him instead, and called new elections for a National Convention.

The Reign of Terror. With the king transferred to the Temple prison in the control of the Paris Commune, the mob went wild again at news of further advances of the Austrian and Prussian armies into France. Probably not stimulated by political agitators for any ulterior purpose but reacting spontaneously to the atmosphere of hatred and fear enveloping the city, the crowd began an indiscriminate massacre of all the prisoners it could find in the city; and in more than a week of slaughter more than half the prisoners in Paris perished, including only a small minority of aristocrats. The elections, held concurrently with the massacres, not surprisingly were ill-attended. Less than one-tenth of those eligible voted, and Parisian voters did so publicly in the Jacobin Club in front of howling onlookers. Paris thus returned a strongly Jacobin delegation headed by Danton; but the provinces again returned the Girondins, who were greatly encouraged by the first victory won by the revolutionary army at Valmy. In the Assembly, the Girondins were soon outmaneuvered. The Jacobins forced them to accept the trial and execution of the king in January 1793; and when the war again turned unfavorable in the spring, after the Convention had added Great Britain, Holland, and Spain to its adversaries, the Jacobins prepared their final showdown. On June 2, a mob, supplied with lists of suspect Girondins and armed with cannon, surrounded the Convention building

The Cells of the Conciergerie, Paris.
During the Reign of Terror, the most important state prisoners, including Marie Antoinette, were imprisoned in the Conciergerie in the months before their trial and execution on the guillotine. (French Embassy Press and Information Division photo.)

and demanded the arrest or resignation of most of the Girondin faction. Most Girondins lost their nerve and fled home; a few were arrested, leaving the Jacobins in control not only of Paris but of the official constitutional authority of the whole country.

The Reign of Terror that followed was nothing less than the dictatorship of the radical leaders of Paris, working through a tight-knit system of committees, of which the most important were the Committee of Public Safety and the Committee of General Security. The most significant member of the Committee of Public Safety was the tough, dogged, dogmatic Maximilien Robespierre, whom Carlyle christened the "sea-green incorruptible," a fanatic devoted to the establishment of a reign of virtue. The Terror was both a desperate effort to save the country from disaster in war, and at the same time a determined plan to remodel French society and even the Frenchman himself. Both goals seemed to require the apparatus of terror—the use of the guillotine and other less rapid methods of annihilation, such as mass drownings, in which up to twenty thousand people died; representatives on mission, sent to the provinces to ensure their loyalty; and open civil war against regions like the Vendée that remained royalist. The war had to be won by organization, however. Universal conscription, the *levée en masse,* was adopted for the first time in history. Strict economic controls to ensure the food supply of the civilian population and the armies, strict apportionment of resources to provide weapons and uniforms, food rationing, and maximum-price laws followed rapidly. The Republic of Virtue was to be achieved by both practical and symbolic reforms. In place of Christianity, first Reason and later the Supreme Being were ordered worshipped. A new calendar, adopted in September 1793, threw out the old months, and replaced them with such charming names as Fructidor, or Fruitful month, and Ventôse, or Snowy Month; and abolishing the Christian Sabbath, the government instituted instead a ten-day week with provision for such civic holidays as Maternal Tenderness Day. The war measures were overwhelmingly successful, and by 1794 the French armies were again in possession of Belgium, the left bank of the Rhine, and Savoy. But success provoked internal scissions in the Jacobin leadership. Robespierre met the challenge to his authority from the followers of Danton, who wanted to relax the terror, and the followers of Hébert, who wanted to intensify it, by executing them all for treason—although it is probable that an ulterior motive was his disapproval of the desire of both groups to line their pockets illegally. Robespierre himself succumbed to a paranoid fear of conspiracy, which terrified the Convention members who assumed that he meant them when he referred to "that collection of factious intriguers, appearing everywhere, turning everything to abuse, seizing the tribune and often public office, who use the education which their advantages under the *ancien régime* gave them to deceive public opinion."[13]

[13] Alfred Cobban, *Modern France. Vol. 1: 1715–1799* (Baltimore: Penguin, 1961), p. 288.

Maximilien Robespierre, by an Unknown Artist. (Alinari photo.)

Overthrow of Robespierre. Robespierre and his few remaining followers had lost the support of the Paris mob that had given them their lease on power. The successful war had not provided bread; the deflection of popular discontent against traitors through the bloodletting of the guillotine was no longer effective, especially as it was obvious to any observer that a majority of the victims were peasants and workers. When the Convention voted to arrest Robespierre on July 26 (8 Thermidor), only three thousand people turned out in response to the tocsin, while the moderates of the Convention put together a force of six thousand from the wealthier Paris sections. Two days later, Robespierre and twenty-two of his followers were beheaded. Paris at once became its pleasure-loving self again, in reaction against the virtue that had been bought at such price. Restaurants, cafés, theaters, and parks, filled with crowds in extravagant new fashions. But a visitor from Geneva, arriving in September, found Paris greatly changed from "the place that I had so long idolized":

> There are some quarters of Paris which seem entirely deserted and you will easily guess that the most abandoned of all is that of the Faubourg Saint-Germain, where among whole streets flanked by Palaces, the only occupied mansions are those occupied by new government departments. . . . In every house into which a revolutionary committee has found its way one seems to recognize the traces of an army of Huns or Vandals. Nor must one forget the great houses transformed and laid waste by the forty-four sections of the Commune of Paris, who grabbed, one after another, the finest houses, which they found unoccupied in their quarters and set up in them their offices and guard rooms. . . . It is when the entertainments are over, toward ten o'clock at night, that the stranger is especially struck by the gloom and destitution of Paris, especially if he has known the city in happier days. . . . One of the things which struck me everywhere in Paris was an odd expression of uncertainty and estrangement visible on all faces. People looked uneasy, defiant, and tormented and some of them haggard and hysterical. I fancy that if a man who has never seen nor even heard tell of Paris, were to come here for the first time, he would be tempted to use the same words as M. de Jussieu used to a certain individual, "Monsieur, I have not the honour to know you but I find you greatly changed."[14]

The Directory and Napoleon Bonaparte. The Convention, and the middle class Directory that took over in 1795, quickly brought Paris under control. The remaining Jacobins were hunted down; the National Guard was restricted to men of property, and only the Guard of the wealthy western sections was used against demonstrations that broke out in April and May 1795. The army was brought into the city, and used under a young general named Napoleon Bonaparte to mow down a royalist crowd with a "whiff of grapeshot" on October 5, the 13 Vendémiaire. Paris had thus lost its radical leaders; the Committee of Public Safety was disbanded; the sections were reorganized to prevent their being centers of future in-

[14] Pernoud and Flaissier, *French Revolution*, pp. 335–38.

surrection, and even the revolutionary Commune government was suppressed. After six years of efforts to direct the course of the Revolution, the majority of the citizens of Paris had probably gained less from the Revolution, and suffered more, than any other segment of the French population.

It was Napoleon Bonaparte who was to restore the dominance of Paris over France, but only when he had made himself undisputed master of both capital and country, a position for which neither his origins nor his age appeared to equip him. Napoleon was born in Corsica only a year after it had been acquired by France, and he spoke Italian better than French. He won a scholarship to military school in France, and like other bourgeois found his advance in the army of the ancien régime blocked by his lack of noble birth. The Revolution removed those barriers, and provided employment for a soldier of talent. In 1793, he made a brief splash as an artillery officer by compelling the British fleet to abandon the port of Toulon. After the whiff of grapeshot endeared him to the Directory, he was entrusted with the army fighting Austria in northern Italy. There, in a brilliant campaign, he utterly routed the Austrian forces; and in a peace he wrote himself, he made northern Italy into a republic and the left bank of the Rhine part of France. He was sent to Egypt the following year, in a campaign aimed at breaking the British hold on the Eastern Mediterranean. Although his campaign was disastrous, and the British Admiral Nelson even destroyed his fleet in the mouth of the Nile, he was fortunate in the even worse performance of the French generals in Europe. In 1799, France was not only losing its previous conquests but was again threatened by invasion. Approached by ambitious politicians inside the Directory who wished to use a popular general and troops loyal to him to forestall both royalists and Jacobins, Napoleon agreed to overthrow the government. He deserted his army, rushed back to France before the news of his debacle in Egypt had been assimilated, and in a quick, bloodless coup, destroyed the Directory. His move was welcomed by the majority of the French people, who gave an overwhelming vote of confidence to the new constitution of the Consulate, which established a barely disguised dictatorship under the First Consul, Napoleon himself.

The Consulate, 1799–1804. Napoleon at once set about providing the benefits the voters had hoped to receive. Within two years he had defeated the Austrians and persuaded the Russians and the British to make peace. His popularity by then was so great, and arrests of possible enemies in Paris so numerous, that in 1802 he was made Consul for life by an even larger majority; and no one was surprised when in 1804 the usual plebiscite sanctioned his change of title from First Consul to emperor. It was during the five years of the Consulate that Napoleon carried through the internal reforms that guaranteed the permanence of many of the changes made by the Revolution, and did so by subordinating the rest of the country

The Madeleine, Paris. In 1806, Napoleon ordered the construction of this temple, modeled upon the Parthenon, as a memorial to the victories of his Grand Army. (French Embassy Press and Information Division photo.)

to Paris. The chaos of governmental administration by the ancien régime with which the revolutionary governments had begun to deal, was finally cleared up; and a coherent group of ministries was created, including those two vitally important instruments of central control, the Ministry of Finances, which controlled taxation, and the Ministry of the Interior, which ensured internal security. Napoleon accepted the administrative division of the country into departments, cantons, and communes, but made all responsive to Paris by appointing all officials from the center rather than having them elected and by ensuring that the prefect who headed the department came from another part of the country. To assure the integration of the governmental programs, he formed the Council of State, a body of legislative experts who were a kind of central cabinet responsible only to him; and he followed their advice in seeking the immediate economic restoration of the country. Revenues were restored by reimposition of many indirect taxes, including the gabelle on salt, and by a less successful effort to ensure that everyone paid direct taxes. Financial centralization was carried through by the foundation of the Bank of France, whose two hundred major shareholders, constituting its governing body, were the elite of the financial bourgeoisie of Paris. Centralization of the legal system was furthered by the issuing of the *Code Napoléon*, a new codification of law that abolished the different provincial laws of France and created an all-embracing body of laws based not on precedent but on reason. Even the centralization of religion was made workable when the pope accepted a concordat giving the state the right to nominate the clergy.

Thus, it is true that Napoleon bound all France together under the control of the government ministries in Paris, and that this control was to be perhaps his most lasting legacy to France. But it is also true that by these controls he justified his claim to have been the heir and the guarantor of the Revolution. To the middle classes, he offered the financial stability, orderly administration, and social mobility for which they had entered the Revolution. To the peasants, he guaranteed the land they had already acquired, accepted in his Code the end of the feudal dues, and restored the Catholic Church. To the working classes, he provided employment, not least because of the demands of his armies for manpower and supplies, and bread. To democrats of all classes, he guaranteed equality before the law and equality of opportunity, religious toleration, the abolition of torture and cruel punishments, and educational opportunity for the intelligent; and he promised the far wider spread of these benefits behind his eagles than had been achieved by the Revolution. To all nationalists, he promised not only national security but territorial expansion and military glory. It was for all these reasons that during the years of Napoleon's hegemony, Paris ceased to be a city in revolution. It was beyond the French borders that cities were in revolution after 1799.

The effects of the French Revolution and of Napoleon on the rest of Europe were far from producing the unalloyed hatred or adoration expressed by a vocal minority who had clear feelings about them. The overthrow of the ancien régime in France undoubtedly stimulated great liberal enthusiasm among would-be reformers in the rest of Europe. But the paradox (for which we should be prepared after seeing the popularity of the philosophes with the enlightened despots) was that the despotic governments, like those of Prussia and Austria, became the most convinced advocates of introduction of certain reforms passed by the National Assembly in France. "Your Majesty!" wrote the reforming minister Hardenberg to the king of Prussia. "We must do from above what the French have done from below." Liberalism thus found some unexpected supporters. The stimulus to nationalism provoked by the conquests first of the revolutionary armies and then of Napoleon was equally paradoxical. Nationalism was stimulated by the positive reforms carried through both by the revolutionary armies and by the governments they helped install. And it was especially stimulated by Napoleon at the very time that it was being encouraged from above, as a weapon against the Revolution and Napoleon, by the governing classes who had the most to lose if nationalism should turn truly liberal.

BERLIN AND NAPLES: HARNESSING OF THE NATIONALIST REVOLUTION

Influence of the French Revolution in Europe. Both Berlin and Naples lay well beyond the early expansion of the revolutionary armies. When the National Assembly made war on Austria and Prussia in 1792, it promised the spread of liberty; but France annexed Savoy and Nice in 1792, Belgium in 1795, and the left bank of the Rhine in 1797. Agitation by minorities of

Karl August, Freiherr von Hardenberg. As chancellor from 1810 to 1822, Hardenberg carried on the modernization of the Prussian state. (German Information Center photo.)

democrats, mostly middle-class in origin, gave the French an excuse, or perhaps a justification, for aiding the establishment of republics in Holland, Switzerland, and northern Italy (the Batavian, the Helvetic, the Cisalpine, and the Ligurian republics). Within this area of direct French control, reaction to the Revolution was already mixed. There was a genuine welcome for the introduction of such reforms as the abolition of feudal rights, the modernization of central and local adminstration, equality of access to legal and governmental positions, freedom of speech, and a reduction in the wealth of the Church. But there was widespread resentment at the annexations and bitterness at the exactions and the general behavior of the French armies. It became increasingly difficult, even for the most uncritical admirers of the changes in Paris, to regard the revolutionary armies as altruistic liberators. It was thus quite easy for the king of Prussia to ignore the ideological threat to his own power from the Revolution; and his ministers were already claiming in 1791 that the aim of the king of reducing the power of his own nobility made him a "democrat in his own way." After the unsuccessful though inexpensive campaign of 1792–1795, Prussia remained neutral until 1806.

In Italy, however, the threat of the Revolution could not be ignored so easily, if only because the French armies had resumed their traditional exploitation of the political division of the peninsula, by defeating the small states individually. In the 1790s, Italy was in as bad a state of political disintegration and military impotence as it had been when Charles VIII invaded in 1494. In the North, the two mercantile republics of Genoa and Venice were run by torpid oligarchies; Milan and Modena were governed directly by the Habsburgs of Austria; Tuscany was ruled as an enlightened ducal despotism by another branch of the Habsburgs; the papal states were stagnant because the papacy rightly equated modernization with an attack on the Church; the Kingdom of the Two Sicilies (Naples and Sicily) was controlled by a repressive monarchy and an exclusive landowning aristocracy. Only the king of Piedmont-Sardinia was showing any inclination to modernize, as the price of survival for a state squeezed between the grindstones of France and Austria. The peasants, who composed the mass of the population, were discontented but politically apathetic, unwilling to take direct action against the city-dwelling aristocrats and gaining a greater share of the land only by hacking out pitiable farms on the inhospitable mountainsides. All reform movements, which in the 1790s meant all movements for the overthrow of the governing classes, for the establishment of efficient state government, and—almost as an afterthought or at least a corollary—for the union of the Italian states, came from a small active middle class within the cities that had been unable to break into the higher levels of society or government. As in Paris, this reforming bourgeoisie was able to bring out onto the streets the mass of city workers, at least in the large cities of Milan, Venice, Genoa, Rome, Naples, and Palermo. But they could only take power with the aid of the French armies. For example, a revolt in Naples in 1792 was encouraged by a visit of a French naval squadron that fraternized with the reformers and helped the formation of two revolutionary societies; but the revolt was broken easily with the arrest and imprisonment of its leaders.

New encouragement for the reformers in Naples was given after Napoleon's victories in Italy in 1796, by the foundation of the Cisalpine Republic, which united around Milan portions of several of the small states of northern

The Palace of Caserta. The poverty-stricken kingdom of Naples was compelled to subsidize such grandiose royal building projects as this vast summer palace, built in 1752–74 in emulation of Versailles. (Italian State Tourist Office photo.)

Italy. In the three years before the Austrians returned, Milan was the center of republican influence in Italy, the citadel of reform to which revolutionaries from all over the peninsula gravitated, a symbolic nucleus for unification, an example of successful constitutional and administrative modernization. It was disillusioning that Napoleon handed the ancient republic of Venice over to Austria in 1797, since, as Wordsworth remarked, Venice was the "eldest child of liberty"; but the example of Milan gave hope for "Cisalpinizing" the rest of the peninsula. Following the murder of a French general in Rome, French troops from Milan occupied the city, and installed republican reformers in power over a Roman republic. When King Ferdinand of Naples attempted to overthrow this republic, the French army moved on down to Naples itself, defeated Ferdinand's army with ease, and set up a Neapolitan republic. As usual in times of stress, Ferdinand retired to Sicily, where the British fleet could defend him. The Neapolitan republic survived only six months, but its brief life highlighted all the problems of liberalism in southern Italy. The king, Ferdinand IV, a Spanish Bourbon, and his queen, Maria Carolina, an Austrian Habsburg, were blindly opposed to change. The Church was the only institution that could reach the peasantry, or indeed even speak their dialect; and it was a peasant army led by a Catholic cardinal that overthrew the republic. The city poor, living in conditions of deprivation unequaled in western Europe, lacked any sympathy for the well-educated, affluent reformers from among the city's professional classes and absentee landlords. Nationalism was nonexistent among the mass of the population, since most did not even know what the Kingdom of the Two Sicilies was, never mind Italy, a country that had never existed. Nevertheless, this isolated, reforming minority prepared the way for change in Italy since, during this short republican experience, they drove out the king, wrote a constitution, took over the administration, and began to analyze if not yet to solve the problems of Naples.

Napoleon and Germany. After Napoleon's seizure of power in 1799, the influence of France, both as a force encouraging liberal change and as an oppressive occupier stimulating nationalist reaction, increased in Germany and Italy. Following the defeat of Austria in 1800, Napoleon had restored the Cisalpine republic, which, renamed the Italian Republic, was left in the hands of Milanese liberals; they continued the liberal policies of the earlier regime. And in the months of peace in 1802–1803, Napoleon made far-reaching changes in Germany. Winning the cooperation of the larger German states by dangling before them the prospect of territorial accessions, Napoleon persuaded the Germans to agree to the abolition of most of the ecclesiastical states, most of the free cities, and all of the principalities of the imperial knights. One hundred and twelve states disappeared, the political geography of Germany was greatly simplified, and thus the number of vested interests opposing its future unification reduced; and by granting Prussia new territories, Napoleon had further strengthened the power that would eventually drive Austria out of Germany. The uneasy truce with

Britain was broken in May 1803, when Napoleon complained that the British had broken their treaty obligations; but the British had also concluded that their interests and Napoleon's were irreconcilable. Napoleon had shown colonial ambitions. After a debacle in his attempt to create an empire in the Western Hemisphere based on Haiti and the Louisiana Territory, he had turned again to Egypt with the possible intention of challenging the British in India. He controlled the Low Countries, which the British regarded as the key to London's security. And he was preparing the military force to extend his domination of Europe from the satellite republics even further into central Europe. For his remaining years as ruler, all Napoleon's plans in Europe were to be shaped, and usually to his own detriment, by the determination of the British to continue war against him until his final defeat. His attempt to invade England in 1805 was frustrated by

Conscripts at the Porte St. Denis in 1807. (French Embassy Press and Information Division photo.)

Admiral Nelson, who refused to be decoyed to the West Indies so that the French invasion barges could cross the Channel, and who put an end to the future possibility of an invasion by destroying the combined French and Spanish fleets off Cape Trafalgar in October. Napoleon, however, had already transferred his armies from the Channel coast to meet the Austrians whom he defeated at Ulm. After taking Vienna, he met the remaining Austrian forces and their Russian allies and annihilated them in the battle of Austerlitz, which, from the point of view of strategy, was his greatest triumph. Prussia which had been on the point of entering the war, was bought off with the cession of Hanover.

Napoleon, however, continued his remodeling of German geography with the formation in 1806 of the Confederation of the Rhine, a federal union of fifteen German states that included Bavaria, Baden, and Württemberg. This section of Germany, proud to have been part of the Roman Empire, conscious of its cultural affinity with France, and suspicious of the militaristic Prussian state, had a greater sense of affinity of its peoples than any other region; and if unification through the absorption of the rest of Germany by one of its most powerful states were to be avoided, the expansion of this confederation into a federal union of all Germany was a feasible alternative. But the confederation offered a direct threat to the ambitions of Prussia and to the self-esteem of Austria; and in 1806 the Prussian king, Frederick William III, finally decided to join the Russians against Napoleon. Outnumbered, outgunned, and outmaneuvered, the Prussians suffered humiliating defeats in the twin battles of Jena and Auerstedt; and Napoleon entered Berlin in triumph. When Russia too was defeated the next year, the mercurial Tsar Alexander met with Napoleon on barges at Tilsit in the River Niemen. Together, they settled the fate of Europe, while Frederick William rode up and down the opposite bank of the river in the rain. Napoleon was finally persuaded not to wipe Prussia off the map. (The blan-

Napoleon Receiving the Queen of Prussia at Tilsit, by F. L. N. Gosse.
(Alinari photo.)

dishments of the Prussian Queen Louise apparently had not effected this; "I am made of oil-cloth, and all this just slides off," Napoleon wrote to Josephine.) It did, however, lose half its territory and population. Its Polish acquisitions were made part of a new Duchy of Warsaw. Part of its German territories and the lands of other princes who had unwisely fought Napoleon were put together as the Kingdom of Westphalia as a throne for Napoleon's brother Jerome. Frederick William returned to a profoundly humiliated Berlin, to embark on a big renovation of what remained of his state.

Revolution from Above in Prussia. The philosophy of the revolution carried out in Prussia mostly under the chief ministers Stein in 1807–1808 and Hardenberg in 1810–1822, was summarized by Hardenberg as early as 1794:

The French revolution . . . has brought the French people a new vigor, despite all their turmoil and bloodshed. . . . It is an illusion to think that we can resist the revolution effectively by clinging more closely to the old order, by proscribing the new principles without pity. . . . Thus our . . . guiding principle must be a revolution in the better sense, a revolution leading directly to the great goal, the elevation of humanity through the wisdom of those in authority and not through a violent impulsion from within or without. Democratic rules of conduct in a monarchical administration, such is the formula. [15]

In short, the revolution that was to be carried out in Prussia from above was to achieve the modernization of the Prussian state. The reforms were to make possible a greater sense of identification of the people with the state; this sense had been lacking because of the barracks mentality demanded by earlier rulers. "We must train the nation to manage its own affairs," wrote Stein, "and to grow out of this condition of childhood in which an ever-restless and officious government wishes to keep the people." [16] It was an impossible ideal, though it represented the last and highest goal of enlightened despotism; but it is worth noting that the French institution that most impressed Stein was the Committee of Public Safety. Modernizing measures were numerous and effective. One of Stein's first actions was the decree emancipating the serfs and granting them part of the land. Physiocratic doctrines were followed in the abolition of the medieval corporations. All professions were opened to all classes, so that nobles were able at last to engage in commerce and industry. A new and extremely effective bureaucracy was founded in 1808. In this way, Stein and Hardenberg hoped to break the ossified structure of Prussian society, enabling the nobles and middle classes to make a greater contribution to the state without impairing its despotism. But it was the military reforms that were the

[15] Cited in Koppel Pinson, *Germany: Its History and Civilization* (New York: Macmillan, 1954), p. 33.
[16] Cited Peter Paret, *Yorck and the Era of Prussian Reform, 1807–1815* (Princeton, N.J.: Princeton University Press, 1966), p. 118.

Karl, Freiherr vom and zum Stein.
As chief minister in Prussia in 1807–1808, Stein began the reforms of Prussia's economic and social system that enabled it to take a leading part in the final defeat of Napoleon. (German Information Center photo.)

most significant. The French revolutionary army was the model. Noble privileges were ended. The planning committee laid down as the new goal: "From now on a claim to officer rank shall in peacetime *be warranted* only by knowledge and education, in time of war by exceptional bravery and quickness of perception. From the whole nation, therefore, all individuals who possess these qualities can lay title to the highest positions of honor in the army." [17] Universal conscription was adopted, after a struggle with the nobility; and service in the army made more humane. To evade the peace treaty's ban on maintenance of an army of more than forty thousand men, troops were called for a month's training at a time, and kept in permanent reserve afterward.

To make these reforms, which were so obviously borrowed from the French, effective in Prussia, it was felt necessary that the people should be inspired with a feeling of nationalism that could be directed against the French; and here the writers, philosophers, poets, and journalists were the key. A very large number of German intellectuals had welcomed the revolution, and many like the philosopher Kant remained admirers to the end. Even Beethoven, who had decided against his first impulse to dedicate the *Eroica* Symphony to Napoleon, returned at the end of his life, in the Ninth Symphony to the ideals of the revolution, by setting to music Schiller's ode to joy, by which he implied freedom.

All men will be brothers
In the shelter of thy wing.

But the violence and the naked self-interest of the conquests disillusioned most of the revolution's former supporters. "Our golden dream is shat-

[17] Ibid., p. 131.

tered," wrote Klopstock. In Berlin, in his famous *Addresses to the German People*, Fichte called for "the devouring flame of higher patriotism, which embraces the nation as the vesture of the eternal, for which the noble-minded man joyfully sacrifices himself, and the ignoble man, who only exists for the sake of the other, must likewise sacrifice himself." [18] Ernst Moritz Arndt was brought to Berlin to become the spokesman of the new nationalism, and it was he who answered the French claim that the Rhine was their natural frontier, with the well-known lines, "Der Rhein, Teutschlands Strom, aber nicht Teutschlands Grenze" (The Rhine, Germany's River but not Germany's Frontier). In Berlin, the deepest emotions of German romanticism were focused on the national struggle—the hatred of reason and of France as the land of the Enlightenment, the worship of the organic community and of the subordination of the individual in the nation, the admiration of the Middle Ages when German society was at its purest. By 1813, at least among the intellectuals and especially among the students and professors of the newly founded University of Berlin, there was a burning feeling of nationalism that had been harnessed in support of the reforms of the Prussian state. It was important because it had inspired the future leaders, but it had not created much of a response in the masses of the German people, in Prussia or outside. The final campaigns in 1813, when the armies of the German states fell on Napoleon's forces after his defeat in Russia, were not a national war of liberation (Befreiungskrieg) by volunteer forces from an aroused German nation, but rather successful attacks by well-trained professional armies on a weakened and demoralized Napoleonic army.

French Rule in Italy. The spread of nationalist feeling in Italy, while even less widespread among the masses in Germany, was equally important in its effects on the politically active minority in the cities. The most lasting effect of French rule was to persuade this minority that internal reform could never be carried out by their former rulers whose stagnant administrations were unfavorably contrasted with the reforms introduced under the French. The kingdom of Italy, which was the former Italian republic renamed to suit Napoleon's imperial pretensions in 1804, was the finest example of the benefits of modernization. Under the viceroy, Eugène de Beauharnais, it was given effective financing, the Code Napoléon, improved education, large-scale public works, expanded exports in agricultural goods, and public order. Moreover, by uniting for a number of years the inhabitants of several formerly independent states, it gave to administrators the experience of working together in a unified administration, and it provided the veterans of its army, who numbered one hundred forty-two thousand by 1815, a sense of common patriotism. There was no revolt against Eugène in 1814, even after the fall of Napoleon; and many in his kingdom would have been pleased to recognize him as king in his own right. The major part of the papal states were eventually annexed to France, and the pope

[18] Pinson, *Modern Germany*, p. 35.

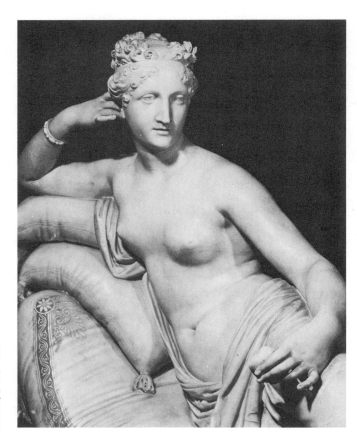

Pauline Bonaparte, by Antonio Canova (1757–1822). Napoleon married his favorite sister Pauline to a leading Roman aristocrat of the Borghese family and then, after they separated, made her princess of the tiny Italian state of Guastalla. (Italian Government Travel Office photo.)

deposed; and the improved administration won a certain grudging admiration from the Roman population. But it was in Naples that the French rulers attempted the most ambitious appeal to Italian nationalism. Ferdinand, who had mistakenly invited the Russians and British to use his ports, was forced to flee to Sicily once more by a French army that invaded in 1806. His territories in continental Italy were made into the Kingdom of Naples, which was given to Napoleon's elder brother Joseph; and when Joseph was promoted to rule Spain in 1808, he passed on his throne to Marshal Joachim Murat, Napoleon's brother-in-law. Joseph was a kindly, though vague administrator; Murat, a vainglorious, shortsighted, but glamorous leader of cavalry. Joseph's legacy to Naples from his brief rule was a new constitution, the Code, the abolition on paper of feudalism, improved roads, and better bureaucrats. The old republicans returned, reconciled to acceptance of a Napoleonic absolutism. Murat while carrying on with Joseph's policies, made a deliberate attempt to court the reformers, and slowly came to consider himself the "liberator of Italy." His own Gascon origins, his rise through the army, and his lack of ease with aristocrats gave him a natural egalitarianism, while his unrestrained exuberance in manner and dress won him a popular following among the Neapolitan crowds. Perhaps suspicious of the ambitions of his wife Caroline Bonaparte, and as defeats crowded in, determined to separate his own fortunes from those of the emperor, he courted the tiny revolutionary groups of the Carbonari and turned increasingly to those Neapolitan councillors in his government who favored a united Italy. Reconciled to Napoleon with the command of the cavalry in the invasion of Russia, Murat decided to abandon him after his defeat; and in 1813 he returned to Naples to bargain with the Austrians on the reward for desertion of Napoleon. He told his army it would fight henceforth for Italian independence; and finally, after hanging on to his throne until Napoleon escaped from exile on Elba, he declared a war for Italian independence in March 1815. Only a few intellectuals supported him, however, and the peasantry ignored his pleas to volunteer. The Austrians quickly defeated his forces, and he finally fled to France where his last hopes were dashed by Napoleon's defeat at Waterloo. In a final gesture, he gathered two hundred men in Corsica for an invasion of Naples, during which he was immediately captured and, on Ferdinand's orders, executed. Murat's own career was an ignominious farce, and probably did disservice to the cause of Italian nationalism. It was in retrospect, when the conservative regimes had been restored throughout the peninsula, that the memory of the changes brought by France became a stimulus to the desire for improved government and national unity.

The Nationalist Revolt. The reaction against French rule was therefore less strong in Italy than in Germany; but the pressure of Napoleon's demands for men and supplies for his armies and for compliance with the Continental

System, the closing of all Europe's ports to trade with Britain as a method of forcing the British to sue for peace to avoid economic disaster at home, constantly increased. Italians, like all the Europeans including the French, eluded the System by smuggling. It was, however, the refusal of Portugal in 1807 and of Russia in 1810 to cooperate that led Napoleon into the military ventures that brought his final defeat. His armies crossed Spain to attack Lisbon, which was protected by British troops under the Duke of Wellington; but Napoleon unwisely attempted to seize control of Spain as well, in order to convert it into a satellite kingdom under his brother Joseph. He thereby provoked a national uprising against the French armies, led by juntas of priests and nobles who proved useful allies of the regular Spanish army and of Wellington's troops in holding down in Spain many of France's best troops for the next six years. From that point, Napoleon was unable to gain any respite. The Austrians declared war on him again in 1809, and he had to scratch together an army of three hundred thousand men, half of them disloyal foreign conscripts, to defeat the Austrians at Wagram. His success disturbed the Russians, who withdrew from the Continental System and massed troops on the Polish border. Napoleon then made his greatest error. With an army of four hundred fifty thousand men he invaded Russia in June 1812. He was able to bring them to battle only once in the march to Moscow across the "scorched earth" the Russian army left behind it, found Moscow in flames, and retreated in growing disorder back to Poland as the winter cold decimated his troops. Only thirty thousand

Victory Parade of the Allies on the Place de la Concorde, April 10, 1814. The parade was given symbolic meaning by being held on the site of the guillotine where Louis XVI was executed. (Bildarchiv. d. Ost. Nationalbibliothek.)

of the Grand Army reached Poland by December. His weakness was the chance for which the Prussians and Austrians had been waiting, to throw their reorganized armies against the green troops he was desperately raising in France. After several indecisive battles, he was badly defeated at Leipzig in 1813; and, when he returned to France to wage a last campaign, his marshals finally demanded that he abdicate. Napoleon sailed in April for the island of Elba, to which his enemies had ceded him sovereignty. They returned to Vienna, where under the chairmanship of Prince von Metternich, the Austrian chief minister, they continued their deliberations on what they should do with France and the Europe it had so drastically reorganized.

What distinguished the meeting in Vienna from the many peace conferences of the previous century, however, was that the statesmen came not only to change boundaries and apportion indemnities but to find methods to deal with intangible enemies—the revolutionary forces of liberalism and nationalism. If the unity of the period 1776 to 1815 lies in the unleashing of those forces, the unity of the years 1815 to 1848 lies in the unsuccessful attempt to restrain them.

SUGGESTED READING

Samuel Bass Warner, Jr.'s *The Private City: Philadelphia in Three Periods of Its Growth* (1968), argues that "the Revolution left the city a tradition of democratic forms and democratic goals grafted upon a society of private economic aspirations." A more optimistic view of Philadelphia as "one of the outstanding urban communities of the century and a center of civilization and culture for the continent," is documented by Carl and Jessica Bridenbaugh, *Rebels and Gentlemen: Philadelphia in the Age of Franklin* (1962). Carl Bridenbaugh's two masterful studies on the colonial cities, *Cities in the Wilderness* (1955) and *Cities in Revolt* (1955) provide a rich survey of life in the five principal colonial cities. A short survey is given by Charles N. Glaab and A. Theodore Brown, *A History of Urban America* (1967), pp. 1–24. In-fighting among Philadelphia's political factions is described by William S. Hanna, *Benjamin Franklin and Pennsylvania Politics* (1964), with no little disparagement of Ben himself. For the revolutionary years in Philadelphia, see David Hawke, *In the Midst of a Revolution* (1961) and Robert L. Brunhouse, *The Counter-Revolution in Pennsylvania 1776–1790* (1942). Struthers Bart, *Philadelphia: Holy Experiment* (1945) makes easy reading.

Among the many delightful travel books, try Andrew Burnaby's *Travels Through the Middle Settlements of North America* (1904); or Marquis de Chastellux, *Travels in North America* (1963). For a thoroughly jaundiced view, see Gottlieb Mittelberger, *Journey to Pennsylvania* (1960).

On the Revolution itself, see Robert R. Palmer, *The Age of the Democratic Revolution. A Political History of Europe and America, 1760–1800: The Challenge*

(1969), which presents the thesis that the American and French revolutions were parts of one great movement. Palmer is supported by Jacques Godechot, *France and the Atlantic Revolution of the Eighteenth Century, 1770–1799* (1965). Bernard Bailyn, *The Ideological Origins of the American Revolution* (1967) argues that colonists saw the changes in British policy as "a deliberate assault launched surreptitiously by plotters against liberty both in England and in America." The approach of the Revolution can be followed in detail in two volumes in the New American Nation Series, Lawrence H. Gipson, *The Coming of the Revolution, 1763–1775* (1954) and John R. Alden, *The American Revolution, 1775–1783* (1962).

The atmosphere of revolutionary Paris can be felt dramatically in many eyewitness reports, such as Arthur Young's *Travels in France* (1969); Gouverneur Morris, *A Diary of the French Revolution by Gouverneur Morris, 1752–1816, Minister to France during the Terror* (1939); Oscar Browning, ed., *Despatches from Paris, 1784–1790* (1910), vol. 2; and especially in the fine collection by Georges Pernoud and Sabine Flaissier, *The French Revolution* (n.d.). All the main documents of the Revolution are to be found in John Hall Stewart, *A Documentary Survey of the French Revolution* (1951). Primary materials have been thoroughly exploited in John Fisher's entertaining *Six Summers in Paris, 1789–1794* (1966) and in a more bloodcurdling way in Stanley Loomis, *Paris in the Terror June, 1793–July 1794* (1964), which focuses on the murder of Murat, the trial of Danton, and the overthrow of Robespierre. For scholarly analysis of the Paris crowds and their motives, one should again consult George Rudé, *The Crowd in the French Revolution* (1959) and Albert Soboul, *The Parisian Sans-Culottes and the French Revolution, 1793–94* (1964).

Attempts to explain the French Revolution by use of an analytical framework into which events are made to fit, more or less, are innumerable; and new attempts at analysis have brought us new insights into the complexity of the Revolution. The historiography of the Revolution is summarized by Gordon Wright in *France in Modern Times: 1760 to the Present* (1960), pp. 107–14. One could also dip into Albert Mathiez, *La Révolution française* (1922–27) for a left-wing rehabilitation of Robespierre, or into Soboul's study of the sans-culottes for a contemporary Marxist view. A persuasive analysis of the Revolution as a series of class revolutions, by aristocracy, bourgeoisie, city crowds, and peasants is given by Georges Lefebvre in *The Coming of the French Revolution* (1947), and in *The French Revolution from its Origins to 1793* (1962). This analysis is equally convincingly dismissed by Alfred Cobban in *The Social Interpretation of the French Revolution* (1964) and in his brilliantly concise survey, *A History of Modern France*, vol. 1: *1717–1799* (1961). Crane Brinton, *The Anatomy of Revolution* (1952) seeks a common pathology in the English, American, French, and Russian revolutions. Palmer's *Twelve Who Ruled: The Year of the Terror in the French Revolution* (1970) looks at the terror from above and not like Soboul and Rudé, from below.

With Napoleon, it is best to begin with a quick survey of the innumerable conflicting opinions of his career, in Pieter Geyl's *Napoleon: For and Against* (1949). Georges Lefebvre's *Napoleon* (1969) is very thorough. J. M. Thompson, *Napoleon Bonaparte* (1952) draws heavily on his published correspondence. A new synthesis of the impact of Napoleon's conquests in Europe is made by F. H. M. Markham, *Napoleon and the Awakening of Europe* (1954) and by Geoffrey Bruun, *Europe and the French Imperium* (1963).

On the impact of the Revolution and Napoleon on Prussia, see George P. Gooch, *Germany and the French Revolution* (1920) for a general introduction and Herbert A. L. Fisher, *Studies in Napoleonic Statesmanship: Germany* (1903). The military reorganization in Berlin is explained in Peter Paret, *Yorck and the Era of Prussian Reform, 1807–1815* (1966), required reading for those who do not know the difference between line battalions and light battalions or why Prussian rifles used plaster bullets. For the bureaucrats, see Hans Rosenberg, *Bureaucracy, Aristocracy and Autocracy: The Prussian Experience, 1660–1815* (1958) and G. S. Ford, *Stein and the Era of Reform in Prussia, 1807–1815* (1922). For a different point of view, see Walter M. Simon, *The Failure of the Prussian Reform Movement, 1807–1819* (1955). The nationalist reaction is described by Eugene N. Anderson in *Nationalism and the Cultural Crisis in Prussia 1806–15* (1939).

The changes in Italy in 1789–1815 are surveyed by Emiliana P. Noether, *Seeds of Italian Nationalism, 1700–1815* (1951) and A. Fugier, *Napoléon et l'Italie* (1947). Eugène de Beauharnais's Kingdom of Italy is described in Owen Connolly, *Napoleon's Satellite Kingdom* (1965), which has a superb bibliography. For Naples, see R. M. Johnston, *The Napoleonic Empire in Southern Italy and the Rise of the Secret Societies* (1904), 2 vols.; Harold Acton, *The Bourbons of Naples* (1956); Owen Connolly, *The Gentle Bonaparte: A Biography of Joseph, Napoleon's Elder Brother* (1968).

Finally, to gain a visual impression of how Napoleon conceived himself as another Roman emperor, see the photographs and sketches of his public works in Paris, which included a column like Marcus Aurelius's, arches of triumph, and plans for a palace for his baby son that would outdo the Palatine, in Marie-Louise Biver, *Le Paris de Napoléon* (1963).

18
THE VIENNA OF METTERNICH

During the first half of the nineteenth century, Vienna was the capital of Europe in two distinct senses. From the foreign ministry in the Ballhaus at the center of the Old City, Prince Clemens von Metternich molded the diplomacy of Europe. In 1815, in his offices, the sovereigns and diplomats of Europe attempted to restore the prerevolutionary world by banning the forces of liberalism and nationalism; and the goal of Metternich's diplomacy was to conserve the achievements of the Congress of Vienna by the continuing repression of those forces whose first victim, he knew, would be the absolutist, multinational Austrian empire itself. But the other Vienna dominated Europe in a more lasting sense. In the great hall of the university, in the Theater an der Wien, or in the ballroom of the palace of Count Rasumowsky, the orchestras and choirs, the opera companies and quartets performed the works of Vienna's composers, most of them adopted citizens, like the artists of rococo Paris, who found the city's atmosphere congenial to their talent. Mozart was buried in Vienna in a pauper's grave in 1791, the year of the first production of *The Magic Flute*. Franz Josef Haydn returned to his native city in 1790, to give it *The Creation* and *The Seasons*. When Beethoven died in 1827, Schubert, Czerny, and the playwright Grillparzer were his torchbearers; Schubert was buried near Beethoven only a year later. But others settled during the coming years—Brahms and Bruckner, and on towards the end of the century Mahler, Hugo Wolf, Richard Strauss. Meanwhile, the tunes that filled the taverns of the Vienna woods or were played by the regiments of the City Guard were the waltzes of the Johann Strausses, father and son, and their rival Joseph Lanner, or the melodies of Viennese light opera like Nicolai's *Merry Wives of Windsor*. In orchestral music, Vienna had no rivals; in opera, it acknowledged only the rivalry of Italy.

Robert Schumann, who had just found Schubert's *Unfinished Symphony* among his unpublished manuscripts, commented in 1840:

The Three Precious Things: Wine, Woman, and Song, by Friedrich von Amerling (1803–1887). Amerling, the favorite painter in early nineteenth-century Vienna, celebrated the sentimental pleasures of the middle classes in the so-called Biedermeier era. (Bildarchiv d. Ost. Nationalbibliothek.)

Bird's Eye View of Vienna, 1769–1774, by Josef Daniel Huber. This extraordinarily accurate view, unrivaled before aerial photography, was the work of a professional artillery officer. (Bildarchiv d. Ost. Nationalbibliothek.)

It is true: this Vienna, with its St. Stephen's tower, its beautiful women, its air of pageantry, girdled by the countless convolutions of the Danube and reaching out to the lush plain which rises gradually into the towering mountains beyond, this Vienna with all its memories of the great German masters, must be fruitful ground for the musician's imagination. . . . In a Schubert symphony, in the clear, rich, romantic vitality of it, I am reminded of Vienna more vividly today than ever and I realize again why this particular environment should have produced such works.[1]

Here is our problem: Why should this city, at least during this particular half-century, have produced such superb music but almost no art or architecture of merit, little science or philosophy, and only one writer of more than local interest? And why should Vienna's other distinction during this period be the leadership of conservative forces throughout the continent? An answer can perhaps be found by consideration of the city's role in the Austrian empire and in Europe as a whole and of the social structure of the city that was formed by performance of that role.

THE BAROQUE LEGACY

Medieval Vienna. During Metternich's years as Austrian chancellor (1809–1848), the physical appearance of Vienna showed clearer evidence of the city's formative experiences during its six-hundred-year history and of its social structure than it does today, after being industrialized and greatly rebuilt in the late nineteenth century. The most striking feature was the wall that surrounded the inner, medieval city, a brick rampart some fifty

[1] Cited in Martin Hürlimann, *Vienna* (London: Thames and Hudson, 1970), p. 74.

feet high that had been extended outwards in the seventeenth century into the complicated pattern of spearheaded bastion perfected by the French for defense against artillery. Here Vienna had blocked the advance of the Turks into Europe, from the siege of 1529 by Suleiman the Magnificent until 1683, when the Grand Vizier Kara Mustapha was compelled to withdraw by a joint imperial-Polish army. A new line of fortifications, the Line Wall, built in 1704, encircled the outer suburbs; but it was only twelve feet high, intended to protect the newer Viennese settlements from Hungarian marauders who disliked their subjection to the Habsburgs and used mainly for collection of customs duties on all goods consumed by the Viennese. The inner wall had been abandoned as a defense, and was used for Sunday walks, bandstands, and coffee shops. When the Austrian army was defeated on the battlefield by Napoleon, he twice found Vienna defenseless, and occupied it without resistance.

Panorama of Vienna in 1830, by Jakob Alt (1789–1872). The eighteenth-century palaces, constructed on the narrow, medieval streets, are dominated by the tall Gothic tower, completed in 1433, of St. Stephen's Cathedral. (Bildarchiv d. Ost. National-bibliothek.)

From above, the inner city still seemed to possess a maze of medieval streets, with the great Gothic tower of the Cathedral of Saint Stephen providing the main point of orientation. The ground plan and a very few churches were all that remained of medieval Vienna, since the Viennese trading classes and craft guilds who had controlled the city in the twelfth and thirteenth centuries had failed to maintain independent urban government. They were hampered by the decision of the Habsburgs that the city they had chosen as their capital in 1278 could not be permitted the inconvenient autonomy of the powerful patriciates of south Germany; the Turkish occupation of Hungary blocked Vienna's primary east-west trade route along the Danube; and the religious wars of the sixteenth and seventeenth centuries damaged its commercial ties with Germany. Worst of all for the Viennese middle classes, who had mostly become Protestant, the Habsburg leadership of the Catholic Reformation in central Europe led to persecution and for many, emigration.

Origins of Viennese Baroque. During the late sixteenth and seventeenth centuries, Vienna was given the indelible mold of the Catholic Reformation and of the baroque civilization that accompanied it. The Jesuits were called to Vienna in 1551 to establish control of higher education and, to a large extent, of architectural style in church building. Vienna welcomed hundreds of Italian architects, painters, stucco-workers, and sculptors, whose domed churches and bulbous towers built for new and old religious orders were visible proof of the dominance of Catholic Reformation religion. The transition from a purely Italian style to a native Viennese, and from the Catholic Reformation to the Enlightenment, was provided by Johann Bernard Fischer, the first of the great Viennese baroque architects. Fischer, after studying for sixteen years with Bernini in Rome, settled in Vienna in 1678 and proceeded to place a more personal imprint on the city than any other architect except, perhaps, his rival Lukas von Hildebrandt. Fischer and Hildebrandt were the architects most responsible for shaping the face of Metternich's Vienna, a city of aristocratic palaces—city palaces with flamboyant facades on the narrow, dirty streets of the inner city, and country palaces in the green belt that lay within the Line wall. The sudden flurry of palace building occured in the fifty years following raising of the Turkish siege of 1683: the Lobkowitz palace of 1685, the Liechtenstein of 1694, the winter palace of Prince Eugen of Savoy in 1695, the Schwarzenberg palace of 1697, the Rasumowsky palace of 1706, the Kinsky palace of 1713 in the inner town, and a galaxy of summer palaces including the two Belvedere palaces of Prince Eugen

The Upper Belvedere Palace, Vienna, by Jakob Alt. The rococo palaces of the Upper and Lower Belvedere were built by Lukas von Hildebrandt as the summer residence of Prince Eugen of Savoy. (Bildarchiv d. Ost. National-bibliothek.)

and imperial Schönbrunn. Besides these luxurious palaces, whose interior decorations brought the arts of rococo to a theatrical climax unexcelled even in Paris, the lesser nobility and the wealthier bourgeois constructed less ambitious but perfectly harmonious private houses of five or six stories, with the same monumental facade and frequently a similar sweeping staircase, but adaptable to leasing to a number of families of different income levels. Thus the aristocratic style spread from the noble quarter throughout the inner city, giving a coherence that impressed visiting foreigners, like the English Dr. Burney who had come in the 1770s to study the state of Viennese music:

The streets of Vienna are rendered doubly dark and dirty by their narrowness and by the extreme height of the houses; but as these are chiefly of white stone [stucco] and in a uniform, elegant style of architecture, in which the Italian taste prevails, as well as in music, there is something grand and majestic in their appearance, which is very striking; and even many of those houses which have shops on the groundfloor, seem palaces above. Indeed, the whole town, and its suburbs, appear, at first glance, to be composed of palaces, rather than of common habitations. [2]

Class Structure of the Habsburg Empire. This multinational nobility in Vienna rested its wealth on ownership of vast landed estates. The Habsburgs themselves were originally archdukes of Austria, and from a nucleus of what is approximately modern Austria, they succeeded in adding, mostly by marriage but occasionally by war, a disparate series of regions bound together only by allegiance to the Habsburg ruler. Of those the dynasty still possessed at the end of the eighteenth century, they had acquired Bohemia in the fifteenth century, reconquered Hungary and Croatia from the Turks at the end of the seventeenth century, retained the Austrian Netherlands and Lombardy instead of the whole Spanish empire in 1715, and taken Polish Galicia in the partitions of 1772 and 1795. The nobility of Poland and Italy was a pre-Habsburg creation; but in all the other regions, the great families, like the Esterhazy in Hungary and the Kolovrat in Bohemia, owed much of their fortune to the land grants of the emperors. Moreover, the empire was based on a fairly simple agricultural system, at least since the reforms of Joseph II, a division of the land between a freeholding peasantry and the great aristocracy. The peasants who worked the nobles' estates were almost entirely under their control, in spite of Joseph's abolition of serfdom. In Hungary alone was there a compromise that permitted the native nobility control over local affairs; in the rest of the empire, the rule of the imperial bureaucracy was complete. Thus the great aristocrats formed a tacit alliance with the emperor, who supported their rule over their peasantry and provided

[2] Cited in Ilsa Barea, *Vienna: Legend and Reality* (London: Secker and Warburg, 1966), pp. 61–62.

Therese, Countess Kinsky, by Elisabeth Vigée-Lebrun. After the Revolution, the French court painter Vigée-Lebrun fled from Paris to find new patrons among the nobility of France's enemies. (Norton Simon, Inc. Museum of Art.)

openings for younger sons in the army, the church, or even the bureaucracy. The aristocracy felt itself part of an international society that revolved around the emperor and found its natural habitat in the court of Vienna.

If the aristocracy was linked by a membership in court society that transcended national origins, the bureaucratic class that developed in Vienna in the eighteenth century was united in its exclusively German origins. The building of the chancery by Lukas von Hildebrandt in 1719 and its extension later by Fischer von Erlach marked the beginning of the bureaucratization of the rule of the empire, and the establishment in Vienna of what soon became its most numerous class of inhabitants. Vienna dominated the administration of the rest of the empire through the cities, also largely German in population; even in Prague and Budapest there were many more Germans than Czechs or Hungarians. The tie was of German language and culture, which was willingly accepted by new recruits to the bureaucracy. For the Viennese middle class, the bureaucracy was the main road to social advancement, which could be charted very easily by the system of ranks; and the bureaucracy, like the aristocracy, revolved around the monarch. A career was not launched until one's title began with the letters K. K., for Kaiserlich-Königlich! The rest of the middle class in Vienna was too small in number for the well-being of the state: a few financiers who had done well from supplying the armies, or participating in royal industrial ventures, or control-

The Library, Hofburg Palace, Vienna. The sumptuous library in walnut and stucco was built by Fischer von Erlach in 1722–1737 to house the great book collection of Prince Eugen of Savoy. (Bildarchiv d. Ost. National-bibliothek.)

ling real estate. The rest of the city's population, who lived in the upper stories of middle-class houses, in tenements in the less fashionable quarters, or in more healthful village houses within or beyond the Line Wall, worked to supply the needs of the court, the bureaucracy, the church, and the army, in small shops, craftsmen's houses, or an occasional mill. They were shoemakers, silk weavers, porcelain workers, builders, the variety of professions that supplied the needs of any large city. Only remarkable was the fact that a city almost exclusively devoted to the supply of a court and aristocracy could support a population of almost three hundred thousand people.

Yet it soon became clear that the whole city revolved around the Hofburg, the rambling palace of seventeen different buildings that stretched along the southwestern edge of the inner city. Here were combined together the remains of a medieval fortress, a late Gothic chapel, a sixteenth century mansion, and the great series of baroque buildings that were built by Fischer von Erlach and Hildebrandt: the Spanish riding school, which was often borrowed for gala state dinners; the imperial library, with the leather-bound volumes of Prince Eugen's private collection; the long row of state apartments, on the Josefsplatz; and the imperial chancery on the Ballhausplatz. Except when the court moved to Schönbrunn for the summer, all ceremonies and entertainments and all governmental decision making was carried on in this complex of buildings. (The deputies of the Diet of Lower Austria, which met in the Landhaus on the Minoritenplatz, had only to stroll one block to the Hofburg when they started the Revolution of 1848.)

Metternich's Vienna was therefore different from the other large capital cities in Europe. It had, until the 1830s and 1840s, slight commercial and almost no industrial importance. It was almost exclusively a social and administrative capital. But the two classes that controlled its life, the multinational aristocracy and the German bureaucracy, were both in their own way alien to the majority of the inhabitants of the empire from which their economic support was drawn; and therefore two possibilities of revolutionary change existed. The one was social revolution, by the peasantry against the great aristocratic landlords, regardless of nationality, and against the emperor, whose power rested on the aristocrats. The other was nationalist revolution, which was most likely to be led by the economically depressed lower nobility or by an aroused peasantry, against German-Austrian dominance. Both fears weighed on Metternich when he assumed the office of chancellor, after Austria's disastrous defeat by Napoleon at Wagram in 1809.

METTERNICH AND THE CONSERVATIVE RESTORATION

It is easy enough to explain the preeminence of Metternich among Europe's diplomats; the difficulty is to understand the weight accorded the Austrian empire.

Metternich's Character and Opinions. Metternich was the supreme exponent of the doctrine of conservatism in internal and foreign relations, at a time when the sovereigns of Europe were grasping desperately for some means to inoculate their subjects, and the subjects of neighboring powers, against the dangerous notion spread by the French Revolution and Napoleon that long-established societies can be remodeled by their less privileged members. Or, put more fairly, Metternich saw himself as the guarantor of the uninterrupted, organic growth of society, as conceived by Edmund Burke in 1790 in his *Reflections on the Revolution in France:*

The state ought not to be considered as nothing better than a partnership agreement in a trade of pepper and coffee, calico or tobacco, or some other low concern, to be taken up for a little temporary interest, and to be dissolved by the fancy of the parties. It is to be looked on with other reverence. . . . It is a partnership in all science; a partnership in all art; a partnership in every virtue, and in all perfection. As the ends of such a partnership cannot be obtained in many generations, it becomes a partnership between those who are living, those who are dead, and those who are to be born. Each contract of each particular society is but a clause in the great primeval contract of eternal society. [3]

"Unmoved by the errors of our time—errors which always lead society to the abyss," Metternich wrote in his *Memoirs*, "we have had the happiness in a time full of danger to serve the cause of peace and the welfare of nations, which will never be advanced by political revolutions." [4] He was admirably equipped for this effort. His father was a wealthy Rhineland count who served the emperor in various diplomatic posts, including governing the Austrian Netherlands. (Winelovers have asserted that Metternich served the great Riesling wine, Schloss Johannisberg, from the family estate near Mainz at the Congress of Vienna, only to be challenged by the French diplomat Talleyrand, who served his own Château Haut-Brion, one of the greatest of the red Bordeaux wines.) His early experiences—study at the universities of Strasbourg and Mainz, stays with his father at Brussels, where he moved among French émigré society, a long visit to England, where he met Burke and other politicians—gave him a knowledge of several European languages and of many leading statesmen; and at the age of twenty-one, he was sent on a mission to Holland for the emperor. Only in 1794 did he see Vienna for the first time, when his parents arranged an advantageous marriage for him with the granddaughter of Chancellor Kaunitz. Then and later, Metternich was realistic about the city in which he was to spend most of his life:

"In Vino, Veritas." The cartoon, printed on a playing-card, shows Metternich as the alien Schloss Johannisberg wine (which he owned) being driven out during the 1848 Revolution by a humbler Viennese bottle. (Bildarchiv d. Ost. Nationalbibliothek.)

Lamentable illusions hang like a thick cloud over the poor city of Vienna. She believes that she holds the same position that Paris occupied in France; she thinks she can dictate to the Empire. It is a gross error. Vienna is merely the outer shell of a nut which constitutes the main body. She is only the leading town in the smallest province of the Empire and she only becomes the capital of it if the Emperor remains Emperor and lives there with the government of the Empire. For her to be the capital it is, therefore, necessary that there should be an Emperor and an Empire. [5]

Fortunately for Metternich, he found the emperor, Francis II (reigned

[3] Edmund Burke, *Reflections on the Revolution in France* (Garden City, N.Y.: Doubleday, 1961), p. 110.
[4] Prince Clemens von Metternich, *Memoirs* (London: Bentley, 1888), I, 175.
[5] G. de Bertier de Sauvigny, *Metternich and his Times* (London: Danton, Longman, and Todd, 1962), p. 165.

1792–1835; he became Francis I of the Austrian empire in 1804, when Napoleon abolished the Holy Roman Empire), a man after his own heart. To Metternich, he appeared "a true father to his subjects . . . in everything loving and seeking only the truth, firm in his principles and just in his opinions." To others, however, Francis, was a born conservative, though perhaps not a reactionary, who amused himself making chain mail and toffee, refused to make use of the bureaucracy left him by Joseph II, ignored recommendations for change, even from Metternich, and relied on red tape in place of decisiveness. Metternich's opponents felt that he had found a perfect master; for Metternich himself, according to the revolutionary Mazzini, was "immobility personified, the Chinese principle in its highest expression, the Status Quo incarnate." Francis gave the elegant, almost too handsome young man a rapid series of promotions: as ambassador to Saxony; then to Prussia; and in 1806–1809, at Napoleon's request, to Paris. From this point until Napoleon was finally sent to Saint Helena, Metternich was in a constant personal duel with the French emperor, a duel in which he had to work out what form of victory would most advance the form of conservatism he desired to see in Europe.

Metternich admired Napoleon for "the remarkable perspicuity and grand simplicity of his mind and its processes. Conversation with him always had a charm for me, difficult to define." But he refused to accept Napoleon's attempts to convince him that he sought legitimacy as ruler of France and that he had crushed the Revolution. Napoleon, Metternich believed, had but "one passion, that of power"; "the object of the universal domination to which he aspired was . . . the establishing of a central supremacy over the states of Europe, after the ideal disfigured and exaggerated in the Empire of Charlemagne." He thus could not be accommodated into the political system Metternich envisaged. The enemies were to change during the next half-century, but Metternich's conviction as he assumed his post in Paris did not: "Napoleon seemed to me the incarnation of the Revolution; while in the Austrian Power which I had to represent at his court, I saw the surest guardian of the principles which alone guaranteed the general peace and political equilibrium." [6]

The Congress of Vienna. This remained his aim when the victorious powers assembled in Vienna in the fall of 1814. Peace with France would be either a revenge or an attempt to establish "the greatest political equilibrium between the Powers." To persuade the powers to accept his views, a propitious setting had to be arranged; Vienna, except for the intermission between Napoleon's flight from Elba and his final defeat at Waterloo, was to be a gigantic festival for the aristocracies of Europe. In the Hofburg, the emperor entertained the tsar of Russia, the kings of Prussia, Denmark,

[6] Metternich, *Memoirs*, I, 65.

Ceremonial Return to Vienna of the Emperor Francis II, June 16, 1814, by Johann Nepomuk Höchle (1790–1835). (Bildarchiv d. Ost. Nationalbibliothek.)

Bavaria, and Saxony, and a host of lesser nobles; forty tables were laid for dinner each night; fourteen hundred horses, with barouches or sleighs, were at their disposition; colorful military parades, equestrian displays in the riding school, fireworks, ice parties, balls in the Grand Hall of the Hofburg, weekly dances at Metternich's, lotteries, amateur theatricals, concerts conducted by Beethoven and a new performance of *Fidelio*, all convinced the Viennese that their city was the most romantic in Europe. The pomp also disguised the fact that the serious discussions of the Congress were taking place in the chancery on the Ballhausplatz among Metternich, British Foreign Secretary Castlereagh, Tsar Alexander I, the Prussian minister Hardenberg, and the persuasive French delegate, Talleyrand, who successfully urged that the Congress would assure stability in Europe by making the restored Bourbon king Louis XVIII popular with his subjects. Saddling France with a punitive treaty would not endear to his subjects a monarch they knew had returned in "the baggage train of the allies."

To achieve equilibrium, a "balance of power," the great states agreed to roughly equal territorial annexations, so that no one of them would become a threat to the others. Their first decision was not to return indiscriminately to the situation of 1789. Metternich was convinced, and remained so, that Austria's primary concern was in Italy, where Napoleonic reforms had left a dangerous residue of both liberal and national resentments. Austria annexed Lombardy, Venetia, and the Illyrian provinces along the Dalmatian coast, and relatives of the emperor Francis were handed Parma, Modena, and Tuscany. In Germany, Metternich wanted the formation of a confederation under the presidency of Austria that would replace the Holy Roman Empire; but to win Prussia's agreement to this Germanic confederation, he had to accept the doubling of the size of Prussia, through the acquisition of territory of its immediate neighbors and of a large part of the left bank of the Rhine. Russia took over an enlarged share of Poland, to which it was supposed to grant internal autonomy as a kingdom of Poland; and it annexed Finland. Britain returned most French colonial possessions, but held on to a line of trading and supply stations on the route to India: Cape Colony on the tip of South Africa, Mauritius in the Indian Ocean, Ceylon, and also Malta in the Mediterranean and Heligoland off the North German coast. The Allies decided to compel France to give up all its territorial annexations in Europe, but not to dismember it as the Prussians were demanding. The second principle underlying the political changes was to establish a number of buffer states around the French borders to prevent future French aggression. The former Austrian Netherlands (Belgium) was united to Holland under the rule of the House of Orange; the Prussians were given the watch on the Rhine; and the kingdom of Piedmont-Sardinia was enlarged by annexation of the former Republic of Genoa, part of Savoy, and Nice. These were the most important decisions made at the Congress of Vienna, and none of them were intended to set the clock back. They were considered necessary, in Castlereagh's words, "to bring the world back to peaceful habits." The principle of "legitimacy," the restoration to power of rulers whose right to their thrones had been demonstrated by long tenure and conservative philosophy, was invoked to justify the return of Louis XVIII to the throne of France, of Ferdinand VII to Spain, and Ferdinand IV to the Kingdom of the Two Sicilies. To ensure the permanence of these agreements, Britain, Austria, Prussia, and Russia signed a Quadruple Alliance in which they agreed to take up arms if the French attempted new aggression or a Bonapartist restoration, and to meet periodically to consider measures "for the repose and prosperity of peoples, and for the maintenance of peace in Europe." The aims of the Quadruple Alliance became blurred in the minds of liberals, and perhaps also of conservative sovereigns, with those of the Holy Alliance, a mystical-sounding agreement that Tsar Alexander I forced the Austrian emperor and Prussian king to join him in signing. Under the influence of Baroness Kruedener, a religious fanatic, the tsar had wanted a high-sounding declaration of repentance and return by the monarch to "an order of things based on the exalted truths of the eternal religion of our Savior." After Metternich had skillfully intervened, he was given, amid the moralistic declarations, the very down-to-earth statement that "regarding themselves as compatriots [the three monarchs] will lend aid and assistance to each other on all occasions and in all places." When the periodic meetings of the great powers led in the following years to repression of liberal movements, it was generally assumed that it was the principles of the Holy Alliance that were being invoked.

Thus, the basis of what, to Metternich's annoyance, came to be called the "Metternich system," as constructed at the Congress of Vienna, was his concept of the solidarity and interdependence of states. "Isolated states exist only as the abstractions of so-called philosophers," Metternich wrote. "In the society of states each state has interests . . . which connect it with the others. The great axioms of political science derive from the recognition of the true interests of *all* states; it is in the general interests that the guarantee of existence is to be found." Revolutionary change within one state therefore affects all other states. "No peace is possible with a revolutionary system, whether with a Robespierre who declares war on châteaux or a Napoleon who declares war on Powers." In the maintenance of a world free of revolutions, the Austrian empire had to play a central part, both in the prevention of revolution beyond its borders and in the preservation of its own internal stability. Metternich was far more successful in the former aim. "Europe I may have governed," he remarked. "But never Austria."

Metternich's View of Austrian Empire. Metternich's power base was the Austrian empire, which in 1815 had a population of about thirty million, of whom a quarter were German-speaking; Prussia's population by comparison was only eleven million, Russia's forty million, France's twenty-eight million. In none of the continental countries had industrialization begun on a large scale; and thus the strength of all these countries lay in agriculture and trade. Austria, after much needed military reforms under General Radetsky, was able to maintain an army that could easily defeat any of the smaller powers of Europe but none of the larger. Metternich was fully aware of the limitation on Austria's action this implied and of the further justification it supplied for maintenance of a system of consultation among the major powers. He constantly opposed any further territorial annexations by Austria, especially adventures to profit from the weakening of the Turkish empire in southeastern Europe. This "saturated" Austrian empire, far from threatening the other great powers, was justified in its international position as a barrier against revolution. In this sense, it was a "European necessity."

Austria's primary international task was to hold down Italy, the country most infected by French revolutionary ideas and by the continuing interference of France itself. In part, Austria's dependence on Italy was economic. Lombardy included the empire's richest agricultural land, in the Po valley, and was the earliest region to industrialize. Trieste was built up as Austria's main port, linked directly across the Ljubljana Gap with Vienna. But the whole peninsula was ripe for revolution. The restored regimes seemed backward after the Napoleonic reforms, particularly the papal administration and the repressive Bourbon rule in Naples. Revolutionary secret societies abounded, especially the Carbonari before 1830 and Mazzini's Young Italy later. Young army officers, professional classes, and businessmen were all determined on the need for modernization, including adoption of more liberal constitutions. And the presence of Austrian occupation troops in Lombardy and Venetia and of the Austrian secret police everywhere made the revolutionary movement anti-Austrian and, by necessity, nationalist. Thus, it was revolution in Italy that led the powers to use the Congress system to authorize armed intervention for the suppression of liberalism. The Quadruple Alliance had met in 1818 at Aix-la-Chapelle, but merely to formalize the ending of the military occupation in France and that country's membership in a new Quintuple Alliance. Two years later, however, army officers and liberal businessmen carried out a successful coup in Spain, where they forced the king to proclaim a new constitution. Intervention by the powers was blocked by the British; but when Neapolitan revolutionaries followed the Spanish example, Metternich persuaded the Prussians and Russians at the Congress of Laibach that Austria should be authorized to crush the Neapolitan

Metternich, by August Weger (1823–1892). (Bildarchiv d. Öst. National-bibliothek.)

revolution before the contagion of revolution spread. This fear seemed justified when revolution also broke out in Piedmont; and the Austrian army, after subjugating Naples without any difficulty, put down the rebels in Turin on its way home. Only the British demurred against this apparently unlimited license to intervene in the internal affairs of other powers.

Suppression of German Discontent. In Germany, Metternich felt almost as strongly the danger of liberal agitation among the army officers, students and professors, and middle-class merchants, especially as there was the danger that the German element in the Austrian empire, on whom both administration and commerce depended, would be willing to abandon the empire to participate in a unified Germany. Germany was as ripe for revolution as Italy, in Metternich's view—a social revolution, to overthrow the noble control of the land; a liberal revolution, beginning in the universities, to emulate the political changes in France; and a national revolution, the most dangerous of all. Metternich's solution was to maintain the old local divisions, at least the thirty-nine surviving states left by the Congress of Vienna, giving them mimimal unity through a form of confederation. His natural allies were therefore the rulers of the small German states. Particularly dangerous was the nationalist fervor whipped up during the final campaigns against Napoleon, and continued with greater violence by the same propagandists, Arndt, Görres, and Turnvater Jahn. Fortunately for Metternich, the Prussian king, Frederick William III, had no liking for popular revolution, even in his favor; and when student associations called Burschenschaften began to get out of hand, burning antinationalist books at the Wartburg in 1817 and celebrating the murder by a student of a conservative dramatist, Metternich got the Prussian king and the other leading princes to agree to the suppression of the student associations. By the Carlsbad Decrees of 1819, the German Confederation banned the Burschenschaften, set up a rigid censorship of the press and the universities, and employed inspectors to find subversives. The next year, the few parliamentary assemblies in Germany were severely restricted in their competence. When several South German rulers were compelled in the uprisings of 1830 to grant constitutions, the Diet acted again, under Metternich's pressure, to reduce their powers; and thus, until 1848, German liberal and national movements found themselves under such severe police controls that they had little opportunity to seek wider support.

Throughout central Europe, therefore, in that band of states comprising the German principalities, the Austrian empire, and the states of Italy that Metternich considered the key to European stability, the forces of nationalism and liberalism were suppressed. In this area, Metternich had secured the establishment of a police regime symbolized by the great jails for political prisoners such as the Spielberg in Vienna, where the Italian revolutionary Silvio Pellico wrote one of the most influential indictments of Metternich's regime, *My Prisons*.

Liberalism and Nationalism in Western Europe. Outside central Europe, Metternich wrestled with less success to maintain the political equilibrium. The French were permitted to put down the Spanish revolution in 1822; but a government so backward was bound to continue to present a cause of instability. When the Greeks revolted against their Turkish occupier in 1821, they presented not only an example of a nationalist revolution but an invitation to Russia to intervene in eastern Europe. It was, however, the French and British who finally joined the Russians in compelling the Turks to recognize Greek independence in 1830, while Metternich looked on in dismay at the incapacity of the administrators appointed by the new king Otto from Bavaria and the amateur politicians of his government. In 1830, the Belgians revolted against their union with the Dutch. Both French-speaking and Flemish-speaking Belgians objected to the predominance given in the new kingdom to its Dutch-speaking subjects; economic policy was felt to discriminate against Belgium; the Catholics complained of Calvinist interference in the schools; the Belgians, who were almost twice as numerous as the Dutch, had the same number of representatives in the States General. Metternich, as well as the Prussian and Russian rulers, would gladly have aided the Dutch king in suppressing the revolt; but both the British and the French objected, and before any decision could be taken, the tsar found himself faced by revolt in Poland, and Metternich, by uprisings in several of the smaller Italian states. Russian troops quickly extinguished the rising in Poland, and Austrian troops invaded Parma, Modena, and the papal states to end revolution there. Meanwhile, however, the French had intervened in Belgium on behalf of the revolutionaries; and in July 1831, the powers recognized Belgian independence under the kingship of Leopold of Saxe-Coburg-Gotha, thus accepting the first important breach of the decisions of the Congress of Vienna.

After the successful Belgian revolt, however, there were no further triumphs for liberalism or nationalism until 1848. Metternich could congratulate himself on the negative achievement that he had sought:

Let anyone look at the situations which Austria and all of Europe confronted between 1809 and 1848 and let him ask himself whether one man's insight could have transformed these crises into health. I claim to have recognized the situation, but also the impossibility of erecting a new structure in our Empire . . . and for this reason all my care was directed to conserving that which existed.[7]

Administrative Immobility in Vienna. This was, however, deliberately ingenuous on Metternich's part, because he had made several efforts to improve Austrian internal administration, and had been blocked by the procrastination of Francis I and by the paralyzing committee government erected to cover the imbecility of his successor, Ferdinand I (reigned 1835–

---

[7] Cited in Henry A. Kissinger, *A World Restored* (New York: Grosset & Dunlap, 1964), p. 213.

Du bist mein lieber Sohn
an dem ich Wohlgefallen habe

"Ferdinand I as the Foundling of the Aristocracy." This political cartoon shows the imbecilic emperor as an abandoned baby fallen into the hands of the aristocracy. (Bildarchiv d. Öst. Nationalbibliothek.)

1848). Metternich admired the Napoleonic system of government, and lacking an emperor of Napoleon's genius, he proposed that a council of state, or Reichsrat, should exercise centralized control of the empire from Vienna. To vitalize such a body, he wanted it broadly representative of the bureaucracy, the aristocracy, and even the provincial diets. Moreover, Metternich recognized that the national problem within the empire could not be solved by mere repression. He wanted to compromise, by giving the local assemblies in the empire more power, at least to advise the emperor; and he encouraged their meetings, thus strengthening the notion that such provinces as Bohemia still possessed a political personality. He went further, by encouraging cultural nationalism, even among the southern Slavs, who in 1914 were to begin the final disintegration of the Austrian empire. At one point, Metternich even proposed that the Austrian empire be governed through a chancery divided into six national groups—Austria, Italy, Bohemia-Moravia-Galicia, Illyria, Hungary, and Transylvania. None of these schemes progressed very far. Metternich himself described what happened to the proposal for a council of state that he made to the emperor in 1811. The emperor put a new version of the plan in his drawer in 1817; ten years later, after a serious illness, Francis told Metternich he had felt guilty of a serious crime toward his chancellor and would take up the reform program when he was convalescent; seven years later, on December 31, 1834,

I went to see the Emperor to present my good wishes for the New Year. "Again you see in me a repentant sinner," the Emperor said, interrupting me. "Your work still has not left my drawer. I give you my word of honor that the year 1835 will not pass without this institution being created. Two months later, the Emperor was dead.[8]

Ferdinand I had epilepsy and rickets, and was mentally unstable. Government was placed in the hands of a committee consisting of his younger brother Lewis, Metternich's bitter rival Kolovrat, and Metternich himself. Paralysis of action was inevitable, and the already stagnant bureaucracy excelled itself in the slow amassing of memoranda on which the committee remained deadlocked. Everyone in Vienna became aware of a sense of waiting for an inevitable breakdown, a feeling described after the revolution began in March 1848 as the *Vor-März,* the pre-March years.

Nationalism and Industrialism in the Austrian Empire. In these years of governmental immobility, two principal changes were transforming the empire from within. The first and most important was the rise of nationalism; the second was the beginning of industrialism. About one-quarter of the empire's population was German, concentrated in the Alps, the plains around Vienna, the cities throughout the empire, and the fringes of Bohemia. Germans had a stake in the preservation of the empire because of their dominance of the bureaucracy and commerce; but many were sympathetic to the idea of linking Austrian Germans with the rest of the German states at the expense of abandoning the non-German regions of the empire. The Magyars of Hungary were made up of half a million aristocrats and almost eight million peasants; they retained a strong sense of national identity, encouraged by their national diet and by control of their own local administration. In the great noble Széchényi, Metternich found a Magyar statesman with whom he could collaborate, for Széchényi wanted to encourage the economic development of Hungary within the unity of the Austrian empire, compelling the landed aristocracy and growing middle class of the Hungarian cities to work together, and pay together, for the roads, bridges, and railroads that would modernize the country. Against him, however, Széchényi found the most vital and persuasive propagandist of the new nationalism, Louis Kossuth, a political journalist of genius who harnessed the national pride of middle-class Hungarians against the German dominance of trade and the professions; and his success created opposition to the Magyars among the Croats and among the Rumanians of Transylvania, whom the Magyars considered they themselves should gov-

[8] Bertier de Sauvigny, *Metternich,* p. 143.

ern. The Poles of Galicia, annexed only at the end of the eighteenth century, felt no sympathy for the Austrian empire; and among the landlords and the intellectuals of the University of Cracow, nationalism appeared to be the key to harnessing peasant support. The Czechs remembered the independent kingdom of Bohemia, whose great Hradčany palace still dominated the skyline of Prague, while in Lombardy and Venetia the doctrines of Mazzini's Young Italy were making great progress among the young people of the cities. The Austrian government's answer to the nationalist movement was suppression; and this was quite successful until 1848 because the movement was concentrated among the intellectual classes, the students and professors, the artists and writers, who thought of nationalism in terms of history or linguistics or literature, that is, for whom nationalism was a cultural phenomenon before it became a political movement. Metternich himself was, probably rightly, contemptuous of professors as revolutionaries:

There are no clumsier conspirators than professors, individually or in groups. Conspiracy is only profitable when it is directed against things and not against dogmas. . . . When political dogmas are involved they must be supported by action, but action means the overthrow of every existing institution and the application of the principle 'out of my way and let me in!' Savants and professors are incapable of this; it is the lawyers who are best suited to it.[9]

But the spread of nationalist ideas in the period before 1848, in conjunction with the desire of liberals to overthrow absolutist regimes that had been restored after the French Revolution or had survived it, was extremely dangerous to the survival of an inefficient empire. What provided the final recruits for revolution was the coming of industrialism in the 1830s and 1840s. By 1848, the suburbs of Vienna, both within and beyond the Line Wall, were dotted with textile mills working for the fashion industry of the city. The city population had expanded by almost a hundred thousand in the period after 1815, the increase composed very largely of immigrants from the rural parts of the empire. In Budapest and the western plains of Hungary, Prague and the mining regions of Bohemia, and the cities of Lombardy, the Austrian empire saw the appearance of an urban proletariat and an industrial bourgeoisie. Deep but generally undirected discontent was prevalent in many parts of the Austrian empire by 1848—with the distribution of the land, with factory conditions, with absolutism and the police-state regime, and with the lack of national independence. The very variety of the forms of discontent was, however, regarded by the Austrian government as a source of its own strength; when the Polish landlords and intellectuals revolted on nationalist grounds in 1846, the government encouraged the Polish peasants to turn on them. Rioters in the Prague factories in 1844 attacked not the Austrian administration but the machines they regarded as responsible for their misery. And even in 1848, when the whole con-

[9] Ibid., p. 60.

Austrian Empire 1815

0 ___ 100 Miles

NATIONALITIES
- Germans
- Magyars
- Serbs and Croats
- Ukrainians
- Poles
- Czechs
- Rumanians
- Slovenes
- Italians
- Slovaks

tinent blew up, the revolutionaries within the empire failed because of their division. Metternich himself could probably have survived even that great series of upheavals if he had not been attacked at the point where he was most vulnerable, by the imperial family itself.

VIENNA IN THE BIEDERMEIER ERA

Viennese Escapism. To most Viennese, the Metternich system provided the kind of tranquility they seemed to want. The years from the Congress of Vienna to the Revolution of 1848 were the Biedermeier era, a time of cozy, somewhat cloying sentimentality, middle-class comfort, family virtues, and kindly self-satisfaction. (The name Biedermeier was first applied in satire, by a German writer who put into the mouth of a naive bourgeois schoolteacher called Gottlieb Biedermeier a number of comic poems expressing simple-minded satisfaction in everyday pleasures. The word soon came to be used to describe the forms of taste of the period in all the German-speaking countries.) To one would-be revolutionary, the Viennese were irresponsibly escapist.

The people of Vienna seem to any serious observer to be revelling in an everlasting state of intoxication. Eat, drink, and be merry are the three cardinal virtues and pleasures of the Viennese. It is always Sunday, always Carnival time for them. There is music everywhere. The innumerable inns are always full of roisterers day and night. Everywhere there are droves of fops and fashionable dolls. Everywhere, in daily life, in art, and in literature, there prevails that delicate and witty jesting. For the Viennese the only point of anything, of the most important event in the world, is that they can make a joke about it.[10]

[10] Cited in Edward Crankshaw, *The Fall of the House of Habsburg* (New York: Viking, 1963), p. 23.

The attitude was a natural reaction to the strain of the years of war with
Napoleon, with two occupations of the city itself and the constant drain
on the city's manpower and resources. But the self-indulgence took a form
totally different from that of, for example, London in the 1660s or Paris
after the Terror. The Viennese withdrew into the family circle. Their
pleasures became those of the family, such as music-making in the evening
with the daughters playing the piano (Vienna being the principal center in
Europe for the manufacture of that instrument) or a group of friends singing
from newly printed song-sheets. Many of Schubert's songs were written
for groups like these, and remained in manuscript until well after his death.
The weekly outing was a trip to the Prater, the parkland to the east of the
city, sprinkled with cafes and dance halls, where the aristocrats rode in
formal procession in their coaches. Furniture too took on the comfortable,
upholstered character of the period, curved and even protuberant, decorated with black lacquer and peasant designs. Greeting cards with simple
rhymes called down the blessings of art and nature on their recipients.
Fashionable paintings showed inordinately charming children, or exquisitely charming lovers, or idealized nature, as in the coveted works of
Friedrich von Amerling. The theater too followed the same pattern. Farces

Biedermeier Greeting Card.
The refrain reads: ''May your
life be spent in flowering
meadows, made happy by the
blessings of sweet nature.''
(Bildarchiv d. Ost. Nationalbibliothek.)

A Child's Portrait, by Friedrich von Amerling. The sweet innocence of childhood was a favorite theme of Biedermeier artists. (Bildarchiv d. Ost. Nationalbibliothek.)

and fairy tales, simple stories of peasants making good and being laughed at for their pretensions, and especially stories in praise of the legendary Vienna were especially popular. "Yes, only one Imperial City; Yes, only one Vienna" was the current hit in 1822. And the greatest escapism of all was the waltz. The dance probably originated among the peasants of southern Germany; but at the end of the eighteenth century it appeared on the stage—best of all in Mozart's *Don Giovanni*—and soon all the chief composers, including Haydn, Mozart, and Beethoven were being called on for dances, especially waltzes, for the balls in the Hofburg and at Schönbrunn. "The people of Vienna were in my time dancing mad," wrote a friend of Mozart's. "For my own part I thought waltzing from ten at night until seven in the morning a continual whirligig; most tiresome to eye and ear—to say nothing of any worse consequences."[11] In the post-1815 period, however, Schubert, writing slow regular waltzes for the dances in the open-air taverns of the Vienna woods or the winter parties in the homes of his friends, created one of the finest of Biedermeier forms—warm, pure, rustic, immediately intelligible and likable. In the 1830s, the dance orchestras became far more elaborate with the enormous success of Josef Lanner and Johann Strauss the Elder. At first playing together, then splitting up to form two rival orchestras, these two were both fine showmen and musicians. Lanner remained gently Biedermeier, delicate, sweet, charming; but Strauss became the demon king of the waltz, frenzied, exotic, irresistible. Lanner and Strauss became the chief tourist attractions of Vienna, until 1844 when Strauss's son and namesake formed his own orchestra and began to compose the most popular waltzes of all.

Absolutism à la Viennoise. Behind the scenes of Biedermeier revelry was the constant presence of the secret police. No absolutism has ever succeeded like the Viennese because no other has persuaded its citizens that spontaneous enjoyment is in the interests of the state. The repression of free thought and the arrest of native agitators and the exclusion of foreign were certainly successful, if excessive. The dramatist Grillparzer was forced to keep much of his writing concealed. "The French have driven out their king," Grillparzer noted in his secret diary, "who tried . . . to break the constitution and turn them into a sort of—Austrians, which, civically and politically, seems to be the worst that can happen to anyone." To Metternich it was desirable that science should be encouraged and the humanities kept down; but even science was unable to transcend the kind of bonds that prevented Austria from producing any philosophy or political science except that of Metternich and his brilliant adviser, Gentz, or any theology or history. The creative urge, and even the desire for enjoyment, was channeled by the state into directions that would release enthusiasms harmlessly. The police department had insisted that the Theater an der Wien stay open after the bread riots of 1805, on the grounds that the "people are accustomed to theatrical shows. . . . In times like these, when the character of individuals is affected by so many sufferings, the Police are more than ever obliged to cooperate in the diversion of the citizens by every moral means. The most dangerous hours of the day are the evening hours. They cannot be filled more innocently than in the theater." And what could be more harmless and moral than music? Metternich himself adored it.

[11] Mosco Carner, *The Waltz* (New York: Chanticleer Press, 1948), p. 18.

Nothing affects me like music. I believe that after love, and above all with it, it is of all things in the world the one that makes me a better human being. Music excites and calms me at the same time. It has the same effect on me as something remembered, it takes me outside the narrow framework in which I live. My heart unfolds; it embraces at one and the same time the past, the present, and the future. Everything comes to life: trouble and enjoyment that is past, thoughts and pleasures to which I look forward with yearning. Music rouses me to gentle tears. It draws my sympathy on to myself, it does me good and it hurts me which in itself is good.[12]

Here at least is a partial explanation why the age of Metternich is also the age of Beethoven, and a partial answer to the question as to how the great rebel in music, the passionate lover of human freedom, could work with the master of the Spielberg.

THE MUSIC CAPITAL OF EUROPE

Vienna as Music Patron. Many factors strengthened Vienna's interest in great music, other than the desire of the secret police for a harmless diversion and the emotional needs of an overworked chancellor. The patronage of the Habsburg family for many generations was probably the most important of all. The founder of the dynasty, Rudolf of Habsburg, was a friend of the medieval troubadors, the minnesingers; and one of the greatest among them, Walter von der Vogelweide, declared, "*In Österreich lernt ich singen und sagen*" (I learned to sing and declaim in Austria). By the sixteenth century, there was a large court orchestra and choir; and from the seventeenth century almost every emperor was not only a proficient musician but a composer as well. Even Metternich's Emperor Francis I played second violin in a weekly quartet; his aunt, Queen Marie Antoinette, had lessons from Gluck before her marriage to the dauphin of France. Both Gluck and Mozart were appointed to the position of Royal and Imperial Court Composer, although for a pittance. Until the end of the eighteenth century and in much smaller numbers later, the great aristocrats followed the musical example of the Habsburgs, maintaining their own orchestras and employing their own Kapellmeister, or resident musician. The most famous example was the Esterhazy family at their estate forty miles from Vienna, where Haydn spent thirty years in uninterrupted intellectual growth. "My prince was always satisfied with my works," Haydn explained later. "Not only did I have the encouragement and constant approval but as a conductor of an orchestra I could experiment, observe what produced an effect and what weakened it, and was thus in a position to improve, alter . . . and to be as bold as I pleased. I was cut off from the world; there was nobody to confuse or torment me and I was forced to be original."[13] All the great families, such as the Lobkowitz, the Starhemberg, the Schwarzenberg, gave entertainments at which the symphonies and concertos of their protégés were per-

[12] Bertier de Sauvigny, *Metternich*, p. 8.
[13] Cited in Egon Gartenberg, *Vienna: Its Musical Heritage* (University Park, Pa.: Pennsylvania State University Press, 1968), p. 33.

formed, although many of them also found it necessary to perform as virtuosos as well. Beethoven's powers of improvisation, one of Vienna's favorite diversions, took him into the palace of Prince Lichnowsky, who, Beethoven laughed, "would like to enclose me in a glass ball so that neither the unworthy nor their breath would touch me." As aristocratic patronage declined in the early nineteenth century, the middle classes became increasingly important as patrons, through the purchase of tickets for public concerts like those of the Vienna Philharmonic Orchestra and for opera performances, and sheet music, although Vienna never offered the financial possibilities of London or Paris. Yet it was significant that throughout Austrian society, from the country towns through the court, there existed the habit not merely of listening but of performing music. In the 1770s, the English musical writer Charles Burney commented over and over at the counterpoint singing of scholars in his inn, of glees sung by soldiers on guard, and especially of the music teachers in the provincial towns: "I went into the school, which was full of little children of both sexes, from six to ten or eleven years old, who were reading, writing, playing on violins, hautbois, bassoons, and other instruments."

Vienna's patronage thus encouraged the influx of musicians from all over Europe. "Vienna is so rich in composers and encloses within its walls such a number of musicians of superior merit," Burney went on, "that it is but just to allow it to be, among German cities, the imperial seat of music, as well as of power." These musicians learned from each other, and thereby increased the overall quality of Viennese music. Again, the most outstanding example was the relationship of Haydn and Mozart, from which Haydn, twenty-four years the senior, profited most. Only after he had studied Mozart's work was Haydn able to achieve the purity of his later string quartets, a debt that Haydn willingly acknowledged; but Mozart repaid it with six great quartets that he dedicated to Haydn. Beethoven arrived in Vienna in 1792 to study with Haydn, but impatient from the start soon transferred to lesser musicians. Beethoven taught Czerny, Schubert studied with the court composer Salieri, and so on. But Vienna acted as a fuser of musical styles in a far broader sense, owing to its geographical and cultural position as the meetingplace of the Germanic and Italian worlds.

Early Development of European Music. Until the Renaissance, music had been largely vocal, the few existing instruments being used to accompany the voice; advances had been made through polyphony, the interweaving of several melodic lines, an art which reached one climax in works of Palestrina in the sixteenth century and another, enriched by the use of harmony and colored by full exploitation of the possibilities of the organ and of the infant orchestra, in the vast output of Johann Sebastian Bach. Polyphony had ruled at the Habsburg court in the sixteenth century; but with the visit in 1618 of the first Italian opera company,

Viennese music was dominated for a century and a half by the Italian pursuit of melody, both in the voice and the orchestra that accompanied it. Italian opera was the most baroque of all the arts, combining illusion, sensuality, grandeur, display. Its high point in Vienna was the production in 1666 of Cesti's opera *The Gold Apple* at the marriage celebration of the emperor; the performance, which lasted five hours, took place in a specially built imperial opera house. The stories were usually classical myths, fairly static in performance but allowing great liberty to the human voice, in the arias, to develop flowing lines of melody and infinite decoration of trills and flourishes. It was the Viennese Gluck who brought this style of opera to perfection in the 1760s with *Orfeo* and *Alceste*. The orchestras had improved in parallel with the development of opera for both technical and stylistic reasons; and this too was essential preparation for Vienna's classical age. The harpsichord, the keyboard instrument used to provide continuo in the opera house, in which the strings were plucked by quills, was the most popular, but the pianoforte, in which the strings were struck by hammers, was invented in 1709 and had been perfected by the late eighteenth century. Bach approved of it, but Haydn and Mozart wrote great concertos for it.

Most important, however, was the development of the orchestral stringed instruments. The violin and the other instruments of the same family, the viola and the violoncello, had already been developed by the sixteenth century; but their manufacture was brought to perfection by such craftsmen as Stradivari and Guarneri, and their possibilities for melody, harmony, and tonal color were more fully exploited when the first eighteenth-century virtuosi, like Tartini, took them up. The oboe and bassoon came into regular use at the end of the seventeenth century, the clarinet and the flute at the end of the eighteenth century. By the time of Handel, therefore, the instruments and their combination in the form of the modern orchestra had been achieved.

Moreover, although the possibilities of the orchestra were first tried out in the opera house, the form in which the Viennese composers achieved their greatest work was the symphony, itself the product of the early eighteenth century. A cantata was, in Italian, something sung; a sonata was something played, but it became in the eighteenth century a technical description of a piece of music of three or four movements—usually fast (allegro), slow (adagio), faster (presto)—in the first of which at least one or two themes are presented, developed, and recapitulated. This form, which had been begun in Italy and developed in Germany, gave to orchestral music a strongly intellectual framework. The listener had to think as well as allow the sounds to wash over him. Within this framework enormous variety was possible, by key change, rhythm, tonal coloring, harmony, and as Mozart was to show, the reintroduction of polyphony; and it was in the working out of the full flexibility of the symphonic form that Vienna's composers established their supremacy in the world of music. These forms, moreover, could be transferred from the symphony to the string quartet, the violin or piano concerto, and the keyboard sonata.

Mozart and Haydn. In the second half of the eighteenth century, Viennese music began to break away from Italian supremacy, by drawing on elements from other parts of the Austrian empire and from Germany. Mozart, for example, who had written his first and unsuccessful opera, *Idomeneo,* on the Italian pattern turned for a different example to the German *Singspiel,* a lighthearted, supposedly native combination of song, speaking, and rapid action. The result was *The Abduction from the Seraglio;* when he combined this convention with that of Italian comic opera, opera buffa, he created a series of characters of unforgettable individuality. In *Don Giovanni,* above all, he created one of the greatest of all operas, perhaps the greatest. Every character is memorable: the timid rogue of a manservant, Leporello, with his list of the Don's amorous conquests ("But in Spain, a thousand and three"); the seduced Donna Elvira, who loves Giovanni in spite of his villainy; the flirtatious country girl, Zerlina, and her boob of a fiancé; the powerful figure of Giovanni himself, with such panache in his fights, his parties, and his love affairs that one feels the identification that is essential to great tragedy. And when the statue of the Commendatore whom Giovanni has murdered comes terrifyingly onto the stage to claim the Don for hell, Mozart drops all pretense of gaiety and, in the darkest of all music, presents the inevitability of damnation.

Commendatore: *You invited me to supper.*
Now you know what you must do in turn.
Give me your answer, give me your answer,
Will you come to supper with me?

Don Giovanni: *No one shall ever be able*
To accuse me of cowardice.
I have decided!

Commendatore: *Will you come, then?*

Don Giovanni: *My heart is strong within me,*
I have no fear of you.
I will come.

Commendatore: *Give me your hand to prove it.*

Don Giovanni: *There it is! Oh!*

Commendatore: *Why do you shudder?*

Don Giovanni: *It is as cold as death.*

Commendatore: *Repent, repent your life of sin.*
Your last moment is near.

Don Giovanni: *No! No! I'll not repent.*
Get away from me.

Commendatore: *Repent! Repent!*

Don Giovanni: *No! No! No!* [14]

[14] Author's translation.

Finally, at the end of his life, Mozart combined the opera buffa with another Viennese institution, the fantastic fairy tales of the popular suburban theater; and in Papageno, of the *Magic Flute,* the cheerful, down-to-earth birdcatcher, he transformed the humble traditions of the Viennese pantomime.

It was Haydn who first revealed the richness that could be achieved in the developing form of the symphony, moving in more than a hundred symphonies from charming studies of the morning and night to the depth of the symphonies he wrote in London toward the end of his life. Mozart was to carry on Haydn's use of the orchestra as the presenter of complex melodic relationships and his use of counterpoint, which he wrote with a purity that has never been matched, as in the Fugue to the *Jupiter* Symphony. But it was Ludwig van Beethoven (1770–1827) who made it the supreme expression of man's greatness and man's loneliness, emotional phrases that are necessary to express the great transition from the Classical to the Romantic age in music.

The Genius of Beethoven. Beethoven came to Vienna first at the age of seventeen, possibly to study under Mozart, but returned to his post in the court chapel of Bonn on the death of his mother. He went again, aged twenty-two, to study under Haydn, and stayed there the rest of his life. By the time he was thirty, he had established himself as the undisputed successor of Haydn and Mozart, patronized by the wealthiest aristocrats but differing from them in doing so entirely as his own master. With Beethoven, the rights of genius were respected for the first time as greater than those of birth. "Prince," Beethoven told his patron Lichnowsky, "what you are, you are by accident of birth; what I am, I am of myself. There are and there will be thousands of princes. There is only one Beethoven." The significance of the remark is not that Beethoven could make it, but that his patrons would stomach it; for that appreciation of the importance of individuality, and of the need to recognize individuality in its most creative form, was a cardinal principle of the new intellectual attitude called Romanticism, whose first persuasive expression came from Rousseau.

Beethoven had always been rough and self-assertive, even in the early period of his success as a pianist and composer; but in 1802, he gave expression, in the will he wrote in the Viennese suburban village of Heiligenstadt, to the deep despair and loneliness that were to give unparalleled intensity to his greatest works of the next decade. He was going deaf, from sclerosis of the inner ear. "What a humiliation," he wrote, "when anyone standing near me could hear at a distance a flute that I could not hear, or anyone heard a shepherd singing and I could not distinguish a sound!" The deafness grew progressively worse, compelling him to give up his public performances and to withdraw inside himself to compose the music he would never hear. In his notebooks, he began to elaborate the largest, most intellectually complex, and most emotionally intense of all the symphonies he would ever compose—first a drama of changing keys, then the melodic themes and their development, then a coda of extraordinary length, to complete, in the first movement of the Eroica Symphony, a total change in the ambitions of instrumental music. In this third symphony Beethoven was concerned with the nature of heroism, at first perhaps the lightning successes of Bonaparte but in reality with his own struggle with infirmity. Throughout the symphony there is a feeling of explosive energy, recalling his famous saying, "I will take fate by the throat." The second movement is a funeral march, but it pulses with an unforgettable rhythm that prepares one for the wild syncopation of the scherzo that follows. The last movement, for which he borrowed the theme of his Prometheus ballet, gained its power from a development in the base by means of a fugue, a polyphonic method of playing themes against each other. In the Eroica, it provided a sense of completeness, of integration of the movements that had never been heard before. Beethoven had overcome the inherent difficulty of presenting as a unity four movements that differed in structure, theme, and mood.

Beethoven had done for the sonata form what the thirteenth-century architects had done for the cathedral—he had created a form in which the profoundest human emotions and thoughts could be expressed as an artistic unity. And he was fully aware that each symphony had to be created as a whole. "I alter a great deal, discard and try again until I am satisfied. And then inside my head I begin to work it out, broadening here and restricting there. . . . And since I am conscious of what I am trying to do, I never lose sight of the fundamental idea. It rises up higher and higher and grows before my eyes until I hear and see the image of it, moulded and complete, standing there before my mental vision." [15] Alternating between works of serenity and repose (the Fourth, Sixth, and Eighth symphonies) and works of storm and conflict (the Third, Fifth, and Seventh symphonies), Beethoven plunged into a decade of driving work, increasing the range of his orchestra with new instruments and new demands on old ones, widening the relationships between the keys he employed, broadening the emotional range he wished to express. By 1815, at the end of what is called his "middle period," Beethoven succumbed for several years to his deafness, bad health, and loneliness, and he wrote little. Then, at the end of his life, he wrote his Choral Symphony, a work on an even larger scale than his Eroica, and the totally different, private exploration of spiritual experience of his last Quartets.

Vienna after Beethoven. Franz Schubert, the last of this great generation of Viennese musicians, died a year after Beethoven in 1828, at the age of

[15] Cited in Ralph Hill, ed., *The Symphony* (Harmondsworth, England: Penguin, 1949), p. 94.

Left, **Ludwig van Beethoven in 1814.** (German Information Center.) Right, **Franz Schubert in 1828.** (Bildarchiv d. Ost. Nationalbibliothek.)

thirty-two. Unlike Beethoven, the Viennese only came to know his greatness years later. They knew him as a writer of superb songs (he wrote 603); but only in the 1840s did they realize that they had failed to appreciate another master of the symphony, the quartet, and ballet music. The Unfinished Symphony was found by Robert Schumann when he started going through Schubert's unpublished papers in 1838; and the *Rosamunde* ballet music was found in an old cupboard by Sir Arthur Sullivan in 1868. Vienna had turned to Strauss and Lanner, to the gaiety of Rossini's *Barber of Seville* and the romance of Weber's *Der Freischütz*. The virtuoso reigned—Paganini on the violin, Liszt on the piano, Jenny Lind in singing. In the period of the pre-March days, Viennese creativity in music went into a hiatus, or at least set its sights lower. "How different our feelings were at leaving Vienna from what they had been when we came," wrote Robert Schumann's wife Clara in 1846, after the Viennese had failed to respond to his music or her playing. "Then we thought we had found our future haven of refuge, and now all our desire for it has vanished." Two years later, Vienna had overthrown Metternich, and the composer Richard Wagner thought the city was reborn:

Vienna, on which I set my eyes once again on a fine bright Sunday enchanted me—I admit it! I found Paris again, only more beautiful, more gay and German. During the sixteen years that have passed since I last saw Vienna the whole city has been renewed: its half million inhabitants, all dressed in German colors, poured through the streets on Sunday as if in celebration—on the Saturday a wavering, incompetent Ministry had been forced out by the People's Committee! . . . And now this opulence! This life! The strange costumes they wear, an entirely new type of hat with feathers and tricolor German hat-bands. On almost every house a German flag. . . . And so it goes on. But everything is gay, calm, and youthful.[16]

The Ouster of Metternich. On March 13, 1848, in the early afternoon, a crowd of students and professors from the University of Vienna gathered in the courtyard of the Landhaus where the provincial diet of Lower Austria was meeting to discuss a reform petition they wished to present to the government. Together, students and deputies then made their way to the Ballhausplatz, the square outside Metternich's chancery building, where a few people began to shout, "Down with Metternich." Workers from the depressed suburbs filtered into the inner city, the crowd became large enough to frighten the Viennese military commander, and he ordered his troops to clear the square. They fired point-blank into the crowd, killing five and turning a good-tempered crowd into a furious mob. The students armed themselves by breaking into the city armory; workers denied entry into the inner city at the closed gates returned to burn down their factories near the Line Wall; and several factions of the crowd presented ultimatums to the government demanding Metternich's resignation by that evening. The state council met in indecision, but Metternich's enemies in the court banded against him, delighted to sacrifice him for

[16] Cited in Hürlimann, *Vienna*, p. 93.

The Ouster of Metternich. This political cartoon of March 15, 1848, illustrates the delight of the Viennese masses at the ignominious flight of Metternich. (Bildarchiv d. Ost. Nationalbibliothek.)

their own supposed advantage. The wily diplomat reminded them that the empire was absolute, and that he could be dismissed only by the imbecilic emperor. The emperor's reply was absolute in its concessions: "I am the Emperor, and it is for me to decide; and I yield everything. Tell the people I consent to all their demands." Metternich at once resigned; and the next night he left Vienna with a false passport and a loan of a thousand ducats from the banker Rothschild. A few days later he explained his fall in the same mixture of perception of administrative reality and blindness to social change that characterized his whole chancellorship: "You know what I have wanted without being able to achieve it. Above all I insisted upon establishing of a *governing power* without which a state cannot be."

The Wave of Revolution. Metternich had failed to realize that his enforcement on most of Europe of a policy of procrastination in meeting widely supported demands for political and social reform had brought the whole continent to a state of revolution, of which events in Vienna were only a small part. The year of revolution began with an uprising in January in Palermo in Sicily against Ferdinand II, which was followed by similar revolts in most of the larger Italian cities. The Parisians revolted against King Louis-Philippe on February 22, and two days later France had become a republic again. On March 3, the Hungarian popular nationalist leader Kossuth gave a dramatic speech, demanding Hungarian autonomy and constitutional reform in the Austrian empire; the diet formulated a new Hungarian constitution after the resignation of Metternich; and the emperor agreed to the changes at the end of the month. Similar demands by delegations of Czechs were granted in April, since the people of Prague had also revolted. Barricades went up in Berlin in mid-March after a clash between troops and a mob, and the king capitulated by calling a constituent assembly and appointing a liberal ministry; and the news from Prussia encouraged uprisings in many of the smaller German states. In all there were some fifty separate revolutions, almost all in large towns; and in every case the governments conceded many of the demands of the revolutionaries. In the spring of 1848, it appeared that Metternich's Europe had disappeared with the downfall of the archconservative. "*Eh bien, mon cher, tout est fini*" (Well, old friend, everything is finished), Metternich remarked after the revolution in Paris. Forces of change common to most of Europe had combined with factors of discontent particular to individual regions to produce universal, but short-lived, revolution.

In part, the revolutionary movement was a revival of the liberalism encouraged by the first French Revolution. The demands of the leaders, who were largely from the intellectual classes and the commercial and industrial middle class, included the abolition of such police controls as censorship and political imprisonment, the grant of a constitution, freedom of speech and assembly, and an end to aristocratic privilege.

In regions like Germany and Italy where a nation was divided into several political units, or like the Austrian empire where several nations were incorporated in one political unit dominated by one nationality, the revolutionaries demanded the formation of nation states, or at least of a nation state dominated by their own particular nationality. Because both liberalism and nationalism were intellectual theories, almost ideologies, they were preached largely by the intellectual classes of the cities, and specifically by university teachers, lawyers, and journalists. In this sense, far more than the first French Revolution had been, the revolution of 1848 was a "revolution of the intellectuals." But, in spite of the charisma of such leaders as Kossuth or Mazzini, more down-to-earth causes of dissatisfaction impelled the working classes to risk their lives in street demonstrations and on the barricades, and brought the peasantry to share in the revolution. Rapid population growth produced social dislocation in both countryside and city. Europe's population grew from 192 million in 1800 to 274 million in 1850. The population of both France and Austria grew by a third. This increase was due to improved medical care, especially of infant children and older people, to an improved food supply through better agricultural metnods and transportation, and to freedom from civil and religious war and internal disorder. In the agrarian lands of Eastern Europe, the pressure of population on limited resources of land produced a stronger resentment of remaining feudal privilege and labor services; throughout Europe, it made efficient farming profitable, encouraged consolidation of estates by purchases and the move of their former owners into the cities which grew in size at a far higher rate than the total population. In the cities the former peasants found inadequate housing, social discrimination, and except in England and Belgium, few jobs. In the Austrian empire, where most of the newcomers to the cities were Slavs, they found racial discrimination as well. They were more vulnerable than ever to the periodic recessions within the capitalist system of production, and especially to the harvest failures like those in potatoes and grain in 1846–1847. For the first time, the workers expressed their grievances in a specific economic demand upon the state, the right to a job.

Revolution's Ephemeral Triumphs. During the first phase of the revolutions, most of the liberal demands were satisfied, and a beginning was made in satisfying the nationalists. By May, new constitutions had been written or were being prepared in France, Prussia and many German states, Austria, Hungary, Bohemia, and several Italian states. Hungary and Bohemia had been promised autonomy; an elected national parliament was meeting in Frankfurt to draw up a federal constitution for the whole of Germany; and the king of Piedmont-Sardinia had been supplied with troops from most other Italian states to fight a war of national liberation against Austria. During the following six months, more radical demands were made by extremists among liberal leaders; the wealthier

The Ceremonial Entry of the Frankfurt Parliament into the Paulskirche, 1848. As a free city, Frankfurt was able to host the nationally elected parliament whose goals were opposed by most hereditary German rulers. (German Information Center.)

among those who had formerly supported the revolutions and the peasantry turned against them, and supported the governments in their decision to crush the revolutions by use of the army. By the end of the year, in most European countries, a new period of reaction had begun. In Paris, the liberal government that took over in Feburary had broken with its working-class supporters by ordering the suppression of the national workshops it had created to provide jobs for the unemployed; and in June, when the Paris crowds seized the working-class quarters, they used the regular army and mobs of peasants, who came by train to the fighting, to bring Paris into submission. The ultimate victor in this political struggle was Napoleon's nephew, Louis Napoleon Bonaparte, who was elected president of the Second Republic in December because an overwhelming majority of the French peasants and bourgeoisie saw in him a "symbol of order." In Prussia in November, the king ordered the return of the regular army to barracks in the city from which they had been withdrawn during the March riots, suspended the meetings of the National Assembly, and in March 1849 contemptuously turned down the Frankfurt Parliament's request that he become "emperor of the Germans." The Frankfurt Parliament itself, an assembly of impractical scholars, lawyers, and businessmen, had written a fine charter of fundamental rights and an advanced constitution, and it had finally brought itself to accept the probable exclusion of

Austria from the unified German states; but it had no armed forces and no authority recognized by the larger German states. When the king of Prussia ordered the Prussian delegates home, several other states followed his example; and the few remaining members finally dispersed in June. With Prussia under control, the king dispatched his army to Dresden, where it restored the king of Saxony, and to Baden and the Rhenish Palatinate to suppress rebellions in western Germany. It was, however, with the aid of the Russians that Austria was to bring its own empire and the rest of Italy under control.

Revolution à la Viennoise.   In Vienna, after the departure of Metternich, the revolution developed a party atmosphere. ''It was the gayest revolution imaginable,'' wrote Grillparzer. ''Favored by the most beautiful spring weather, the whole population filled the streets all day long'' [17] When the emperor announced on March 15 that he was granting a constitution, the whole inner city was illuminated. But the new cabinet was full of reactionaries, the new constitution was issued without consultation with

[17] Cited in Barea, *Vienna*, p. 194.

Viennese Fashions in 1848.   (Bildarchiv d. Ost. Nationalbibliothek.)

the diet, and the city's garrison had been doubled with troops who were
advertising their arrival by pitching tents in the open land around the wall
of the inner city. Even a more liberalized constitution issued in May
stated: "Workmen paid by the day or by the week, domestic servants,
and persons receiving public assistance are not eligible to vote for candidates standing for the Chamber of Deputies." A huge crowd of workers,
students, and the National Guard marched on the Hofburg on May 15 to
present a new petition, during which the army terrified the court by frater-
nizing with the marchers. The emperor was then removed to the imperial
palace in Innsbruck by the leading courtiers, to get him away from the influence of the Viennese revolutionaries; but the government felt compelled
to agree to universal suffrage and a one-chamber legislature for the whole
empire. Meanwhile, the workers had been slightly appeased with a public
works program of road construction and waste reclamation, a concession
to their demand for the "right to work."

The success of the Viennese revolution was, however, dependent on
concurrent success of the revolutions in the other parts of the empire;
and there the Austrian forces were commanded by ruthless, efficient,
conservative soldiers. General Windischgrätz pulled his troops out of
Prague in June, leaving the city in the hands of students and workers.
A week later he bombarded the city into submission. In Italy, Field Marshal
Radetsky defeated the king of Piedmont at the decisive battle of Custozza
on July 26, and broke the revolt in Lombardy by taking Milan. The Magyars
of Hungary, who had refused to grant to the Serbs and Croats in the section
of the empire they controlled any form of national autonomy, were faced by
revolt, supported by the new governor of Croatia, Colonel Jellachich.
In September, Jellachich began to march on Budapest. To support him,
the imperial government in Vienna ordered part of the Viennese garrison
to Hungary, to help crush the government of Kossuth which most of the
Viennese revolutionaries felt to be their indispensable support. Demonstrations to stop the trains leaving with the troops for Hungary began on
October 6; railroad lines were pulled up, and telegraph wires cut; and
when the government turned loyal troops against the crowds, the mob
succeeded in lynching the minister of war. Windischgrätz and Jellachich
were then ordered to march against Vienna.

For three weeks, Vienna was besieged by the imperial armies, and
was defended only by bands of university students, impoverished workers
and craftsmen, and a few idealistic bourgeois. At first the defenders tried
to hold the Line Wall, converting the poor houses along it into bastions.
But Windischgrätz repeated his Prague tactics, and bombarded the central
city for several days. A Hungarian army sent to relieve the city was beaten
back without difficulty, and in the final assault on October 30 the imperial
armies broke through the Line Wall in the morning; and in the afternoon,
after severe fighting at the Burgtor near the imperial palace, the inner city
was taken. Windischgrätz then turned his troops loose on the population,

permitting looting and indiscriminate savagery. Although only twenty-five people were officially executed, it is probable that several thousand were killed. Martial law was imposed, thousands were jailed, and informers encouraged to denounce the untrustworthy. The city thus suffered from the worst kind of civil war, a kind of family struggle symbolized by the split in the Strauss family. Johann Strauss the Elder wrote his "Radetsky March" to celebrate the fall of Milan; Johann Strauss the Younger played his "Revolution March" and "Songs of the Barricades" daily on the ramparts of the inner city during the October siege. He was to spend the next two decades creating his own myth of a Vienna that existed in his imagination, the Vienna of the "Blue Danube," the "Tales of the Vienna Woods," and his last, "Wiener Blut."

Restoration of Absolutism. The new imperial cabinet under Prince Schwarzenberg moved to restore efficiency to Austrian abolutism. The emperor Ferdinand was persuaded to abdicate in favor of his eighteen year-old-nephew, Francis Joseph, who was to govern for the next sixty-eight years. New law courts and government ministries were instituted. Internal customs barriers were ended, to make the Austrian empire into one of the world's largest economic units, and thus encourage capitalist industrial development. And most important of all, the remaining feudal rights of landlords, such as judicial powers over the peasants and the right to demand forced labor were abolished, so that the peasant became free to own land and equally free to be forced, by economic necessity, to sell his land and move to the cities. A new efficient absolutism based on an alliance with the upper middle class was thus the first internal result of the Viennese revolution. In dealing with the rest of the empire, no progress was made toward a solution of the nationality question. The constituent assembly's suggested constitution providing national and local autonomy was ignored. The demands of German nationalists were foiled by reintroduction of the German Confederation of 1815. And the remaining centers of revolt were soon defeated. The aid of one hundred forty thousand Russian troops was needed to bring about the defeat of the Hungarians; but in Italy, Radetsky besieged Venice by land and sea, driving it into defeat with starvation, cholera, and shelling. Rome, where a republic had been set up in 1849, led by Mazzini and defended by the charismatic guerrilla hero Garibaldi, was captured by a French army dispatched by the new French president, Louis Napoleon Bonaparte.

Thus liberalism and nationalism had failed to triumph over the Metternich system. Liberal leadership had been idealistic but impractical. Nationalism had proved itself to be a divisive force, even between movements whose goal was nationalism; and quarrels among different nationalities had been one decisive cause of the failure of the revolutions. Industrialism had been sufficiently far advanced to create an impoverished proletariat in certain large cities, but insufficiently advanced for the working classes to be numerous enough to create a revolutionary movement of their own. Industrialism indeed had provided the railroad and the telegraph and the big guns by which the reactionary government forces could subdue the revolutions. Would-be organizers of liberal, nationalist, or social revolutions were thus forced into a period of reassessment of both aim and technique, which is one of the main themes of the next half-century. The restored court society of Vienna had little appeal to the statesman it had so gladly sacrificed at the beginning of the revolution. Metternich was perfectly at home in London, where he found a society surprisingly akin to his own ideals, "a calm of which the continent has lost even the memory, and for which it ought in its own interest to find a taste again." But his wife was restless, and in 1851 he returned to Vienna, from which he continued to offer the governments of Europe his own suavely reasoned advice, which was sought by everyone from the British foreign secretary to the sultan of Turkey. Nothing had changed, he felt, with his fall from power: "My disappearance from the stage has not influenced things; it may be reduced to this: There is one man less but not one need or one necessity less."

SUGGESTED READING

Ilsa Barea, *Vienna: Legend and Reality* (1966) is a delightful reconstruction of the city's social history, combining literary sources with sound historical documentation; the Biedermeier period receives specially sympathetic treatment. Arthur May describes the physical appearance of Vienna in 1848 in the opening chapter of *Vienna in the Age of Franz Josef* (1966). A brief history with fine photographs is given by Martin Hürlimann, *Vienna* (1970). The intellectual background of eighteenth-century Vienna is painstakingly dissected in Robert A. Kann, *A Study in Austrian Intellectual History: From Late Baroque to Romanticism* (1960).

Among the general works on Austrian history, A. J. P. Taylor's *The Habsburg Monarchy, 1809–1918* (1948), though concentrating almost exclusively on political and diplomatic history, is still the most useful. Arthur May, *The Age of Metternich, 1814–1848* (1963) is brief but old-fashioned. There is no good economic history of the Austrian empire in English, but some information can be gleaned from Shepard Clough and Charles W. Cole, *An Economic History of Europe* (1952). The agrarian situation is profoundly analyzed in Jerome Blum, *Noble Landowners and Agriculture in Austria* (1948).

On Metternich, there is an abundance of material, too much of it polemical. The chancellor is his own best advocate, in his *Memoirs,* edited by Prince Richard Metternich (1888), and in the superbly chosen quotations that form the major portion of G. de Bertier de Sauvigny, *Metternich and His Times* (1970). Helene du Coudray, *Metternich* (1936) and Constantin de Grünwald, *Metternich* (1953) are a bit romanticized, but have useful primary materials. Henry A. Kissinger's *A World Restored* (1964) is an exciting and evocative analysis of the diplomacy through

1829. Enno E. Kraehe, *Metternich's German Policy*, vol. 1, *The Contest with Napoleon, 1799–1814* (1963) is a standard treatment of the early years. The Congress of Vienna is reconstructed by Harold Nicolson, *The Congress of Vienna, A Study in Allied Unity, 1812–1822* (1946) and Charles K. Webster, *The Congress of Vienna, 1814–1815* (1934). The atmosphere of the year can be sampled in John Fisher, *Eighteen Fifteen: An End and a Beginning* (1963), which describes a football match organized by Walter Scott and the breakthrough across the Blue Mountains of Australia as well as the Congress.

Musical Vienna can be enjoyed in Egon Gartenberg's *Vienna: Its Musical Heritage* (1968) and Hans Gal, *The Golden Age of Vienna* (1948). For scholarly analysis of the Viennese classical age of music, see Alec Robertson and Denis Stevens, eds., *The Pelican History of Music*, vol. 3, *Classical and Romantic* (1968); W. H. Hadow, *The Oxford History of Music*, vol. 5, *The Viennese Period* (1904); and Paul Henry Lang, *Music in Western Civilization* (1941). On individual composers, there are fine biographies by Alfred Einstein of *Gluck* (1945), and *Schubert* (1951). See also Einstein's *Music in the Romantic Era* (1947). For Haydn, consult Karl Geiringer, *Haydn: A Creative Life in Music* (1946). For Beethoven's life, but not his music, Alan Pryce-Jones has a short biography, *Beethoven* (1957); J. W. N. Sullivan, *Beethoven* (1949) is a fine analysis of the music. Mosco Carner, *The Waltz* (1948) compares the dance kings.

The revolutions of 1848 throughout Europe are ably dissected in Priscilla Robertson, *The Revolutions of 1848* (1952); and in François Fejtö, ed., *The Reopening of an Era, 1848: A Historical Symposium* (1948), in which Robert Endres (pp. 253–80) deals with the revolution in Vienna. For a detailed study of events in Vienna, see R. John Rath, *The Viennese Revolution of 1848* (1957). Arnold Whitridge covers the fall of Metternich in *Men in Crisis: The Revolution of 1848* (1949). Lewis B. Namier, *1848: The Revolution of the Intellectuals* (1946) is particularly good on Germany.

19
THE INDUSTRIAL REVOLUTION

The political history of the years from the American Revolution to the revolutions of 1848 was marked by the rise of liberalism and nationalism and the unsuccessful attempts to suppress them. The economic history of this period was shaped by the completion of the first phase of Europe's industrialization, the "revolution of coal and iron," which began in England in the late eighteenth century and spread to the continent in the three decades following the Congress of Vienna. Industrialization involved changes greater than Western society had ever undergone: the replacement of human and animal power by machinery of infinitely greater effectiveness; the exploitation of largely unused natural resources, especially those in the subsoil; the supplanting of the craftsman by the factory; the conversion of the majority of the laboring population from peasants to an urban proletariat and the relegation of agriculture to a minor role compared with industry in the production of economic wealth; the depopulation of the countryside and the urbanization of life; an unprecedented growth in population; the unification of the world through new means of transportation and communications; the appearance of an entrepreneurial middle class that replaced the aristocracy as the possessor of the major portion of society's wealth; antagonism between employer and worker that varied from union-owner bargaining to open class war; and perhaps most important of all the development and application of new political ideologies conceived as a solution to the problems inherent in industrial society. These generalizations take body when we consider Manchester, the city universally recognized in the early nineteenth century as the prototype of the new society.

"From this foul drain the greatest stream of human industry flows out to fertilize the whole world," wrote Alexis de Tocqueville, after visiting Manchester in 1835. "From this filthy sewer pure gold flows. Here humanity attains its most complete development and its most brutish, here civili-

MANCHESTER AND THE ORIGINS OF THE INDUSTRIAL REVOLUTION

A Manchester Cotton Mill, 1842.

zation works its miracles and civilized man is turned almost into a savage." [1]
The reason that Manchester enjoyed and endured this mixed blessing was
obvious to all observers: Lancashire, with Manchester as its industrial
heart, had adopted the modern factory system. Everything de Tocqueville
observed was the result of that one essential change.

Manchester lay on the edge of the plain of southwestern Lancashire,
where the prevailing westerly winds from the Atlantic hurled rain-heavy
clouds against the steep slopes of the Pennine range. It was for long a
pleasant market town bringing a taste of urban amenity to a backward
agricultural region. A sixteenth-century visitor called it "the fairest, best
buildid, quikkest and most populous toun of all Lancashire," but then it
had little competition in attractiveness from the scrawny fishing village of
Liverpool or the gloomy fortress of Lancaster. The changes in the rest of
Britain made it possible for Manchester, from the 1770s on, to capitalize
on its natural if hitherto unappreciated advantages—its humid climate, its
access to water power, the availability of labor from its depressed countryside, its outlet to the sea through the great natural harbor of Liverpool, perhaps even the thrifty and uncompromising Protestantism of its inhabitants.

Prerequisites for Industrialization in Britain. By 1770, Britain alone
possessed all the factors necessary for an "industrial revolution," a phrase
first used in the 1820s to show that the industrial changes taking place were
of the same magnitude as the political changes introduced by the French
Revolution. Geographically, it was ideally suited to becoming a great
industrial power. No point in Britain is more than seventy miles from the
sea. Fine harbors existed on every coast—Glasgow, Liverpool, Bristol,
Southampton, London, Newcastle, among many. Distances were so small
and natural barriers so negligible that where rivers were inadequate for
inland transportation by water, canals could be constructed with relative
ease and profit. Rich, accessible deposits of raw materials were awaiting
exploitation: coal in Tyneside near Newcastle, in Lancashire near Manchester, in Staffordshire near Birmingham, and in South Wales; iron ore,
along the eastern and southern slopes of the Pennines; even the clay that
was to be made into the Wedgwood pottery of Etruria. Easily harnessed
water power was provided by the steep streams of the Pennine range, such
as the Ribble, the Tees, and the Irwell.

Economically, it possessed the instruments necessary for making use of
these natural advantages. In the two centuries since it had first challenged
the Spanish on the seas, Britain had built the largest merchant marine in
the world, perhaps as many as six thousand ships employing a hundred
thousand seamen; and these ships were engaged in a regular trade, not only
with the British colonial empire but with the Baltic, the Turkish empire, the
Spanish and Portuguese colonies, and West Africa. The East Indiamen were

[1] Cited E. J. Hobsbawm, *Industry and Empire: An Economic History of Britain since 1750*
(London: Weidenfeld and Nicolson, 1968), p. 27.

The Industrial Revolution in Britain, about 1840

even sailing to China. With great commercial expertise, the merchant classes of England had thus accumulated capital, for which insufficient investment opportunities existed in commerce itself. So too had the enterprising noblemen who were converting English agriculture, through the "enclosure" of the open fields and common pasture, from predominantly subsistence farming to a capitalistic agriculture geared to profit making through sale on a nationwide market. This conversion, incidentally, had changed the social structure of English farming from a landowning peasantry to a threefold structure of landowning aristocracy, tenant farmer, and hired laborer. The excess capital in the hands of the mercantile and the agrarian nobility was mobilized through the development of a fine banking system—a central national bank in the Bank of England founded in 1694 and a large number of private banks, including such long-lived institutions as Barclay's and Martin's. The function of the banking system in the industrialization of Britain was to transfer money accumulated largely in the South and West to the North, especially from the 1820s when large-scale

Coal Miners at Work, 1871.
Mining conditions improved
very slightly during the nineteenth century. Coal was still
dug by hand, but light was
provided by a safety lamp,
and children drove pit ponies
instead of pulling the carts
of coal themselves. (*The
Graphic*, January 28, 1871.)

investment in iron and coal and in railroads seemed inviting. Experience
in formation of joint-stock companies for such trading ventures as the
Muscovy company and even for the Bank of England had provided financial
knowledge and safeguards that could be applied in the formation of industrial companies, and indeed had accustomed many to the uses that could
be made of ''risk capital.''

Not only did the agricultural improvements provide surplus capital for
reinvestment; their most significant effect was to make possible greater
productivity both per man and per acre. Fallow was no longer necessary,
with the improved crop rotation, especially through the use of clover and
turnips, which not only restored the fertility of the soil after wheat-growing
but also provided fodder for animals. The wasteful strips in the open fields
were gone, and the laborer no longer lost hours in moving between his
scattered holdings. Improved breeding of animals, especially cattle and
sheep, enormously increased the contribution of livestock to agricultural
income. By the mid–eighteenth century, only one-third of Britain's population worked in agriculture, and it was only in the 1780s that Britain for
the first time was unable to feed its population from home production. As
a result of the agricultural changes, combined with a continual rise in the
total population caused principally by improved diet and medical care, a
large number of the rural workers became redundant; and since they no
longer lived on family farms, they were unable to remain underemployed
at home, like their counterparts on the continent, but went on poor relief
or sought employment in the industry of the cities. The agrarian changes

thus provided laborers for the factories and much of the food to feed them.

Finally, the political and social climate, an intangible but significant factor, was conducive to industrialization. As a result of the constitutional struggles of the seventeenth century, the government was stable and in the hands of the upper classes. The upper classes, however, respected and encouraged through legislation the talent for making money; and possession of wealth was a guarantee of upward social mobility, though not always at the pace its owner might have wished. The power of the state, to some extent its army but largely its navy, was available for the extension overseas of Britain's economic interests, as was clearly displayed when, in the Seven Years' War, the government accepted that Britain's national interest was to prevent the East India Company from being ejected from Bengal. All of these factors contributed to the success of that dour, self-confident, forceful capitalist who became known throughout England as the Manchester Man.

The First Textile Inventions. Manchester had been a textile town at least since the sixteenth century; but it was mostly woolen goods, spun and woven in the cottages of the neighboring villages by peasant families, that constituted the bulk of trade. Slowly, the product became more varied with the introduction of linen from Ireland and silk from Damascus, and especially of cotton. Fustians (a mixture of cotton from Cairo and linen), and calico (cloth of cotton from Calcutta), and muslin (manufactured from cotton of Mosul in Iraq) were exported to many parts of Europe and especially to Africa. The cotton merchants in Manchester at the beginning of the eighteenth century were therefore aware of the potential market for cotton goods, based on the comfort and wearing quality of cotton cloth compared with wool, and of the inability of spinners to keep up with the weavers, especially those who had started to use a weaving machine called the Dutch loom, imported from Holland in 1660. The industrial revolution began when inventors in or near Manchester invented machines for speeding the process of spinning and weaving and Northern businessmen put them into use in factories.

This first phase of industrialization did not require great scientific knowledge in the inventors nor large capital investment from the manufacturers. The first of the Lancashire inventors, John Kay, was a weaver who worsened the imbalance between the efficiency of spinning and weaving by inventing the "flying shuttle," an ingenious combination in which the operator was able, with one hand, to control two hammers that tapped a shuttle on wheels from side to side across the lengthwise threads of the loom. Not only could cloth be woven faster, but for the first time a piece could be made wider than the operator's outstretched arms. When the flying shuttle was widely adopted in the 1760s, the Society for the Encouragement of Arts and Manufactures of London was so struck by the need of comparable productivity in spinning that it offered two prizes for "the best invention of a machine that will spin six threads of wool, flax, cotton, or silk, at one time, and that will require but one person to work it and to attend it." The desired invention was patented in 1770 by James Hargreaves of Blackburn, a cotton town near Manchester, who turned his dual skills as carpenter and weaver to making a machine that could spin eight threads at once. Within twenty years, twenty thousand of these "spinning jennies" were in use in England, and the spinning wheel had almost disappeared from Lancashire. (Hargreaves does not seem to have won the Society's prize, however, and his invention was pirated by others.) The application of water power to spinning followed shortly after, when Richard Arkwright invented the "water frame" at Preston, twenty miles from Manchester. Arkwright was a barber and wigmaker, whose business acumen drove him into not only invention but the large-scale merchandising of his product. For Thomas Carlyle, whose popular writings in the 1830s blackened the fame of Manchester's capitalists for all England, he was typical of the industrial exploiter, a "plain, almost gross, bag-cheeked, pot-bellied Lancashire man, with an air of painful reflection, yet also of copious free digestion. . . . Oh, reader, what a historical phenomenon is that bag-cheeked, pot-bellied, much enduring, much inventing barber!" Arkwright went on to become the richest cotton spinner in England, and his factories became the model for the whole textile industry. When Samuel Crompton of Bolton invented his "mule," a combination of the water frame and the spinning jenny, the spinners at last exceeded the output of the weavers, and moreover were able to produce all varieties of cotton thread from coarse and strong to the

Spinning Cotton. In this Manchester factory, water power was applied to drive the cotton "mules," in which one worker could supervise the spinning of a large number of threads.

Weaving Cotton. In a Manchester factory like this one, frequent accidents were caused by the unprotected belts of the power looms.

most delicate muslin. Thus, the first phase of the revolution in cotton production was in cotton spinning; and by 1800, Manchester had become the leading city to apply the inventions in factory production. Arkwright himself built the first spinning mill in Manchester in the 1780s; by 1802, there were fifty-two such mills. Twenty years later, one-quarter of all the cotton spindles in Britain were in Manchester. By then, weaving sheds were being added to the spinning mills to accommodate the final major invention of this technological revolution, the power loom of Edmund Cartwright, a Leicestershire clergyman who was stimulated by conversation with some Manchester businessmen to invent the needed weaving machine. His own ingenuous description shows just how amateurish such an inventor might be:

It struck me that . . . since there could only be three movements which were to follow each other in succession, there could be little difficulty in producing and repeating them. . . . To my great delight, a piece of cloth, such as it was, was the product. As I had never before turned my thoughts to anything mechanical, either in theory or practice, nor had even seen a loom at work, or known anything of its construction, you will readily suppose that my first loom was a most rude piece of machinery. The warp was placed perpendicularly, the reed fell with the weight of at least half a hundredweight, and the springs which threw the shuttle were strong enough to have thrown a rocket.[2]

[2] Cited in John Sanders, *Manchester* (London: Rupert Hart-Davis, 1967), p. 66.

The Bridgewater Factory.
The factory was located where
the Liverpool and Manchester
Railway crossed the Duke
of Bridgewater's Canal.

Canals, Steam Engines, and Railroads. The growth of Manchester's cotton industry stimulated other forms of industrial progress. As early as 1759, the duke of Bridgewater, whose estate at Worsley a few miles to the north had rich coal deposits, determined to become the main supplier to the growing city by cutting a canal from the underground galleries in Worsley to the heart of Manchester. He called in James Brindley, a brilliant though almost illiterate engineer, who in two years organized the cutting of the canal, even though the first stages were 550 feet below ground and an aqueduct had to be built to carry the canal 40 feet above the river Irwell. The canal, the first true canal in Britain, halved the price of coal in Manchester, and was regarded by contemporaries as a marvel of engineering. Brindley followed it by linking Manchester to the river Mersey and thus to the port of Liverpool with the Bridgewater Canal, 42 miles long. Manchester thus started the rest of the country on a mania of canal building, which by the beginning of the nineteenth century had linked the chief industrial centers of Britain with each other and with their ports, and perhaps most important of all, had connected the North and South of England with the Grand Trunk Canal. This canal and its branches, Brindley's greatest and last undertaking, linked Manchester, the Midlands, London, and the western ports on the river Severn.

Apart from good transport, the cotton industry required power. Steam engines had been in use since the early eighteenth century to pump water out of coal mines; but in 1769, James Watt, a scientific-instrument maker at the University of Glasgow, invented the first engine that used steam power rather than atmospheric pressure to drive the piston of his engine. It economized greatly on the use of fuel, and as he later showed, could be converted from up-and-down to rotary motion. In a long and profitable partnership with a Birmingham businessman, Mathew Boulton, Watt sold engines to most of the mining districts of Britain. The principal customer proved to be the cotton mills of Lancashire, although Manchester was also developing its own foundries and engineering works that supplied it with an independent brand of steam engine. In the last quarter of the eighteenth century, three times as many steam engines were used in textile mills as in the mines.

Manchester too stimulated the most far-reaching application of the steam engine—to railroad transportation. Railways, that is, parallel metal rails on which trucks were pulled, had been used in the mines since the 1700s, and a complicated steam locomotive had been used in a few cases. In 1829, George Stephenson, an engineer from the Tyneside mines, perfected a locomotive called the Rocket, in which steam pressure was applied, in rotary motion, to drive a piston connected directly to the wheels. Stephenson was commissioned by the Liverpool and Manchester Railway Committee to link the two cities by railroad; and at a famous competition on a specially built piece of track at Rainhill, half way between Liverpool and Manchester, he demonstrated that his Rocket could travel at 29 miles an hour pulling a 13-ton load. At the official opening of the railroad a year

Stephenson's Rocket. The first railroad engine, demonstrated in 1829, harnessed the power of the steam boiler by linking cast-iron pistons to the two back wheels. (Loan Collection, Free Library of Philadelphia.)

later, attended by the whole government, the Rocket had the unfortunate distinction of running down and killing the Home Secretary in the first fatal railroad accident. As with the Bridgewater Canal, the success of the Liverpool and Manchester Railway set off a new transportation mania. By 1843, nineteen hundred miles of railroad had been constructed in Britain, and all the main cities were linked more effectively than they had ever been by canal. Moreover, as we shall see later, the railroad had enormously increased the use of coal and iron, thereby introducing a second phase of the industrial revolution, in which cotton would no longer be king.

Manchester's Overseas Trade. Overseas, too, the influence of Manchester's cotton merchants was strongly felt. Vast quantities of the raw material were needed. In 1785, ten million pounds of cotton were imported; in 1850, five hundred eighty-eight million. At their peak, cotton imports accounted for one-fifth of all British imports. For most of the eighteenth century, the West Indian islands supplied the bulk of Lancashire's needs; and the cotton trade thus increased the need for African slaves in those islands and magnified the profits of the merchants of nearby Liverpool who supplied them. From the 1790s, however, the southern states of the United States of America became the main cotton supplier, after Eli Whitney's invention of the gin had made possible the use of the American brand of short-stapled cotton. By 1830, three-quarters of the cotton imported by Britain was grown on the slave plantations of the southern United States. The British cotton industry was largely responsible for the spread of cotton plantations from the Old South into the Gulf states and the Mississippi valley in the early nineteenth century and for making slavery pay. The effect of exports of cotton goods was also considerable. In Europe, British cotton goods were able for half a century to delay the growth of native cotton industries because, as a Lancashire cotton millionaire explained, "We can spin both cheaper and better, and we can print not only cheaper and better. . . . With respect to colours and taste, I think we are on a par with any other country." But war and trade barriers restricted the growth of British exports to Europe; and the cotton industry became largely dependent on exports to the underdeveloped parts of the world, many of which were part of the British empire, or soon to be. Latin America took more British cotton than Europe after gaining its independence from Spain; the native Indian industry collapsed before Lancashire's competition; and Lancashire shirts were worn by West Africans, those at home and the slaves in the West Indies, by the citizens of the Turkish empire, and even by Chinese peasants. Cotton established a form of economic imperialism, in which native industries of unprotected countries were severely restricted and concentration on production of raw materials for the industry of the developed countries encouraged. Some writers have held that the large share of the underdeveloped world in the markets for British cotton goods impelled the British government to seek an extension of its territorial empire; but even in the case of India, it has been hard to prove that the cotton manufacturers could not have extended their sales without political controls.

The Manchester Businessman. What most impressed contemporary observers about the growth of Manchester's industry was the entirely new type of society it seemed to have created. Manchester was divided into two social classes, between whom there appeared to be no bonds of any kind except what Carlyle called the cash nexus. And what is more, both classes in Manchester, the millowners and the workers, were new to England. To many, the millowner represented a vital, sound new force in English life. Without the cotton plants, wrote one of them, "those majestic masses of men which stretch, like a living zone, through our central districts, would have had no existence; and the magic impulse which has been felt during that period in every department of national energy, which has affected more or less our literature, our laws, our social condition, our political institutions, making us almost a new people, would never have been communicated."[3] Such self-made men included the early socialist theorist Robert Owen, who began in Manchester with £100, and eventually was able to pay £84,000 in cash to pay off his factory. But they were probably represented better by the industrialist whom Friedrich Engels described in a famous anecdote:

One day I walked with one of these middle-class gentlemen into Manchester. I spoke to him about the disgraceful unhealthy slums and drew his attention to the disgusting condition of that part of the town in which the factory workers lived. I declared that I had never seen so badly built a town in my life. He listened patiently and at the corner of the street at which we parted company, he remarked: "And yet there is a great deal of money made here. Good morning, Sir!"[4]

The Manchester businessmen were deeply and personally involved in the production of the factories. Many had begun their careers as spinners or weavers themselves, others as manufacturers of textile equipment, still others as brokers of raw cotton or the finished goods. They knew every detail of the process of manufacture, worked enormously long hours themselves, took risks with their capital, and demanded very high profit margins from their investment. Their driving energy impressed the older landed aristocracy when they saw it in action in the great propaganda machine of the Anti–Corn Law League, which Manchester erected in the 1840s to force Parliament to end protection of England's wheat farmers. And they so impressed contemporary novelists in the 1840s and 1850s that some of the most unforgettable figures, perhaps because they were so exaggerated,

[3] Cited in Asa Briggs, *Victorian Cities* (Harmondsworth, England: Penguin, 1968), p. 100.
[4] Cited in E. J. Hobsbawm, *The Age of Revolution: Europe, 1789–1848* (London: Weidenfeld and Nicolson, 1962), p. 182.

were the Northern businessmen of such novels as Disraeli's *Coningsby*, Mrs. Gaskell's *Mary Barton*, or Charles Dickens's *Hard Times*. In Josiah Bounderby of Coketown, Dickens sought to isolate through exaggeration the extraordinary character of the new businessman:

He was a rich man: banker, merchant, manufacturer, and what not. A big, loud man, with a stare, and a metallic laugh. A man made out of coarse material, which seemed to have been stretched to make so much of him. A man with a great puffed head and forehead, swelled veins in his temples, and such a strained skin to his face that it seemed to hold his eyes open, and lift his eyebrows up. A man with a pervading appearance on him of being inflated like a balloon, and ready to start. A man who could never sufficiently vaunt himself a self-made man. A man who was always proclaiming, through that brassy speaking-trumpet of a voice of his, his old ignorance and his old poverty. A man who was the Bully of humility.[5]

To most contemporary social critics, Dickens's picture rang true. The well-to-do of Manchester lived in Alderley Edge on the outskirts of town, facing the lovely moorland countryside. Henry Adams saw them in 1861, "all country houses on the outskirts of the town, so that for miles about one meets long and very pretty roads lined with villas and parks, which leave the city proper very dull and gloomy, from the want of handsome private houses."

Condition of the Workers. The rest of the town had spread haphazardly in acres of slums, built for a quick profit by local builders. The worst was Irish Town, built for immigrants several floors below the level of the rest of the city; but most of the working-class housing was little better. An early nineteenth-century economist described how Irish Town and the other sections of Manchester were built:

These towns . . . have been erected with the utmost disregard of everything except the immediate advantage of the speculating builder. A carpenter and builder unite to buy a series of building sites (i.e. they lease them for a number of years) and cover them with so-called houses. In one place we found a whole street following the course of a ditch, because in this way deeper cellars could be secured without the cost of digging, cellars not for storing wares or rubbish, but for dwellings of human beings. Not one house of this street escaped the cholera. In general the streets are unpaved, with a dungheap or ditch in the middle; the houses are built back to back, without ventilation or drainage, and whole families are limited to a corner of a cellar or a garret.[6]

Working conditions in the factories were as bad, as a series of governmental inquiries in the early 1800s proved. Child labor was at first regarded as essential to profitable operation. At first, apprentices were picked from

[5] Charles Dickens, *Hard Times* (Boston: Houghton Mifflin, 1894), p. 14.
[6] Nassau Senior, cited in J. L. and Barbara Hammond, *The Town Labourer, 1760–1832: The New Civilisation* (London: Longmans, 1932), pp. 43–44.

orphans on parish relief. Then, child labor spread more widely among the children of the millworkers. The children usually began work at the age of six, spending from 6 A.M. to 7 or 8 P.M. in the factories, with half an hour for lunch and an hour for dinner, six days a week. They were used to join broken threads in the spinning machines, to sweep up waste cotton, or to replace bobbins of thread. Children were regularly beaten to keep them awake; they had constant lung trouble from breathing the fine cotton fluff. The first important attempt to remedy their condition, the Factory Act of 1819, was itself a comment on attitudes to child labor because it merely forbade the employment of children under nine years of age and restricted working hours of children under eighteen to ten and a half hours a day. Inspection was left to the local justices, who were frequently retired factory owners. In the 1830s and 1840s, many commissions appeared in Manchester and the other industrial cities to study working conditions of all laborers, produced a large number of case studies and some statistics, and publicized the appalling conditions they found. The most famous report, *On the Sanitary Condition of the Labouring Population of Great Britain in 1842,* showed that the average age of death of ''mechanics,

Child Labor. As this popular London magazine shows, half a century after the first Factory Act, very young children were still employed in unhealthy, heavy work at the mines. (*The Graphic,* June 10, 1871.)

labourers, and their families" in Manchester was 17, compared with 38 in a completely rural area taken for comparison. And even the well-to-do of Manchester suffered from the unsanitary condition of the city, since "professional persons and gentry, and their families" died at an average age of 38 compared with 52 in the rural county.

Recently, economic historians have shown that real wages in England were rising during the nineteenth century—by twenty-five percent between 1800 and 1825; by forty percent between 1825 and 1850. But this did little to palliate the discontent of the working classes. Manchester was known as a caldron constantly ready to boil over. Frequently the workers smashed the machines they held responsible for their condition. Occasionally, particularly during the wars with France after the Revolution, they rioted for bread. Elementary unions were formed among the cotton spinners as early as the 1790s, and they organized sporadic and fairly ineffective strikes. But widespread mob disorder was common. The worst occurred in 1819, when troops fired into a crowd of demonstrators, killing ten and injuring hundreds, in what came to be known as the Peterloo massacre. But ten years later, the troops were unable to disperse the crowds that constantly re-formed after every charge; and in 1842 the city was given over entirely, during the Plug Plot riots, to a vast mob augmented by rioters who had swarmed in from all the neighboring cotton towns. There was thus, during the first half of the nineteenth century, the constant fear of genuine insurrection in Manchester. "Here there seems no sympathy between the upper and lower classes of society," wrote a Manchester newspaper in 1819. "There is no mutual confidence, no bond of attachment." It was this vision of Manchester that Engels was to present to Karl Marx, when they met in Paris in 1844; and it was Manchester more than any other place they had in mind when they penned the *Communist Manifesto*:

Our epoch, the epoch of the bourgeoisie, possesses, however, this distinctive feature: it has simplified the class antagonisms. Society as a whole is more and more splitting up into two great hostile camps, into two great classes directly facing each other: Bourgeoisie and Proletariat.

Character of the Industrial City. With Manchester and the other great industrial cities of northern England, especially during the first fifty to seventy years of their expansion, a new form of urbanization had thus occurred. Here were cities devoted entirely to economic production. Until the 1850s, almost all building in Manchester itself consisted of factories, warehouses, and mass housing; and its social structure was equally simple. That is to say, two-thirds of its population were wage earners, mostly engaged in the cotton industry; the rest was composed of a service population of shopkeepers, lawyers, doctors, and the "merchants," comprising not only the millowners but owners of engineering companies and trading companies, and the bankers. From the 1840s on, when Manchester's character as a Coketown was irrevocably formed, the city began to receive

Manchester Town Hall. Completed in 1877 at a cost of one million pounds, the neo-Gothic hall was modeled upon the great wool halls of fifteenth-century Flanders. (British Tourist Authority photo.)

a few of the urban amenities that had made life in, say, Constantinople or Paris constantly interesting and at times even pleasant for the mass of inhabitants. Three public parks were opened in 1846; Manchester's university employed its first five professors in 1851, and a year later a free library was started. An exhibition of paintings from private collections was held in 1857 and it attracted over a million visitors; and its musical director, Charles Hallé, stayed on to found in Manchester one of the world's great symphony orchestras. Finally in 1868–1877, the town fathers spent a million pounds in constructing a monstrous Gothic town hall that would symbolize the city's devotion to local self-government. Manchester thus slowly and belatedly built a cultural life for itself amid the gloom of its factory chimneys; and its evolution was typical of the industrial city.

This evolution can be explained in part by the lack of governmental controls. Manchester had no municipal government and no representation at all in Parliament until the 1830s. No form of zoning or even of sanitary controls was exerted over the early builders, and so expansion was completely dictated by the desire to make a quick profit. Moreover, until the first Factory Act, no form of governmental control was exerted over working conditions, and the efforts of workers to better their own conditions by unionization were forbidden by law. Most house building had to cater, as a result, to a working population paid close to subsistence wages. Here the philosophy of laissez-faire accepted sincerely by the industrialists played an important part. Britain's economic theorists from the time of Adam Smith had taught that the economic system followed its own natural laws and that when it was left free from governmental interference the greatest economic productivity resulted. The industrialists believed in simple lessons taught by the economists. Adam Smith had proved the value of free trade. Ricardo had taught the "iron law of wages," that "the natural price of labor is that price which is necessary to enable the laborers, one with another, to subsist and perpetuate their race, without either increase or diminution." Malthus had shown that improvement in the standard of life increases population, which negates the increase in the standard of life, and that therefore population, or at least the working-class population, will always be at subsistence level. These comfortable theories were summarized in Ricardo's statement, "the pursuit of individual advantage is admirably connected with the universal good of the whole."

Moreover, the traditional elements that had made city life more urbane and more humane were largely lacking. The churches played a very subordinate role. The nonconformists (that is, Protestants who did not accept the Church of England) built their chapels in functional red brick, like warehouses; and their preachers, especially the Methodists with their visions of a heavenly paradise that would follow this earthly hell, were often held to be more effective at quenching the desire for revolutionary change than the police forces. The Church of England, comfortably entrenched in the rich livings of the rural South, barely penetrated the North. The aristocracy, the force that had given the baroque city so much of its character, kept its town houses in London, but saw no reason for building similar homes in Manchester or Liverpool, even when they owned large parts of the city's acreage, as Lord Derby did in Liverpool or the duke of Bridgewater in Manchester. The industrial cities augmented the agricultural income of the aristocracy, who were thus able to extend throughout the nineteenth century the lavish life on their country estates without the need to penetrate the maelstrom of the northern cities.

Finally, the massing of industry ravaged the natural environment. The use of coal for power and for home fires filled the air with grime, and the mining towns near Manchester with mountains of slag. The rivers were polluted with chemicals from the dyes used in printing the textiles and every other kind of waste. The river Irwell at Manchester was graphically described by a mid-nineteenth-century novelist:

The hapless river—a pretty enough stream a few miles up, with trees overhanging its banks and fringes of green sedge set thick along its edges—loses caste as it gets among the mills and print works. There are myriads of dirty things given it to wash, and whole wagon-loads of poisons from dye houses and bleachyards thrown into it to carry away; steam boilers discharge into it their seething contents, and drains and sewers their fetid impurities; till at length it rolls on—here between tall dingy walls, there under precipices of red sandstone—considerably less a river than a flood of liquid manure.[7]

[7] In Lewis Mumford, *The City in History* (New York: Harcourt, Brace & World, 1961), pp. 459–60.

The factories needed the best sites along the rivers for water power or transportation. The railroads followed the river valleys for ease of construction, slashed gashes through hillsides, and cut vast swathes right into the center of town. And the whole city reechoed constantly to the sound of the mills, the steam engines, and the trains. Noise pollution had become normal.

Manchester had become the prototype of the unplanned industrial city, the creator of wealth and the producer of material goods on a scale unknown in history, and—at least until the mid-nineteenth century—one of the ugliest of man's creations. "Every day that I live," wrote an American in 1845 after visiting Manchester, "I thank Heaven that I am not a poor man with a family in England."

On the continent of Europe, industrialization lagged behind the British pace; but by the middle of the nineteenth century, Belgium, parts of France, the Rhineland and Saxony, some cities in Lombardy, and a few small regions of the Austrian empire were enjoying the mixed blessing of the eruption of their own Coketowns. Engels had seen the waters of the Wupper River polluted with textile dye from the mills of Elberfeld where Germany's first spinning jenny had been installed, and watched the disappearance of "the fresh and vigorous popular life, which existed almost all over Germany." The city of Lyons in southern France was seized by thirty thousand silk weavers in 1831, in protest against their inadequate wages. Belgian mining towns like Liège and Namur were as foul as any in the Rhondda valley of South Wales, and no factory acts had been considered necessary to alleviate intolerable working conditions.

Drawbacks to Industrialization on the Continent. Certain factors common to all Europe helped retard the beginning of industrialization; and to these disadvantages individual countries added their own peculiar impediments. War and internal revolutions had thrown the European economy into recurrent chaos, discouraging the investment of risk capital or the movement of the labor force from the land. Most governments had regarded the growth of cities as a danger to public order and had tried to discourage it. Communications by land were atrocious, as few new roads had been built since the time of the Roman Empire. Water transport was hindered by political barriers, which also discouraged the canalization of rivers crossing borders. Customs duties hampered not only foreign trade but internal trade as well; and governments were reluctant to give up one of their most reliable sources of income. Whereas luxury goods, as medieval trade proved, can be sold at many times their original cost and can thus absorb large costs for transportation and duties, the products of the industrial revolution that are intended for the mass consumer market cannot; and thus the large-scale sale of heavy goods like coal and iron and of manufactured goods only became possible on the continent with cheap transportation and reduction of supplementary costs in tolls or customs. In a broader sense, this implied that the industrial revolution was only possible when a large, unified market

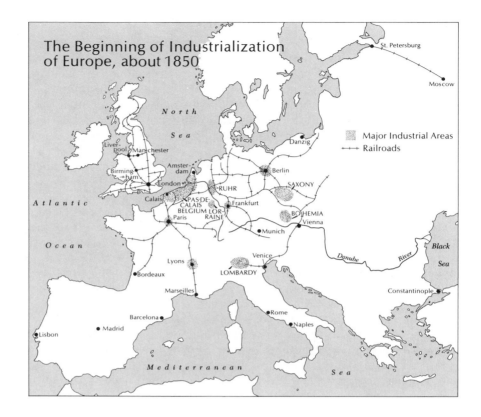

The Beginning of Industrialization of Europe, about 1850

existed; and the political fragmentation of Germany and Italy was thus an economic impediment as well as a nationalist grievance. Political fragmentation was particularly disastrous to the development of the European coal industry, because Europe's greatest coal deposits lay in a great crescent stretching from northern France to the Ruhr in Germany, broken up regardless of economic logic between France, Belgium, the Netherlands, Luxembourg, and Prussia. The only significant deposit of iron ore on the continent, in French Lorraine, was cut off from the coal deposits of the Saar by national hatred of French and Germans and from the French coal of the Channel coast by lack of transportation. The other great coalfield, in Silesia, was isolated both physically and fiscally from the rest of Germany. The continuing restrictions of the guilds on new economic activity, which were still powerful through much of Europe, prevented the introduction of the factory system in the older cities, while the genuine preference of many peasants like those in France to go hungry on their own land rather than in the cities prevented the growth of a large labor market. Even the attitude of the middle classes who made money in commerce discouraged industrialization, since most preferred to put their profits in the more socially remunerative investment of land, while those who did invest in industrial projects wanted to keep them small, in their family possession, and stable rather than expansive. But the most discouraging factor was Britain's industrial progress, which had given it an enormous lead in capture of markets, in technical improvements, and in mobilization of capital. It was hard for any other country to compete with the British in quality, or price, or well-established market organization. Where they had a choice, consumers forgot to be patriotic, and preferred British goods to the products of the infant native industries.

Beginning of Industrialism in Europe. In a small way after 1815, and on a large scale after 1830, certain regions of the continent underwent an industrial revolution of their own because conditions were more favorable than in the nineteenth century. No major war disturbed the continent's stability, and the sporadic uprisings were soon suppressed. Population growth was as rapid as in England, and increased the overpopulation, and thus the underemployment, of the villages, and poverty-stricken farm laborers began drifting into the cities. Many governments were determined to emulate the effective administration enforced by Napoleon, and to stimulate the modernization of their economies by state action. Foremost among these were the governments of the united Netherlands, Prussia, and France after the 1830 revolution. Such governments sponsored industrial expositions, subsidized inventors, founded technical and scientific schools, and paid for official inspection tours abroad. Capital was more easily mobilized for investment in industrial enterprises with a great improvement in the banking system, partly the foundation of national banks but especially of joint-stock banks, which created the Belgian coal industry, for example. Moreover, the British, seeking lucrative investment for the profits of their own industrial revolution, began to make large amounts available for continental industrialization, especially for investment in the supposedly secure profits from railroad building. Transportation seemed to many the key to creation of an industrial revolution on the continent, and a start was made in road building, river dredging, and canal construction. For example, France had 1,200 kilometers of canal by the time of the abdication of Napoleon I, the canal builder; the restored Bourbons added another 900; and the middle-class government of Louis Philippe added 2,000 before the 1848 revolution. The introduction of the steamboat was especially important in developing river transportation, and for use in short sea crossings, of the English Channel and the Baltic, for instance. As in England, however, it was the railroad that linked the continental suppliers and markets together. The Belgian state took the lead, by constructing two intersecting lines across the country, one from Holland to France, the other from Germany to the Channel coast. France and Germany were somewhat slower; but in the 1840s the French produced an ingenious plan whereby the state would provide the roadbed, tunnels, and bridges, and private companies the rolling stock and rails. A centrally planned system, with Paris at its hub, was well

**The Third-Class Carriage, by
Honoré Daumier.** (The
Metropolitan Museum of Art.
The H. O. Havemeyer
Collection. Bequest of Mrs.
H. O. Havemeyer, 1929.)

under construction by 1848 and was completed by the 1860s, in spite of
the early fears expressed that frightened cows would give no milk and passengers in tunnels would catch pleurisy. Less fearful of such perils, the
Germans created their network a decade earlier than the French, so that the
philosopher Treitschke could boast: "It was the railroads which first dragged
the nation from its economic stagnation. . . . With such power did they
break in upon all the old habits of life, that already in the forties the aspect
of Germany was completely changed." The rural East of Germany, in
particular, was united to western Europe, finding new markets for its agricultural produce and a psychological impact that had never before penetrated the aristocratic estates of the broad eastern plains.

The economic environment was therefore more favorable to industrialization; but the most difficult moment in a process of economic growth,
in Professor Walt Rostow's phrase, is the "takeoff" into sustained growth,
"the interval when the old blocks and resistances to steady growth are
finally overcome." In Europe, a first stimulus was provided by acquisition
of British machines and skills. In part this was achieved by industrial espi-
onage, since the export of the most important machinery, except steam
engines, was forbidden by law until 1842, or by study of British technical
periodicals. But many British skilled workers emigrated·to the continent

to enjoy the high wages paid them for instructing native workers in their skills, including operation of the flying shuttle and the spinning jenny and the new techniques in iron manufacture like puddling. Other British managers and entrepreneurs saw that they could make a fortune more rapidly in the uncompetitive continental environment than in Britain. British businessmen engineers built the railroad from Paris to Rouen, opened the great Hibernia coal mines in the Ruhr, modernized the cotton industry of Normandy, and built the largest engineering concern in the world in the 1830s at Seraing in Belgium. Europeans were very soon making their own inventions or improving those brought from England; and among these pioneers were some of the founders of the great industrial fortunes of the nineteenth century. Friedrich Krupp of Essen, for example, made crucible cast steel in the early 1800s; the Borsig company of Berlin developed an improved locomotive in the 1830s; the de Wendels of Lorraine pioneered in introducing the integration of the various stages of iron making. These were only a few of the greatest names among the thousands of entrepreneur capitalists who were determined to become continental counterparts to the Manchester man.

Thus, by the middle of the century, the relative economic position of Britain and the continental countries had shifted, although not yet dramatically. Britain was still producing half of the iron and cotton cloth and two-thirds of the world's coal; half of its population lived in towns. Belgium, however, the most thoroughly industrialized country of the continent, greatly resembled Britain. It had a highly developed coal-mining and iron-manufacturing industry in the central towns from Mons to Liège, and a large-scale textile industry for both cotton and woolen goods. The French had developed the coal mines of the Channel coast and were beginning to exploit the rather poor quality iron ore of Lorraine; they had several isolated but highly organized centers of iron production, such as Le Creusot in central France, and a thriving textile industry in Alsace. In Germany, a start had been made in opening up the coal mines and developing an iron industry in the Ruhr and Saar and in Saxony, but textile manufacture was still spread throughout the country among millions of small craftsmen. Small-scale industry, especially textiles or iron, had begun in northern Italy, Bohemia, and western Hungary, and around Vienna.

Social Impact of Industrialism. The change in the character of society affected Europeans in various ways. To those who had loved the placid life of the eighteenth century, it was depressing. "Wealth and speed are things the world admires and for which all men strive," wrote the seventy-six-year-old Goethe. "Railways, express mails, steamboats, and possible means of communication are what the educated world seeks. . . . Actually this is the century of clever minds, of practical men who grasp things easily, who are endowed with a certain facility, and who feel their own superiority to the multitude, but who lack talent for the most exalted tasks. Let us as far as possible retain the ideals in which we were raised. We and perhaps a few others will be the last representatives of an era which will not soon return." To others more attuned to the spirit of enterprise, it was a time of unlimited possibilities. Even the German railroads had romantic possibilities:

For these rails are bridal bracelets,
Wedding rings of purest gold;
States like lovers will exchange them,
And the marriage-tie will hold.[8]

But industrialization on the continent was producing the same problems that had shocked the observers of Manchester. The Prussian king was informed in 1828 that early work in the factories of the Rhineland had so stunted the population of his western provinces that they could no longer fill their quota of army recruits; eleven years later, the employment of children under nine in Prussia was forbidden. In 1839, Louis Blanc had begun his famous indictment of early French capitalism, *The Organization of Work,* with the startling announcement: "The other day a child was frozen to death behind a sentry-box in the heart of Paris, and nobody was shocked or surprised at the event." Europeans, like the British, had realized belatedly that industrialization was a phenomenon whose social consequences were so disruptive that they required widespread political action. But there were irreconcilable differences of opinion on the action needed.

POLITICAL PANACEAS FOR INDUSTRIALIZATION

Liberalism. The most natural reaction to industrialization on the part of those who profited from it was to justify its workings. The upper middle classes adopted the doctrine of liberalism whose principal tenet, at least so its opponents claimed, was summarized in the French Premier Guizot's advice to those who wanted a lower property qualification for voting: "Enrichissez-vous" (Get rich). This helpful doctrine had been given a convincing formulation by the great English economist Adam Smith (1723–1790) in his great book *The Wealth of Nations,* published in 1776. Smith had argued that men had the unique ability to trade, that is, to exchange material goods in order to increase the well-being of both parties to the bargain. In a state of perfect freedom from interference, some men realize that certain goods are more in demand than others and exert themselves to profit from that demand. These entrepreneurs develop new resources or create new patterns of trade for the purpose of bettering themselves by satisfying demand. Competition among suppliers increases quality and prevents excessive profit making. When one demand is satiated, the entrepreneurs seek new demands to satisfy. The consumer, with his ability to buy or not to buy, is therefore king of the economic system. The worker,

[8] Cited in Theodore S. Hamerow, *Restoration, Revolution, Reaction: Economics and Politics in Germany, 1815–1871* (Princeton, N.J.: Princeton University Press, 1966), p. 8. Reprinted by permission of Princeton University Press.

with his ability to sell his labor or not sell it, is also theoretically master of the wage structure, since competition among employers for labor enables the worker to choose the wage rates that satisfy him. Yet the consumer too is protected, since the demands of the workers must not force the price of goods above what the consumer can afford to pay. Therefore a harmony of interests of consumer, employer, and worker exists, Smith argued, when the working of the economic system is not falsified by government interference, tariffs or other restrictions on international trade, or monopolies of producers. The role of government is to protect society from foreign attack, to ensure internal order and justice, and to create such large-scale public works as roads that the individual cannot erect alone.

This theory was incorporated into David Ricardo's *Principles of Political Economy* published in 1817, which became the gospel of the early-nineteenth-century liberals. Ricardo, however, was clear that Smith had been too optimistic in thinking this natural system to be harmonious. Ricardo saw that the classes of society were of necessity antagonistic, and that in particular the wages of the working class would always remain at the approximate level necessary for subsistence alone. Taking up the theory of Thomas Malthus in his *Essay on the Principle of Population* (1798), Ricardo showed that an expanding economy merely supports an expanding population, and the natural tendency was for the expanding population to exceed the food supply. Faced with starvation, the working class would be compelled to reduce its size until its share of the wealth of society was again exactly what was needed for subsistence. But the landlord receives rent and the capitalist profits from the wealth produced by labor; and these two groups would also be in conflict over their share of society's wealth. Ricardo's sympathy lay with the capitalist whose enterprise produced wealth and not with the landowner who, in his view, did little to justify his share.

Conflict of Conservative and Liberal in England. This conflict was dramatized in England from 1815 to 1846. The conservatives, composed of the aristocratic landlords, the Church of England, and the army, were represented by the Tory party that held office from 1815 to 1830. The general attitude of the Tories was to favor agriculture, especially in their passing of the Corn Law of 1815, which banned the importation of foreign grain until the English price rose to eighty shillings per quarter, and to maintain a mercantilist economic policy. The liberals, who were mainly but not exclusively in the Whig party, were composed of the older commercial classes, the new industrialists from the North, and many of the professional classes. The liberals wanted cheap food for the working classes (and thus lower wages), by abolition of the corn laws and the end to all other forms of state interference in the economic system, such as tariffs. But they also demanded a change in the British electoral system, which was a strange hodgepodge of anachronisms inherited from the Middle Ages. The new industrial cities, like Manchester and Birmingham, had no parliamentary representation; many boroughs sending members to Parliament had little or no population, and were in the "pocket" of some great landowner; no constituency had more than a few thousand voters, and they were usually bribed. The liberal demand, however, was for a property-owning democracy; Parliament had to be made responsive to the wishes of the industrial middle class who were described by one of their principal theorists as "the wisest part of the community." Power seesawed between the conservatives and the liberals, usually represented by the Tories and Whigs; but on many crucial issues, conscience or self-interest drove large numbers to cross party and even class lines. The Tories repealed the Combination Acts forbidding workers to form trade unions, and Tories were the leaders of the movement for reform of working conditions in the factories. The Whigs forced through the reform of Parliament in 1832, which gave representation to the industrial cities but introduced so restricted a franchise that only twenty percent of the population had the vote. In 1846, their pressure and fear of an uprising following famine in Ireland compelled a Tory prime minister to repeal the corn laws. And by the middle of the century, Britain enjoyed almost free trade, a symbol of the triumph of the liberalism of the upper middle classes.

Birmingham Town Hall. The Hall, erected in 1835, expressed Birmingham's civic pride by its derivation from the temple of Jupiter Stator in Rome. (British Travel Authority photo.)

Revolution of 1830 in France. A similar victory seemed to have been won by the French liberals when, in the revolution of 1830, they succeeded in forcing the abdication and flight of the Bourbon king, Charles X. Under the Bourbon restoration (1815–1830), France had been governed largely by the landed aristocracy and for their benefit—both the old nobility and the new nobility of Napoleon. The electorate, restricted to a hundred thousand voters, chose conservative majorities who compensated the émigré nobles, revived the powers of the Catholic Church, and restricted civil liberties. The "middle-class monarchy" of Louis Philippe (reigned 1830–1848), representing an electorate of two hundred thousand through a cleverly written law that gave the franchise to well-to-do businessmen and less wealthy but politically reliable doctors, lawyers, and professors, carried through the ideal liberal program. Almost all the members of the government were recruited from the bankers and industrialists of the *haute bourgeoisie*. State interference in the economic system was reduced to almost nothing, except for the suppression of workers' uprisings and the planning of the railroad network. Few laws to reform working conditions were passed, and none were enforced. The elections were managed by corruption, and all changes in the electoral system refused. Paris seemed to have become the plaything of the aristocrats of the new society—the bankers, the railroad builders, the textile manufacturers, and the manipulators of government bonds. In the rest of Europe, the liberals remained in close alliance with the other discontented groups in society, because power was held by the conservative allies of Metternich. The essential difference of goal and interest between the upper-middle-class liberal and the political, social, and nationalist reformers was hidden in their common suppression. In Britain and France, however, where the liberals had triumphed, their early supporters were soon converted into their principal enemies.

Radicalism. The so-called radicals or democrats held that the liberal mistake was its restriction of the suffrage to their own class. They held that the solution of society's ills was the extension of universal suffrage and the taking of political power by the people. This program was expounded in England by a brilliant political pamphleteer, William Cobbett, and it received widespread popular support in the difficult times following the end of the Napoleonic wars. The government's answer was repression—the Peterloo massacre of 1819 and the Six Acts that restricted public meetings and the freedom of the press. In the renewed distress of the 1830s and 1840s, these demands were voiced again by the Chartists, a working-class movement that campaigned for universal manhood suffrage, annual parliaments, equal electoral districts, and payment of members of Parliament. With increasingly extremist leadership, the Chartists presented petitions to Parliament with millions of signatures; held huge demonstrations; promised general strikes; and finally alienated not only Parliament but many of their own more peaceable supporters.

Paris became the center of radicalism on the continent, welcoming exiled reformers of every description. In France, the lower middle classes were most frustrated by the restriction of the suffrage, and they found leadership among the intellectual classes, notably the poet Lamartine, and political journalists in demanding a republic. In 1847–1848, the radicals created the French equivalent of the Chartist petitions, a series of "reform banquets" in which leading opposition deputies called for a broadened suffrage and salaries for deputies. With industry in depression the radical leaders were able, in February 1848, to overthrow the liberal government and to turn France briefly into a republic with universal suffrage. Lamartine himself took office as president of the provisional government of the second French republic on February 24. In June, when he was compelled to use the army to suppress the workers of Paris, it was made dramatically clear that for one section of the population political solutions of the radical variety were inadequate for dealing with social problems. Social problems required socialist solutions.

Early Socialist Theory. The theory of socialism had existed long before the industrial revolution. In *The Republic*, Plato had suggested common ownership of property, including wives and children; and the early Christians laid considerable emphasis on the sharing of wealth. In the sixteenth century, writers of books about perfect lands, such as Sir Thomas More in *Utopia*, frequently abolished private property; and Rousseau blasted private ownership of land in one of his most famous passages:

The first man who, having enclosed a piece of land, took it into his head to say: "This belongs to me," and found people simple enough to believe him, was the true founder of civil society. What crimes, wars, murders, what miseries and horrors would have been spared the human race by him who, snatching out the stakes or filling in the ditch, should have cried to his fellows: "Beware of listening to this impostor; you are lost if you forget that the fruits belong to all and that the earth belongs to none." [9]

The French peasantry proved how little Rousseau had understood them by using the Revolution to stake themselves a plot of land, rather than to communalize it; and the only genuine opponent of private property during the Revolution, Gracchus Babeuf who led an insurrection in 1796 to achieve a communistic society in place of the Directory, was denounced by informers and executed. Only when the progress of industrialization had begun to create the large agglomerations of factory workers, a proletarian class, and an equally identifiable class of bourgeois employers, who actually practiced the doctrine that the workers can never rise above subsistence level, did modern socialist theory begin.

[9] Cited in Alexander Gray, *The Socialist Tradition: From Moses to Lenin* (London: Longmans, Green, 1947), p. 81.

Utopian Socialism. Initially, socialism began as an emotional reaction against the results of the industrial revolution and the inequity in the sharing of the products of industrialism between worker and capitalist. It was also a reaction against the worthlessness of the industrial way of life in the new cities, where freedom was given to the individual to seek profit regardless of the public good and thus to some extent even of his own. It was not a reaction against industrialization itself but a demand for its better regulation and use. One of the first and most influential socialists was the factory owner Robert Owen, who made a fortune by the age of twenty-eight from spinning mills in Manchester and then bought the largest mill in Scotland, New Lanark, which he attempted to make into a model socialist community. Owen showed, to the amazement of industrialists all over Europe who came to see his achievement, that a factory could be attractively designed, that workers could be given decent homes and free schools, that wages could be higher than the competitors', without a loss of profits. In New Lanark and later in the United States at New Harmony, Indiana, he set up working examples of reconciliation between the classes; and he tried to show that the new industrial society could be created by the gradual proliferation of communities of this type. These two ideas were widely popular among the socialists of the first half of the nineteenth century, who for their unrealistic idealism were called by Karl Marx the "utopian" socialists. Owen himself became disillusioned, and went on to attempt to better working-class conditions through a national trade-union organization and later through the establishment of consumers' cooperatives; but his ideal of the voluntary organization of society into harmonious industrial communities was taken up by the French writer Charles Fourier (1772–1837), an eccentric traveling salesman with a passion for amateur mathematics. Fourier held that society should be organized in groups of 1,620 people because in such a group the work to be done can be matched to the natural inclination of all the members. (Children, who like playing in dirt, would clean the streets.) In these groups, called phalanstères, all work would be cooperative, but the profits would be shared unequally between labor, capital, and "talent." Although Fourier reportedly went home at noon every day for ten years to meet any capitalist willing to invest in his phalanstères, no one ever came.

Far more influential in France were the followers of Claude de Saint-Simon, a nobleman who had fought in the American Revolution, and turned to science and history to find a more harmonious method for organizing society. Saint-Simon was significant as a theorist because he taught his followers that industrial society could be collectively planned for the benefit of all. He felt that the French Revolution had done good work by destroying obsolete institutions; the moment had come to create the new institutions. For that, *les oisifs* (the lazy), who were the nobles and soldiers, should be overthrown; control of administration and government should be placed in the hands of *les industriels* (manufacturers and bankers), who would work in favor of the unpropertied class, "*la classe*

la plus nombreuse et la plus pauvre''; and the general moral and intellectual well-being of society was to be safeguarded by an elite of intellectuals and artists. In this way, society would be run for the benefit of the
poor by those most capable of providing those benefits. Saint-Simon
also threw out innumerable other ideas that were taken up by the bankers
and industrialists who served Louis Napoleon Bonaparte when he became
emperor (1852–1870)—the building of the Suez canal, the founding
of credit institutions, the employment of technocrats in government;
but after his death his followers turned his creed into a wild Messianic
religion, with a Universal Father who spent a somewhat unwholesome
length of time in search of the Universal Mother.

The transition to the view that the working class cannot be reconciled
to the bourgeoisie but must overthrow it was made by Pierre Joseph Proud-
hon (1809–1865), the only utopian theorist in France of working-class
origins. Like Rousseau's *Social Contract*, Fourier's main work, *What Is
Property?* (1840), made his fame with its opening paragraph:

If I were asked to answer the following question: What is slavery? *and I should
answer in one word,* It is murder, *my meaning would be understood at once.
No extended argument would be required to show that the power to take from a
man his thought, his will, his personality, is a power of life and death; and that
to enslave a man is to kill him. What, then, to this other question:* What is property?
may I not likewise answer, It is theft, *without the certainty of being misunderstood;
the second proposition being no other than a transformation of the first?* [10]

Property must disappear; possession should be given to those who do the
work, but only for as long as they work. Society would become a group
of federations of producers; and as later anarchists would hold, the power
of the state would become unnecessary.

Louis Blanc and the National Workshops.   Among the utopian socialists,
Louis Blanc (1811–1882) was the only one to find a government willing
to put his ideas into practice. In his *Organization of Work* (1840), he had
satirized the supposed freedom of the worker to offer his labor to the
employer who would pay him best.

*What is competition, relative to the workers? It is work put up to auction. An
entrepreneur has need of a worker: three present themselves. . . . How much for
your work? . . . Three francs: I have a wife and children. . . . Good, and you?
Two and a half francs: I have no children, but I have a wife. . . . Marvellous.
And you . . . Two francs are enough for me: I am single. . . . You get the job.
The transaction is over: the bargain is concluded. What will become of the two
proletarians who are excluded? It is to be hoped that they will allow themselves
to die of hunger. But suppose they become thieves? Have no fear; we have police-*

[10] Cited in Albert Fried and Robert Sanders, *Socialist Thought: A Documentary History* (Garden City, N.Y.: Doubleday, 1964), p. 201.

men. And murderers? We have the hangman. As for the most fortunate of the three, his triumph is only provisional. If there should come along a fourth worker sufficiently sturdy to fast every other day, wages will slide down to the bottom; there will be a new pariah, a new recruit for the convict-prison, perhaps! [11]

The worker, Blanc claimed, had the right to work; the state's duty was to help him to do so by creating "social workshops." The workshops would receive their initial capital from the state, would provide ideal working conditions and good wages, and would therefore attract the best workers away from private industry. The private capitalist, finding himself uncompetitive with the social workshops, would turn his business over to the state, and thus in time the whole of industry would be organized into prosperous, cooperative units.

During the February revolution of 1848 in Paris, Blanc and another working-class leader entered the provisional government, and pressed Lamartine and the democratic members to provide work for the unemployed through national workshops. But the democrats, who had little faith in social reform, sabotaged the scheme by refusing to put Blanc in charge and by providing meaningless work. When one hundred twenty thousand unemployed flocked into Paris to join the workshops, the government lost its nerve, ordered their dissolution, and when the Parisians again took to the barricades, sent the regular army against them. In the bloody June days, the first confrontation took place between the democrats who wanted political reform and the social reformers; and in this battle of the streets, the conservatives and liberals joined forces with the democrats in crushing the proletarian Reds. The June Days effectively killed utopian socialism as a method of solving the evils of industrialism; class reconciliation and the gradual adaptation of society to industrialization through cooperative units of production were regarded as idealistic relics of little use in the class war that had been laid bare by General Cavaignac's reconquest of Paris. The doctrine for the new age was scientific socialism, better known after its founder as Marxism.

MARXISM

Perhaps the most important event of the year 1848 was the publication, by a small group of German socialists, of a short pamphlet called *The Communist Manifesto*, written by Karl Marx (1818–1883) and Friedrich Engels (1820–1895). At the time only a few hundred people read the manifesto; it is now part of the official political philosophy of more than a billion people. Marx and Engels had provided the socialist movement with a theory of history, a materialist philosophy, an economic explanation of class conflict, and a blueprint for a new society. And they had given the working-class leaders a specific role in hurrying along the process of history, in exacerbating class conflict, and in realizing the new society.

[11] Cited in Gray, *Socialist Tradition,* pp. 221–22. Translation modified.

Karl Marx. Although delicately poetic in appearance when young, Marx later developed the girth and beard befitting the strong-willed patriarch of a revolutionary workers' movement. (German Information Center photo.)

The Philosophy of Marx. Marx was born in Trier on the Franco-German border, the son of a Jewish lawyer who had converted to Christianity when his son was six; but Marx was marked by a sense of Messianic isolation that many have attributed to generations of rabbinic ancestors. He studied law at the Universities of Bonn and Berlin, but swept away by the attractions of Hegelian philosophy, he changed fields, and after receiving his doctorate sought unsuccessfully a university post in philosophy. The first principles of Marxism were formulated in his argument with the followers of Hegel on the philosophy of history. Marx agreed with Hegel that history is a dynamic process, or dialectic, that moves forward through a series of conflicts: any given state of society (the thesis) produces its own opposite (the antithesis), and the conflict between the two leads to their amalgamation (the synthesis). Hegel, however, had seen the process of history as the working out of God's purpose, the realization of the Absolute Idea, which, Hegel apparently decided, had been achieved in the Prussian state. Such abstractions dissatisfied Marx, and he found the antidote in the materialist philosophy of Feuerbach. The dialectical process of history, Marx decided, was determined by economic forces, not by abstract ideas.

Dialectical Materialism. By 1845, Marx had formulated the two key ideas by which to apply this theory to actual historical events. The method of production at any time dictates the character of social relationships and the politics, law, and even the values and spiritual beliefs of a society. Medieval society, for example, believed in chivalry, the Church, and so on because it was based on agricultural production by unfree labor. Moreover, in the productive process there have always been two classes, the exploiter and the exploited, who are in political terms the ruler and the oppressed. The conflict of classes is the dialectic of history. The constant change in the means of production through technological advance, pressure of population, and so on, ensured that new classes would constantly arise to challenge the dominance of the established ruling class. Plebeian had challenged patrician; the journeyman, the guildmaster; the serf, the baron. But the most important challenge was the attack of the commercial and manufacturing bourgeoisie on the feudal ruling class, which was an attack of a moneyed class on a landed class.

Here Marx's acquaintance with Engels, whom he met in 1842 but only got to know while Engels was working on *The Condition of the Working Class in England*, provided him with the down-to-earth details of the contemporary conflict of the bourgeoisie and the class it had itself created, the proletariat. After Marx failed to get a faculty position in philosophy, he took up newspaper writing for a couple of years. But, hounded by the censors, he moved on to Paris and later to Brussels, and finally, after the failure of the Rhineland revolution in which he participated, to London. His knowledge of the proletarian up to that point was largely theoretical, although he was already burning with moral outrage. Engels provided him with the details of factory life, of slum conditions, of cyclical crises, that fed the passion with which, in the late 1840s, Marx analyzed the character of the proletariat. The working class, "instead of rising with the progress of industry, sinks ever deeper beneath the social conditions of his own class. The laborer becomes the pauper, and pauperism increases even more rapidly than population and wealth." Marx, however, was much more than a polemicist, and he wanted to explain the condition of the proletariat in the broadest economic conditions. The poverty of the worker was explained by the labor theory of value. A product was only "so much congealed labor-time"; but the capitalist sold the product for several times more than he paid the worker in wages. The difference, "surplus value," the capitalist took for himself, as a blatant form of exploitation. As a result of competition among the capitalists, however, their numbers were being constantly reduced, while the size of the proletariat was constantly growing. While the proletariat was thus growing in strength, the capitalists themselves would find that the crises in the system would grow in number and intensity, thereby preparing the moment when the proletariat would be able to seize power themselves.

The Proletarian Revolution. The Marxist theory of revolution was already complete in *The Communist Manifesto*. Although the process of economic change was inevitably working toward the victory of the proletariat over the bourgeoisie, that day could be hastened by well-timed revolution. Preparation for such a revolution was the work of a professional elite of working-class leaders. Once the bourgeoisie had been overthrown, the working class would set up a dictatorship of indefinite length, which would set about putting an end to the dialectical process of history by creating a classless society. When no classes existed, presumably there could be no further conflict of classes. Slowly the workers' attitude to material things was to be transformed. During the stage when ideas carried over from capitalism were still prevalent, wages would be paid in accordance with the amount of work done, although already, since the state would have taken possession of all means of production, no capitalist would exist to appropriate surplus value for himself. When the new society was a reality, the slogan would be "from each according to his ability, to each according to his need." In this society, man would therefore have been transformed in his very nature; and such institutions as the police and the army would be unnecessary. The organs of the state would be gradually allowed to wither away. "The government of persons is replaced by the administration of things and the direction of the process of production."

A German Workers' Meeting in 1890. (German Information Center.)

To Marx and Engels, the industrial revolution, and in fact the rise of the bourgeoisie, had been of enormous benefit to the human race because they had destroyed the feudal society, and simplified the class relationship to the point where the proletariat could take power. In the classless society they envisaged, the vast productive power of industrialism would be used for the benefit of the workers who alone produced the wealth. There have been many criticisms of the theories of Marx and Engels—that they overemphasized the materialist motivation of human beings and ignored such driving forces as patriotism, or religion, or even chance; that the foundation of the dialectic in changes in means of production was to link it to human initiative and not to material forces; that the emphasis given to surplus value ignored the contribution of the capitalist to the creation of wealth; that the assumption of the inevitable crisis of capitalism and the reduction in the number of capitalists has not been borne out by events; and especially that class war and violent revolution is an inhuman way to rescue mankind from inhumanity. But the doctrine had a revolutionary appeal and an intellectual logic that had been lacking in earlier Socialist theory, and the spread throughout Europe of Coketowns was providing Marx and his followers with the vast proletarian army to which they had spoken in the *Manifesto*.

SUGGESTED READING

Nineteenth-century Manchester is considered a symbol of the new industrial city by Asa Briggs, in *Victorian Cities* (1968), pp. 88–138. In this superb introduction, Briggs weighs particularly the reasons for the fictional treatment of Manchester and the value of such an approach. For graphic portrayals of industrial life, see Charles Dickens, *Hard Times;* Elizabeth Gaskell, *Mary Barton;* Benjamin Disraeli, *Coningsby;* and Kathleen Tillotson's study, *Novels of the Eighteen-Forties* (1954). Friedrich Engels's slashing study, written when he was twenty-four, *The Condition of the Working-Class in England* is still a fascinating document of Manchester's contribution to the formulation of communist attitudes.

For some scholarly enquiries into the character of Manchester business, there are Arthur Silver, *Manchester Men and Indian Cotton, 1847–1872* (1966); Michael M. Edwards, *The Growth of the British Cotton Trade, 1780–1815* (1967); and Arthur Redford, *Manchester Merchants and Foreign Trade, 1794–1858* (1934). For Manchester's economic theories, see W. D. Grampp, *The Manchester School of Economics* (1960). A fine overview of Manchester's history and geography is given in C. F. Carter, ed., *Manchester and its Region* (1962); especially useful is W. H. Chaloner's chapter, "The Birth of Modern Manchester", pp. 131–46, which also, like Briggs, has a useful bibliography. Leon S. Marshall discusses the public reaction to the coming of industrialization in *The Development of Public Opinion in Manchester, 1780–1820* (1946).

For the origins of the industrial revolution in England, brief surveys are provided by Arthur Redford, *The Economic History of England (1760–1860)* (1957); and T. S. Ashton, *The Industrial Revolution, 1760–1830* (1964). Paul Mantoux, *The Industrial Revolution in the Eighteenth Century* (1961) is still the fullest and most serviceable account, and has much incidental detail on Manchester. Fine synthesis from the left-wing point of view is given by E. J. Hobsbawm, in *Industry and Empire: An Economic History of Britain since 1750* (1968), and in more abbreviated form in *The Age of Revolution: Europe 1789–1848* (1962), pp. 27–52. For the early nineteenth century, see John H. Clapham, *An Economic History of Modern Britain: The Early Railway Age, 1820–1850* (1930) and W. O. Henderson, *Britain and Industrial Europe 1750–1870* (1954) for the British influence on European industrialization. Modern economic techniques are applied to the study of economic growth in Phyllis Deane and W. A. Cole, *British Economic Growth, 1688–1959: Trends and Structure* (1962). Many case studies are evoked in J. L. Hammond and Barbara Hammond, *The Town Labourer, 1760–1832: The New Civilisation* (1932), and relevant anecdotes are cited by John Sanders, *Manchester* (1967).

W. O. Henderson, *Britain and Industrial Europe 1750–1870* (1965) traces the direct influence of British inventions, entrepreneurs, and capital in creating industrialization on the continent. Henderson deals more fully with the industrial revolution in France, Germany, and Russia in *The Industrial Revolution on the Continent* (1967). Among the old-fashioned economic histories that are still useful and that one could profitably consult are Herbert Heaton, *Economic History of Europe* (1936) for continentwide treatment of various economic sectors, such as transportation, banking, and currency, and Shepard B. Clough and Charles W. Cole, *Economic History of Europe* (1952) on business organization. David S. Landes, *The Unbound Prometheus: Technological Change and Industrial Development in Western Europe from 1750 to the Present* (1969) is a fine up-to-date survey, with a particularly useful analysis of "continental emulation" of British industrialization. Landes's book is an enlarged version of his chapter in the valuable *Cambridge Economic History of Europe*, vol. 6, *The Industrial Revolutions and After: Incomes, Population and Technological Change* (1965), in which W. A. Cole and Phyllis Deane (pp. 1–55) assess the impact of industrialization on the growth of national incomes. Arthur Birnie's short *An Economic History of Europe 1760–1939* (1962) is useful on social reform. Everyone should read Walter W. Rostow's brilliant little book, *The Stages of Economic Growth: A Non-Communist Manifesto* (1960), which presents his theory of the "takeoff" into sustained economic growth.

Much recent work in economic history, and particularly in the history of the industrial revolution, has drawn so heavily from economics that it claims to be the "new economic history." To sample this approach, see R. M. Hartwell, ed., *The Causes of the Industrial Revolution* (1967) and Simon Kuznets, the economist on whose studies the new economic historians have depended so largely, *Modern Economic Growth: Rate, Structure, and Spread* (1966). Phyllis Deane considers the first century of industrialization in the new economic framework of theories of growth in *The First Industrial Revolution* (1965).

John H. Clapham, *The Economic Development of France and Germany 1815–1914* (1963) is urbane and very readable; Rondo E. Cameron, *France and the Economic Devolopment of Europe, 1800–1914* (1966) emphasizes international finance. Two basic accounts of France's slow industrialization are A. L. Dunham, *The Industrial Revolution in France, 1815–1848* (1953) and Shepard B. Clough, *France: A History of National Economics, 1789–1939* (1939). Theodore S. Hamerow relates economic development to political change in *Restoration, Revolution, Reaction: Economics and Politics in Germany, 1815–1871* (1966). The importance of the German customs union is assessed in W. O. Henderson, *The Zollverein* (1959).

The doctrines of nineteenth-century liberalism are ably abbreviated in John Plamenatz, ed., *Readings from Liberal Writers, English and American* (1965); but the most persuasive approach is to go directly to Adam Smith, *Inquiry into the Nature and Causes of the Wealth of Nations* and John Stuart Mill, *On Liberty* (many editions). Guido de Ruggiero, *The History of European Liberalism* (1927) contrasts the different versions in France, Germany, and Italy. On the political democrats, see Asa Briggs, ed., *Chartist Studies* (1960); Mark Hovell, *The Chartist Movement* (1925), old but reliable; and John Plamenatz, *The Revolutionary Movement in France, 1815–1871* (1952).

Jürgen Kuczynski, *The Rise of the Working Class* (1967) is a fascinating dissection, from a left-wing point of view, of the nature of the working class, presenting international similarities and national differences. E. P. Thompson, *The Making of the English Working Class* (1963) analyzes the structure of the laboring class and its sense of class consciousness. An excellent selection of documents of socialist theory is made by Albert Fried and Ronald Sanders, eds., *Socialist Thought: A Documentary History* (1964); one should, however, read *The Communist Manifesto* somewhere, perhaps in Karl Marx and Friedrich Engels, *Basic Writings on Politics and Philosophy* (1959), edited by Lewis S. Feur. Early socialist theory is surveyed, but with inadequate commentary, in G. D. H. Cole, *Socialist Thought*, vol. 1, *The Forerunners, 1789–1850* (1955); and Alexander Gray, *The Socialist Tradition: From Moses to Lenin* (1947). Edmund Wilson, *To the Finland Station: A Study in the Writing and Acting of History* (1940) is incisive in relating personal experiences to social history, particularly for Marx and Engels. Two fine lives of Marx are Isaiah Berlin, *Karl Marx* (1948) and Franz Mehring, *Karl Marx* (1962).

20
THE LONDON OF VICTORIA

If in the first half of the nineteenth century Manchester was regarded as the prototype of the unplanned industrial city, in the second half of the century London fascinated the West as the first example of the "world city." This new form of city was characterized primarily by a very large population spread over a very large area; by 1900 Greater London had a population of over six million inhabitants spread over more than a hundred square miles. This spread of the city had been made possible by the mechanization of transport. The construction of the railroads from the 1830s made possible the middle-class commuter and the development of suburbia. The dispersion of the poorer classes was made feasible first by the underground railroad in 1865, and then in the 1880s by the laying down of rails in the streets themselves for horsedrawn trams and later for electrically powered cars. Secondly, the world city's population was drawn from the whole world. London's population was constantly augmented by the influx of great numbers of migrants, from within Britain and abroad. The railroads brought into London the dispossessed and the ambitious of the countryside and the northern cities, as well as the poor and politically oppressed from the South and East of Europe; the steamship brought migrants from the empire, Indians and Chinese above all. Thirdly, the world city had direct industrial and commercial ties to the rest of the planet. The steamships brought into the Port of London eight million tons of goods in 1880, compared with only 800,000 at the beginning of the century; and Baedeker was sending visitors to see the warehouses that could store 200,000 tons of goods. "Nothing will convey to the stranger a better idea of the vast activity and stupendous wealth of London," he wrote, "than a visit to the warehouses, filled to overflowing with interminable stores of every kind of foreign and colonial products." Fourthly, the world city was deeply involved in the internal affairs of the other nations of the world. For Victorian London, this involved a dual responsibility. It was the

Ludgate Hill, by Gustave Doré (1833–1883). Doré, the leading French book illustrator in the nineteenth century, captured both the vitality and the suffering of London life in engravings for Blanchard Jerrold's *London: A Pilgrimage* (1872).

**"London Going Out of Town
—Or—The March of Bricks
and Mortar," by George
Cruickshank (1792–1878).**
Cruickshank's engraved carica-
tures made mordant comment
on the ecological disaster of
uncontrolled urban expansion.

administrator of a growing colonial empire and the undisputed leader of
a group of self-governing dominions; and as its industrial supremacy
and its naval might made it, at least until about 1870, the major power
in the world, it was a necessary participant in all important world affairs.
Indeed at times its attitude seemed well summed up by the popular music
hall song:

*We don't want to fight
But by Jingo, if we do
We've got the men, we've got the ships,
We've got the money too.*

The change in London in the nineteenth century was due to the conversion
of an industrial, commercial and administrative capital to a new world
role; and its physical adaptation was made possible by the application
of a new technology to the needs of urban life.

**THE TASTE OF
VICTORIAN
LONDON:
THE CRYSTAL PALACE**

The word *Victorian* was coined in 1851, when Victoria had already been
on the throne for fourteen years and the dark days of the Hungry Forties
were over. In that year, the nations of the whole world were invited
to send exhibits of their industrial and artistic skills to London for display
in the first international exhibition ever held. Throughout the year, poetry
was utilized for some revealingly Victorian purposes:

*Gather, ye Nations, gather! From forge, and mine, and mill!
Come, Science and Invention; Come, Industry and Skill!
Come with your woven wonders, the blossoms of the loom,
That rival Nature's fairest flowers in all but their perfume;*

Come with your brass and iron, Your silver and your gold,
And arts that change the face of earth, unknown to men of old.
Gather, ye Nations, gather! From ev'ry clime and soil,
The New Confederation, the Jubilee of toil. [1]

For Britain itself, competition with the best the foreigner could produce
was a sign of self-confidence not only in its industrial achievements but
in its artistic superiority as well. The Great Exhibition symbolized the
end of the years of disillusionment and the full assertion of Britain's renewed
self-esteem.

Social Tension in Britain, 1815–1848. The years between the defeat
of Napoleon at Waterloo in 1815 and the continentwide revolutions in
1848 had not been years of social peace in Britain. The predominant
mood had been a state of disquiet for the future of British society, due to
either a distrust of British institutions or fear for their survival. It is true
that the industrial revolution was continuing unabated, passing from a
transformation of textile production to an industrialism of railroads, coal,
and iron. Industrial production rose at an average of thirty-seven percent
each decade. Yet the working classes were continuously discontented
and intermittently riotous. In the 1830s and 1840s, bad harvest combined
with the tariff on imported wheat to keep food prices high; downturns in
the business cycle, uncontrolled by government action, produced severe
unemployment; and there was even a fall in the real wages of those who
had jobs. The reform measures that were finally passed in the 1840s,
such as the Factory Acts and the repeal of the Corn Laws, were little more
than palliatives. Only higher wages and more secure employment could
end working-class misery.

Discontent with the country's political institutions had been focused
on the method of electing the House of Commons. The Reform Bill of
1832 had at last spread representation to the industrial cities, and had
given the wealthier middle classes suffrage. But only one man in five had
the vote; and no women had the privilege. The general discontent with the
nature of parliamentary representation had even, in the early part of the
century, extended to include the monarchy itself. George III had been
totally insane in the last years of his reign. His son George IV (reigned
1820–1830) was interested only in buildings, food, and clothes. William IV
(reigned 1830–1837) was, in the words of *The Spectator*, ''a weak, ignorant,
commonplace sort of person.'' Little more was expected of Victoria when
she ascended the throne at the age of eighteen, unprepared by education
or background for her new responsibilities. The people of London, as
The Times commented, ''saw the monarchy in Queen Victoria, and pledged
themselves that for their own sakes they would uphold it, with the help

[1] John W. Dodds, *The Age of Paradox: A Biography of England, 1841–1851* (Westport, Conn.:
Greenwood Press, 1952), p. 443.

Burning of the Houses of Parliament, by Joseph Turner (1775–1851). The reformed parliament ordered construction of a far more grandiose meeting place after a fire in 1834 destroyed the palace where it had met since 1547. (Philadelphia Museum of Art. Photograph by A. J. Wyatt, Staff Photographer.)

of their Sovereign, so—if not, they would preserve the monarchy, in spite of an ill-advised monarch."[2]

As for the empire, which was to become the chief source of national pride by the end of Victoria's reign, only the working classes showed any interest. In the 1830s, over 100,000 persons emigrated annually; in the 1840s, over 200,000. Their destinations were Canada, Australia, New Zealand, South Africa, and also the United States. The government fought small wars, like the Opium War in China, to increase trade facilities, and permitted both governmental and private agencies to expand their territorial hold in India and South Africa. But for the general public the disillusionment that had followed the loss of the American colonies persisted.

Character of the Mid-Victorian Age. By 1851, the discontent with industrialism and with the country's political institutions had been alleviated, and the first glimmerings of interest in empire were being roused by the activities of antislavery groups and explorers. From about 1848 to the

[2] David Thomson, *England in the Nineteenth Century* (Harmondsworth, England: Penguin, 1950), p. 169.

crash of 1873, the mid-Victorian age knew steady and real prosperity. Its basis was the expansion of the heavy industries linked to coal, iron, and steel, especially for the building of railroads, steamships, and other forms of heavy engineering. The beginning of industrialism on the continent made the developing countries there major importers of British coal, iron and steel, and heavy engineering products until they themselves, from the 1870s, could challenge Britain's position as the workshop of the world. Capital accumulated in the earlier phases of the industrial revolution now sought new openings for profitable investment in new forms of industry and in overseas investment. Britain became the world's banker as well as its manufacturer. Even the farmers found that they could profit from the growing home market by capital investment in land or mechanical improvements, and ceased to regret the repeal of the Corn Laws. Free trade was welcomed as the common philosophy of both industrial and agricultural classes, and a climate of opinion thus came to exist that was favorable to the capitalist expansion. Even working-class wages rose faster than the rising prices that were themselves acting as an inflationary stimulus to the economy. Money wages probably rose fifty-six percent between 1850 and 1874. Taken in relation to the rise in prices, the average working-class family probably received about ten percent more in real wages. The rise was sufficient to blunt the discontent of the poorer people.

One important factor strengthening faith in Britain's political institutions was the sense of relief at having avoided the upheavals that rocked the continental capitals in 1848. British governments, even if elected by a minority of the country's population, had answered demands for reform with bills ranging from the abolition of slavery in the British empire (1833) to the institution of a ten-and-a-half-hour working day in the factories (1847). Moreover the predominant liberal ethic was against the increase in state controls, and hence minimized the significance of widespread political participation. London itself lacked an effective local government, and even an adequate water supply and sanitary system, and efforts to provide them received little public support. "We prefer to take our chance of cholera and the rest," wrote *The Times*, "than be bullied into health." Even minor attempts at parliamentary reform in the 1850s died for lack of interest.

To this renewed acceptance of the validity of Britain's political institutions, Victoria herself had contributed substantially. From the moment of her accession, Victoria showed the qualities that were to remain with her throughout her reign: a sense of duty, a conviction of moral righteousness, and a deep feeling for her country. "Since it has pleased Providence to place me in this station," she wrote in her diary, "I shall do my utmost to fulfil my duty towards my country; I am very young, and perhaps in many, though not in all things, inexperienced, but I am sure, that very few have more good will and more real desire to do what is fit and right than I have." Her marriage in 1840 to the earnest young German prince, Albert of

Saxe-Coburg-Gotha, helped her find her political role. Albert was well-educated and intelligent. He had grasped the significance of the monarchy's new functions, which combined a small amount of political manipulation with an unlimited responsibility as the emotional and ceremonial focus of a people in social turmoil. It was Albert whose growing domination over his wife forced Victoria to take an interest in matters that had previously bored her, such as science and literature and even industrial progress. As Victoria accepted the necessary transition of power to men with whom she had little personal sympathy, she pursued family interests with her nine children, visits to the seaside and the country with the family, and admiration of Albert's plunge into the world of British industry.

Victoria and Albert, Photographed about 1860. (The Granger Collection.)

The Crystal Palace. In 1849, Albert hit upon the idea of the Great Exhibition, "to give us a true test and a living picture of the point of development at which the whole of mankind has arrived in this great task of applied science and a new starting point from which all nations will be able to direct their further exertions." The prince's idea was approved by the Royal Society, and won the financial backing of industry and the general public, who subscribed £200,000 as guarantee. A Royal Commission of architects and engineers was appointed to plan the building and exhibits. Out of 234 plans submitted, the commission, urged by the prince, eventually picked the most original design of all, a massive greenhouse designed by the head gardener of a northern duke. Joseph Paxton, however, was no mere gardener, but an engineer, railroad director, newspaper promoter, and imaginative architect in glass and iron. He offered a building 1,848 feet long, 408 feet broad, and 66 feet high, tall enough to cover the old elm trees already occupying the chosen site in Hyde Park. It was composed of mass-produced and standardized parts, including over 6,000 15-foot columns and over one million square feet of glass. It could be erected in seventeen weeks; and it could be, and was, dismantled and re-erected in another part of London when the exhibition was over. In spite of many fears expressed over the building's durability, it survived until 1936. The completed building found few detractors. All of the thirteen thousand exhibitors had ample space; and so did six million visitors from all over the world, who gazed in fascination, as described by Lord Tennyson, on

> . . . the giant aisles   Steel and gold, and coal and wine,
> Rich in model and design;   Fabric rough or fairy-fine . . .
> Harvest-tool and husbandry,   And shapes and hues of Art divine!
> Loom and wheel and enginery,   All of beauty, all of use,
> Secrets of the sullen mine,   That one fair planet can produce.[3]

To Victoria, it was Albert's greatest triumph, "the *greatest* day in our history, the most *beautiful* and *imposing* and *touching* spectacle ever seen, and the triumph of my beloved Albert." The Queen was right in thinking that the exhibition summarized the aspirations of her time. She had little idea how diverse would be the judgments of later ages on the contents of her Crystal Palace and on the state of mind and taste that they epitomized.

Purpose of the Great Exhibition. The mixed motives of the Victorians, the ingenuous combination of altruism, moral striving, and material selfishness that the Great Exhibition illustrated, was summarized by Albert himself when he tried to win the support of London's business and civic leaders for his idea. "We are living at a period of most wonderful transition, which tends rapidly to accomplish that great end, to which, indeed, all history points—the realization of the unity of mankind. . . . The products of all quarters of the globe are placed at our disposal, and we have only to choose which is the best and cheapest for our purposes, and the powers of production are intrusted to the stimulus of competition and capital." The exhibition was a monument to the belief in progress, to mankind's inevitable upward drive to self-improvement and material productivity, under God's guidance, which, as the Archbishop of Canterbury misguidedly noted, had

[3] Nikolaus Pevsner, *High Victorian Design: A Study of the Exhibits of 1851* (London: Architectural Press, 1951), p. 12.

The West Nave of the Crystal Palace, London. Paxton's design for a vast greenhouse of cast-iron struts and glass panels provided space for 13,000 displays at the Great Exhibition of 1851. (*Illustrated London News,* Sept. 6, 1851.)

brought "peace within our walls and plenteousness within our palaces." The exhibition's organizers in fact genuinely believed that the display would convince foreigners of the good sense of peace and international collaboration through the doctrine of free trade. But the exhibition was also intended to promote internal peace in England by glorifying honest work and the trustworthy laborer. The prince was president of the Society for the Improvement of the Labouring Classes, and he had a model home for the working classes erected near the entrance to the exhibition. The workers were encouraged to come from their northern slums by special excursion train to see the wonders of the exhibition after the entrance price had been reduced to a shilling; and their good humor and behavior delighted the city's well-to-do and reinforced their satisfaction with England's social system.

For all its moral message, the exhibition was above all a display of the application of artistic taste to objects of utility. The exhibition was divided into four categories: raw materials, machinery, manufactures, and fine arts. Even among the first category there had been a lapse of taste, with glass imitating wood, clay as artificial marble, and papier-mâché substituting for brass. But the machinery produced the most extraordinary, and the most popular, examples of extravagance. The display included some functionally designed machinery like McCormick's reaping machine, gas cooking ranges, electric clocks, and the electric telegraph; there were also steam engines in Ancient Egyptian style, others with Greek Doric columns, yet others in cast-iron Gothic. No style appeared pure, but elements of many crept in jovial juxtaposition together, as in a partially Elizabethan sideboard

made entirely of rubber by the gutta-percha company that had just started
tapping the sap of Malayan trees. Victorian taste in fact was gloriously
eclectic. Period revivals were the foundation of its styles in art and architecture, and every style was represented in the exhibition. Bastardized
baroque and rococo predominated in industrial exhibits; in the fine arts,
however, Gothic easily carried the day.

**Prince Albert's Model Lodging
House.** The Society for the
Improvement of the Labouring
Classes erected this workers'
house opposite the Exhibition
as an example for employers.
(*Illustrated London News,*
June 14, 1851.)

Period Revivals in European Art. The revival of period styles had begun
a full century earlier. After the domination of rococo and classicism (see
Chapter 15), there had first been a revival of pure Greek forms that caused
country parks of the English aristocracy to be filled with Doric temples, and
that influenced the finest of all English pottery makers, Josiah Wedgwood.
After the Greek came a Gothic revival, accompanied by an emotional attachment to the dark mysteries of the Middle Ages, which was conceived
as an age of faith and emotion in utter contrast with the materialism of the
eighteenth century. Gothic motifs were seized for country houses. Living-
room ceilings branched out into fan vaulting, and fireplaces built with can-
opied statue niches. With the romantic movement a further element, the
rejection of industrialism, was added to stimulate the revival of period styles.
Any period before industrialism appeared aesthetically valuable, most of all
to the great industrialists themselves, who applied this conclusion not only
to the design of their homes and the art they bought for them but even to
the very machinery they were manufacturing. George IV, while still prince
regent, introduced Hindu architecture in the fanciful pavilion he built at
the seacoast in Brighton. The Germans popularized the neo-Greek style
for public buildings in the 1820s and then experimented with neo-Renaissance palaces and high Gothic cathedrals. The French revived their own
Renaissance, which soon drove out the Roman style that Napoleon I had

Contrasts, by Augustus Welby Pugin (1812–1852). (Below) "Catholic Town in 1440." (Above) "The Same Town in 1840." Pugin sought to show that the ruin of the English city was due to Protestantism as much as to industrialism.

favored, although by the midcentury they had almost come full circle with a revival of baroque. The English borrowed both the French and German revivals, and continued seeking their own past to reconstruct; they found it in their own Elizabethan and Jacobean buildings. Architects filled their pattern books with buildings of almost every conceivable style, and the patron picked whatever style appealed to him either for its own intrinsic merits or for some religious or literary association it might have for him.

Architecture of Nineteenth-Century London. The London in which the Crystal Palace stood was already a showcase of period revivals by 1851. During the building boom of the last hundred years no single style had predominated at any time. Fortunately for London, until at least 1830 the stylistic experiments had been relatively successful. John Nash's white stuccoed terraces lined the monumental mall that led to Buckingham Palace, overlooked the picturesque new Regent's Park, and ran along the great curve of Regent's Street north from Piccadilly Circus. The abandonment of red brick radically changed the appearance of the aristocratic sections of London:

Augustus at Rome was for building renowned
And of marble he left what of brick he had found;
But is not our Nash, too, a very great master,
He finds us all brick and leaves us all plaster.

Meanwhile, the romantic movement's admirers were turning the squares and parks into bowers that would have pleased Rousseau; the Gothic admirers were raising on the banks of the Thames the vast facade and irregular towers of the Houses of Parliament; the neo-Greeks were putting up the British Museum and the central courtyard of Euston railroad station, proclaimed as the eighth wonder of the world; and the great London clubs and many of the banks were going up as imitation Florentine palaces. In the well-to-do districts, the result was a surprisingly charming hodgepodge.

Carlton House Terrace, London. The monumental terraces of John Nash (1752–1835) imposed a plan of linked boulevards upon the confused growth of central London. (British Travel and Holidays Association photo.)

The Gothic Revival. In the year of the Crystal Palace, Gothic was probably the most popular of all these competing styles. Pugin, who designed the medieval court at the Crystal Palace, had indicated the way with his *True Principles of Pointed or Christian Architecture*. Ruskin was praising the medieval centuries, in *Seven Lamps of Architecture*, for their purity of faith as reflected in their art. Thomas Carlyle was directing the historians back to the heroes of the Middle Ages, while Walter Scott was thrilling the readers of his novels with the broad sweep of distant battles and crusading kings. Many took the Gothic apostasy to its logical conclusion, and were converted to Catholicism. Six years before the Great Exhibition, John Henry Newman, who had been a leading member of the Oxford Movement's struggle to reemphasize the Church of England's role as the upholder of Catholic traditions of worship, became a Roman Catholic; and he shook Victorian England later with his classic autobiographical defense of his conversion, *Apologia pro Vita Sua*.

Outside the Catholic Church things are tending . . . to atheism in one shape or other. What a scene, what a prospect, does the whole of Europe present at this day! and not only Europe, but every government and every civilisation through the world, which is under the influence of the European mind! Especially, for it most concerns us, how sorrowful, in the view of religion, even taken in its most elementary, most attenuated form, is the spectacle presented to us by the educated intellect of England, France and Germany! Lovers of their country and of their race, religious men, external to the Catholic Church, have attempted various expedients to arrest fierce wilful human nature in its onward course, and to bring it into subjection . . . but where was the concrete representative of things invisible, which would have the force and toughness necessary to be a breakwater against the deluge?[4]

Even the painters themselves published their own of rejection of everything that had preceded the High Renaissance. In 1848, a group under the leadership of Dante Gabriel Rossetti founded the Pre-Raphaelite Brotherhood, and set the style for the whole of the 1850s with their bright colors, affectedly innocent tableaux of religious or rural scenes, and grotesque re-creations of scenes from the medieval chronicles. The tragedy of Victorian taste is due to a remarkable degree to their love for history. The Victorians, while taking pride in their material achievements in industrial production and in the huge spread of their cities, refused to develop an architecture or an art or a functionalism of design that would correspond to their new technology and their new materials.

It is thus not surprising that Queen Victoria should have found pleasure in the gloom of Pugin's Medieval Court in the Crystal Palace. Years later, when the last traces of the Crystal Palace had been removed from the lawns of Hyde Park, and a memorial to Albert, dead in 1861 at the age

---

[4] John Henry Newman, *Apologia pro Vita Sua* (London: Dent, 1934), pp. 221–24.

The Albert Memorial, London.
The Prince, who is surrounded
by 178 statues of musicians,
poets, and artists, is shown
holding a catalog of the Great
Exhibition. (British Travel
and Holidays Association
photo.)

of forty-two, was to be erected on its site, it was in Victorian Gothic that
the 175-foot high canopy with its 178 life-size figures was erected. Albert
was to look forever over the scene of his greatest triumph.

THE EAST END OF LONDON

Albert died of typhoid fever, a reminder that even the highest in society
could not ignore the debased conditions of sanitation and housing in which
the mass of London's population lived. Buckingham Palace was connected
with the poorer districts of London by its sewers and it shared their water
supply; and the aristocracy of the new mansions of Belgravia or Regent's
Park were prey to the epidemics of typhus, cholera, typhoid, and febrile
influenza that swept the poorer districts. In the 1840s, a tough-minded
reformer called Edwin Chadwick dramatized the plight of the poor by
publication of a large number of official reports on the state of public
health in the unsanitary cities and especially in London. Chadwick's
studies were followed over the next half-century by a large number of
detailed, well-documented exposés, of which the most influential was
the seventeen-volume *Life and Labour of the People in London* (1886–
1903) of Charles Booth, a philanthropic Liverpool shipowner. During the
same time, some of England's greatest novelists, with Charles Dickens

preeminent among them, found among the teeming poor of London the subject matter for their stories. The problems of urban growth were thus approached in a unique, double-barreled way: in the reports, the problems were analyzed in meticulous depth and feasible solutions proposed, while the novelists prepared the public for acceptance of these solutions by making the problems comprehensible in human terms.

The Slums of London.   The mushroom growth of nineteenth-century London had been responsible for many of its problems. London had developed from two nuclei, Westminster where the king resided and Parliament met, and the City of London where the port, trading companies, and financial offices were situated. By the end of the eighteenth century, when London had a population of about 800,000, the two nuclei were joined in a continuous band of buildings, with the thoroughfare called the Strand joining the older sections. Much of the expansion (see Chapter 15) had been in aristocratic or middle-class quarters, but already London possessed the slum areas that fascinated painters like Hogarth. They were small, however, compared with those that sprang up in the first forty years of the nineteenth century when London's population increased by a million. Better medical care, including vaccination and hospitals, accounted for some of the rise. New employment opportunities were provided by huge

**Over London—by Rail, by
Gustave Doré.**

new docks and by the expansion of London's own industries like foodstuffs, drink, building materials, and soap. Service industries grew to supply the growing numbers in commerce and administration. The bulk of the new population lived in the boroughs to the east of the City, down both sides of the river from the Tower of London in what came to be called the East End. While the aristocracy were building their town houses in the elegant squares and crescents near Westminster in the West End, about one-third of London's population lived in Stepney, Poplar, Bethnal Green, Bermondsey, and Southwark in the oppressive squalor that Chadwick described in 1842 in his *Report on the Sanitary Conditions of the Labouring Classes.*

This contrast of West and East ends, which increased during the century, fascinated both English and foreign observers. The reason was obvious. "I was yesterday . . . over the cholera districts of Bermondsey," the novelist Charles Kingsley wrote his wife in 1849. "And, oh God! what I saw! People having no water to drink—hundreds of them—but the water of the common sewer which stagnates full of . . . dead fish, cats and dogs, under their windows." Owing to an almost total lack of public administration in the newer areas—London did not get a city government until 1888—there were few public services. Water, often polluted, was supplied by nine private companies at a profit, and usually was turned on only a few

**Dudley Street, Seven Dials,
by Gustave Doré.**

**The Southwark Waterworks,
by George Cruickshank.**
"Salus populi suprema lex"
(The People's Health is the
Highest Law) is Cruickshank's
comment on the use of the
polluted Thames River for
London's drinking water.

hours a day three times a week. Drainage was inadequate; uncovered ditches emptied the cesspools into the river Thames, which became, in *Punch's* words, a "foul sludge and foetid stream." Cemeteries were overcrowded, and bodies buried above street level; shallow graves were inadequately provided, in pest fields and plague pits, for victims of the epidemics. No controls were extended to housing contractors, who threw up the slums called rookeries. The author of one report found 1,465 families in an area near London's most fashionable church, living in 2,174 rooms with only 2,510 beds among them. But it was Dickens, in *Bleak House*, who permitted the London bourgeois to follow Kingsley's advice: "Go, scented Belgravian, and see what London is."

Jo lives—that is to say, Jo has not yet died—in a ruinous place, known to the like of him by the name of Tom-all-Alone's. It is a black, dilapidated street, avoided by all decent people; where the crazy houses were seized upon, when their decay was far advanced, by some bold vagrants, who, after establishing their own possession, took to letting them out in lodgings. Now, these tumbling tenements contain, by night, a swarm of misery. As on the ruined human wretch, vermin parasites appear, so these ruined shelters have bred a crowd of foul existence that crawls in and out of gaps in walls and boards; and coils itself to sleep, in maggot numbers, where the rain drips in; and comes and goes, fetching and carrying fever, and sowing more evil in its every footprint than Lord Coodle, and Sir Thomas Doodle, and the Duke of Foodle, and all the fine gentlemen in office, down to Zoodle, shall set right in five hundred years—though born expressly to do it.

Working Conditions of the London Poor.   The vast numbers of poor were
compelled to seek work in conditions of great hardship.   The worst exploitation did not take place in factories but among small employers, particularly
in the clothing trade where so-called sweated labor was normal.   Women
and children worked at sewing in their homes for very small wages;
they received four shillings and sixpence for sewing a dozen shirts.   'As
a result of the lack of regular employment, thousands turned to trades
like hawking and others less legal.   Henry Mayhew, in his very influential
book *London Labour and the London Poor* (1861) estimated that there were
13,000 street traders, many of whom he interviewed.   They included the
children called mud-larks, who scraped the Thames mud for scraps of
coal dropped by the barges; sellers of sheeps' trotters, ham sandwiches,
flowers, and birds' nests; and costermongers, who sold fish, fruit, and
vegetables.   There were also the dredgers, who went into the river for
dead bodies, and the sewer hunters, who searched for bottles or iron that
could be sold.   Mayhew's books became a mine for novelists like Kingsley
and Dickens; but Mayhew's own ear for the language of the interviewed and
the illustrations he published were as effective as any novel in waking
the conscience of London.   His twenty-two-year-old birds'-nest seller
told him:

*Mother died five years ago in the Consumption Hospital at Chelsea, just after it
was built. I was very young indeed when father died; I can hardly remember him.
He died in Middlesex Hospital: he had abscesses all over him; there were six-and-
thirty at the time of his death. . . . I'm a very little eater, and perhaps that's the luck-
iest thing for such as me; half a pound of bread and a few potatoes will do me for the
day. If I could afford it, I used to get a ha'porth of coffee and a ha'porth of sugar
and make it do twice. Sometimes I used to have victuals given to me, sometimes
I went without altogether; and sometimes I couldn't eat. I can't always.*[5]

It was hardly surprising then that crime, especially theft, was rampant.
The police believed that some 20,000 children were being trained in
thieving in the 1860s, in the way Dickens described in *Oliver Twist*.
Prostitution was widespread.   Gambling was a full-time profession for
10,000 people.   By the 1880s, it was common for reformers to compare
the London slums unfavorably with the jungles of central Africa being
described contemporaneously by England's explorers and missionaries.
General Booth's *In Darkest England and the Way Out* began with the
comment, "The lot of the Negroes in the Equatorial Forest is not, perhaps,
a very happy one, but is it so very much worse than that of many a pretty
orphan girl in our Christian capital?"[6]

Metropolitan Reform.   The authors of these reports were clear on the
reforms needed to remedy the problems of unplanned urban growth.

[5] John L. Bradley, ed., *Selections from London Labour and the London Poor* (Oxford: Oxford
University Press, 1965), p. 116.
[6] Cited in Asa Briggs, *Victorian Cities* (Harmondsworth, England: Penguin, 1968), pp. 313–14.

They did not condemn the whole structure of capitalist society as the Socialist reformers were doing, but as practical men, they suggested practical reforms. London needed public construction and maintenance of a network of drains and sewers; public provision of pure water; slum clearance and provision of decent public housing; and public asylums for the insane and public hospitals for the indigent sick; and above all it needed a metropolitan government to deal with the problems of the whole sprawling area in a unified way. Slowly the reformers gained their way. In the 1850s, there was established a Metropolitan Board of Works, which began a large-scale building program and sanitary improvements. Parks were purchased. Burial boards, an asylums board, a school board, and finally in 1888 a London County Council were created. Life was still hard for the London poor, as the riots known as Bloody Monday in 1886 and Bloody Sunday in 1887 demonstrated. But a start at least had been made in remedying the most blatant grievances.

CHARLES DICKENS: THE NOVELIST AS SOCIAL REFORMER

The English Novel. In making the general public aware of these problems and receptive to a solution, the novelists of the mid–nineteenth century played a significant part. By then, the novel had been developed into a perfect vehicle for this task, although its history had been relatively short. Only a hundred years earlier, with the publication of Samuel Richardson's *Pamela*, the modern form of novel had been invented. There had obviously been story-telling in prose for two millennia at least, in Apuleius's *The Golden Ass,* for example, and the Arabian *Tales of a Thousand and One Nights*. But in London in the mid–eighteenth century, writers used the story in prose to probe human motivation and explore individual character, and to present a reconstruction of all the varieties of contemporary life, as they engaged in a dramatic form of infinite complexity. With Henry Fielding, who was a magistrate in the Bow Street law court and head of the equivalent of the London police, the great variety of the London underworld first entered the English novel; and in his masterpiece *Tom Jones*, after the rollicking scenes of bucolic life in the West Country, we are thrown into the rough slums of London that Hogarth depicted in *Gin Lane*. By 1836, when Charles Dickens had swept his way to fame by depicting the meeting of Mr. Pickwick and his inimitable valet, Sam Weller, in the fifteenth number of the serialization of *The Pickwick Papers*, the novel had won a vast public among the middle-class patrons of the monthly magazine and the lending library. With Jane Austen, it had explored the art of showing subtleties of character through the niceties of conversation; with Walter Scott, it had spread itself over vast panoramas of time and space, becoming the instrument for the Romantic movement's re-creation of the imagined dramas of medieval life; with Disraeli, it had begun to explore the nature of English class distinction. But Dickens was able to create a world in his novels that for many of his readers had a greater reality and coherence, and thus a more poignant message, than the necessarily restricted sphere of their own daily lives.

London at the Time
of Charles Dickens

0 ½ Mile

Dickens's London. For them, Dickens described the parts of London they had never known, or gave meaning to the parts they did. In *Bleak House*, it was the law courts along the Strand and the lawyers' chambers in Lincoln's Inn Fields, characterized by the fog that penetrates everything. "Fog everywhere. Fog up the river, where it flows among green aits and meadows; fog down the river, where it rolls defiled among the tiers of shipping and the waterside pollutions of a great (and dirty) city. Fog on the Essex marshes, fog on the Kentish heights. . . . And hard by Temple Bar, in Lincoln's Inn Hall, at the very heart of the fog, sits the Lord High Chancellor in his High Court of Chancery." In *Oliver Twist*, it is the dark recesses along the river bank where Fagin's gang lurks, where "the old smoke-stained storehouses on either side rose heavy and dull from the dense mass of roofs and gables, and frowned sternly upon water too black to reflect even their lumbering shapes." And there is the den in the slums where Fagin trains his boys as pickpockets, "these foul'd and frowsty dens, where vice is closely packed and lacks the room to turn." Mr. Pickwick is consigned to a debtors' prison, just as Dickens's own father had been:

"Ohr," replied Mr. Pickwick, looking down a dark and filthy staircase, which appeared to lead to a range of damp and gloomy stone vaults, beneath the ground, "and those, I suppose are the little cellars where the prisoners keep their small

quantities of coals. Unpleasant places to have to go down to, but very convenient, I dare say." "Yes, I shouldn't wonder if they was convenient," replied the gentleman, "seeing that a few people live there, pretty snug." . . . "My friend," said Mr. Pickwick, "you don't really mean to say that human beings live down in those wretched dungeons?" "Live down there! Yes, and die down there, too, very often!" replied Mr. Roker; "and what of that? Who's got to say anything agin it?"

The Londoners of Dickens. But even more than he did with places, Dickens brought alive a vast gallery of London characters. His anger blazed against the heartless and irresponsible among the middle classes. Mr. Snawley abandons his stepchildren to Mr. Squeers's nightmarelike school of Dotheboys Hall, in *Nicholas Nickleby:*

"Not too much writing home allowed, I suppose?" said the step-father hesitating.
"None, except a circular at Christmas, to say they never were so happy, and hope they may never be sent for," rejoined Squeers.
"Nothing could be better," said the step-father, rubbing his hands.

Unscrupulous lawyers abound in his pages. It is through the machinations of the firm of Dodson and Fogg that Mr. Pickwick finds himself in the Fleet prison. In *Bleak House,* the trial of Jarndyce v. Jarndyce has been prolonged for years, the symbol of the profitable legal procrastination of the court of chancery, "which has its worn-out lunatic in every madhouse and its dead in every churchyard." The bureaucrats who froze an army to death in the Crimean War appear as the Tite Barnacles of the Circumlocution Office in *Little Dorrit.* There is the cheap, hyocritical crook, like Uriah Heep in *David Copperfield*; and in *Oliver Twist* the violent, unthinking thief, like Bill Sikes, and Fagin, the almost likable trainer of pickpockets and psychological master of outcast children. Only occasionally is there an oasis of quiet and good will, like Pickwick's Christmas with the Wardles at Dingley Dell. Usually Dickens's characters cannot avoid the great swelling tide of social injustice and the human malice that grows in such a system. For all his humor, Dickens's London was a place where the sufferings of human beings needed remedy. His method, which was to create innumerable scenes of the great macrocosm of metropolitan life, and then to multiply the effect by showing those scenes through the eyes of a large number of characters, was perfect for his task.

Dickens was able to bring alive the different worlds of London, and especially those in need of reform—the prisons, hospitals, mortuaries, slums, poorhouses, schools, countinghouses, law courts, hustings, ministries, factories, shipyards, cab stands, fishmarkets. "Heart of London," he wrote, "I seem to hear a voice within thee that sinks into my heart, bidding me, as I elbow my way among the crowd, to have some thought for the meanest wretch that passes, and, being a man, to turn away with scorn

and pride from none that wears the human shape." In spite of his sentimentality and sensationalism, or perhaps because of them, Dickens impressed on his huge reading public his own vision of a London in which
the mechanism of society had not kept up with the needs of its diverse
humanity. He was the reformers' finest ally.

The reformers had another ally, however, that spread through Victorian
society even more pervasively than the writings of Dickens—the sense of
the obligations of religion. Religion was probably the most powerful force
in nineteenth-century England until it was challenged by the doctrines of
science, or more accurately until it challenged them.

VICTORIAN RELIGION

Evangelicalism and the Oxford Movement. In the early years of the
century, the reforming forces within organized religion were to be found
in the dissenting sects (that is, those branches of Christian worship, such
as the Methodists or Congregationalists, who dissented from the beliefs
or form of worship of the Anglican and the Catholic churches) or in the
evangelical, or reformist, wing of the Anglican church. By Victoria's reign,
"evangelicalism" had come to denote an attitude of moral rectitude, an
emphasis on the sense of sin and of the need for self-improvement, and a
reliance on Bible reading and strict religious observance regardless of
whether the evangelical was an Anglican or a dissenter. The most famous
of the early evangelicals had been the Clapham Sect, named after the
village just outside London where the members met. Their leaders, especially William Wilberforce and Lord Shaftesbury, had successfully fought

**Night in the East End, by
Gustave Doré.**

a number of crusades for social reform that had culminated in the abolition of the slave trade in 1807 and slavery in the British empire in 1833; in the factory acts of the 1830s and 1840s; and in the banning of all public amusement on the Sabbath. The changes that accompanied the parliamentary reform of 1832 and the establishment of municipal governments after 1835 strengthened the evangelical movement, bringing its adherents to power in the local districts and increasing their influence in parliament.

"Evangelical morality," as Noel Annan has shown, "was the single most widespread influence in Victorian England. . . . It spread through every class and taught a clear set of values."[7] The evangelicals felt that they experienced God personally, in their daily emotional communication with him; they knew from their conversion that they were saved; and they were confident that they had the power, and knew they had the duty, to go into the world to do God's work.

In the 1830s, however, the main body of the Church of England was stirred from a somnolence due to anachronistic organization and clerical indifference by a very different type of religious enthusiasm from evangelicalism, the Oxford Movement. Many of the leaders of the movement sprang from the evangelical groups, found in their upbringing a sense of religious certainty, and then rejected evangelicalism for its inability to accept the Catholic origins of the Anglican church, or even Catholicism itself. In *Tracts for the Times,* the preachers of the Oxford Movement demanded a return to the deep devotion of the seventeenth-century church, with its emphasis on authority, ritual, liturgy, and ecclesiastical decoration. By 1840, this "High Church" revival had roused great interest, which was not dissipated when several of its most influential leaders, like Newman, were converted to Roman Catholicism.

Popular Attitudes toward Religion. When a religious census was taken in 1851, it showed that over seven million people attended church that day, of whom just over half went to Anglican services. The census, which shocked many by showing that only half the population had gone to church, proved conclusively that religious attendance was a matter of class standing or even of income. The worst attendance was recorded in the slums of the East End of London and in the industrial cities of the North. In Bethnal Green, for example, only 6,000 out of 90,000 residents went to church. The Congregationalists admitted that they could attract "congregations of tradesmen, but never of artificers." Catholics knew that they had too few churches for their adherents, especially for the large numbers of Irish immigrants. The reaction was a new effort from the 1850s by all denominations to reach the poor through church building, increases in numbers of clergy, founding of church schools and Sunday Schools, and genuine missionary activity, which included the support of revivalist preachers from the United States and in the eighties the founding of the

---

[7] Noel Annan, *Leslie Stephen* (London: McGibbon and Kee, 1951), p. 110.

Salvation Army. Thus, from the 1860s there was a strong religious revival that affected the poorer sections of society and combined with the movement for the simultaneous improvements of their material conditions. It is ironic that the most dramatic example of the strength of the religious revival was the Victorian sabbath. In many middle-class homes, diversions like cards, music, dancing, and reading anything other than the Bible were forbidden. Screens were even put in front of pictures in Ruskin's house. All public amusements were closed, which caused more hardship on the poor than anyone else, as Dickens complained in *Little Dorrit*.

Everything was belted and barred that could possibly furnish relief to an overworked people. No pictures, no unfamiliar animals, no rare plants or flowers, no natural or artificial wonders of the ancient world—all taboo with that enlightened strictness, that the ugly South Sea gods in the British Museum might have supposed themselves at home again. Nothing to see but streets, streets, streets. Nothing to breathe but streets, streets, streets. Nothing to change the brooding mind, or raise it up. Nothing for the spent toiler to do but to compare the monotony of his seventh day with the monotony of his six days, think what a weary life he led and make the best of it—or the worst, according to the probabilities.

There are many possible explanations of this religious enthusiasm. Religion brought a sense of hope and of self-importance to many who felt ignored by the political and economic system. It provided emotional release—to some through the vestments and rituals of the High Church or of Catholicism, to others through revivalism or evangelicalism. It canalized the moral forces that sought remedy for social injustice. For some, like the architect Pugin, it was a reaction against the values of an industrial age. For most, it coincided with the Victorian belief in self-improvement, preached by everyone from the self-made businessman to the costermonger of Mayhew. Above all, the religious revival succeeded because it was led by a number of men of extraordinary personality and often of great intellect, such as John Keble, who began the Oxford Movement; the Catholic converts Newman and Manning; Charles Booth, who founded the Salvation Army; Thomas Arnold, who made religion a bulwark of boarding-school education; the novelist Charles Kingsley, who preached Christian socialism; and Charles Spurgeon, who brought the poor of the London borough of Southwark into the Baptist church by the thousands. It is against the background of this religious revival that one must place the great furor that followed Charles Darwin's publication of his views on evolution in 1859.

Progress in Chemistry. Science had already made great advances during the late eighteenth and early nineteenth centuries without causing much commotion in religious circles. Some of the first important breakthroughs were made in chemistry because laboratory experimentation had become greatly refined. Chemists like the French pioneer Antoine Lavoisier and the English experimenter Joseph Priestley concentrated on Aristotle's

**THE CONFLICT
OF SCIENCE
AND RELIGION**

theory that matter comprised four elements (earth, air, water, and fire), and they were able to prove, after oxygen had been isolated in 1774, that phenomena such as burning and rusting involved a combination of some element with oxygen. By 1800, Aristotle's concept had been thrown out, and the scientists were successfully beginning to draw up a list of the basic chemical elements. Lavoisier himself had identified thirty-two; Priestley had discovered many of their basic combinations, such as sulphur dioxide, carbon monoxide, and many acids.

After 1800, however, a big advance was made by considering the elements as composed of atoms. John Dalton, an English schoolteacher, suggested in 1802–1808 that the nature of compounds (that is, combinations of elements) could be described by ascertaining the weight of the atoms of the elements forming each compound. Dalton was correct in assuming that future progress lay in ascertaining the exact atomic weight of the different elements, although he mistakenly assumed that the simplest compound of two elements would contain only one atom of each element. During the following sixty years, chemists were able to designate the atomic makeup of a large number of compounds, both by letters (CO_2 = carbon dioxide = a molecule made up of one atom of carbon and two atoms of oxygen) and by structure based on the grouping of the atoms in the molecule. The practical uses of chemistry won it instant acceptance in industry. Although its principal uses became apparent after 1850, before that time chloride of lime had been used for bleaching textiles, coal gas for illumination, ether and chloroform occasionally as anaesthetics, carbolic acid for cleansing, vulcanized rubber for waterproofing. High explosives evolved through the discovery of nitrocellulose in 1846. Organic chemistry was one primary force in industrial progress in the second half of the nineteenth century.

The Study of Energy.   Equally important advances were made, with equal public acceptance, in the study of energy. In the eighteenth century, scientists had been unable to find the connection between heat, light, electricity, and magnetism, namely, that they were all forms of energy that could be transformed into mechanical work. Instead, they assumed that heat, electricity, and so on were substances, material fluids that flowed into and out of other material substances but that were weightless. These weightless substances were called imponderables. A hot body was said to contain the imponderable called calorific fluid; an electrified body, electric fluid; a magnetic body, magnetic fluid. The idea of calorific fluid was rejected after the experiments of Benjamin Thompson, Count Rumford, at the end of the eighteenth century. Rumford was able to show that heat in unlimited quantities could be produced by friction, and that since matter cannot be produced limitlessly, heat cannot be matter. By the 1830s it was generally conceded that light was not a substance but rather a wave motion of energy. And in the 1840s, through the work of an English physi-

cist, James Joule, and a German, Hermann von Helmholtz, the converti-
bility of one form of energy into another, such as electricity into heat, was
demonstrated quantitatively. Helmholtz then formulated the important
law of the conservation of energy, that energy can be changed from one
form into another but the total amount of energy in the world will always
remain the same. This conception was especially fruitful when applied to
chemistry industrially, where the transformation of one form of energy into
another was basic to many processes; and it reached its most effective use
in the twentieth century with the harnessing for destructive as well as for
peaceful uses of the energy contained within the atom.

This fundamentally important work in chemistry and physics roused
little or no opposition within the churches, whose beliefs, at least since the
seventeenth century, no longer encompassed unchanging dogma on the
chemical or physical universe. With biology, however, the situation was
radically different, as Darwin discovered.

Biology in the Early Nineteenth Century.   At the beginning of the nineteenth century, not only theologians but scientists had accepted the view
that all species of plant and animal life had been created at one time and
were immutable. The majority of churchmen assumed that the description
of the creation given in the Bible, in the *Book of Genesis*—the creation by
God of the earth and all living things upon it in six days, at a time about
4000 B.C.—was literally correct; and they laid special emphasis on the
superior position accorded to man. "And God said, Let us make man in
our image, after our likeness and let them have dominion over the fish of
the sea, and over the fowl of the air, and over the cattle, and over all the
earth, and over every creeping thing that creepeth upon the earth." But
the churches also taught God's continuing interference in the world he had
created, the imposition of purpose or rationality upon the changes occurring
in this world, and in particular the safeguarding of man's role as God's
supreme creation.

Darwin's work was to challenge first, the notion that God had created
immutable species; second, that man had always been the highest form
of creation; and third, that change in the biological world was the product
of a purpose, and especially of a divine purpose. Darwin's work was made
possible by advances in a number of fields related to the explanation of
the material universe and its plant and animal life. Geologists in particular
had shown that the strata of the earth's crust had been laid down in successive geological epochs lasting perhaps millions of years, and that the
strata could be identified by the fossils they contained. The French botanist
and biologist Lamarck, classifying plants and invertebrates at the botanical
gardens in Paris, had concluded that species change because of the need
to adapt to their environment; and he had suggested, wrongly, that they pass
these acquired characteristics on to their offspring. The giraffe had developed a long neck, according to Lamarck, by stretching to reach higher

tree branches. Lamarck was ridiculed for his views, and Darwin's own grandfather, who had suggested that "all warm-blooded animals have risen from one living filament," was ignored. The idea of evolution, however, had stimulated a number of scientists, whose work began appearing during the following thirty years; and views identical to Darwin's were reached by a British naturalist in Malaya at the same time. Science, in short, was prepared for the theory of evolution, if religion was not. Darwin caught both popular and learned fancy, however, by combining long, first-hand preparation, painstaking research and experimentation, and a large and factual presentation of his views.

Darwin and the Theory of Evolution. Darwin, at the age of twenty-two, had signed on as naturalist with the surveying ship *Beagle,* which for five years (1831–1836) sailed in the South Atlantic and South Pacific and eventually circumnavigated the globe. From the start he made vast collections, of fossils dug from the cliffs of the Cape Verde Islands, of extinct toxodons as large as elephants in Argentine riverbeds, of the fish of the South Pacific. But it was in the Galapagos Islands off the coast of Ecuador that he found the most startling evidence of the mutation of species. On these small islands many species bore close resemblance but also marked differences to species on the coast six hundred miles away. "It was most striking to be surrounded by new birds, new reptiles, new shells, new insects, new plants, and yet by innumerable trifling details of structure and even of the tones of voice and plumage of birds to have the temperate plains of Patagonia, or rather the hot dry deserts of Northern Chile, vividly brought before my eyes." Even more remarkable in his view, however, was the clear difference in animals, like the tortoises, and birds, like the finches, from island to island. On his return he lived on his private income, and methodically worked through his findings, conducted new experiments, and published specialized books and papers on subjects like coral reefs and barnacles. He was struggling with the enormous intellectual task of imposing an intelligible pattern on the origin of all living and all extinct things and their relation to each other and to their environment. His theory was finally presented in 1859 in his book *On the Origin of Species by Means of Natural Selection, or the Preservation of Favoured Races in the Struggle for Life.*

Darwin began by pointing out that species change, as can be shown by considering domestication of animals and plants; selective breeding had produced the racehorse, for example. But species also varied in nature; and this, he felt, could only be explained by the results of a struggle for existence which is the result of the tendency of all living groups to multiply their numbers. "As many more individuals of each species are born than can possibly survive; and as, consequently, there is a frequently recurring struggle for existence, it follows that any being, if it vary however slightly in any manner profitable to itself, under the complex and varying conditions

of life, will have a better chance of surviving, and thus be *naturally* selected. . . . Natural Selection almost inevitably causes much Extinction
of the less improved forms of life, and leads to what I have called Divergence of Character."[8] This divergence Darwin felt was due to the existence of "variants," or variations, which made a plant or animal adapt to
its environment more effectively. Birds that had coloring that camouflaged
them survived; others did not. These variations were "accidental," extremely small differences of one organism from another, whose origin
Darwin could not explain but which accumulated in those species that
proved fittest in the struggle for survival. The theory suggested that all life
was being continually perfected in its adaptation to the environment.
But as Jacques Barzun points out, "the sum total of the accidents of life
acting upon the sum total of the accidents of variation thus provided a completely mechanical and material system by which to account for the changes
in living forms." The notion of a divine purpose in the universe was
unnecessary, at least from the biological point of view. The most startling
consequence of Darwin's theory that species evolved from a common
ancestor was its application to man. Although he himself did not immediately point out the "evidence of the descent of man from some lower
form," many of his opponents were at once aware of this necessary corollary. To his demolition of the literal interpretation of the Bible and his
construction of a purely mechanical world, Darwin had added as a final
ignominy that man was biologically related to all invertebrates, and especially to monkeys.

The Battle over Evolution. A storm of protest arose on publication of
Origin of Species, led by the bishop of Oxford, who accused Darwin of
"a tendency to limit God's glory in creation." The theory of natural selection, the bishop claimed, "contradicts the revealed relations of creation
to its Creator," and "is inconsistent with the fulness of his glory." Roman
Catholic leaders agreed with the Anglicans. According to Cardinal Manning, Darwin's view was "a brutal philosophy—to wit, there is no God, and
the ape is our Adam." And similar denunciations rang out from noncon-
formist pulpits. Their fears seemed justified when many leading intellectuals, like Leslie Stephen, publicly declared their loss of religious faith
under the impact of the *Origin of Species.* The controversy dragged on for
more than thirty years, during which the ecclesiastical opposition gradually
lost its fervor. By the 1890s, Darwin's views had come to be generally
accepted among the educated groups in society, and in the thinking of
many, Darwin had taken his place beside Newton as the man who had
provided the laws governing a whole field of scientific knowledge. To
Darwin's triumph more than any other factor must be attributed the reverence for science that characterized late Victorian London.

---

[8] Cited in Philip Appleman, ed., *Darwin* (New York: Norton, 1970), p. 103.

THE VICTORIAN
EMPIRE

The Late Victorian Malaise. Mid-Victorian prosperity came to an abrupt halt with the financial crash of 1873, which was followed by fifteen years of depression in agriculture, greatly reduced profits in industry accompanying a decline in the rate of economic growth, and violent antagonism between workers and employers. But by the beginning of the 1870s there were many other signs that the late Victorian period would be very different in character from the two stable decades ushered in by the Great Exhibition. Economically, Britain was being challenged by foreign competitors, both abroad and in her home market itself. The United States and Germany especially threatened her world monopoly of cheap, mass-produced manufactured goods; and at that very time the British working classes, organizing through trade unions and moving toward Socialist political leaders, were determined to better their own conditions of life and to gain a greater share of the national revenue. The Reform Bill of 1867, which had extended the vote to the working classes of the cities, had provoked new uncertainty not restricted to the well-to-do; and the adoption of the secret ballot in 1872 and the extension of the vote to the rural workers in 1884 put squarely before England the challenge of making its newly democratic system work. In the political sphere, big changes followed: a vast increase in the duties of local government, a democratization and increase in the

Communist Working Men's Club, London. The left-wing parties provided the workers, many of whom were exiles, not only with the radical newspapers of the continent but with a social meeting place as well. *(Illustrated London News,* Jan. 6, 1872.)

powers of the central bureaucracy, the extension of public education, the abandonment of many of the dogmas of liberalism. The tranquility of Parliament, shocked by the presence of a Socialist in tweed jacket and cap, was further disturbed by the speed with which reformers demanded the adoption of social change and by the widespread strikes that backed these demands. The refusal of the House of Lords to accept a proposed redistribution of income through capital gains taxes and supertaxes in 1911 was the culmination of a rearguard action fought by conservatives against the reformers; and their opposition was broken only by the threat of swamping the House of Lords with new, reform-minded peers. The movement for home rule in Ireland, which became increasingly violent at the end of the century, further exacerbated the political divisions in the country. In this atmosphere of economic and political tension, only one endeavor seemed to catch the imagination and swell the pride of the majority of the country's population. The acquisition of a new empire between 1870 and 1890 appeared to advance the cause of science and to extend to the benighted overseas the solicitude of a revivalist religion. Acquisition also provided investment opportunities for the nation's surplus capital, captive markets for its industrial production, ports for its warships, and an infusion of national pride at a time of external challenge to Britain's hegemony. The new imperialism was for the late Victorians an escape from their problems at home.

Origins of the New Imperialism. The first and lasting imperial love of the Victorians was for the colonies settled by Britons. Until the 1870s, the overseas territorial expansion of which they most approved was in Canada, Australia, New Zealand, and South Africa. These territories, the Victorians felt, were peopled by men of British tastes and political experience, with comprehensible desires as consumers, realistic goals as exporters, and reliable habits as businessmen. These areas—and the former British colonies that had become the United States—were the principal recipients of British overseas emigration and of capital investment. Moreover, the grant of self-government to these territories had proved a completely satisfactory way of ending the burden of colonial rule without breaking any valuable ties. The Dominion of Canada had been formed in 1867; Australia had four self-governing colonies by 1861; New Zealand received its autonomy in 1854 and Cape Colony in South Africa in 1872. This pleasing and mutually profitable relationship helped preserve a certain affection for empire during the long period of questioning that followed the American Revolution.

The possession of India, however, taught a very different imperial lesson. It showed that a country, alien in race and religion and unsuitable for British settlement or for anglicization, could be a profitable area for investment, provided that military and administrative control was firmly maintained. One-fifth of Britain's overseas investments had been made in

The British Army on the March in India. *(Illustrated London News,* Oct. 7, 1848.)

India by the 1880s, and almost one-fifth of Britain's exports were sold there. Possession of India gave the British a controlling position in most of the local trade of East Asia. India supported an army of 250,000 men, with limitless reserves, that was used without compunction to enforce British wishes throughout Asia; and from its ports the British navy patrolled the great trade routes from East Asia and Australia to Britain. And perhaps most magnetic of all India's inducements to imperialism, it conferred a strange, exotic glamor on the nation and the monarch that possessed it. India appealed to the imagination of the imperialist. Benjamin Disraeli (prime minister, 1874–1880), an exotic creature himself, flamboyant in appearance and baroque in language, had proclaimed the monarchy as the center of a new imperialism in a famous speech in the Crystal Palace in 1872. Three years later, as premier, one weekend when the banks were closed, he had borrowed four million pounds from the Rothschild family to buy the controlling shares in the Suez Canal to safeguard the route to India;

and he had handed it to the aging Victoria as a personal trophy: "It is just settled. You have it, Madam." And in 1876, he had persuaded Parliament to name her empress of India. That night, she came out of her widow's mourning, and decked herself in huge, uncut jewels sent her by the Indian princes of her new empire. It was the Indian contingent that raised the excitement of the crowd watching the great Jubilee procession make its colorful way to Saint Paul's Cathedral in 1897 behind a band playing *Three Cheers for India*—the squadron of Indian Lancers manned by bearded Sikhs and Pathans, forty princes of the native states who cantered three abreast, diamond-clad rajas, their wives in golden cloth. And it was an Indian-born Englishman, Rudyard Kipling, who did most to bring alive for the English the color and intoxicating scents of their Indian possession. His first stories of life of the English in India, *Plain Tales from the Hills* and *Soldiers Three,* and his rollicking, colloquial poems like *Barrack-Room Ballads* caused a sensation. With his deep, simplistically moral commitment to empire and his ability to conjure up battles on the sultry plains of India, the tough unromantic chores of the young Englishman struggling to bring law beyond the reaches of civilization, and sympathetic portraits of Indians like Gunga Din, Kipling made India the best known part of the empire.

The fact that they already possessed an empire thus prepared, and in some way predisposed the British, to imperial action. Far more, however, than the example of India was driving the British into Africa and the Far East by the 1870s. With Africa, the leading impulses during the preceding two decades had been missionary activity and scientific curiosity. The former was of course linked with the antislavery movement. Largely as a result of the continuing pressure of the evangelicals and the humanitarian societies, British ships patrolled the coasts of East and West Africa to intercept slave traders. But the philanthropists were aware that they would have to strike inland if they were ever to put an end to the sale of Negro slaves by Arabs along the valley of the Nile and in the markets of Zanzibar, or by native chieftains along the rivers of West Africa. After the British government set up the Gold Coast Colony in 1874, for example, the Aborigine Protection Society of London persuaded them to put an end to slavery in the surrounding regions. Among the hundreds of missionaries sent out to bring Christianity to the Africans, the most famous was Dr. David Livingstone, who penetrated the unknown heart of Africa as a medical missionary in the 1840s. His books, like *A Narrative of an Expedition to the Zambesi,* told of the sufferings of the slaves in the hands of the Arabs, and brought his readers a personal sight of massacres like that of a tiny village on the Congo River by Arab slavers:

Shot after shot continued to be fired on the helpess and perishing. Some of the long line of heads [of Africans in the river] disappeared quietly: whilst other poor creatures threw their arms high, as if appealing to the great Father above, and sank. . . . As I write I hear the low wails on the left bank over those who are slain,

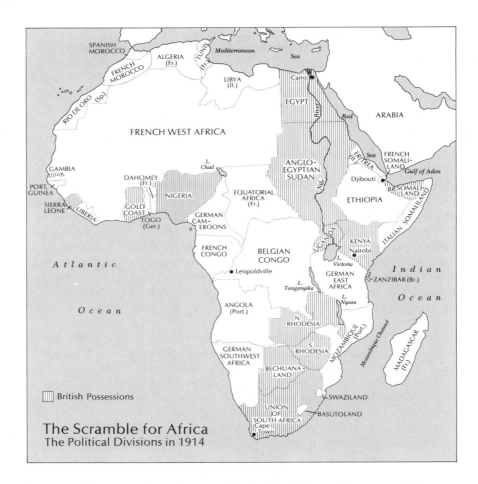

The Scramble for Africa
The Political Divisions in 1914

*ignorant of their many friends now in the depths of the Lualaba river. Oh, let Thy
kingdom come! No one will ever know the exact loss this bright sultry summer
morning. It gave me the impression of being in Hell.*[9]

Most explorers, however, were patronized not by the missionary societies
or by the newspapers but by scientific societies, such as the Royal Geographic Society of London. As early as 1866, Burton and Speke were sent
out on one of the first important explorations of East Africa with the aim of
discovering the sources of the Nile. During the next thirty years, expedition
after expedition brought back to England increasing knowledge of the great
lake region of East Africa and the Nile valley and of the torrid hinterland that
lay up the great rival valleys of West and Central Africa. No region of the
world interested the scientists of Victorian London more than this heart of
the Dark Continent, which was supplying the biologist and the ornithologist

[9] Alan Moorehead, *The White Nile* (New York: Harper, 1960), pp. 108–9.

with new specimens, the anthropologist with data on unspoiled tribes, and
the geologist with new access to the mineral wealth of the earth.

The businessmen soon joined the scientist in exploring the potential
of the opening region; and many people came to believe that they were
the principal gainers from empire. In 1902, an English economist named
John A. Hobson argued in the influential study *Imperialism* that the primary
forces behind imperialism were the industrialist and the finance capitalist. The industrialists needed captive markets for "the excessive capitalist
production over the demands of the home market." The inequitable
division of the national revenue left in the hands of the capitalists a surplus
that they could not use at home because of the restriction on consumption
and that they therefore sought to invest in the newly acquired colonies.

"Manchester, Sheffield, Birmingham, to name three representative cases,"
Hobson wrote, "are full of firms which compete in pushing textiles and
hardware, engines, tools, machinery, spirits, guns, upon new markets. . . .
Certain sectional interests . . . usurp control of the national resources and
use them for their private gain." These ideas were even more widely

The Slave Market in Zanzibar.
The island of Zanzibar off
the coast of East Africa was
the chief market for slaves
captured in the interior by
Arab traders. Zanzibar was
made a British protectorate
in 1890. (*Illustrated London
News,* June 8, 1872.)

popularized by Lenin, in his *Imperialism: The Highest Stage of Capitalism* (1916). For Lenin, this stage was marked by the struggle of monopoly companies growing constantly fewer in number who are engaged in a feverish search for raw materials and for profitable investment but who would end in mutually destructive confrontation. "The economic essence of imperialism," he concluded, "must be characterized as capitalism in transition, or, more precisely, as dying capitalism." In assessing the validity of these arguments, historians have little difficulty in showing that most of the colonies acquired at the end of the nineteenth century were not profitable. They accounted for little of the increase in trade during the period 1870–1914; barely one-eighth of Britain's investments at that time went to the dependent colonies, including even India; and very few British people chose to migrate to Africa or Asia. But it is also clear that the business community expected colonies to be profitable and that therefore the desire for profit, if not its actual achievement, was a definite motive force in the new imperialism.

Advertisement for Lipton's Tea. Large British companies established tea plantations on the hills of Ceylon, which had been brought under British control in 1833. (*Illustrated London News,* November 27, 1897.)

It was rare, however, to find even a private businessman engaging in the colonial venture without a firm conviction of national pride and superiority and even of mission that made him conceive his business ventures as a contribution to national glory and human betterment. Statesmen and businessmen joined in the pursuit of economic self-interest in the name of national power and glory. The brilliant young parliamentarian

Charles Dilke had popularized this double conception in *Greater Britain*, in which he portrayed a world benevolently dominated by an Anglo-Saxon master race. Disraeli had forced his Conservative party to endorse imperialism as a matter of policy, and had inextricably involved Britain in the affairs of Egypt. And the colonial secretary, Joseph Chamberlain, a tough imaginative Birmingham businessman, had in 1895–1903 worked on the principle, he said, that the job of the Colonial and Foreign Office was to find new markets and defend old markets, and the task of the War Office and Admiralty to protect commerce on land and sea. He sincerely thought that Britain was the trustee of civilization, and he had joined with the South African premier, Cecil Rhodes, in seeking to bring all Africa from the Cape to Cairo under British control.

London as an Imperial Capital. All these impulses to empire—religious philanthropy, scientific curiosity, economic self-interest, national assertiveness—were gathered together in the city of London. London, like seventeenth-century Amsterdam, possessed the institutions that could turn national impulses into governmental policy, and its ruling class was still sufficiently small and homogeneous for the ideas of one group to penetrate rapidly. In London were the offices of the most important missionary organizations, all of which acted as pressure groups in forcing the government into the realization that Christianity and commerce could only extend securely with governmental protection. They included the Baptist Missionary Society, the London Missionary Society, the Church Missionary Society for Africa and the East, and the Wesleyan Methodist Missionary Society, all of which had been active for almost a century in Africa, India, and the South Seas. In close contact with the missionaries were the scientific societies, for example, the Royal Geographic Society, and more blatantly expansionist groups like the Royal Colonial Institute, the United Empire Trade League, and the Imperial Federation League. These societies gained strong supporters in both major political parties, especially when it became clear to Parliament that, startled by the rise on the continent of great new powers like Germany, the British public was turning its affections and ambitions toward the colonial empire.

By 1870, imperialism had become good politics. "Our great empire has pulled us out of the European system," declared one Conservative leader. "Our foreign policy has become a colonial policy." But the politicians who voted the rapidly increasing funds for imperial expansion and defense were not merely responding to the pressure of their constituents. Products almost without exception of the boarding-school training devised by Dr. Arnold, the famous headmaster of Rugby School, they saw their class, who staffed the Indian civil service and commanded the colonial armies, as Christian gentlemen disciplined from youth for command of colonial peoples. Such feeling gave a moral veneer to the more down-to-earth interests in empire expressed by the businessmen of the City. Grouped within a mile of the Bank of England were the most significant of all London's pressure groups, the companies who demanded the profitability of empire, and whose very solidity seemed to guarantee it. Here were the great commodity exchanges, such as those for rubber and tea on Mincing Lane, diamonds in Hatton Garden, wool in Coleman Street; the Royal Exchange, where much insurance was issued by firms like Lloyd's; the Foreign Exchange, which dealt in all the world's currencies as well as gold and silver; and the Metal Exchange, which established the world price for most metals. Nearby in the maze of narrow streets were foreign banks, joint stock companies, shipping offices, insurance companies, stockbrokers, shipping suppliers, all of whom in some way participated in the imperial venture.

The combination in one place of all these institutionalized interest groups provided the main impetus to imperialism. "The key of India is not Herat or Kandahar," said Disraeli. "The key of India is London."

Acquisition of a New Colonial Empire. Britain, however, was far from unique in its desire to acquire new colonies; and in its attempt to expand into Africa and East Asia it found itself in competition with the French, the Belgians, the Portuguese, the Italians, and the Germans. Even the United States decided to "take up the White Man's Burden," as Kipling bade it to do, at the end of the century; and Russia began to put pressure on Iran, Afghanistan, and China. The same motives, though in differing degrees, affected all these would-be imperialists. All believed that it was necessary to acquire raw materials, markets, and outlets for population while they were still available. All believed they needed strategic bases, additional sources of manpower, and even the imponderable advantages of prestige provided by the acquisition of colonial territory. The European powers were sending out missionaries, such as the French White Fathers and the Belgian Catholic missions in the Congo, and subsidizing explorers such as Karl Peters, who explored the Congo, and De Brazza, who penetrated equatorial Africa. Finally, the European governments were also under pressure from colonial societies, such as Germany's Society for Commercial Geography and the Promotion of German Interest Abroad and the Pan-German League.

But Britain was easily able to outdistance its rivals. To maintain its control of the Suez Canal, it established a protectorate over Egypt in 1882, and soon extended its rule southward to the Sudan. From Cape Colony in South Africa, which Britain had taken from the Dutch in 1806, the British pushed northwards, interrupting the Portuguese attempt to join up their territories of Angola and Mozambique. Bechuanaland was taken in 1885, Rhodesia in 1889, and Nyasaland in 1893. In 1899–1902, in three years of brutal fighting in the Boer War, the British forced the

independent states of the Transvaal and the Orange Free State, inhabited
by descendants of the original Dutch settlers of South Africa, called Boers,
to join in a Union of South Africa. Since the British had also established
themselves on the east coast in British East Africa and Uganda, it seemed
that the dream of controlling Africa from Cape to Cairo was near realization.
The German East Africa Company, however, succeeded in establishing itself
in German East Africa; and Germany also took a large area of West Africa
and the arid wastes of German Southwest Africa. The Congo valley with
its great deposits of copper, lead and gold and its valuable rubber, cotton,
and ivory, had been annexed as the Congo Free State under the personal
control of the Belgian King Leopold II. Although the British were able

greatly to expand their holdings in the Gold Coast and Nigeria, the French
became the masters of most of North and Central Africa, while the Italians
took Libya and a scrap of Somaliland. By 1900, only one-tenth of Africa
had not been annexed by the European powers, whereas twenty-five years
previously only one-tenth was in European possession.

In the Far East, the attention of the imperialists was divided between the
South Pacific and China. In both areas, Britain took the lead. It annexed
the Fiji Islands in 1874, and it shared in the division of New Guinea with

**British Troops Campaigning in
the Ashanti Wars.** (*Illustrated
London News,* March 21,
1874.)

**British and Indian Princes in
the Jubilee Parade.**
(*Illustrated London News,*
June 26, 1897.)

the Germans and the Dutch in 1885. By the end of the century, Germany was in possession of the Marianas and the Caroline Islands. France had extended its hold from Tahiti to include the whole of the Society Islands and the Marquesas, and was sharing the New Hebrides with Britain. And the United States, after the Spanish-American War of 1898, had not only annexed Porto Rico in the Caribbean but had also, somewhat unwillingly, acquired the Philippine Islands. In China, Britain had acquired Hong Kong in 1842, following a brief war, and had forced open a number of ports to European trade. By taking Burma, it also shared in the amputation from China of tributary states. The French had completed their conquest of Indochina in the 1880s, and the Japanese, who had defeated China in 1894–1895, annexed Korea and Formosa.

Thus, in the last thirty years of the nineteenth century, the European powers had vastly increased their colonial possessions. Britain, the greatest gainer, had added to its empire over four million square miles with a population of sixty-six million. In the outburst of self-congratulation with which the propagandists of imperialism dazzled public opinion at home, the problems that had been acquired along with the new colonies were largely ignored, and for Queen Victoria's Diamond Jubilee in 1897, the British organized the most glamorous celebration of the imperial age.

Jubilee Day, 1897.   For weeks, London was filled with the representatives of empire—princes of India, gold diggers from Australia, Chinese police from Hong Kong, overweight Maoris and Dyak headhunters, Sudanese horsemen, Fijian princesses, and eleven prime ministers of the self-governing colonies.   The conquerors of empire were accorded a suitable precedence, especially Lord Roberts who had subdued Afghanistan; and the power of empire was emphasized with a special demonstration of the new Maxim gun.   For the last time before the self-confidence was swept away by the First World War, the people of London gave themselves up to an imperialist euphoria so explosive that even Rudyard Kipling felt called to rebuke them:

If drunk with sight of power, we loose
Wild tongues that have not Thee in awe,
Such boastings as the gentiles use,
Or lesser breeds without the Law—
Lord God of Hosts, be with us yet,
Lest we forget—lest we forget! [9]

This ill-timed moralizing merely reduced Kipling's popularity.   In 1897, Londoners believed with some reason that theirs was the greatest of world cities.

Four years later, Victoria was dead; Victorian was soon a word of opprobrium; and London gave itself up, under the leadership of King Edward VII, to its own *belle époque*, to the uninhibited pleasures of the Edwardian age.

SUGGESTED READING

Francis Sheppard's *London 1808–1870: The Infernal Wen* (1971) is a fine reconstruction of all aspects of the city's life, with special attention to the money market, the transport revolution, and public health questions.   The bibliography is indispensable for further study.   Aldon D. Bell, *London in the Age of Dickens* (1967) has many details of the aspects of the city that interested Dickens, such as the law courts and the slums.   Different quarters of the city are examined in more specialized fashion by H. J. Dyos, *Victorian Suburb: A Study of the Growth of Camberwell* (1961); Ruth Glass, ed., *London: Aspects of Change* (1964), on the role of the Irish immigrant; James Bird, *The Geography of the Port of London* (1957); and Peter Hall, *The Industries of London since 1861* (1961).   The architecture of each borough of London is described with extraordinary clarity and grace in Nikolaus Pevsner, *London*, vol. 1, *The Cities of London and Westminster* (1957) and vol. 2, *London Except the Cities of London and Westminster* (1952).

[9] *Rudyard Kipling's Verse: Definitive Edition* (London: Hodder and Stoughton, 1940), p. 329.

The best introduction to the Victorian age is perhaps G. M. Young's *Victorian England: Portrait of an Age* (1936); and for good textbooks one can turn to David Thomson, *England in the Nineteenth Century* (1950); Asa Briggs, *The Making of Modern England, 1783–1867: The Age of Improvement* (1959); and Robert K. Webb, *Modern England: From the Eighteenth Century to the Present* (1968). For portraits of the leading Victorians, one can savor the malice of Lytton Strachey in *Five Victorians* (many editions); Asa Briggs, *Victorian People* (1954) is especially good on Thomas Hughes, headmaster of Rugby School, and on Benjamin Disraeli, who is treated more fully in the fine biography by Robert Blake, *Disraeli* (1967). Two strong-willed ladies are admirably described by Elizabeth Longford, *Queen Victoria: Born to Succeed* (1965) and Cecil Woodham-Smith, *Florence Nightingale* (1951). Prince Consort Albert is best understood through the Great Exhibition, as analyzed in Nikolaus Pevsner, *High Victorian Design: A Study of the Exhibits of 1851* (1951).

The social reformers' achievements are weighed by David Owen, *English Philanthropy 1660–1960* (1965). The motives of the evangelicals are sparklingly outlined in Noel Annan's *Leslie Stephen* (1951). The great work of Henry Mayhew can be sampled in John L. Bradley, ed., *Selections from London Labour and the London Poor* (1965).

The literature on Charles Dickens is even more voluminous than his own writings. Good introductions that deal specifically with the London scene as perceived by Dickens are J. Hillis Miller, *Charles Dickens: The World of His Novels* (1959), and Angus Wilson, *The World of Charles Dickens* (1970), which is beautifully illustrated. Dickens's own essays dealing with London are collected by Rosalind Valance, ed., *Dickens' London* (1966), with illustrations by George Cruickshank. But it is better to turn to the novels themselves, especially *The Pickwick Papers* for the debtors' prison; *Bleak House* for the law courts; *Oliver Twist* for the slums called rookeries; *Nicholas Nickleby* for the private schools; and *Little Dorrit* for the government bureaucracy.

The role of religion in Victorian life is reassessed in J. Kitson Clark, *The Making of Victorian England* (1962), and K. S. Inglis, *Churches and the Working Class in Victorian England* (1963). Augustus W. Pugin, the Gothic reviver, showed in *Contrasts* how architecture should incorporate the medieval Catholic spirit, and Cardinal John Henry Newman described his spiritual pilgrimage to Catholicism in *Apologia pro Vita Sua*. Darwin's great work *On the Origin of Species* is placed in its position in the evolution of scientific thought in Philip Appleman, ed., *Darwin* (1970); while his intellectual development is assessed in Jacques Barzun, *Darwin, Marx, Wagner: Critique of a Heritage* (1958), and Gertrude Himmelfarb, *Darwin and the Darwinian Revolution* (1959). For the battle over evolution, see W. Irvine, *Apes, Angels, and Victorians* (1959).

The most delightful introduction to imperialism without shame, or at least with nostalgia, is James Morris, *Pax Britannica: The Climax of an Empire* (1968), which contains a glorious exposé of life in India's summer capital of Poona. More conventional histories of the empire include D. K. Fieldhouse, *The Colonial Empires* (1966), and A. L. Burt, *The Evolution of the British Empire and Commonwealth from the American Revolution* (1956). The intellectual roots of imperialism are analyzed by A. P. Thornton, *The Imperial Idea and Its Enemies: A Study in British Power* (1959). The economic basis of imperialism is denied by L. H. Gann and Peter Duignan, *Burden of Empire* (1967); the strategic significance of Africa is emphasized by John T. Gallagher and Ronald I. Robinson, with Alice Denny, *Africa and the Victorians* (1965). The explorers of East Africa fight every kind of misfortune, including each other, in Alan Moorehead, *The White Nile* (1960). But one understands the spirit of empire best by reading the poems of Rudyard Kipling or the novels of George A. Henty (choose any of his eighty best-sellers).

For the relief that set in after Victoria passed on, that outburst of Edwardian good spirits, see James Laver, *Manners and Morals in the Age of Optimism, 1848–1914* (1967) or J. B. Priestley, *The Edwardians* (1970).

21
FIN DE SIÈCLE

In the 1870s and 1880s, Europeans were sharply aware of an acceleration in the pace of change. A new epoch, both exciting and frightening in its promise, was opening. Germany and Italy were both united as nation-states in 1871, after centuries of disunity (see Chapter 22); and their future role in the European balance was still uncertain. The European powers were beginning to scramble for control of the undeveloped regions of the world, in a movement that promised immense returns but also the possibility of war among the imperialists. But the average European was more aware of the social and economic changes that impinged upon his own daily life; and these were enormous. A population explosion was taking place that increased the total number of Europeans from 261 million to 418 million, in spite of the emigration of over 30 million. This rise in population occurred principally in the cities of western Europe and of Russia. The urbanization of life, the grouping of vast populations in modern industrial cities composed largely of factories, offices, and houses, was perhaps the most marked phenomenon in social history; and this agglomeration was made possible by revolutionary technological advances and by the reorganization of the capitalist method of running the economy. Accompanying these changes, and undoubtedly greatly influenced by them, was an intellectual transformation as far-reaching in its effects on science, medicine, music, painting, and philosophy as any in Western history. The magnitude of the leap forward is evident if one considers intellectuals active in this period, among them Einstein, Freud, Picasso, Schoenberg, Max Weber, Proust, and Nietzsche. These years were among the most seminal in all Western history; and although every part of the continent contributed to the general achievement, two cities were universally recognized as the most exciting embodiment of the end-of-the-century spirit, of *fin de siècle*. In the Paris of the *Belle Epoque* and in the Vienna of the aging Francis Joseph, the nineteenth century came to a resplendent

Sunday Afternoon on the Island of La Grande Jatte [detail], **by Georges Seurat (1859–1891).** (Courtesy of the Art Institute of Chicago.)

climax and the twentieth century made a fittingly iconoclastic debut. "The world has changed less since Jesus Christ," commented the French poet Charles Péguy in 1913, "than it has in the last thirty years."

The incoherent vitality of Paris was captured the same year by another French poet, Cendrars, whose broken idiom is itself symptomatic of the artistic reaction to the new age:

It's raining electric light bulbs
Montrouge Gare de l'Est subway North-South river boats world
Everything is halo
Profundity
In the Rue de Buci they're hawking l'Intransigeant *and* Paris-Sports
The airdrome of the sky is on fire, a painting by Cimabue [1]

URBANIZATION OF THE WEST

The Population Explosion.   During the nineteenth century, the European population expanded faster than that of any part of the globe except those regions inhabited by European migrants. In 1800, Europe's population was one-fifth of the total population of the world; by the end of the century it was one-quarter. This growth affected all parts of Europe. Russia's population for example increased 89 percent, reaching 142 million by 1914. Italy's population increased from 26 million to 36 million, giving it a density of 118 people per square kilometer. Britain, whose population had increased from 26 million to more than 40 million, had a population density of 172 per square kilometer.

The most important cause of this rise in population was the fall in the death rate. Great medical advances were made in the last quarter of the century, especially for the prevention of typhoid, cholera, typhus, and plague. The provision of more and better hospital care, the use of anaesthesia, better hygienic control in operations, improved laboratory techniques for the diagnosis of bacteria, new public health codes—all increased the expectancy of life. Between 1880 and 1900 in France, for example, the mortality rate of infants was reduced from 184 per thousand to 159. Food supply too was greatly improved. The railroad and the steamship made it easier and cheaper to supply the population with food from distant areas and in greater variety. In the early part of the century the expanded production of the potato provided food for the poor, although even the potato crop could fail, as the Irish famine of 1846 showed. By the end of the century even the working classes were buying fats made of vegetable oils, more and varied vegetables, citrus fruits, and pasteurized milk and cheese. Better-built houses and apartments supplied with running water and with coal heating cut the impact of winter epidemics, although in some of the densely packed slums of the larger cities mortality rates among the very poor may even have increased. At least until 1880,

---

[1] Roger Shattuck, *The Banquet Years* (New York: Random House, Inc., 1968), p. 337.

there was also an increase in the birth rate, which rose in some countries
by as much as a half. A large family became the rule partly because,
owing to improved health, married couples had a longer life together.
But beginning in France quite early in the century, in Britain about 1880,
and in Germany about 1910, there was a marked fall in the birthrate as
a result of voluntary family planning. Although this process was at first
most evident in the upper and middle classes, the habit of keeping down

**Vaccination in the East End
of London, 1871.** Smallpox
vaccination helped reduce the
death rate in England by one-
fourth in 1850–1900. (*The
Graphic,* April 8, 1871.)

the size of the family spread among the less well-to-do, as they realized
that their young were going to survive more frequently. The average size
of the family in Britain, for example, fell from 5.9 to 2.8 persons between
1870 and 1914. By 1914, however, birth control had not markedly reduced
the rate of population growth because it had not caught up with the aging of
the population caused by the decline in mortality.

The great mass of this new population was born in the cities, or made
its way there. In Germany, the increase of the population of the cities
equaled exactly the increase in the total population. In France, where
the population was growing more slowly, the increase in the size of Paris
alone was the equivalent of half the country's total increase. The vast
expansion of the cities was not restricted to western Europe or even to
the industrialized areas. By 1900 there were already 17 cities in European
Russia with over a hundred thousand inhabitants. The population of

Warsaw in Russian Poland increased by half a million between 1870 and 1900. And there were many centers in eastern Europe with over a quarter of a million, among them Riga, Bucharest, Odessa, and Budapest.

Mechanization of City Transport. There was a great similarity in the character of the development of both the new centers and of the expanding older cities. The most novel feature of the city in this period was the mechanization of its transport. First came the steam railroad. In London, a first great swathe of railroad cuttings, viaducts, sidings, and freight yards had been inflicted by the construction of the London and Birmingham railway, which was finished in 1838, and by the end of the century the iron roads snaked off in every direction from the huge Gothic or classical railroad stations. The stations had even begun to acquire a certain glamor of their own. In *Howard's End,* the novelist E. M. Forster spoke of the meaning for his heroine of the different stations:

Like many others who have lived long in a great capital, she had strong feelings about the various railway termini. They are our gates to the glorious and the unknown. . . . In Paddington all Cornwall is latent and the remoter west; down the inclines of Liverpool Street lie fenlands and the illimitable Broads; Scotland is through the pylons of Euston; Wessex behind the poised chaos of Waterloo. Italians realize this, as is natural; those of them who are so unfortunate as to serve as waiters in Berlin call the Anhalt Bahnhof the Stazione d'Italia because by it they must return to their homes. And he is a chilly Londoner who does not endow his stations with some personality, and extend to them, however shyly, the emotions of fear and love.[2]

But much the same could be said of any of the great metropolises. In Paris, the Gare Saint Lazare meant trips to the Channel resorts or to England; the Gare de Lyon, the escape to the Riviera. In Vienna, the Südbahnhof meant journeys to Budapest and the Balkans. In Saint Petersburg, the overnight express from Moscow arrived at the Nikolaevsky Station, where Anna Karenina parted from Prince Vronsky on the arrival of her husband; and it was at the Finland Station that the Bolsheviks met Lenin in April 1917 on his return from exile in Switzerland, a moment that immortalized that railroad station in the history of Communism. Steam locomotives were used in New York City on the New York and Harlem railroad as early as 1839; in 1871, travelers to Chicago and California bought their tickets beneath a vast series of cupolas of iron and glass at Grand Central Station; and from 1910, Florida passengers waited in the ancient Roman basilica of Pennsylvania Station under a 150-foot-high vault. In all, Europe's railroad mileage increased from 66,000 to 172,000 in the last thirty years of the nineteenth century, and brought every major city and most minor ones into the transportation network.

The railroad exercised a direct effect on the character of the city itself, not only by linking its factories to distant sources of raw materials and markets, but by making possible a dispersion of the population from the heart of the historic city to nearby villages and towns, which rapidly became the nucleus of true suburbs. Since it was first the middle classes and then, with the introduction of commuter fares toward the end of the century, the more prosperous among the workers who could afford to take the train to work, there was already a physical separation of the classes of the city's population on a scale that had never been known before. For most of the city's population, however, a far more important change was the laying down of rails for omnibuses, which were horse-drawn from the 1860s and driven by electricity from the 1880s. In very large cities, the surface transportation was supplemented by the underground railroad. London built

[2] E. M. Forster, *Howard's End* (New York: Knopf, 1951), p. 16.

The Bayswater Omnibus, London, by George William Joy (1844–1925). (The Trustees of the London Museum.)

the first underground line, mostly a few feet below the ground, and its success in persuading people that it was not dangerous to travel underground was so great that twelve million passengers were carried in 1864. Other cities were slower in following London's example. Boston constructed its system in 1895, Paris in 1900, New York in 1904. Many cities, particularly in the United States, found it cheaper, if more disagreeable for nearby inhabitants, to build elevated railroads that passed on viaducts of steel girders along already existing streets, usually in the poorer quarters of town. With the elevated railroad and the subway, the most inexpensive and effective form of public transport had been invented, since the trains could carry between forty and sixty thousand passengers an hour, a number at least five times greater than that possible by any public transportation on the street and forty times greater than that for the automobile.

The transportation revolution created the working-class suburb. Huge new areas of closely packed tenements grew up on the edges of all the large cities of the West, no longer restricted to the linear development enforced by the railroad line that had created an aristocracy of commuters—the Main Line of Philadelphia or the London-to-Brighton commuters, for example. With little municipal control, free-enterprise builders threw up blocks of flats. In Berlin, six- and seven-story tenements were built around tiny courtyards with little provision for air or light. In Vienna, it was legally permissible until 1929 to build an eight-story building covering eighty-five percent of the land site. Many cities developed for their working classes new areas that had been previously left as uninhabitable because they were low-lying, subject to flood or disease, or marshy. Budapest extended from the charming hill settlement of Buda, with its palaces, churches, and medieval houses, across the Danube to the flatlands of Pest, which soon became the industrial, commercial, and working-class section of the city, a pattern followed by many cities, such as Cologne, Warsaw, and Bordeaux. The spatial separation of the different classes of the population undoubtedly slowed down the demand for urban improvements in sanitation, public health, housing, education, and cultural amenities. The inhabitants of the villas of Hampstead on the edge of London or of the chalets of the Buda hills could separate themselves morally and physically from the smoke and grime. Physical separation became an alternative to municipal improvements for a laissez-faire society.

The Boulevard Builders. Not all cities developed at this time without planning, however, nor were all population movements centrifugal. Since the development of military technology had made the city walls and their land-consuming fields of fire useless for the city's defense, from the mid-nineteenth century most large continental cities began to pull down their fortifications. As the land laid bare was usually municipally or nationally owned, large-scale plans of rebuilding, and often of urban beautification, were adopted, with very beneficial results for the inner city's inhabitants. A glance at the map of almost any European city will show an encircling band of broad roads, or boulevards, which are usually tree-lined and backed by substantial middle-class houses or apartments, built on the site of the walls. The most lavish example of redevelopment in this area was in Vienna, whose walls were pulled down in 1857. In their place a wide series of boulevards swung in a circle around the medieval city. This Ringstrasse, opened in 1865, was sixty yards wide and two and a half miles long, lined with trees and illuminated with gas burners. Between the boulevards were pathways for pedestrians, and on the outer edge, many public gardens. The Ringstrasse became the setting for a grandiose, though occasionally unprepossessing, display of Habsburg imperial architecture. For the next quarter of a century, a medley of massive architectural styles were developed along the Ring, first the neo-Renaissance opera house and university, then a Gothic town hall, a classical imperial parliament, and finally two garish hybrids for art and science. "The entire Ringstrasse affected me like a fairy tale out of the Arabian Nights," Adolf Hitler commented after living there a generation later.

In Paris, where Louis XIV had already dismantled the city walls in the seventeenth century, the pattern of broad tree-lined boulevards had been created early. But during the Second Empire of Napoleon III, in the third quarter of the nineteenth century, the prefect of Paris, Baron Georges Haussmann, rode roughshod over opposition from vested interests and urban aesthetes alike to set a new example in the modernization of the medieval and baroque sections of the European city. He built vast underground sewers to carry off the storm water. On the eastern and western borders he created two huge parks, the Bois de Vincennes and the Bois de Boulogne, that were to act as the lungs of Paris. He drove new boulevards through the heart of the most crowded slums sections of the city, even if it necessitated tearing down old palaces or churches. Along his boulevards he laid down strict regulations for the height and style of apartment buildings, although they were to be erected by free-enterprise builders. Unfortunately, regulations stopped at the facade, and the interiors were frequently cramped and unhygienic.

Improvements in Urban Amenities. There were, however, many other ways in which the quality of the urban environment was improving. Gas and electricity were introduced for street lighting between 1880 and 1900. Clean water was made available in all parts of the city through reservoirs and aqueducts. In America though not in Europe, the ideal of one water closet per family had been largely achieved by the end of the nineteenth century. Public baths were built, and private enterprise began to cater on a large scale to the enjoyment of the working classes. The end of the nineteenth century saw the building of the great popular theaters, the music halls and vaudevilles, along Shaftesbury Avenue in London, the Boulevard Montmartre in Paris, and Broadway in New York, and after 1895, when the first movie was shown in Paris, increasing numbers of movie houses. Catering to an even larger audience were the sports fields.

The Regent Street Quadrant at Night, London, by Francis Forster. (The Trustees of the London Museum.)

Soccer games in London as early as 1900 attracted over a hundred thousand people. A third of a million Parisians would turn out to gamble on the races at Longchamps and Auteuil in the Bois de Boulogne. By 1876 when the National League was formed, most big American cities sported a baseball arena. The increase in value of real wages of the working classes, as well as the rise in their demand for quality and variety of goods, led to the invention and spread of the department store. Until the nineteenth century, shops were small and specialized; or else, in small towns, they tried to sell everything. Early in the nineteenth century, the ingredients of the department store were put together. Price labels in shop windows appeared for the first time in 1820. Plate-glass windows had been introduced by 1850. Drapers led the way by diversifying their stock, and were followed closely by the large-scale food sellers. Gaslight and the plate-glass window gave scope to the window dressers, and created the new phenomenon of the window shopper. In the great capital cities first, and then in the provinces, the department store became a palace of light. Already by 1900, enchanted emporia had been created on Fifth Avenue in New York, on Regent Street in London, on the Boulevard Haussmann in Paris, the Leipzigerstrasse in Berlin, and even on the Nevsky Prospekt in Saint Petersburg.

It was, however, still the factory and the office building that gave the predominant character to the new urbanism. The creators of wealth created the urban landscape.

THE OLD AND THE NEW INDUSTRIALISM

Coal, Iron, and Textiles. The first industrial revolution had been based on coal, iron, and textiles. Its principal source of power had been the steam engine. Its main form of transportation had been the canal and then the railroad. As a result, the cities that grew up during this first industrial revolution had been massed around the sources of coal and iron, or near water power. Up to 1870, the agglomeration of the industrial population in Europe had taken place principally around the Pennine chain in England and the coal mines of South Wales and along the great belt of coal deposits that ran from the Ruhr valley in Germany across Belgium and Luxembourg into the Channel region of northern France. In the United States, urban growth had been concentrated on the eastern seaboard and the Great Lakes and the Allegheny regions. Because of their large working-class population and their position as the arbiters of financial and commercial power, the capital cities, too, had expanded, regardless of the absence of nearby sources of raw materials, and all had acquired large industrialized suburbs. In all these places, the pattern of urbanization had been similar. The factories had been constructed where possible near water, monopolizing the lake or river frontage; water washed or cooled their products and swept away their effluent. Or else they grouped near the freight yards of the railroads or the slag heaps of the mines. Workers' homes were scattered in the unused spaces between them or on hillsides too steep for factory construction.

Between 1870 and 1914, this first industrial revolution continued its vertiginous expansion. In countries where it was already established, as in Britain, France, Germany, and the United States, it achieved new heights of productivity, but it also spread rapidly to other parts of Europe and to restricted areas of South America, Africa, and Asia. Thus the basis of the industrial growth of the late nineteenth century was primarily a continuation of the first industrial revolution. Coal remained central to the expansion. British coal production, for example, increased 150 percent; French, 300 percent; German, 800 percent; and American, 1,700 percent. New mines were opened in the Donets basin in Russia and Silesia in Germany. Pig-iron production expanded at a similar rate, and new ore mines were opened in areas like the German-occupied Lorraine. While Britain maintained its supremacy in textile production, new competitors such as Italy and Russia appeared. Finally, the railroad construction was vastly expanded, especially in countries like the United States, Canada, and Russia, with vast hinterlands to open up. The first transcontinental railroad in the United States was opened in 1869, in Canada in 1875, and in Russia in 1905. This expansion produced urban results similar to that in Manchester half a century earlier. Houses, factories, marshalling yards, and urban amenities of Pittsburgh, Saarbrücken, or Dnepropetrovsk were little different from their English forerunners.

The Second Industrial Revolution: Steel.   Nevertheless during this period an important series of new industries was created, largely by the application of new scientific knowledge that greatly increased the scale of industrial production, diversified its output, and changed the character, even in some instances for the better, of the industrial city. Probably the most important of the new processes to be perfected was the manufacture of steel. Steel was an enormously versatile metal, far tougher than the wrought iron used in the first half of the nineteenth century. It was made by combining iron and carbon, and its qualities could be varied by the addition of small quantities of other metals such as tungsten and manganese. Following improvements in the blast furnace used to convert iron ore into pig iron, in 1856 an English scientist named Henry Bessemer developed an inexpensive method of making steel by blowing air through molten pig iron in a lined steel container. Then, to remedy the lack of quality controls in the Bessemer process, the open-earth, or Siemens-Martin, process was invented in the 1860s. Scrap iron was mixed with pig iron in a reverberatory furnace in which air and a gaseous fuel were introduced at very high temperatures; the process was slow, but produced high-quality steel and moreover had the advantage for countries short of ore of using scrap metal. In 1878, the Thomas Gilchrist process was perfected to permit the use of the high-phosphorus ores such as those of Lorraine. Finally, at the beginning of the twentieth century, the electric furnace, which produced steel by passing an electric current through the resistant mass of materials inside the electric furnace, was adopted in countries poor in coke and high in hydroelectric power. World steel production had reached more than sixty million tons by 1914, a one-hundred-twentyfold increase from half a century earlier. Steel replaced iron for railroads, steam engines, cable, and most forms of machinery. It was used in the construction of larger and lighter steamships, which finally replaced the sailing ship as the principal form of ocean transportation. It made possible the sewing machine, which had replaced handsewing by the 1870s, and was soon applied to the mechanization of shoe production. It transformed the office with the typewriter in 1878 and the tabulating machine in 1890. Steel made it possible for Daimler-Benz to develop the first gasoline-driven automobile in 1886, although the effects of this invention were only felt on a large scale after the First World War. And it also changed the basic form of city building, making it possible to replace wood, brick, and stone with the steel beam and girder and with ferro-concrete.

Early Automobile. Primitive internal combustion cars were put on sale in the 1890s. Many had only one cylinder and carried two passengers.

There had already been glimpses of a new form of architecture in the first half of the century when engineers rather than architects were called on to design iron suspension bridges, like Adam Clark's bridge across the Danube at Budapest, and when Paxton designed the Crystal Palace in iron and glass. A whole church had been constructed of iron in Paris in 1854, but its architect had been ridiculed. The United States took the lead in recognizing the potential of steel architecture. The first use of a steel skeleton for a facade was the Home Insurance Company building of 1884 in Chicago. The style was ideal for warehouses, department stores, and factories; and in the work of Louis Sullivan (1856–1924), Chicago for a brief period led the world in architectural innovation. By 1914 factories were finally being illustrated in architectural magazines, a symbolic change in itself. The great innovator Walter Gropius had designed a steel and glass frame factory in Germany as early as 1911. The Marshall Field wholesale warehouse (1895) in Chicago was a model of the use of steel framing to create large interior spaces. Albert Kahn, a German immigrant, designed a complete factory under one roof in his Packard Motor Company plant and in the Highland Avenue factory of the Ford Motor Company, where Henry Ford produced the first Model T. French architects had pioneered in the use of concrete for apartment blocks, garages, theaters, and even had proposed a design for a whole industrial city in concrete. It was the use of steel in the skyscraper that most changed the appearance of the American city. The first electric elevator had been used in 1889, and from then American buildings could, as the French said in awe, become "sky-scratchers." As early as the 1850s, Americans had been building solid stone skyscrapers up to twenty stories using hydraulic elevators. By the 1890s, riveted steel frames had been developed, and in 1913 the Woolworth Building in New York City, the tallest building in the world, reached sixty stories.

Woolworth Building, New York. The 792-foot tall tower, the highest building in the world when completed in 1913, was built for the five-and-ten-cent store tycoon, Frank W. Woolworth. (Fine Arts Commission, The National Archives.)

Electricity. Electricity was second only to steel in changing the appearance of the city. Electricity had been known in classical times, but the only use it had ever been put to before the nineteenth century was in shocking guests at parties in eighteenth-century salons. Benjamin Franklin, however, had caught electricity from the skies with his lightning conductor, and he and several Italian scientists had begun serious experiments as to the nature of this mysterious force. In the nineteenth century, theory, experiment, and application had advanced together. Alexander Volta invented the Voltaic pile, the first battery that gave a steady supply of electricity. Sir Humphrey Davy discovered how to decompose certain solutions in water by the process of electrolysis, which was eventually applied to the electroplating of metals. But electricity could only be used as a source of power when the relationship between magnetism and electricity was understood. The Englishman Michael Faraday produced the first electrical motor by applying the principle of electromagnetic induction; he used a magnet spinning inside a wire coil to produce a current of electricity. Shortly after, the American inventor Samuel Morse was able to apply such a motor to the invention of the electric telegraph. In the 1870s, an important advance came with the invention of the turbine for generating electricity. The turbine converted moving water or steam into mechanical energy, and had been used on a large scale in the Alps to harness water power. Water turbines of this kind were linked to electrical generators; by them, the mechanical power generated in the water turbine was converted into electrical energy. Even more power was produced, however, when Charles Parsons in the 1880s used steam to drive a turbine, a process that was soon used to drive ships. Other machines made it possible to supply alternating current to factories and to transmit electrical power over long distances. Although the invention of the incandescent gas mantle in 1886 prolonged the use of gas lighting for another generation, the use of electricity as the main form of lighting was assured with the invention of Joseph Swann in England and Thomas Edison in the United States of the electric-light bulb, based on the principle that electricity passing through a filament of metal can be made to heat the filament to incandescence. Electricity, in short, became an important source of power and of light for the expanding industries.

By 1914 the use of electricity was evident in every part of the city, not least in the innumerable wires that crisscrossed the city skies. Streetcars drew their power from trolleys attached to overhead electric wires. Streets, factories, theaters, and many houses were illuminated with the new light bulbs, prolonging the hours of business, making urban life cleaner and safer, and removing some of the drudgery and inconvenience of the oil lamp and candle; and there were signs, small as yet but pregnant with promise, of the transformation in everyday life that would occur when the household electrical appliance was brought within the reach of the average consumer. The radio, the phonograph, the refrigerator, the washing machine, and the electric heater had all been invented by 1914.

The Advantages of Electricity [left], **The Disadvantages of Electricity** [right]. As electricity came into wide public use in the 1880s, the streets of all Western cities were festooned with innumerable wires and cables.

It was, however, the telephone that most captured the imagination of the fin de siècle generation. To the exquisite sensibility of the French novelist Marcel Proust, it was an "angel-voice":

We are like the person in the fairy-tale to whom a sorceress, on his uttering the wish, makes appear with supernatural clearness his grandmother or his betrothed in the act of turning over a book or shedding tears, of gathering flowers, quite close to the spectator and yet ever so remote in the place in which she actually is at the moment. We need only, so that the miracle may be accomplished, apply our lips to the magic orifice and invoke—occasionally for rather longer than seems to us necessary, I admit—the Vigilant Virgins to whose voices we listen every day without ever coming to know their faces, and who are our Guardian Angels in the dizzy realm of darkness whose portals they so jealously keep; the All Powerful by whose intervention the absent rise up at our side, without our being permitted to set eyes on them; the Danaids of the Unseen who without ceasing, empty, fill, transmit the urns of sound; the ironic Furies who, just as we were murmuring a confidence to a friend, in the hope that no one was listening, cry brutally: "I hear you"; the ever infuriated servants of the Mystery, the umbrageous priestesses of the Invisible, the Young Ladies of the Telephone.[3]

[3] Marcel Proust, *Remembrance of Things Past,* vol. 5, translated by C. K. Scott Moncrieff (London: Chatto & Windus, 1952), p. 177. Reprinted by permission of Chatto & Windus and Random House, Inc.)

Chemistry. The inventions in chemistry were less evocative in their appeal, but no less pervasive in their effects. The main industrial uses of chemistry in the first half of the nineteenth century had been in the adaptation of sulphuric acid and chlorine to heavy industry and textile production. In the second half of the nineteenth century, however, chemistry advanced over a broad front. Paper was made from wood pulp instead of from linen and rags. Rayon, artificial silk, was developed from wood pulp. Metal alloys diversified the forms of metal available, especially the different kinds of steel. Black and white photography was invented in 1870, and cameras were marketed commercially in the 1880s. But the two chief developments in the chemical industry were the production of cheap alkalis and the invention of synthetic dyestuffs. Alkalis, especially soda ash, were needed on a very large scale for soap and textile manufacture, as well as for the bleaching power used in papermaking. The Solvay process, perfected in the 1870s, reduced the cost of the manufacture of soda ash and prevented the wastage of by-products. The first synthetic dyestuff, mauve, was isolated in England in 1856, and thereafter German scientists produced a whole series of artificial colorings that were far more reliable and lasting than natural dyes. Vast sales of dyestuffs made the German chemical industry boom, to become the largest in the world. The great chemical companies like Badische Anilin, Höchst, and Agfa built on their primacy in synthetic dyestuffs to develop other organic chemical products, explosives, lacquers, celluloid, photographic plates, and artificial fibers. They also turned to the study of agricultural chemistry and produced artificial fertilizers.

The impact of chemistry was most obvious in the inexpensive products it made possible. It was no longer necessary for city dwellers to wear black, because now the colors would not fade from their ready-made clothes. Cheap paper helped the development of a vast new communications industry, including inexpensive newspapers and the magazines—which became even more popular when in the 1880s they could carry the latest photographs that the ubiquitous journalists had snapped with their Kodak or Zeiss cameras. Improvements in canning made wider supplies of fruit and vegetables available at all times of year, improving the diet of the poor. But as always there was a heavy price to be paid. The destructive power of the new chemistry was obvious in the explosives of the Swedish Alfred Nobel. The environmental destruction was also enormous, for few chemical factories controlled the disposal of their waste products. In the neighborhood of the industrial cities, the chemical factories spewed out their sulphur, hydrochloric acid fumes, and calcium. Chemical-producing cities like Widnes on the River Mersey in northern England were topped with a noisome dome of blue and yellow fumes, and their houses were filmed with sulphur powder.

Edison-Archimedes-Kamera.
Heinrich Ernemann, Dresden.

Edison-Röntgen-Kamera.
Heinrich Ernemann, Dresden.

Edison Camera. George Eastman's development of a daylight-loading film in the 1880s made low-cost photography available to the general public for the first time.

The Change in Business Organization.   Vast changes in the organization of business made possible the technological changes of the second industrial revolution and were in turn encouraged by these technological changes. The new industrial techniques and the improvement in transportation of heavy and bulky products, the growing competition, and the speed with which supply was overtaking demand on the world market made anachronistic the small family-owned firm or partnership by which most industrial firms had been run until the 1870s. Industrial production and distribution had now to be carried out by large-scale organizations. The most obvious example where industrial concentration was necessary was in the manufacture of steel. By combining in one series of interlocked operations the production of iron into pig iron in the blast furnace, the conversion of pig iron into steel, and the stamping or shaping of the final products, heat loss was minimized and waste products utilized; and to these basic processes could also be added the coking of coal. Cost could be further reduced by the ownership of mines for coal and iron ore and of ships, cokeries, freighters, and sales agencies. This combination was the secret of the success of the Krupp Company in Germany, which expanded from a work force of 16,000 in 1873 to 70,000 by 1913, of Schneider-Creusot in France, and especially of Andrew Carnegie in the United States. Similar considerations led to the concentration of the chemical industry, with Imperial Chemical Industries in England and Badische Anilin in Germany as leading examples.

Large-scale production was also encouraged by economy of scale. Large companies could operate with smaller profit margins. Item for item they could undercut smaller companies and often, in open competition, drive them out of business. As a result, very frequently many companies in comparable lines of production merged in what is known as horizontal integration. The normal method by which companies in a similar line of business joined together was in a holding company or trust, such as the Standard Oil trust of John D. Rockefeller or the dynamite trust of Alfred Nobel. Where companies did not actually merge, they frequently formed informal groups, called cartels, to fix prices and avoid costly competition by sharing markets among themselves. The lead was taken by the steel companies of northern Europe and was followed rapidly by other cartels among bankers, shipping owners, munitions manufacturers, chemical and metal producers, and even whiskey distillers.

In this way the number of industrial units and thus the number of individual owners declined drastically. In Germany, for example, the number of industrial organizations employing five people or less declined by half while the number of those employing fifty or more doubled.

A major change in the character of banking from industrial to financial capitalism accompanied the change in industrial organization. In the early years of the industrial revolution, most capital for expansion had been provided by the capitalist himself from his profits. Short-term working capital to enable him to buy raw materials had been provided by merchant banks. But in the nineteenth century companies appealed to the public directly for their savings, through the sale of stock. These joint-stock companies could only be created on a large scale when the government permitted them the principle of limited liability, which meant that the management of the company was not held personally responsible for the debts of the company for which they worked. Britain was the first to grant limited liability in 1825, and was followed by the United States, France, and Germany. From the time of the 1870s, joint-stock manufacturing companies were created for public utilities and for insurance companies, banks, and most forms of transport. From 1900, the joint-stock company extended to most forms of manufacture, and thus enabled the small investor and the insurance companies and savings banks to channel their investment into the business sector. Management of the larger companies was increasingly divorced from control by their stockholders who often preferred to have their capital handled by investment banks that took a controlling role in company administration. As a result, the great investment banks— some of them in the hands of private families like the Rothschilds; others, vast enterprises drawing on the savings of millions of people, like the Darmstädter Bank in Germany—wielded enormous power, not only over finance but over industry as well.

The Aristocracy of Wealth. The profits accumulated in the hands of leading industrialists and bankers dwarfed those of any previous period of history. Every branch of industry, commerce, and finance produced its elite of wealth, who in an age of increasing nationalism among the masses, formed a kind of supranational aristocracy who met constantly in the pursuit of business and pleasure; and slowly the industrialists and bankers amalgamated with the older landed aristocracy to form a relatively homogeneous European ruling class. The United States was prolific in the production of this new type of capitalist. When the Scottish immigrant Andrew Carnegie sold out his steel holdings to the United States Steel Corporation, he was paid $250 million. The railroads formed great fortunes like those of the Vanderbilts of the New York Central Railroad or the Stanfords of the Southern Pacific; and the banking empire of John Pierpont Morgan made its founder a Midas among financiers, as a result of his wizardry in moving among investments in steel, shipping, communications, insurance, mining, and munitions. Marshall Field had expanded a dry-goods store in Chicago into one of the world's largest retailing companies. These were, of course, the builders of the banks, offices, factories, and working-class housing that composed most of the new urban expansion. But the great capitalists, although they all possessed vast country estates, were still city dwellers, like the Parisian aristocracy of the eighteenth century or the Florentine patriciate of the fifteenth century. With their city mansions, they added variety, and even at times charm, to the landscape of the city.

In New York City, their town houses advanced northward from Washington Square to the upper reaches of Fifth Avenue; in San Francisco they looked down on their business enterprises from the heights of Nob Hill; in Paris, they overlooked the Bois de Boulogne or the Avenue Foch.

These nouveaux riches were not, however, divorced from the older landed aristocracy. In some cases, the older aristocracy became involved in industry themselves: Lord Derby in England, for example, owned most of the riverfront in Liverpool and a number of mines in the South Lancashire coalfield. Others, such as the old families of the Austro-Hungarian empire like the Karolyi in Hungary or the aristocrats of Russia, remained extremely wealthy from the exploitation of their agricultural estates and could equal in wealth and outshine in blood the upper bourgeoisie. In many cases, wealth brought social equality. Queen Victoria happily accepted the hospitality of the Rothschilds. Often equality was the result of marriage, especially of American heiresses to impoverished European nobility. Usually fusion was the result of the mingling of social mores—education at the same schools, membership of the same regiment and club, attendance in the restricted balconies at the horse races or opera.

The whole of Europe became the playground of this elite of wealth and breeding. During the season the capital cities were transformed with balls, plays, banquets, and horseraces. The English season set the pattern and was emulated by all the capitals of Europe. In July, one French visitor commented, it seemed as if "a race of gods and goddesses descended from Olympus upon England . . . to live upon a golden cloud, spending their riches as indolently and naturally as the leaves grow green."[4] To the novelist John Buchan, looking back on it, it seemed like a dream:

London at the turn of the century had not yet lost her Georgian air. Her ruling society was aristocratic till Queen Victoria's death and preserved the modes and rites of aristocracy. . . . In the summer she was a true city of pleasure, every window box gay with flowers, her streets full of splendid equipages, the Park a show ground for fine horses and handsome men and women. The ritual went far down, for frock-coats and top-hats were the common wear not only for the West End, but about the Law Courts and in the City. . . . Looking back, that time seems to me unbelievably secure and self-satisfied. The world was friendly and well-bred as I remember it, without the vulgarity and the worship of wealth which appeared with the new century.[5]

Out of season the well-to-do entertained each other at their country homes for grouse-shooting, or else they met for a round of parties at their favorite vacation towns. Most favored were the spas, Biarritz on the Atlantic coast of France, Marienbad and Karlsbad in the Sudeten highlands of what is now Czechoslovakia, or Baden-Baden on the edge of the Black Forest.

[4] Cited in Barbara Tuchman, *The Proud Tower* (New York: Macmillan, 1966), p. 16.
[5] John Buchan, *Memory Hold the Door* (London: Hodder and Stoughton, 1940), pp. 92–94.

Boat-Races at Henley. The annual regatta at Henley was the occasion for London society belles to display their newest summer costumes. (*Illustrated London News,* June 27, 1874.)

But the seaside resorts, especially those of the French and Italian Riviera, drew their clientele to the gingerbread fantasies of seafront hotel and casino. The Americans and Russians shared in these passions. The wealthy of America took their waters at Hot Springs, Virginia, and relaxed by the ocean in the mansions on the cliffs of Newport, Rhode Island. Russians sunned themselves at Yalta and safeguarded their livers at Piatigorsk, although they were often to be found also in the playgrounds of western Europe. The character of this society fascinated the period's novelists, stimulated the new sociology to some of its most acute analysis, and provoked social reformers into theory and action.

The rapid pace of industrial, scientific, and social change stimulated the period's intellectuals to undertake a searching analysis of their world, questioning not only the nature of society but also the nature of man and of matter. European novelists of the realist school of the 1850s and 1860s had already begun a searching portrayal of the character of the new industrial society and especially of the problems of the bourgeois in his struggle upward in the pursuit of material success. Deeply impressed by the progress of science and technology, they had rejected the exaggeration, the sentimentality, and the unreality of the Romantic writers, and had determined instead to apply scientific methods in their approach to the human being, his physical setting, and his social relationships. They considered their method experimental, an attempt to combine all data, ugliness as well as beauty, corruption as well as heroism, to place human

THE WRITER AS SOCIAL ANALYST

beings in an exactly described situation and to observe the results. They were convinced that the philosopher Auguste Comte (1798–1857) had correctly described the progress of human society as passing through three stages—primitive theological; a more advanced metaphysical; and the final scientific, or positivist, stage, in which by the observation of phenomena and the collection of scientific fact exact laws for all knowledge from mathematics to sociology (a word he invented) could be established. In 1856, when Gustave Flaubert published *Madame Bovary,* the unsentimental portrayal of an intelligent woman trapped in the inanity of provincial life, he created the first genuine masterpiece of realism. After Flaubert, the realist novelists insisted on absolute accuracy and enumeration of physical details of the environment, the painstaking portrayal of human emotions and thoughts, and the analysis of such influences as heredity and social restriction.

Emile Zola (1840–1902) brought the realistic approach to its most extreme. He explained his theories in 1880 in *The Experimental Novel,* in which he argued that "the writer is part observer and part experimenter. In him the observer provides the facts as he has seen them, decides the point of departure, establishes the firm ground on which the characters will move and phenomena develop. Then the experimenter appears and sets up the experiment, I mean to say causes the characters to move and act in a particular story, in order to show that the succession of facts will be such as the determinism of the phenomena that are being studied demands."[6] With Zola, the realistic school of novelists merged in the naturalist. He himself set the pattern of analysis by studying, not a few individuals but a whole family, in his twenty novels, which he called the Natural and Social History of a Family under the Second Empire. But in spite of the prolific material details, these novels still rang with the outraged morality of a Dickens, as when Zola dealt with prostitution in *Nana* or the sufferings of the workers in *Germinal.*

It was only in the last two decades before the First World War that the naturalist novelists produced their most balanced and searching works, when the reaction against the excesses of social realism had combined with a greater interest and knowledge regarding the human character. The Russian playwright Anton Chekhov explored the vacuity and the ineffectiveness of the provincial Russian gentry. The Norwegian dramatist Henrik Ibsen, (1828–1906), laid bare the false values of the middle classes, as in *An Enemy of the People,* when a whole town whose livelihood is dependent on their spa rises up against the doctor who has discovered that their waters are harmful to the spa's visitors. At the end of the century the brothers Heinrich Mann (1871–1950) and Thomas Mann (1875–1955) gave classic portrayals of the decadence of the bourgeois class. They had been brought up in Lübeck, where the middle classes had failed to keep up with modern

[6] Cited and translated by Eugen Weber, *Paths to the Present* (New York: Dodd, Mead, 1962), p. 167.

progress, and saw their city slipping into irretrievable decay. For Heinrich, the middle class deserved savage satirization. In his novel *Der Untertan (Little Superman),* he followed the progress of Diederich Hesselring, a petty bourgeois haplessly enamored of the upper-class Germans, who despise him. At the moment when Diederich has sold out his factory at a ridiculously low price to the local governor, he is rewarded with an imperial medal, the Order of the Crown Fourth Class.

A blue ribbon could be seen hanging from Karnauke's pointed fingers, and beneath it a cross, whose gold rim sparkled. . . . Ah, what an uproar and congratulations! Diederich stretched out his two hands, an ineffable joy flowed from his heart to his throat, and he began to speak involuntarily, before he knew what he was saying: "His Majesty . . . unprecedented graciousness . . . modest services . . . unshakable loyalty." He bowed and scraped, and as Karnauke handed him the cross, he laid his hands on his heart, closed his eyes, and sank back, as if another stood before him, the Donor himself. Basking in the royal approval Diederich felt that salvation and victory were his. . . . Authority kept its pact with Diederich. The Order of the Crown, fourth class, glittered. It was an event, foreshadowing the William the Great monument and Gausenfeld, business and glory! . . .

Like a man of iron he stood before her [his wife], his order hanging on his breast; he glittered like steel. "Before we go any further," he said in martial tones, "let us think of His Majesty, our Gracious Emperor. We must keep before us the higher aim of doing honor to His Majesty, and of giving him capable soldiers." "Oh!" cried Guste, carried away into loftier splendors by the sparkling ornament, "Is it . . . really . . . you . . . my Diederich."[7]

In 1913, however, the novel that portrayed the peculiarities of society had been enriched with an exploration of the role of the unconscious and of the changing experience of time, by the great French writer Marcel Proust (1871–1922). Proust, the son of rich parents who spoiled him, made a vigorous and fairly successful attempt to reach the upper levels of Parisian society. Before the death of his mother in 1905, he wrote a few unimportant sketches. A chronic invalid, he cloistered himself after 1905 in a bedroom lined with cork, probing in his writing the character of a society that had disillusioned him and the nature of his own self. The first volume of his massive novel, *A la recherche du temps perdu (Remembrance of Things Past),* caused little sensation; the second volume, published in 1919, was recognized as a modern classic. The following volumes, published mostly posthumously, won him acclaim as one of the greatest novelists in all French literature. At one level, the novel was a superb portrayal of the weaknesses and the idiosyncrasies of French middle and upper classes at the turn of the century. He created an unforgettable gallery of portraits of the minor nobility and the rising bourgeoisie: the graceful aristocrat Saint Loup, the hostess Madame Verdurin, the witty Marquis de Villeparisis, the fanatically prideful Baron de Charlus.

[7] Heinrich Mann, *Little Superman,* (New York: Creative Age), pp. 241–42.

**Robert Comte de Montesquiou-Fezensac,
by James McNeil Whistler (1834–1903).**
This prominent society figure is now
best remembered as one of the models
for the character of Baron de Charlus
in Proust's *Remembrance of Things Past.*
(Copyright The Frick Collection,
New York.)

But above all there is the duke of Guermantes, with his wealth and his vanity and his vulgarity, and the duchess of Guermantes, who floats through so much of the novel as an unattainable dream:

Mme de Guermantes had sat down. Her name, accompanied as it was by her title, added to her corporeal dimensions the duchy which projected itself round about her and brought the shadowy, sun-splashed coolness of the woods of Guermantes into this drawing-room, to surround the tuffet on which she was sitting. I felt surprised only that the likeness of those woods was not more discernible on the face of the Duchess, about which there was nothing suggestive of vegetation, and at the most the ruddy discoloration of her cheeks.... Her eyes ... held captive as in a picture the blue sky of an afternoon in France, broadly expansive, bathed in light even when no sun shone; and a voice which one would have thought, from its first hoarse sounds, to be almost plebeian, through which there trailed, as over the steps of the church at Cambrai or the pastry cooks in the square, the rich and lazy gold of a country sun.[8]

But Proust had done far more than pick up the social analysis of Thomas or Heinrich Mann. He changed the whole character of novel writing

[8] Proust, *Remembrance of Things Past,* V, 278.

by displaying the unconscious workings of the mind, the forgotten memories that can be touched off by a sudden, unimportant event, as when the taste of a little cake called a madeleine soaked in tea evoked for him the whole of his childhood. But above all he examined the character of time, the elasticity of its nature relative to the emotions and experiences of the individual, the fusion of the past with the present. With Proust it was the inner world that was worth knowing, and it too could only be understood in relation to the experiences in time that remained perpetually in one's unconscious memory.

The novelists had sapped the faith in bourgeois society by exposing its hypocrisies and the shallowness of its pretensions. The new science of psychology was even more disturbing to the belief in man's rational control of his environment, since it suggested that man was driven by motives that lay beneath the conscious mind.

THE ANALYSIS OF MAN

Sigmund Freud. From the mid-nineteenth century, medical experimenters had made considerable progress in the knowledge of the mind by concentrating on the relationship of physiology to psychology. The French doctor Philippe Broccart had shown that the front lobe of the brain controls the speech. Other psychologists who were called behaviorists had experimented on the behavior of animals, attempting to find which physical stimulations produced psychological responses. The most famous of these was Ivan Pavlov, who had conditioned dogs to salivate when a bell rang as an indication of food. But it was essential to get beyond the physiological and the rational factors in man's behavior. The explanation of the unconscious mind was undertaken by Sigmund Freud (1856–1939), a Viennese doctor whose ideas took a formative role in twentieth century culture because he combined scientific genius, literary skill, and stubborn ambition. He was the child of a German-Jewish family from Moravia, which after financial troubles, had moved to Vienna when Freud was four years old. Although Freud lived in Vienna until the last years of his life, he claimed never to like the city. "I never felt really comfortable in the town. I believe now I was never free from a longing for the beautiful woods near our home in which," he wrote, linking his feelings immediately to the Oedipus complex, "(as one of my memories from those days tells me) I used to run off from my father, almost before I had learned to walk."[9] Although constantly short of money and developing a desire for recognition and the security that success brings, he entered the university as a medical student, but finding he disliked the physical aspects of medical practice, he devoted himself to neurology. Slowly, under the influence of professors with whom he worked in Vienna and in Paris, he abandoned the physical explanation of nervous disorder. In the famous case of Anna O., who was paralyzed

[9] O. Mannoni, *Freud* (New York: Pantheon, 1971), pp. 8–9.

by hysteria, he succeeded in curing her physical symptoms by persuading her through hypnosis to dredge up unhappy events of her childhood. Since hypnosis did not work with all his patients, Freud developed the method of free association of ideas, a technique for permitting the patient to reveal, with the doctor's aid, the forgotten experiences that Freud was convinced lay in their unconscious mind.

Theories of Freud. It was essential for the physician, Freud decided, to discover in the unconscious the thoughts or wishes that, because they were incompatible with the "ethical, aesthetic and personal pretensions of the patient's personality," had been repressed. Since those repressed ideas were still active, causing pain and even physical symptoms, Freud employed not only the free association of ideas stimulated by the questions of the doctor, but also the interpretation of dreams and of unconscious acts such as forgetting names or movements of the body, which were "clues to the hidden complexes of the psychic life." But, as Freud was well aware, he had to explain the origin of the memory that remained in the unconscious. He had already decided that the primary impressions were sexual, and that they had existed in earliest childhood. "He found in himself love of the mother and jealousy of the father," and claimed that it was universal in early childhood. This, he said, was why the play *Oedipus Rex* was so gripping. The Greek myth "seizes upon a compulsion that everyone recognizes because he had felt traces of it in himself. Every member of the audience was once a budding Oedipus in fantasy, and this dream-fulfillment played out in reality causes everyone to recoil in horror, with the full measure of repression which separates his infantile from his present state." [10] He went on to theorize that personality could be understood in an almost physical sense as the conflict between the *ego*, the reason that directs a man's adaptation to his environment, and the *id*, the primary instinct that drives a man to erotic and aggressive thoughts. The ego was the rider, the id the horse that had to be directed. But the ego had also to deal with the *superego*, the sublimation of the image of the parent that a child had constituted inside himself as a set of moral goals. For Freud, the task of the ego was enormous because it had to sublimate or direct into permissible or socially useful channels the drive of id; and, where it failed, the suppression of those drives could produce neuroses.

Influence of Freudian Psychology. Freud's main psychological ideas were quite well known by the First World War. Freud went much further, attempting to relate the whole development of society to the work of the unconscious, but few people would accept him as the analyst of all human development. As the analyst of the individual, however, he soon gained widespread acceptance. His ideas were the starting point for other psy-

[10] Ibid., p. 46.

chologists, such as Carl Jung, who eventually substituted the will for power as the primary drive in place of the sexual urge. The influence of the new psychology was deeply pervasive. In the widest sense, it sapped the liberal belief in man's rationality and his ability to govern himself through rational process. It destroyed much of the Victorian belief in such matters as parent-child relations, the role of women, and the respect due to authority. To the creative mind, it offered an enormous hope. To some political theorists, the knowledge of man could be the beginning of a wiser theory of the state. To social reformers, it was a key to a healthier society. To the artist, it was the long-dreamed-of key to human motivation. By presenting a character's stream of consciousness, it became possible for the novel to break out of its established narrative form. To Proust, James Joyce, and Virginia Woolf, and to poets like T. S. Eliot and W. B. Yeats, the psychologist had opened a startling new world.

The discoveries of the great physicists between 1890 and 1914 were perhaps even more momentous in their effect on established ideas, for they destroyed the very concept of nature as described by laws that scientists like Newton had so successfully uncovered. Nature implied the existence of absolute and distinct space, time, matter, energy, and velocity. By 1914 it had been demonstrated that matter and energy are interchangeable; that matter is not composed of indivisible atoms but that all atoms are themselves composed of electrically charged particles; and even that mass increases with velocity.

THE ANALYSIS OF MATTER

Origins of the New Physics. The new physics was the product of simultaneous advance in many fields of experiment and theory. Experiments in the nature of radioactivity were carried out in the 1890s by Wilhelm Roentgen, who discovered X rays, and by the French scientists Pierre and Marie Curie, who showed that radium emits energy. By 1913, several scientists had demonstrated that the atom, far from being solid, was constructed something like a solar system with a positively charged proton, or nucleus, surrounded by negatively charged electrons. Ernest Rutherford was able to prove the truth of his ideas experimentally by bombarding a nitrogen atom to reduce the number of its electrons in such a way as to change it into a hydrogen atom. He had thus succeeded in changing one element into another, the dream of the medieval students of alchemy. Knowledge of the behavior of the electron was dependent on Max Planck's quantum theory, which he had announced in 1905. Planck held that energy is emitted in small groups, or quanta, in a series of discontinuous ejections rather than in a continuous stream; moreover, because of the extremely small size and rapid movement of these particles it is impossible to state the precise position of the particles but only the probability of their being in a particular place. Science would have to accept the uncertainty principle, that one cannot observe the exact position of speed of particles but only predict the probability of a certain result.

Albert Einstein (1879–1955). (U.S. Information Agency photo.)

The Theory of Relativity.   Albert Einstein, a German-Jewish theoretical physicist, in his special theory of relativity of 1905 and the general theory of relativity of 1916, succeeded in producing a unified explanation of the phenomena of the physical world.   There is no such thing as absolute space, time, or motion, Einstein held.   Space is not filled with a weightless substance called ether against which motion can be measured, as scientists had theorized, and thus there is no absolutely stationary space.   All motion is relative to the speed at which the observer himself is traveling.   Einstein showed, moreover, that even mass is dependent on velocity, since it increases as its speed increases.   Finally, Einstein concluded that mass and energy are interconvertible, and that their relationship is defined by the equation, $E = mc^2$ (energy equals mass multiplied by the square of the speed of light).   His conclusion that the conception of space and time would have to be replaced by a four-dimensional space-time continuum was incomprehensible to all except a few physicists, but his ideas on the curving nature of space received wide popular, if uninformed, admiration when his prediction was proved correct that in a solar eclipse light rays passing near the sun would be bent.   Thus, by 1914 physicists had taken their share in disturbing man's conception of himself.   If space, time, and motion no longer could be accepted as external reality, what certainties were left?

THE ANALYSIS OF SOUND   In music and painting, Vienna and Paris continued to exert their predominance, by the magnetism of their way of life, by the ease of personal communication they afforded to artists, by the living they afforded, and by the presence of an interested audience.   There was a sense of the brilliant end of a great epoch about Vienna. In part, the tone was set by the Emperor Francis Joseph himself, unbendingly determined in the face of continual personal tragedy to act out the kindly, aloof role of father of his people. Tall, upright, white-mustached, *der alte Herr* had been a part of Vienna for sixty years, and the occasional glimpses of him brought alive a memory of an older empire. When the emperor appeared briefly at aristocratic balls, noted a Russian diplomat, "it was not to lead for a fleeting moment the life of a mere mortal but to represent the majesty of the sovereign." Everyone in Vienna gave himself up to nostalgia, created in a self-deception so patent as to be doubly charming. Johann Strauss had died, but his place had been taken by Franz Lehar, an equally effective dream maker, whose *Merry Widow* was produced in 1905. Even more than in the Biedermeier era, Vienna lived off itself, its houses filled with engravings of its own streets, its winegardens echoing to songs celebrating its beauty, its conversation filled with the stories of its own characters.

Brahms, Bruckner, Mahler. Audiences who filled the new opera house on the Ringstrasse were satisfied that they too were carrying on and developing to fulfillment the great tradition of classical music their grandfathers had patronized. Johannes Brahms (1833–1897), who had settled in Vienna in 1863, was regarded as having mastered the counterpoint of Bach and the symphonic structure of Beethoven. His First Symphony won him the highest praise possible for Viennese audiences. This, wrote a critic, was a "Tenth Symphony, alias the First of Johannes Brahms. . . . But I believe it is not without the intelligence of chance that Bach, Beethoven, and Brahms are in alliteration." Four years after Brahms's arrival, Anton Bruckner (1824–1896) had come from the Austrian provinces. A disciple of Richard Wagner, he was a writer whose vast cadences and enormous spaciousness appealed to the audiences of the 1870s. His orchestration was so lush that Brahms found it personally offensive. Bruckner sought to create whole forests, rollicking rustic dances of peasants in iron-shod boots, gigantic storms, and galloping huntsmen. With him the emotional coloring of romantic music reached a new immensity that could only be accepted by a spacious age. And after Bruckner had come the even more expansive music of Gustav Mahler (1860–1911). As the conductor of the opera and of the philharmonic orchestra, he had a far more expert knowledge of the instruments of the orchestra than Bruckner; and in his Eighth Symphony, known as the Symphony of the Thousand, because it required a huge orchestra and chorus, he seemed to be reaching out to introduce into symphonic music that combination of voice and instrument that found an ideal in opera. However, in spite of all the choral and orchestral embellishments of his music, Mahler was developing a new form of symphonic expression. Especially in the Ninth Symphony of 1909, he plunged deep inside his personality, writing music at once cynical, overbearing, wistful, delicate, and tragic.

Atonal Music: Schoenberg. Mahler's work nevertheless lay within the accustomed tradition of Western music, which was written on a seven-tone scale with major and minor keys. The revolt against tonality was begun by Arnold Schoenberg (1874–1951), a widely talented composer from a middle-class Jewish family. Schoenberg was dissatisfied with everything, from the way babies were brought up to the local streetcars; and he suggested remedies for all his discontents. He began as a composer with a sparsely orchestrated tone poem, *Transfigured Night*, a morality play in which a man forgives a woman for bearing a child that is not his own, and by his generosity transfigures the night. The eery clarity of the moonlit night is suggested by a new form of harmony, which, together with the nature of the story, shocked the first audience in 1899 into uproarious ridicule. By 1908, Schoenberg and two young followers, Alban Berg and Anton Webern, had begun to abandon altogether the traditional conception of keys. The result was the strange, disturbing sound of atonality, which Schoenberg preferred to call "floating tonality." Schoenberg argued that the traditional sounds based on rules giving preference to specific notes, such as the tonic, and the laying down of rules for the progression from key to key, were stifling. All notes should be equal, he argued, and that would be achieved if a twelve-tone scale were used. The notes would be related to each other in a "series," or tone row, in which none of the twelve notes could be repeated until the other eleven had been played. This tone row in a set sequence would be repeated with various changes of orchestration or volume, and could be used with all kinds of mathematical variants, such as backward or upside-down configurations. It was impossible for most people to distinguish the tone row being used, and the music seemed to the uninitiated to have a completely shapeless character. But Schoenberg had in fact created a totally new sound, which, he argued, the audience should learn to hear.

Berg and Webern. But it was Berg, a student of Schoenberg from 1904, who won for the new music its widest, if still restricted, audience. In his two operas, *Wozzeck,* a savage attack on the savagery of war, and *Lulu,* a Freudian fantasy littered with the dead bodies of ineffectual lovers, Berg showed that the action of the operatic stage could emphasize the drama inherent in the moderate use of atonality. Webern, with a doctorate in musicology from the University of Vienna, was a natural disciple of Schoenberg. To him, the atonal scale appealed because of its ability to express in the most compressed form the deepest of emotions. His total written work can be played in three hours; one string quartet lasts one minute. With the same mathematical ability and the same fascination with the nature of numbers as Schoenberg, he was able to create works of extraordinary ingenuity. The twelve-tone scale appealed to him, he said, because one does not need a chord to end the music; and in accordance with this principle, after surprising his listeners by the fact that no note seems at first to relate to any other note, his music simply stops.

"Der Rosenkavalier". But even the young had to recognize that Vienna had found itself again not in Schoenberg or Berg, but in the collaboration of its finest poet, Hugo von Hofmannsthal (1874–1929) and its new operatic genius, Richard Strauss (1864–1949). Strauss was unrestrainedly and successfully romantic. Hofmannsthal belonged to a group of writers called Young Vienna, who met nightly in the Cafe Griensteidel to reinvigorate Viennese literature, drawing to it the analysis of human motives and of mental aberration. They called themselves expressionists because they wished to reveal the inner mental states of their characters. It was the miracle of Viennese music that Hofmannsthal was able to write an operatic libretto that at once, in the character of the Marschallin, summed up that moment of fragile beauty and self-awareness when a charming woman feels the first cold breath of age. It is hardly fanciful to think that the immense popularity of *Der Rosenkavalier* in Vienna was due to the fact that the Viennese saw in the Marschallin, and heard in the elusive waltzes of Strauss, the dilemma of their own aging city:

I too can remember a young girl
Who, fresh from the convent, was ordered into holy marriage.
Where is she now? Yes,
Look for the snows of yesteryear!
How can I say it so lightly?
But how can it really be
That I was that little Resi
And that some day I shall be an old woman.
An old woman, the old Marschallin!
"Take a look, there she goes, old Princess Resi!"
How can this happen?
How can our dear God do this to us?
When I am still the same as ever.
And if He must do this
Why does He let me see the change
Ever so clearly? Why doesn't He conceal it from me?
That's all such a secret, such a very great secret.
And yet we are here to endure it.
And in the "How"—
There is what makes the difference.[11]

A golden glow suffuses all reminiscences of Paris at fin de siècle, as though then more than at any other time in its role as the incubator of the European intellect Paris had combined intense creativity with the most seductive charm of daily living. To the Austrian novelist Stefan Zweig, who arrived there in 1904 at the age of twenty-three, it was an "exhilarated and exhilarating Paris":

**PARIS
DURING
LA BELLE
EPOQUE**

[11] Hugo von Hofmannsthal, *Der Rosenkavalier*, Act I. Author's translation.

Nowhere did one experience the naive and yet wondrously wise freedom of existence more happily than in Paris, where all this was gloriously confirmed by beauty of form, by the mildness of the climate, by wealth and tradition. Each one of us youngsters took into himself a share of that lightness and in so doing contributed his own share; Chinese and Scandinavians, Spaniards and Greeks, Brazilians and Canadians, all felt themselves at home on the banks of the Seine. . . . Oh, how easily, how well, one lived in Paris, particularly if one were young. . . . The only difficult thing was to stay home or to go home, especially when it was spring and the lights shone soft and silvery over the Seine, and the trees on the boulevards were beginning to bud, and the girls were wearing bunches of violets which they had bought for a penny. But it was not necessarily spring that put you in a good mood in Paris. [12]

Paris was truly the artistic heart of Europe, and few artists or writers could stay away for long. In Paris, they fed on each other, stimulating each other to new experiments and to more sustained effort of imagination and relaxation. From America came Henry James and Gertrude Stein; from Russia, Stravinsky, Diaghilev, and Kandinsky; from Belgium, Maurice Maeterlinck; from Italy, Modigliani; from Switzerland, Le Corbusier; from Spain, Pablo Picasso; and from Germany, Rainer Maria Rilke. Thus, Paris led the West in painting and poetry and was second only to Vienna in music. Yet in 1871, Paris had been besieged by Germans and then ravaged by civil war; France had agreed to a German occupation that would last until a huge war indemnity had been paid; and a prolonged political struggle seemed imminent over the constitutional structure of the country. Why did the capital of such a country succeed in attracting so much talent and permitting them to work so successfully?

Shadows on the Belle Epoque. One ignores the realities of the Belle Epoque if one fails to establish at the start the unfavorable factors that had to be overcome, ignored, or in a few cases seen as a source of stimulation. The republic, established in 1871 and slowly given a constitution over the next decade in a piecemeal set of laws, was extremely unstable. On the right, two groups of monarchists sought the restoration of the Bourbon and the Orleans dynasties. When those hopes faded in the 1880s, not least for lack of a suitable pretender, conservative groups turned in some desperation to the ideal of a soldier-savior, a man on horseback; but their candidate, General Boulanger, turned out to be an adventurer without backbone. After 1900, far more activistic and authoritarian groups appeared on the right to challenge the authority of the republic, the most influential being the Action Française. The parties in the center, on whom the stability and indeed the survival of the republic depended, were debilitated by quarrels among themselves that did not allow any government to form a stable majority for long, and were often brought into disrepute by unsavory scandals. On the left, radical groups increased in

[12] Stefan Zweig, *World of Yesterday* (New York: Viking, 1943), pp. 127–28, 130.

strength, especially because of the slowness of reform—the first law
enforcing sanitary standards in factories was not passed until 1903, and
only in 1906 were employers compelled to give workers a day of rest
each week. Georges Sorel preached the doctrine of direct action for the
overthrow of bourgeois society by the general strike. The homes of Paris
magistrates and even the Chamber of Deputies rocked to the bombs of
anarchists.

The Dreyfus Affair. Even more disruptive was the Dreyfus affair, which
split the whole of French society into two irreconcilable factions for
almost twenty years. Dreyfus, the only Jewish officer in the French general
staff, was convicted of selling French military secrets to the Germans, and
even though he protested his innocence, he was sent to Devil's Island.
Leading intellectuals were finally convinced by evidence brought by Dreyfus's brother and a few officers that Dreyfus had been convicted on forged
evidence, and that the army because of its anti-Semitism had hushed up
the affair. Eventually a coalition of the center and the left forces in French
politics forced a reconsideration of the case, and in 1906 Dreyfus was found
innocent. But the damage had been done, in every sphere of French society.
The painters Monet and Degas quarreled, and never spoke again. Writers
like Barrès took public issue with Zola and Anatole France. A wave of
anticlericalism broke against the Church for the part played by the Assump-
tionist fathers in accusing Dreyfus. Trust in the army was poisoned, as the
full details became known. For Proust, in whose novel the Dreyfus affair
constantly recurs, the whole affair was irrational: "When we find systems
of philosophy which contain the most truths dictated to their authors, in
the last analysis, by reasons of sentiment, how are we to suppose that in a
simple affair of politics, like the Dreyfus case, reasons of this order may
not, unknown to the reasoner, have controlled his reason."[13] Whatever
then the reasons for the preeminent cultural position of Paris at the fin de
siècle, they were not political stability, economic or social harmony, or
racial tolerance.

The Appeal of Paris. Paris was the unparalleled setting for a society of
extraordinary individualism and complexity. Haussmann had made many
of its glories visible, by removing the accumulation of broken-down buildings that had blocked its finest monuments and by constructing the long
vistas that opened the city to the sky. He had helped clean the city, too,
freshening its air with his parks and its gutters with his sewers. In spite
of the industrial expansion, the painters of Paris could still appreciate the
unique clear, grey light of the Ile de France, not only in the surrounding
towns like Barbizon but in the very heart of Paris itself, as the street scenes
of Camille Pissarro showed. But the city's population was part of the

---

[13] Proust, *Remembrance of Things Past,* V, 407.

Au Moulin Rouge, by Henri de Toulouse-Lautrec (1864–1901). In the famous Montmartre cabaret, the artist is seated at the right of the table with his friends, while in the background, the dancer La Goulue knots her orange hair. (Courtesy of the Art Institute of Chicago.)

fascination. The almost total centralization in Paris of French government, commerce, banking, publishing, theater, and scientific and medical research had siphoned off into the city an extraordinary proportion of the country's talent. It had also concentrated in the city a great proportion of the country's wealth; and much that was not earned in Paris was spent there. Hence the first impression Paris presented was of a well-to-do city, which supported a unique number of great restaurants, boutiques, racecourses and racing stables, playhouses, international exhibitions, and art galleries and museums. This was of course due to the most conspicuous consumption of the era, uninhibited and self-congratulatory. This spate of spending provided a regular source of entertainment for most of Paris, and it was surprisingly hard for reformers to rouse resentment against it. With Edward VII at Maxim's, Sarah Bernhardt at the Théâtre de la Nation, and the king of Serbia at the Jockey Club, even the intellectuals had to enjoy the spectacle; painters like Degas or Renoir in particular delighted in portraying the rich fabrics of a couple in an opera box or the bright panorama of the races in the Bois de Boulogne.

But this extravagance of life was only tolerable because there was a general improvement in the standard of living of the whole Parisian population, which became especially marked after 1900. For all except the poorest working-class districts, wages left something over for entertainment, and the general Parisian population was as determined to enjoy itself as the well-to-do was. Working-class Paris attended the races, although in the grassy oval in the middle of the track rather than in the stands. As Renoir showed, they enjoyed boating parties on the river Seine, or as Seurat portrayed in his pointilliste paintings, a swim at the island of Grande Jatte. They filled the great open-air dance halls like those being opened on the slopes of Montmartre, especially the Moulin de la Galette where Toulouse-Lautrec found them waltzing beneath the gas lights. Everyone attested to the joy in being alive, the joie de vivre that affected everyone in Paris. It was especially in the music hall and the cafe that Paris achieved a kind of social unity. The cafe with its tables scattered across the sidewalks of the newly opened boulevards became a substitute for the declining salon. Although there were still a few grandes dames to carry on the traditions of the eighteenth century, it was in the famous cafes, like the Napolitain and the Weber, that the intellectuals held court. Impressionist painting worked out its credo around the tables of the Cafe Guerbois and the Nouvelle Athènes, where the composer Eric Satie later became cafe pianist. There was little opportunity for conversation in music halls like the Moulin Rouge or the Chat Noir, where a throaty-voiced singer called Yvette Guilbert was singing for Emile Zola and his friends and a cancan dancer known as La Goulue was being drawn by Toulouse-Lautrec.

It was perhaps this intermingling in conditions of almost total artistic freedom of personality and talent—with a mildly open-handed government free in the provision of low-paying sinecures to artists and writers, and an interested if not exceptionally open-handed audience—that brought the talented to Paris. They lived in small, inexpensive apartments, some in the streets leading up to Montmartre, others in the maze of the Left Bank. In *The World of Yesterday,* Stefan Zweig described the group he had known in 1904, and emphasized the stunning impression of genius created on him by the sculptor Rodin:

You never know a people or a city in depth and its most hidden qualities through books, nor even the most persistent poking about in its nooks and crannies, but only through its best people. It is only through an intellectual friendship with the living that one gains insight into the true connection between folk and land. . . . All these young French poets, like the rest of the people, lived for the joy of living in its sublimest form, the creative joy in work. How the simple human integrity of these newly won friends revised my idea of the French poet. . . . [Later he met the sculptor Rodin.] Rodin was so engrossed, so rapt in his work that not even a thunderstroke would have roused him. His movements became harder, almost angry. A sort of wildness or drunkenness had come over him; he worked faster and faster. Then his hands became hesitant. They seemed to have realized that there was nothing more for them to do. Once, twice, three times he stepped back without making any changes. Then he muttered something softly in his beard, and placed the cloths gently about the figure as one places a shawl around the shoulders of a beloved woman. . . . In that hour I had seen the eternal secret of all great art, yes, of every mortal achievement, made manifest: concentration, the collec-

**The Call to Arms, by Auguste Rodin
(1840–1917).** (Philadelphia Museum
of Art.)

tion of all forces, all sense, that ecstasis, *that being-out-of-the-world of every
artist. I had learned something for my entire lifetime.*[14]

Paris in short appeared to offer an immensity of experience, as Guillaume
Apollinaire showed:

But ever since then I've known the flavor of the universe

I'm drunk from having swallowed the entire universe
On the quay from which I saw the darkness flow and the barges sleep

Listen to me I am the throat of all Paris
And I shall drink the universe again if I want

Listen to my songs of universal drunkenness.[15]

It was in this exhilarating atmosphere that the writers, painters, and musicians of Paris embarked on half a century of experimentation at an ever
increasing tempo, leaving behind not only the more conservative patrons
of art but the majority of the public as well.

[14] Ibid., pp. 134, 136, 148–49.
[15] Shattuck, *Banquet Years*, p. 313.

Impressionism. During the first three quarters of the nineteenth century, Paris had seen three major artistic movements rise to general acceptance and then fall before their critics—romanticism, realism, and naturalism. In the 1870s, the exponents of the naturalist school, such as Zola in the novel or Courbet in painting, were still defending an approach to art that was almost scientific in character. A number of young painters who had gathered around Courbet in the 1860s were determined, however, to carry the study of reality beyond Courbet's view that "painting is essentially a concrete art and does not consist of anything but the representation of real and concrete things." The camera could achieve this goal only too well. The first big step away from the accurate representation of concrete objects was taken by the group of painters who became known as impressionists, a word first used as abuse but later taken as an accurate description of their attempt to capture the immediate impression on their visual sense of external reality. Above all they were interested in the effect of light and color in the creation of an impression. The leading impressionist painter, Claude Monet, showed how little he was interested in a specific scene and how his real subject matter was the change of light in different atmospheric conditions, by painting several different pictures of the same scene under differing light conditions, whether his subject was haystacks, water lilies, Saint Lazare railroad station, or the South Church at Amsterdam. He and Alfred Sisley were especially interested in the play of light upon water, since here the disassociation from the concrete object is most striking. Sisley profited from widespread flooding in the Seine valley in 1876, for example, to paint series of pictures of flooded streets and meadows. The technique of the impressionists was to avoid sharply drawn design through use of line, and instead to lay down broad dabs of color, which seen from a distance would fuse in the eye of the onlooker to give him both a sense of perspective and an enhanced sense of the scintillating character of the colors themselves. This technique could be transferred from landscapes outside Paris to the streets themselves, as Camille Pissarro demonstrated; or to the beauty of the female body, clothed or unclothed, as Auguste Renoir showed. But it was also effective in giving the true sparkle of the haunts the impressionists loved in Paris, the cafes and their patrons, backstage at the theater, or the skating rink. The first exhibitions of the impressionists were met with disbelief, or with scorn at their apparent inability to finish a painting properly; and it was a rare critic, like Jules Laforgue, who understood what they were trying to achieve. "The Impressionists," he wrote, "abandoned the three supreme illusions by which the academic painters lived—line, perspective, and studio lighting. Where the one sees only the external outline of objects the other sees the real living lines, built not in geometric forms but in a thousand irregular strokes which, at a distance, establish life. Where one sees things placed in regular perspective planned according to theoretical design, the other sees per-

South Church at Amsterdam, by Claude Monet (1840–1926). Monet's love of the play of the light on water led him to paint such scenes as the floods around Paris and the canals of Amsterdam. (Philadelphia Museum of Art, Photograph by A. J. Wyatt, Staff Photographer.)

spective established by a thousand trivial touches of tone and brush and by the varieties of atmospheric states."[16]

The heyday of the impressionists lay between their first independent exhibition in 1874 and their last joint show in 1886. By then their conception of the artist's task as the record of the fleeting sense impressions had been challenged by several painters who collectively are known as the post-impressionists. Paul Cézanne, the leader of this new school, argued that the artist must go beyond the transitory moment to the eternal. Through mental discipline the artist must impose his own conception upon a subject he is painting. This implied in part a return to line, form, and strict design; in part, the intellectual involvement of the painter in his scene. Cézanne, determined increasingly to discipline his subject matter, became convinced that the answer lay in geometry, in the reduction of nature's vastness of form to the elementary shapes of the sphere, the cone, and the prism. In the landscapes that he painted in the Provence hills, the impressionist vision slowly changes until one reaches a landscape that is almost an abstract design.

For Paul Gauguin, the son of a well-to-do bourgeois family who finally abandoned the artificial world of France altogether to find his own reality among the unspoiled primitive landscapes and peoples of the South Seas,

[16] Phoebe Pool, *Impressionism* (New York: Praeger, 1967), p. 178.

Haystacks, by Vincent van Gogh (1853–1890). Even in a black and white drawing, van Gogh could present the intense, vibrant heat of a landscape in Provence. (Philadelphia Museum of Art, Photograph by A. J. Wyatt, Staff Photographer.)

the emotional dominance of the painter was the essential task. "Where do we come from? What are we? Where are we going?" he would constantly ask. His answer was an almost mythical presentation of the life of the South Sea islanders, in whose innocence he claimed to see a sense of reality that civilized Europe had lost. Henri Rousseau, known as Le Douanier Rousseau because he was a customs official, found a similar purity in the countryside outside Paris, which he depicted with a childlike sense of the primitive forces at work even in a suburban meadow. But it was Vincent van Gogh, a Dutchman who moved to spend the last tormented years of his adult life in the south of France, who was most successful in making the technical elements of painting, the colors themselves, into symbols expressing an inner view of truth. "To express the feelings of two lovers by a marriage of two complementary colors, their mixture and their oppositions, the mysterious vibrations of tones in each other's proximity. To express the thought behind a brow by the radiance of a bright tone against a dark ground. To express hope by some star, the ardor of being by the radiance of a setting sun." [17] But as the accompanying photo shows, Van Gogh could express the same intensity of insight even in a black and white drawing, where the sharp flare of the emotion might be caught in the movement of branches or the waving of grass. Van Gogh comes close, as he intended to do, to the nature of music and of poetry, at the time when both were striving to achieve reality through the use of symbols.

[17] Cited in Weber, *Paths to the Present,* p. 202.

Symbolism.   The symbolist school of poetry was a French creation, another aspect of the attack on realism.   To get away from the detailed, concrete presentation of a purely rational perception, they hit upon the qualities of the symbol, which they valued for its intensity.   The Christian church had used heaven and hell as symbols; the poet would achieve a similar effect, for himself at least, by using words that *evoked* for him certain passionate experiences, memories, or unconscious reactions.   Wagner, they felt, had succeeded in doing this in music, not least by his use of the *leitmotiv*.   The poet must use words in the manner of a musician.   ''De la musique encore et toujours'' (Music ever and always), wrote Verlaine:

Music ever and always
Let your verse be the object flying on high
That one feels to be fleeing from a soul in freedom
Toward other skies and other loves.

Let your verse be the great adventure
Flying high on the sharp wind of morning
Which floats scented with mint and with thyme . . .
And the rest is literature.[18]

Or as Mallarmé put it, ''Since Wagner, Music links up with Verse to form Poetry.''   When he himself wrote a poem on the fleeting experiences of a faun on a summer afternoon, it lent itself at once to the evocative music of Debussy's *L'Après-midi d'un faune.*

Fauvism, Cubism.   By 1900, in short, there seemed to be a kind of common purpose among the artists, poets, and musicians at work in Paris.   As usual, the victory of an idea—illustrated by the admission of the impressionists and post-impressionists to the Great World Exhibition of 1900 and their ready sales to American collectors, if not yet to French—was followed by a reaction.   The artists in revolt were nicknamed *les fauves,* or the wild beasts, because the violence of their approach to art was something entirely new.   The leader of the Fauves was Henri Matisse, who explained their daring use of brutal discordant colors as a search for expression.

Expression to my way of thinking does not consist of the passion mirrored upon a human face or betrayed by a violent gesture. The whole arrangement of my picture is expressive. The place occupied by the figures or objects, the empty spaces around them, the proportions, everything plays a part. Composition is the art of arranging in a decorative manner the various elements at the painter's disposal for the expression of his feelings.[19]

If Paris found the colors of Matisse and Georges Rouault disconcerting, it was even more shocked by the first exhibition of cubist painting in 1907,

---

[18] Author's translation.
[19] Cited in Herbert Read, *A Concise History of Modern Painting* (New York: Praeger, 1968), p. 38.

Mechanical Element, by Ferdinand Léger (1881–1955). In this cubist painting of 1920, Léger has used black, white, and gray and three-dimensional design to present the essence rather than the outward appearance of the machine. (Philadelphia Museum of Art, Photograph by A. J. Wyatt, Staff Photographer.)

in which Pablo Picasso, an émigré from Spain, displayed *Les Demoiselles d'Avignon*. Picasso at the time was influenced by Cézanne's geometric landscapes, and he had adapted the geometric approach to the human figure. Not only did Picasso and the other cubists who joined him at this time, including Georges Braque and Fernand Léger, seek out geometric structures but they deliberately fragmented their subjects, as though they were being viewed in a mosaic of mirrors. From this they moved to the even greater distortion of the collage, which made possible a representation of the unconscious mind. Fernand Léger explained what they were trying to achieve:

Trees cease to be trees, a shadow cuts across the hand placed on the counter, an eye deformed by the light, the changing silhouettes of the passers-by. The life of fragments: a red finger-nail, an eye, a mouth. The elastic effects produced by complementary colors which transform objects into some other reality. He fills himself with all this, drinks in the whole of this vital instantaneity which cuts through him in every direction. He is a sponge: a sensation of being a sponge, transparency, acuteness, new realism.[20]

[20] Ibid., p. 88.

What had been achieved was in fact the takeoff point for all modern art. The picture had been finally liberated from its relationship to its subject. The painter had passed from the representation of an object to the interpretation of an object and finally to the idea suggested by an object; and the painting now existed in its own right as a free association of images from the artist's own mind that have become objective reality themselves in the painting. From that point it became possible to embark on even more revolutionary forms of art. Even before 1914, the principles of surrealism, dadaism, futurism, and abstract art were being worked out.

For Paris, however, its artists were now increasingly an isolated and incomprehensible coterie. When Stravinsky's *Rites of Spring* brought its wild rhythms and disturbing story of human sacrifice to the stage in 1913, the music could not be heard for the jeers of the audience.

SUGGESTED READING

Adna F. Weber supplies the statistics of urban growth, and suggests reasons for the vast expansion, in *The Growth of Cities in the Nineteenth Century* (1963), while E. A. Wrigley relates population growth to industrialism in *Population and History* (1969). An excellent survey of the economic growth of all western Europe is given by David Landes, *The Unbound Prometheus: Technological Change and Industrial Development in Western Europe from 1750 to the Present* (1969); Peter N. Stearns, *European Society in Upheaval: Social History since 1800* (1967) is useful on the composition of the working classes. For the improvements in city life, one should consult the studies of individual cities, such as Sheppard's *London, 1808–1870: The Great Wen,* which does look beyond the carbuncular aspects; David H. Pinckney, *Napoleon III and the Rebuilding of Paris* (1958); Barea, *Vienna,* cited earlier, and Gerhard Masur, *Imperial Berlin* (1970).

Nineteenth-century urban growth is explained in Robert E. Dickinson, *The West European City: A Geographical Interpretation* (1951), and dramatized in Arnold Toynbee, *Cities on the Move* (1970). Urban improvements are questioned in Lewis Mumford, *Technics and Civilization* (1934) and also in his *The City in History.*

The technology of the second industrial revolution is described in S. J. Singer et al., eds., *A History of Technology, vol. 5: Late Nineteenth Century, 1850–1900* (1958) and T. K. Derry and T. I. Williams, *A Short History of Technology* (1961). On steel, see N. G. B. Pounds and W. N. Parker, *Coal and Steel in Western Europe* (1957); on electricity, *Singer,* cited above, pp. 177–234; and on chemistry, L. F. Haber, *The Chemical Industry in the Nineteenth Century* (1958). The changes in business organization can be followed in H. J. Habbakuk, *American and British Technology in the Nineteenth Century* (1962); William C. Cochran and William Miller, *The Age of Enterprise* (1961); and C. J. H. Hayes, *A Generation of Materialism, 1871–1900* (1941).

Among the many novels that deal with the social changes of fin de siècle, see Marcel Proust's *Remembrance of Things Past* (1951), translated by C. K. Scott

Moncrieff; E. M. Forster, *Howard's End;* Heinrich Mann, *Little Superman* (1945); Thomas Mann, *Buddenbrooks;* Roger Martin du Gard, *Jean Barois* (1949); John Galsworthy, *The Forsyte Saga;* and of course the vast output of H. G. Wells, including *Kipps* and *Tono Bungay,* which, if prolix, at least gives his view of the evolution of London. For a succinct and often biting summation of this society, see Barbara W. Tuchman, *The Proud Tower* (1962).

For an introduction of intellectual currents of this period, one might begin with H. Stuart Hughes, *Consciousness and Society: The Reorientation of European Social Thought, 1890–1930* (1961) or George L. Mosse, *The Culture of Western Europe: The Nineteenth and Twentieth Centuries* (1961). Freud's life is succinctly explained, with ample quotations from the doctor himself, in O. Mannoni, *Freud* (1971); the standard biography is Ernest Jones, *The Life and Work of Sigmund Freud,* which has been abridged by Lionel Trilling and Steven Marcus (1961). For a biographical approach to the new physics, which is perhaps the best method for a layman to cope with the complexity of relativity and quantum theory, there is Leopold Infeld, *Albert Einstein: His Work and Its Influence on Our World* (1950) and B. L. Cline, *The Questioners* (1965).

Vienna at century's end as a formative intellectual milieu is described by Carl Schorske, "Transformation of the Garden: Ideal and Society in Austrian Literature," *American Historical Review,* July 1967, pp. 1283–1320. The books on Viennese music listed in Chapter 18 may be supplemented by Paul Collaer, *A History of Modern Music* (1961); but they should be accompanied by a playing of such pieces as Schoenberg's *Variations for Orchestra,* or better yet, Berg's opera *Lulu.*

The Belle Epoque is charmingly evoked through the lives of Alfred Jarry, Henri Rousseau, Erik Satie, and Guillaume Apollinaire, in Roger Shattuck, *The Banquet Years* (1955). The journey of the writers from romanticism to naturalism is traced by Cesar Graña, *Modernity and Its Discontents: French Society and the French Man of Letters in the Nineteenth Century* (1967). On symbolism, see Edmund Wilson, *Axel's Castle: A Study in the Imaginative Literature of 1870–1930* (1943) and C. M. Bowra, *The Heritage of Symbolism* (1943). Stefan Zweig describes the intoxicating effect of Paris on a young writer in *The World of Yesterday* (1943); Igor Stravinsky relates his explosive experiences in the unreceptive world of Parisian music, in *Autobiography* (1936). On the impressionist painters, see the solid work of John Rewald, *The History of Impressionism* (1962) or the lighter Phoebe Pool, *Impressionism* (1967). Later developments from Cézanne through surrealism are explained by Herbert Read, *A Concise History of Modern Painting* (1968). Finally, to enjoy the full overromanticized feeling of the gaieté parisienne, one could browse in the music halls described by Jacques Castelnau, *Belle Epoque* (1962); or glance at the fine old photographs in Jean Roman's *Paris: Fin de siècle* (1960), with a delightful text translated by James Emmons.

22

THE BERLIN OF THE KAISER

Emperor William the Second of Germany (reigned 1888–1918), known to subjects and enemies alike as The Kaiser, was realistic about the attractions of his capital city, although not notably realistic in most of his other pronouncements. "The glory of the Parisians robs the Berliners of their sleep," he told his chancellor when he suggested in 1892 that Berlin hold a world's fair. "Paris is the great whorehouse of the world; therein lies its attraction independent of any exhibition. There is nothing in Berlin that can captivate the foreigner, except a few museums, castles, and soldiers. After six days, the red [guide-] book in hand, he has seen everything, and he departs *relieved,* feeling that he has done his duty. The Berliner does not see these things clearly, and he would be very upset if he were told about them. However, this is the real obstacle to an exhibition." [1]

The kaiser's Berlin, whatever it may have lacked in the more obvious tourist attractions, had progressed enormously since the mid–fifteenth century, when one of its first Hohenzollern rulers had chosen it for the capital of his Mark of Brandenburg. At the time it consisted of little more than twin trading settlements, Berlin-Kölln on the two banks of the insignificant Spree River, and a castle that provided protection against marauding barons and an outpost for the drive against the Slavs across the sandy wastes of the North German plain. It had been laid in ruins during the Thirty Years' War, and was only saved from insignificance by the forceful genius of the Great Elector, Frederick William I (reigned 1640–1688). He gave his state of Prussia, now enlarged to include territory on the Rhine and the province of East Prussia on the Baltic, a large standing army, adequate revenues, a peasantry subdued to their Junker landlords, and a thriving industrial base which was mainly the work of French Calvinist

---

[1] Gerhard Masur, *Imperial Berlin* (New York: Basic Books, 1971), pp. 125–26.

Emperor William II of Germany. (German Information Center photo.)

779

refugees. The role of Berlin as the garrison center of the Prussian state was further emphasized by King Frederick William I (reigned 1713–1740), a rough brute whose pet ambition was to possess the tallest regiment in Europe and who despised the refinements of French culture that his son, Frederick II (reigned 1740–1786) appeared to prize above the military virtues. Frederick, as we saw in Chapter 16, was adept in combining military adventures and territorial aggrandizement, notably in Silesia and western Poland, with the patronage of the arts and music; and by the end of his reign, Berlin and the neighboring town of Potsdam shared in a small, subdued way in the architectural and artistic advances of the rococo age.

By 1786, Berlin, with a population of almost 150,000, was a moderately attractive representative of the many princely capitals of a Germany divided into more than three hundred states. Each of the rulers of the previous century and a half had left his imprint on the growing city. The wife of the Great Elector had laid down the city's most famous avenue, Unter den Linden, that drove toward the west from the castle. The castle itself received a new baroque facade when the Great Elector's successor, Frederick I, who had won the title of King, decided to let Germany's finest architect and city planner, Andreas Schlüter, make Berlin worthy of its new royal status. Frederick II, however, created on both sides of the Unter den Linden one of the great eighteenth-century squares, the Forum Fredericianum.

Unter den Linden, Berlin.
(German Information Center photo.)

On one side of the street was the classical facade of his brother's palace, which was soon converted into the University of Berlin. Facing it was the new opera house, a domed Catholic church, and the curving facade of the royal library. With the completion of Frederick's Forum, Berlin possessed a monumental center of great dignity; and the preeminent importance of Unter den Linden was emphasized with the construction in 1788–1791 of the Brandenburg Gate.

City Palace, Berlin. The great baroque architect, Andreas Schlüter, designed the principal facade for this palace, which was the residence of the Hohenzollern family from 1470 to 1918. (German Information Center photo.)

For the next generation, the classical revival replaced the rococo; and the style was created that was to dominate throughout the nineteenth century. Monumental Berlin of the nineteenth century was to be, its architects hoped, a synthesis of Athens and Rome, which corresponded to some extent to the rulers' belief that Berlin could be a combination of spirit *(Geist)* and strength *(Macht)*. The Brandenburg Gate was a Doric version of a Roman triumphal arch. The guardhouse, or Neue Wache, had a Parthenon-like portico as entry to a square Roman fortress. The Old Museum, built by the architect Karl Friedrich Schinkel, who was perhaps more responsible than any other person for the appearance of the heart of Berlin,

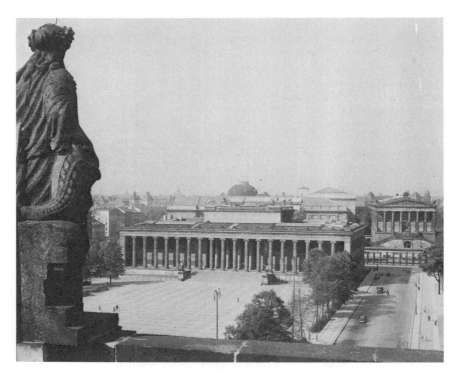

Old Museum, Berlin. From the palace, one could see on Museum Island the Ionic facade of the Old Museum, the domed, neo-baroque Kaiser Friedrich archaeological museum, and the Corinthian exterior of the National Gallery. (German Information Center photo.)

was a long basilica, like Julius Caesar's in Rome, masked by a facade of Ionian columns; it marked the beginning of a totally new concept for Berlin and a lesson to other cities, the Museum Island in the Spree River, dedicated by the king as a "sanctuary of Art and Learning" and developed during the next hundred years into one of the three or four greatest museum complexes in the world.

For most of the nineteenth century, however, Berlin's development, though extensive, was lackluster. After the brief period in which Prussia led the national revolt against Napoleon and the political and intellectual life of Berlin itself was reinvigorated by the reforms of Stein and Hardenberg and the intellectual life by the Humboldt brothers, it slumped into its own Biedermeier quiescence. Germany's intellectual life was centered still in Weimar, where Goethe held sway until 1832, although Hegel and his disciples were teaching (among others to Karl Marx) the philosophy of the dialectic and the embodiment of the absolute in the Prussian state. In Prussia, after the king had dismissed the reforming ministers in 1819, those who sought change had to find it in economics rather than politics. In the Rhineland provinces Prussia had acquired in 1815, the first great ironworks and engineering companies were created in the 1830s and 1840s. In Berlin itself, the Borsig locomotive works was the forerunner of several large engineering plants, stimulated especially by the construction of railroads and by the formation of a customs union, or *Zollverein*, joined by most German states. By 1848, Berlin's population had reached 400,000 people, many of whom lived in dismal slum conditions in the new suburb of Moabit. Neither industrialization nor political repression had turned the Berliners into effective revolutionaries, however, as the anarchist Bakunin complained in 1840:

Berlin is a fine town, excellent music, cheap living, very passable theater, plenty of newspapers in the cafes.... In a word, splendid, quite splendid—if only the Germans weren't so frightfully bourgeois. Yesterday I noticed a sign outside a shop: the Prussian eagle above and below a tailor ironing. And underneath the following couplet:

> *Under thy wings*
> *Quietly, I can do my ironing.*[2]

The failure of the 1848 revolution in Berlin and the concurrent collapse of the attempt to unify Germany through the Frankfurt Parliament were, however, the necessary prerequisite to Berlin's seizure of its role as the unifier of Germany, and thus to its transformation into the imperial capital of a country forcibly unified by Prussian military might. It is a moot question whether Prussia would have played an important part if the liberal reformers of 1848 had succeeded in creating a democratic German state; it was certain that in a state unified by blood and iron, Prussia would be the unifier.

Throughout the 1850s, however, the Prussian government seemed unwilling to recognize that the failure of the Frankfurt Parliament was its own opportunity. The king, Frederick William IV (reigned 1840–1861) was slowly succumbing to the mental sickness that made it necessary for him to hand over power to his brother William I (reigned 1861–1888) three years before his death. The highest positions in society and politics were held by the landed aristocracy, and especially by the semifeudal gentry from East Prussia and the Mark of Brandenburg, who had little interest in western or southern Germany. The middle classes, elated with the rapidity of Prussia's economic growth under the stimulus of vast railroad construction, were increasingly aware of the benefits of economic unification in Germany but disoriented as to possible methods of achieving it. Their more well-to-do members were given representation in the Prussian parliament, but they could do little except make muted protests at the police powers that seemed necessary to enforce the paternalism of the Prussian bureaucracy and its Junker overlords. Until 1860, Prussia turned inwards politically, the conservative reaction excluding any ambitious attempt to challenge the power of an equally reactionary Austria in the German Confederation. In 1861, however, the liberals in the Prussian parliament used their power over the state finances to block the adoption of a new reorganization of the army that would have increased the term of conscription from two to three years and abolished the civilian militia.

---

[2] John Mander, *Berlin: The Eagle and the Bear*, trans. modified (London: Barrie and Radcliff, 1959), p. 76.

A situation of constitutional deadlock resulted, in which the king and his conservative advisers accused the liberals of attempting to gain control of the state and were regarded in turn by the liberals as seeking to militarize it. King William's way out of the impasse was the appointment of a new chief minister, Count Otto von Bismarck, who in nine years converted Berlin from the capital of a Prussian kingdom of eighteen million to the capital of a German empire, the Second Reich, with almost forty million inhabitants.

FROM ROYAL TO IMPERIAL CAPITAL, 1862–1871

"Prussia is henceforth absorbed into Germany," the Prussian king had declared in 1848. By 1871, Prussia had swallowed up Germany, preferring to follow Bismarck's own maxim that in Germany pike eats carp. To carry through this design Bismarck had to overwhelm the liberal opposition inside Prussia, create a modernized army, harness the nationalism of North Germany behind Prussia, defeat Austria and eject it from Germany, and stimulate the South German states to desire unification under Prussia by leading them to victory in a war against France. But he had perhaps unguardedly summed up his program more pithily the day before he dismissed the recalcitrant parliament. "It is not by speeches and majority resolutions that the great questions of our time are decided," he said. "That was the great mistake of 1848 and 1849. It is by blood and iron."

Cavour's Unification of Italy. After he had succeeded in unifying Germany, Bismarck's solution won over many of his critics, and came to appear as the only feasible course of action. The revolutions of 1848 in Germany and Italy had been led by idealistic and frequently inexperienced middle-class reformers who had been convinced that liberal political change, including universal suffrage and representative government, would accompany the national integration of the more than thirty states in Germany and the eight states of Italy. The attempt to combine nationalism and liberalism had led to the defeat of both. The liberal reformers had quarreled among themselves; they had been unable to find any solid basis of military strength to set against the armies of Radetsky or Wrangel because they had outraged possible nationalists among the monarchs and landed aristocrats; and they had been unable to carry through economic and social reforms that would have won the lasting backing of the proletariat.

After 1848, the leadership of the Italian nationalist movement fell into far more realistic hands than those of Mazzini, Manin, or Garibaldi. Count Camillo Cavour, who became chief minister of Piedmont-Savoy in 1852, coldly and painstakingly planned Italy's unification by his own state and its royal family, the one native Italian dynasty in the peninsula. He groomed Piedmont for stardom, modernizing its industry and its military forces, emphasizing its constitutional copying of England, and seeking reliable allies against Austria. He found an ally in the new French emperor, Napoleon III, who in his youth had even joined one of the Italian revolutionary groups and now sought to create a client state for France in an en-

THE CITY: FROM THE BAROQUE TO THE INDUSTRIAL AGE

Throughout most of Europe in the eighteenth century, the city remained in the pre-industrial age. City functions were largely unchanged since the Renaissance, and the city still showed the dominance of the court and aristocracy, the bourgeoisie, the army, and the church. The appearance of the great eighteenth-century cities was faithfully recorded by Antonio Canaletto. Canaletto specialized in views of Venice, but in the middle of the century during a stay in London he painted *The Thames and the City From Richmond House,* showing the capital in the last years before it felt the impact of industrialism.

In that last century before the upheavals precipitated by the French Revolution, the monarchs of Europe indulged in a spree of palace building, dotting the great cities and the surrounding countryside with vast architectural extravaganzas. In South Germany and Austria in particular, the rococo style of decoration achieved a refinement unparalleled elsewheré as can be seen in the ballroom of a merchant's home in Augsburg. In Russia, the Italian architect Bartolomeo Rastrelli built the summer palace of Tsarkoe Selo (top) for the Empress Catherine II. The Empress of Austria, Maria Theresa, also called in Italian architects to complete her summer palace of Schönbrunn (bottom right) on the outskirts of Vienna. She laid out fountains, lawns, alleys of trees, and parterres of flowers in direct emulation of Louis XIV's palace of Versailles.

In Britain, however, the first industrial revolution of textiles, coal, and iron was already bringing profound changes to the rapidly expanding cities of the Midlands and the Pennine Hills, of South Wales and central Scotland. As in *Southeast View of Sheffield* (top) by William Ibbitt and at the *Nant-y-Glo Ironworks* (bottom) in South Wales, shown here in the 1780s in a painting attributed to German Robertson, the countryside was being transformed into a smoking inferno.

By the mid-nineteenth century, Europe and the United States had followed the British lead, and the chimney landscape had sprouted there too, as Vincent van Gogh showed in his *Industrial Landscape* of 1886 (above).

For many, the new industrialism was an inchoate force, as J. M. W. Turner attempted to show in his *Rain and Speed, The Great Western Railway* (top opposite page), in which the passage of the steam locomotive blurs the physical image of the city.

For some, even the railroad had its own glamor and excitement, not least to the Impressionist painter Claude Monet, for whom the billowing smoke in the *Gare Saint-Lazare* (bottom opposite page) created the ever-changing light he loved to depict.

The greatest Western cities adapted to the changes brought by industri-alism, and became World Cities. Their architecture absorbed the style of every past age, and merged it with the omnipresent evidence of the industrial age. The palatial railroad stations and their adjoining hotels, such as the neo-Gothic *St. Pancras Hotel and Station* (detail) by John O'Connor in 1884, epitomized the soaring aspirations and the slumping taste of the newly enriched bourgeoisie.

Yet, by the end of the nineteenth century, many of the great cities appeared to have created a new and widely exciting way of life, in spite of the harsh living and working conditions of the majority of their populations. At fin de siécle, there was an undeniable optimism about life for the citizens of such metropolitan centers as London, Vienna, and especially Paris. The comings and goings on the streets of Paris, as on the *Boulevard des Italiens* (bottom), delighted a painter like Camille Pissarro. Even noisier and more jovial crowds flooded *Place Pigalle, La Nuit* (top), painted by Pierre Bonnard, and the neighboring cabarets and music halls of Montmartre.

Following the Communist takeover of power in 1917, the cities of Russia witnessed a social revolution of great intensity. Their streets became the backdrop to a new type of urban pageantry, especially on May Day, as in Leningrad, when the workers turned out in the millions to salute the memory of their revolutionary leaders.

Yet the very future of the city remained uncertain. Two world wars had brought irreparable damage to many of the great Western cities. In the economic recovery after 1945, most of the cities of Europe and North America faced new and unprecedented problems of overcrowding, congestion, pollution, and even, it was suggested, of dehumanization created by the prosperity itself. At times, it seemed that the very viability of city life had been brought into question.

larged Piedmont. After years of skillful propaganda among the various nationalist groups inside Italy and of bargaining with Napoleon, Cavour provoked Austria into war with Piedmont. At once his carefully laid plans were implemented. France came to the aid of its aggrieved ally Piedmont, and on its behalf defeated the Austrian armies in Lombardy. Well-orchestrated nationalist uprisings took place in the central states of Italy, whose populations demanded unification with Piedmont. When Garibaldi conquered Naples and Sicily without Piedmont's support or authorization, a Piedmontese army was sent to compel him to hand over his newly won possessions—which, to Cavour's relief, he did peacefully and with panache. By 1860, Piedmont had thus been able to unite all Italy except Venice and part of the papal states under its king, Victor Emmanuel I; the price paid had been the cession of Savoy and Nice to France; Austria, the great obstacle to Italian unification from the year 1815, had collapsed ignominiously.

The Unification of Italy
1859–1870

Area unified in 1859
Added in 1860
Added in 1866
Added in 1870

The lesson of Piedmont's success for Germany was obvious. In 1859, a national association was formed in Frankfurt for the purpose of putting Prussia at the head of a similar unification movement in Germany. Economists formed the Congress of German Economists to agitate for economic unity. Jurists formed an all-German association for a unified German legal system. Protestants pressed for the ouster of Catholic Austria and unification under Protestant Prussia. Historians argued that the whole political evolution of Germany pointed to the leadership of Prussia. Heinrich von Treitschke regretfully pointed out that the Italians had displayed far clearer insight into the national goals of their struggle than the Germans: "Whoever . . . has not lost his understanding of true human greatness must gaze at this wonderful spectacle with utmost joy, how within fifty years a nation, sunk to the lowest moral depths, has raised itself to honorable unity and readiness to self-sacrifice, and has become a political reality."[3] Much of this outpouring of nationalist feeling in 1859–1862 in favor of Prussian leadership was liberal rather than conservative or militarist in orientation; and Bismarck, the most sagacious of political observers, was prepared to profit from the nationalist atmosphere created by the liberals while at the same time denying their aspirations within Prussia, secure in the belief that they would eventually return to his support after success.

Bismarck Unifies Germany.   Bismarck was clear both as to methods and goals for Germany's unification. In background and in character, he stood for authoritarianism. "I am no democrat and cannot be one!" he said. "I was born and raised as an aristocrat." He had grown up on the family estates in Pomerania; and he never forgot that he was above all a Junker who despised public opinion. He was also unshakably though realistically loyal to the Prussian monarchy. "I take the king in my own way, I influence him, trust him, guide him, but he is the central point of all my thinking and all my action, the Archimedes point from which I will move the world." Far from being isolated as a rural squire, however, Bismarck had studied law in Göttingen and Berlin, and had gained international political experience as a Prussian representative to the German Confederation in Frankfurt and later as ambassador to Saint Petersburg and Paris. From this experience he had drawn the conclusion that Germany was too small to include both Prussia and Austria and that eventually the outcome would be settled on the battlefield. He prepared for that day with extraordinary skill and duplicity.

When parliament refused the olive branch he offered them (he literally offered them an olive branch that he had brought from Avignon), he ordered the state's tax collectors to collect the past taxes anyway, and gave the army organizers, Von Roon and Von Moltke, the credits to supply the army with the needle-gun and steel-barreled artillery from the Krupp factory.

[3] Cited Koppel S. Pinson, *Modern Germany: Its History and Civilization* (New York: Macmillan, 1959), p. 114.

He manipulated Austria with great cunning. After winning Russian friendship by encouraging it to crush a revolt in its Polish territories in 1863, he lured Austria into a war against Denmark to prevent the incorporation into the Danish kingdom of the two largely German-inhabited duchies of Schleswig and Holstein, and then persuaded the Austrians to administer Holstein while Prussia ran Schleswig. Criticism of Austrian management of Holstein was to be Bismarck's goad that would bring Austria to the exasperation necessary for it to declare war on Prussia. Before that point was reached, he continued with his clever diplomatic preparations for the isolation of the unwary victim. In vague but plausible promises made to Emperor Napoleon III at Biarritz, he indicated that French neutrality in a war between Prussia and Austria might be rewarded with territory along the Rhine. He astounded, and to some extent disarmed, the German liberals by proposing that the German Confederation should be given an all-German parliament elected by universal suffrage. He made a secret treaty with the Italian government promising it Venetia if it attacked Austria from the south in the event of an Austro-Prussian war within three months'

German Unification
under Bismarck

Prussian in 1862   United in 1871
United in 1866–1867   Annexed in 1871

0 ——————— 100 Miles

time. And he reassured world opinion that his aim was not to bring Austria or southern Germany into Prussian control, merely "that part of Germany which is united by its genius, its religion, manners, and interests to the destiny of Prussia—the Germany of the North." In 1866, the German Confederation supported Austria's demand that it declare war on Prussia for occupying Holstein, which Bismarck had claimed to be necessary to

Prince Otto von Bismarck (1815–1898).
Even as chancellor of a united Germany,
Bismarck prided himself upon preserv-
ing the simplicity and directness of an
East Prussian Junker. (German Informa-
tion Center photo.)

protect it from Austrian misgovernment. The Austrian army was badly armed, and hampered by inadequate railroads. It was defeated within seven weeks at the decisive battle of Königgrätz. Bismarck, who had sat with King William I on horseback watching his rising excitement and disregard for danger, found that the martial experience had given the king and his general staff an unwise desire to humiliate the Austrians with an occupation of Vienna and annexation of Austrian territory. "We are just as quickly intoxicated as discouraged," he wrote to his wife, "and I have the ungrateful task of pouring water in the foaming wine, and to make them see that we are not living alone in Europe, but with three neighbors still." He was successful in winning light terms for Austria, although he insisted that Italy, which had entered the war as stipulated only to be defeated, should be given Venetia. For the North German states, however, he demanded annexation to Prussia, under the poorly disguised form of membership in a new North German Confederation with Berlin as its capital. By 1866, the territory under Prussian control had increased by four and a half million people, while Austria was definitively driven out of internal German affairs.

Bismarck then dropped the pretense that his ambitions extended only to North Germany. A war with France would, in Bismarck's eyes, serve several purposes. It would strike a paralyzing blow at Germany's "heredi-tary enemy," from whom the German-speaking territory on the Rhine an-nexed by Louis XIV in the seventeenth century could be retaken. It would end the opposition to unification of North and South Germany of France, the country most affected.   And it could be used to entice the South German states into a military alliance under the leadership of Prussia, which if successful in battle might well be the prelude to political unification. It still seems distorted logic—and criminal irresponsibility—to embark on a major war in which 135,000 French soldiers and 40,000 German soldiers would be killed, to effect the unification of North and South Germany; but Bismarck's policy worked to perfection.   He goaded Napoleon III into declaring war on Prussia by publicizing his refusal of Napoleon's demands for compensation in Luxembourg or in Belgium, by promoting the candidacy of a member of the Hohenzollern family for the throne of Spain, and by doctoring a telegram from William I describing a conversation with the French ambassador to make it appear that the Prussian king had snubbed him rudely.   The telegram arrived on July 13, 1870, when Bismarck was dining with his army leaders, Von Moltke and Von Roon.   All were despondent that, with plans for the invasion of France in complete readiness, the French seemed unwilling to give them the desired declaration of war. According to Bismarck:

In the presence of my guests I reduced the telegram by deleting words, but without adding or altering a single word. . . .   The difference in the effect of the shortened text of the Ems telegram as compared with that of the original was not the result of stronger words but of the form, which made the announcement appear decisive.

After I had read the condensed version to my two guests, Moltke said:

"Now it has quite a different ring.   In its original form it sounded like a parley. Now it is like a flourish of trumpets in answer to a challenger." . . .

I went on to explain:

"If, in execution of his Majesty's order, I immediately communicate this text, which contains no changes in or additions to the telegram, not only to the newspapers but also by wire to all our embassies, it will be known in Paris before midnight. Not only on account of its contents but also because of the manner of its distribution, it will have the effect of a red flag on the Gallic bull . . ."

This explanation drew from both generals a metamorphosis into a more joyous mood, whose liveliness surprised me.   They had suddenly recovered their desire to eat and drink.[4]

This masterful manipulation of public opinion brought the crowds out on the streets of Paris and Berlin in a war-hungry mood.   The French declared war; the South German states placed their armies at the disposal of the Prussian command; the main French armies were defeated within three months, and Napoleon captured; and in May 1871 the new French government ceded Alsace-Lorraine to Germany and agreed to pay an indemnity of five billion francs.

[4] Cited in Louis L. Snyder, *The Blood and Iron Chancellor: A Documentary Biography of Otto von Bismarck* (Princeton, N.J.: Van Nostrand, 1967), pp. 185–86.

"What Bismarck Means by German
Unity," by Honoré Daumier.

In January, however, Bismarck had prevailed on the South German
states to unite with the North German Confederation, thereby creating a
unified German state; and at the culminating ceremony of creation of
the Second Reich, the German princes proclaimed William I as German
emperor in the Hall of Mirrors in the Palace of Versailles. William himself objected vehemently to becoming emperor, preferring the title *King
of Prussia*; and he ignored Bismarck ostentatiously at the ceremony.
In spite of these personal tensions, Bismarck ensured that the ceremony
should have the requisite grandeur for the re-creation of the German
empire. He enjoyed the symbolism of using the palace of the French kings,
the recognition of the emperor by the German ruling houses and not by
a parliamentary assembly, and especially the presence of the army, which
supplied officers from all sixty of the units surrounding Paris. The new
emperor returned to Berlin on June 16, 1871, passing through a garlanded
Brandenburg Gate to a vast cheering welcome from the crowds in Unter den
Linden. Berlin, the imperial capital, was about to enjoy the exhilarating
boom of the founding years of the new empire, the *Gründerjahre*.

**The Return of William I
to Berlin on June 16, 1871.**
The Brandenburg Gate and
the buildings on Unter Den
Linden were festooned with
ribbons and flowers to welcome the victorious armies
back from the Franco-
Prussian war.

"Essential for the state is a capital city to act as a pivot for its culture,"
Heinrich von Treitschke proclaimed in his self-appointed role as guide to
the new nation's position in history. "No great nation can endure for long
without a center where its political, intellectual, and material life is concentrated, and its people can feel united." That center could only be Berlin.
Other cities such as Hamburg or Frankfurt were better located; others
such as Munich or Dresden were more beautiful and more cultivated.
But since Prussia had absorbed Germany, Prussia's capital would have to
be transformed into a worthy capital of the Reich.

BERLIN DURING THE GRÜNDERJAHRE: CREATION OF AN IMPERIAL CAPITAL

Monumental Berlin. Preparation had already been made in the 1860s
for the replanning of Berlin. Until then the city had been surrounded
by a wall some eighteen feet high, erected during the wars with Napoleon,
which had been used for collecting local tolls. With its demolition the
expansion of the city to engulf the nearby villages became possible.
Several great avenues already existed that could become the axes of future
development, notably the Kurfürstendamm, which led from the beautiful
Tiergarten park on the edge of the old city to the lovely woods of the
Grünewald, and the Charlottenburgerstrasse, which prolonged Unter den
Linden toward the summer palace of the Prussian kings. It was even
given a general development plan in 1863, the last it was to have for
more than half a century, and to this the newer sections owed wide tree-
lined streets. Undoubtedly, the example of Haussmann's transformation of
Paris inspired many of these city planners, although they could do little
with the inner city itself. Here only piecemeal improvements were made:

a huge city hall in an odd mixture of native Brandenburg and Italian Renaissance styles; a monumental square called the Königsplatz, whose central feature was a tall, ugly Victory Column (*Siegessaüle*) begun in 1864 to celebrate the defeat of Denmark and further elaborated to immortalize the victories over Austria and France; and a number of vast, half-classical railroad stations around the old city boundary, such as the Lehrter station of 1869 and the Potsdam station of 1870, which helped link the capital to its new possessions.

There was surprisingly little monumental building carried out to accommodate the demands of imperial administration or even imperial pretensions. The most grandiose building erected was a new home for the imperial parliament, the Reichstag, on the edge of the Königsplatz—a vast neoclassical building completed in 1894. William I made no pretense of seeking to enhance the glamor of a title he had never wanted; but his grandson William II sought in his own idiosyncratic way to give a little monumental sparkle to the subdued setting bequeathed him by his ancestors. He laid out a new Victory Avenue leading to the Victory Column, and flanked it with thirty-two marble statues of the principal rulers of the House of Hohenzollern, from Albert the Bear to William I.

Cathedral, Berlin. This monstrous church—344 feet long, 374 feet high—was built in 1894–1905 in the style of the High Renaissance, as a demonstration of the grandeur of Germany's capital city. (German Information Center photo.)

Although William paid for it himself as a gift to his people and thought it had made Berlin the most beautiful city in the world, most Berliners found it a masterpiece of grotesquely bad taste. The two vast churches he erected were little better. The cathedral, built near the palace on the site of Frederick the Great's cathedral, which was pulled down, was intended to outdo Michelangelo's Saint Peter's in size, color, and decoration. The Kaiser William Memorial Church, built in commemoration of his grandfather at the head of the Kurfürstendamm, was a massive, neo-Romanesque creation, which many later felt looked more picturesque after 1945 in ruins. Only the new museums being added to the museum island managed to harmonize with the older Schinkel buildings; and the tourist would have forgiven them almost any outrage against good taste because in them Wilhelm Bode, the director of Berlin galleries, was accumulating one of the greatest collections of the world's art, especially the findings of the great German archaeologists who were laying bare the buried cities of the Near East. These treasures included the Altar of Pergamum, the Processional Way and Ishtar Gate of Babylon, and the Market Gate of Miletus; and their acquisition was directly favored by the kaiser who admired, and understood, archaeology.

Economic and Commercial Expansion.   But the main changes in Berlin's appearance were the result of the economic and commercial expansion that followed unification. The population of Berlin expanded at great speed. It had reached a million by 1875, two million by 1900, and four million by 1914. Many of the newcomers were immigrants from the East of Germany, especially Silesia and the Polish provinces, although the freedom of movement in united Germany persuaded many non-Prussians to move to Berlin rather than emigrate abroad. As was true of all big cities of the late nineteenth century, a physical separation of the classes occurred. The new workers moved into overcrowded tenements, called *Mietkasernen* (rental barracks), in the area to the north of the Spree River, first in the slums of the Moabit district and then, as the big factories moved into the countryside, in the outer districts to the north and east. Little provision was made by the city for inspection of their living conditions, and the only interference was when the police drove workers out of shantytowns that grew up outside the city limits. It was in these areas of working-class discontent that the Socialist party found ready support. The aristocracy came to Berlin only for court functions, and most of them preferred to live on their country estates, where they could still cultivate the old Prussian virtues of discipline and thrift; in Berlin they composed only a small percentage of the population. The middle classes were sharply split between the *Bildungsbürgertum* (intellectual middle class) and the *Besitzbürgertum* (propertied middle class); and with the passion for classification that characterized all German society, they too were minutely subdivided according to the social prestige of their employment. The former included the university professors, bureaucrats, and other professionals, many of whom liked to live in what was called the Old West, a quiet charming area on the edge of the Tiergarten park. They were thus separated from the money-making middle class, whose most successful members bought themselves plots in the leafy suburbs of Grünewald, and erected ostentatious palaces in Gothic or Renaissance style. The majority of the businessmen lived in new stuccoed apartment buildings near the Kurfürstendamm, in an area that one industrialist labeled "Chicago on the Spree."

A great rash of offices and factories was erected by this middle class during the Gründerjahre. After unification, the financial center of Germany passed from Frankfurt to Berlin. This was due in part to the fact that the five-billion-franc indemnity paid by France was channeled through Berlin, and much of it remained there. It was also due in part to the foundation of new banks by industrial companies already in Berlin, and the transfer of central offices of banks to be near the location of political power and also in close touch with the new imperial bank, the Reichsbank. Berlin thus became the center of the great speculative mania that gripped the German people in the euphoria of unification, and led them to shift capital from savings banks into stocks, real estate ventures, and railroads, only to lose much of it in the crash of 1873. Berlin too was becoming the chief manufacturing city in Germany, and by the time of the great industrial exhibition in 1886, it produced seven percent of the nation's industrial production. The greatest Berlin industries were the heavy engineering industry, with companies like Borsig that turned out enormous steam engines, locomotives, and machine tools; the electrical appliance industry, virtually monopolized by Siemens and the General Electrical Company (AEG); and the chemical industry, whose best known firm was AGFA. But there were many others, including textiles, rubber, printing, and food-processing. Berlin became a great industrial city in which the majority of its inhabitants had no connection at all with its function as a capital.

The great economic expansion of Berlin was only possible because of the enormous boom felt throughout Germany during the Second Reich. By 1914, Germany had become the greatest industrial power in Europe. The country was rich in natural resources, especially in the coal of the Ruhr basin and the iron ore of newly acquired Alsace-Lorraine. It had superb communications: rivers that were readily navigable, fine canals, and a great railroad network linking the agricultural east with the industrial west. It had a good supply of labor, its population increasing from forty to sixty-eight million between 1870 and 1914; and its working population was the best-educated in Europe. Its banking system had been designed to further industrial growth. The banks put little money into government bonds but invested in long-term operations that they themselves could supervise. As small banks were merged into larger by the 1890s to produce several giants, especially the four "D Banks" (Deutsche Bank, Diskonto

Gesellschaft, Dresdener Bank, and Darmstädter Bank), the bankers were able to use their great power to force the formation of trusts in industrial production too, especially in those large-scale operations such as mining and engineering where great capital investment was required. Trusts were supplemented by the great cartels, especially in coal and steel manufacture, which claimed to maintain stability of production and employment by their rigid supervision of prices and markets. The German economy thus enjoyed only a few years of liberal economic policy immediately after the founding of the empire; for free competition was soon restricted both by the competitors themselves and by the state. Nevertheless, the results were staggering. Between 1871 and the First World War, coal production rose from 30 million tons to 191 million, steel production from almost nothing to 13 million tons. Moreover the average German had profited personally from this growth. His real income had risen from 352 marks a year to 728, a remarkable achievement in view of the population growth. This vast economic growth was the foundation for the growth of Berlin; and it was the awareness of the power of this newly acquired wealth that inspired much of the rhetoric of Berlin, both official and unofficial, in the years before the war.

The mood of Berlin was satirized as early as the 1870s by an English visitor, who found "Berlin wird Weltstadt" (Berlin will be a world city) on everyone's lips:

Stock Exchange, Berlin. The Stock Exchange, built in 1859–1864, had a fine Doric colonnade overlooking the River Spree. It was demolished after 1945. (German Information Center photo.)

"We have vanquished the modern Babylon," said the orators of the bier hallen . . . . "Paris is at our feet like the dragon beneath the lance of St. George. She was the capital of the world; she is fallen. Berlin will take her place. The mode of Paris will become that of Berlin. . . . We will inundate the world with Moltke cravats, and Bismarck collars, manufactured in Berlin. The products of Paris and Vienna are condemned for the future. We have already 800,000 inhabitants, next year we shall have 900,000, and the year after that a million. We have outdistanced St. Petersburg and Vienna, we shall soon pass before Constantinople, then Paris, and afterwards commence to compete with London." *

Bismarck and the Creation of a Political Capital. Economic power gravitated naturally toward political power; and Bismarck had determined that political power should be concentrated in Berlin. He had been forced to make a large number of concessions to persuade the rulers of South Germany freely to join a united Germany; the separate states of the federal union ran their own law courts, police, education, and most fiscal matters, and in time of peace the South German states controlled their own armies. But the central government ran foreign affairs, the navy and the wartime army, customs, and colonies. Bismarck had ensured above all that Prussia,

* Henry Vizetelly, *Berlin under the New Empire*, vol. 1 (London: Tinsley 1879), pp. 164–65.

William I (reigned as king of Prussia 1861–1888 and as German Emperor, 1871–1888). (German Information Center photo.)

and specifically its king and chancellor, should control the central government. The king of Prussia was the hereditary emperor. In the upper house, or Reichsrat, Prussia had seventeen out of the fifty-eight seats. The lower house, or Reichstag, appeared to be a genuine legislative body, elected by universal manhood suffrage, but it had no power over foreign policy or the military, could not force the resignation of the chancellor, and was limited to its control over the budget. Most power of the state lay in the hands of the imperial chancellor, appointed by the emperor and dismissible only by him, and aided not by a cabinet but by deputies. Bismarck had in fact created a constitutional situation in which he himself seemed indispensable, except for the remote chance of his dismissal on a whim of the emperor.

Yet Bismarck did not intend to run a constitutional absolutism. He wanted to work with the Reichstag, creating in Berlin a genuine give-and-take between the government and the representatives of the people, whatever parliamentary manipulation was necessary to achieve harmony. For the first seven years after unification, he put together a coalition of Liberals and conservative Reich party members who approved of his policy of unifying the country through such measures as introduction of uniform coinage, national law codes, a national bank, and internal free trade. At the same time, he catered to the secularism of the Liberals by beginning a campaign known as the *Kulturkampf* (the culture struggle) to reduce the powers of the Catholic Church in Germany. Bismarck, however, encountered vast opposition from the Catholics of the South and only succeeded in encouraging the growth of the Catholics' political party, the Center party. With his usual realism, he concluded that the forces of separatism among the princes of South Germany were no longer his primary obstacle, but rather the Liberal allies who had encouraged an anti-Catholic policy while obstinately refusing to give the imperial government greater powers of military appropriations. He decided that "honest if clumsy Prussian policemen with spurs and dangling sabers could not catch up with smooth and light-footed priests moving through back doors and bedrooms," and he stopped the campaign against the Church, and struck an alliance with the Center party and Conservatives. From then on, he abandoned liberal economics, ended free trade, and introduced a number of protective measures for both industry and agriculture. But his concept of political stability based on a moderately conservative coalition required that he inoculate the growing working classes against the disruptive Socialist theories being preached to them by the Social Democratic party. Here in fact was the basic class struggle in Berlin itself—a conflict of an alliance of Junkers and middle classes with the workers, which Heinrich Mann epitomized in *Little Superman* when Diederich, the new bourgeois, is overjoyed to see the mounted police charge down the demonstrating workers on Unter den Linden. The imperial answer to discontent, for Bismarck or for the kaiser, is the ultimate reliance on the power of the state.

As Diederich sees the kaiser ride out amid the crowds, Mann describes his reaction:

There on the horse rode Power, through the gateway of triumphal entries, with dazzling features but graven in stone. The Power which is beyond the reach of hunger, spite and mockery! Against it we are impotent for we all love it! We have it in our blood, for in our blood is submission. We are an atom of that Power, a diminutive molecule of something it has given out. Each of us is as nothing, but massed in ranks as neo-Teutons, soldiers, bureaucrats, priests, and scientists, as economic organizations and unions of power, we taper up like a pyramid to the point at the top where Power itself stands, graven and dazzling. In it we live and have our being, merciless towards those who are remote beneath us, and triumphing even when we ourselves are crushed, for thus does power justify our love for it! [5]

Bismarck therefore outlawed the Social Democratic party; but he tried at the same time to win over the workers to his paternalistic state by passing a program of state socialism. Between 1883 and 1889, he gave Germany some of the most advanced welfare legislation in the world, including sickness insurance, accident insurance, old age and disability insurance.

The end result of Bismarck's policies was pernicious for German democracy. The weakness of the Reichstag brought it into disrepute with the people at large, and ensured that few first-rate men would seek election to it, while his own arbitrary control of executive power had a similar effect on the recruitment to the highest ranks of government. The mass of the population felt alienated from the whole process of politics, not least because Prussia itself still retained the old system of voting by class. Bismarck had made Berlin the political capital, but he had so restricted the exercise of political power that large numbers of Germans thought of themselves as unpolitical. "Bismarck has broken the nation's backbone," wrote Theodor Mommsen. "The injury done by the Bismarck era is infinitely greater than its benefits. . . . The subjugation of the German personality, of the German mind, was a misfortune that cannot be undone."

Berlin, Fulcrum of European Diplomacy. After 1871, Bismarck was determined that Berlin should be the arbiter of European diplomacy because only in that way could he safeguard the achievements of his years of war. His principles for running Europe's diplomacy were simple and realistic, based upon *Realpolitik*, or the clearheaded calculation of relative positions of power. Germany, he told Europe's suspicious governments, was a "satiated" power. Its role as the greatest economic and military power on the continent was to dominate the structure of alliances by which the major states sought support for their aims in foreign policy and assured themselves of military backing in the event of war. There were only five powers that Bismarck considered important: Germany,

[5] Heinrich Mann, *Little Superman*, trans. Ernest Boyd (New York: Creative Age, 1945), p. 45.

Russia, Austria-Hungary, France, and Britain. Germany must therefore always be "one of three on the European chessboard"; and it must try, as a subsidiary goal, to prevent the remaining two from allying. One of those two would inevitably be France, which was smarting not only over its defeat but over the annexation of Alsace-Lorraine, which Bismarck was slowly coming to see as a mistake. France must therefore be isolated at all costs.

The most natural alliance appeared to be between the three authoritarian emperors of central and eastern Europe. In 1872, the suspicious tsar intimated to Bismarck that he would like to be invited to Berlin during the state visit of the Emperor Francis Joseph of Austria. The city was thus able to give a first demonstration of its ceremonial function as Europe's new arbiter. The monarchs were feasted in the royal palace, entertained to ballet in the opera house, and given an open-air concept in Unter den Linden, where eleven people were unfortunately trampled to death. But military display predominated, some of it theatrical—the German emperor wore an Austrian uniform with a Russian scarf, and his son a Russian uniform with an Austrian medal—but most of all, it taught the lesson of German might, especially the parade of the regiments that had defeated Austria in 1866. The Three Emperors League was duly concluded the next year as an agreement to put down internal subversion and to consult on problems in Europe. The lack of substance in the agreement was demonstrated, however, when Bismarck erected a big new fortress, Posen, near the Russian border and in 1875 when the tsar returned to Berlin to pressure the German government to drop what he considered were plans for a preventive war against France.

The Congress of Berlin in 1878 was a far more effective demonstration of the new prestige of Germany in international affairs. During the previous year, the Russians had defeated the Turks, ostensibly in support of the independent Slavic states of Serbia and Montenegro and of the Greek Orthodox Bulgars, who were under Turkish oppression. Although the Russians were stopped before they could take Constantinople, which appeared their main goal, they imposed crushing peace terms that forced Turkey to recognize the creation of a large Bulgarian state and to cede other territories to Russia and its allies. To Austria, this settlement imposed a threat to its own ambitions to expand in the Balkans, and to Britain it was a dangerous disturbance of the balance of power. Fearful of the possibility of war between Austria and Russia and convinced, he said, that the Balkans were not worth the bones of a single Pomeranian grenadier, Bismarck invited the powers to meet in Berlin with himself in the position of an "honest broker." For the city of Berlin, the Congress of 1878 had much the same distinction that the Congress of 1815 had for Vienna or the Congress of 1856, which ended the Crimean War, for Paris; it recognized the central position of Germany in the international system. The powers sent their foremost statesmen—England, Prime Minister

Disraeli; Russia, its Chancellor Gorchavov; Austria, the foreign minister, Andrássy; France, its foreign minister, Waddington; and ministers and ambassadors came from Italy, Turkey, and the Balkan states. Bismarck dominated the negotiations, and in many ways dictated the terms of the final settlement. Moody, sick, bloated, he appeared to many a man unnecessarily petulant and outspoken; and except to Disraeli, to whom he unburdened himself about his sovereign, the courtiers, and the socialists, he provoked considerable resentment. With the Russians, this was to be expected, since he compelled them to give up many of their acquisitions and to settle for the creation of a much smaller Bulgarian state. The Austrians were conciliated somewhat with the administration of Bosnia and Herzegovina, which Serbia had hoped to annex. The British were handed Cyprus because it was on the route to the Suez Canal. The French, whom he openly courted at the congress, were encouraged to move into Tunisia, which would bring them into conflict with the Italians and divert them from Europe. Bismarck's extraordinary summation of his own goals, which explains why the Congress of Berlin made little progress toward a lasting peace in the Balkans, was that "it would be a triumph for our statesmanship if we succeeded in keeping the Eastern ulcer open and thus jarred the harmony of the other Great Powers in order to secure our own peace."

From the high point of his diplomatic influence in 1878, Bismarck's strategy went rapidly downhill. Although he continued to seek alliance with the Russians, as in the Reinsurance Treaty of 1887, he had decided to base Germany's security on a secret alliance with Austria, signed in 1879, and on the German army, which was expanded in 1873, 1880, and especially in 1887, when the standing army was increased to almost half a million men. With his policy predicated upon a possible conflict with Russia and a certain confrontation with France, he made a mistake by agreeing in 1883–1885 to go along with the commercial classes' demand for a share of the colonial world. Inevitably this move into Africa and the South Pacific would bring Germany into conflict with Britain, and would determine the German government eventually to challenge Britain on the seas. Thus, the final judgment of these years when Bismarck attempted to shape Europe's diplomatic relationships from Berlin must be that he failed. The structure that he created was too intricate and too self-serving to last, if less astute leaders were called on to handle its excessive ingenuity.

Bismarck had long expected that the son of William I, Crown Prince Frederick, would eventually appoint ministers of a different political caste from himself. But when William I died at the age of ninety-one, in 1888, his son was already struck by cancer, and ruled for only ninety-one days. He was succeeded by his own son, William II, whose grossly inflated sense of his own abilities gave him the courage to dismiss Bismarck in March 1890. That night at dinner, Bismarck declared that William II was "the man who will certainly ruin the Empire."

Under the reign of the kaiser, Berlin showed a divided personality, which was an exaggerated form of the character of the whole of the German Reich. During these years the intellectual and cultural life of the city finally achieved a kinship in quality and inventiveness with that of the other great Western capitals. But at the same time, the government of the Reich remained under the influence of the military, whose massive forces were placed at the disposal of an irresponsible emperor and mediocre politicians. Under Bismarck, there had been little of this schizophrenia. Berlin had remained the somber, hard-working, disciplined city it had been as capital of Prussia; and its imperial dignity had done little to improve the quality of its intellectual life. Under William II, however, the question could be seriously raised: Which was the real Berlin—the Berlin of Einstein and Max Planck, of Gerhart Hauptmann and Stefan George, of Max Reinhardt and Oskar Kokoschka? or the Berlin of Admiral von Tirpitz, Count von Schlieffen, and General von Moltke?

THE SCHIZOID BERLIN OF WILLIAM II

The Berlin of William II

Intellectual Liberation of Berlin. Official Berlin can take no credit for the city's great achievements after 1890. William II himself had strong and decidedly unenlightened views on culture. He regarded himself as the arbiter of taste, as he explained when he dedicated the Hohenzollern statues in the Siegesallee:

To us, the German people, ideals have become permanent possessions, whereas among other peoples they have been more or less lost. Only the German nation is left, and we are called upon to preserve, cultivate and continue these great ideals, and among those ideals is the duty to offer to the toiling classes the possibility of elevating themselves to the beautiful and of raising themselves above their ordinary thoughts. If art, as so frequently happens now, does nothing more than paint misery more ugly than it is, it sins against the German people.[6]

For that reason, when the judges wanted to award Gerhart Hauptmann the Schiller prize for his play *The Sunken Bell,* which unsparingly portrayed the misery of the working class, the kaiser ordered instead that the prize be given to a historical play by a nonentity. For him, historical plays were the great uplifter of the working class, and could "inculcate respect for the highest traditions of the German Fatherland." He felt much the same about sculpture, as the Siegesallee showed. And in art he was an unabashed opponent of every modern tendency. The Academy of Fine Arts was governed for thirty years by Anton von Werner, who painted huge photographic scenes whenever the Hohenzollern family or the German government had done anything it wanted preserved for posterity. The museum entrusted with the patronage of contemporary artists, the National Gallery, was so out of date that the more forward-looking artists seceded in 1898, and formed the *Sezession* group, whose impressionist paintings were labeled by the kaiser as "art from the gutter." The break was thus official; artists and writers who refused the stultifying conservative standards of official art could expect no patronage from the court or the government.

[6] Masur, *Imperial Berlin*, p. 211.

National Gallery, Berlin. Built in 1865–1876 in the form of a Corinthian temple to house the work of contemporary artists, the Gallery suffered from the conservative taste of its directors. (German Information Center photo.)

Richard Wagner (1813–1883). (German Information Center photo.)

Wagner and Strauss. Court interference was least effective in music, because the break with tradition was led by Richard Wagner. Wagner was certainly in harmony with the spirit of the Second Reich in his desire to bring the German people to a new spiritual and cultural rebirth based on a revival of its medieval legends and its folk spirit. But even Wagner also remained the man who had taken part in the 1849 revolution in Dresden, a self-appointed prophet who felt that he had to tear down all conventional society. At the end of his greatest work, *The Ring of the Nibelungen,* he wrote lines, which he never set to music, that expressed his whole philosophy: "Not goods nor gold nor divine splendor; not house nor estate nor lordly pomp; not the treacherous convenant of gloomy treaties nor the hard law of hypocritical custom: blissful in lust and woe, love alone sets you free." The redeeming power of love, that ignored all convention, was to be celebrated again and again in his operas, most notably in *Tristan and*

Isolde; but the anarchism implied was too strange a message for the Hohen-zollern monarchy to accept. In musical style, Wagner was even less conventional. Having written two operas *(Rienzi* and *The Flying Dutchman)* in the grand operatic tradition of Italy, he invented a new art form, the *Gesamtkunstwerk,* which combined music, drama, poetry, and the visual arts into one overpowering experience intended to regenerate its audience. *Tannhaüser* in 1845 and *Lohengrin* in 1848 revived the tales of medieval German grandeur. He then turned to the four operas that were to compose *The Ring* cycle, in which the characters of Germanic folk legend, Wotan, Siegfried, Brünnhilde, and the Walkyrie, became for him strange cosmic creatures protesting against his own age. In *The Ring* the gods have been mastered by chaos itself. "What I deeply loathe I give to thee as my heir, the futile splendor of the Divine: let thine envy greedily gnaw it up," Wotan howls to the Walkyrie. In technique, he explored new harmonies and rhythms refusing to give his gift of melody full play but disciplining it to the demands of his music drama. Only in 1864 did he find the fame and fortune that he considered his due, when the king of Bavaria became his patron, and sponsored the building in Bayreuth of his own opera house, which was to be the shrine of the Wagner cult that soon spread over all Europe except to Berlin. In 1870, Berlin jeered *The Mastersingers;* Bismarck ignored its composer, even though the large pension he was paying the king of Bavaria from his secret state funds made possible that mad king's patronage of Wagner.

Prussian State Opera, Berlin. This late-nineteenth century photograph shows the re-modelled facade of Frederick the Great's Opera House and the sparse traffic on Unter den Linden before the automobile. (German Information Center photo.)

In the 1870s, however, in the battle between the followers of Brahms
and of Wagner that convulsed the Berlin music world, Wagner slowly
triumphed. His acceptance opened the way for Richard Strauss, in spite of
the kaiser's profound disapproval of his musical style and his operatic
plots. As director of the Royal Opera orchestra, Strauss was able to modernize programs, bringing in the music of Mahler and Berlioz; and he was
even able to present his own operas after they had been tried out in the
more liberal atmosphere of Dresden. Even then, he had to make compromises to meet the demands of the kaiser. To produce the sultry, erotic
scenes of *Salome,* with its dance of the seven veils and the final aria of
Salome to the severed head of John the Baptist, he had to permit the star
of Bethlehem to illuminate the night sky as reassurance to the kaiser's wife.
Even then the kaiser was heard to remark after the performance, ''That's
a nice snake I've reared in my bosom.'' And the charming *Rosenkavalier*
had to be modified to make the buffoonery of Baron Ochs acceptable to
the court.

Max Reinhardt and the Free Stage.   In the drama, Berlin was able to surge
ahead more quickly because the kaiser's interference was minimal. The
middle classes, and especially the large Jewish population of Berlin, felt
the need for the presentation of modern drama of the highest quality, and
saw the opportunity in the lightening of the censorship and licensing
laws that followed unification. The result was the Free Stage (*Freie Volks-
bühne*) movement, which built its own theater and presented a new form
of naturalist drama, of which the plays of Gerhart Hauptmann were the
best examples. His play *The Weavers,* with its harsh presentation of conditions of the Silesian poor, brought the Socialist laborers into the theater
audience, and so shocked the kaiser that he had the imperial arms removed
from the theater after it had the effrontery to perform the play. The Free
Stage's forward-looking impetus was further increased by the appointment
of the great young director Max Reinhardt, who gave Berlin the dramatic
version of Wilde's *Salome,* Ibsen's *Ghosts,* and a host of other plays by
such modern dramatists as Wedekind, Gogol, and Schnitzler. Reinhardt
set the fashion, and by 1900 almost thirty theaters had been founded to
meet the Berlin bourgeois' thirst for straight drama. Even before 1914,
Berlin had become one of the most creative theatrical centers of Europe,
to which, after the four-year madness of the World War, Germany's
brightest minds would instinctively gravitate. The Berlin of 1920 characterized by the playwright Carl Zuckmayer is recognizably the same Berlin
as that of the last years of the Second Reich:

*This city devoured talents and human energies with a ravenous appetite, grinding
them small, digesting them or rapidly spitting them out again. It sucked into itself
with hurricane force all the ambitious in Germany, the true and the false, the*

nonentities and the prize winners, and, after it had swallowed them, ignored them. . . .

We called her proud, snobbish, nouveau riche, uncultured, crude. But secretly everyone looked upon her as the goal of their desires. Some saw her as hefty, full-breasted, in lace underwear, others as a mere wisp of a thing, with boyish legs, in black silk stockings. The daring saw both aspects, and her very reputation for cruelty made them the more aggressive. All wanted to have her; she enticed all; and her first reaction was to slam the door in the face of every suitor. . . . [The best minds] encountered her scepticism, her skittishness and disdain; usually they were rudely rejected several times before they could make good their claim to her attentions.

But once they had done so, their triumph might be absolute. To conquer Berlin was to conquer the world.[7]

Expressionism. For poets and painters, the same unexpected attraction was exercised by the imperial city. Their most memorable movement was expressionism, a name applied to those who tried to go beyond the surface explored by the impressionists or naturalists to a deeper, psychological reality. In a sense, such great German poets as Stefan George and Rainer Maria Rilke were part of this movement, but they were only infrequent visitors in Berlin and preferred Paris or Munich. Others stayed, however, finding in the bleakness of the northern city a suitable setting for the anguish with contemporary society that they tried to express. The poem *The War*, for example, written by Georg Heym in 1912, saw in the cities of the West the prowling figure of the coming catastrophe:

Resurrected is he from ancient sleep,
Risen once more from the vaulted deep,
Tall and unknown in the twilight he stands
And he pulps the moon in his two black hands.

For through the cities' evening noises wade
The stranger's dark presence and his frosty shade—
And all the whirling markets stiffen to ice.
All's quiet. Each looks around and no man knows. . . .

A city went under in that yellow smoke
Jumped into the abyss and never spoke . . .
But giant-like above the glowing ruins
He stands who thrice his bright torch turns

Above the ragged clouds' storm-scattered light
Towards the icy wilderness of the night
And sets the darkness blazing like a witch
Above Gomorrah's sea of burning pitch.[8]

[7] Carl Zuckmayer, *A Piece of Myself*, trans. Richard and Clara Winston (New York: Harcourt Brace Jovanovich, 1970), p. 217
[8] Cited in Mander, *Berlin: The Eagle and the Bear*, p. 113.

The painters, too, tried to express the alienation of the artist in the city, seeking new techniques to show the suffering of the city poor, the loneliness of the night streets, and the savagery of the new industrialism. Already by 1914, Berlin was viewing the first works of the leaders of the avantgarde in the interwar years, among others Oskar Kokoschka and Käthe Kollwitz, whose illustrations for *The Weavers* was denied the gold medal awarded it by the jury because her style was so displeasing to the kaiser's court.

University of Berlin. Deeply traditional, hierarchical, and conservative, the University of Berlin nevertheless made a great contribution to Berlin's intellectual life. In physics, in particular, with Planck and Einstein, it could lay claim to leadership of the new research. In economics, it had Werner Sombart, an outspoken critic of modern capitalism whose social conscience had failed to keep up with its productive advances. In philosophy, it had Wilhelm Dilthey, who taught that ideas had to be studied as the expression of a particular historical situation rather than in the abstract. It was however the historians who were most responsible for enshrining the Germanic state as the highest fulfillment that could be achieved by the combined efforts of German individuals, for what has been called Germanophilism. The great historian Leopold von Ranke, professor of European History at Berlin from 1825, had already taught the importance of the state as "a living thing, an individual, a unique self" and politics as "the field of power and of foreign affairs." From here his many disciples at the university had carried the emphasis on state power to imply a justification of the extension of the controls of the Prussian state, and had seen their duty as historians to attempt to influence the political process in that direction. Heinrich von Treitschke's annual course on politics proclaimed the need of the state for increasing its power, if necessary by military victories which were to be construed as moral triumphs. The ultimate expression of this view came during the World War, when Otto von Gierke, one of Berlin's leading legal historians, wrote in *The German Folk Spirit in the War,* "If we achieve our war aims the triumph of our arms will bring about the triumph of the truth. For in world history success utters the decisive word. Even those formerly incapable of being taught this will now realize that success in war is not an accident, but rather the outcome of eternal laws, in which God's rule reveals itself." In this way, the intellectuals gave an ideological justification, which the middle classes and in 1914 even the working classes accepted, for the predominance in the new Germany of the Prussian military tradition and of its upholders, the Junkers.

The Barracks City. Even in the vast new industrialized Berlin the military were ubiquitous. The kaiser set the example, for nothing pleased him more than to wear one of his large collection of uniforms. He appeared at a dinner of the Berlin Motor Club wearing the uniform of a general of engineers, and rumor had it he dressed as an admiral for a performance of *The Flying Dutchman*. But his favorite was a cuirassier's outfit, with polished breastplate and helmet topped with a golden eagle. His language reflected the same preoccupation with military accoutrements and frequently proved a diplomatic embarrassment to his country, as when he spoke of his mailed fist or of himself as a knight in shining armor. But at times his pronouncements had a more sinister ring: "In the present social confusion it may come about that I order you [army recruits] to shoot down your own relatives, brothers or parents, but even then you must follow my orders without a murmur." And again, "The only nations which have progressed and become great have been warring nations. Those which have not been ambitious and gone to war have been nothing." Army officers were compelled to appear always in uniform, except on the rare occasions when they might visit an art exhibit of which the kaiser disapproved. Members of the bourgeoisie were encouraged to don uniforms themselves by the fact that the only way into society was to be an officer of the reserve. The rest of the population was drafted into uniform by the conscription laws. With many exemptions, young men were drafted into the infantry for two years or the artillery for three, and then were kept in the first reserves until the age of 39 and the second reserves until 45, during which time they were hammered into the military mold by career N.C.O.s, known as the *Feldwebel*.

The central role of the army was symbolized by the Watch House on Unter den Linden. A French writer who taught the imperial family described it in 1882 as "the moral and symbolic center of Berlin, as well as its topographic center. Located in the middle of the Avenue of the Linden Trees, between the university and the arsenal, opposite the two palaces and the opera, it is a sort of Roman castrum, a low grey temple with a triangular pediment with bas-reliefs and a portico with six columns." Inside was a permanent guard ready at a moment's notice to rush out to present arms to any carriage of the imperial family, babies included, that might pass by. But the army was everywhere. "Berlin swarms with soldiers," wrote Henry Vizetelly. "Perhaps no other capital in Europe presents such a military aspect. Regiments sallying forth in spick and span brightness, or returning to barracks half-smothered in the dust or bespattered by the mud picked up during the morning's manoeuvres, orderlies mounted or on foot hurrying to and fro between the different ministries and public offices, squads in charge of waggons," all composed the permanent garrison of Berlin. In 1875, Vizetelly listed within the city limits two regiments of Grenadiers of the Guards, the First Foot Guards, the Fusiliers of the Guard, the Riflemen of the Guard, the Pioneers of the Guard, the railroad battalion, the Cuirassiers of the Guard, the First and Second Dragoons of the Guard, the Second Uhlans of the Guard, the Third Squadron of the Garde du Corps, and two regiments of field artillery. Their castellated barracks rose from the flat fields surrounding the city, giving substance to the saying that in

North Germany there were no cathedrals but only barracks and arsenals. But Berlin was also the central training point for the leaders of the German army. The Central Cadet School trained one third of the officers in the Prussian service; specialized training was provided by the United Artillery and Engineer School; advanced scientific education was given to selected officers in the War Academy. But by far the most important of the army's buildings was the Red House, the group of red brick buildings on one side of the Königsplatz occupied since 1871 by the general staff. Behind the stone-dressed walls, with their bellicose decorations of helmets, eagles, and mythological warriors, the strategy of the German army was planned, and the advice, and many critics would say the orders, of the army for the emperor prepared.

The German General Staff. The power of the general staff derived from the German constitution, which gave the Reichstag control only over certain parts of financing and administration and made the army and navy responsible directly to the emperor. William II was available for regular consultation more frequently to his military than his civilian advisors, and the chief of the general staff saw him at least once a week. It was not only the constitutional duty of the military representatives to explain their desired policies directly to the kaiser, but his manner of work and his own need for constant flattery made him receptive to all forms of backstairs influence. There were even times, as in 1888–91 when the chief of the general staff was being groomed as the leader of a coup d'etat to establish full military control of the government. The military were able to force one chancellor, Caprivi, who was a general himself, to resign; and during the chancellorship of Prince Hohenlohe, military intrigues led to the dismissal of a war minister, a foreign minister, and an interior minister. The army had become "a state within the state," and indeed seemed to be carrying on the long tradition summarized by an eighteenth-century historian that Prussia was not "a country that had an army, but an army that had a country which it used as a billeting area." Even Bismarck had had great difficulties with the general staff, as when he attempted to force it to accept his doctrine of the political advantages of limited war; and after 1871 the assumption of the planners in the Red House was still that a short decisive war achieving total victory was the goal of military planning. From 1879, Von Moltke drew up annual plans for a double deployment against France and Russia; and as the French fortification lines along the frontier of Alsace-Lorraine grew stronger, the need to be ready for a decisive blow in the West became the general staff's preoccupation. At times, they discussed the need of preventive war, of an attack on the French before they could gain strength for the war of revenge that the annexation of Alsace-Lorraine had made inevitable, and even of an attack on the Russians.

The general staff itself expanded to meet the demands of its growing duties. From sixty-four officers in 1857 it expanded to two hundred and thirty-nine when Von Moltke resigned in 1888. Its technical facilities multiplied. "In this vast factory," wrote a French observer, "war is prepared just like some chemical product; within these walls all the various directing strings that regulate the German army are made to meet in order to be under the control of one master-hand, so that the troops in fact scarcely march a step, explode a cartridge, or fire a cannon shot without orders from here, while not so much as a military gaiter button can be sewn on anywhere in Europe without a note being taken of it." Three geographical sections of the general staff studied the armies of possible enemies; a subsection studied foreign railroads; trigonometrical and topographical sections prepared perfect maps of areas of possible military operations; there was even a section for military history so that none of the lessons of past wars should be forgotten.

In 1899, Count Alfred von Schlieffen, a meticulous, proud, professional soldier of disastrously limited political vision, became chief of the general staff, and at once began to elaborate plans for the expected two-front war. Germany has the advantage, he wrote, "of lying between France and Russia and separating these allies. . . . Germany must strive, therefore, first, to strike down one of the allies while the other is kept occupied; but then, when the one antagonist is conquered, it must, by exploiting its railroads, bring a superiority of numbers to the other theater of war, which will also destroy the other enemy." To carry through this apparently simple scheme, he became convinced that Germany would have to deal with France first and that this could only be achieved by invading it through neutral Belgium. The plan was complete by 1905. The war, according to Schlieffen, would begin with a two-pronged attack of German forces on France, the right wing that would pass across northern Belgium being seven times stronger than the left wing, which would engage the French in Alsace. In six weeks, in which every day's campaign was carefully orchestrated in advance, the French line would be broken and the major French armies encircled. The decisive victory would be followed by the transfer of the majority of German strength to the Russian front. Schlieffen assumed that the six Belgian divisions would not fight, and that Britain would not enter the war to defend Belgium, dangerous miscalculations due to his lack of interest in political considerations. His successor at the general staff accepted the basic Schlieffen plan, but decided to modify it to strengthen the left flank at the expense of the right, a decision that may have prevented the German army in 1914 from achieving a decisive breakthrough.

By 1905, then, the role of the army in German politics had become a major threat to the peace of Europe. According to Gordon Craig, "Schlieffen and Moltke [his successor] devised, and imposed upon the German army, the most rigid operational plan which had ever been accepted by any modern army, and one, moreover, which had dangerous

Count Alfred von Schlieffen (1833–1913). As head of the General Staff, Schlieffen prepared the plan for a lightning attack on France through neutral Belgium which, with modifications, was used in 1914. (German Information Center photo.)

political implications which were never fully understood by the political leaders of the country or for that matter, by the soldiers themselves."[9]

After the defeat of France, Bismarck's somewhat unrealistic view of the European state system had envisaged Germany as a disinterested power, concentrating on safeguarding what it possessed and in suppressing the tensions provoked by the quarrels of the other, less satisfied powers. The Triple Alliance of Germany, Austria-Hungary, and Italy, cemented in 1882 and backed by the occasional renewals of the platonic friendship with Russia, had been the central strut of his diplomatic structure. But even before Bismarck had been forced from office, his basic assumption that Germany need not be a direct participant in the colonial disputes or in the struggle to profit from the weakness of the Turkish empire had been jettisoned; and after 1890, Germany found itself centrally involved in almost all the major disputes in Europe and beyond. In every international crisis, the swashbuckling oratory of the kaiser was thus able to exacerbate, if not directly to cause, the international tension that came to be known as the "dry war."

Many internal forces were pushing the Berlin government to take a more active role in international affairs. The power of the army to influence

THE KAISER'S EBULLIENT RIDE TO ARMAGEDDON

[9] Gordon Craig, *The Politics of the Prussian Army, 1640–1945* (New York: Oxford University Press, 1964), p. 256.

policy, a direct result of the constitution, had been reinforced by the military predilections of the kaiser himself, while the Reichstag's financial controls were exercised only once every seven years until 1893 and every five years thereafter. From 1898, when the Reichstag passed the first naval bill creating a war fleet, a new pressure group was created in Berlin. Under Navy Secretary Alfred von Tirpitz, the Ministry of the Navy, backed by such groups as the Navy League and the Pan-German League, began to press for a more active role overseas. They found considerable public backing, especially as the middle classes considered the navy more democratic than the army; and this enthusiasm was fanned by an adroit program of public relations, in which Von Tirpitz sponsored lectures, organized public tours of the new ships, sent free pamphlets into the schools, and even paid for suitable novels about the navy. The program created prosperity for the shipbuilders of the great port cities like Hamburg and Bremen, and was welcomed by the shipyard workers. In the kaiser it had its greatest supporter. "Our future lies on the water," he declared. The program was of course a direct challenge to Great Britain—the second navy bill of 1900 envisaged a fleet of thirty-eight battleships, which according to Von Tirpitz's "risk theory" would be large enough to inflict such serious damage on the superior British fleet that it would never be attacked.

This fleet also seemed a necessary adjunct to the great merchant marine that was being constructed to enable Germany to find the export markets needed for its vast new industries. Between 1887 and 1912, German exports had risen 185 percent, German imports by 243 percent. Here was an unfavorable trade balance that had to be rectified. The great German banks and the new trusts were also vitally interested in expanding their opportunities overseas, and in the developing regions of Europe. Subsidiaries of the central banks were springing up in Rumania, Brazil, and German East Africa; railroads, mines, and oil-drilling throughout the world from China to Venezuela were financed by them; the trusts were purchasing ever larger supplies of raw materials from outside Europe. These economic forces formed a further pressure group in Berlin that sought more effective governmental foreign involvement. They were effectively organized for applying pressure in Berlin through such groups as the General Federation of German Industrialists and the Union of German Mining and Ironworks Owners; and many of their leaders were friendly with the kaiser himself. The close fusion of the aims of industrialists and politicians was achieved in the years after 1900. The construction of the Berlin-to-Baghdad railroad, begun under the sponsorship of the Deutsche Bank in 1899 and supported with great enthusiasm by the kaiser, led even more directly to tension with Britain and Russia, when the Germans used it to exercise strong political controls over the Turkish empire.

The drive for colonies was even more effective in isolating Germany. Germany had seized parts of East and Southwest Africa in the 1880s. In the 1890s it had turned to the South Pacific, with the acquisition of some

Samoan islands, and had even attempted to establish a base in the Philippines. When the Germans finally took a Chinese port for themselves in 1897, the kaiser enlivened the occasion with one of his most blustering speeches, since the Yellow Peril to Europe was one of his constant fears. "Thousands of German Christians will breathe again when they see the ships of the German navy in their vicinity," he said, "hundreds of German merchants will shout with joy in the knowledge that the German Empire has at long last set foot firmly in Asia, hundreds of thousands of Chinese will shiver if they feel the iron fist of the German Empire lying firmly on their back."

There was thus in existence in Berlin a tacit coalition of the kaiser, army and navy officials, great businessmen and banks, which was to a large extent supported by the middle classes and even some sections of the working class, which felt that Germany's material interests were involved in a successful resolution of almost all the important international crises. This did not imply that Germany plotted the First World War, or was solely responsible for its outbreak; but it did imply that Germany would not exercise a restraining influence when crises broke out.

International Crises and the Alliance Structures. The main breakdown in Bismarck's planning was the conclusion of the Franco-Soviet alliance in 1894. Although the kaiser had refused to renew the Reinsurance Treaty with Russia in 1890, he had warned his cousin Nicholas II of Russia of the dangers of allying with France: "Take my word for it, Nicky . . . the curse of God lies heavy on that nation. Heaven has imposed a sacred duty . . . on us Christian kings and emperors—to uphold the divine right of kings." Russia, however, was increasingly convinced that the French alliance must be the mainspring of its policy, as German provocation against it mounted, with tariffs on Russian wheat and German penetration in China, and especially with German opposition to its plans in the Balkans. Russia joined with France in a military convention by which they agreed to come to each other's aid if attacked by Germany, and to begin coordinated military planning for the coming war. Germany's naval expansion persuaded the British to seek a French alliance as well, which took the form of a loose agreement known as an Entente Cordiale. In 1907, the British swallowed their distaste of Russian autocracy, and signed a similar agreement with the Russians. There were thus in existence two alliance systems, of which the German seemed by far the weaker—Italy had made it clear it would not fight against France; and the Austro-Hungarian empire, if reliable as an ally, was more likely to be a source of provocation than an element in keeping the peace. But the strength of the German army and economy seemed to the German government to outweigh these weaknesses; and in fact most statesmen in Europe concluded that they had created a genuine balance of power that would be a guarantee of the peace on which continuance of the existing social structure depended. "Nations and Empires crowned with princes and potentates rose majestically on every side," wrote Winston Churchill, "lapped in the accumulated treasures of the long peace. All were fitted and fasted, it seemed securely, into an immense cantilever. The two mighty European systems faced each other glittering and clanking in their panoply, but with a tranquil gaze. A polite, discreet, pacific, and on the whole sincere diplomacy spread its web of connections over both. A sentence in a dispatch, an observation by an ambassador, a cryptic phrase in a parliament seemed sufficient to adjust from day to day the balance of the prodigious structure." [10] The balance made every crisis seem manageable, and thereby in itself contributed to the coming of war.

Crises in Morocco and the Balkans. The system was tested in two important areas. The French, having followed Bismarck's invitation by moving eastwards from Algeria into Tunisia, had begun in the 1900s to look westwards as well, into Morocco. The British had agreed to give them a free hand; but in 1905, the kaiser landed in Tangier and emphasized that he recognized the Sultan as an "independent ruler," while the German government demanded that the French give up their plans on Morocco. German intervention forced the calling of an international conference at Algeciras in 1906, in which the Germans were supported only by Austria-Hungary and Morocco; and the French were given permission to take over the Moroccan police and to run its state bank, measures that were obviously the preliminary to its becoming a French protectorate. The crisis had strengthened the Franco-British alliance without any corresponding gain to Germany. In 1911, the Germans precipitated a new crisis by sending their gunboat *Panther* to the Atlantic port of Agadir in protest against the French occupation of the Moroccan capital city of Fez. They were finally fobbed off with some small pieces of the Congo, and Morocco became a French protectorate. Throughout the crisis, however, the diplomats had been appalled that they all seemed to be threatening to wage a war that none of them wanted. To avoid such a situation again, all powers determined on greater armaments and on closer military coordination with their allies.

Meanwhile in the Balkans, Austria and Russia were moving closer to conflict. Since the Congress of Berlin in 1878, the Bulgarians had looked to the Russians to help them complete their national independence from the Turks; and the Serbs hoped for Russian aid in gaining control of Bosnia-Herzegovina, which the Austrians had just brought under their administration. Austria, on the other hand, feared all nationalist movements in that region, in part because it saw the area as the only region open to its territorial expansion but principally because it was afraid that the success

[10] Winston S. Churchill, *The World Crisis* (New York: Scribners, 1924), p. 199.

of the South Slavs in creating a large nation-state under Serbia would simply encourage the subject nationalities within the Austrian empire to seek independence. Not only would Bosnia-Herzegovina and Slovenia join a South Slav state, but the Poles would seek the re-creation of Poland, and the Czechs, Moravians, and Ruthenians would seek one or more independent states; and the whole fragile structure of the Austro-Hungarian empire would fall apart. Both Russia and Austria felt it essential to act quickly, since in 1908 a Young Turk revolution threatened them with the modernization and the reassertion of Turkish power. That year, the Russian foreign minister agreed to allow Austria to annex Bosnia-Herzegovina permanently in return for his agreement to Russian naval use of the straits through Turkey from the Black Sea to the Mediterranean. Austria annexed the provinces without warning, and the ensuing international protests were so great that the Russian foreign minister denied his agreement and forgot his demand for passage through the straits. The Serbs appealed to the Russians for help in an immediate war against Austria, but were told to bide their time: "Your day of joy will come." But perhaps the deciding factor in the crisis had been the German decision to back up Austria, regardless of international opinion. The chancellor had even gone to the extent of dispatching an ultimatum to Russia demanding that it accept the annexation, which merely confirmed the general impression in Europe that Germany was seeking hegemony on the continent.

In 1912, a new Balkan crisis erupted when Serbia, Montenegro, Bulgaria, and Greece suddenly attacked Turkey in order to seize most of its remaining possessions in Europe, and they were so successful that they had to be stopped from capturing Constantinople by intervention of the major powers. The victors then quarreled over the disposition of the spoils, and the greatest gainer, Bulgaria, was attacked in a second Balkan war by Serbia, Greece, Rumania, and Turkey. In August 1913, after Bulgaria had been thoroughly defeated, Serbia and Greece split Macedonia between them; Rumania expanded southwards down the Black Sea coast; Albania was recognized as an independent state. The Balkan wars had caused further tension between Russia and Austria. The Germans had, however, persuaded Austria not to come to the aid of Bulgaria, while the English had pressed the Russians not to allow the Serbians to become too ambitious. But such restraint was achieved only with great difficulty, and from 1912 all the statesmen of the great powers became infected with a sense of the inevitability of war among them in the near future. The kaiser was particularly gloomy about "the fight to the finish between the Slavs and the Germans," since the Gauls and the Anglo-Saxons would aid the Slavs. Foreboding over the possibility of war compelled the very powers that had urged restraint on their allies to make greater protestations of support lest the long-standing alliances fall apart on the very edge of the catastrophe. Thus, when the final crisis was precipitated in June 1914 by the murder of the heir to the Austrian throne at Serajevo in Bosnia by a terrorist trained in Serbia, the diplomats were more anxious to reassure their allies than to end the tension with their enemies.

The Serajevo Crisis.   The murder provided an excuse for Austria to begin the preventive war it had long desired against Serbia, because it suspected, correctly as it turned out, that the murder had been planned at high levels of the Serbian government for fear the reformer Franz Ferdinand would win the loyalty of the South Slavs inside the Austrian empire.   The military gained the upper hand in Vienna, and persuaded the government to issue so strong an ultimatum to the Serbian government that it could not accept it without losing its independence.   When the ultimatum was rejected, the Austrian army bombarded Belgrade, secure in the knowledge that the kaiser, with his chancellor's acquiescence, had agreed that war with Serbia was inevitable and had promised German aid if Russia came to Serbia's aid.

During the next critical days, war between the great powers became inevitable because none of the governments, neither the emperors nor the civilians, dared refuse the mobilization orders that their military staffs demanded.   The Russian government ordered general mobilization on July 30, 1914, which in German eyes was tantamount to a declaration of war.   The German government demanded that the Russians cancel their mobilization, and when no reply came declared war on Russia on August 1. They also sent an ultimatum to France, demanding that France guarantee its neutrality in the coming fighting by handing over several border fortresses to Germany, which was refused.   It was a greater surprise when the Belgian government refused to give German troops permission to pass across its territory.   Nevertheless, on August 3 Germany declared war against France, and invaded Belgium according to the split-second timing of the Schlieffen plan.   The British, who had been hesitating, found the violation of Belgian neutrality sufficient reason for declaring war on Germany.

Thus Germany found itself involved in a war for which it would, when defeated, be held principally responsible by its victors.   The debate over German responsibility has exercised historians since 1914; but several factors stand out.   The international system, based on the maintenance of a balance of power among competing alliance systems, was far less stable than its creators believed.   One reason for the instability was the misunderstanding of the nature of modern war, when armies are supplied and transported by the products of industrialism; few statesmen or military planners conceived of a war lasting more than a few months.   Hence all military planning assumed the need of short, strictly organized schedules of attack; and even those who followed Norman Angell's argument in *The Great Illusion* (1909), that modern war would destroy the societies that waged it, felt that this was an additional reason why war would have to be short. There were even some leaders found to argue that war was a social good, reviving the creative spirits of jaundiced nations, as well as a necessary instrument in the struggle for existence among nations, which was the international equivalent of the Darwinian conception of evolution. Some statesmen, especially in England, may have lost control of events; but the most recent evidence seems to show that by 1914 most civilian states-men had come to agree with their military leaders that their goals could only be achieved by war. In this respect, the blame for the war can be dis-tributed fairly impartially among all the belligerents.

It is perhaps for this reason that Berlin experienced a sense of relief on July 31, when the kaiser declared from the palace balcony that "the sword has been forced into our hand." The mobilization order the next day filled Unter den Linden with cheering crowds and officers standing erect in their cars waving their handkerchiefs. The crowds sang "Now Thank We All Our God" in the Palace Square, and roared for the kaiser, who told them, "I know no parties any more. Only Germans." The Social Democrats, every one of whom the kaiser had once declared to be "an enemy of the Empire and Fatherland," reciprocated by voting the war credits. Like clockwork, the men of military age in Berlin reported to their units, were issued uniforms and weapons, and within hours were sitting in railroad wagons moving westwards. In the general staff building, the oiled machine hummed effectively, even though its chief, Von Moltke, had been in tears briefly when the kaiser had cheerfully told him to abandon the attack on France and transfer the troops against Russia instead, only to rescind the order shortly after. The kaiser himself, however, was far from optimistic. White, haggard, and exhausted, he saw that the encirclement of Germany had been achieved. "The world will be involved in the most terrible of wars," he lamented, "the ultimate aim of which is the ruin of Germany." Two weeks later, he left Berlin for the Army headquarters at Koblenz, to await the results of the Schlieffen plan. "The Kaiser is never going to ride on a white horse with his paladins through the Branden-burg Gate as conqueror of the world," the financier Walter Rathenau re-marked. "On the day he did so, history would have lost its meaning."

Failure of the Schlieffen Plan. In just over a month of fighting, two deeply disturbing features of the war were evident even to the generals who had unleashed the first campaigns: a quick victory was impossible, and the human and material losses incurred as a result of the industrializa-tion of war preparation were on a scale never before seen. The Schlieffen plan had at first seemed to go according to schedule. Although the Bel-gians had declared war rather than allow the Germans passage across their borders, their great fortresses had not proved a big obstacle. The right wing had swung along the Channel coast to enter France on August 27, and at one time were within forty miles of Paris. But the British had supplied an unexpectedly large expeditionary force, which helped strengthen the French center; the Russians penetrated into East Prussia and thus compelled

THE FIRST WORLD WAR

German Advance–Aug./Sept., 1914   German Front–December 1914
Furthest German Advance, 1914   Furthest German Advance, 1918

The Western Front
1914–1918
0   50 Miles

the Germans to detach part of their forces from the western to the eastern front; and the poor leadership of Von Moltke had allowed his two armies on the Belgian front to lose contact. The French commander Joffre seized his opportunity to counterattack, and threw in his reserve against the dangerously extended German line to the east of Paris. In the first Battle of the Marne, the Germans were forced to retreat to the line of the river Aisne, where they were able to establish a strong defense line. By November, when the winter rains began and operations literally bogged down, the war of rapid movement originally planned by the generals had turned into a slogging match between entrenched armies, disposed in double lines of ditches behind barbed wire barriers along a front that stretched all the way from the Channel coast to Switzerland. These lines were to move only a few miles for the next four years.

This stalemate was the result of enormous losses on both sides. The British lost half of their professional soldiers in the defense of one city, Ypres. In only four days of fighting in the Battle of the Frontiers, the French army had suffered 140,000 casualties; in the first sixteen months, over 600,000 of their soldiers had been killed. German losses were on a similar scale, as army commanders threw in troops in senseless bayonet charges. At the fort of Liège, a Belgian officer related, the Germans "made no attempt at deploying but came on line after line, almost shoulder to shoulder, until as we shot them down, the fallen were heaped on top of each other in an awful barricade of dead and wounded that threatened to mask our guns." By the end of the Battle of the Marne, German casualties were 650,000. It was, however, in the trenches that the full horror of the war became evident. The lines became steadily more elaborate, stretching miles back to the rear with communication trenches, dugouts, command posts, fortified bastions, machine-gun nests, and camouflaged artillery. Normal military activity consisted of exchange of rifle fire or throwing of grenades, accompanied by planned artillery barrages. But at frequent intervals the army commanders mounted massive assaults intended to drive back the enemy over a long salient, or less frequently, to establish a breakthrough in his line that would enable him to be attacked from the rear. Such attacks began with a long artillery barrage intended to blow away the enemy's barbed wire, flatten his front trenches, and destroy his morale. Then, at first light of dawn, the attacking army, usually carrying heavy packs and fixed bayonets, would go "over the top" in long lines that walked slowly, in rapidly diminishing numbers, toward the enemy's trenches. Occasionally, poison gas would be hurled ahead of them, but

Western Front, France. As the First World War dragged on, the topsoil of battlefields in France was pulverized by artillery barrages; and soldiers often drowned in the shell-holes. (French Embassy Press and Information Division photo.)

it would often blow back into their own faces. No more vicious or militarily ineffective method of slaughter could have been imagined. Throughout 1915, the French mounted a "war of attrition," a series of attacks at different points of the German line that achieved nothing except punishing losses for both sides. In 1916, the Germans attempted to break the French line by capturing the pivotal fortress of Verdun; although they failed to capture it, they lost 336,000 men in the attempt. To the suffering of the fighting, the weather added a new element. As the bombardments destroyed the foliage and even the topsoil along the four-hundred-mile front, the rains turned the land surface into a kind of moonscape of muddy pools, from which bodies protruded and in which men drowned. Disease was spread among the troops by rats and polluted food and drink. "We are not in fact leading the life of men at all," wrote one young soldier, "but that of animals living in holes in the ground and only showing our heads outside to fight and to feed."

The War in the East. The front in the East was more mobile, but the sufferings were no less great. The kaiser had been appalled in 1914 when the Russian army had penetrated his "lovely Masurian lakes" in East Prussia, but a new team of generals, Hindenburg and Ludendorff, had driven the invaders back at the Battle of Tannenberg. The German armies

Field Marshal Paul von Hindenburg (1847–1934). Hindenburg was made chief of the General Staff in 1916, and given supreme command of the forces of Germany and its allies. (German Information Center photo.)

had then been able to relieve the Austrians at the southern end of the line by attacking in central Poland, and by the end of 1914 the front had been briefly stabilized on a long curving line from East Prussia to Lodz in central Poland and on to the Carpathian Mountains and the Black Sea. The next year, however, the Germans took command of the whole front, and mixing their divisions with Austria's far less reliable troops, hit the Russians in Galicia in May at a time when they were disorganized, hungry, and badly armed. Russian casualties by September, when the Russian army had been pushed back almost 200 miles into Russia itself, were a million. Nevertheless, in 1916, even though the attempt by the British to seize the Dardanelles and Constantinople to open a direct route to Russia had failed, the Russians put together another vast army, with which they recouped many of their territorial losses. But cost in lives and materiel of the 1916 campaign brought Russia to revolution the following March; and although Russia did not officially stop fighting until the Bolshevik revolution in November, its contribution to the Western allies during 1917 was not great. In March 1918, with the conclusion of the Treaty of Brest Litovsk with the new Bolshevik government of Russia, the Germans appeared to have won an enormous triumph, by forcing Russia to give up Poland, the Baltic states, Finland, the Ukraine, all of which became German satellite states.

The Broadening of the War. The original combatants continually pressured other powers to join the war, as new means of breaking the balance of strength between them. Japan entered the war against Germany in 1914, simply to seize the German possessions in China and the Pacific. Turkey had entered the war on Germany's side at the end of 1914, as a consequence of the great economic influence Germany had come to exercise there before the war. Italy, which had denied that the Austrian attack on Serbia compelled it to enter the war under the obligations of the Triple Alliance, had succumbed to secret British offers of territorial compensation from Austria; in 1915, it entered the war on the side of the Entente, only to suffer dreadful losses in battles in the snows of the Italian Alps. The Bulgarians joined Germany and Austria in September 1915, to take a share in the disintegration of Serbia. The Rumanians joined the Entente in 1916 in the hopes of taking part of Hungary. But the most important new belligerent was the United States, which declared war on Germany in April 1917 after the Germans began unlimited submarine warfare against neutral ships entering the war zone around Britain. American supplies, and in 1918 American manpower, were to be the decisive factors in blunting the last German offensives in the West.

The Last Campaigns. During the last months of the war in 1918, the stalemate in the West was broken, and a war of movement again became possible. The introduction of the tank by the British finally rendered the

Soldiers of the U.S. 132nd Infantry at Forges, France, in 1918. Although the American army fought for less than a year, it lost 106,000 men. (U.S. Signal Corps.)

trench lines penetrable. The use of the airplane not only made small-scale bombing possible but gave far more accurate reconnaissance information. Shock troops employed by the German high command were often able to break through the Western lines, and cause havoc in selected areas in the rear. But the chief factor was Ludendorff's decision in the spring of 1918 to throw all Germany's remaining strength into one big effort to defeat France. For four months, from March to June 1918, Ludendorff struck without respite at different sections of the front, but one by one the blows were parried—by the French, the British, and the Americans. When in June the Germans tried once again to march down the Marne to Paris, they were thrown back; and all their fronts began to collapse at once, in Bulgaria, Turkey, Serbia, Italy, and along the whole Western front. In October, Ludendorff informed the kaiser that the war was lost, and that an armistice should be sought immediately. One was signed on November 11, but not by the kaiser, who had been compelled to abdicate two days earlier.

Berlin had seen little of the kaiser during the years of war, since he had preferred to wander by royal train from one headquarters to another, rarely consulted by the military and largely protected from the realities of the front. Propaganda pictures of him were taken from time to time in a specially constructed trench in the park of his requisitioned villa at Spa; and he showed his continuing taste for bellicose rhetoric with such recommendations as "Take no prisoners" and "We know our goals, our rifles cocked and traitors to the wall." But he had become increasingly an unreal figure to Berliners, who were concerned with staying alive through the years of universal shortage. In spite of fine organization of supplies, through a special war raw materials department, a central purchasing company, and an imperial grain office, supplies for the home front gradually dwindled. Such products as tea, coffee, or sugar, slowly vanished. Ersatz, or substitute, supplies were made with great ingenuity—sausages from nuts, coffee from barley, soap from sand. In the harsh Turnip Winter of 1916, even potatoes were hard to obtain, and many people had to live on turnips. Clothes had to be constantly repaired, because wool and cotton were unobtainable. From 1916, morale began to break, as the reports of the suffering at the front, of the apparently endless fighting, and of the incredible losses, became widely known. The reaction of the conservative groups, both military and business, was to demand national unity, which in fact became a method of avoiding democratization of power. In the Reichstag, however, a majority was formed that pressed for a constitutional change to make the government responsible to the elected representatives of the people. In 1917, in the famous Peace Resolution, they demanded peace without annexations. Although the resolution was ignored, for the first time a coalition of moderate right-wing groups, of the Catholic Center, and of the Social Democratic party had been formed that in November 1918 was able to take over power when the kaiser was ousted.

Friedrich Ebert (1871–1925). A trade union leader and Social Democratic deputy, Ebert became first President of the Weimar Republic in 1919. (German Information Center photo.)

In late October 1918, spontaneous uprisings began in the German navy and in the seaport towns. Revolutionary committees of soldiers and workers were formed in towns like Kiel and Wilhelmshaven. In November, Munich was seized by left-wing revolutionaries, and Bavaria declared a separate republic. Within two weeks, every one of the minor princes of Germany had been driven from his throne; and mobs of workers and soldiers began to fill the streets of Berlin itself. Officers were occasionally assaulted, and their epaulets removed. Red flags appeared on some buildings. But the abdication of the kaiser removed the principal source of grievances of most of the workers, and the proclamation of a German republic under Social Democratic Chancellor Ebert promised a new beginning. When a Communist revolt did break out in Berlin in January 1919, it was suppressed with considerable bloodshed by a Social Democratic minister of the interior.

It was thus an ironic epilogue to the days of imperial Berlin that it was not the kaiser but a Socialist who welcomed the return of the Berlin divisions on December 11 as they marched through the Brandenburg Gate to become a guarantee against social revolution. "I salute you," Chancellor Ebert shouted to the defeated army, "who return unvanquished from the field of battle." It was a remark worthy of the kaiser himself.

SUGGESTED READING

Berlin is a city about which it is hard to be nostalgic, especially as so many of the imperial buildings were destroyed in the Second World War. But Gerhard Masur has painstakingly assembled the most salient information on the city's life under Bismarck and William II, in *Imperial Berlin* (1970), while John Mander, *Berlin: The Eagle and the Bear* (1959) evokes the literary and artistic background. Observant visitors from abroad do much to give a feeling for Berlin society, especially the thorough, whimsical, and informative volumes of Henry Vizetelly, *Berlin under the New Empire: Its Institutions, Inhabitants, Industry, Monuments, Museums, Social Life, Manners, and Amusements* (1879). Poulteney Bigelow, an American who lived much of his life in Prussia, has left *Prussian Memories, 1864–1914* (1915), and J. F. Dickie, pastor of the American Church, paints a sympathetic picture of the kaiser in *In the Kaiser's Capital* (1912). For daily life, especially of the army, see Pierre Bertaux, *La Vie quotidienne en Allemagne au temps de Guillaume II en 1900* (1962). The musical life of the capital, seen through the career of Richard Strauss, is sardonically described by Barbara Tuchman, in *The Proud Tower* (1962). Good novels that illustrate the life of Berlin include Theodor Fontane, *Effi Briest*, and Heinrich Mann, *Little Superman*. For memoirs of writers who spent part of their lives in Berlin, see Carl Zuckmayer, *A Part of Myself* (1970), and Stefan Zweig, *The World of Yesterday* (1943).

On the unification of Germany, the most reliable studies are Otto Pflanze, *Bismarck and the Development of Germany: The Period of Unification, 1815–*

1871 (1963); C. W. Clark, *Franz Josef and Bismarck: The Diplomacy of Austria before the War of 1866* (1934); Eugene N. Anderson, *The Social and Political Conflict in Prussia, 1858–1864* (1954); and Erich Eyck, *Bismarck and the German Empire* (1958). Bismarck tells his own story, with considerable reliance on hindsight, in *Bismarck, the Man and Statesman* (1899), while Louis L. Snyder, *The Blood and Iron Chancellor: A Documentary-Biography of Otto von Bismarck* (1967) relies mostly on excerpts from primary accounts to create a biography. Finally, Werner Richter, *Bismarck* (1965) makes entertaining reading. J. Alden Nichols, *Germany after Bismarck: The Caprivi Era, 1890-1894* (1958) shows the political struggles that followed the dismissal of Bismarck.

The best biography of William II is Michael Balfour's *The Kaiser and His Times* (1964). Virginia Cowles, *The Kaiser* (1963) concentrates largely on the man himself, thus permitting many of the kaiser's outbursts to be compared with his later version of the events in *The Kaiser's Memoirs* (1922). The kaiser is placed in the gallery of doomed monarchs in Edmond Taylor's well-documented *The Fall of the Dynasties: The Collapse of the Old Order, 1905–1922* (1963).

The role of the army in German politics is thoroughly elucidated in Gordon A. Craig, *The Politics of the Prussian Army, 1640–1945* (1964) and Walter Goerlitz, *History of the German General Staff, 1657–1945* (1953), while Hans Kohn, *The Mind of Germany: The Education of a Nation* (1958) demonstrates the power of Germanophilism as a support for militarism. The nationalism that arose from cultural crisis is studied by Fritz Stern, *The Politics of Cultural Despair: A Study in the Rise of the Germanic Ideology* (1965).

The causes of World War I have been the subject of continual debates since 1914. A very full account of the principal events is given by Luigi Albertini, *The Origins of the War of 1914* (1952–1957), but Lawrence Lafore, *The Long Fuse: An Interpretation of the Origins of World War I* (1965) is more sparkling. The whole controversy over Germany's expansionist aims was reopened by Fritz Fischer, with *Germany's Aims in the First World War* (1967), which painstakingly shows that civilian as well as military leaders were obsessed with turning the war to the profit of Germany. The influence of the war on German society is discussed by Gerald D. Feldman, *Army Industry and Labor in Germany, 1914–1918* (1966), the front line graphically reconstructed by Barbara Tuchman, *The Guns of August* (1962), and Alistair Horne, *The Price of Glory: Verdun, 1916* (1963). Erich Maria Remarque's best novel, *All Quiet on the Western Front* (1970), first published in 1928, gains its authenticity from the author's own experiences, but one should contrast it with Ernst Jünger, *Storm of Steel* (1929) to understand the attraction some found in trench life.

23

THE MOSCOW
OF LENIN AND STALIN

On the night of March 9-10, 1918, Vladimir Ilyich Lenin, the chairman of the Council of People's Commissars, which had governed Russia since the successful Communist seizure of power the previous November, reversed Peter the Great's momentous decision to move the capital of Russia from Moscow to his new city of Saint Petersburg. Traveling secretly by train in fear of assassination attempts by political enemies from the Socialist Revolutionary party, the whole government was transferred back from the western outpost on the Neva to the heart of old Muscovy. Within a few weeks, Lenin and his ministers were established in cramped, uncomfortable quarters in the old Court of Chancery building in the Kremlin, where in symbolic austerity they planned the strategy of victory in the civil war then raging and the simultaneous transformation of Russian society.

There were many reasons for the move back to Moscow. Saint Petersburg was vulnerable to attack from Finland and Estonia. The Communist leaders needed a central position from which to organize the defense of the territory they controlled against the White, or counterrevolutionary, forces. But Lenin was also aware that Moscow, for the great majority of Russians, had never ceased to be the true capital of a unified country. Saint Petersburg had represented the alien, Westernized veneer that differentiated the possessing classes from the masses. "We are good revolutionists," Lenin told them, "but I don't know why we should feel obligated to prove that we also stand on the heights of foreign culture."[1] The buildings of Moscow, and especially of the Kremlin, represented an older, truer Russia, "white and shining little mother Moscow"; and it was essential that Moscow should take the lead, and be the finest example, of the revo-

[1] Davis Shub, *Lenin* (Baltimore: Penguin, 1967), p. 377.

Lenin in Red Square, Moscow. Lenin transferred the newly-formed Communist government from Petrograd to the Moscow Kremlin in March 1918. (Tass from Sovfoto.)

lutionary change in Russian society that the new leaders were determined to bring about.

In the brief isolation of his first-class compartment on the train journey to Moscow, Lenin wrote an essay, *The Principal Tasks of Our Time*, summarizing his views of the importance for humanity of the events of the previous weeks and of the changes he was about to introduce:

In our day the history of humanity has reached one of those immensely great and difficult turning points, of vast—and one may add without the least exaggeration of world-liberating—significance. . . . It has been given to Russia to have observed with clarity, and with extraordinary sharpness and anguish to have lived through, one of the most sudden turns of history, the turn which leads away from imperialism to the communist revolution. In a few days we utterly destroyed one of the most ancient, powerful, barbaric, and ferocious monarchies. . . . From one end of our immense country to the other we have seen the victorious and triumphal march of Bolshevism. We have raised up the lowest strata of the toiling masses, who were oppressed by Tsarism and the bourgeoisie to freedom and independence. We have inaugurated and strengthened the Soviet Republic, a new kind of stage, immeasurably superior and more democratic than the best of the bourgeois parliamentary republics. [2]

The fascination of Moscow's history during the twentieth century is thus not merely to see the rise of another world city, struggling with the problems of industrialism, mushroom growth, and technological change, but rather to see the experience of a great, old city, steeped in a traditional culture, meeting the demands of a political and social experiment of unparalleled intensity. To study Moscow is to observe the Communist revolution at once from above and from below.

FROM THE COMMUNIST MANIFESTO TO THE NOVEMBER REVOLUTION

After the failure of the 1848 revolutions, socialism made only small numbers of converts for the next three decades. Marx himself retired to the reading room of the British Museum, where he concentrated on the great theoretical exposition of his views in *Capital,* the first volume of which appeared in 1867, and on a number of analyses of the revolutionary struggles he had witnessed in France. He helped set up the first International Workingmen's Association, or First International, in London in 1864, whose purpose was to spread socialist ideas among workers' organizations throughout the world; but after quarreling bitterly with Michael Bakunin (1814–1876), whose anarchist followers believed that the state should be replaced in a violent upheaval by associations of producers, Marx allowed the International to die peacefully in New York in 1876. Anarchism never became a serious rival to Marxism, in spite of the magnetic personality of Bakunin himself. It did find followers in the less developed countries of Europe and a few individual terrorists in the developed. Assassinations of leading statesmen that were supposed to be the prelude to the abolition of the state

[2] Robert Payne, *The Life and Death of Lenin* (New York: Simon and Schuster, 1964), pp. 456–57.

machinery became common toward the end of the century—the murders carried out by anarchists included those of the president of France in 1894, the prime minister of Spain in 1897, the empress of Austria in 1898, the king of Italy in 1900, the president of the United States in 1901, and another prime minister of Spain in 1912. But while anarchism appealed to peasants in Spain and Italy who wanted to seize the estates of the aristocracy and at times to Spanish and French industrial workers who felt denied their rights to organize, it never became a serious alternative.

Gradualist Socialism.   Marx's views were, however, being challenged far more seriously by moderate leaders who sought to ameliorate the condition of the working classes without destroying the capitalist system by violence. The most innocuous and most immediately effective plans for worker action were laid by the cooperative movements. In England and at the end of the century in Germany, consumers joined to run their own retail stores, on the pattern of the shop opened by workers in Rochdale in northern England in 1844. In France and later in Scandinavia, agricultural producers and some artisans formed producers' cooperatives to cut out the middleman in bringing their products to market. Trade unions, however, proved far more effective than cooperatives in changing working conditions. After 1886, the unions began to give up their emphasis on self-help through accident and sickness insurance programs, and to take strike action against their employers on a large scale. Long bitter strikes were carried out by such groups as the London match girls and dockworkers, the Belgian glass workers, and the French forestry employees; and at the end of the century it looked for a short time as though the French trade union movement would attempt to seize power through a general strike, as advocated by the "syndicalist" writer, Georges Sorel. Most labor unions, however, were satisfied to concentrate on the improvement of the salaries and working conditions of their members, and they were so successful in this goal that they soon developed a large dues-paying membership and a professional body of bureaucratic organizers. In Germany, by 1914 there were four million trade union members; in France, one million; in Britain, about two million.

Only rarely did the trade unions move directly into politics, as when the British Trade Unions Congress helped found the Labour Representation Committee in 1906. Most unions concentrated on improvement of material conditions within the capitalist system, and ignored both the political parties that wanted gradual change in the economic system and those that wanted its revolutionary overthrow. It thus fell to political organizers, who were frequently disaffected members of the middle class rather than workers themselves, to spread the socialist doctrine that the worker should not merely gain a greater share of the produce of his society but ought eventually to gain control of the means of production. Most socialist leaders confessed to adhere to the teachings of Marx, at least to his theories of the class struggle and of dialectical materialism. But from the 1860s, socialists were divided into those who believed socialism could be achieved by working through democratized political machinery and those who believed in the revolutionary seizure of the state. The first important organization pledged to parliamentary activity on behalf of the workers was Ferdinand Lassalle's German Workingman's Association of 1863, which merged in 1875, with a more revolutionary group from southern Germany called the German Social Democratic Labor party. By their Gotha program, the two groups agreed to found a German Social Democratic party to engage in a big campaign for representation in the new German Reichstag, where by parliamentary means they proposed to advance the socialist cause. They were very successful, in spite of the harassment of Bismarck's antisocialist laws. Under the leadership of the former carpenter August Bebel, they succeeded in enrolling a million members, and building up a huge organization that included publishing houses, newspapers, beer halls, insurance companies, and educational clubs. By 1903, it was by far the largest party in the Reichstag. Their success persuaded many of their members, led by the theorist Eduard Bernstein, to demand that the party "revise" its ideology, to accept openly what they were tacitly recognizing, that Marxism was out of date. In particular, the "revisionists" demanded that the party give up talk of inevitable class war, of the dictatorship of the proletariat, and of the revolutionary seizure of power, and concentrate instead on the gradual transformation of society. The party refused to make this open break with Marx's teachings, but continued to act as though Bernstein were correct. The British Socialist intellectuals, grouped in the Fabian Society, had already rejected the violence of Marxism, and the British Labour party founded in 1900 was avowedly gradualist in its methods and goals. In France, the great Socialist orator Jean Jaurès was practicing much the same philosophy, as the majority of the Socialist deputies in the Chamber were also doing. By the end of the century, orthodox Marxism, according to the tenets of the Communist Manifesto, appeared to be restricted to a vocal but uninfluential fringe of fanatics. It might have remained so, if the collapse of the Russian monarchy had not given one of those small groups the opportunity to take power in the largest state in Europe.

Lenin and the Bolshevik Movement. The Russian Social Democratic Labor party had been founded in 1898 on strictly Marxist principles, largely because the political repression in Russia made the idea of a reforming Socialist party that would work within the existing political system ludicrous. Its leaders were compelled to live in exile in Switzerland, from which they smuggled their propaganda into Russia. When the party held its second congress in 1903, partly in a grubby flour mill in Brussels and later in stifling trade union halls in London, the expected harmony within the party was shattered by a long dispute over doctrine and tactics. A brilliant, self-confident young lawyer named Vladimir Ilyich Ulianov (1870–1924), who used the pseudonym Lenin, challenged

Vladimir Ilyich Lenin (1870–1924).
(U.S. Information Agency.)

the view of several older leaders of the party, that Russia would pass through a long capitalist phase in which the Socialists would collaborate with the bourgeois and that the Socialist party should broaden its membership as widely as possible in preparation for that phase. Lenin believed that the party must cut short the bourgeois phase of the revolution, and that to do so it must itself become an elite of disciplined, professional revolutionaries. On the crucial vote, whether the party should be limited as Lenin proposed to those who were active members of one of its organizations, or broadened to include those who gave "regular personal cooperation under the guidance of one of its organization," Lenin won a two-vote majority. He immediately labeled his faction the Bolsheviks (or "majority") and his opponents the Mensheviks (or "minority"), politically useful labels even when they were no longer accurate. The congress thus left Lenin in undisputed control of one faction of a tiny party led by exiles; but from this position of political leverage he saw the method of gaining power. He wanted, Trotsky remarked, not the "dictatorship of the proletariat" but "dictatorship over the proletariat." The future of the revolution in Russia would be the creation of one leader of political genius.

Lenin was the son of a school inspector from a town on the Volga. His elder brother was hanged for attempting to assassinate the tsar when Lenin was only sixteen; and embittered against the regime, Lenin himself joined a terrorist organization at the University of Kazan. He was expelled, but managed through independent study to get his law degree from the University of Saint Petersburg. He was, however, far more interested in theoretical Marxism than in law, and within four years he was arrested for trying to convert the workers to socialism. He spent three years in exile in Siberia, and then in 1900 was permitted to go into exile in Switzerland. From his own experience with the Russian police, he was convinced that terrorist methods were useless; and from his attempts at propagandizing the masses, he had concluded that "by their own efforts the working class can only arrive at a trade union mentality." He was able to spread these views as editor of the party newspaper *Iskra*, but in 1902 he poured his whole philosophy of revolution, in a bitter, sarcastic, visionary steam of ideas, into his finest book, *What Is to Be Done?* He dismissed freedom as the banner under which the workers are exploited and predatory wars fought. He lashed out at those who gave the revolutionary leaders advice without joining them, and he sketched his concept of the small revolutionary elite infiltrating all the levels of society from the postal services even to the police and the imperial court. But above all, he proclaimed that the proletarian revolution would begin in Russia: "The destruction of the most powerful bulwark of European and (we may even say) of Asiatic reaction, would surely make the Russian proletariat the vanguard of the international proletarian revolution."

The Beginning of Russian Industrialization. Such a prophecy seemed idle dreaming when Lenin wrote it. Russia was by far the most backward of all the big European countries. Peter's Westernization had not included any sharing of political responsibility; and at the end of the nineteenth century, political parties were still forbidden, and Russia possessed no central representative body. The only institutions where self-government was permitted were the *zemstvos*, or local government bodies, established in 1864, where the more liberal-minded among the aristocracy and the middle classes struggled to improve local economic conditions. Any attempt to move beyond such narrow tasks brought immediate intervention from the vast police force, whose informers were ubiquitous. The political immobility was reinforced by the resilience of the entrenched bureaucracy, a system of vested interests opposed to any change in the absolutist system and in particular to any form of popular accounting for its own actions. When the tsar issued the Emancipation Proclamation in 1861, it seemed that at least through the abolition of serfdom the Russian peasantry would enjoy vastly improved conditions. Yet the peasantry had remained tied to the land through their membership in the village commune, which had communal responsibility for payment of taxes and of the installments for purchase of the land. In 1870, 85 percent of the population was engaged in agriculture, and the figure had dropped only to 75 percent by 1914. The farms were too small, techniques of farming too backward, marketing arrangements primitive, living conditions pitiable. Thus many who sought revolutionary change in Russia believed that it must come from the peasantry. At first, in the 1860s and 1870s, this populism was emotional and leaderless; but after 1873 many idealistic intellectuals joined a "to the people" movement, working in the villages to make the peasants willing to seize political authority in their own localities. The peasants remained unmoved, and were probably shocked when a populist murdered Tsar Alexander II with a bomb in 1881. A new attempt was made to reach the peasantry by the Socialist Revolutionary party, founded in 1902, which also took up the terrorist tactics of the later populists.

The beginning of industrialization in Russia in the 1890s vastly increased the need, and the possibility, for political change. The building of railroads from the 1870s had provided a first stimulus to the iron industry, especially in the Donets basin; in the 1890s, concerned with the military need for rapid transportation to the west, the government had doubled railroad mileage. Textile production, which accounted for one-third of all Russian industrial output at the end of the century, was encouraged by placing heavy tariffs on imports, as was the engineering industry. Foreign capital and foreign industry were welcomed, especially in 1892–1903 while Count Witte was finance minister. Both the French government and private French investors poured money into Russia from the 1890s on, financing among other things the building of the Trans-Siberian railroad; and more than two hundred foreign companies began operations. The government also attempted to provide a labor force for the factories, two-fifths of which employed more than a thousand people, by making it easier for the peasant to leave his village community. Although many returned home for the harvest weeks, large numbers of peasants moved into the industrial cities, where they often lived in the factory itself or in barracks nearby. Their wages were so low that women and children were compelled to work also, and only in 1882 was the first law passed that restricted child labor. Russia, in short, was experiencing belatedly the rise of a proletariat and the largely unregulated expansion of its urban centers. It was among these groups that the Bolsheviks found their crucial support.

Capitalist Moscow. The main locations of Russian industry by 1900 were the coal and iron basin of the Donets, the oil region of Baku on the Caspian Sea, newer cities like Rostov-on-Don, and especially in the suburbs of Saint Petersburg and Moscow. The rise of industry in Moscow compensated for its loss of political importance to Saint Petersburg, and throughout the second half of the nineteenth century its growth paralleled that of its rival. Moscow had only 360,000 inhabitants in 1860, but this number had risen to 1.7 million by 1917. While Saint Petersburg was the seaport and heart of the shipbuilding industry, Moscow was the railroad hub and

Moscow Before the Reconstruction of the 1930s. In the middle distance can be seen the elaborate turrets of the Kremlin wall and, within, the bulbous domes of its four cathedrals. (U.S. Information Agency.)

the main railroad engineering center; Saint Petersburg concentrated on foreign trade, Moscow on the home market; Saint Petersburg engaged in cotton spinning and making of yarn, Moscow in the finishing of textiles. Moscow's central position in a region devoted largely to textile mills was somewhat similar to Manchester's; and Lenin himself pointed out that "if Russia is to be compared with West European industrial countries (as is often done here), then these countries should be compared with just this one area, for it alone has conditions approximately similar to those of the industrial capitalist countries."[3] The people of Moscow took pride in this expansion. In 1881, the playwright Ostrovsky noted that "Moscow's population is predominantly commercial and industrial. . . . Moscow is perpetually young, and is being continually rejuvenated; through it the great might of the people keeps surging into Russia. . . . Everyone who has brains and strength of character, everyone who has discarded the bast sandals and the home-spun coat, strives to live in Moscow."[4]

There was however an important change in the social character of the city. The boyars, whose old ways Peter had determined to uproot, were gone, to be replaced by a new aristocracy of merchants, who bought up the old aristocratic homes or built new ones in wildly imaginative period

[3] Yuri Saushkin, *Moscow* (Moscow: Progress Publishers, 1966), p. 53.
[4] Ibid., pp. 53–54.

revivals. Up to the 1850s, Moscow had enjoyed a harmonious mixing of styles. For two centuries, from the building of the Kremlin in the late fifteenth century to the accession of Peter, it had been decorated with a wide variety of boyar homes and Orthodox churches, many of them colorful fantasies in a style called Moscow baroque, a whimsical composition of cupolas, octagonal steeples, false gables, and fantastic brickwork. In the eighteenth century, this style gave way to a sober modification of the rococo palaces of contemporary France, and Russian rococo in its turn was superseded by a heavy Greek and Roman revival. But with the influx of the new capitalists from the surrounding cities, many of the older buildings in the city center were torn down to make way for new mansions in many different styles, such as neo-Byzantine, neo-Renaissance, and neo-Pskovian. The results are still startling, even after acquaintance with the oddities erected around London or Berlin; and the private mansions were far less exuberantly revivalist than the railroad stations, the polytechnical museums, the art galleries, or the Hall for the city Duma. Moscow in short had adopted the appurtenances of all the great capitalist cities of the West, covering them with a thin veneer of motifs drawn from a conscientiously discovered past. The factories and the workers barracks were relegated to the outer suburbs, well beyond the city's official boundary at the Kamer-Collegium wall; and it was here, in October 1905, that some half a million workers began a big strike that culminated in December in the seizure of the largest cotton mill, the Tryokhgornava Manufaktura of Presnya.

The 1905 Revolution in Saint Petersburg and Moscow. The uprising of 1905 had begun in Saint Petersburg in January when striking workers were shot down by the hundreds on the square in front of the Winter Palace as they tried to present notice of their grievances to the tsar. A general strike proclaimed by the workers of Saint Petersburg was soon respected by all the other large industrial cities of Russia including Moscow; and it was followed by peasant uprisings in which many landlords were murdered. The crew of the battleship *Potemkin* mutinied in June; and many soldiers and sailors joined spontaneously with the workers in informal committees for political action, called *soviets*. The tsar's concessions were piecemeal and insincere: he first granted a consultative assembly, then election by restricted suffrage, then a broader franchise with a ministry responsible to the parliament, and finally secret universal suffrage. With the grant of constitutional government, most middle-class reformers and peasants declared themselves satisfied; and thus, when the principal Social Democratic leaders reached Russia in November, it was to witness the final repression of the workers' revolt rather than to take command of a revolution. The Soviet of Workers' Deputies of Saint Petersburg, which had been formed in October, was suppressed after only fifty days, and its leaders arrested. The peasants were cowed by shootings and burnings. But the greatest repression took place in Moscow, where about eight thousand workers threw up barricades and maintained a sniping battle with the local troops until, after nine days, the tough Semionovsky Guards and artillery were sent from Saint Petersburg. The new troops bombarded the workers into submission, and killed over a thousand men, women, and children.

Boris Pasternak, in his novel *Doctor Zhivago*, described the Cossacks scattering a procession of workers just before the uprising:

When the dragoons charged, the marchers at the rear first knew nothing of it. A swelling noise rolled back to them as of great crowds shouting "Hurrah," and individual screams of "Help!" and "Murder!" were lost in the uproar. Almost at the same moment, and borne, as it were, on this wave of sound along the narrow corridor that formed as the crowd divided, the heads and manes of horses, and their saber-swinging riders, rode by swiftly and silently.

Half a platoon galloped through, turned, re-formed, and cut into the tail of the procession. The massacre began.

A few minutes later the avenue was almost deserted. People were scattering down the side streets. The snow was lighter. The afternoon was dry like a charcoal sketch. Then the sun, setting behind the houses, pointed as though with a finger at everything red in the street—the red tops of the dragoons' caps, a red flag trailing on the ground, and the red specks and threads of blood on the snow. [5]

Collapse of the Tsarist System, 1906–1917. The 1905 revolution left behind only a vague constitution, and as Lenin said, the "revolutionary education" of the Russian people. The tsar might have turned the constitutional changes to his own advantage by striking an alliance with the moderate elements within the new parliament, or Duma. But he was a weak, stubborn man, unable to conceive of the end of autocracy and deeply influenced by the irresponsible chidings of his insensitive wife, Alexandra. He turned more and more to right-wing reactionaries, like the anti-Semitic Black Hundreds, and allowed the debauched monk Rasputin, who had won the tsarina's blind devotion by his power to stop the bleeding of her hemophiliac son, to nominate worthless ministers to his government. The powers of the first two Dumas were strictly circumscribed, the suffrage for the third sharply restricted. As a result, the parliament became a purely consultative body whose recommendations were largely ignored. The tsarist autocracy fell back on its old pillars of support—the bureaucracy, the aristocracy, the Church, and especially the army. It failed to realize that the industrialization of Russia, which continued at a frenzied pace in the last decade before the First World War, was increasing the strength of the middle classes, who sought parliamentary power, and of the industrial proletariat, who demanded a betterment of their conditions in some urgent manner that was still to be defined.

[5] Boris Pasternak, *Doctor Zhivago*, trans. Max Hayward and Manya Harari (New York: Pantheon, 1958), pp. 36–37.

Russia's entry into war with Germany, Austria-Hungary, and Turkey in 1914 destroyed the basis of the power of the tsar. The government mobilized sixteen million men, and threw them into battle against the efficient German forces without adequate weapons, ammunition, food, uniforms, medical supplies, transport, or leadership. When the tsar himself took personal command at the front in 1915, it increased the incompetence of the military command, and threw the government in Saint Petersburg (now renamed Petrograd) into the purblind control of his wife and Rasputin. By 1916, the aristocracy itself was estranged from the tsar; two aristocrats even murdered Rasputin, and others spoke of overthrowing the tsar himself. The bureaucracy was demoralized by the incompetence and inconsistency of the changing ministries; and the tsar and his ministers refused to give greater powers to such local authorities as the zemstvos, who were sincerely trying to further the war effort. In 1915 they prorogued the Duma, which had supported the mobilization, because it demanded the institution of parliamentary responsibility as the sole method of winning the war. Above all, the tsar lost the support of the army, which for almost three years had fought with extraordinary bravery and terrible losses against superior German forces. During 1916, the army slowly began to disintegrate, with over one and a half million deserting. It was by then no longer a reliable instrument for the repression of discontent among the peasants and workers at home. For the peasants, the war was an unmitigated disaster, for which they provided the majority of the manpower slaughtered. Their farms were turning to waste for lack of workers, seeds, and fertilizer, their animals taken to feed the armies. But it was among the workers of the cities that the sufferings and the discontent were greatest.

The greater part of industry had been turned over to war production, so that the supply of consumer goods had almost ceased. Food was scare because of the disorganization of the railroad system and breakdown of the farms. Fuel was almost impossible to obtain in the long winters. And the cities were growing in size, as workers were drafted into the munitions factories, and the barracks swelled with new recruits for the armies. The uprising in March 1917 was a spontaneous demonstration against conditions that had become intolerable in the cities, not a planned revolution; and from October 1916, when 150 mutinous soldiers had been executed for firing on the police instead of on demonstrating workers, Petrograd had been in constant tension.[6] In March, however, furious housewives attacked bakeries and foodshops in a "bread riot." The workers came out on strike, and forced the closing of all the factories. On the third day of the rioting, some troops refused to support the police

---

[6] The Bolsheviks adopted the Gregorian calendar on February 14, 1918, which would have been February 1 on the old Julian calendar. Thus, the March Revolution actually began on February 27, 1917 by the Julian calendar, and the November Revolution on October 25. The two revolutions are therefore often referred to as the February and the October revolutions.

against the crowd. On the fifth day, March 12, the Volinski Guards regiment, ignoring its officers, marched to the neighboring barracks with its band playing the Marseillaise, persuaded the other troops to join the revolt, and during the rest of the day was joined by almost all the regiments in the capital. At the same time, the factory workers again formed a Soviet of Workers' Deputies, which set up office in one wing of the Tauride Palace, where the Duma parliamentarians were setting themselves up as an alternative government to the tsar's. The Duma executive committee collaborated with the Soviet long enough to bring Petrograd back to order the next day. Then, on March 14, the Duma representatives declared themselves to be the provisional government of Russia, and at their demand, the tsar abdicated, on March 15. He was brought as a virtual prisoner first to his palace outside Petrograd and later to Siberia, where in July 1918 he and his whole family were murdered by Communist guards.

Tsar Nicholas II (reigned 1904–1917). The Tsar was photographed in the captivity of Communist troops in December 1917, seven months before his murder. (U.S. War Dept. General Staff photo.)

From the March to the November Revolution, 1917. After the March Revolution, freedom in Russia was complete but chaotic. The legal power lay in the hands of the provisional government as the representative of the constitutionally elected Duma. But while granting such traditional rights of parliamentary democracies as freedom of speech and assembly, the middle-class leaders who controlled the provisional government failed to meet the people's primary demands for peace and land. Although the government was headed after July by a fiery charismatic leader, Alexander Kerensky, from the Socialist Revolutionary party, it remained procrastinating and unrealistic. Kerensky even believed that a great new offensive he launched against the Germans would solidify the country in his support, whereas it simply increased the number of desertions to over two million. A committee was formed to study the land question, but the impatient peasants began to seize the land themselves and to murder their landlords. While failing to gain the support of the soldiers and the peasants, the provisional government was even less likely to win the trust of the workers, who were forming their own committees throughout the country on the pattern of the Petrograd soviet. These soviets slowly became the real power in the cities, controlling local administration and constantly interfering with the enforcement of the orders of the provisional government. The chaos was compounded, however, by the fact that the leaders of the soviets, who were mostly Mensheviks and Socialist Revolutionaries, in the early weeks after the March Revolution did not wish to seize power. They collaborated with the provisional government and thus disgusted their own supporters, who in July rioted on the streets of Petrograd against them. The way to power was thus open to the one Socialist faction that could offer self-confident leadership in bringing about revolutionary social change.

Lenin had lived in poverty in Switzerland during the first years of the war, supporting himself with literary jobs and fulminating against the working classes, who had allowed the capitalists to use them as cannon fodder in a war in which they had no class interest. When the news of the March Revolution reached him, Lenin tried frantically to find a way to get back to Russia. To his surprise he was given a comfortable passage across Germany in a sealed train by the German government, which saw correctly that the Bolsheviks would attempt to force Russia to withdraw from the war. He arrived at the Finland station in Petrograd on April 16, where a great crowd was waiting for him, and he at once placed himself at the head of the most radical elements of the revolution: "The people needs peace; the people needs bread; the people needs land. And they give you war, hunger, no bread—leave the landlords still on the land. . . . We must fight for the social revolution, fight to the end, till the complete victory of the proletariat. Long live the world social revolution!" Nevertheless, it took months of organization before the Bolsheviks were able to win over the city workers. Lenin, liberally supplied with funds by the German government, was able to spread his views through the newspaper *Pravda* and in vast numbers of pamphlets, and to put together workers' armed forces, called Red Guards. His supporters were able to win controlling positions on factory committees and in the district soviets, as disgust with the moderate leadership grew. When the forces of a Cossack general, Kornilov, moved against Petrograd in the hope of destroying the provisional government, the Bolsheviks led the organization of the city's defense. They even won supporters in the local dumas of Petrograd and Moscow, and thus they felt that by November, when an assembly of representatives of soviets from the whole country was to meet, they would have a majority. At that point, Lenin announced that the moment for the seizure of power had come. The execution of the coup was left to Trotsky, who was then the president of the Petrograd Soviet. In a perfectly planned operation on the night of November 6, detachments of the Red Guards and the regular army seized the main government buildings. The only bloodshed occurred in the attack on the Winter Palace, where a few loyal troops tried to defend the provisional government. The next morning Lenin announced a new government, the Council of People's Commissars, with himself as chairman. The council's first decrees announced the state's expropriation of all land and its distribution to those who worked it, and demanded immediate peace without annexations. There was surprisingly little opposition at first to this seizure of power. Kerensky, who had escaped in disguise, was unable to rally any support in the army. Most of the big cities had recognized the new government within a month; and the other parties, like the Mensheviks and the Socialist Revolutionaries, tried to oppose the Bolsheviks by boycotting the meeting of the Congress of Soviets. Only in Moscow was there a dramatic clash.

The November Revolution in Moscow. Perhaps the most exciting and the most beautiful description of Moscow in 1917 is given by the writer Konstantin Paustovsky in his autobiography, *The Story of a Life.* As a young newspaper reporter on the eve of the March Revolution, he had found a dejected, rebellious city, isolated in the wilderness of the unchanging Russian countryside, "woods filled with bandits, unusable roads, decayed old settlements, ancient peeling churches, little horses with manure stuck to their skin, drunken fights, cemeteries with overturned gravestones, sheep living inside the peasants' huts, snotty children, straitlaced monasteries, God's fools clustered on church porches, markets filled with rubbish and the squeal of pigs and obscene cursing, decay, poverty, and thievery. And through all this wilderness around Moscow, where the wind whistled in the bare birch twigs, could be heard the repressed agonizing crying of women. They were crying for their soldiers—mothers and wives, sisters and sweethearts."[7] The overthrow of the tsar brought elation, and instant excitement, and disorderly change. Through a cold spring of hailstorms, the people of Moscow debated endlessly in the open air; and it seemed to

[7] Konstantin Paustovsky, *The Story of a Life,* trans. Joseph Barnes (New York: Pantheon, 1964), p. 462.

Paustovsky that the debaters were slowly dividing into two camps, the
"camp of the Bolsheviks and the workers, and the camp of the Provisional
Government, of the intelligentsia, of men who seemed to have the highest
sort of principles but who turned out to be boneless distraught people. . . .
The state was falling to pieces like a handful of wet mud."

*The idyllic aspect of the first days of the Revolution was disappearing. Whole
worlds were shaking and falling to the ground. . . . On the walls of buildings the
wind ruffled dozens of posters. The air was filled with the kerosenelike smell of
printer's ink, and the smell of rye bread. The army brought this second village
smell with it. The city was filled with soldiers pouring back from the front in spite
of Kerensky's strident orders.*

*Moscow was transformed into a turbulent military camp. The soldiers settled in
around the railroad stations. The squares in front of them were wreathed in smoke
like the ruins of a conquered city. This was the smoke not of gunpowder but of
cheap tobacco. . . . The whole city was on its feet. Apartments were empty.
People spoke at meetings for nights on end, loafed sleepily around the streets, then
sat down and argued in public squares on the sidewalks. . . . Four months had
gone by since the Revolution, but the excitement had not died down. Anxiety
still filled people's hearts.*[8]

Fighting began in Moscow two days after the successful assault on the
Winter Palace in Petrograd. At first, the Bolsheviks held the Kremlin itself,
where they had installed a Military Revolutionary Committee, but the city
government and most of the army officers and cadets of the military colleges
remained loyal to the provisional government. In a quick blow, the city
government's Committee of Public Safety seized the Kremlin, and shot the
soldiers defending it. By the evening of November 9, the whole of the
center of the city was in the hands of the Whites; but all the industrial
suburbs were loyal to the Bolsheviks. Moreover, armed workers were
pouring in from the surrounding towns, so that on November 13 the Reds
were able to resume their offensive on the center of the city. After many
hours of constant fighting with rifles, machine guns, and hand grenades,
the Whites were driven back into the Kremlin itself. Paustovsky, who had
been trapped for days in his lodgings in the middle of the fighting, emerged
into the shattered streets. "Frozen blood lay in a ribbon on the stones
around our gate. The buildings, riddled by machine-gun fire, were dropping
sharp shards of glass out of their windows, and you could hear it breaking
all round us. . . . It was all over. Through the cold dark there came from
the Tverskoi the sounds of a band, and singing.

Nobody gives us our salvation
Not God, the Tsar, nor anyone.
We will win our liberation
With a power all our own."[9]

[8] Ibid., pp. 487, 489.
[9] Ibid., p. 505.

Meanwhile, artillery had been called in to bombard the Kremlin, that holiest of all Russian shrines. According to John Reed, an American Communist journalist who had been following the revolution in Petrograd, the news shocked all Petrograd: "Thousands killed; the Tverskaya and the Kuznetsky Most in flames; the church of Vasili Blazheiny a smoking ruin; Usspensky Cathedral crumbling down; the Spasskaya Gate of the Kremlin tottering; the Duma burned to the ground. Nothing that the Bolsheviki had done could compare with this fearful blasphemy in the heart of Holy Russia." He found most of the rumors exaggerated, however, when he reached Moscow three days later. But the mass burial by the Kremlin wall of the five hundred workers killed in the fighting was for him an unforgettable experience:

Through all the streets to the Red Square the torrents of people poured, thousands upon thousands of them, all with the look of the poor and the toiling. A military band came marching up, playing the Internationale, *and spontaneously the song caught and spread like wind-ripples on a sea, slow and solemn. . . . A bitter wind swept the square, lifting the banners. Now from the far quarters of the city the workers of the different factories were arriving, with their dead. They could be seen coming through the Gate, the blare of their banners, and the dull red—like blood— of the coffins they carried. . . . All day long the funeral procession passed, coming in by the Iberian Gate and leaving the Square by way of the Nikolskaya, a river of red banners, bearing words of hope and brotherhood and stupendous prophecies, against a background of fifty thousand people—under the eyes of the world's workers and their descendents forever.*[10]

LENIN'S MOSCOW

When Lenin transferred the government to Moscow in March 1918, the city had already experienced the startling pace with which the Bolsheviks were "cutting away whole layers of a way of life," as Paustovsky wrote, "throwing them away, and laying the basis for a new life. It was still hard to imagine what this new life might be. The change took place so unexpectedly that our very existence sometimes lost its reality and seemed as unstable as a mirage."[11]

The Land Decree had permitted the peasants to take over the land, and only in the summer of 1918 were they compelled to hand over part of their produce to feed the cities. In the first weeks, even the members of the Council of People's Commissars lived on sour cabbage soup and black bread. All the banks were nationalized, although small withdrawals by private citizens were still permitted. The factories were handed over to the control of workers' committees, and an eight-hour day for workers instituted. All potential sources of rivalry to the Bolshevik leaders were destroyed. The popularly elected Constituent Assembly, chosen on November 25, was allowed to meet only once, since the Socialist Revolutionaries held a majority of the seats. The city dumas and the local zemstvos were both abolished. Opposition newspapers were banned. The only par-

[10] John Reed, *Ten Days that Shook the World* (New York: Modern Library, 1935), pp. 257–58.
[11] Paustovsky, *Story of a Life,* p. 506.

Arrest of a Political Prisoner by the Secret Police (Cheka). The Cheka was created in December 1917 as a terrorist force against the political opponents of the Revolution. (U.S. Information Agency photo.)

ties other than the Bolshevik party that were allowed to operate were the Socialist Revolutionaries and the Mensheviks. The Church was separated from the state, and its functions drastically reduced. Its lands had already been confiscated, and its other possessions soon passed into the hands of the state. Terror was accepted as an essential instrument of government. "Do you really think that we shall be victorious," Lenin asked, "without using the most cruel terror?" On December 20, the Cheka, the Extraordinary Commission for Combating Counter Revolution and Speculation was created, under Felix Dzerzhinsky. It was a secret political police, with power of immediate arrest and punishment. Finally, only six days before the move to Moscow, the Bolshevik representatives signed the Treaty of Brest Litovsk with Germany, by which they bought peace at a very high price—the loss of one quarter of Russia's territory and over sixty million people. Lenin believed, however, that he had saved the revolution; Germany's gains, he foresaw, would be ephemeral.

Once installed in the Kremlin, the Bolshevik government showed even in its living quarters that the confused improvisations of the early days in the Smolny Institute in Petrograd, where government ministries consisted of trestle tables in overcrowded halls and the state treasury was kept in a wardrobe in Lenin's room, were over. Lenin himself had a five-room apartment, with a large reception room where the Council of People's Commissars could meet, and a private telephone system by which he could be in immediate contact with army or the local Bolshevik leaders. The other commissars all had apartments nearby, and ate together in a large Kremlin mess hall. It was close-knit, relatively efficient, and ostentatiously austere. The three hundred leaders who lived within the Kremlin permitted almost no one to penetrate the closely guarded walls, because of the constant danger to which they felt exposed not only from aristocratic and bourgeois elements but even from within the revolutionary movement. The most dangerous of the attacks came in July 1918, when the left-wing Socialist Revolutionaries attempted to overthrow the government and murder Lenin. They began by murdering the German ambassador in hope of forcing a renewal of the war with Germany, occupied the Cheka headquarters and arrested Dzerzhinsky, and bombarded the Kremlin. Trotsky however brought up loyal troops in time, and the insurrection was mastered and its leaders executed. After September, when the head of the Cheka in Petrograd was assassinated, Lenin unleashed the secret police on a wave of terror intended to cow all opposition, even though he had restrained it somewhat after the attempt on his own life the previous month.

War Communism.   The terror and the isolation seemed the necessary protection of men engaged in a gigantic social experiment in the midst of civil war. The most extensive changes were brought about by a policy known as war communism. By this policy, Lenin proposed to bring about total control over the economic life of every individual in Russia. After a

Streetside Market, Moscow.
Sale of private possessions continued throughout the 1930s in open-air markets, in spite of state control of the retail trade. (U.S. Information Agency photo.)

few months of untrammeled enjoyment of their newly acquired lands, the peasants were forced to hand over a large portion of their produce to the state, which became the sole distributor and stockpiler of foodstuffs. The farms, which they had expected to own, were declared to be state property. The workers' committees ceased to be the management of the factories, and the Communist party took over the nationalized companies under the instructions of a central economic committee within the Kremlin. All foreign trade and all internal trade were brought under state control, and a system of regimentation of labor introduced. Workers had to possess a passport; if they did not work, they did not receive a ration book for food; workers could be drafted to jobs where they were needed, although the most menial tasks were reserved for the bourgeoisie. Private wealth was severely restricted, by confiscation of the most obvious luxuries like paintings and furs and by banning of the inheritance of private property. All apartment buildings were taken over, and "living space" assigned according to need.

The Civil War. Realization of the full import of these measures by the possessing classes and the peasantry helped to produce the civil war. A base for counterrevolution had been provided by the intervention of the Western allies for the ostensible purpose of protecting the large quantities of supplies they had sent to Russia. The British moved into the Arctic ports and Baku, the French into Odessa, the Japanese and later the Americans into Vladivostok. Anti-Bolshevik, or White, regimes were encouraged in these areas. But many other opposition groups were organized around the periphery of the great central region where Bolshevik control was firm. Minority nationalities like the Cossacks and the Ukrainians joined forces in the South. In the Urals and Siberia, a second army was formed under Admiral Kolchak. In the Baltic states, White forces were joined after 1918 by demobilized German soldiers of the so-called Free Corps. The civil war seriously threatened Bolshevik control. At one time, the armies of General Denikin, moving from the Ukraine, reached to within 250 miles of Moscow, and those of Yudenich from Estonia penetrated the outer suburbs of Petrograd. Conditions in the cities under Bolshevik control were fearsome. Famine, typhus, riots, and looting made life uncertain for all. Medical supplies ran short in the Kremlin policlinic itself. In April 1918, Trotsky, as commissar for war, persuaded the government to institute universal military service for workers and peasants, and to use tsarist officers under close political supervision to command them. From then on, young party workers from Moscow were taken with Trotsky to the front, where they were used to stiffen the fighting resolve of the rank and file, and they were soon followed by thousands of workers from the industrial suburbs. Slowly the new army grew in size and efficiency, reaching 800,000 by the end of the year and three million before the end of 1920. The Whites quarreled among themselves, and made their cause

The Russian Civil War

0 _____ 300 Miles

Controlled by Bolsheviks
Occupied by Allied troops
Major thrusts by White generals

KOLCHAK FORCES

YUDENICH FORCES

DENIKIN FORCES

unpopular by restoring the land to its former landlords and by vicious executions. Trotsky profited from his central position, moved his armies by railroad with great logistic genius, and in two years had broken all three White armies. The last White and foreign forces were evacuated from Russian soil in 1922. By then, the older order in Russia had capitulated to the new. Two million Russians had fled into exile. The political opposition was broken. But the economic chaos was complete. The true opposition remaining was the passive resistance of peasant and worker to the nationalizing state that demanded work with no reward. Half the workers of Moscow had moved back into the countryside where they could find food; industrial production for the country as a whole was down to fourteen per cent of prewar figures. But the final blow was the revolt of the sailors at the Kronstadt naval base in March 1921, which convinced the realistic Lenin that he had to pull back from massive socialization for a while.

The New Economic Policy. The New Economic Policy of 1921–1928 permitted the peasant to sell his produce for whatever price he could get, in order to restore some form of consumer goods that middlemen, soon known as NEP men, could bring into the cities to sell. With goods for purchase, the worker was encouraged to put in longer hours in the factory, thereby restoring the productivity of industry. But the "controlling heights of industry" remained in the hands of the state; no industries were denationalized. The policy worked. The famine of 1920–1921, in which as many as five million died, was alleviated. Slowly agricultural and industrial production returned to prewar levels, and the popularity of the Communist government rose with it.

Leon Trotsky (1879–1940). Trotsky was photographed in 1920, when he was directing the organization and strategy of the Communist forces in the Russian civil war. (The National Archives.)

Rise of Stalin. Lenin himself, however, had suffered a paralytic stroke in 1922, which for the last two years of his life left him able to understand but unable to command. He watched with frustration the rise to prominence in the party of a tough, maneuvering Georgian, named Joseph Vissarionovich Dzugashvily and called Stalin, who was using his role as general secretary of the party to make himself rather than Trotsky the heir to Lenin's power. In an addition to the political testament he had written for the party's guidance after his death, Lenin tried to give warning against Stalin. On December 24, 1923, he cautioned that "Comrade Stalin, having become general secretary, has concentrated enormous power in his hands, and I am not sure that he always knows how to use that power with sufficient caution." On January 4, 1924, two weeks before his death, Lenin added a postscript: "Stalin is too rude, and this fault, entirely supportable in relation to us Communists, becomes insupportable in the office of General Secretary. Therefore I propose to the comrades to find a way to remove Stalin from that position and appoint to it another man who in all respects differs from Stalin in one characteristic—namely, more patient, more loyal, more polite, and more attentive to comrades, less capricious, etc." Having created a dictatorship, Lenin had at the last moment become aware of the abuses to which it could be put. After his death on January 21, 1924, his body was embalmed, and placed in a wooden mausoleum in Red Square; in 1930, the present mausoleum of granite and porphyry was inaugurated. Lenin had become a figure of religious awe, visited by millions every year. The damaging testament was suppressed by the party Central Committee, however, and Stalin dominated even the burial ceremonies.

Lenin's Funeral, January, 1924. Stalin [left front] and members of the Politburo lead Lenin's funeral cortege through Red Square. (Sovfoto.)

Within four years, Stalin had destroyed his opposition and was unchallenged ruler of Russia. Stalin had been a successful but not an outstanding revolutionary leader before 1917. After being educated in a seminary, he had become a professional Bolshevik organizer, working underground and being frequently arrested. He played only a minor part in the November Revolution, and was given the peripheral post of commissar of nationalities in the first Council of People's Commissars. But by his ability to handle multifarious details of administrative work, he slowly became indispensable in the party apparatus, and without Lenin's realizing his intention at first, he used the powers of general secretary to fill all the provincial and many central party offices with new men dependent entirely on him. While Lenin was dying, Stalin had forged an alliance with Zinoviev and Kamenev, the party chiefs of Petrograd and Moscow, to isolate Trotsky; and he was able to persuade the Central Committee to dismiss Trotsky from the post of war commissar in 1925, from the Central Committee in 1927, and from the Party itself in 1929. Trotsky went into exile, where he fulminated against the Stalinist regime until, on Stalin's orders, he was brutally assassinated in 1940. With Trotsky defeated, Stalin turned against his allies. Kamenev and Zinoviev were expelled from the party in 1927, and all of the original associates of Lenin soon followed. By 1928, Stalin felt prepared to change the whole direction of the party's policy in Russia; in the First Five-Year Plan, he would hurl it into the Iron Age.

Moscow in the 1920s. During the 1920s, at least after the inauguration of the New Economic Policy, life in Moscow had been materially adequate and socially exciting. Food and a minimum amount of consumer goods had percolated back, through the agency of the NEP men. The trade unions had been permitted to stand up for workers' rights, and could even bargain for higher wages. Many small workshops had been opened by artisans. Although little housing was being built, cramped quarters were available for most people by a sharing out of rooms in the larger buildings. Educational opportunities were being opened to all workers, with the opening of a new nine-year polytechnic school for all children and free schooling through the age of seventeen. In intellectual life, too, there was much exciting innovation. The nationalized theaters had been placed under the supervision of an experienced director, Vsevolod Meyerhold, who determined to throw over the classical in favor of a proletarian theater. He did away with curtains, footlights, and even costumes, changed scenery in sight of the audience, and filled the stage with vast spectacles of workers in revolutionary action. The movie houses showed the masterpieces of directors like Sergei Eisenstein, who gave many younger Russians their lasting impression of the revolutionary days with his film *October*. The NEP permitted private publishing of books, with the result that many imaginative novels of the revolutionary struggles and of the civil war were produced. Some writers, such as Alexei Tolstoy and Ilya Ehrenburg, who had gone into exile, came back. To Ehrenburg, life in Moscow during the time of the New Economic Policy was a strange mixture of idealism and materialism:

I was astonished when I saw Moscow again. I had gone abroad in the last weeks of War Communism. Everything looked different now. Ration cards had disappeared, people were no longer 'registered.' Administrative personnel was greatly reduced and no one was working out grandiose projects. . . . Old workers and engineers were painfully getting production on its feet. Consumption goods had made their appearance. The peasants had begun to bring poultry to the markets.

**Boys in Moscow During the
Famine of 1921.**

*The Muscovites had grown fatter and were more cheerful. I was both pleased and
saddened. . . . From the point of view of the politician or the production expert the
new line was correct; we know now that it produced what it was intended to produce. But the heart has its reasons: NEP often seemed to me to have a sinister
grimace.*[12]

The NEP men, he found, were dancing to the phonograph records of
Paris and London, wearing bright tight-fitting suits, eating huge meals in
restaurants, and driving around town in smart drozhkys. The young, he
thought, were an idealistic new generation, romantic in "the bold attempt
to mass-produce tangible myths, in series," in the factories and schools.
The party, he claimed, remained puritanical, worked fourteen hours a day,
and "ate humble rissole in the canteen." By 1926, he felt "the stifling,
brutal life of NEP's last years was being played out. Everybody traded in
everything, wrangled, prayed, swilled vodka and, dead drunk, fell like
corpses in the gateways. The yards were filthy. Vagrant children huddled
in the cellars."[13] In 1928, Stalin brought a sharp surgical end to this
epoch.

**STALIN'S
IRON AGE**

First Five-Year Plan, 1928–1932. The First Five-Year Plan had been
under discussion for three years, and when presented to the party congress
it was elaborated in enormous detail. Stalin had returned to the original
plans of 1917 of total socialization of the Russian economy, but he had
linked them to a newer and perhaps more important concept: the Communist state was to become a totalitarian machine for the forced industrial-

[12] Ilya Ehrenburg, *Truce 1921–33* (London: MacGibbon and Kee, 1963), pp. 66, 69.
[13] Ibid., p. 139.

ization of an underdeveloped country. Principal emphasis was placed on accelerated growth of heavy industry, especially coal and iron, heavy engineering, and electrification. Vast new centers of industry were to be created, notably in the Urals and Siberia. Large numbers of workers were to be transferred to such new cities as Magnitogorsk in the Urals, while others, including the inmates of labor camps run by the secret police, were to be employed on building roads, railroads, and canals. Detailed production goals were laid down for every branch of production, which had to be met if managers wanted to avoid demotion or even imprisonment and if workers wanted to eat; and rewards, mostly verbal, were given to those who exceeded their norms. The industrialization of agriculture was conceived as a necessary accompaniment to the growth of heavy industry. Tractors were to be produced to mechanize the countryside. The maze of inefficient individual peasant holdings was to be replaced by large consolidated farms called collectives *(sovkhoz* and *kolkhoz),* in which the peasants would be paid laborers. Each collective farm would also be assigned a quota, and would be allowed itself to consume only what it produced beyond that quota. Increased production in the countryside would enable the growing urban population of the industrial centers to be fed, and would free many peasants to become industrial workers. Since almost no material incentives would be provided for the worker, consumer

A Tractor on a Collective Farm in the 1930s. (U.S. Information Agency.)

goods being kept at the absolute minimum, a vast propaganda effort would be needed, to persuade the worker that he was building for the future. In subordinating his own immediate well-being to the needs of the state's industrialization, the Soviet citizen would not only be creating a new civilization but would be changing his own personality as well. The Five-Year Plan would help create a new Soviet man.

Urban Growth during the Five-Year Plan.   The Five-Year Plan vastly accelerated the urbanization of Russia.   Moscow itself grew to a population of 3.9 million by 1935, and its industrial base was changed from predominantly light industry concentrated on textiles to engineering industries, especially automobile parts, tractors, machine tools, and precision instruments.   The new migrants in Moscow were usually uprooted peasants, torn from their farms by the collectivization program and largely unskilled in industrial trades and unaccustomed to the tedious discipline of factory life.   Even in the capital city they found living accommodations barbaric, several families often crowding into a single room and kitchen, and they reacted with drunkenness, indiscipline on the job, and absenteeism. In the Urals and beyond rather than in Moscow, however, the most dramatic scenes of the great urbanization were played, because there a great mixing occurred of the unwilling peasant population with an enthused idealistic aristocracy of labor, many of whom were young workers persuaded by the government's propaganda to build socialism in the wilderness.   "Komsomols [young Communists], fired with enthusiasm, set off for Magnitogorsk or Kuznetsk," wrote Ehrenburg.   "They believed it was enough to build huge factories to create an earthly paradise.   In freezing

The Opening of a New Factory, 1928. During the Five-Year Plans factory openings were celebrated as national triumphs of the working class.

January metal scorched the hands. People seemed to be frozen to the marrow; there were no songs, no flags, no speeches. The word 'enthusiasm,' as so many others, has been devalued by inflation, yet there is no other word to fit the days of the First Five-Year Plan; it was enthusiasm pure and simple that inspired the young people to daily and unspectacular feats.'' [14] There were of course the thousands of ''specials,'' the former kulaks or well-to-do peasants who were drafted into the factories and supervised by the secret police, but on the job there was little to choose between their conditions and those of the average worker. John Scott, a young American who went out to Magnitogorsk in 1931 to work as a welder and see the new state in action, described in *Behind the Urals* (1942) the creation of this vast city in the steppes of Siberia by workers who reported at six in the morning in a temperature of forty-five degrees below zero; he noted the ragged clothes and insufficient food, the constant political interference in technical plans, the huge waste of lives from inadequate safety precautions and poor materials. The enthusiasm ran thin, he reported; the ''population was taught by a painful expensive process to work efficiently, to obey orders, to mind their own business, and to take it on the chin with a minimum of complaint.'' The town they created was far from beautiful. In 1933, Magnitogorsk was a harsh, grey, dusty maelstrom of half-finished blast furnaces and wooden barracks. By 1940, it was beginning to have pretensions to urban amenity, with broad paved streets, large five-story apartment buildings, fountains, childrens' playgrounds, orchestras and singing societies, and a system of schools ranging from nurseries to a teachers' college and a mining and metallurgical institute.

Magnitogorsk, while one of the largest new cities, was only one of many. Throughout the Urals and Siberia, new cities were created— Krivoy-Rog, Kursk, and Gornaia-Shorii for iron mining; Krasnoiarsk, Irkutsk, and Novosibirsk for steel and heavy engineering; Frunze, Pavlodar, and Omsk for agricultural machinery. Great new dams, like that at Dnieprostroy on the Dnieper River, not only provided hydroelectric power to wide areas but also provided a nucleus around which steel, chemical, and aluminum factories were grouped. The Second Five-Year plan, for 1933– 1937, carried on the expansion of these new centers, especially the iron- and steel-producing cities, and also increased the emphasis on machine tools, nonferrous metals, and transportation. Not only were the railroad lines to be given a second track and many new lines constructed, but rivers were to be widened, new canals like the Moscow-Volga canal built, and a highway network begun. A third plan, in 1938, had similar goals, but had to be shelved during the war. The success of these plans in turning Russia into a highly industrialized state and in transferring the center of Russian industry from the West into the Urals and Siberia is undoubted,

[14] Ibid., p. 221.

**The Opening of the Dnie-
prostroy Dam, 1932.** The
foodline in the foreground
is testimony to the price
Russian workers paid for
great public works, such as
this dam and power station
on the Dnieper River. (U.S.
Information Agency.)

even though very few of the unrealistic goals of the plans were actually
met. Steel production, for example, did reach 17 million tons by 1937,
from only 4 million in 1928; coal production was 128 million tons compared with 31.

Collectivization of Agriculture.   The collectivization of agriculture, which
was regarded as the necessary accompaniment of these industrial changes,
was only carried through, however, at the cost of class war in the countryside, the death of between five and ten million peasants, and a huge new
famine in 1930–1931. To force the peasantry to bring their livestock, machinery, and land into collective farms, Stalin turned the poorest peasants
against the kulaks, the well-to-do peasants, who numbered just under
a million. Then, to bring the mass of small proprietors into the collectives
as well, he found that he had to use the Red Army against them. Recalcitrant
peasants were machine-gunned into submission, and sent by the millions
into Siberia or forced labor camps. The peasants replied by burning down
their own houses and killing (and eating) their livestock. Collectivization
continued, however, and by 1930 over half the Russian landholdings had
been collectivized. By 1938 the process was almost complete. But the
economic consequences had been disastrous. Half of Russia's horses
and cattle and two-thirds of its pigs and sheep had been slaughtered.
But this time it was not the cities but the peasantry that starved, since the
government forced the compulsory delivery of quotas. The peasants began
to flock into the cities, much as the government desired, to provide the unskilled labor for the construction of the new industrial plants. In spite
of its adverse results on food production, Stalin had therefore achieved his
main goal for the countryside. He had brought under control the one sector

**Peasants on a Collective
Farm in the 1930s.** In spite
of desperate opposition, almost
all of Russia's agricultural
population had been grouped
on collective farms by 1938.
(U.S. Information Agency.)

of the economy and of the population that had resisted the direct controls
of the state. Socialized cities and individualistic farming could not continue
side by side.

The determination to encourage industrialization in the East of Russia
and to restrict the growth of the cities of European Russia was confirmed
in 1931, when the Party Central Committee defined Moscow's position
in the new state. To avoid "creating huge cities with an agglomeration of
a great number of enterprises in the existing urban centers," and especially
to prevent the building of new industrial enterprises in Moscow itself,
the city's population was not to grow beyond five million. To achieve
this, not only were no new factories to be started in Moscow but unsanitary
old ones were to be moved 50 to 100 kilometers away; special passports
were required for residence in Moscow; and frequently after slum clearance,
the inhabitants of the cleared areas were moved out of Moscow. Within
these limits, Moscow was to become a showplace of the new workers'
society, especially as it would be the main center visited by all the delegations from foreign countries, tourists, and journalists. In Moscow the
superiority of the Socialist society had to receive physical demonstration.

**MOSCOW
DURING
THE IRON AGE**

Ten-Year Plan for Moscow. Various options were considered in dealing
with the largely unplanned city. According to the detailed announcement of the Ten-Year Plan (1935):

*Moscow, which for many centuries had developed in chaotic fashion, reflected,
even in the best years of its development, the barbaric character of Russian capitalism. The narrow and crooked streets, the districts intersected by a multitude of*

*lanes and blind alleys, the uneven distribution of buildings between the center
and the outskirts of the city, the center encumbered with warehouses and small
enterprises, the low, decrepit houses huddled together, the haphazard distribution
of the industrial enterprises, railroads and other branches of economy and public
service, hinder the normal life of the rapidly developing city, particularly in respect
of traffic, and make imperative a radical and planned reconstruction. . . .*

*The Central Committee of the Party and the Council of People's Commissars
reject the projects of preserving the present city intact as a museum-city and of
creating a new city outside the limits of the present one. The Central Committee
of the Party and the Council of the People's Commissars also reject the proposals
to demolish the existing city and to build a new city in its place according to a
totally different plan. . . . It is necessary to retain the historical outlines of the city,
but radically to replan it by coordinating the network of its streets and squares. . . .
The hilly contours of the city, the Moscow river and the Yauza river, which intersect
the city in different directions, the fine parks of Moscow—all these individual
sections of the city in all their variety taken as a whole make it possible to create a
truly socialist city.*[15]

The control by the state of all property rights made wide-scale planning
possible on a hitherto unknown scale. By decree all suburban areas were
to be annexed to the central city as "reserve city land," to which the city
building codes would be applied. A green belt of forests and parks ten
kilometers in width was to be preserved around the built-up area to "serve
as a reservoir of fresh air for the city and a place of recreation for its inhabitants." The rivers were to be banked with granite-faced walls, and
broad streets constructed along their length as the city's main throughways;
and architecturally harmonious apartment buildings and public offices
were to be constructed along them. A new large area beyond the Lenin
hills was to be annexed, and developed into apartments to relieve the city's
congestion. Impressive public buildings were to be constructed on the
main squares, in front of the railroad stations, at principal intersections,
and at viewpoints above the Moscow River. A central heating system for
the whole city was to use steam from turbines at the new electric power
plants; an underground pipe and cable system was to combine telephone,
telegraph, light and power cables, gas and water mains, to give ease to
access and to remove the visual annoyance of wires and pipes above
ground. Finally, vast provisions were to be made for the improvement of
the living conditions of the workers. Schools, outpatient hospitals, dining
rooms, kindergartens, nurseries, theaters, cinemas, clubs, hospitals, and
stadiums were to be located at central points in groups of apartment
buildings. Like all the other planning of the Iron Age, it was immensely
ambitious and could only be achieved in part.

Socialist Realism in Moscow Architecture. Much of the reconstruction
went according to plan. The streets were widened and covered with

[15] E. D. Simon, *Moscow in the Making* (London: Longmans, Green, 1937), pp. 184–85.

**A New Apartment Building
and a Traditional Wooden
Home in Moscow during the
1930s.** (U.S. Information
Agency.)

asphalt, and the river embankments built. Many of the new public buildings, built from the 1920s until the mid 1930s, were in the most advanced
styles then being adopted only on a small scale in Western Europe. Le
Corbusier, for example, was consulted on the replanning of Moscow, and
he designed several buildings, including the airy, glass-fronted Centro-
soyouz for the Moscow cooperatives. Soviet architects themselves drew
inspiration from the ideas of Gropius and the Bauhaus organization in
Weimar Germany; and exciting new buildings in concrete and plate glass
were designed for such functions as palaces of labor, the offices of the
newspaper *Pravda*, the Moscow planetarium, and workers' apartments
and clubs. In the planning of the suburban towns around Moscow, the
urbanists engaged in a fruitful debate between those who favored concentration of population and those who wanted to scatter apartment houses
among the forests, and for a while the adherents of the "Green City" concept were able to give free play to their ideas of scattering the workers and
their automobiles (still to be constructed) among the fresh air of the green
belt.

Between 1931 and 1935, however, these creative ideas of architecture
and urbanism were stifled. The official policy of the state in all the arts
was declared to be "Socialist realism." The definition itself was somewhat
misty: "In architecture, Socialist realism means the intimate union of
ideological expression with the truth of artistic expression, and the effort
to adapt every building to the technical, cultural or utilitarian demands

Rejected Designs for the Palace of Soviets, Moscow. The victory of Socialist Realism in architecture was assured with the rejection of designs influenced by contemporary West European design. (U.S. Information Agency.)

which are its own." In practice, under the cultural controls of Stalin and his collaborator Zhdanov, architectural style was to return to a monumentalism based on a mingling of period revivals. At first the "realist" architects turned to safe and undemonstrative Italian Renaissance models, especially the airy villas of Palladio in northern Italy. Nonfunctional pilasters and heavy balconies and balustrades, inside and outside, were in some curious way supposed to express artistic wishes of the Soviet worker. Palladio was followed by a vast medley of other styles, including Greek, Roman, Florentine, neo-Muscovite, and baroque, all characterized by high ceilings, sculptured fountains, inset columns, and vast glistening candelabras. The victory of the realists over their opponents, who were condemned as "formalists" and thus politically as well as architecturally unreliable, came with the competition for a great central Palace of the Soviets. The "formalist" Guinzburg designed an ascetic composition of sharp angles, in plain white concrete, surmounted by a huge dome in glass. The "realists" who won the competition projected a series of superimposed drums, placed upon a vast colonnade like the death temple of an Egyptian dynasty, topped with a gigantic statue of Lenin. It was taller than the Empire State Building and the Eiffel Tower, and was intended to become the central point of the whole Moscow skyline. Its construction was interrupted by the Second World War, and its foundations later turned into the largest swimming pool in Moscow. But the victory of the realists was assured, and until Stalin's death in 1953, the architecture of Moscow turned to ever more grandiose variations on the "wedding-cake style" invented during the 1930s.

The Moscow Subway. The most notable examples of the new realist style were to be found in the main stations of the Moscow Metro, the subway begun in 1931 as the supreme demonstration of the Socialist state's urban preoccupation. The party had ordered completion of the first section of the Metro by November 1934 for the seventeenth anniversary of the Revolution, and no expense in money, labor, or risk was spared to achieve the goal. The first section was to cost half a billion rubles, at a time when the Five-Year Plan was appropriating less than that each year to the industries making consumer goods. The head of the work was Nikita Khrushchev, a former mine worker from the Ukraine who, after proving himself in local politics, had been brought to Moscow as a protégé of Kaganovich, first secretary to the Moscow City Party Committee and as such, responsible for Moscow's administration. For a while Khrushchev had headed the Red Presnaya district of Moscow, making his name in the Party by organizing a "Stalin Estafette," a campaign for forcing more work out of the laborers of his district. He turned the same methods to forcing completion of the subway, where workers in three shifts were falling behind in their efforts to drive the underground tunnels through dangerous brown mud under houses that frequently collapsed. "At the construction sites as everywhere," Khrushchev warned them, "mere words are not enough. We need a Bolshevist organized system, clearness of purpose, knowledge of the matter, and ability to fulfill without fail the plan assigned by the party and Government. . . . Under the influence of self-seekers who have wormed themselves into our construction sites, some workers have begun to think along the following lines: why don't we try to get our norms revised downwards? Pernicious and disorganizing aspirations of this kind must be severely put down." [16] He himself plunged into the waterlogged shafts, inspecting the work, raising the norms, threatening and cajoling. In spite of his efforts and those of thousands of Young Communists who were used for unskilled work, the first section was a year late in completion. But it immediately became the showplace of the new city, because never before had subway stations been decorated with porphyry, granite, bronze, marble, mosaics, statues, bas-reliefs, and crystal candelabras. It was ironic that the style of Socialist realism in architecture should have been outlawed two decades later by Khrushchev, the constructor of the Moscow subway. In the Decree on Eliminating Waste in Building Design in 1955, Khrushchev noted:

[16] Lazar Pistrak, *The Grand Tactician: Khrushchev's Rise to Power* (New York: Praeger, 1961), pp. 82–83.

*Completely unjustified tower-like superstructures and numerous decorative col-
onnades, porticos, and other architectural excesses borrowed from the past have
become characteristic of apartments and public buildings, as the result of which
state funds have been overexpended on housing construction in the last few years
to an extent that would have provided many million square meters of living space
for the working people. . . .*

*An improper architectural trend is also evident in the design and construction
of railroad stations, and manifests itself in the erection of palatial stations. In spite
of their great cost, these stations do not provide the essential comforts for passengers.*[17]

Socialist Realism in Art and Literature.   The same crackdown on innovation was evident in both painting and literature in the 1930s. During the
1920s many Communist leaders had believed that the writers should be
permitted to move slowly toward the new society as, in Trotsky's famous
phrase, "fellow travelers"; and without strict controls over their style,
Soviet writers had succeeded in producing literature of considerable
quality. Vladimir Mayakovsky had become the poet hero of the revolution,
declaiming to vast crowds such verses as "I love the hugeness of our plans,
The boldness of our mile-long strides." Isaac Babel had recovered the style
of the great nineteenth-century novelists in his *Red Cavalry* of 1926. Yevgeny
Zamyatin was able to read aloud his satirical fantasy *We,* and to publish
his less pointed short stories. Boris Pilnyak had drawn upon the style of
the Parisian symbolists in his novel *The Naked Year* (1922). And the
efforts of the militant Association of Proletarian Writers to force the more
independent literary figures to proletarian themes had even been rebuked
by the Central Committee. In 1930, everything changed. Mayakovsky,
finding himself under sharp criticism and despairing of the new political
controls, committed suicide, after writing one last poem:

*I am also fed up
With the agit-prop; [Department for Agitation and Propaganda]
I too could compose
Ballads about you—
It is pleasanter and pays more—
But I forced myself
By planting my foot on the throat of my own song.*[18]

The Central Committee turned on Pilnyak and Zamyatin with the accusa-
tion that they had published works abroad, and thus these two leading
writers were made scapegoats as a warning to the rest. Stalin himself
intervened in the literary debate with letters of warning to writers who had
failed to strike a suitable propagandist note. The nature of his intervention
can be understood from a letter he wrote to a poet about the latter's critical
verses, published in *Pravda,* on Ukraine miners. "You announce to the

[17] Ibid., p. 99.
[18] Cited in Marc L. Slonim, *Soviet Russian Literature: Writers and Problems, 1917–1967* (New
York: Oxford University Press, 1967), pp. 27–28.

whole world that Russia in the past was a vessel of filth and indifference," Stalin raged, "and that present-day Russia is no better, that laziness and the desire to 'sit on the stove' are to all intents and purposes national characteristics of the Russian people—and that means, of Russian workers— who after accomplishing the October revolution did not cease to be Russians. And you call that Bolshevik criticism! No, my honored Comrade Demyan, that is not Bolshevik criticism but a slander on our people. It is the degradation of the USSR, the degradation of the proletariat of the USSR, the degradation of the Russian proletariat. And after that you expect the Central Committee to be silent! Just who do you take us for?" [19]

All writers were grouped into one organization, the All-Union Organization of Associations of Proletarian Writers, whose head was brother-in-law of the chief of the secret police. There was to be a "draft of shock-workers into literature." Writers were to exalt the goals of the Five-Year plans. Many did, publishing such novels as *Cement, Energy, The Big Assembly Line,* and *Hydrocentral.* Occasionally a fine novel was created in these difficult conditions, such as Michael Sholokov's *Virgin Soil Upturned.* But almost all experimentalism was condemned, and in the late 1930s some of the best of the earlier Soviet writers such as Isaac Babel and Boris Pilnyak died during imprisonment. In painting and sculpture, Socialist realism wiped out all creativity, leaving behind only the gigantic monumentalism of exuberant muscular workers exultant in the completion of superhuman tasks in industry and agriculture.

All aspects of life had to be mobilized for the strengthening of the Russian economy. "No, Comrades, the pace must not be slackened," Stalin had declared in 1931.

To slacken the pace would mean to lag behind; and those who lag behind are beaten. We do not want to be beaten. No, we do not! Russia . . . was ceaselessly beaten for her backwardness. She was beaten by the Mongol Khans, she was beaten by the Turkish Beys, she was beaten by the Swedish feudal lords, she was beaten by the Anglo-French capitalists, she was beaten by the Japanese barons, she was beaten by all—for her backwardness. . . .

We are fifty or a hundred years behind the advanced countries. We must make good this lag in ten years. Either we do it or they crush us. [20]

The disciplining of intellectuals was only the forerunner of a major search for disloyalty within the Communist party itself that began in 1934. The purge and punishment of disloyal elements took place in every section of the country, but its most dramatic events were enacted in Moscow, with the secret police as the producers of the drama and the purged as principal actors.

The purge was already a frequently used device within the Russian Communist party by 1934. There had been at least four big purges during the 1920s. A sweep of those held responsible for the shortcomings of the

THE GREAT PURGES

[19] Max Hayward and Leopold Labedz, eds., *Literature and Revolution in the Soviet Union, 1917–1962* (New York: Oxford University Press, 1963), p. 56.
[20] Cited in Edward Crankshaw, *Khrushchev: A Career* (New York: Viking, 1966), pp. 76–77.

collectivization program was carried out in 1930, and yet another in 1933 to "achieve a higher ideological standard of party members." Following the assassination in Leningrad on December 1, 1934, of Stalin's presumed heir, Sergei Kirov, however, a purge unparalleled in its scope and savagery began. Khrushchev later suggested that Stalin was responsible for Kirov's murder, and used it as an excuse to impose a new regime of terror against former critics and possible rivals. The murder of Kirov was held to be the work of supporters of Zinoviev and Kamenev, with whom Stalin had earlier allied to oust Trotsky; and they and thousands of their supposed accomplices were arrested in 1934–1935. In August 1936, the most important of the Old Bolsheviks suddenly emerged, briefly, from the prisons of the NKVD (the new designation of the secret police), for a show trial, in which most of them confessed to organizing terrorism against Stalin, to working for Trotsky, and to having murdered Kirov. They were immediately executed, but their confessions were held to have implicated even more of the original Bolsheviks who had been Lenin's collaborators. A second show trial was held in January 1937, in which all seventeen prisoners confessed that they were guilty of sabotage, collaboration with Germany and Japan, and plots to dismember the Soviet Union. Thirteen were executed, the others disappeared. That summer, the purge was extended to the highest levels of the Red Army, and the chief of the general staff and Civil War hero Marshal Tukachevsky and a large number of other commanders were found guilty of treason, and executed. Finally, a fourth show trial in March 1938 of the remaining Old Bolsheviks led to the execution of eighteen more prominent leaders, including even a former head of the secret police.

The public trials caused a tremendous sensation. The spectacle of Lenin's most trusted collaborators, including all the members of his Politburo except Stalin and Trotsky, confessing to crimes they could not possibly have committed, implied that their minds had been broken. Khrushchev, in his denunciation of Stalin in his secret speech to the Twentieth Party Congress in 1956, charged that physical torture had been used. "Confessions of guilt of many arrested and charged with enemy activity were gained with the help of cruel and inhuman tortures," Khrushchev explained.

Facts prove that many abuses were made on Stalin's orders without reckoning with any norms of Party and Soviet legality. Stalin was a very distrustful man, sickly suspicious; we knew this from our work with him. He could look at a man and say: "Why are your eyes shifty today?" or "Why are you turning so much today and avoiding looking me directly in the eyes?" The sickly suspicion created in him a general distrust even toward eminent party workers whom he had known for years. Everywhere and in everything he saw "enemies," "two-facers" and "spies."

Possessing unlimited power he indulged in a great willfulness and choked a person morally and physically. A situation was created where one could not express one's own will.

When Stalin said that one or another should be arrested, it was necessary to accept on faith that he was an "enemy of the people." Meanwhile Beria's gang, which ran the organ of state security, outdid itself in proving the guilt of the arrested and the truth of materials which it falsified. And what proofs were offered? The confessions of the arrested, and the investigative judges accepted these "confessions." And how is it possible that a person confesses to crimes which he has not committed? Only in one way—because of application of physical methods of pressuring him, tortures, bringing him to a state of unconsciousness, deprivation of his judgment, taking away of his human dignity.[21]

The terror was not restricted to the upper levels of the Communist hierarchy or even to the Party itself. It spread on a huge scale through all levels of society, with punishment varying from execution or labor camp to ejection from the Party or loss of job. A balance sheet is impossible. But some of the prominent statistics speak for themselves. Of 1,966 delegates to the Seventeenth Party Congress of 1934, 1,108 were arrested. Of 139 members and candidates of the Party's Central Committee in 1934, 98 were arrested and shot. Over one and a half million members and candidate members were dropped from the Party. Half the officer corps of the army were arrested. Perhaps five percent of the entire population were arrested for some length of time, and over eight million sent to labor camps. No one could feel safe, no matter how loyal his past or even how blank his mind. In Magnitogorsk, John Scott found thousands had been arrested, mostly at night, and that "people were afraid of anyone and anything foreign." George Kennan, attached to the American embassy in Moscow, saw that a "terrible cloud of suspicion and violence, of sinister, unidentifiable terror and *sauve qui peut* denunciations, began to gather over Russia. . . . If in earlier stages of the development of Soviet power there had been vestiges of belief that society would be genuinely benefited by all the cruelty and suffering, here, in the Russia of the purges, was cynicism, shamelessness, contempt for humanity—all triumphantly enthroned." And Ilya Ehrenburg, returning to Moscow from the Spanish civil war in 1937, was amazed and disoriented at the ubiquitous fear and suspicion. The composer Prokofieff told him, "Today one must work. Work's the only thing, the only salvation." At the newspaper *Izvestia,* they had stopped putting nameplates on the doors: "Here today and gone tomorrow," a messenger girl explained. Meyerhold's theater had been closed, and he himself was soon arrested. Ehrenburg only got back to Spain after sending two personal letters to Stalin. The most inexplicable suffering, however, was that of apolitical citizens, like the Leningrad typing-pool superviser, Olga Petrovna, in Lydia Chukovskaya's heartbreaking little book, *The Deserted House.* Her son, a loyal Komsomol worker, is implicated by a former schoolmate's confession in a plot he knows nothing of; Petrovna slowly breaks down in the misery

---

[21] Cited in Basil Dmytryshyn, *USSR: A Concise History* (New York: Scribner's, 1965), p. 419.

of the faceless oppression. She has to line up for days on end to gain ten-second interviews with clerks in the prosecutor's office. She is denounced in the typing pool, and compelled to resign her job. Friends cross the street to avoid her. Her neighbors plot to take her room. Finally, when a letter is smuggled to her from her son begging her to intercede, she realizes that her action would only increase his own troubles. In a gesture of ultimate despair, she burns the letter.

The effect of the purges went very deep. At the political level, it had removed all important critics of Stalin's policies, and had reinforced his dictatorship at all stages of the Party hierarchy. But it was in the armed forces that most deleterious effects were observed, as the purges not only removed the most competent of the older generation but deprived their replacements of the willingness to take personal initiative. The poor performance against the Finns in the Winter War of 1939–1940 and the early defeats by the Germans during the invasion of 1941 were due, to an important degree, to the weakening of the officer corps.

May Day in Moscow in the 1930s. The first day of May was designated as a festival of the laboring classes by the Second Socialist International in 1889, and has been celebrated as one of the principal holidays in the Soviet Union. (U.S. Information Agency.)

What then was the meaning of the Soviet experience two decades after the revolution? Both Communist apologists and Western observers were in agreement that a vast social and political revolution had taken place and had made possible one of the most gigantic experiments in the remodeling of a society ever undertaken. But what had occurred? There were many for whom the essence of the experiment was the reimposition of the tyranny of one man, now far greater in its controls over the individual citizen because of the physical controls available to the twentieth-century state. To some, Stalin was thus the reincarnation of Russia's historic tyrants, a new Ivan the Terrible; to others, he was the inevitable product of the Communist insistence on the elite's leadership of the proletarian dictatorship that Lenin had made the key idea of bolshevism, the pig who turns into an exploiting farmer himself as in George Orwell's fable *Animal Farm*. For others, the foremost feature of the two decades was the industrialization of an underdeveloped country. Again, however, the industrialization could be interpreted in several ways. For the official apologists in Soviet Russia itself, the industrialization carried through in the Five-Year plans was a highly successful method of speeding up the transition that Marx had described, from capitalism to the ultimate state of communism via an intermediate period of socialism. By 1936, it was held that Russia no longer needed the dictatorship of the proletariat, since class antagonism had vanished; and Russia was about to achieve the final Communist society. Both Soviet and Western observers, however, felt that this forced industrialization through the political control of the Communist party had lessons for other underdeveloped countries. The Soviet regime claimed that the success of their experiment proved that communism was not only the necessary instrument for the end of exploitation in industrialized societies like those of Western Europe but a means by which the underdeveloped regions of the world, namely Asia, Africa, and South America, could achieve not only a more just society but also begin the process of economic development. Finally there were others who looked primarily at the human impact of the revolution. To some, it was a gigantic tragedy, in which human life had been lost on a terrifying scale to satisfy the whims of an autocrat who cynically based his power on a pseudo-ideology. To others, it was an exciting experiment in human brotherhood, in the creation of a new type of man who would lack the economic greed, the self-interest, and the ruthlessness inculcated by the struggle for survival in capitalist society. The very possibility that this might be occurring drew visitors to Moscow by the millions during the 1930s, and it gave the average Russian a tiny ray of hope throughout the darkest days of the purges that a better society was in the making. Without that hope—and the deep-rooted attachment to Russia itself—the Bolshevik experiment must have been hurled away in the torrent of suffering that the Second World War was about to inflict on the Russians.

SUGGESTED READING

Nothing betters the superb vignettes of life in Moscow during the first three decades of the twentieth century in Boris Pasternak's *Doctor Zhivago* (1958), but Konstantin Paustovsky's memoirs, *The Story of a Life* (1964) is a close rival. Moscow is more effectively approached through the reminiscences and novels of Russian and foreign writers than through a more academic treatment. Ilya Ehrenburg, in *Men, Years— Life* (1963) not only gives short portraits of almost all Europe's leading literary figures but does so against a background of Europe's political upheavals, most of which he witnessed personally. Yevgeny Zamyatin's *We* (1924) is a fantasy about the world after the revolution, in which everyone has become a number. It provided inspiration for George Orwell's *1984* (1949) and Aldous Huxley's *Brave New World* (1932), both of which are in part comments on the Russian revolution. The American Communist reporter John Reed gave an exciting account of the November Revolution in Petrograd and a description of Moscow immediately after the revolution in *Ten Days That Shook the World* (1919); Eugene Lyons was stationed as reporter in Moscow in 1928–34, as he relates in *Assignment to Utopia* (1937); and George F. Kennan, *Memoirs, 1925–1950* (1967) summarizes the atmosphere of Moscow on the eve of the purges. The mundane suffering of ordinary people during the 1930s is captured in Lydia Chukovskaya's, *The Deserted House* (1967), while Stalin's daughter, Svetlana Alliluyeva, gives a view of life inside the Kremlin hierarchy in *Twenty Letters to a Friend* (1967).

Anatole Kopp, *Power and Revolution: Soviet Architecture and City Planning 1917–1935* (New York: A. Braziller, 1970), translated by Thomas E. Benton, is the best treatment of the exciting innovations in architecture and city planning in Moscow during the 1920s. E. D. Simon et al., *Moscow in the Making* (1937) describes the new city plan and comments on the nature of Moscow city government under the Communists. For the building of the subway, one should read the biographies of Nikita Khrushchev, such as Lazar Pistrak, *The Grand Tactician: Khrushchev's Rise to Power* (1961) or Edward Crankshaw's somewhat polemical *Khrushchev: A Career* (1966), or see Z. Troitskaya, *The L. M. Kaganovich Metropolitan Railway of Moscow* (1955). Valentin Gonzalez (El Campesino) tells of his work on the later section of the subway in *Listen, Comrades: Life and Death in the Soviet Union* (1952). For short summaries of Moscow's city growth, see the two surveys published in the Soviet Union, Yuri Saushkin, *Moscow* (1966) and the very fine *Moscow: Architecture and Monuments* (1968) of M. Ilyin. Peter Hall, *The World Cities* (1966) concentrates on city planning for the future. For a pictorial view of Moscow in 1928, see Alexys A. Sidorow, *Moskau* (1928).

For broad analyses of the causes of the Russian revolution, see M. T. Florinsky, *The End of the Russian Empire* (1961), which emphasizes the role of war; Bernard Pares, *The Fall of the Russian Monarchy* (1939), in which he explains from personal acquaintance the breakdown of all the social forces that supported the tsardom; and Theodore von Laue, *Why Lenin? Why Stalin?* (1971), an admirably condensed attempt to "view the emergence of Russian communism as an integral part of European and global history." The detailed events of 1917 can be followed in N. N. Sukhanov, *The Russian Revolution, 1917: A Personal Record* (1955); Leon Trotsky, *The History of the Russian Revolution* (1932–33); William H. Chamberlin, *The Russian Revolution, 1917–1921* (1935); Robert V. Daniels, *Red October* (1967); and Alexander Kerensky, *The Kerensky Memoirs* (1965). On the civil war, see David Footman, *Civil War in Russia* (1961). Among the many solid biographies of the Bolshevik leaders, one might browse in David Shub, *Lenin: A Biography* (1966) and Robert Payne, *The Life and Death of Lenin* (1964), both of which are rich in primary materials; or try Adam B. Ulam, *The Bolsheviks* (1965), which is primarily about Lenin. Isaac Deutscher has provided two indispensable studies, his two-volume life of Trotsky, *The Prophet Armed, 1879–1921* (1954) and *The Prophet Unarmed, 1921–1929* (1959), and *Stalin: A Political Biography* (1949). E. H. Carr's enormous study of the first decade of Communist rule, which eschews narrative in favor of political and economic analysis, is composed of *The Bolshevik Revolution* (1951–53), *The Interregnum, 1923–1924* (1954), and *Socialism in One Country, 1924–1926* (1961). The capture during the Second World War of the documents from the Soviet archives in Smolensk made it possible to reconstruct in detail the process of Communist takeover of a big city, which is summarized in Merle Fainsod's excellent *Smolensk under Soviet Rule* (1958).

On the Five-Year plans, see William H. Chamberlin, *Russia's Iron Age* (1934), by a perspicacious reporter; John Scott, *Behind the Urals: An American Worker in Russia's City of Steel* (1942), a very well-written account of Magnitogorsk during the 1930s; and Fedor Belov, *A History of a Soviet Collective Farm* (1955), a personal account of the collectivization of agriculture. Overall industrial results are collated in Naum Jasny, *Soviet Industrialization, 1928–1952* (1961).

Marc L. Slonim provides a short survey of the main figures of Soviet literature in *Soviet Russian Literature: Writers and Problems, 1917–1967* (1967), which can be compared with the Soviet view of the same writers in K. Zelinsky, *Soviet Literature: Problems and People* (1970). The papers of a fine symposium covering the whole development of Soviet literature are collected in Max Hayward and Leopold Labedz, eds., *Literature and Revolution in Soviet Russia, 1917–1962* (1963). Abram Tertz (Andrei Siniavsky) condemns the Stalinist influence on literature in *On Socialist Realism* (1960).

For various verdicts on communization as a human experience, see the comments of the English Socialists Sidney and Beatrice Webb, *Soviet Communism: A New Civilization* (1944); Milorad Drachovitch, ed., *Fifty Years of Communism in Russia* (1968); and Klaus Mehnert, *Soviet Man and His World* (1962).

24
FROM WAR TO WAR, 1919-1945

During the 1920s, Paris once again exercised political and cultural hegemony in the West. Its intellectual preeminence was well deserved. Not only did its own artists and thinkers continue that great creative flowering that began during the Belle Epoque before the war; but it became the haven for foreign intellectuals whose native urban centers could not compete with the City of Light as congenial environments for creative activity— for many of Russia's intelligentsia fleeing the Bolshevik revolution; for Viennese and Hungarians who found that Vienna and Budapest had turned provincial with the loss of their status as imperial capitals; for Italians escaping from Mussolini's fascism; and for Americans disgusted with the materialism of the Roaring Twenties back home or merely unable to leave the city that had entranced them as soldiers during the war. But the political hegemony of Paris was essentially unreal. It was due to the temporary abasement of Germany and to the isolation from the international system of the two major world powers—the United States, retreating in revulsion against further costly intervention in European affairs, and a quarantined Soviet Union, concentrating its efforts on recovering from the civil war and on building socialism in one country.

The Great Depression of 1929–1933 exposed the unreality of French hegemony, however, by destroying the prosperity that had lulled the other powers into accepting France's pretensions. The depression persuaded France and its principal ally, Britain, of their own economic weakness and military incapacity, and thereby attuned them to accept appeasement of military aggressors; it further increased the unwillingness of the United States to risk expensive commitments to the European powers; and it brought to power in Germany the Nazi party, which under Adolf Hitler was to use the vast economic and military resources of Germany for premeditated aggression. Thus in the 1930s, the center of political hegemony in the West passed from Paris to Berlin, from the capital of the Third Re-

Nuremberg in 1945. When the American army captured Nuremberg in 1945, it found 90 percent of its buildings destroyed. (U.S. Office of War Information.)

public to the capital of the Third Reich. In Berlin was a society that was in many ways the antithesis of everything that Western civilization had created in the previous two thousand years, the Nazi totalitarian state based on perverted racist doctrines of a sadistic madman.

THE LAST HEGEMONY OF PARIS

Paris Peace Conference of 1919. The armistice agreement of November 11, 1918, that finally brought an end to the fighting of the First World War, was greeted by the citizens of the victorious powers with a mixture of relief and jubilation. Siegfried Sassoon expressed the general delight with a poem that began:

Everybody suddenly burst out singing
And I was filled with such delight
As prisoned birds must find in freedom.[1]

That night the crowds went wild in London's Trafalgar Square, on the Champs Elysées in Paris, and in Times Square in New York, to celebrate the end of the bloodletting. Sixteen million people had died as a result of the war, and another twenty million had been wounded. The French army had mobilized over eight million men, and three-quarters of them had been killed or wounded; one-twentieth of the French population had died.

Armistice Night, by George Benjamin Luks (1867–1933). (Collection of the Whitney Museum of American Art, New York.)

[1] From "Everybody Sang" by Siegfried Sassoon. Copyright 1920 by E. P. Dutton, renewed 1948 by Siegfried Sassoon. From *Collected Poems* by Siegfried Sassoon. All rights reserved. Reprinted by permission of The Viking Press, Inc. and George Sassoon.

Georges Clemenceau, by Auguste Rodin. Rodin's craggy bronze captures perfectly the ferocity of the "Tiger," as Clemenceau was called. (Philadelphia Museum of Art.)

Britain and Italy each had had losses of a million men; and the United States, 126,000. The Allied victors had spent $156 billion, the defeated Central powers $63 billion. The French premier, Clemenceau, the sharp-tongued Tiger who had lashed France to final victory, slowly came to dominate the proceedings of the peace conference, which began in Paris in January. In Lord Keynes's malicious but essentially truthful picture of him in *The Economic Consequences of the Peace* (1919), Clemenceau appears as the epitome of the cynical, Machiavellian, Old World statesman, whose primary preoccupation is to prevent the foolish unrealistic scruples of the American president, Woodrow Wilson, from stopping the permanent debilitation of Germany. In a classic passage, Keynes summed up Clemenceau and his vision of France:

He felt about France what Pericles felt of Athens—unique value in her, nothing else mattering; but his theory of politics was Bismarck's. He had one illusion—France; and one disillusion—mankind, including Frenchmen, and his colleagues not least. His principles for the peace can be expressed simply. In the first place, he was a foremost believer in the view of German psychology that the German understands and can understand nothing but intimidation, that he is without generosity or remorse in negotiation, that there is no advantage he will not take of you, and no extent to which he will not demean himself for profit, that he is without honor, pride, or mercy. Therefore you must never negotiate with a German or conciliate him; you must dictate to him. On no other terms will he respect you, or will you prevent him from cheating you. But it is doubtful how far he thought these characteristics peculiar to Germany, or whether his candid view of some other nations was fundamentally different.[2]

With that premise, it was easy to justify territorial dismemberment and economic exactions from Germany. Alsace and Lorraine were returned to France, and it was handed the mining region of the Saar for fifteen years. The reconstituted Polish state was given the Polish Corridor, a broad strip of territory separating East Prussia from the main body of Germany. The German colonial empire was divided among the Allies, and its merchant fleet shared out as reparations. During the following two years, it was to pay $5 billion in reparations; the total amount to be paid was finally settled at $31 billion. To ensure the military weakness of Germany, its army was to be reduced to 100,000 men; the left bank of the Rhine and a strip fifty kilometers wide on the right bank were to be permanently demilitarized; and occupation troops, mostly from France, were to be stationed in the Rhineland for fifteen years. The Germans were appalled by this dictated settlement, which they labelled the *Diktat,* but were compelled to accept it unchanged under the threat of Allied invasion. Their representatives appeared at the Palace of Versailles on June 28, 1919 to give ceremonial atonement to the French for Bismarck's choice of the same Hall of Mirrors for the declaration of the German empire in January 1871. Harold Nicolson described the ceremony in his diary that evening:

Through the door at the end appear two huissiers with silver chains. They march in single file. After them come four officers of France, Great Britain, America and Italy. And then, isolated and pitiable, come the two German delegates, Dr. Müller and Dr. Bell. The silence is terrifying. Their feet upon a strip of parquet between the savonnerie carpets echo hollow and duplicate. They keep their eyes fixed away from those two thousand staring eyes, fixed upon the ceiling. They are deathly pale. They do not appear as representatives of a brutal militarism. . . . Suddenly from outside comes the crash of guns thundering a salute. It announces to Paris that the second Treaty of Versailles [the first being the treaty of 1871 at the end of the Franco-Prussian War] had been signed by Dr. Müller and Dr. Bell. Through the few open windows comes the sound of distant crowds cheering hoarsely. . . . We kept our seats while the Germans were conducted like prisoners from the dock, their eyes still fixed upon some distant point of the horizon.[3]

Equally momentous changes were being ratified in other suburban palaces of Paris that spring. The peace conference had also sanctioned the dismemberment of the Austro-Hungarian and Turkish empires. It gave to the new state of Czechoslovakia not only the Czech provinces of Bohemia and Moravia, Slovakia, and the Ukrainian province of Sub-Carpathian

[2] John Maynard Keynes, *The Economic Consequences of the Peace* (New York: Harper Torchbook, 1971), pp. 32–33.
[3] Harold Nicolson, *Peacemaking* (London: Constable, 1934), pp. 366–71.

Ruthenia, but also the border province of the Sudetenland, where almost three million Germans lived. Serbia expanded to become the South Slav state of Yugoslavia. The aggrieved Hungarians were left with a small state of only eight million inhabitants. Poland, in addition to the formerly German territories of the Polish Corridor, was permitted, after four years of fighting with Soviet Russia, to annex a large strip of territory in White Russia. The Turks lost the Arab provinces in the Middle East, Britain taking up mandates over Palestine, Iraq, and Jordan, and France over Lebanon and Syria. Finally, the independence of Finland, Estonia, Latvia, and Lithuania, granted at the Treaty of Brest Litovsk, was left undisturbed.

Thus a line of new or remodeled states stretched from the Arctic to the Mediterranean in place of the three great empires that had collapsed during the war. Although these states all possessed fine written constitutions, they were economically backward, socially divided, and politically unstable. Eastern Europe had become a political vacuum inviting the intervention of Germany from the west and Russia from the east. Its social divisions gave the Fascist states allies in the landed aristocracy and the well-to-do bourgeoisie, and gave to Communist Russia supporters among certain sections of the industrial proletariat and the farming population. Eastern Europe

Central Europe
between the Wars

— · — German Empire, 1914
|||||||| Russian Empire, 1914
•••••• Austro-Hungarian
Empire, 1914
Territorial losses
of the empires:
1918–1923

became the greatest threat to the maintenance of a workable balance-of-
power system during the interwar years.

French Enforcement of the Treaty of Versailles.   The French soon discovered that they would be the chief enforcers of the treaty from which
they had the most to gain.   The American Senate refused to ratify the Treaty
of Versailles; and the United States did not even join the League of Nations.
The French therefore sought to build up an alliance system with Poland,
Czechoslovakia, Rumania, and Yugoslavia.   As long as Germany remained
quiescent, these alliances with states whose military strength was grossly
overestimated appeared to give France the ability to threaten Germany
with a two-front war.   The French therefore felt strong enough for several
years to use military force to ensure that Germany kept the obligations
imposed upon it by the Treaty of Versailles.

In response to what they regarded as deliberate default on reparations
payments, the French took over the customs collection at the German

border, moved into several Rhineland towns, and finally in 1923, occupied the vast industrial region of the Ruhr. The Germans replied with passive resistance. All industries closed down, transportation stopped, and government workers refused to collaborate. For months, the French tried desperately to break the resistance by arresting leaders of the general strike, using soldiers to run essential services, and confiscating industrial produce. The German currency collapsed; Communist coups were attempted in several industrial cities; Hitler made a first attempt to seize power in Munich; separatist movements attempted to gain autonomy for the Rhineland. But France found the occupation of the Ruhr too costly. Its own currency began to waver, owing to the burden of the occupation army and the total cessation of reparations payments. It finally, in 1924, accepted American intervention through the Dawes Plan, which scaled down German reparations payments and guaranteed large American loans to back the currency and industrial recovery.

The Years of Hope, 1924–1929. After the crisis of 1923–1924, Europe enjoyed half a decade of economic prosperity, in which French hegemony was expressed in the organization of various schemes of international cooperation. Largely through the work of French Foreign Minister Aristide Briand, the Germans were persuaded to accept the permanence of their new border with France, at a dramatically harmonious meeting of the British, French, and German foreign ministers in the Swiss lakeside town of Locarno in 1925. The Germans were welcomed to the League of Nations; they joined with almost every nation in the world in signing the vapid declarations of international good will contained in the Kellogg-Briand peace pacts of 1928; and they even debated for a time joining with France in a European federal union. The continuance of this "spirit of Locarno" was, however, dependent on the economic prosperity that in the late 1920s was making territorial losses seem far less significant than enjoyment of the material benefits of the new industrial productivity.

The prosperity of 1924–1929 was real. Throughout Europe, there was a general stabilization of the currencies, which led many countries to revert to the gold standard. Technological advances, many of them the result of the war, were creating whole new industries, among them automobile and airplane manufacturing, artificial fibers, chemical fertilizers, electrical appliances, and oil and its by-products. Older industries were being revitalized by new methods of organization. The number of cartels increased enormously, especially in Germany where the new giants included the great chemical trust, I. G. Farben, and Europe's largest steel trust, Vereinigte Stahlwerke; and a number of conglomerates were formed. "Americanization" of production included the use of management consulting firms, the introduction of time-and-motion studies, and especially widespread attempts at standardization of parts and use of the conveyor belt for mass production. Spending on public works projects and on public housing gave a boost to the construction industry and stimulated the production of cement, timber, brick, and paintstuffs. The increase in real wages acted as a stimulus to the consumer industries, from such items as cosmetics, which became an important industry at this time, to processed foodstuffs.

There were, however, many precarious features underlying this prosperity. Agriculture never knew the prosperity of the cities. Even among the industrial population, unemployment remained high during the best years of the prosperity. In England, for example, it never sank below one million, roughly one-tenth of the working population. Many of the cartels were unstable structures that fell apart in times of economic recession, destroying smaller companies that might have been able to survive on their own initiative. The dependence of Europe on American loans, many of them short-term, and on the continuance of large American imports from Europe, was especially risky. The American economy was based on overextended credit and the collapse of this credit structure would inevitably produce vast repercussions in Europe as short-term loans would be called in, new loans would diminish, and the market for European exports would be greatly restricted.

The Depression of 1929–1933. The depression was precipitated by the Wall Street crash of October 1929, which in a few weeks reduced the value of the American industrial stocks by half. Five thousand American banks failed; farm prices collapsed; industrial companies cut back on work forces, thereby further reducing the demand for goods. Within three years, American unemployment had reached twelve million. The industrial areas of Europe were the first to feel the effects of the American crash, especially those which had borrowed heavily from American banks. In May 1931, the greatest Austrian bank, the Credit-Anstalt, which held two-thirds of Austria's assets, collapsed. The panic immediately spread through parts of Eastern Europe, for which the Credit-Anstalt had been banker. Panic-

Crowds Outside the Stock Exchange on Wall Street after the Crash of October 1929.
(U.S. Information Agency.)

stricken depositors withdrew their savings, precipitating more bank failures. Industries reduced production and laid off workers; and desperate governments made matters worse by decreeing economy measures and higher taxes that increased the recession. The huge German bank, the Darmstädter National, failed shortly after the Credit-Anstalt, and a similar depression spiral soon affected Germany. Unemployment rose steadily until it hit six million in 1932. In Britain, where the Bank of England was paying out over $12 million in gold each day, the Labour government resigned, and was replaced by a National Government that took Britain off the gold standard. Economy measures failed to halt the recession, however, and England's unemployment rose to over two and a half million.

France at first escaped the worst effects of the depression. Its agriculture had absorbed many of the unemployed industrial workers who had gone home to the family farms; and it had reduced the impact of unemployment by sending home thousands of foreign workers. But in 1932, France, too, felt the depression. Tourism, especially from the United States, was greatly reduced; export markets, particularly for French luxury goods, had been closed; agricultural prices and income were dropping. The customary budget surplus had been replaced by a deficit of 6 billion francs. Governments began to fall like ninepins; in 1932–1934 there were six different governments. France slowly lost the belief in its own economic strength and in its military importance that had given it the self-confidence to attempt to dominate the European state system throughout the 1920s. It turned in on itself, occupied with the problems of economic recovery and of political instability. And in 1930, almost as a symbol of their loss of confidence, the French began construction of the Maginot Line, steel and concrete fortifications intended to halt any German invasion along the whole border from southern Belgium to Switzerland.

The Golden Twenties: A Second Belle Epoque. At the time the Maginot Line was begun, an equally symbolic change took place in France's cultural life; the literary expatriates began to go home. The second Belle Epoque was over.

Paris was especially exhilarating to intellectuals and artists in the 1920s since so many of the innovations that had been ignored or scorned when they were conceived in the last years before the World War were now accepted and admired by the members of the educated public. They followed Picasso as he moved from cubism back to figurative painting and then on into surrealism, in which the distorted images of the subconscious mind were presented as a new form of artistic understanding. They paid increasingly high prices for the more easily appreciated works of Utrillo and Bonnard, and showed new appreciation of the experiments in cubism that Braque and Léger continued to make. Even dadaism, the cult of nonsense invented by the Rumanian expatriate Tristan Tzara, found its advocates. Dada called for the rejection of all established styles, the rejection of reason, the overthrow of authority, the expression of the immediate im-

Three Musicians, by Pablo Picasso (1881–). In his Cubist painting of 1921, Picasso forces the viewer to re-create for himself the original subject, while the artist stimulates his understanding of its inner meaning. (Philadelphia Museum of Art, Photograph by A. J. Wyatt, Staff Photographer.)

pulse or thought or emotion. For literary innovation, too, there was a new receptivity. Although Proust had died in 1922, the remaining volumes of *Remembrance of Things Past* continued to appear until 1927, to constant acclaim. André Gide (1869–1951), praised by the dadaist and surrealist writers, was recognized as the master literary craftsman of the generation. In his *Journals* and especially in the novel *The Counterfeiters* (1926), he wrestled, in a severely disciplined classical manner, with the problem of reconciling man's hidden drives with the demands of society. For him, the individual consciousness had rights that were denied it by rigid social convention, rights that he justified by slowly revealing to the public his own inner deviations. Behind Gide followed a group of younger writers, all bent on trying new forms of experimentation. Among them were surrealists like Paul Eluard and Louis Aragon, whose experimentation finally took political form and brought them into the Communist party. In music, Stravinsky had conquered, and the scandal of the first performance of *The Rites of Spring* was forgotten. He again worked with Diaghilev and the Ballets Russes, who, reassembled in Paris after the war, turned to ever more innovative styling, exploring the unconscious in dance forms, and rejecting the conventionally pretty for stark, angular effects of lighting or choreography.

Paris became home to a group of young American expatriates who combined determination to enjoy Paris to the full with the discipline for producing fine writing. They formed almost a world of their own on the Left Bank, living in cold uncomfortable flats six or eight floors up, making do on pickings from occasional journalism or sale of a short story, re-creating the "Vie de Bohème" with a consciousness and a vivacity that exceeded even that of the fin de siècle. The shrill awareness of the precarious nature of their good fortune, of the still inexplicable brutality of the war that lay behind them, and of the uncertainty of the political future was captured by F. Scott Fitzgerald in books like *The Great Gatsby,* and by Ernest Hemingway in *The Sun Also Rises.* It remained a constant in their daily lives, as Hemingway described it later in his superb little memoir *A Moveable Feast.* "Paris was a very old city and we were young and nothing was simple there," Hemingway wrote, "not even poverty, nor sudden money, nor the moonlight, nor right and wrong nor the breathing of someone who lay beside you in the moonlight." The wild cacophony of their lives comes through in all the writing of this Parisian generation of Americans—in the disconnected phrases of the poems of e e cummings, in the cinematic sequences of John Dos Passos, and especially in the myriad themes of *Ulysses,* the masterpiece by the Irishman James Joyce, who was recognized by the whole American colony as the commanding genius among them.

Ernest Hemingway (1898–1961). (U.S. Office of War Information.)

With the depression and the appointment of Adolf Hitler as German chancellor in 1933, this frenetic age of literary creation came to an end, or rather changed character. Politics became increasingly important, even to France's literary and artistic figures who had tried most vigorously to avoid its entanglement. During the 1930s, all groups in French society found that they had to come to terms with the phenomenon of Fascism, both in its internal manifestations as a right-wing threat to French democratic institutions and especially as an external danger embodied in Hitler's Third Reich.

Suppression of the Spartacus Uprising in Berlin, January 1919. German troops, using a tank borrowed from the British army, move through a working-class section of Berlin. (French Embassy Press and Information Division photo.)

RISE OF FASCISM

In 1919 most West European leaders felt that the main threat to the stability of their political and social institutions was the Bolshevik regime in Russia. But by 1923, all Communist attempts to take power had failed. The Spartacus uprising of German Communists in January 1919 had been put down with bloody violence by the freelance bands of demobilized soldiers called the *Freikorps*. The Communist regime installed in Hungary under Bela Kun was ousted by a monarchist Rumanian army in November 1919, after only six months in power. And various sporadic Communist uprisings in the industrial cities of Germany between 1920 and 1923 were repressed by the regular army. By 1923, it was obvious that the hope of a continent-wide proletarian revolution, which Lenin and Trotsky had believed might occur at the end of the war, had been disappointed. Yet as Communism receded as an immediate threat to the democratic governments it was replaced by the challenge of Fascism, a right-wing totalitarian movement that took power in Italy in 1922, and in 1933–1939 in one form or another seized control of most of the governments of central and eastern Europe.

Triumph of Italian Fascism. Benito Mussolini (1883–1945) had been a Socialist agitator before the First World War; he had thrown his considerable talents as journalist and orator into organizing Italian migrant labor and into opposing Italy's war to seize Libya in 1911. During the First World War, however, he changed course completely, demanding intervention by Italy, serving in the army himself, and glorifying the moral benefits of war in raising the spiritual caliber of the nation. At war's end, he formed a political movement called *fasci di combattimento* (fighting bands) to channel the discontent of demobilized soldiers against the Reds, who were sponsoring, or at least acquiescing in, seizure by the workers of the North Italian factories, and against the spineless democratic government. By 1922, Mussolini had laid down the propagandist slogans that were to bring him to power. Man exists for the state, and is not fully alive unless he is part of the state. Man must sacrifice himself for the state; the highest form of sacrifice occurs in war. Democracy is a form of dictatorship of the majority, and must be replaced by the rule of an elite guided by a leader, a *Duce*. The Duce embodies in himself the will of the nation, and thus can never be wrong in any of his actions: "Il Duce ha sempre ragione" (The leader is always right) he later emblazoned on every wall in Italy. The nation is a body that exists permanently in time, binding together the generations of past and future; the present Italian generation must re-create the glories of the Roman Empire. The new Italy must make the Adriatic an Italian lake and the Mediterranean into "our sea"; and it must win "sun and earth" in the colonial territories of Africa.

Mussolini Working at His Desk in the Palazzo Venezia, Rome. (U.S. Information Agency.)

In the social turmoil of 1919–1922, many discontented middle-class people turned to the Fascist movement to rouse them from what Mussolini called the "red plague." In October 1922, Mussolini felt strong enough to proclaim a March on Rome by every Fascist in Italy. Only about 10,000 of his black-shirted followers finally made it to the capital, but the government resigned in terror. Mussolini was then invited by King Victor Emmanuel II to form a government, all the legal forms being scrupulously respected.

During the next seven years, he painstakingly destroyed all opposition. Rival political parties found their offices destroyed; and their leaders were beaten up in the streets or arrested. One leading Socialist was brutally murdered and his body flung in the Tiber. A new election law gave a majority of the seats in parliament to the party that won the greatest number of votes. The resultant Fascist-controlled parliament abolished all other political parties. All judges were replaced with loyal Fascists; trade unions turned into Fascist corporations; and all local government made directly responsible to the central government. Recalcitrant opponents were exiled to prison islands off the coast of Italy or sent into remote villages in the southern mountains. Mussolini's greatest success was to make a concordat with the papacy, which from the time of Italian unification in 1871 had refused to have any dealings with the new Italian state. In return for large financial concessions, continuing Church influence on Italian education, and the recognition of the formal independence of the tiny Vatican City as a separate state, the pope agreed to establish diplomatic relations with the Fascist government.

During the 1920s, Mussolini achieved considerable popularity at home without causing much opposition abroad. His public-works policies, which included draining of marshes, building new roads, and construction of many public buildings, helped maintain employment. Big companies found the Fascist government willing to give them a free hand in industrial planning, and to help them by keeping the labor force disciplined. Bombastic speeches restored national pride without exacting a high price. Mussolini seemed to have made dictatorship respectable; and to many conservative Europeans, his regime, and those of the military dictator Primo de Rivera in Spain from 1923 to 1930 and of the military-backed presidency of Antonio de Oliveira Salazar in Portugal established in 1926, were models of firm, anti-Communist government.

Nazi Movement in Germany. The National-Socialist (Nazi) movement in Germany had a more brutal vigor and sinister leadership, although many of the tenets of its ideology were similar to those of Italian Fascism. It was the brainchild of a sallow, dark-eyed young Austrian with a fine command of emotive oratory and a bundle of neurotic hatreds. Adolf Hitler's most lasting obsession, his hatred of the Jews, was probably acquired during his early days in prewar Vienna, where, denied admission to the Academy of Fine Arts by what he felt to be Jewish prejudice, he was forced to earn a meager living by manual labor, house painting, and selling little picture postcards he painted of Viennese buildings. The Jews came to represent "the evil spirits leading our people astray," the inspiration for the modern art and music he despised, the cosmopolitan bourgeois elite that dominated Viennese life. By 1913, he considered the Jews poisonous dregs in the pure Aryan blood.

In 1914, he enrolled in a Bavarian regiment and in four years of service on the western front, acquired an admiration for war, in which "individual interest—the interest of one's own ego—could be subordinated to the common interest." When he returned to Munich, his aim was an ideology backed by ruthless physical force. In 1919, he joined a small group of anti-Semitic amateur politicians, renamed it the National-Socialist German Workers party, and made himself its leader, or *Führer*. By 1923, he had gathered around himself many of the party's future leaders, including scar-faced Ernst Röhm, who put together the brown-shirted storm troops of the Sturm-Abteilung (SA), Rudolf Hess and Hermann Göring. At that time he carried out his first and only attempt to seize power by force. With a force of about three thousand men, he arrested the Bavarian government during a Munich beer-hall rally, but fled the next day when his storm troopers were routed by determined police action. He was arrested, put in jail for eight months, and used the time to write his memoirs, *Mein Kampf*.

When he emerged from jail, Germany was feeling the first elation of returning prosperity, and the Nazis made little progress in winning support. Hitler devoted himself to careful grooming of his party for a semilegal conquest of power. He showed great skill in developing propaganda devices, such as banners, the swastika, armbands, jack-boots, disciplined hordes of marching men, and innumerable hate-provoking slogans. His ideology took form as a consistent political doctrine that could be easily grasped by the unsophisticated public. All nations were part of a racial hierarchy, he held, in which superiority was dependent on quality of blood. The Jews were an impurity in the German blood that would have to be removed; the Slavs were subhuman *(Untermenschen)*, and their future was to act as laborers for the Germans. All Germans should live in the German fatherland, especially those who had been forcibly separated by the territorial annexations of the Treaty of Versailles. Germany itself, however, was too small for the German people, which needed living space *(Lebensraum)* that it would find in the return of Germany's colonial empire and especially by expansion into the vast plains occupied by the Slavs of Poland and Russia. Germany should be governed by a new elite, the Nazi party, under a Führer; then it would recognize those qualities that were necessary for its own greatness. To be a National Socialist, his propaganda chief Josef Goebbels wrote, meant nothing less than "Kampf, Glaube, Arbeit, Obfer" (struggle, belief, work, sacrifice), ideal qualities for the service of a totalitarian state.

The depression of 1929–1933 gave the Nazis their opportunity to capitalize on the discontent of six million unemployed, of white-collar workers who had lost their savings, of conservatives sickened of the indecisiveness

of the Weimar regime, and of industrialists who feared the advance of Socialism and Communism. By 1932, the Nazis were the largest party in the
Reichstag; and in January 1933, Hitler was able to force his appointment
as chancellor. That night, the Nazis gave Berlin a spectacle that dwarfed
any demonstration of William II's day. The French Ambassador, André
François-Poncet, later described the scene:

*In massive columns, flanked by bands that played martial airs, [the Nazi storm-
troopers] emerged from the depths of the Tiergarten and passed under the triumphal
arch of the Brandenburg Gate. The torches they brandished formed a river of fire,
a river with hastening, unquenchable waves, a river in spate sweeping with a
sovereign rush over the very heart of the city. From these brown-shirted, booted
men, as they marched by in perfect discipline and alignment, their well-pitched
voices bawling warlike songs, there arose an enthusiasm and dynamism that were
extraordinary. The onlookers, drawn up on either side of the marching columns,
burst into a vast clamor. The river of fire flowed past the French Embassy, whence,
with heavy heart and filled with foreboding, I watched its luminous wake; it turned
down the Wilhelmstrasse and rolled under the windows of the Marshal's palace.*

*The old man [President Hindenburg] stood there leaning upon his cane, struck by
the power of the phenomenon which he had himself let loose. At the next window
stood Hitler, the object of a very tempest of cheers, as wave upon wave kept surging
up from the alleys of the Tiergarten.*[4]

Berlin, from William II to Hitler. Nowhere did Hitler's advent to power
strike more chillingly than in Berlin itself, for the capital was enjoying its
most scintillating period of creativity. Since 1918 there had been a new
freedom of expression, particularly of the sardonic wit for which the Berliner had been noted throughout Germany, and an unleashing of all kinds
of social inhibitions, which found expression in jazz, gaudy night clubs,
drugs, and drunkenness: "Berlin transformed itself into the Babel of the
world," wrote Stefan Zweig. The multiplicity of political parties gave vigor
to a political debate that had been sadly unrealistic during most of the
Second Reich. The University of Berlin entered its most fecund period;
its professors included Friedrich Meinecke in history and Einstein and
Planck in physics. One of the main training schools in the new art of
psychoanalysis was the Berlin Psychoanalytical Institute, which produced
many of the decade's greatest psychologists. But it was in the arts that
Berlin especially excelled. With forty theaters, two great orchestras, three
operas, one hundred and twenty newspapers, and most of the great publishing houses, it centralized German culture without stifling it. Bertolt Brecht,
the innovative left-wing playwright, moved to Berlin in 1925, to join in the
collaboration with Kurt Weill that three years later produced *The Three-
penny Opera.* Georg Grosz and Käthe Kollwitz were revealing the suffer-
erings of the poor in spare, heartbreaking sketches. The expressionist
painters, including the notable immigrants Wassily Kandinsky and Paul

[4] André François-Poncet, *The Fateful Years* (New York: Harcourt Brace, 1949), p. 48.

Klee, were experimenting with the use of color and abstract design to represent what has been intuitively rather than intellectually understood. The
films above all struck out in new directions, from the dark cruelty of *The
Cabinet of Dr. Caligari* (1920) to the pacifist *All Quiet on the Western
Front* (1930).

Beneath the surface in Weimar Germany, however, there was a sense
of desperation that was alien to the spirit of Paris. The recurrent economic
crises, especially the great inflation of 1923 and the depression-provoked
unemployment of 1929–1933, made everyone skeptical of the future, and
left them with a deep distrust of the capacity of the republican politicians.
The atmosphere of the last years before Hitler was captured by the English
novelist Christopher Isherwood, who eked out a mean existence among
the worst Berlin slums during the collapse of the Weimar Republic, in *The
Last of Mr. Norris* (1935) and *Goodbye to Berlin* (1939). Visiting Isherwood
in his scrofulous neighborhood, the poet Stephen Spender found "there
was a sensation of doom to be felt in the Berlin streets."

*In this Berlin, the poverty, the agitation, the propaganda, witnessed by us in the
streets and cafes, seemed more and more to represent the whole life of the town, as
though there were almost no privacy behind doors. Berlin was the tension, the
poverty, the anger, the prostitution, the hope and despair thrown out on to the
streets. . . .*

**The Potsdamer Platz, Berlin
in the Early 1930s.** (German
Information Center photo.)

[We] became ever more aware that the carefree personal lives of our friends were facades in front of the immense social chaos. There was more and more a feeling that this life would be swept away. When we were on holiday at Insel Ruegen, where the naked bathers in their hundreds lay stretched on the beach under the drugging sun, sometimes we heard orders rapped out, and even shots, from the forest whose edges skirted the shore, where the Storm Troopers were training like executioners waiting to martyr the armed and self-disarmed.[5]

Hitler's Berlin. The Nazis changed the atmosphere of Berlin in a few weeks. At first life went on as usual, many people expecting the Nazis, once in power, to moderate their propagandist attacks on such groups as the Jews. In February, however, the Reichstag building was set on fire, possibly by a crazed Communist put up to the job by the Nazi storm troopers, and the incident was used as an excuse for suspending guarantees of individual liberty and for banning the Communist party. In March, Hitler forced through the Reichstag the Enabling Act, which granted him power to govern by decree for four years, a power he used shortly after to ban all political parties except the Nazis, to destroy the trade unions, and to bring the law courts under Nazi control. In June 1934, he purged his own party of possible opposition elements by murdering several hundred storm troop leaders in the "Night of Long Knives." Finally, when Hindenburg died in August 1934, Hitler himself took the offices of both president and chancellor. Within eighteen months, he had exceeded the powers Mussolini had accumulated in twelve years.

The Nazis made it evident to Berlin that they were serious, humorless renovators who intended to wipe out what they felt were Jewish cultural depravities of the Weimar period. During the next six years, there was an exodus of many of Germany's leading intellectual and artistic figures, including Heinrich and Thomas Mann, Gropius, Grosz, Kandinsky, Zweig, Zuckmayer, Einstein, and thousands of others. The Nazis welcomed the exodus, and turned to the creation of a distinctively Nazi culture. Atonal music, abstract painting, and stream-of-consciousness literature were banned. Hitler's taste in music ran to Wagner and a few light operas, although Wilhelm Furtwängler and the Berlin Philharmonic continued to give superb performances of the most established classics. The approved taste in art, a robust naturalism similar to that of the contemporary socialist realism in Russia, was displayed in Munich in 1937, in the exhibition of German art that was run parallel to a show of decadent art, including post-impressionists and abstract painters. In architecture, the steel and concrete structures of Gropius and his followers were replaced by a monstrous neobaroque style, in which Hitler himself, the architect manqué, took constant interest.

Hitler had grandiose plans for making Berlin a worthy capital of the vast empire he proposed to win for Germany. He admired the remodeling

---

[5] Stephen Spender, *World within World* (London: Hamish Hamilton, 1951), pp. 129–31.

of Vienna in the 1860s, but thought the finest of all urban planners was Haussmann, who had remodeled Paris for Emperor Napoleon III. At times he may have toyed with the idea of creating a great new capital city in an uninhabited part of Germany, to put himself on the level of Peter the Great; but he soon decided that Berlin was the only suitable setting for the monumental vistas he had in mind. Albert Speer, his architect during the 1930s, claimed that Hitler's desire to outdo any previous buildings—a larger Arc de Triomphe, a wider and longer Champs Elysées, a statue bigger than the Statue of Liberty, even a suspension bridge bigger than San Francisco's Golden Gate—was not only egomania but a matter of policy. He wanted to "transmit his time and its spirit to posterity," because his buildings would represent the rebirth of national grandeur after a period of decline. He began with the theatrical settings for the huge party rallies in Nuremberg, moved on to a large remodeling of the chancellery, and kept Speer at work for almost a decade on models of the vastest city rebuilding ever undertaken. "Berlin is a big city," he told Speer, "but not a real metropolis. Look at Paris, the most beautiful city in the world. Or even Vienna. Those are cities with grand style. Berlin is nothing but an unregulated accumulation of buildings. We must surpass Paris and Vienna." [6] His plans called for a three-mile long avenue, with a domed hall at one end several times larger than Saint Peter's Cathedral in Rome and an Arch of Triumph at the other

[6] Albert Speer, *Inside the Third Reich: Memoirs* (New York: Macmillan, 1970), p. 75.

Nazi Party Rally, Nuremberg. The annual rally of several hundred thousand party members was carefully planned to impress onlookers with the irresistible power of the Nazi movement. (The National Archives.)

four hundred feet high. Beside the great dome, around a new Adolf Hitler Platz, were to be grouped the main buildings of the Third Reich: a new chancellery, that for the High Command of the Armed Forces, and the Reichstag building.

The majority of Germans found Hitler's first six years in office an exciting and gratifying time. Most of the six million unemployed were back at work within three years. The rearmament program, the public works projects, which included the famous freeways, or Autobahn network, the conscription of workers into labor battalions, the provision of inexpensive open-air vacations, the general sense of purpose and strength displayed by the new regime, won Hitler widespread support. Although concentration camps had been set up and the secret police, the Gestapo, were active, most people were able to convince themselves that the Jews were in most cases being permitted to leave the country without molestation. The industrialists were pleased to be given a free hand in a program of concentration of ownership, and were made prosperous by large-scale state contracts for armaments. But the Germans did not follow Hitler gladly into war; and as it became evident in 1938–1939 that he was bent on military adventures, his popularity dipped so greatly that Nazi officials had difficulty in assembling enthusiastic crowds when Hitler appeared in public. By then, however, all opposition inside Germany had been cowed, and the Germans could only follow him sullenly into war. Fortunately for them, the disarray among Germany's future conquerors was to make his early victories cheap.

THE COMING OF THE SECOND WORLD WAR

Hitler's Foreign Policy. Hitler's first aim was to overthrow the Treaty of Versailles. This implied the withdrawal of Germany from the League of Nations and its disarmament conferences, the return of the Saar to Germany, large-scale rearmament, the remilitarization of the Rhineland, and the return to Germany of the territories incorporated into the new Polish state. The restoration of Germany's prewar position was only the preliminary, however, to the goal of achieving the reunification of all German blood and German land *(Blut und Boden)* within the Third Reich. The immediate goal, apart from the restoration of the Germans of Poland and the Free City of Danzig, was the annexation to Germany of the Sudetenland of Czechoslovakia and the whole of Austria; but the "Germanness" of Alsace-Lorraine, Luxembourg, and Slovenia would eventually require their return to Germany. Finally, Hitler considered that this Greater Germany would need *Lebensraum* (Space to Live), which it would find at the expense of the supposedly inferior races in the East of Europe, the Slavs of Poland and Russia. In *Mein Kampf,* he had announced:

We put an end to the perpetual Germanic march towards the south and west of Europe and turn our eyes towards the lands of the east. We finally put a stop to the colonial and commercial policy of prewar times and pass over to the territorial policy of the future. But when we speak of new territory in Europe today, we must

*principally think of Russia and the border states subject to her. Destiny itself seems
to wish to point out the way for us here. . . . This colossal empire in the east is ripe
for dissolution.*[7]

The Policy of Appeasement. Only strong concerted action by the Western
democracies—Britain, France, and the United States—in coalition with the
Soviet Union could have blocked Hitler's expansionist ambitions. The
Western democracies however were in disarray. The United States alone
possessed the economic resources and the population adequate to meet
the German challenge; in 1919, its population was 105 million compared
with 59 million in Germany. But the experience of the First World War
had left Americans isolationist; and, as late as 1937, President Franklin D.
Roosevelt was unable to rouse any public support for measures that would
quarantine military aggressors in Europe. Britain and France were thus left
as the sole bulwark against Hitler in the West. The British, however, were
struggling to overcome their economic problems at home, and felt incapable of making any primary military effort in Europe. The First World
War had cost them one-quarter of their national wealth; the general strike
of 1926 had brought the country to the verge of social war in the streets;
and no government dared take action that would increase the level of unemployment. Britain's political leaders, vapid Socialists like Ramsay Mac-
donald and insensitive businessmen like Stanley Baldwin, were unable to
provide the kind of inspiring direction that alone could have persuaded the
British people of the need of new sacrifices to meet a renewed German
danger in Europe. The French were facing great political disruption at
home. Large numbers of right-wing groups, many of them sympathetic to
Nazi Germany, were threatening to overthrow the failing democratic structure and its scandal-stained practitioners; on the left, the Communists had
made great headway in gaining control of the trade unions and in gaining
electoral support. With a shaky political system, a depressed economy, and
an atrociously anachronistic military leadership, France relied on the supposed impregnability of its Maginot Line.

Stalin was well aware of Hitler's ultimate intention of attacking Russia.
Many of Russia's war industries were being transferred to the Urals and
beyond, and high priority given to the needs of the army. Russia joined
the League of Nations in 1934, and attempted to negotiate a security pact
for most of the East European countries. Both the British and French governments remained distrustful of Stalin's intentions, and the purge trials
in Moscow, especially those of the top military leadership, seemed to them
to be making Russia's military alliance less valuable. No grand alliance
therefore existed that could stop Hitler.

Aggression by Stages, 1933–1939. Hitler's first infringement of the Treaty
of Versailles occurred in March 1935, when he announced that Germany

[7] Alan Bullock, *Hitler: A Study in Tyranny* (New York: Harper Torchbook, 1964), p. 318.

was rearming. He picked the Heroes' Memorial Day, commemorating the two million soldiers killed in World War I, for the announcement, arranged a picturesque ceremony in the opera house, where Beethoven's Funeral March was played, and succeeded in creating in Berlin an atmosphere of euphoria. He was certain at that point, however, that no action would be taken against Germany. In 1931, the Japanese had invaded the Chinese province of Manchuria, and the League of Nations had taken no action beyond passing a vote of censure. Poland, the keystone of the

Nazi Parade for Prince Paul of Yugoslavia in Berlin, June 2, 1939. Paul, the Regent of Yugoslavia, sought close relations with Nazi Germany, but was overthrown in 1941, two days after joining the Axis alliance. (The National Archives.)

French alliance system in Eastern Europe, had signed a ten-year nonaggression pact with him in 1934, and good relations were being established with the right-wing regimes in Rumania, Bulgaria, and Hungary.

The next year world attention shifted to Italy's aggression—the invasion of the poor, almost defenseless African state of Ethiopia in October 1935, during which Mussolini sent tanks, dive-bombers, and poison gas against tribesmen armed mostly with spears. The League of Nations was shocked, not least by the impassioned appeal to them for aid by the Ethiopian emperor, Haile Selassie, and agreed to impose economic sanctions on Italy. Since no embargo was put on oil and since the Suez Canal remained open to Italian ships carrying troops and military supplies, the embargo proved to be a farce. Within eight months, Italy was in complete control of Ethiopia. Just before the Ethiopian war ended, Hitler made a daring infringement of the Treaty of Versailles. On the night of March 7, 1936, when only the nucleus of Germany's new army had yet been created, against the advice of the general staff, he moved a division of troops into the demilitarized areas of the Rhineland. Three brigades were stationed close to the French border, in a direct challenge to France's will to resist him. The Poles demanded that the French act; together they could raise ninety divisions. Hitler himself admitted that "the forty-eight hours after the march into the Rhineland were the most nerve-wracking of my life. If the French had then marched into the Rhineland we would have had to withdraw with our tails between our legs."[8] The French were unable to persuade the British to move, and contented themselves with a diplomatic protest.

In July, the opening of the Spanish Civil War (1936–1939) gave Hitler's armed forces the opportunity to try out their new techniques. Spain had been tottering on the verge of military insurrection since it became a republic in 1931, because the Republicans included not only moderate middle-class liberals but a wide array of extremists, including Communists, Trotskyites, and Anarchists, many of whom wanted to use the new government to attack the great landowners and the Church. When in February 1936 a Popular Front government of moderate Republicans, Socialists, Communists, and Anarchists won a small majority in the elections, the army in Spanish Morocco, under the leadership of General Francisco Franco, decided to revolt. In July, the armed forces seized most of the South and West of Spain; the Republicans were left with the industrialized triangle of the East, including the big cities of Madrid, Valencia, and Barcelona, and an army consisting mainly of workers. Mussolini intervened at once on the side of Franco, sending him large numbers of airplanes and trucks, and seventy thousand men. Shortly after, Hitler too decided that Franco's political opinions were close enough to his own to justify the dispatch of aid, mostly in the form of planes, pilots, tanks, and technicians. In October, Stalin decided to aid the Republican side, and thereby transformed the

[8] Bullock, *Hitler*, p. 345.

civil war into an international ideological war. Russian military supplies, experts, and political commissars reached Spain in large numbers by the end of the year; volunteers pouring in from all over Europe and America were organized by the Communists as International Brigades. Once again, the British and French stood aside helplessly. The Republicans were unable to hold out against the forces of Franco and his Italian and German allies. Madrid fell in March 1939 after a heroic defense, and thousands of refugees poured north across the Pyrenees to an uncertain exile in France. Franco at once set up a rigidly authoritarian regime, in which prominent positions were given to Spanish Fascists.

While the British and French were distracted by the Spanish war, Hitler had begun the second part of his program, the absorption into Germany of all people of German blood. In 1938, he summoned the Austrian Chancellor Kurt von Schuschnigg, to his mountain retreat in the Bavarian Alps, and demanded that he remodel his government to include three Austrian Nazis. When Schuschnigg surprised him on returning to Vienna, by ordering a plebiscite so that Austrians could demonstrate that they did not want to be united to Germany, Hitler gave orders for the German army to invade Austria. Schuschnigg was forced to resign, an Austrian Nazi was made chancellor, and Hitler entered Vienna to a conqueror's welcome on March 14. For him, it was a personal revenge for all the humiliations of the years before the First World War, to see the Ring filled with cheering crowds and to be received in the Hofburg palace of the Habsburg dynasty. The plebiscite, conducted by the Nazis in both Germany and Austria, gave ninety-nine percent approval of the union of Germany and Austria. Although the Treaty of Versailles expressly forbade such a union, Britain and France were again unable to interfere. The French were in the middle of a cabinet crisis; the British prime minister, Neville Chamberlain, told Parliament with amazing candor that "nothing could have arrested what actually has happened—unless this country and other countries had been prepared to use force." Chamberlain had accepted Hitler's claim that he wanted only to permit Germans to return to their fatherland; and in November, at the Munich conference, he and the French prime minister agreed to permit Hitler to take the Sudetenland of Czechoslovakia, even though it contained most of the country's border fortresses. German troops moved in on October 1, 1938, meeting no resistance from the Czechs. Chamberlain told the British that he had won "peace in our time." His error was brought home to him the following March when the German army invaded the main body of Czechoslovakia. In April, Mussolini followed Hitler's example, by annexing Albania. Finally driven into action, the British and French guaranteed that they would come to the military aid of Poland if, as seemed likely, it should be attacked by Germany.

The spineless betrayal of Czechoslovakia by the British and French persuaded Stalin that he must safeguard Russia's interests at their expense if necessary, and he entered negotiations with the Germans that culminated,

Stalin with German Foreign Minister Ribbentrop. The Soviet premier was photographed in Moscow at the signing of the Nazi-Soviet Non-Aggression Pact in August 1939. (National Archives photo.)

in August 1939, in the signature of the Nazi-Soviet non-aggression pact. To gain Russian neutrality during his attack on Poland, Hitler agreed to add to the pact a secret, additional protocol, which, as amended in October, gave Russia the right to establish a "sphere of interest" that included the eastern third of Poland, Estonia, Latvia, Lithuania, Finland, and the Rumanian province of Bessarabia. Hitler then ordered the attack on Poland to begin on September 1; the British and French governments, somewhat to his surprise, declared war on Germany in defense of Poland on September 3.

The eruption of what everyone recognized to be the beginning of a new world war caused elation nowhere—not even in Berlin. The American journalist William Shirer, crossing Unter den Linden on his way to broadcast the news of the dawn attack on Poland to the United States, was struck by the apathy of the people on the streets. Workers on a new building for the chemical trust did not buy the extra newspaper editions that the newsboys were hawking, and even the handpicked Reichstag seemed dazed and unresponsive. In France, there was a sense of dull despair at the inevitability of the new destruction. The writer Simone de Beauvoir noted in her diary: "Unthinkable prospect: another day after this, and another, and another—much worse, too, for then we shall be fighting. Only stopped from crying by the feeling that there would be just as many tears left to shed afterwards."[9] In London, air-raid sirens sounded within minutes of the declaration of war; and Winston Churchill was probably not alone in his reaction: "As I gazed from the doorway along the empty street and at the crowded room below, my imagination drew pictures of ruin and carnage and vast explosions shaking the ground; of buildings clattering down in dust and rubble, of fire brigades and ambulances scurrying through the smoke, beneath the drone of hostile airplanes."[10] As in no previous war, the cities of the West lay vulnerable; in 1939 it was hard to predict whether the scourge of air warfare would spare any, on either side. The destruction, as W. H. Auden envisaged it in *The Age of Anxiety,* was ubiquitous and impartial:

Dull through the darkness, indifferent tongues
From bombed buildings, from blacked-out towns,
Camps and cockpits, from cold trenches,
Submarines and cells, recite in unison
A common creed, declaring their weak
Faith in confusion. The floods are rising;
Rain ruins on the routed fragments
Of all the armies; indistinct
Are friend and foe, one flux of bodies
Miles from mother, marriage, or any
Workable world.[11]

THE SECOND WORLD WAR

The German Onslaught, 1939–1941. The first city to suffer the destructive powers of air bombing and artillery bombardment was Warsaw. The rapidity of the German attack enabled them to destroy most of Poland's five hundred planes before they could leave the ground. Stuka dive-bombers supported the tank columns in attacks on the immaculate but ineffective cavalry of the Polish army, strafed fleeing civilians, and struck at the central core of the Polish capital. Within a week the main body of the Polish army had been destroyed; Cracow, Poland's second city, fell on September 6; and Warsaw fought heroically until September 27, when it too surrendered. The Russians moved into Poland on September 17, and annexed the eastern third of the country. Poland had fallen before any British or French troops could come to its aid. In the West, where a small British expeditionary force had been dispatched to France, there was inactivity along the whole front. That quiet winter, when the French played cards in the airy cellars of the Maginot Line fortresses, came to be called the Phony War, the *drôle de guerre;* to the Germans, it was a *Sitzkrieg,* very different from their *Blitzkrieg* attack on Poland.

---

[9] Simone de Beauvoir, *Prime of Life* (Harmondsworth, England: Penguin, 1965), p. 361.
[10] Winston S. Churchill, *The Second World War* (Boston: Houghton Mifflin, 1948), I, 408.
[11] W. H. Auden, *The Age of Anxiety* (London: Faber and Faber, 1948), p. 91. From *Collected Longer Poems.* Reprinted by permission of Faber and Faber Ltd. and Random House, Inc.

The German Onslaught
1939–1941

When Britain and France failed to seek peace, Hitler ordered preparation for a major invasion of the West in the spring of 1940. As a preliminary to that attack, however, he decided to carry through a quick,
inexpensive occupation of Denmark and Norway, to safeguard his ore
supplies from Sweden and to prevent the British from sealing the Baltic.
German troops met no resistance in Denmark, whose flat lands and open
cities were indefensible; Norwegian resistance was overcome within
five weeks, and Hitler was ready to attack westwards on May 10.

With an army of 136 divisions, Hitler launched simultaneous attacks
on the neutral countries of Holland, Belgium, and Luxembourg. The Dutch,
whose neutrality had not been broken since 1815, fought back savagely
against superior forces, and it was decided, on May 14, to make an exemplary punishment of the city of Rotterdam. German bombers struck at
the heart of the old city, killing eight hundred civilians, making 78,000
homeless, and destroying, among many other historical treasures, the home
of the philosopher Erasmus. On the fifth day of fighting, the Dutch army
surrendered. A second and larger German force entered Belgium from the
city of Aachen, and captured Brussels. After eighteen days of resistance,
the Belgian king, Leopold, against the advice of his government, ordered
his troops to stop fighting. The British and French armies, which had
been rushed to the aid of the Belgians, found themselves in a trap when
the main German armored divisions emerged from the Ardennes mountains
and the Moselle valley, broke through the French lines at Sedan (where
Bismarck had captured Napoleon III in 1870!), and swung north to isolate

the British and French forces on the Belgian border. The trapped armies withdrew to the beaches of the tiny French port of Dunkirk, where they were saved from annihilation by a strange armada of tiny sailboats, tugboats, and fishing vessels that sailed from England to evacuate them to the warships waiting offshore. About 300,000 soldiers were carried back to England, but one-third of the impoverished evacuation fleet was destroyed. It was a great defeat, but Britain had at least saved its only trained soldiers.

The German attack resumed on June 5, with 143 German divisions now facing 65 French and 2 British divisions. The French people were fatalistically accepting defeat. Army leaders in the cabinet demanded surrender. Nazi sympathizers welcomed the invaders. Paris, undefended and abandoned by the government, was occupied on June 14. On June 16, Marshal Pétain, hero of the defense of Verdun in 1916 and now the main proponent of defeatism, became premier and at once sought a cease-fire. For Hitler, the moment was one of his greatest triumphs. He forced the French to sign an armistice agreement—which left Pétain's government in control of the southern third of France only—in the same railroad car in the clearing at Compiègne where Marshal Foch had presented the armistice terms to the Germans on November 11, 1918. At the end of the month, Hitler visited Paris for the first time. He found a silent city, from which more than half the population had fled as refugees. Giant swastika flags flew from the Chamber of Deputies. The Hotel Crillon on the Place de la Concorde had been turned into the German headquarters. German tanks were drawn up along the entry to the Champs Elysées. German soldiers with cameras were acting like excited tourists. Hitler followed their example, went up the Eiffel Tower, surveyed the city from the terrace of the Sacré Coeur church in Montmartre, and spent a long time gazing at Napoleon's tomb in the Invalides. "That was the greatest and finest moment of my life," he remarked later.

Hitler proved surprisingly reluctant to authorize a full-scale invasion of England after the fall of France. He feared that the cost of getting an army across the Channel would not be justified by the expected gains; and he wanted no delay in his coming attack on Russia. He therefore authorized an invasion only if a preliminary air assault proved effective. The British, however, were quite well prepared to throw back the Luftwaffe planes. They had between seven hundred and eight hundred fighter planes of superior quality to the German, and were equipped with the new invention of radar, which gave them advance warning of where and in what strength the Germans were attacking. The Channel was a formidable barrier, in view of British naval strength, and the British army was increasing in size daily. British morale had improved enormously since the appointment of Winston Churchill as prime minister in May. In his first important speech as prime minister, reporting the evacuation from Dunkirk, he had struck a note of proud defiance:

*Even though large tracts of Europe and many old and famous states have fallen or
may fall into the grip of the Gestapo and all the odious apparatus of Nazi rule,
we shall not flag or fail. We shall go on to the end, we shall fight in France, we
shall fight in the seas and oceans, we shall fight with growing determination and
growing strength in the air, we shall defend our island, whatever the cost may be,
we shall fight on the beaches, we shall fight on the landing-grounds, we shall
fight in the fields and in the streets, we shall fight in the hills; we shall never surrender, and even if, which I do not for a moment believe, this island or a large
part of it were subjugated and starving, then our Empire beyond the seas, armed and
guarded by the British fleet, would carry on the struggle, until, in God's good time,
the New World, with all its power and might, steps forth to the rescue and the
liberation of the Old.* [12]

Through late August and September, the German air force sustained heavy
losses; but many of their planes got through, especially after Hitler ordered
the bombing of England's large cities in retaliation for the bombing of
Berlin. Deaths of civilians increased, and large parts of the slum dwellings
of the East End, the docks of the Pool of London, and the old blocks around
Saint Paul's cathedral in London were destroyed. In the North, industrial
cities like Liverpool, Manchester, Coventry, and Sheffield were heavily
damaged. But the attacks had failed. In October, Hitler began to transfer
his troops to the East. "Russia must be liquidated. Spring, 1941. The
sooner Russia is smashed, the better," he ordered.

Unfortunately for Hitler, his invasion of Russia was delayed by the
need to come to the aid of his ally Mussolini whose troops had invaded
Greece in October 1940. When the Yugoslavs refused to allow German
troops to cross their territory, he unwisely expanded his Balkan operation even further, to include "Operation Punishment" against the Yugoslavs.
Between April 6 and 23, 1941, both Yugoslavia and Greece were defeated,
without major losses to the Germans except the crucial loss of one month's
time in the invasion of Russia. German troops attacked Russia, along its
whole border from Finland to the Black Sea, at dawn on June 22, 1941, a
month behind schedule.

Stalin had made little preparation to meet this invasion. He had taken
over Estonia, Latvia and Lithuania, and the Rumanian province of Bessarabia in 1940; and as a result of the Winter War against Finland (November 1939–March 1940), the Finnish threat to Leningrad had been
removed by the annexation of the Finnish province of Karelia. He had
slightly increased the number of divisions on the Polish border. But he
had gone to extraordinary lengths to avoid giving provocation to the
Germans, supplying them with food and raw materials and forbidding
any of his military staff to prepare even defensive strategy for repelling a
German attack. Russia's industry was not even put on war footing. Although Stalin later claimed he had gained two years to prepare for the

---

[12] Churchill, *Second World War*, II, 118.

invasion by making the nonaggression pact of 1939, his new territorial acquisitions were overrun by the Germans in a few days. By December, German forces were in the suburbs of Leningrad and Moscow, and a third German army was driving across the Ukraine toward the oilfields of the Caucasus. But the coming of the Russian winter stalled the German troops just short of their objectives; the lost month in the Balkans had been crucial. Instead of permitting the Germans to install themselves until spring in fortified defense shelters, as they had hoped, Stalin mounted a massive counterattack of forces that had regrouped beyond Moscow, and drove the Germans back up to two hundred miles. The possibility of German defeat was suddenly glimpsed, especially as that month the United States, with its Pacific fleet heavily damaged by a surprise Japanese attack on Pearl Harbor in the Hawaiian Islands, declared war not only against Japan but against its allies Germany and Italy.

The Beginning of the Allied Counteroffensive, 1942–1943. In November 1942, the Americans and British launched a three-headed attack on French North Africa, which was ruled by the Vichy government of France. In many ways, however, the invasion worsened the French political situation. German troops occupied the whole of Vichy France when the invasion began, and Pétain was compelled henceforth to use officials more sympathetic to German demands. French North Africa was without a legal government, and Roosevelt and Churchill were divided over possible candidates. Roosevelt favored General Giraud, a professional soldier with no political ambitions; Churchill supported General Charles de Gaulle, a brilliant, thorny, ambitious leader, who had originally made his name as a theorist of tank warfare. In June 1940, de Gaulle had fled to London where he had proclaimed himself the leader of continuing French resistance to the Germans through a movement called Free France. Several French colonies declared their allegiance to his movement, and it was clear by 1942 that de Gaulle regarded himself as the sole claimant to rule French North Africa and eventually France itself. "I was France," he remarked later, by way of explanation. In spite of Roosevelt's intense dislike of this prickly genius, de Gaulle slowly emerged as one of the greatest and most farsighted statesmen of the twentieth century. Resistance leader Emmanuel d'Astier summed up the reasons for his magnetism:

In three days I have seen him make unequal use of his three weapons: prestige, secrecy, and cunning. His cunning is mediocre, but his secrecy, supported by a natural, icy prestige derives from: his height? . . . Or from his appearance, which is always so typical of himself, like a portrait of himself, a picture showing a lack of sensitivity to the warmth of life? Or from his inspired voice, its broken cadences emerging from an inanimate body lacking in all animal warmth, a voice issuing from a waxwork? Or from his aloofness from his fellow men? Or from his language, always too infallible even when his thought is not, approximating in certain of his utterances to the great sermons of the eighteenth century? Or from his remoteness, his expressionless body and his few gestures which, in the last analysis, are as solemn and inevitable as his adjectives? . . . I do not know. He remains a

*mystery, this man, motivated by one historical idea, the greatness of France, and
whose single voice seems to replace all others, the voice of God, man, progress
and all ideologies.* [13]

At the Casablanca conference (January 1943), Roosevelt and Churchill
agreed that Giraud and de Gaulle should be joint presidents of a committee controlling French North Africa and the French army; but de Gaulle
soon took sole command. It was also agreed that the next Allied military
operation should be an amphibious invasion of Sicily from North Africa;
this began in July 1943.

The Germans withdrew to southern Italy, where they prepared a defense
line north of Naples, using the monastery of Monte Cassino as the principal
defense barrier across the route to Rome. The invasion of Italy drove
the Fascist Grand Council to vote for Mussolini's resignation on July 25.
The next day he was arrested, and replaced as premier by an old, conservative soldier, Marshal Pietro Badoglio. In a few hours, Italian Fascism
was dismantled. Badoglio, however, did not sign an armistice with the
Allies until September. By then, Hitler's troops had occupied the whole
of Northern Italy. Mussolini, rescued by German paratroops, was rein-
stalled in the North as puppet ruler of a German-dominated Italian Social
Republic. The Allies did not break the line at Monte Cassino until May
1944, and they were blocked at the Gothic line north of Florence until April
1945. Thus Italy suffered more heavily after the armistice than before.
Italians in the North were compelled to fight against the Italian army in
the South; heavy reprisals were taken by the Germans against the Resistance
movement, and vast destruction of roads, bridges, railroads, factories,
homes, and art treasures occurred in the bombing and the northward
advance of the Allies.

On the Russian front, Hitler had mounted new offensives in 1942
to capture the oil fields of the Caucasus, the Donets industrial basin,
and the communications center of Stalingrad on the river Volga. Stalin,
however, was determined for reasons of prestige not to abandon the city
that carried his name, and for identical reasons, Hitler was determined
to take it. Thus the Battle of Stalingrad (September 1942–January 1943)
commanded the greatest resources both sides could muster, with hand-to-
hand fighting taking place in every block of the city as the Germans drove
in. Soviet forces succeeded in surrounding 200,000 German troops in
the ruined city. After weeks of suffering from artillery bombardment,
frostbite, starvation, and lack of medicine, the Germans—against Hitler's
express orders—surrendered; they then numbered 91,000. The Russian
victory was the turning point of the war. After Stalingrad, the Russian
attack increased in momentum. By July 1943, the Red Army had taken
Kharkov, Orel, Smolensk, and Kiev, and by January 1944 they were in
the Baltic states in the north and Odessa in the south. Hitler's "Fortress
Europe" was collapsing.

[13] Emmanuel d'Astier, *Seven Times Seven Days* (London: MacGibbon and Kee, 1958),
pp. 132–33.

Allied Advances
1943–1945

Attack on Hitler's "Fortress Europe," 1944. On June 6, 1944, D-Day, a vast sea- and airborne force composed of American, British, Canadian, and French troops struck at the beaches of Normandy and in spite of harsh resistance succeeded in putting 130,000 men ashore by nightfall. During the next week, the Allied armies took control of fifty miles of coast, and landed over 300,000 men. In August, a second invasion force landed in the South of France, and moved rapidly northwards up the Rhone valley to establish a common front across France with the rapidly advancing armies from Normandy. The Resistance forces in Paris rose spontaneously on August 19, and in a week of street fighting took possession of large parts of the city, losing over 3,000 men. But on August 25, French and American armored detachments forced their way into the city; that afternoon, General de Gaulle, whose authority had been universally recognized as each section of France was liberated, strode down the whole length of the Champs Elysées acclaimed by a crowd of millions in triumphant apotheosis. By the end of September 1944, most of France was in Allied hands, and the German border had been penetrated in several places.

The Russians had attacked in June 1944 in coordination with the D-Day invasions, and by July they had driven Finland from the war and were established in the heart of Poland, close to the inner defense line that the Germans were establishing between Warsaw and Budapest. Russian

actions during the remainder of 1944 have been the subject of considerable
controversy. On August 1, 1944, the underground forces in Warsaw, which
were sympathetic to the anti-Communist government-in-exile in London,
rose in rebellion against the Nazis, in the hope of taking possession of
the capital before the Red Army could install a pro-Communist regime.
Within three days, the underground was in command of most of Warsaw;
but the Germans counterattacked, using dive-bombers and heavy artillery.

The Russians refused aid to the Poles, in what they claimed was a criminal,
anti-Russian adventure, and even refused to allow British planes to land
on Russian-controlled airfields to supply the Poles. After sixty-three days
of fighting, the poor remnant of the Warsaw underground surrendered
to the Germans a city totally ruined. Only in January 1945 did the Red
Army take Warsaw. Meanwhile, Stalin detached several large armies to
conquer the Balkans. Rumania was taken by September 5 and Bulgaria by
September 9. Russian tanks then advanced into Yugoslavia to meet
the communist partisans of Marshal Tito, who had been fighting in the
western mountains. By December 1944, the Red Army was in the suburbs
of Budapest, which fell the following February.

**Sniper Fire on the Place de la
Concorde, Paris, August 26,
1944.** (French Press and
Information Service.)

The Big Three at Yalta, February 1945. High-ranking officers stand behind Prime Minister Winston S. Churchill, President Franklin D. Roosevelt, and Premier Josef Stalin. (U.S. Office of War Information.)

Yalta Conference. When Churchill and Roosevelt met with Marshal Stalin at the Yalta conference in the Russian Crimea (February 1945), they found that there was almost nothing they could do to halt the communization of Eastern Europe. Marshal Tito had enormous popular support in Yugoslavia for the imposition of a Communist regime through his partisan movement. Albania was already in the hands of a Communist-dominated National Liberation Army, which, after driving out the Italians and Germans, had set up a provisional government under the veteran Communist, Enver Hoxha. Coalition governments in which the Communists held crucial ministries were in power in Rumania and Bulgaria, which were both occupied by the Red Army. Poland was ruled by a provisional government installed by the Red Army, which refused to have any relations with the Polish government in London. Only in Greece, where Churchill had used British troops in December to break the Communist underground armies, had a pro-Western government been put in power. Roosevelt, moreover, wanted two major concessions from

Stalin—agreement to the final details of a United Nations Organization
that was to be set up at war's end and Russian participation in the final
stages of the war against Japan, which, Roosevelt had been warned, might
cost up to a million American casualties. Stalin agreed to both Roosevelt's
proposals, and in return was promised the grant to Russia of the Japanese
territories of southern Sakhalin Island and the Kurile Islands and a lease
on the Chinese city of Port Arthur. In Eastern Europe, Stalin made no
concessions of any significance, merely promising free elections and the
representation of the London Poles in the Polish government.

Götterdämmerung in Germany, 1945. Shortly after the conference,
both western and eastern fronts sprang to life again. The Germans were
fighting a last, desperate struggle under the goad of the SS and the ravings
of Hitler, who, especially since the unsuccessful attempt in July 1944 to
kill him with a time bomb, was a physical, demented wreck, held up only
by injections from a quack doctor. Germany itself had been subject to
continual pounding from the air since 1942, when the British air force
had decided to break German morale by bombing the civilian population

**The Bombing of Berlin, June
1944.** This photo, taken by
an American bombing crew,
may be compared with the
street plan of Berlin on p. 801.
Central Berlin, with
Museum Island and Unter
den Linden, can be dis-
tinguished in the bottom left
corner. (U.S. Office of War
Information.)

out of their homes. In 1943, they had dropped firebombs on Hamburg nightly for a week, destroying most of the city and causing a million inhabitants to flee. American planes dropped even heavier loads on oil supplies, railroads, and factories, but in the last months, their destruction became almost indiscriminate. Small baroque cities, like Würzburg, which had little military value, were destroyed in a few minutes. In spite of this pounding, German morale remained largely unaffected. More important, the German economy continued to produce in ever greater quantities the materials of war. In 1945, Hitler still had armies of seven million men, and was beginning to deploy long-range rockets against England. The force ranged against the Germans was, however, over-whelming. By April, Eisenhower had captured the great industrial area of the Ruhr, and his troops had reached the Elbe. He then drove south-westwards to prevent the establishment of a Nazi redoubt in the Alps, leaving the final assault on Berlin to the Russians.

The Red Army, meanwhile, had finally captured Warsaw and Budapest in February. The northern armies broke through the defenses of Danzig, and moved toward Berlin. Günter Grass, in *The Tin Drum*, described how his hero, the dwarf Oskar, saw the burning of Danzig's medieval streets:

After that we seldom emerged from our hole. The Russians were said to be in Zigankenberg, Pietzgendorf, and on the outskirts of Schidlitz. There was no doubt that they occupied the heights, for they were firing straight down into the city. Inner City and Outer City, Old City, New City, and Old New City, Lower City and Spice City—what had taken seven hundred years to build burned down in three days. Yet this was not the first fire to descend on the city of Danzig. For centuries Pomerelians, Brandenburgers, Teutonic Knights, Poles, Swedes, and a second time Swedes, Frenchmen, Prussians, and Russians, even Saxons, had made history by deciding every few years that the city of Danzig was worth burning. And now it was Russians, Poles, Germans, and Englishmen all at once who were burning the city's Gothic bricks for the hundredth time. Hook Street, Long Street, and Broad Street, Big Weaver Street, and Little Weaver Street were in flames; Tobias Street, Hound Street, Old City Ditch, Outer City Ditch, the ramparts and Long Bridge, all were in flames. Built of wood, Crane Gate made a particularly fine blaze. In Breechesmaker Street, the fire had itself measured for several pairs of extra-loud breeches. The Church of St. Mary was burning inside and outside, festive light effects could be seen through its ogival windows. What bells had not been evacuated from St. Catherine, St. John, St. Brigit, Saints Barbara, Elisabeth, Peter, and Paul, from Trinity and Corpus Christi, melted in their belfries and dripped away without pomp and ceremony. . . . Only the West Prussian Fire Insurance Building, for purely symbolic reasons, refused to burn down. [14]

The Russians mounted their final attack on Berlin on April 16; within nine days the city was surrounded; and Hitler, living his last days amid the remnants of his hierarchy in an underground concrete bunker beneath the bombed out chancellery, prepared to take the remaining inhabitants

[14] Günter Grass, *The Tin Drum* (Greenwich, Conn.: Fawcett, 1962), pp. 378–79.

of Berlin to their deaths with him. "If the war is to be lost, the nation also will perish," Hitler declared. "This fate is inevitable. There is no need to consider the basis even of a most primitive existence any longer. On the contrary, it is better to destroy even that, and to destroy it ourselves. The nation has proved itself weak, and the future belongs solely to the stronger eastern nation. Besides, those who remain after the battle are of little value; for the good have fallen." [15] Through incessant air raids and artillery bombardment, the Russian forces fought into the city block by block until they were close enough to shell the chancellery itself. Hitler dictated his last will and testament, married his mistress Eva Braun, and then on April 30, joined her in suicide. Their bodies were cremated in the chancellery garden. Goebbels poisoned his six children, and shot his wife and himself. On May 2, the Russians took the chancellery, and at the opposite end of the Unter den Linden, raised the red flag over the Brandenburg Gate. The final German surrender was signed in ceremonies at Rheims on May 8 and in Berlin on May 9.

Defeat of Japan. At its greatest extent, the Japanese empire, conquered in the months following Pearl Harbor, comprised a million and a half square miles of territory and 140 million people. It included most of China, Hong Kong, Borneo, the Dutch East Indies, Malaya, Burma, Guam, Wake Island, and the Philippines. The American counterattack had begun in the summer of 1942 when an attempted Japanese invasion of New Guinea was foiled; but the campaigns were slow and expensive, involving bloody battles for small Pacific islands that Japanese suicide troops held with fanatical obstinacy. But the capture of the Mariana Islands in June 1944 brought the American bombers within reach of the home islands of Japan, and the Philippines were retaken in the spring of 1945. Savage Japanese resistance on the atoll of Iwo Jima, 750 miles from Japan, inflicted 27,000 casualties on the American attackers, however, and gave promise of the formidable losses that would be incurred in invading Japan itself. For this reason, President Roosevelt felt the promise of Russian intervention against Japan that he had won at Yalta was crucial. In July 1945, however, Harry S Truman, who had become president at Roosevelt's death in April, was informed that the team of scientists who had been attempting for four years to develop an atomic bomb, had finally succeeded. Although warned that the United States possessed a weapon of terrible destructive power, the Japanese government refused to surrender; and Truman ordered the dropping of the first atomic bomb, on the port city of Hiroshima on August 6, 1945. The explosion killed over 70,000 people immediately, and most of the city was laid waste. Two days later, the Soviet Union declared war, and invaded Manchuria. Even then, the Japanese military refused to surrender, and a second atomic bomb was dropped on Nagasaki, killing 36,000 people. At that point, Emperor

---

[15] Bullock, *Hitler*, p. 775.

Hirohito finally intervened, and ordered his government to seek an armistice, which was signed on a warship in Tokyo Bay on August 28, 1945. After almost six years of fighting, the guns finally fell silent.

The Destruction of the Second World War. The destruction of the Second World War dwarfed even that of the First. Seventeen million soldiers and at least as many civilians had been killed. Mass murder, carried through in concentration camps like Dachau and Auschwitz, that the Nazis had set up throughout occupied Europe, had brought about

The Freeing of Prisoners at the Wöbbelin Concentration Camp, Near Berlin. (U.S. Office of War Information.)

the death of at least six million Jews and hundreds of thousands of other victims—members, or suspected members, of Resistance movements, many of the East European intelligentsia, gypsies, the chronically sick. Populations had been uprooted on a gigantic scale. Eleven million prisoners of war and forced laborers had been deported to Germany. Six million Germans had been driven from the Oder-Neisse territories Russia had handed to Poland, and up to two million more were being driven out of the other East European states. And these vast movements of populations were taking place across a continent in ruins. The bombing, the artillery bombardments, and the street fighting, had inflicted damage equaled only by the Thirty Years' War. Some cities, like Warsaw, Budapest, and Berlin had suffered destruction of ninety percent of their buildings; and many lovely smaller cities, especially in Germany, Poland, and Russia, had been totally wasted. Moreover, the economic structure was in shambles. Canals were blocked, bridges blown up, and railroads unusable. A scorched earth policy, adopted by both Germans and Russians, had ruined most of the Ukraine's industrial plants, many of the Caucasus oil installations, and huge agricultural areas. Even where factories had not been destroyed, they were working with worn, out-of-date equipment. Sewers were flooded, dams destroyed, electricity and telephone lines down. At the end of the war, one hundred million Europeans were on the edge of starvation; agricultural production had fallen by as much as two-thirds of prewar levels, industrial production by at least a half in many areas. Only the United States appeared to have emerged from the war with its resources enhanced and its vigor undiminished; and many Europeans began to ask, though reluctantly, if the future of Western civilization lay with the colossus across the Atlantic, the heir to a Europe that had gone to its own suicide.

SUGGESTED READING

The atmosphere of the Paris peace conference of 1919 is admirably described in Harold Nicolson, *Peacemaking 1919* (1933); its conclusions are blasted with literary and economic genius by John Maynard Keynes, *The Economic Consequences of the Peace* (1920) and defended by Etienne Mantoux, *The Carthaginian Peace* (1946) and Paul Birdsall, *Versailles Twenty Years After* (1941). Arno Mayer's *Politics and Diplomacy of Peacemaking* (1967) is a challenging reappraisal from a New Left viewpoint, that seeks to cast Wilson primarily as an opponent of Bolshevism. C. A. Macartney and A. W. Palmer, *Independent Eastern Europe* (1962) surveys the results of the conference's work in the new states of Eastern Europe; the political struggles of the Weimar Republic in Germany can be untangled in Erich Eyck, *A History of the Weimar Republic* (1962–63), and S. William Halperin,

Germany Tried Democracy (1946); the chaos of French politics is made clear in René Rémond, *The Right in France* (1972) and Denis W. Brogan, *France under the Republic* (1940). The coming of the depression in America is dramatically described in John K. Galbraith, *The Great Crash, 1929* (1955), its effects in Europe in W. Arthur Lewis, *Economic Survey, 1919–1939* (1949).

The savor of the American literary colony in Paris during the 1920s is caught by Ernest Hemingway, *A Moveable Feast* (1964) and John Dos Passos, *The Best Times* (1966). Simone de Beauvoir describes Jean Paul Sartre and his circle during their early days as little known writers, in *Memoirs of a Dutiful Daughter* (1962) and *The Prime of Life* (1962). H. Stuart Hughes explores the social thought of Parisian intellectuals in *Consciousness and Society* (1958) and *The Obstructed Path* (1968).

On the phenomenon of Fascism, Ernst Nolte, *Three Faces of Fascism* (1966) provides a complex philosophical and sociological explanation; Hannah Arendt, *The Origins of Totalitarianism* (1966) traces the progression from anti-Semitism through imperialism to the totalitarian state in Russia and Germany. Mussolini's career is well documented in Sir Ivone Kirkpatrick, *Mussolini: A Study in Power* (1964), which lacks the ideological background that can be found to some degree in Herman Finer, *Mussolini's Italy* (1935). The standard biography of Hitler is Allan Bullock's *Hitler: A Study in Tyranny* (1952), but for economic and social changes it should be supplemented by David Schoenbaum, *Hitler's Social Revolution: Class and Status in Nazi Germany, 1933–1939* (1966) and Franz Neumann, *Behemoth: The Structure and Practice of National Socialism* (1944). On the reasons for Hitler's success in taking power, see the useful symposium of Maurice Baumont et al., *The Third Reich* (1955), and especially William S. Allen's account of the takeover of one town, *The Nazi Seizure of Power* (1955). On the army, see J. W. Wheeler-Bennett, *The Nemesis of Power: The German Army in Politics, 1918–1945* (1953); on Himmler's SS, consult G. Reitlinger, *The S.S.: Alibi of a Nation, 1922–1945* (1957); on the concentration camps, see Eugen Kogon, *The Theory and Practice of Hell* (1950). The cultural aspirations of the Third Reich can be measured in Barbara M. Lane, *Architecture and Politics in Germany, 1918–1945* (1968) and Albert Speer, *Inside the Third Reich: Memoirs* (1970), but should be compared with the tense creativity of the Weimar period, as seen in Peter Gay, *Weimar Culture: The Outsider as Insider* (1968). A less admiring view of Weimar from the inside, however, is provided by Christopher Isherwood's novels, *The Last of Mr. Norris* (1935) and *Goodbye to Berlin* (1939) and in the memoirs of Stephen Spender, *World within World* (1951).

The policy of appeasement is sharply criticized in A. L. Rowse, *Appeasement: A Study in Political Decline, 1933–39* (1963) and Lewis Namier, *Diplomatic Prelude, 1938–39* (1948), and explained in Arnold Wolfers, *Britain and France Between Two Wars* (1940). American policy is roundly condemned by William Appleman Williams, *The Tragedy of American Diplomacy* (1962), and calmly analyzed in Jean-Baptiste Duroselle, *From Wilson to Roosevelt: Foreign Policy of the United States, 1913–1945* (1963). Keith G. Feiling's *The Life of Neville Chamberlain* (1946) is informative but oversympathetic.

Winston Churchill and Charles de Gaulle have given classic accounts of the war from their personal vantage points, the former his six-volume *The Second World War* (1948–1953) and the latter his three-volume *War Memoirs* (1958–60).

The best short accounts are Cyril Falls, *The Second World War: A Short History* (1948) and Basil Liddell-Hart, *The Second World War* (1972). Nazi occupation policies are described in Arnold and Veronica M. Toynbee, eds., *Hitler's Europe* (1954), and the Russian takeover in Eastern Europe is summarized in Hugh Seton-Watson, *The East European Revolution* (1956). Gordon Wright, *The Ordeal of Total War, 1939–1945* (1968) is particularly strong on the economic, psychological, and scientific dimensions of the struggle.

25
NEW YORK CITY:
THE CRISIS OF THE METROPOLIS

The most impressive characteristic of New York City throughout its history has been its intensity. In 1906, the English novelist H. G. Wells saw New York's material progress as "something inevitable and inhuman, as a blindly furious energy of growth that must go on. . . . New York's achievement is a threatening promise, growth going on under a pressure that increases, and amidst a hungry uproar of effort." [1] New York City intensified many of the most characteristic features of the American experience—the mingling of ethnic groups, the escape of the immigrant from the imprisonment of economic or social deprivation, the encouragement of productivity in every field by the lure of vast material reward, the unrestricted freedom of capitalist enterprise, the abandonment of the old in favor of the excitement of the new. The result was a city endlessly renewing itself, in population, in talent, in physical appearance, and in character. To the great French architect Le Corbusier, New York was "a city in the process of becoming. Today it belongs to the world. Without anyone expecting it, it has become the jewel in the crown of universal cities. . . . Crown of noble cities, soft pearls, or glittering topazes, or radiant lapis, or melancholy amethysts! New York is a great diamond, hard and dry, sparkling, triumphant." [2] Perhaps the height of confidence and even enjoyment of this creation was reached in the decade after the First World War. Then, the Soviet poet Mayakovsky could stand on Brooklyn Bridge, and see around him in microcosm the achievements of all America:

[1] Cited in Bayrd Still, ed., *Mirror for Gotham: New York as Seen by Contemporaries from Dutch Days to the Present* (New York: New York University Press, 1965), p. 278.
[2] Ibid., p. 335.

The Vertical City. The Empire State Building, completed in 1931, dominates the skyline of mid-town Manhattan. To the right is the Pan Am Building, constructed over Grand Central Station on Park Avenue. (New York Convention and Visitors Bureau photo.)

911

I clamber,
> *with pride,*
>> *on to Brooklyn Bridge.*
As a beauty-drunk artist
> *thrusts his eyes*
into a museum-madonna
> *love-gazing sharp-edged*
so I,
> *enveloped*
>> *in star-studded skies,*
look
> *at New York*
>> *through Brooklyn Bridge.*
New York,
> *oppressive and stuffy*
>> *by nightfall,*
forgets
> *its oppression*
>> *and straining heights,*
and only a few
> *household ghosts shine sprightful*
in the shimmer
> *of windows' transparent fires. . . .*
If
> *this world of ours*
>> *should come to an end,*
and our planet
> *in chaos*
>> *burst into bits,*
and one thing
> *alone*
>> *remained of men*
this spanning earth's ruins uprearing bridge—
then,
> *as from a tiny*
>> *needle-thin bone*
a museum
> *restores*
>> *a giant brontosaurus,*
a centuries-hence
> *geologist*
>> *from this bridge alone*
could
> *recreate*
>> *the days now before us.*
"This very
> *paw of steel,"*
>> *he would say,*
"oceans and prairies
>> *united,*

from here

Europe swept

to the west-far-away,

putting

Indian feathers

to windy flight. . . .

I know--

by these lines of electric strands—

this

was the epoch

that followed steam.

Here

people

the skies

in aeroplanes spanned,

here

people

orated

by radio-beam.

Here

life

for some

was comfort unalloyed,

for others—

a desperate

drawn-out howl. . . ."

I stare,

as an Eskimo out-stares an express,

drinking it in,

like a drowning man air.

Brooklyn Bridge—

yes . . .

is something

beyond compare! [3]

Yet from the crash of 1929 and especially in the quarter-century following the Second World War, the often predicted self-destruction of New York City was recognized by all its inhabitants to have begun. Large migrations had produced racial tension. The three million most recent immigrants to the city, the blacks and the Puerto Ricans, were unable to break out of their poverty. The intellectual life of the city was being stifled by the harshness of living conditions. The constant rebuilding seemed to have bereft the city of the charm of the old, replacing it with a new that was aesthetically sterile and humanly restrictive. The freedom of productive enterprise had

[3] "Brooklyn Bridge," from *Mayakovsky,* trans. Herbert Marshall (New York: Hill and Wang, 1965), pp. 336–40. Reprinted by permission of Hill and Wang and Dobson Books Ltd.

The Brooklyn Bridge, New York City. The skyscrapers of the big corporations grouped on lower Manhattan can be seen beyond the 1,595-foot span of New York's first suspension bridge. (Trans World Airlines photo.)

led to the pollution of the city's air and water and the strangling of its streets in traffic. And the violence of the city's life, which French novelist Paul Morand in the 1920s could describe as "New York's supreme beauty, its truly unique quality [which] gives it nobility, excuses it, makes its vulgarity forgettable," [4] had become intolerable, driving out the middle classes to the suburbs and turning the central core of the city into a residence only for the very poor and the very rich. "What oppresses New Yorkers today," a prominent New Yorker commented in 1971, "is a double sense of diminution: first, that the mundane problems of life in their city become daily more difficult; and second, that the unique element in New York that compensated for its hardships—the pride of cosmopolitan citizenship—is wasting away. Manhattan—the cosmopolis—the world city—has begun to lose its quality." [5]

In part, the change in the character of New York City has been the result of peculiarly American conditions of government, of economic policy, and of society. But its difficulties are, in an advanced form, those of any

[4] Paul Morand, *New York* (New York: Henry Holt, 1930), p. 315.
[5] Roger Starr, "The Decline and Decline of New York," *New York Times Magazine,* Nov. 21, 1971.

world city. For that reason New York raises some vital questions on the future of the city in the preservation and expansion of civilization. In the most elementary form, the question arises whether the world city can maintain even a minimum of tolerable living conditions for its people—in housing, public services, employment, clean air and water, and individual safety. This problem is compounded by the fact that the individual city no longer stands isolated in the countryside but forms part of an urbanized region of increasing size. New York stands in a contiguous belt of cities and suburbs stretching from southern New Hampshire to northern Virginia that has been aptly labeled Megalopolis. In the second place, the question arises whether the world city is still the most effective unit for the production of wealth in present and future technological conditions. And finally, most apposite to our present inquiry, the question is posed whether the world city can continue to be the center of intellectual creativity that cities have been in the 2,500 years we have surveyed.

"When we get piled upon one another in large cities," Thomas Jefferson had warned in 1787, "we shall become as corrupt as in Europe, and go to eating one another as they do there." At that time, there seemed little threat of such cannibalism, since the line of tiny towns that had played so large a part in organizing the Revolution (Chapter 17) were still countrified in appearance and character and were dependent for their expansion on trade in the agriculture of their hinterland. The first federal census of 1790, which classified as urban twenty-four towns of more than 2,500 inhabitants, found they contained only 5 percent of the country's population. New York, the second largest city, had only 24,000 inhabitants at the time of the Revolution. Moreover, until 1820 the percentage of Americans living in towns of more than 2,500 did not exceed 7.2 percent; and the towns remained devoted primarily to shipping by sea and river and secondarily to finance and small-scale manufacturing. The choice in 1790 of an undeveloped meadowland on the banks of the Potomac River for Washington, the federal capital, further ensured that, in contrast with the situation in European states, no large commercial city would be stimulated in its growth by the presence of the central government.

**AMERICAN URBAN
DEVELOPMENT,
1790–1860**

Causes of Urban Expansion. After 1820, American urbanization proceeded rapidly. By 1860, one-fifth of the country's population lived in towns of more than 2,500 inhabitants; there were 101 cities with more than 10,000 inhabitants, eight with more than 100,000, and one, New York, with more than a million.

The impetus to city growth had come from the acquisition and the populating of the continent beyond the Allegheny Mountains. The western lands between the Mississippi River and the Alleghenies had been ceded to the federal government by the states of the eastern seaboard, and opened to orderly settlement by the Land Ordinance of 1785. The purchase of the Louisiana Territory from Napoleon by President Jefferson in 1803 extended the territory open to American settlement to the Rocky Mountains, and brought to the United States the flourishing port city of New Orleans, a possible rival for the Atlantic ports in the shipment of the South's important exports of cotton. Spain had been compelled to cede Florida in 1819; Texas had been annexed in 1845, following its revolt from Mexico; a compromise agreement with Britain had given the United States the Oregon Territory in 1846; and finally, war with Mexico in 1846–1848 had completed American control of the continent as far south as the Rio Grande River. A whole continent had thus become available for settlement. Total population, fed by a high birth rate and an open-door immigration policy, rose by one-third every decade, from seven million in 1810 to thirty-one million in 1860; the flood of immigrants arriving between 1830 and 1860 accounted for about five million of this growth.

This growing population, most of which wanted agricultural land, drove the frontier of settlement continually westwards, first into the trans-Allegheny West at the end of the eighteenth century, and then into the Midwest, the trans-Mississippi South, and the Oregon territory, in the first forty years of the nineteenth century. California boomed after the gold rush of 1849. The Great Plains were settled in the 1860s and 1870s. Even though many of the farmers had imagined they would build an idyllic, self-sufficient existence, the opening of this vast acreage of agricultural land proved to be a direct stimulus to the rise of cities. The agriculture of the South, conducted principally by slave labor on big plantations, had always been oriented to large-scale markets, usually overseas. At first, products had been diversified, including wheat, corn, horses, pigs, sugar, and cotton. From about 1820, however, especially due to the purchases of the Lancashire textile industry, cotton became the supreme cash crop not only in the old South but in newer states like Alabama and Arkansas. Cotton encouraged the growth of the cities through which it was shipped, notably New Orleans and New York, and the rise of manufacturing cities to supply the Southern planters with tools and consumer goods. In the "Middle Border" region, the vast fertile territory stretching from Indiana in the east to Nebraska in the west and from Minnesota in the north to Kentucky in the south, agriculture rapidly became big business, in part to supply the Cotton Kingdom of the South with wheat and meat, in part to supply the eastern American cities and the industrialized regions of Europe. The mechanization of farming in this area made the farmers customers for such city-produced machinery as reapers and threshers, for textiles and household goods, and for such city services as bank loans, insurance, warehousing, and commodity exchanges.

Commercial agriculture in the West and South in turn made those regions a lucrative market for mass-produced industrial goods from the East, which embarked upon an industrial revolution from the 1820s. New England led the way with textile mills for cotton and to a lesser degree woolen goods, whole new towns like Lowell in Massachusetts being created along the rivers that supplied both water and power. The midwestern cities followed, with factories for processing of agricultural products—mills for flour and meal, distilleries for spirits, breweries for beer, and packinghouses for meat; while the manufacture of agricultural machinery was concentrated in such cities as Chicago and Cincinnati. The iron industry, although still small compared with Britain's, expanded rapidly to supply the manufacturers of steamboats, railroads and locomotives, telegraph wires, and textile machinery. By 1860, industrial production had almost reached $2 billion; and two million people were employed in industry.

Agricultural and industrial advances were made possible by a revolution in internal transportation, which itself was responsible for much urban growth. American roads, while useful for the pioneers moving westward, were unsuited to large-scale transportation of bulky goods, and until about 1850 most goods moved by water, partly on the great rivers like the Mississippi and the Ohio, partly on the many canals constructed in the 1830s and 1840s. But the railroad triumphed from the end of the 1840s, and by 1860 inland water traffic was in decline.

The proliferation of cities by 1860 was a major change from forty years earlier, when one-third of all city dwellers lived in New York or Philadelphia. New Orleans had boomed with the cotton trade; Chicago, from which 5,000 miles of railroad track branched out in all directions, had become the railroad hub of the continent; Pittsburgh, ideally located on the junction of the Allegheny and Monongahela rivers, was manufacturing the goods bought by the westward migrant hordes; Cleveland, aided by lake and canal transportation, was building a big iron industry; Boston had found new strength as the financial and marketing center of the New England textile industry. But New York, in spite of this competition, had established a preeminence that appeared unassailable.

New York's Economic Preeminence. New York's natural advantages were very great. Manhattan Island was situated on a large sheltered bay, with channels forty-five feet deep at the piers, a rocky bottom that made dredging unnecessary, and freedom from ice and fog. The Hudson River and its tributary the Mohawk led directly into a vast hinterland, and gave easy water access to the western frontier. New York merchants were ambitious and skillful in profiting from these advantages. In January 1818, four Quaker merchants inaugurated the first regularly scheduled transatlantic packet schedule, promising that their ships would sail as announced, whether full or not. This Black Ball Line, operating sleek, fast, comfortable sailing ships, was an immediate success; and was followed by opening of similar service along the coast to New Orleans. For the commodity trade, the city operated an auction system, in which, contrary to the practice of other cities, merchants were guaranteed that goods would be sold to the highest bidder. Direct contacts were established with foreign markets. In Britain, the New York auctioneers took charge of export goods directly from the manufacturer; in Latin America, resident agents were established; in the American South, they took over much of the shipment of cotton and

View of New York in 1852 and **View of New York in the 1960s.** In 1852, Manhattan still resembled a European city. By the late 1960s, half a century of skyscraper-building had given it a unique profile among world cities. (Above, The Eduard W. C. Arnold Collection, Lent by the Metropolitan Museum of Art, Photo courtesy Museum of The City of New York. Below, New York Convention and Visitors' Bureau photo.)

provision of the necessary services like maritime insurance. But the greatest single addition to New York's economic strength was the construction in 1817–1825, of the Erie Canal, which linked the Hudson River directly with the Great Lakes.

Its position as the nation's greatest wholesaler compelled New York to become also the nation's greatest financial center. Commercial banks sprang up to finance the shipment of Southern cotton and the purchases of imports and manufactured goods by Western suppliers. Maritime coverage was supplied by insurance companies. Securities specialists set up the New York Stock and Exchange Board in 1817. The presence of the markets and of a large work force made manufacturing profitable. Shipbuilding was carried out on the East River. Heavy engineering factories supplied steam engines and locomotives. The raw materials passing through New York harbor began to be processed in the city. Raw sugar was turned into molasses and rum, hides into boots and saddles. Meat was packed, textiles turned into ready-made clothes. Finally, the possibility of employment encouraged a good proportion of the immigrants, most of whom reached America through New York, to stay in the city.

This vast growth inevitably changed the character of New York. In 1821, one English visitor could report that there were "no dark alleys, whose confined and noisome atmosphere marks the presence of a dense and suffering population, no hovels, in whose ruined garrets, or dank and gloomy cellars crowd the wretched victims of vice and leisure, whose penury drives to despair, ere she opens them to the grave." By 1860, this pleasant picture was no longer true, if it ever had been. The physical separation of rich and poor had accelerated the decay of many poorer areas. As Lower Manhattan was turned over almost exclusively to business, the well-to-do moved northwards, the wealthiest constructing fine brownstone mansions on Fifth Avenue north of Washington Square. The middle classes were scattering, many of them commuting by steam ferry to Brooklyn or New Jersey or by horse-drawn streetcar to the new blocks just south of Forty-second Street. The working classes—mostly immigrants, since the foreign-born composed almost half the city's population—tended to group in the most run-down sections, especially on the East Side, though the poorest of all lived in shanties just north of the built-up area on Forty-second Street. Death rates, which rose from one death per 46.5 persons in 1810 to one in 27 in 1859, were proof of the overcrowding, the lack of sanitation, and the inadequate medical care of a large section of the population, who were swept away by typhoid, typhus, cholera, consumption, yellow fever, and even plague. Thus, for most immigrants to New York, the New World failed to offer the bright prospects they had expected; and the presence of pauperized immigrants huddled in city slums was to become one of the outrages most widely advertised by the city reformers of the next thirty years.

There was as yet little cultural vitality to the city. Columbia University had less than two hundred students; there were only three theaters; the favorite museum was Barnum's collection of oddities. The city's character

New York City

To George Washington
Bridge ~0.7 mile

THE
BRONX

HARLEM

QUEENS

Queensboro
Bridge

Queens
Midtown
Tunnel

Times
Square

Lincoln Tunnel

NEW JERSEY

Hudson River

JERSEY CITY

Holland Tunnel

Greenwich Village
Union Sq.
Gramercy Park

Chinatown
Lower East Side

Williamsburg
Bridge

Wall St.
Battery Park

Manhattan Bridge

Brooklyn Bridge

Ellis Island

Governors Island

Upper New York Bay

BROOKLYN

Millionaires'
Mansions,
1860–1916

KEY

1. Carnegie Hall
2. City Hall
3. Columbia University
4. Empire State Building
5. Fulton Fish Market
6. Grand Central Station
7. House of Seagram Bldg.
8. Lever House
9. Lincoln Center
10. Madison Square Garden
11. Metropolitan Museum of Art
12. Museum of the City of New York
13. Museum of Modern Art
14. Pennsylvania Station
15. Rockefeller Center
16. Waldorf-Astoria
17. Woolworth Bldg.
18. World Trade Center

New York City

0   1 Mile

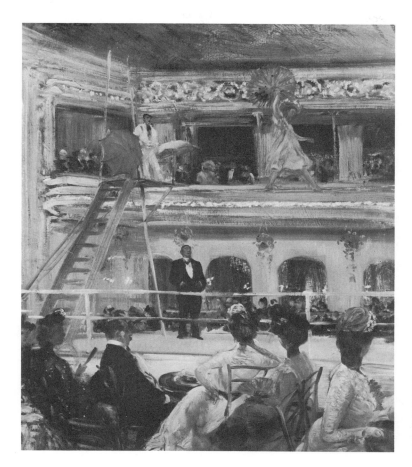

Hammerstein's Roof Garden, by William James Glackens (1870–1938). Hammerstein was the most exuberant theatrical impresario in early twentieth-century New York. (Collection of Whitney Museum of American Art, New York.)

was unabashedly shaped by the hurried creation of material prosperity. Even then however, the city's energy found admirers among the literati, including the poet Walt Whitman, who loved the "tall masts of Manhattan," in the

City of hurried and sparkling waters! city of spires and masts!
City nested in bays! my city![6]

In 1870, Whitman still found New York and Brooklyn irresistible:

The splendor, picturesqueness, and oceanic amplitude and rush of these great cities, the . . . lofty new buildings, facades of marble and iron, of original grandeur and elegance of masses, with the masses of gay color, the preponderance of white and blue, the flags flying, the endless ships, the tumultuous streets, Broadway, the heavy,

[6] "Manahatta," from Walt Whitman, *Leaves of Grass* (Garden City, N.Y.: Doubleday, 1948), p. 395.

*low, musical roar, hardly ever interrupted, even at night; the jobbers' houses, the
rich shops, the wharves, the great Central Park and the Brooklyn Park of hills. . . .
these, I say, and the like of these completely satisfy my senses of power, fulness,
motion, &c and give me, through such senses . . . a continued exaltation and absolute fulfilment. Always, more and more . . . I realize . . . that not Nature alone is
great in her fields of freedom and the open air, in her storms, the shows of night and
day, the mountains, forests, seas—but in the artificial, the work of man too is equally
great—in this profusion of teeming humanity—in these ingenuities, streets, goods,
houses, ships—these hurrying, feverish, electric crowds of men, their complicated
business genius (not least among the geniuses,), and all this mighty, many- threaded
wealth and industry concentrated here.[7]*

THE INDUSTRIALIZATION OF AMERICA, 1860–1914

In the half-century following the outbreak of the Civil War (1861–1865),
America's urbanization continued at an ever faster pace. By 1910, over
forty-five percent of the population lived in towns of over 2,500 inhabitants;
and for the first time, the census bureau classified as metropolitan twenty-
five cities with a central-city population of over 200,000. New York, in
spite of its five million population, had become *primus inter pares*, one
metropolis among many although still by far the largest.

American Industrialization. Agriculture played a smaller part in the
stimulus of urbanization in the second half of the nineteenth century than
in the first. Certain cities did expand in service of the agricultural communities. The opening of the Great Plains to large-scale cattle ranching
was primarily responsible for the growth of Kansas City as a cattle market
and meat-packing center. Other cities specialized in processing agricultural goods: Milwaukee made beer; Minneapolis, flour; Memphis, cotton-
seed oil. The building of the railroads to the Pacific, beginning with the
completion of the Union Pacific line in 1865, led to the development along
the railroad of many cities that specialized in handling the products of
the newly opened agricultural regions, especially the rich production of
the central valley of California. But industry was outdistancing agriculture
as the source of the nation's wealth. By the end of the century, industrial
production was valued at over $11 billion, agricultural production at only
$8.5 billion. Until about 1880, the extractive industries had been the
greatest source of nonagricultural wealth. The most dramatic of the mining
ventures were the gold rushes to California after 1849 and to Colorado
after 1858, the silver rush to the Comstock Lode in Nevada in 1859, and the
new gold rush to the Black Hills of South Dakota in 1876. But the search
for precious metals, whose seams soon ran out, was followed by more
lasting discoveries, such as copper in Montana and the even more important iron ore fields in Michigan and Minnesota. The United States,
however, only became a primary producer of iron and steel after Andrew
Carnegie's company adopted the Bessemer process for steelmaking in
1873. Twenty-two years later, American steel production had surpassed

[7] Cited in Still, *Mirror for Gotham*, pp. 200–1.

Britain's; and vast steel factories were going up along the shores of the Great Lakes, at Pittsburgh, and in the southern Appalachians.

After 1880, the United States rushed from the first industrial revolution into the second. Steel was adapted to an infinity of uses in both heavy and light engineering. It was used for new types of railroad cars, for the framework of buildings, and after the 1890s for the automobile; for the telegraph, the telephone, and from the 1880s, for electric light and power; and it made possible new forms of office equipment, like the typewriter and the business machine. As in Europe, the chemical industry expanded with fertilizer production and dyestuffs. And perhaps most significant for the future, after the tapping of the Titusville oil fields in Pennsylvania in 1859, the refining of oil became a principal industry, which within only twenty years was almost completely monopolized by John D. Rockefeller's Standard Oil Company.

New York's Changing Economic Function. New York could not maintain its hegemony after 1860, as industry diversified and spread to new and distant regions of the country, new sources of finance became available in metropolitan centers, and a number of new and more efficient ports were created not only on the Pacific and Gulf coasts but on the East coast as well. The port of New York slowly lost its predominant importance in the city's economy. The railroads replaced coastal shipping; the growing manufacturing capacity at home reduced the share of imports in the nation's consumption; shipbuilding could not be carried out economically in the overcrowded city. After the 1880s, New York's share of the nation's manufacturers also began to decline. For many industries it was hampered by distance from raw materials. The very efficiency of the railroad networks made it possible for producers in the Midwest or West to undercut New York producers of items like flour, glass, lumber, machine tools, and beer. The great new automobile industry found it profitable to locate in the Midwest, near both raw materials and big markets; and this industry drew to it other subsidiary industries like rubber and glass.

New York proved its continuing vitality, however, by concentrating on those manufacturing industries for which transportation costs were relatively unimportant. Above all, it became the nation's chief producer of ready-made clothing, aided in this expansion by the shift from homemade to ready-to-wear clothing and by the arrival in New York of several million immigrants from eastern and southern Europe who would work for little wages in the city's sweatshops. By 1910, the apparel industry was employing 236,000 New Yorkers. A second form of adaptation was the concentration in New York of the book and periodical publishing industry, which had previously been located primarily in Boston; this was aided particularly by the migration to the city of many European intellectuals, especially Jews who were driven out by the persecutions that began in the 1880s and continued through most of the twentieth century.

Still more important than manufacturing, however, was New York's primacy as the financial and service center of the expanding national economy. Life insurance companies were almost always located in downtown Manhattan, near Wall Street, from the Civil War on, partly because they were permitted to use their funds for speculation, partly to be near the nation's largest single market for sale of insurance. Banks continued to maintain their central offices in the same area, and thus exerted an attraction on large companies who needed constant contact with the money market. The change in the capitalist system, discussed in Chapter 20, from industrial to financial capitalism, was directly beneficial to New York. Many of the great trusts that controlled huge industrial empires throughout the country were dominated in whole or in part by large New York banks, and thus of necessity they also located their central offices in New York. The need for direct communication with customers, bankers, or even rivals persuaded many other industrial companies to establish themselves in New York, and they in turn were followed by other organizations depending on them, such as trade unions or research institutes. This proliferating industrial and financial bureaucracy in turn created new satellite companies in New York such as real estate, architectural and construction companies, advertising agencies, and engineering consultants. Finally, New York expanded its retail sales outlets, remaining the nation's largest shopkeeper. Great department stores were constructed just to the north of the financial district, the most impressive being the neighboring Macy's and Gimbel's. Luxury shops proliferated from Thirty-fourth Street north.

A New City Profile. New York's appearance changed rapidly as it sought to meet the demands of its new economic functions. The skyscraper was the answer to the demand of the financial and industrial organizations for the proximity that was essential to their efficient conduct of business. In New York, brick and mortar construction provided a massive base for buildings as high as eleven stories in the 1870s; but with the adoption of steel frame construction, there began a competition for height that can only be compared with the rivalry of the cathedral builders of thirteenth-century France. By the 1890s, New York had a skyline, with six buildings over 300 feet high and one, the Park Row Business Building, 392 feet high. The assembling and dispersal of the hundreds of thousands of people who worked in the skyscraper canyons required miracles of urban transportation. From 1867, the elevated railroads began to carry the clanking, filthy steam-powered trains between the houses on the city's poorer streets, providing an efficient alternative to the five main street railways whose carriages were drawn by horses. Only in 1904, with the improvement of the electric railroad, was the first New York subway constructed, from City Hall to 145th Street. To New Yorkers, the most exciting improvement in their transportation network was the link of Manhattan to Brooklyn provided by the Brooklyn Bridge, a mile-long suspension bridge that carried two railroad lines, four lanes of traffic, and a footpath.

View of New York in 1870.

The housing to which the trains and trolleys carried New York's workers was more varied than even that of prerevolutionary Paris. The existence of an aristocracy of wealth, of the tycoons of railroads, banks, steel works, and real estate, was blatantly evident in the new homes going up along Fifth Avenue from Forty-sixth Street to Seventy-second. Here were palaces, in every style from French Renaissance to debased Byzantine, belonging to the Vanderbilts (New York Central), the Astors (real estate, after an early fortune in fur trade), Jay Gould (finance), and Collis P. Huntington (Southern Pacific), and many others of the inner group called the Four Hundred, a title invented in 1892 after Mrs. Astor sent out exactly four hundred invitations to a ball at her home. This social elite indulged in conspicuous consumption on an almost unparalleled scale, supporting the great hotels (or even running them, in the case of the Astors' Waldorf-Astoria), dining at Delmonico's or the Brunswick restaurant, attending the Metropolitan Opera House. Most middle-class New Yorkers sought to live in the long terraces of brownstone houses, but often had to settle for less commodious wooden-frame structures that speculative builders were erecting beyond Central Park or in Brooklyn.

Over one and a half million poor people lived in tenements, a form of barrackslike building invented in the 1850s that could house some five hundred people in a structure lacking plumbing and heat. From the 1870s, a law requiring bedrooms to have a window led to the construction of tenements shaped like dumbbells, with a small, putrid passage five feet wide supplying air and light to all inside rooms. The plight of these tenement dwellers was exposed in 1888 in Jacob Riis's *How The Other Half Lives;* his photographs were an even more scalding testimony than his text. In a famous passage Riis, himself an immigrant from Denmark, described the ethnic pattern of these tenement dwellings:

Battery Court, by Jacob Riis (1849–1914). As a newspaper reporter Riis was familiar with conditions of the New York poor and tried to stir the public conscience with his books and photographs. (The Jacob A. Riis Collection, Museum of the City of New York.)

*A map of the city, colored to designate nationalities, would show more stripes than
on the skin of a zebra, and more colors than any rainbow. The city on such a map
would fall into great halves, green for the Irish prevailing in the West Side tenement
districts, and blue for the Germans on the East Side. But intermingled with these
ground colors would be an odd variety of tints that would give the whole the appearance of an extraordinary crazy quilt. From down in the Sixth Ward, upon the
site of the old Collect Pond . . . the red of the Italian would be seen forcing its way
northward along the line of Mulberry Street to the quarter of the French purple on
Bleecker Street and South Fifth Avenue, to lose itself and reappear, after a lapse of
miles, in the "Little Italy" of Harlem, east of Second Avenue. Dashes of red, sharply
defined, would be seen strung through the Annexed District, northward to the city
line. On the West Side the red would be seen overrunning the old Africa of Thompson Street, pushing the black of the negro rapidly uptown, against querulous but
unavailing protests, occupying his home, his church, his trade and all, with merciless
impartiality.*[8]

[8] Charles N. Glaab and A. Theodore Brown, *A History of Urban America* (New York: Macmillan, 1967), pp. 139–40.

**Crowds at New York City
End of the Brooklyn Bridge
during Rush Hour, 1904.**
(U.S. Office of War In-
formation.)

A Sweatshop in Ludlow Street, by Jacob Riis. In the "sweating" system widely used in New York, an employer supplied materials to workers in their homes, and paid extremely low prices by the piece for their work. (The Jacob A. Riis Collection, Museum of the City of New York.)

Almost as shocking as the city-condoned horror of the tenements was the governmental neglect of normal city functions. Almost no controls were placed on any form of real estate development, whether for factories, stores, or residences. The creation of Central Park was a fine exception to the neglect of provision of open space. Pollution of the waterways was unrestricted. Streets were poorly paved, if at all. Lighting was inadequate. Garbage collection and sewage disposal was completely inadequate. "No one as yet has approached the management of New York in a proper spirit," Rudyard Kipling commented in 1892, "that is to say, regarding it as the shiftless outcome of squalid barbarism and reckless extravagance." New York's streets, he went on, were "first cousins to a Zanzibar foreshore, or kin to the approaches of a Zulu kraal." New York was the prototype of crooked city government in the late nineteenth century. Mayor William M. Tweed, the "Boss," and his Tammany Hall ring of crooked cronies, created an organized political empire based on disciplined control of the immigrant groups, which was able to bilk the city of over $100 million.

The Progressive Reformers. The situation in most American cities worsened between 1900 and 1914, during the last great migratory wave, which brought more than nine million people from the poorer regions of Europe, mostly Italy, Russia, the Balkans, and the Austro-Hungarian empire. Yet at the same time the reformers of the Progressive movement found widespread support for their demand that the most blatant injustices in American society, of which the "Shame of the Cities" was notorious, should be remedied. New York was of necessity in the eye of the Progressive hurricane. Its skyline and its mansions were the product of many of the most significant economic achievements of the last half-century—the opening of the continent, the creation of the world's most productive industrial system, the mobilization of vast capital resources for the multiplication of wealth, the provision of work for the fastest growing population on earth. But New York also represented the price America had paid—the perversion of democracy into bossism, the widening of the gulf of rich and poor, the abuse of natural resources for private profit, the failure to protect the individual citizen against the power of the large private company.

The Progressive movement therefore demanded far more than municipal reform, although that was one of its main battle cries; it demanded reform at the national level as well. Through the presidencies of Theodore Roosevelt, Taft, and Wilson, much was achieved in developing the powers of the national government to curb private business; and state governments had taken similar action. Among the many steps taken were Roosevelt's efforts to break up the trusts and to regulate the railroads and foodpacking industries, and Wilson's introduction of an income tax and of banking system reform through the creation of the Federal Reserve system in 1913. At the city level, the changes were immediate, in part because the "muckraking" journalists concentrated much of their effort in exposing city corruption. The power of Tammany Hall had been broken by the end of the century. Some improvement in tenement housing was forced by creation of a tenement house department. A few more parks were provided. And New York was even given its first city plan in 1912 and its first zoning regulation in 1916. The achievements were minor, but it was at least a start that seemed to many reformers to promise that New York too might become a "City Beautiful."

From the First World War to shortly after the end of the second, New York was appreciated not only as the center of the wealth-creating segment of American society but as a genuine cosmopolis. At last, it had become one of the world's great centers of civilization.

THE REWARDS OF INTENSITY: NEW YORK BETWEEN THE WARS

The Skyscraper City. By the time the hundred-and-second story of the Empire State Building had been completed in 1932, New York was recognized as having created for itself in about thirty years an architectural char-

acter as distinct as that which Pericles gave Athens or Ivan the Great gave
the Moscow Kremlin. Moreover, its appearance was totally representative
of the culture that created it. The buildings represented the enormous
financial power of the great corporations, the two hundred or so giant
companies that dominated the American economy but were run by faceless administrators instead of the flamboyant millionaires of the previous
generation. The tallest of the buildings followed the pattern of the Gothic-
topped shaft of the Woolworth Building (1913), failing in any way except
in size and engineering prowess to create a genuinely new architectural
style. The great towers ended in the skies in Roman temples, or Strozzi
palaces, or even Mayan pyramids, the efflorescence of meaningless detail
due principally to the architect's need to give to the skyscraper of the
American Telephone and Telegraph Company (1924) or of the McGraw
Hill Publishing Company (1931) or of the Chrysler Automobile Company

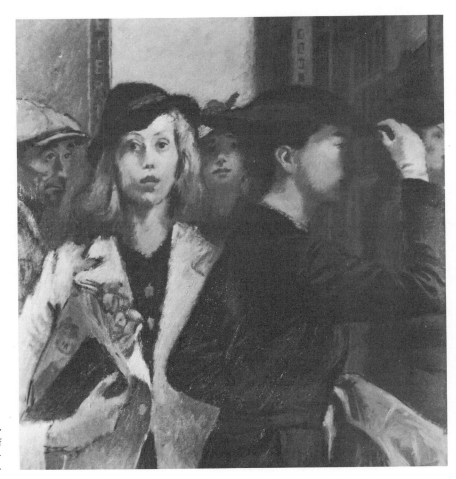

**Office Girls, by Raphael Soyer
(1899–   ).** (Collection of
Whitney Museum of Amer-
ican Art, New York.

(1929) a distinctive, recognizable outline. Next to the pillars of the sky-scrapers, New York developed an unfortunate aberration, the setback silhouette, or "ziggurat," in which, in pursuit of light and air for the street, the upper stories of the cube-shaped buildings were narrowed. Only occasionally were skyscrapers grouped in balanced relationship, leaving space at their base for pedestrians to enjoy malls, gardens, or even ice rinks, as in the Rockefeller Center (1931–1940).

Yet the two clusters of skyscrapers, the older grouping on the tip of Manhattan that struck the imagination of the visitor arriving by ocean liner, and the uptown grouping between Thirty-second Street and Central Park, were immensely exciting. They had created a sharp, rectangular city, whose verticality was enhanced by the dry sparkle of a sky that was still clear to view, a city that to the English poet Rupert Brooke "gave a kind of classical feeling, classical, and yet not of Europe. . . . that characteristic of the great buildings of the world, an existence and meaning of their own." The skyscrapers had finally hit the scale required by the physical grandeur of Manhattan's setting, the long southward sweep of the Hudson River, the "bright, breezy bay" that Henry James admired, and the granite out-croppings that were still impressive along Riverside Drive or across the river in the Palisades of New Jersey. Throughout the 1920s, European writers, artists, and architects came to be amazed, and to swell the book-stores of Paris and London with their accounts of the new metropolis. The best qualified commentator of all was perhaps the town planner Le Cor-busier, who deliberately shocked New Yorkers by telling them that their skyscrapers were too small. They had found the solution to urban con-gestion, he said, the "Cartesian skyscraper" in which three to four thou-sand people could be concentrated on two and a half acres, using only eight to twelve percent of the ground and leaving the rest free for parkland and people. But they had not built it. In New York, Le Corbusier charged, skyscrapers were put up as "acrobatic feats, a banner in the sky, a fire-works rocket, an aigrette in the coiffure of a name henceforth listed in the financial Almanach de Gotha." But even he had to admit that New York was a "beautiful catastrophe," especially at night:

The night was dark, the air dry and cold. The whole city was lighted up. If you have not seen it, you cannot know or imagine what it is like. You must have had it sweep over you. Then you begin to understand why Americans have become proud of themselves in the last twenty years and why they raise their voices in the world and why they are impatient when they come to our country. The sky is decked out. It is a Milky Way come down to earth; you are in it. Each window, each person, is a light in the sky. At the same time a perspective is established by the arrange-ment of the thousand lights in each skyscraper; it forms itself more in your mind than in the darkness perforated by illimitable fires. The stars are part of it also— the real stars—but sparkling quietly in the distance. Splendor, scintillation, promise, proof, act of faith, etc. Feeling comes into play; the action of the heart is released; crescendo, allegro, fortissimo. We are charged with feeling, we are intoxicated; legs strengthened, chests expanded, eager for action, we are filled with confidence.

New York City by Night.
(Trans World Airlines photo.)

That is the Manhattan of vehement silhouettes. Those are the varieties of technique, which is the springboard of lyricism. The fields of water, the railroads, the planes, the stars, and the vertical city with its unimaginable diamonds. Everything is there, and it is real.[9]

The New Bohemia. The New Yorkers who responded most enthusiastically to the excitement of the upward-thrusting city preferred, however, to live in the oases in which the older, horizontal city had not yet been torn down. In the years immediately preceding the First World War and in the interwar years, gathered in a Bohemian world whose center was the walk-up flats of Greenwich Village to the south of Washington Square, New York's literary figures pushed into the forefront of the literary revolution.

New York had attracted America's literary giants before. In the 1840s, Melville, Irving, and Poe had moved there; in the 1880s, it had attracted Edith Wharton, Walt Whitman, and Mark Twain, and fleetingly, Henry James. Artists and sculptors had found occasional patronage from the society leaders for portraits or house decoration. But unlike the patriciate of Florence or the aristocracy of Paris, the Four Hundred of New York had done little to foster the cultural life of their city. They had bought their paintings in Europe, usually old masters that were secure investments. Only at the very end of the century did any of the vast wealth of Fifth and Madison avenues spill over to the cultural benefit of other New Yorkers. In 1895, the New York Public Library was formed by amalgamating three privately endowed libraries, including the Astor collection. The Metropolitan Museum of Art had been limping along since 1870, but only blossomed after completion of its new home on Fifth Avenue in Central Park in 1902. The Metropolitan Opera House only became a financial

[9] Cited in Alexander Klein, ed., *The Empire City*, trans. Francis E. Hyslop, Jr. (New York: Rinehart, 1955), p. 448.

and artistic success after a great showman, Maurice Grau, attracted the wealthy to the Diamond Horseshoe of his rebuilt theater, giving them for the opening performance in 1903 the young Enrico Caruso in *Rigoletto.* But it was the advent of the mass audience for books, newspapers, theater, and radio, that changed the character of literary New York. For perhaps the first time it became easy for a writer at a relatively young age to make his living from writing; a single best-seller, like Sinclair Lewis's *Main Street,* published when he was thirty-five, could set a writer up for years. Journalism provided alternative employment in lean times, and the theater offered new sources of riches and instant success.

The objective of the "lost generation" of writers, as Gertrude Stein had labeled them, was to express in contemporary language the American scene, breaking with the European models that had still lingered on in the classical writers of the nineteenth century. The effort had begun with several older writers who had come to New York before the First World War. Theodore Dreiser's first novel, *Sister Carrie* (1900), had shocked its publisher into stopping its distribution, but Dreiser had gone to explore such facets of New York life as *The Financier* (1912) and *The Titan* (1914). Dreiser set the pattern of lashing out at the city he loved in spite of its shortcomings in *The Color of a Great City* (1923); Dreiser pinpointed the city's attraction to the novelist: "The thing that interested me then as now about New York—as indeed about any great city, but more definitely New York because it was and is so preponderantly large—was the sharp, and at the same time immense, contrast it showed between the dull and the shrewd, the strong and the weak, the rich and the poor, the wise and the ignorant. . . . the number from which to choose was so great here that the strong, or those who ultimately dominated, were so very strong, and the weak so very, very weak—and so very, very many." To F. Scott Fitzgerald, writing in the 1920s, the gaudiness and the underlying tragedy of the carnival atmosphere permeating New York offered the theme suited to his style and his character; and he became the exponent of the Jazz Age, of such people as treated in *The Beautiful and the Damned* (1922), one of his best books. John Dos Passos picked up the Dreiser indictment of America, especially in his trilogy *U.S.A.* (1930–1936). John Steinbeck settled for a time, after the success of *Tortilla Flat,* writing on about California, but he found the atmosphere of the city more conducive to hard literary work than that of any other place.

Of all the writers who capitalized on the separation that New York gave from a rural background, the most vociferous was Thomas Wolfe. Beginning with *Look Homeward, Angel* in 1929 and ending with *You Can't Go Home Again* (1940), Wolfe told the story of his own flight from the poverty of the North Carolina hills and his battle with New York:

For the first time his vision phrased it as it had never done before. It was a cruel city, but it was a lively one, a savage city, yet it had such tenderness; a bitter, harsh and violent catacomb of stone and steel and tunneled rock, slashed savagely with

White Way, by John Sloan (1871–1951). The section of Broadway above Times Square was known as the Great White Way because of the profusion of flashing electric signs from advertisements and theaters. (Philadelphia Museum of Art.)

light, and roaring, fighting a constant ceaseless warfare of men and of machinery; and yet it was so sweetly and so delicately pulsed, as full of warmth, of passion and of love as it was full of hate.[10]

The artists too were gathering in Greenwich Village, where one millionaire at least had set out to help contemporary artists. Gertrude Vanderbilt Whitney established her studio, and in 1908 displayed such innovating painters as George Bellows and John Sloan; in 1913, these painters had shocked the conservative art patrons with the Armory Show's postimpressionist, cubist, and abstract art. During the interwar years, American art came to be accepted by wealthy collectors. The Museum of Modern Art opened in 1929 under Rockefeller patronage. The Whitney studio was replaced by the Whitney Museum of American Art in 1931.

Finally, in communications and popular entertainment, New York reigned supreme with the one exception of movie-making, which its climate compelled it to yield to Hollywood. Its newspapers ranged from the

[10] Cited in V. S. Pritchett, *New York Proclaimed* (New York: Harcourt Brace & World, 1965), p. 5.

world's finest reporting in the *New York Times* to the most yellow; Broadway, illuminated by the new electric lights, had become the Great White Way, with shows ranging from Eugene O'Neill's *Mourning Becomes Electra* (1931) to the Ziegfeld Follies. Tin Pan Alley songsters were turning out jingles for the new radio stations; soap opera was being manufactured on a mass-production basis; jazz and ragtime bands were proliferating as rapidly as the speakeasies that legal prohibition of the sale of alcoholic drinks had fostered.

Dreiser in the early 1920s described a "poor, half-demented, and very much shriveled little seamstress" who told him she preferred poverty in New York to a fifteen-room mansion in the country: "The color and noise and splendor of the city as a spectacle was sufficient to pay her for all her ills." Slowly in the decade following the Wall Street crash in 1929 and with growing speed following the Second World War, the rewards of New York life ceased for many to compensate for the difficulties of living there; and New York faced, in an aggravated form, specifically American social problems and also the universal problems of a mid-twentieth-century metropolis.

THE EMERGENCE OF THE METROPOLITAN DILEMMA

The Migration from Europe. New York had always been a city of immigrants, but it had never been a melting pot. The pattern had been of attempted social and economic discrimination against new immigrant ethnic groups by older established groups and of eventual breakthrough by the new groups to higher positions of employment and better living conditions. In short, there was a pattern of upward social mobility by successful ethnic groups. Until the 1840s, almost half of the city's population were of British stock, and this "old stock," assimilating to itself other white groups such as the Dutch and the French, never ceased to dominate the city's business life. They were at the top of the economic hierarchy; in 1970, they still held controlling positions in banks, insurance companies, and large corporations. In the 1840s, large-scale immigration by Germans and Irish completely changed the city's ethnic pattern. By 1850, the Irish constituted one-fifth of New York's population; by 1890, one-quarter. In the 1870s, they grabbed control of the city's political life, and hung on to it for sixty years, running a corrupt but egalitarian machine, giving temporal power to the Catholic Church, and monopolizing such city functions as the police. During this period, most of the Irish were able to work upwards from manual labor into white-collar jobs, and they moved outwards geographically from the East Side to Brooklyn and the Bronx. The German-born already composed sixteen percent of the population by 1855, and the tide swelled as Bismarck's unification drove many opponents of Prussia and of compulsory military service to emigrate. The Germans were able to demand a share in political power with the Irish, to better themselves even faster, and to move out more quickly from the slums of Lower Manhattan.

The second great wave of immigration, of Italians and South and East European Jews, began in the 1880s and lasted until 1924, when immi-

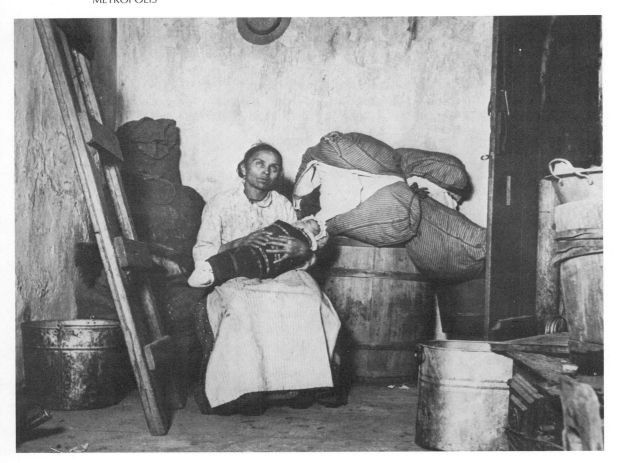

Italian Ragpicker and her Child in a New York Tenement, by Jacob Riis. (The Jacob Riis Collection, Museum of the City of New York.)

gration restrictions were sharply imposed. By 1920, the Italians, mostly former peasants from the poverty-stricken areas of southern Italy and Sicily and their offspring, composed fourteen percent of New York's population, and soon rose to one-sixth. The Italians remained remarkably stable in their choice of neighborhood, unlike other immigrant groups, preferring with new affluence to upgrade their houses and apartments rather than move to a new neighborhood. Until the 1960s, therefore, Manhattan retained its Italian quarters around Greenwich Village and in East Harlem, and Italians shared with Jews most of the new suburbs opened in the 1920s and 1930s on the subway lines in the Bronx, Queens, and outer Brooklyn. By the 1940s, the Italian-American community had the leadership, the financial resources, and the organization to challenge the Irish political control of the city, and the group as a whole was beginning to pull away from the unskilled laboring jobs into more skilled occupations and small business operation. By the 1960s, the third-generation Italian-Americans were breaking through, by superior education, into openings in government and business administration, advertising and entertainment.

The upward Jewish movement in occupational status was achieved a generation earlier than the Italian, largely through the emphasis on higher education. The earlier Jewish immigrants, the Sephardic Jews from Spain and Portugal who came in the seventeenth century and the German Jews who arrived in the mid–nineteenth century, were relatively well-educated and prosperous on arrival, and had little difficulty in establishing themselves, especially in the retail trade. The million or more Yiddish-speaking Jews from eastern Europe who arrived from the 1880s and soon brought the Jewish segment up to one-quarter of the city's population, also made very rapid progress in light industry, retailing, the garment industry, and professions like law. Their socialist background also made them turn to labor organization. In housing, they moved as rapidly as possible out of the East Side ghetto, on into the new suburbs of the 1920s and 1930s in the outer boroughs, and after the Second World War even further out to outer Queens and beyond on Long Island.

Black and Puerto Rican New Yorkers. In spite of the opposition felt by all immigrant groups and in spite of the continuing social discrimination, all these earlier immigrant groups felt that American society as exemplified by New York offered in time the possibility of economic and social betterment. This situation was radically changed, however, with the migration into New York of large numbers of blacks and Puerto Ricans, to whom the clumsy but effective methods of advancement of previous migrant groups seemed closed.

Very few blacks had left the South in the half-century following emancipation, in spite of the pattern of legal segregation and economic discrimination that had been imposed after Reconstruction. Beginning with the First World War, however, in which almost half a million black soldiers served overseas, a vast migration northwards and westwards began. By 1930, the black population outside the South was 2.3 million, and about 300,000 of these were living in New York City. By 1940, there were 450,000 in the city; by 1950, 748,000; by 1960, one million; and by 1970, 1,700,000 or about twenty percent of the total population. Faced by segregation in the housing that was available, the black community in the 1920s was concentrated in Harlem, the area extending roughly from 110th Street north to 155th Street, and from Eighth Avenue east to the East River. Harlem had been one of the finest neighborhoods of New York after the railroads opened it as a suburb in the 1830s, and it had wide avenues, theaters, shops, apartment houses, and private brownstone homes. In spite of overcrowding and unemployment, during the 1920s Harlem became the gathering-place of black writers, musicians, actors, and political speakers, a much adulated black counterpart of the white Greenwich Village downtown. Tourists from all over the world poured in to taste its exotic ways.

Only rarely did they reach the depth of comment of the Spanish poet Federico Garcia Lorca, in his *Ode to the King of Harlem:*

Ah Harlem! Ah Harlem! Ah Harlem!
There is no anxiety comparable to your oppressed scarlets,
to your blood shaken within your dark eclipse,
to your garnet violence deaf and dumb in the penumbra,
to your great King, a prisoner with a commissionaire's uniform. . . .
Ah, masqueraded Harlem!
Ah, Harlem, threatened by a mob wearing clothes without heads!
Your rumor reaches me.
Your rumor reaches me, crossing tree trunks and lifts.
Across the grey plates
where your cars float covered with teeth
across the dead horses and the minute crimes.
Across your great despairing King,
whose beards reach the sea.[11]

The unreality of the specious optimism about Harlem was swept away with the depression, which reduced the number of menial jobs for which blacks were employed, and put sixty percent of its population on relief. Continuing migration from the South combined with the poverty of those already there led to increasing dilapidation of the buildings, particularly since landlords made little effort to renovate ghetto housing. The postwar migration simply helped create new ghettoes in other boroughs of New York, especially in the Bedford-Stuyvesant area of Brooklyn. Residential segregation was repeated in the new areas of black settlement, as whites moved out whenever a sizeable black population settled. Public housing, provided by the city government, did little to help the situation, since fewer units were constructed than were torn down in the slum clearance projects and since most of the buildings were poorly designed and constructed. New York, though on a slower scale than other large cities, began to show the phenomenon of the flight of the whites to the suburbs and the continuing growth of the nonwhite population in the central city. The segregation of the black neighborhood was accentuated by poverty due to unemployment or the low level of paid employment, which made it impossible for the black residents to afford better accommodation in another area. The deteriorating situation was due in part to deliberate discrimination against blacks at all levels of employment from unionized labor up; in part, to the lower educational levels achieved by black schoolchildren as the consequence of family background, school quality, and social incentive; and in part to the reduction of the number of jobs available in New York in manufacturing and commerce. Whatever the reason, it was evident by 1970 that New York in particular, and American society in general, was not

[11] Federico Garcia Lorca, *Selected Poems.* Copyright 1955 by New Directions Publishing Corporation. Reprinted by permission of New Directions Publishing Corporation.

offering to the black the same chance of personal betterment that had been enjoyed by earlier immigrant groups.

The riots in Harlem in 1964 dramatized the frustration of the dwellers in this ghetto where almost half of the housing was officially classified as deteriorated or dilapidated and the median family income was $3,500 a year. Accompanied as it was by riots in many of the country's other ghettoes, it indicated the centrality in American urban life of the racial—and not of the ethnic—problem, and of the inefficiency of all attempts to solve it.

In New York, the difficulties of the blacks were also experienced by the Puerto Ricans, who, after their island had been annexed by the United States in 1898, had possessed the freedom to move to the continental United States regardless of immigration restrictions. Few took advantage of this right until the depression of the 1930s hit the island's own staple agricultural product, sugar; by 1940, there were 70,000 Puerto Ricans in New York, concentrated mostly in *El Barrio* of East Harlem. When cheap airplane service was introduced after the Second World War, the migration became a flood. In 1960, there were over 600,000 people born in, or the children of parents born in, Puerto Rico, constituting eight percent of New York's population. By 1970, the Puerto Ricans constituted eleven percent of the population, and had spread from East Harlem to several other sections of Manhattan, including the old East Side, and many sections of Brooklyn, Queens, and the Bronx, including the already overcrowded Bedford-Stuyvesant area. The Puerto Ricans found enormous difficulty in coping with life in New York because most of them had poor education, were accustomed to agricultural labor, and had extremely large families as a result of a birthrate twice that of the city's white population. Although those trained in the industrialization programs initiated in Puerto Rico itself in the 1950s were better able to find employment, the majority of the group were less able than the blacks to find work. They thus found themselves condemned to the same, or worse, types of housing as the black population; they competed for the same types of manual labor, and were subject to demeaning dependence on an overstrained welfare system.

Thus, New York displayed in all its complexity the racial problem that was gnawing at the vitality of all American city life. Large sections of the central core of the city had become ghettoes for racial minorities. Previously successful channels of upward social mobility, such as schooling, small-scale enterprise, and even political involvement, had failed to raise the economic level of those minorities. A worsening crime rate among the deprived or alienated inhabitants of the ghetto had increased the flight from the central city. The financial plight of a city government grappling with the problems of its poor had been exacerbated by the inability to draw on the financial resources of the white suburbs, by inadequate financial backing from a rurally dominated state government, and by ineffective federal intervention in the city's difficulties. As the sociologist Nathan Glazer has pointed out, "Almost every urban problem in the United States has a racial dimension, and the racial dimension in almost every problem is the key factor."[12] For this reason, the pressing problem of the deterioration of the city common to all the metropolitan centers of the West—overcrowding, urban sprawl, environmental pollution, inadequate transportation, psychological alienation—was made worse in the United States by the imposition on it of the unsolved racial problem.

THE CRISIS OF THE WORLD CITY

While the racial problems of New York are best understood as part of a national problem, all other aspects of its urban crisis are best understood in relation to the difficulties of all the great urban agglomerations of the West. At the base of these difficulties is always growth of population; the concentration of that population in cities, and especially in great metropolitan centers; and the consequent pressure on the resources of the city, from its schools and houses to its air and water.

Although the population of the industrialized Western countries, as compared with that of the underdeveloped regions of the world, grew less quickly in the post-1945 period, it did not level off, as many demographers had confidently predicted it would. Instead, after the expected "baby boom" that followed the Second World War, the birthrates settled at far higher levels than before the war. For Europe as a whole, the population rose from 393 million in 1950 to 427 million in 1960 and 462 million in 1970; the population of the United States rose from 150 million in 1950 to 176 million in 1960 and 204 million in 1970. This growth in population was accompanied by a large-scale exodus from farming, caused in part by the inability of small farmers to compete with mechanized well-capitalized farms and by the reduced number of laborers required on those farms. To those who left the land unwillingly, the city provided alternative employment or at worst, welfare payments; to the majority, however, it offered better pay and a more interesting life. Hence not only the absolute size of the urban population increased, but also the percentage of the population living in urban areas. In the United States, the urban percentage of the population rose from 51 percent in 1920 to 70 percent in 1960.

What is significant, however, was the more rapid growth of the larger metropolitan centers than the urban population as a whole. The great city, as we saw, was the natural point of concentration of government, administrative offices of business and finance, a vast pool of white-collar labor, educational and entertainment resources, communications industries, and the service industries supplying the needs of an urban agglomeration. Occasionally the process could be modified by deliberate governmental intervention, as when the Soviet government attempted to discourage the growth of Moscow, or the British government founded new satellite cities to siphon off the growth of London. But a far more common characteristic

---

[12] Nathan Glazer, ed., *Cities in Trouble* (Chicago: Quadrangle Books, 1970), p. 9.

was the spatial expansion from a central city or group of cities to produce
a vast semi-urbanized hinterland, such as that stretching around the cities
of the Ruhr basin in Western Germany and especially that of the Eastern seaboard of the United States, from Boston to Washington, D. C., a form of expansion that posed new types of problems in urban existence.

Pollution of the Environment.   The most obvious effect of the concentration in large cities of huge numbers of people, their homes, their work,
their transportation, and their entertainment, was the pollution of the
environment.   The air above the West's cities had been blackened with coal
smoke throughout the nineteenth century, both from homes and factory
chimneys; but by the mid–twentieth century, with the decrease in the use
of coal as a home fuel and governmental restriction on inefficient forms
of combustion, other causes of air pollution had taken coal's place.   By
far the worst was the automobile, which in the 1960s was pouring out
10,000 tons of carbon monoxide daily into the skies of New York as
well as many other gases, such as nitrogen oxide.   In cities where the utility
companies burned fuel oil to produce electricity, sulfur dioxide was released; in New York, which used poor-quality imported fuel oil, the sulfur
dioxide in the air was twice that of other big cities.   Industrial companies
contributed their own toxic substances; from metallurgical plants came
sodium and calcium flourides and arsenic compounds; from chemical
plants hydrogen, chlorine, sulfur dioxide, and many other compounds.

**Start of the New York to
Paris Auto Race at Times
Square, New York, on
February 12, 1908.**   (Photo-
graph by Byron, The Byron
Collection, Museum of the
City of New York.)

Eighty tons of heavily polluted dust were calculated to fall on every square mile of Manhattan each day; and the situation was infinitely worse at times when the weather compounded the chemical problem, either by sunshine working photochemically on hydrocarbons or by inversion layers that prevented the polluted air from being blown away. All western cities were experiencing smog alerts by the time of the 1950s. In London, four hundred deaths were attributed to the smog of 1962, and a similar number in a two-week period of smog in New York in 1963. The annual price in health was incalculable; but medical researchers noted that the average New Yorker breathed as many cancer-inducing hydrocarbons each day as if he were smoking two packs of cigarettes.

Pollution of the neighboring waters was just as obvious a problem. At the beginning of the 1960s, seventy million Americans had no sewers, and many of these lived in the suburban areas around the big cities, where the use of septic tanks overloaded the receiving capacity of the soil. Many big cities channeled their sewage into lakes and rivers, with little preliminary treatment; New York flushed half a billion gallons of raw sewage daily into the surrounding rivers. Industrial wastes were even more dangerous to health; and as a result many cities, with New York in the forefront, found themselves short of drinking water even though vast rivers flowed on their threshold. In the 1960s, sixty percent of Americans were supplied with water that had already been used once or more for sewage and industrial waste disposal; and this water, although safe for health, had been so treated as to be unpalatable. The effect of noise pollution was also unmeasurable though obviously great. The noise level of an industrial city was shown to be at least three and a half times greater than that of the countryside; in New York, with its congested buildings, tall canyons, piled-up traffic, and constant construction, it was considerably worse.

In the same category as air, water, and noise pollution, the environmentalists grouped the spoliation of the natural environment within the bounds of the city. The need for parks in the central areas of the city and of easily reached green space around was recognized early, but as a consequence of the predominant role of private entrepreneurs in the American city, little provision was made for satisfying this need; little more was provided in Western Europe; and the planned provision of green space in the Soviet designs of urbanization has often been ignored, as by the dacha builders in the Moscow Green Belt. New York had been given Central Park; but most of the amenities due to location—the views and access to the rivers, the use of the waters for swimming and fishing, even the architectural grandeur of the juxtaposition of fine buildings and broad waterways as in Saint Petersburg—were lost.

The Crisis of Urban Transportation. Attempts to improve transportation within the city and its surrounding region often resulted in the further spoliation of the environment. The greatest damage was wrought by de-

New York City Traffic.
(Weaner Wolff from Black
Star, New York City.)

pendence on the automobile as a form of transportation, in the United
States from the 1920s and in Western Europe from the 1950s. The railroad had already done enormous damage to the beauty of the older cities;
the acceptance of the right of the automobile driver to entry into the heart
of the city did more. Quite apart from the pollution of the air, the automobile was held by American planners to require high-speed freeways
cut through downtown sections of the city, large spaces for parking lots
or garages, and bridges and tunnels for entry. In European cities, these
enormous roads were rarely built inside the city, with the result that though
the fabric of the old city was preserved, as in Rome or Paris, the congestion
of the narrow spaces between the old buildings was infinitely worse than
any congestion in American streets (though not worse than congestion
on American freeways and bridges). More than one-third of the surface
of Manhattan was devoted to streets and freeways! For the average motor-
ist, who had already made a fixed investment in his automobile and its
insurance, the cost of commuting by car was usually less than the cost
of railroad transportation, and was more comfortable by far than travel by
subway or bus. Hence public transportation facilities declined drastically
after 1945 in quality and in patronage. The New York subways had to
be taken over by the city as early as 1940, and by 1953 they were losing
$100 million a year. The Long Island Railroad went bankrupt in 1949
and required massive aid to stay in operation at all. Most of the other
commuter lines were providing run-down service and losing huge amounts
doing so.

The Insatiable Land Hunger of Suburbia. The automobile and the truck accelerated the change in the spatial pattern of urban life that had begun when the commuter railroad, the subway, and the streetcar made possible the first suburbs. Vehicles propelled by internal combustion energy made feasible not only the location of the workers' homes at considerable distances from their work but their dispersion over the countryside, since they were no longer restricted to the area within a short distance of fixed public transportation. Even if all workers lived within 20 miles of the center of a city, they would have at their disposal an area of 1,250 square miles.

The decline of living conditions in the central parts of the city was an important factor in driving those who were able to move into the outer suburbs, but there were other influences that drew whites to suburbia: the availability of space, both in house and yard, at a lower price than in the city; the lower taxes and newer and better schools; the virtual exclusion of low-income groups; the access to open countryside; and the more natural aspect of the suburb itself. The suburb had a homogeneity that was lacking in the central city where all groups of the population had to live a short distance from their work. It was usually constructed, for obvious financial reasons, by a large-scale contractor developing a former piece of farmland with houses of similar design on similar lots sold at a similar price. Suburban government protected that homogeneity by zoning laws, especially laws requiring the building of single-family residences on lots of a prescribed minimum size and prohibiting multifamily dwellings of the price that the central city's poor could afford. Thus the homogeneity of the suburb increased the homogeneity of the central city, leaving the latter increasingly to the nonwhites and the poor.

Many retail and service industries followed the homeowners, as the huge suburban shopping centers and the bankruptcy of many central stores testified. But large-scale transportation by truck, especially along the freeway network, enabled many manufacturing companies to leave the central cities, especially the large companies that were independent of the ancillary services of the small specialized companies that tended to group in the heart of the city. Finally, even the administrative offices of large companies began to be removed from the congested center, as modern methods of communication made physical proximity no longer essential for financial and business administrators. This dispersion of economic activity within the suburbs made possible further dispersion of housing, and thus increased the area of land developed for suburban housing. The process of spatial expansion, which most urban planners felt was only in its infancy in the early 1970s, was already beginning to link previously separated metropolitan centers. The Greek city planner Constantinos Doxiadis has predicted that by the end of the twenty-first century

all the great metropolitan centers of the world will have coalesced to form
a continuous urbanized band across all the economically viable portions
of the globe, an urbanized territory that he calls Ecumenopolis.

New York differed from most American metropolitan centers, and was
similar to the great European cities, in that most of the workers in the central
city—roughly eighty-six out of a hundred—had resigned themselves to
taking public transportation to work; suburbia had spread, nevertheless.
New York could be divided into three sections—a central core, the interwar suburbs, and the postwar suburbs. The downtown business section,
the slums, and the oases where the very wealthy lived formed the central
core. Opened up by the subway and the tunnels under the Hudson, the
interwar suburbs extended in a great circle roughly five to fifteen miles
from Times Square and had a density of 10 to 12 single-family apartments
per acre. The third section, postwar suburbia, stretched between 15 and 25
miles or more from Times Square and had a density of only about 1.5
houses per acre. The low density of the outer suburbs was due in part to
the fact that perhaps three-quarters of the land was still undeveloped for
housing, in part to the zoning requirements, which had raised the minimum
homesite in some parts to as much as two acres. This outer suburban ring
showed all the criticized defects of such development—the proliferation
of local governments that are able to keep out both nonwhites and poor
whites; the removal of the most affluent from the taxing power of the city
where they work; the wasteful use of open space for housing and the
failure to provide for public enjoyment of green areas; the standardization
of taste, from the house itself to standards of behavior. For sociologists,
suburbia became a new laboratory, in which they could explore the values
and the social mores of a new form of society; for the novelist, it became a
gold mine, whose depiction could occasionally produce fine literature.

Megalopolis. The outer suburbs of New York link with those of Philadelphia to the south and Bridgeport and New Haven to the northwest, forming part of the megalopolis described by the French geographer Jean
Gottmann, "an almost continuous stretch of urban and suburban areas
from southern New Hampshire to northern Virginia and from the Atlantic
shore to the Appalachian foothills." Gottmann pointed out that in this
area "we must abandon the idea of the city as a tightly settled and organized unit in which people, activities, and riches are crowded into a very
small area clearly separated from its nonurban surroundings. Every city
in this region spreads out far and wide around its original nucleus; it grows
amidst an irregularly colloidal mixture of rural and suburban landscapes;
it melts on broad fronts with other mixtures, of somewhat similar though
different texture, belonging to the suburban neighborhoods of other
cities. . . . So great are the consequences of the general evolution heralded
by the present rise and complexity of Megalopolis that an analysis of this

region's problems often gives one the feeling of looking at the dawn of a new stage in human civilization."[13]

Gottmann found the future of New York and of its megalopolitan region bright, in part because of the very coalescence of the society of the five-hundred-mile seaboard. He recognized that it had already achieved "*on the average,* the richest, best educated, best housed, and best serviced group of similar size (i.e. in the 25-to-40 million-people range) in the world"; the greatest concentration of universities and cultural facilities in the United States; administrative predominance in economics and politics; and the most important position on earth as a crossroads where people, ideas, and goods must pass. But he also noted that this region was pioneering in a totally new urban process, as novel as that which affected England during the industrial revolution. In particular, he isolated a revolution in land use, which included the abolition of the distinction between the city and the country, movement of goods and people on a hitherto unknown scale, and dispersal of population; "new patterns of intense living," represented not by density of population but by density of activity; and an integration of personal contacts throughout the region, indicated by the scale of such "flows" as telephone calls, highway and air traffic, and movement of goods. Megalopolis, Gottman felt, possessed the ability to deal with the problems arising from its novel form of society. New forms of regional government, conceived on a scale that would relate to the density of contact within megalopolis were needed. A massive attack on environmental pollution with the highest technology available should be combined with renewed emphasis on spatial planning, to preserve the amenities of the rural landscape and to promote the most efficient use of land for productive or residential purposes. The taxation structure within the area of megalopolis would have to be renovated, and state and federal resources committed on a greater scale to the cities. Major programs for breaking the cycle of poverty within the inner city must be implemented. And most difficult and important of all, there would have to be a beginning made, by whatever means were available, in the reduction of racial tension and improvement in the conditions of racial minorities. There were few New Yorkers, however, who shared his optimism.

**THE CONTINUING
VITALITY
OF THE
TROUBLED CITY**

In spite of the overwhelming pessimism of those who have experienced New York's growing problems in the quarter-century after 1945, the city's vitality remained undeniable. Its port was the second largest in the world, exceeded only by Rotterdam and carrying twice the freight handled by London. A large number of corporations chose to move into the city, especially in the boom years of the late 1950s, when forty-two million square feet of office space was constructed, notably along Third Avenue and in the Wall Street area being redeveloped by the big banks; and yet

[13] Jean Gottmann, *Megalopolis: The Urbanized Northeastern Seaboard of the United States* (New York: Twentieth Century Fund, 1961), pp. 3, 5, 9.

another boom, which showed signs of being excessively speculative, led
to the construction of even more office buildings after 1969. Although some
large corporations moved out, in the aggregate New York gained in the
number and size of companies settling there, not only banks, insurance
companies and stock-brokerage houses but such related companies as
advertising, corporate law offices, management and engineering consultants, and representatives of large foreign companies. In particular, the
central position of New York finance in world trade, at least until the revival of Western Europe in the late 1950s, was responsible for a further
increase in the expansion of employment in the downtown region.

The great building boom, at least in office construction, brought into
the city the finest architects who had ever worked there. The emphasis was
no longer on maximum height as a source of corporate individuality, but
rather on new use of materials, to bring out the surface quality in stone or
concrete or the reflections of light or other buildings in glass; on variety
through grouping, not only of several buildings but of parts of one building;
and the use of curtain walls that could be machine-made and assembled
in panels. Frank Lloyd Wright's Guggenheim Museum (begun in 1956), in
cream-colored concrete, was an exercise in the combination of natural
form, here the swirl of a nautilus shell, with the rough surface texture of
cream-colored concrete. Totally different were the glass-walled sky-

**Interior of the Guggenheim
Museum, New York, by
Frank Lloyd Wright (1869–
1959).** Wright's design,
inspired by a nautilus shell
and executed in concrete,
is an outstanding example of
his ability to use natural
forms and contemporary
materials. (New York Convention and Visitors Bureau
photo.)

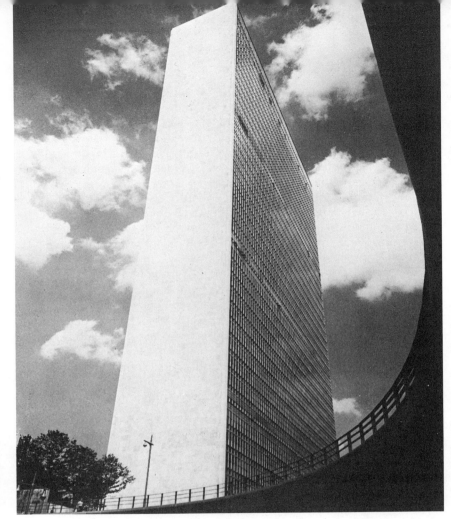

United Nations Secretariat Building, New York. Le Corbusier's influence is reflected in the first of the city's glass-walled sky-scrapers. (Trans World Airlines photo.)

scrapers, beginning with the unbroken thirty-nine stories of the United Nations Secretariat building (1950) and progressing with Gordan Bunshaft's Lever House (1951), which seems to float upon its supporting pillars. The most beautiful of all the curtain-wall skyscrapers was, however, the Seagram building, erected in 1958 by Mies van der Rohe. Not only was half the site given to a garden patio with fountain pools and green marble benches, but the curtain wall, made of bronze with amber glass, achieved the architect's goal of creating a sensation of free-flowing space within the building. Although other buildings erected on Park Avenue failed to meet the standards of Lever House or the Seagram building, nevertheless the harmony of their glass walls had created a new focus of architectural excitement in the city.

The other arts also have continued to flourish. The Broadway theater not only produced a long series of glamorous musicals, but also the dramatic surgery of Eugene O'Neill, Tennessee Williams, and Edward Albee. In

Grayed Rainbow, 1953, by Jackson Pollock (1912–1956). In Pollock's "action" paintings, the swirling lines and color are used to create a sense of driving energy.

painting in particular, the New York artists struck out in a multitude of personal ways. Until the mid-1950s, the prevailing style was abstract expressionism, or "action painting," a kind of imageless energetic expression of personal intuition. Jackson Pollock led the way with shimmering, agitated fields of color; Willem de Kooning combined mastery of savage color with a surrealistic imagery; Mark Rothko set out to purify painting of the organic forms visible even in surrealism and from 1947 created brilliantly colored compositions of parallel masses of varying density. By 1955, the abstract expressionists had become popular and even well-paid. In reaction to them, younger artists sought new forms of expression, and brought back the exploration of human and material reality. Perhaps the most shocking to the public were the pop artists like Andy Warhol and Claes Oldenburg, who used such means as comic strips, newspaper pages, multiple images like movie film, and banal subject matter like soup cans and hamburgers, to comment on everyday reality. George Segal forced a new perception of human beings in relation to their surroundings by modeling people in plaster casts. Others became preoccupied with the machine, presenting machinery with human character and human beings as mechanical objects; Robert Stankiewicz's sculpture is an example. Artistically, New York had rarely been as creative; but there was a disturbing sense of violent protest about some artists and of delight in chaos about others that seemed to many to be a true mirror of the state of the city. The postwar artist had no message of comfort.

SUGGESTED READING

Two collections of engravings and historical photographs form the best introduction to the development of New York. John A. Kouwenhoven's *The Columbia Historical Portrait of New York* (1953) covers the whole sweep of the city's history; Grace M. Mayer, *Once Upon a City* (1958) is impressionistically organized, but draws on the superb photographs of the Byron family, made in 1890 to 1910. No good synthesis of the city's history exists, but there are some useful studies of different periods. They include Sidney I. Pomerantz, *New York: An American City, 1783–1803* (1965); Robert G. Albion, *The Rise of the New York Port* (1939); Seymour J. Mandelbaum, *Boss Tweed's New York* (1965), which sees Tweed as a "symbol of a society with a primitive communications network"; Allan Nevins and John A. Krout, ed., *The Greater City, New York, 1898–1948* (1948). The economic and social character of the city was thoroughly analyzed, and predictions made on its future growth, in the New York Metropolitan Region Study undertaken by the Graduate School of Public Administration of Harvard University. Among the nine volumes of its findings are Edgar M. Hoover and Raymond Vernon, *Anatomy of a Metropolis* (1959); Oscar Handlin, *The Newcomers* (1959); Robert M. Lichtenberg, *One-Tenth of a Nation* (1960), a particularly interesting examination of the relationship of the city's to the nation's economy; and Raymond Vernon, *Metropolis 1985* (1960). New York necessarily figures prominently in all the urban histories of the United States, including Charles N. Glaab and A. Theodore Brown, *A History of Urban America* (1967); Blake McKelvey, *The Urbanization of America: 1860–1915* (1963) and his *Emergence of Metropolitan America, 1915–1966* (1968); and Constance McClaughlin Green, *American Cities in the Growth of the Nation* (1957).

Good collections of contemporary comments on the city provide invaluable insights into the human character of the city. Bayrd Still, *Mirror for Gotham: New York as Seen by Contemporaries from Dutch Days to the Present* (1956) makes good use of the comments of European visitors; Alexander Klein, ed., *The Empire City: A Treasury of New York* (1955) concentrates on the perceptions of recent American literary figures.

Among the rich variety of memoirs and novels dealing with New York life, for the late nineteenth century there is Edith Wharton, *The Age of Innocence* (1948); Rudyard Kipling, *Letters of Travel (1892–1913)* (1920); and Walt Whitman, *New York Dissected* (1936). For the Jazz Age of the interwar years, Le Corbusier's "voyage to the land of timid people" is described in *When the Cathedrals were White* (1947); Federico Garcia-Lorca's expressed views in both prose and poetry in *Poet in New York* (1955); the French writer Paul Morand composed a novelistic guidebook in *New York* (1930); Ford Madox Ford characterized its intellectual life in *New York Is Not America* (1927). E. B. White, *Here Is New York* (1949) was absorbed by the city's mysterious quality, and so was V. S. Pritchett, *New York Proclaimed* (1965), in which Evelyn Hofer's photographs find beauty in the Bowery and elegance in coffeeshop plastic.

The racial problem in New York is described by Nathan Glazer and Daniel Patrick Moynihan, in *Beyond the Melting Pot: The Negroes, Puerto Ricans, Jews, Italians, and Irish of New York City* (1970). The early history of Harlem is portrayed by Gilbert Osofsky, *Harlem: The Making of a Ghetto* (1966), and by James Weldon Johnson, *Black Manhattan* (1930). The plight of the black in the ghetto is explained in Robert Weaver, *The Negro Ghetto* (1948), and made palpable in such books as James Baldwin, *Nobody Knows My Name* (1961) and Malcolm X, *Autobiography* (1965). On the growth of suburbia, see Leo F. Schnore, *The Urban Scene: Human Ecology and Demography* (1965); on the suburbanite, see C. Wright Mills, *White Collar: The American Middle Classes* (1951) and Auguste C. Spectorsky, *The Exurbanites* (1955). Herbert J. Guns takes a positive view of suburban living in *The Levittowners* (1967); Jane Jacobs makes a plea for the central city in *The Death and Life of Great American Cities* (1961) and *The Economy of Cities* (1969). The geographer Jean Gottman presents his view of the new form of social organization appearing in America in *Megalopolis: The Urbanized Northeastern Seaboard of the United States* (1961). The general urban crisis is discussed in Nathan Glazer, ed., *Cities in Trouble* (1970) and Irwin Isenberg, *The City in Crisis* (1968); the particular plight of New York is blasted in Richard J. Whalen, *A City Destroying Itself: An Angry View of New York* (1965). Yet perhaps New York's artists provide the most telling comment upon the impact of mechanization, of standardization, and of meaningless violence, which have been three of their favorite themes. See Andy Warhol's montages of automobile accidents in John Coplans, *Andy Warhol* (1970); Rauschenberg's distorted cityscapes in Andrew Forge, *Rauschenberg* (1966); or Oldenburg's giant hamburgers in Barbara Rose, *Claes Oldenburg* (1970).

26
THE CONTEMPORARY AGE

"They fought the enemy," wrote the American poet Marianne Moore, of the soldiers in the Second World War. "We fight/fat living and self-pity. Shine, O shine/unfalsifying sun, on this sick scene."[1]

The desolation left by the Second World War seemed to many in the West to be spiritual as well as material. Not only had there been immense destruction of the productive capacity so painfully built up in a century of industrialization and of an even older cultural heritage, but the malaise sank deeper into the Western consciousness, marked above all by a sense of personal involvement in the vast inhumanity of the preceding decade. The Soviet poet Yevtushenko expressed this feeling in his meditation on *Babiy Yar*, a hillside near Kiev where thousands of Jews were massacred:

Over Babiy Yar
there are no memorials.
The steep hillside like a rough inscription.
I am frightened.
Today I am as old as the Jewish race.
I seem to myself a Jew at this moment.
I, wandering in Egypt.
I, crucified. I perishing. . . .
Over Babiy Yar
rustle of the wild grass.
The trees look threatening, look like judges.
And everything is one silent cry.
Taking my hat off
I feel myself slowly going grey.

[1] Reprinted with permission of the Macmillan Company from *The Complete Poems of Marianne Moore* by Marianne Moore. Copyright 1951 by Marianne Moore.

Avenue of the Americas, New York. (Trans World Airlines photo.)

And I am one silent cry
over the many thousands of the buried;
am every old man killed here,
every child killed here.[2]

The problem of reconstruction was therefore of many dimensions. The physical damage had to be repaired, and the economy modernized. The traditional forms of society had to be changed, either by democratic modification or by revolutionary overthrow, to meet the demands of dissatisfied segments of that society. But there had also to be spiritual stock-taking, a coming to terms with the past and the formulation of a new sense of cultural identity. And this challenging task had to be undertaken in a time of unparalleled tension. Even before the Second World War had ended, the Soviet Union and the United States confronted each other in an ideological conflict that soon divided Europe once again into two armed camps, both possessing continually growing mastery of the destructive power of nuclear energy. The economic and social reconstruction of Europe had to be undertaken under the direct influence of this confrontation of opposing ideologies. Eastern Europe was compelled to create a new form of society on the pattern of the Soviet Union; Western Europe re-

Dresden in 1947. Two years after the destruction of the lovely capital of Saxony in one night of fire-bombing, reconstruction had barely begun. (U.S. Information Agency.)

[2] Yevgeny Yevtushenko, *Selected Poems,* trans. Robert Milner-Gulland and Peter Levi (Harmondsworth, England: Penguin, 1962), pp. 82–83.

vived its prewar political and economic structure, with some modifications, with the aid of the United States. The predominance of Europe and North America in the international state system was challenged by the re-emergence of China as a world power, and by the winning of independence by most of the European colonial territories in Asia and Africa. Both Communist and non-Communist powers in the industrialized West thus found themselves cast as the "haves" in a world of "have-nots," as rich nations challenged by the overpopulation and underdevelopment of the rest of the world. In this situation of tension, the material basis of Western civilization was rebuilt with extraordinary success; but the spiritual unease seemed only to intensify. In the 1970s, Western civilization was still uncertain of its course.

The Age of the Continent State. A totally new balance of forces characterized the West after 1945. In the interwar years, the chief states of Europe had been able to maintain an illusory predominance in world politics because the two most powerful states in the world, the United States of America and the Soviet Union, had withdrawn into isolationism—the one to avoid military involvement like that of the First World War, the other to carry through its social revolution. But from the moment those two continent states entered the Second World War, their overwhelming military and economic power dwarfed that of the other combatants. Only Germany was able to compare with them because it had already gained control of the resources of a large part of a continent itself. Stalin had summarized the situation with his usual succinctness at the Yalta conference when he remarked that great powers put an army of five million men into battle.

Both the Soviet Union and the United States derived their predominance from control over a vast continental landmass containing enormously rich natural resources and inhabited by a large population. Both nations possessed almost unlimited supplies of coal, iron ore, oil, natural gas, lead, copper, zinc, sulphur, and potash. Both had huge forests and agricultural land in climatic zones varying from the Arctic to the subtropical. Both had invested heavily in the most advanced technology for their heavy industry and in the scientific education of their managers and engineers. Both had economies that were internally integrated; no barriers existed in either to the free movement of goods, capital, or labor. Both had populations three times the size of the largest European state. By contrast with these giants, the largest European state, Germany, had a population of only about sixty million. The European continent was divided into twenty-nine states, whose boundary lines cut across natural economic units such as coal fields and even cities, and slashed natural lines of communication. Thus the European powers gravitated inevitably to the orbit of one or the other of the superpowers in the immediate postwar years.

**THE OPENING
OF THE
COLD WAR**

Stalin's Last Years, 1945–1953. In Russia, Stalin reimposed strict Party controls at the end of the war, and forced the weary population to prepare once again for a confrontation with the capitalist powers by re-creating the war-damaged heavy industry and modernizing the military machine. To maintain the necessary discipline, controls as harsh as those imposed in the 1930s were reintroduced. Soldiers who might have been infected with Western ideas during the campaigns in Europe were transferred to Siberia. Several minority nationalities inside the Soviet Union who were suspected of having shown sympathy to the Germans were moved from their homes to newly colonized areas of the East. Intellectuals were once again forced into subservience by Andrei Zhdanov, Stalin's leading aide, whose *Zhdanovschina* punished any guilty of betraying the ideals of Socialist realism, of expressing admiration for the West, or of failing to emphasize Russia's overwhelming superiority in all cultural and technical achievement. Behind this whole program of isolation of the Russian people from outside influences was the growing tyranny of Stalin, who once again, as at the time of the purge trials of the 1930s, was lashing out at his closest collaborators. As Khrushchev pointed out in his secret speech to the Party Congress in 1956, "After the war . . . Stalin became even more capricious, irritable and brutal; in particular his suspicion grew. His persecution mania reached unbelievable dimensions. Many workers were becoming enemies before his very eyes. After the war, Stalin separated himself from the collective even more. Everything was decided by him alone without any consideration for anyone or anything."[3] The secret police, renamed the MVD, under its sinister head, Lavrenti Beria, engaged in widespread arrests, deportations, and executions. Up to five million people may have been sent to labor camps in the Arctic and in Siberia, to suffer the purgatory that Alexander Solzhenitsyn described in *One Day in the Life of Ivan Denisovich* (1962). At enormous cost to the Russian people, Stalin was thus able to act in foreign affairs from a position of strength.

Communization of Eastern Europe. The political allegiance of Eastern Europe was determined by the advance of the Red Army. By 1944, Russia had already reannexed part of Finland, Estonia, Latvia, and Lithuania, and the Rumanian province of Bessarabia; and in 1945 it had taken the northern section of East Prussia and the Czech province of Sub-Carpathian Ruthenia. These areas were to remain integral parts of the Soviet Union. Beyond this boundary, however, the Soviet government was determined to create a line of friendly governments, both to safeguard its own security and to extend the Communist revolution; the interests of Russia went hand in hand with the extension of communization to Eastern Europe.

In Yugoslavia and Albania, the native Communist leaders, Tito and Hoxha, were able to organize genuinely popular revolutionary movements

---

[3] Cited in Basil Dmytryshyn, *USSR: A Concise History* (New York: Scribner's, 1965), p. 429.

that combined resistance to the German and Italian invaders with attacks on the representatives of the former possessing classes. The Russian army had swept briefly through eastern Yugoslavia, but had established no form of Russian political controls, since communization was already assured. In the other states of Eastern Europe, however, the Communists were a minority whose hold on the poorer classes was strongly challenged both by the Social Democrats and by various peasant or small-holder parties. In these countries, the occupation by the Red Army made possible direct Russian interference.

In Poland, the anti-Communist resistance forces had attempted to seize control of Warsaw in August 1944, but had been destroyed by the Germans in two months of savage street fighting. Thus, there was little organized opposition to the Communist-controlled provisional government, which was installed in power after the capture of Warsaw at the beginning of 1945. Attempts by the Polish Peasant party to reorganize in 1945–1947 were thwarted by the Communist minister of the interior and the police. In the elections of 1947, the Peasant party was declared to have won only 28 seats to the government bloc's 394. By 1948, Poland was firmly in the control of a coalition of Communists and left-wing Socialists; its industry was almost totally nationalized; its large estates had been annexed though not yet collectivized.

The pattern of communization of Poland was repeated, with only minor variations, in Rumania and Bulgaria. After the Red Army had invaded Rumania in August 1944, the government had been placed in the hands of a coalition government, in which the Communists were in a minority. The following January, however, the Communist leader Gheorghiu-Dej apparently received instructions from Moscow to begin an all-out attack on the coalition government, by organizing demonstrations in the factories and in Bucharest itself. When the government attempted to suppress a mass Communist demonstration in the main square of Bucharest, the Red Army troops disarmed the Rumanian forces, and the Soviet representative, Vishinsky, forced the king to accept a new, Communist-dominated government. Using the ministry of the interior, the Communists were then able to terrorize the other parties; in elections in 1946, they gained an overwhelming majority; in 1947, Iuliu Maniu, the seventy-four-year-old leader of the Peasant party, was condemned to solitary confinement for life. The new government at once embarked on massive industrialization and the collectivization of agriculture. In Bulgaria, the coalition government established after the invasion by the Red Army in September 1944 soon lost its meaning, as the non-Communist parties were purged and many of their leaders arrested. By the end of 1945, the Communist party leader Georghi Dimitrov had forged for himself a position of dominance, which he maintained until his death in 1949. Revered as the Bulgarian Lenin, he was embalmed and placed in a mausoleum similar to Lenin's in the main square of Sofia.

Hungary and Czechoslovakia at first appeared to resist the pattern of communization being imposed on the rest of Eastern Europe. In Hungary, free elections held in 1945 gave a majority to the popular small-holder party. Once again, however, the Communists used their control of the ministry of the interior to cow the opposition; and they were able to bring the police, the bureaucracy, and the trade unions under their control without difficulty. In 1947, the leader of the Small-holder party was taken into custody by the Red Army, and died in imprisonment; and in elections in 1949 the official government candidates won ninety-five percent of the vote.

It was, however, the communization of Czechoslovakia that caused the greatest sensation in the Western Europe and the United States. President Eduard Beneš, whom the Red Army had restored to power in 1945, was a confirmed democrat who had nevertheless displayed sympathy throughout his career for the Soviet Union. Moreover, he had formed a genuine coalition government, in which the communist leader Klement Gottwald had become prime minister but in which the foreign ministry was in the hands of Jan Masaryk, the son of the country's founder. No police controls had been exerted over the non-Communist parties, and parliamentary debate was free. The Communist party, however, had gained control of most of the local police, the trade unions, and units of the army; and thus in February 1948, they were able to force Beneš to accept a Communist-controlled government by using workers' militia to seize government offices, and to occupy the headquarters of non-Communist political parties.

Stalinallee, East Berlin. Built in the Soviet style of Socialist Realism in 1952–1964, the Stalinallee (now the Karl-Marx-Allee) was intended to be a showplace of Communist urban planning. (German Information Center photo.)

Masaryk, who had stayed on as foreign minister, was found in the courtyard
of his ministry a month later with a broken spine. Beneš resigned in June
and died shortly thereafter; and following elections that gave them an
eighty-nine percent majority, the Communists established a monolithic
regime, purged up to half their own party and hanged several of its former
leaders, and clamped down police-state controls.

Finally, in its zone of occupation in Germany, the Soviet Union had
moved rapidly to ensure Communist dominance. The pillars of the old
society, the great landowners and the industrialists, had been dispossessed
immediately, and their property brought into state ownership. The non-
Communist parties, although permitted to reorganize, were under constant
harassment; and the Soviet commander-in-chief, Marshal Zhukov, personally intervened to dismiss two of their principal leaders. The provincial governments and in 1949 the new central government were placed
in the control of the Socialist Unity Party, in which the Communists had a
large majority; and compliance with the Party's program was ensured by the
Soviet secret police and by East Germany's own state security service and its
militia, the Volkspolizei, or Vopos.

Defection of Yugoslavia, 1948. The most dramatic demonstration of the
resentment aroused in Eastern Europe by the Soviet Union's control of the
process of communization occurred in 1948, when Yugoslavia broke its
ties with Russia. Tito had apparently been the most convinced of the
Soviet satellites up to that time. But resentment had been building up in
Yugoslavia against the Soviet-Yugoslav joint-stock companies, against the
Soviet technicians and military advisers who had disparaged Yugoslav
planning and attempted to infiltrate the Party and the secret police, and
especially against Russian interference with Yugoslav expansionist aims
in the Balkans. After Russia had withdrawn its advisers, the Yugoslav and
Soviet leaders engaged in a doctrinal battle, in which Tito was eventually
blasted as a heretic. "The leaders of the Communist Party of Yugoslavia,"
Stalin wrote, "have taken a stand unworthy of Communists, and have begun
to identify the foreign policy of the Soviet Union with the foreign policy
of the imperialist powers. . . . Instead of honestly accepting this [Soviet]
criticism and taking the Bolshevik path of correcting these mistakes, the
leaders of the Communist Party of Yugoslavia, suffering from boundless ambition, arrogance and conceit met this criticism with belligerence and
hostility." As a result, Yugoslavia was expelled from the newly founded
international Communist Information Bureau (Cominform), and attempts
were made to persuade dissident Yugoslav Communists to overthrow Tito.
Soviet pressure failed, because Tito's internal popularity and firm controls
were unassailable, while his military forces would have made direct intervention against him very costly. Moreover, the Western powers came at
once to his aid, with loans and surplus food supplies, thus creating an
isolated example of an alternative road to Communism to that of the Soviet
Union.

Formation of the Western Bloc. The United States assumed leadership of a Western bloc dedicated to the containment of further Communist expansion with considerable reluctance. In 1945–1947, it had tried to give up responsibilities in Europe by demobilizing most of its forces and cutting off programs of direct aid. The communization of Eastern Europe, the con-

Brandenburg Gate, East Berlin. The boundary between the Soviet zone and West Berlin cut across Unter den Linden behind the Gate, leaving the historic center of Berlin in Communist control. (German Tourist Information Office photo.)

tinual disagreements with Russia over the administration of occupied Germany and Austria, the revival of Communist insurgent forces in Greece, the growth of the Communist parties of France and Italy during the postwar economic distress—all these factors combined to convince President Truman that the United States government had to take firm action to prevent the further spread of Communism in Europe. In 1946, the American military government in Germany stopped sending dismantled factories to Russia as reparations, and an attempt was made to win over the West Germans to membership in a Western bloc by promising them self-government. In March 1947, Truman offered American financial and technical aid to Greece and Turkey, under a new doctrine that guaranteed American willingness to "help free peoples to maintain their institutions and their national integrity against aggressive movements that seek to impose upon them totalitarian regimes." Three months later, Secretary of State Marshall offered large-scale financial aid to all of the countries of Europe for their reconstruction; his offer was accepted only by the non-Communist countries, who were thus differentiated from the Communist bloc not only by their dependence on the United States but by their growing prosperity. In 1949, the American government took the lead in a military alliance, the

North Atlantic Treaty Organization, composed of Canada and ten European countries, by which all members promised to act together to repel any armed attack on them in the North Atlantic area. The formation of NATO brought a stalemate in the confrontation of Russia and the United States in Europe. Only West Berlin, a Western outpost more than a hundred miles inside East Germany, provoked big disagreements between the blocs—primarily because it offered a route of escape for refugees from East Germany. Once that route had been closed with the erection of the Berlin wall in 1961, West Berlin ceased to be a principal source of tension between the two blocs. In 1972, it was even possible for West Germany and the Soviet Union to recognize that the political changes brought about by the Second World War were unalterable in the immediate future; the Treaty of Moscow of 1972 between West Germany and the Soviet Union, which recognized the German loss of the Oder-Neisse territories and East Prussia, was almost the equivalent of a peace treaty ending the Second World War; and it promised a relaxation of tension of the Cold War in Europe.

Collective Leadership in Russia and the Thaw. In January 1953, the arrest of the leading doctors in the Kremlin was regarded as the opening of a new purge of the Soviet hierarchy; but Stalin suffered a fatal stroke two months later, and on March 9 his embalmed body was entombed next to Lenin's in the mausoleum on Red Square. Only then could the long-delayed political reconstruction take place within Russia.

Power in Russia was assumed by the "collective leadership" of representatives of the elites of Soviet society—the Party, the army, and the industrial bureaucracy. Together, they ousted Beria from control of the secret police, and had him secretly executed. The doctors' plot was denounced as a fabrication of the secret police, and thousands arrested in the last years of Stalin's life were released. Greater legal safeguards for Soviet citizens were guaranteed, and a relaxation of international tension promised. Within the Soviet satellites in Eastern Europe, there was to be a relaxation of police powers, more freedom for national diversity, and a rehabilitation of those previously purged. Thus, Stalin's death was welcomed throughout Europe as the harbinger of a "thaw" in Stalinist autocracy.

Definite progress was made toward political liberalization. Inside Russia, many of the prisoners in the labor camps were released, and the powers of the secret police slightly restricted. Denunciation of the "cult of the individual" reached its height in Khrushchev's de-Stalinization speech in 1956; and controls over intellectuals were considerably lightened. As a result, the literary magazine *Novy Mir* was able to publish a number of stories sharply critical of party or governmental administrators; novels like Vladimir Dudintsev's *Not By Bread Alone* dared to assert that "someone who had learned to think can never be deprived of freedom". Soviet film

**THE SOVIET BLOC
AFTER STALIN**

makers produced some of their most penetrating work, including *The Cranes Are Flying* and *Ballad of a Soldier*. It was however in the East European satellites that the ferment of liberalization took its most explosive form.

The first reaction to the lightening of controls was sporadic outbursts of violent protest against the harshness of living and working conditions. Raising of work norms provoked a general strike in East Berlin that spread to most of the other cities of East Germany. Government buildings were set on fire, and Russian troops attacked. The uprising was defeated only when the Russians sent three armored divisions into East Berlin. To avert such uprisings, the new Russian collective leadership recommended to the satellite governments increases in consumer goods and lightening of work norms, and in several cases, it forced the ouster of unpopular governments. Except in East Germany, the other Communist regimes all adopted some form of collective leadership, and reduced the powers of the secret police. In Poland and Hungary in particular, this leniency encouraged great political ferment within the Communist parties and workers' organizations and among intellectuals. In Poland, factory workers rioted in the town of Poznan in June 1956, and perhaps a hundred were killed by the police and hundreds were arrested; but, shortly after, control of the Polish Communist party was taken by a group headed by Wladislaw Gomulka, which was demanding greater internal liberalization. The Soviet government considered direct military intervention to prevent Gomulka's coming to power. Their troops moved into position near Warsaw, and Khrushchev flew there to browbeat Gomulka in October. His blustering proved unsuccessful, in face of Gomulka's threat to use the Polish army against the Russians and to call the whole country out in revolt; but it also seems clear that Gomulka persuaded Khrushchev that his policies would not endanger the security of the Soviet Union. Khrushchev acquiesced in the appointment of Gomulka as head of a new Polish government, and Gomulka's slight lightening of domestic controls prevented Polish unrest from turning into armed revolt.

Soviet Suppression of the Hungarian Uprising, 1956. In Hungary, however, discontent boiled over in October 1956. Workers and students united in Budapest in an armed uprising, murdering party officials and the secret police and attacking Russian tanks that patrolled the streets with rifles and Molotov cocktails. The revolt spread to the rest of Hungary, and the Hungarian army joined the rebels. In the face of a popular Communist revolution, supported by workers' councils and led by a popular Communist leader, Imre Nagy, the Russians withdrew their troops from Hungary, and appeared willing to acquiesce in the premiership of Nagy. For ten days there was self-congratulation throughout the country. Non-Communist political leaders were admitted to the government; freedom of speech and of the press was permitted; the security police were disbanded. Nagy however made the mistake of announcing Hungary's withdrawal from the

Warsaw Pact, the military alliance of Russia and the East European countries organized in 1955. On November 2, Soviet troops moved back into Hungary in great strength; and two days later, in face of desperate resistance from every element of the population, their tanks seized control of the main government buildings in Budapest. The Soviet troops installed Janos Kadar as premier in place of Nagy who, after being guaranteed a safe conduct out of the country, was arrested and later executed. Mass arrests and deportations followed, although about 200,000 Hungarians were able to flee to the West.

Political Stabilization in Eastern Europe after 1956. Khrushchev was bitterly criticized by Party opponents for provoking the revolt in Hungary by his policy of de-Stalinization; but he was able to fight off the attack of the "anti-Party" group in 1956, and for the following seven years to maintain personal control of both Party and government. Nevertheless, he continued his policy of de-Stalinization of some aspects of Soviet life. Membership in the Party was broadened to include many more representatives of the workers and peasants. The bureaucratic elite, the educated and well-paid Soviet bourgeoisie, whom Milovan Djilas called the "New Class," were compelled to achieve closer contact with the workers by a law requiring two years of manual labor before entry to higher education. A new criminal code abolished categories such as "enemy of the people." Literary controls varied according to Khrushchev's whims, but literature continued to show considerable freedom and versatility—if not in the sanctioned publications at least in the underground press and in manuscripts sent abroad, such as Boris Pasternak's *Dr. Zhivago*. The most effective commentary on the relative liberalization of Khrushchev's regime was the ease with which he was overthrown in 1964, by a vote of the Presidium led by Leonid Brezhnev and Alexei Kosygin taken during his absence on vacation, and the permission granted him to retire unmolested to his country home outside Moscow. The new collective leadership made few political changes, although controls over intellectual life were somewhat stiffened. In spite of a few attempts to set Brezhnev ahead of the other leaders, a fairly genuine form of collective rule seemed to have been accepted.

The evolution of government in Eastern Europe during this period of stabilization was quite varied. At one extreme was the regime of Party Secretary Walter Ulbricht in East Germany, which refused all except the most superficial forms of de-Stalinization. Few amnesties were granted; the secret police remained active; and large numbers of Russian troops provided firm backing for the repressive policies of the regime. Gomulka in Poland, to the great surprise of those who had hailed his triumph in 1956 as proof of Poland's right to seek its own road to Communism, soon embarked on a "retreat from October," a reimposition of harsh political controls through a strictly purged Communist hierarchy. He suppressed the independent-minded workers' councils, slapped restrictions on the freedom of the universities, and resumed the campaign to restrict the activity of the Catholic Church. He did not, however, force collectivization of agriculture, and Poland remained the East European country with the highest proportion of independent farmers. Gomulka's greatest error, however, was his handling of industrial policy; his continued emphasis on heavy industry, refusal to increase living standards for the workers, and continuance of overcentralized planning finally provoked nationwide riots in December 1970. Beginning in the seaport town of Gdansk, the former German city of Danzig, they spread throughout the country even though the government cordoned off the city with tanks. After several days of arson, looting, and shooting, Gomulka himself was forced to resign his position as Party secretary; and a new government promised immediate material concessions to reestablish workers' confidence. No far-reaching political reforms were envisaged, or even apparently demanded, however; a change in the political leadership was acceptable to Russia because it involved no basic change in political course.

Hungary and Bulgaria managed to maintain a central position. Kadar, after an initial period of repression following his elevation to power by the Russians, cautiously began to relax his regime. From 1960, amnesties were granted to political prisoners, and some freedom given to writers. The professional classes and intellectuals were persuaded that non-Communist opinions would not be held against them in administrative or scientific work; "He who is not against us is with us," Kadar explained. Relatively free elections for local governmental positions were permitted. With the rise in living standards that was achieved in the late 1960s, Hungarians who had originally regarded Kadar as a traitor were beginning to regard him as an acceptable leader within the limits imposed by Russia. Bulgaria, after the strict rule of Dimitrov, had known an even more repressive regime under a Moscow-trained Communist, Vulko Chervenkov, who seemed to most Bulgarians the archetype of Stalinist ruler. His successor, Vulko Zhivkov, was a cautious, moderate man who sought better economic relations with the West, welcomed hundreds of thousands of tourists to the Bulgarian beaches along the Black Sea, and allowed a modified form of profit-and-loss accounting to be used as stimulus to industrial production.

Rumania and Czechoslovakia on Independent Roads to Communism. Throughout the 1950s and 1960s, the Rumanians moved slowly and successfully out of the direct control of Russia. Even before Stalin's death, the Moscow-trained leaders of the Communist party were ousted by those who had remained in the underground opposition at home, led by Gheorghe Gheorghiu-Dej, whose predominance remained unchallenged inside Rumania until his death in 1965, in spite of Soviet efforts to unseat him. Gheorghiu-Dej refused to accept the economic role assigned to Rumania by the Council for Mutual Economic Assistance (Comecon), an economic union of the East European Communist countries and Russia whose purpose was to harmonize the region's economic planning. Instead of agreeing to concentrate on agricultural and oil production, he ordered "rapid and all-round industrialization," and sought aid from the West in planning new factories and in investment loans. Little by little, he threw off Russian influences. Russian troops left the country in 1958; compulsory study of the Russian language was dropped in the schools; and the subordinate nature of the Rumanian party to the Soviet in international Communism, the much-vaunted Father-Party and Son-Party relationship, was denied. Gheorghiu-Dej's successor, Nicolae Ceausescu, was an even more convinced nationalist, who even dared attack the necessity of the Warsaw Pact and the wisdom of dividing Europe into two opposed military blocs. In spite of numerous signs of Soviet displeasure with the Rumanian display of independence and occasional movements of troops around its borders, Rumania maintained its precarious autonomy without direct interference because it remained strictly orthodox in its communization of Rumanian society. Whatever independence Rumanian leaders showed, no dissension from the Party line was permitted internationally.

The Czechoslovak experiment in liberalized Communism, introduced in 1968 by the new Party secretary, Alexander Dubcek, was a far more direct challenge to the supremacy of the Soviet model of Communism. It permitted widespread decentralization of industrial decision making, introduced considerable freedom of the internal market, almost completely ended controls over freedom of expression, and permitted open criticism of the Soviet Union. The whole country seemed to bloom, with a new-found confidence in itself and its government; and many Communists in the West European countries began to proclaim that the Czech evolution was a proof of the humanity at the basis of Communist ideals. To the leaders of the Soviet Union, Dubcek's attitude was doubly dangerous—Czechoslovakia was renewing its traditional Western ties and moving to a position of neutrality in the Cold War; and it was permitting such internal political liberalism and encouraging such capitalistic industrial experiments that its society was ceasing to be genuinely Communist. In August 1968, Soviet armored columns, supported by troops from East Germany, Poland, and Hungary, invaded Czechoslovakia, and occupied the whole country. The liberalization was immediately halted, and the control of the party's hard-liners reimposed. Dubcek was kept as Party leader as a slight sop to Czech sentiments until April 1969, when he was replaced by Gustav Husak, a Slovak Communist willing to carry through the repression demanded by the Russians.

Once again in the invasion of Czechoslovakia, the Soviet Union had made it clear that within its security zone in Eastern Europe no major internal deviation from the Soviet model of Communism would be permitted unless, like Yugoslavia, the country was sufficiently distant and well-armed to make direct military intervention excessively costly.

Defection of Albania and the Sino-Soviet Confrontation. In 1961, tiny Albania proved that defection from the Soviet Union was also possible with the help of a powerful ally, in this case, China. By 1960, both the Albanians and the Chinese were outraged with the Russian leaders, the Albanians because of their courtship of Tito and their insistence on de-Stalinization in Albania, the Chinese because of Russian insistence on the superiority of their own version of Communism and of their own strategy for coexistence with the West. In 1960–1961, the discontent was voiced openly with various vituperative attacks on each other by Russian and Chinese leaders; and when Albania openly sided with China, Russian aid was cut off, technicians called home, and the Russian submarine base in Albania closed down. The Albanians, ousted from Comecon, turned to the Chinese for technical and financial aid, which was at once dispatched. Within a few months, Albania was ostentatiously posing as China's principal ally in Europe. The split between the Chinese and the Russians intensified as the Chinese sought allies within the East European bloc and among the West European Communist parties and the nonaligned countries. The Soviet Union began to mass large forces along its border with China, where brief fighting broke out in 1969. In short, the Chinese refusal to accept Russian leadership in the world Communist movement had transformed the bipolar world dominated from 1945 by the United States and Russia into one in which "polycentrism," the existence of several centers of power, became possible.

POLITICAL RECONSTRUCTION OF WESTERN EUROPE

Foiled Idealism of the Resistance Movements. The Resistance movements in Western Europe during the German occupation had envisaged a political renovation on a vast scale that the members would undertake at the end of the war. For the Communist parties, the ideal was the remodeling of society on the Soviet model; but in spite of their popularity in 1945 due to their exploits in the underground fighting, the Communist parties remained a minority in all the West European countries. The non-Communist groups, mostly Socialist or Christian Democratic in orientation, laid the blame for the Second World War not only on the Nazi regime but on the ineffectiveness of their own ruling classes and anachronistic constitutional machinery that they manipulated. Some went further and claimed that the political sickness of Europe, which had inflicted upon it two major wars in only a quarter of a century, was due to the existence of the nation state itself; and they proposed that Europe seek the unification of its peoples in one federal state. All of these ideas were disappointed. As Western Europe was liberated country by country, largely by American and British armies, old constitutions were restored or new ones written, so similar to the old as to be indistinguishable. Most of the prewar leaders who had not been compromised by collaboration with the Germans reappeared and resumed their accustomed places in the parliamentary hemispheres of the individual nation states. Even the monarchies were restored without much opposition, although the Belgian King Leopold was finally compelled to abdicate in 1951 as atonement for his role in ordering the Belgian army to surrender in 1940. Above all, no attempt was made to form any kind of federation, on the ground that such planning was utopian when the needs of economic reconstruction were so urgent.

Weaknesses of Constitutional Renovation. The failure to modernize the political structure had baleful consequences that were felt for most of the postwar period. In France and Italy in particular, new constitutions were written that perpetuated the multiparty regimes of the late nineteenth century. Governments could only be formed by complicated compromises among Party leaders; they lacked clear programs, and were overthrown for trifles; constant juggling of ministerial positions among a small inner group of party bosses caused public disenchantment with the whole political process. The disenchantment increased the appeal of parties on the extreme left and on the right who denied the validity of the constitutional process itself, and hence were never included within the process of alternation of power. In Italy, for example, the Communists with twenty-five percent of the vote and the right-wing parties with ten percent were almost invariably excluded from power, with the result that over one-third of the population felt themselves permanently disfranchised. In Belgium, the politicians failed to adjust the representative machinery to the need for providing both French-speaking and Flemish-speaking citizens with a sense of just representation in the parliament and government, and encouraged the tension between the two communities that verged at times on civil war. Even the Dutch seemed unable to make a parliament dominated by only two principal parties workable; prolonged cabinet crises were the result of inability of either party to win a clear majority. Even in West Germany, which adopted a new constitution in 1949 drafted by brilliant constitutional lawyers determined to overcome the weaknesses of the Weimar constitution, power was monopolized by the seventy-three-year-old Konrad Adenauer, who emulated Bismarck by creating a *Kanzlerdemokratie* (chancellor democracy), until being forced out of office in 1963. When Charles de Gaulle became president of France in 1958, under a new constitution that had been tailor-made to meet his objections to multiparty democracy, his own presidential powers proved to be so grandly conceived that the French electorate remained estranged from the political process. This estrangement helped provoke the rioting in Paris in 1968 among students and workers, which was followed by the resignation of de Gaulle himself after the electorate refused to give him a vote of continuing confidence on a referendum. In short, both multiparty systems and strong rule by a president or a chancellor proved unsatisfactory—the one for its incoherence, the other for its lack of responsiveness to public opinion.

Creation of the Welfare State. One area in which the restored governments of Western Europe achieved a great popular success was in the provision of a vast range of social services. From the end of the nineteenth century the state had taken responsibility for various insurance programs for industrial workers; and in the interwar years the Scandinavian countries had begun to apply a moderate program of socialization that included public ownership of utilities, operation of hospitals, and insurance coverage for sickness, accidents, and old age. But after 1945 almost every European country, regardless of its constitutional system, adopted important programs for state provision of health care, housing, increased educational opportunities, and various forms of direct financial aid.

Britain's Labour government embarked on the broadest of these programs in 1945. Basing its program on recommendations for the elimination of "want, ignorance, squalor, and disease" drawn up during the war by the Liberal leader, Lord Beveridge, it determined that every citizen should receive a national minimum standard of living. Monetary payments were made to help large families, and numerous other payments were made by the state for maternity costs, sickness, pensions, and educational expenses. Against great opposition from the medical profession, the Labour government created the National Health Service, which was to provide everyone in the country with medical, dental, surgical, and hospital care without limit of cost, in return for payment of a small weekly fee. Within three years, 95 percent of the population and 90 percent of the doctors had enrolled in the program. Public housing was constructed on a very large scale, so that eventually one in four of the population lived in housing constructed by one of the public authorities. Educational opportunity was opened to all, by making primary and secondary education free and by provision of scholarships to all needy students in higher educational institutions. For the first time in British history, entrance to the universities became dependent largely on ability.

Similar programs were instituted in most of the continental European countries. In the two to three years following the war, the Communists usually cooperated with Socialist and Christian Democrat parties in setting up social security systems. In France and Italy, insurance programs were usually preferred to outright socialization of medicine; the system of payments was unified under the state and gradually extended to include all segments of the population. Family allowances were paid to aid dependent children. Schools and public housing were constructed; and continual interference maintained over hours of work, paid vacations, and factory conditions. In Sweden, social security expenses absorbed one-third of the national budget; in France and Italy, employers contributed as much as one-third of a worker's wage toward social security benefits.

This increase in the powers of the state over the life of the individual citizen was usually welcomed. Many right-wing politicians even claimed that the true predecessor of the welfare state had been the Fascist or the National Socialist state, which had also set out to provide similar benefits. Most Europeans recognized that the welfare program was simply a necessary extension of state services, which implied no specific ideological commitment.

In no sphere was the lack of strong, popularly supported political leadership more obvious than in the bitterly contested process of decolonization. It was evident at war's end that the European hold on the millions of colonial subjects had been severely weakened. In Asia, the Japanese had driven the armies of all the colonial powers out in ignominious defeat: the United States from the Philippines; the British from Hong Kong, Malaya, and Burma; the French from Indochina; the Dutch from Indonesia. Nationalist movements had sprung up in those areas, sometimes in alliance with the Japanese, sometimes opposing them; and with Japanese withdrawal in 1945, many of these areas were left in the hands of native liberation movements. European rule had therefore in most cases to be restored by force.

THE TRAGEDY OF DECOLONIZATION

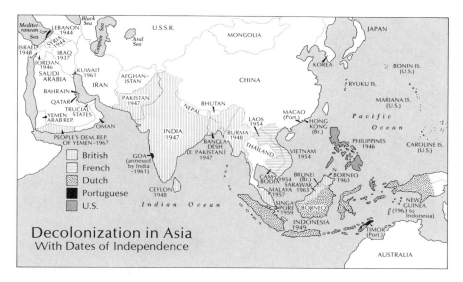

Decolonization in Asia
With Dates of Independence

American and British Decolonization. There were exceptions. The American forces were welcomed back to the Philippines in part because of the clear agreement, which was respected, that independence would be granted at the end of the war. The British Labour government had come to power in 1945 with the goal of giving independence to Britain's colonial possessions as rapidly as possible, not only because it disapproved of colonialism on moral grounds but because it regarded them as military and economic liabilities. It gave up Britain's mandates in the Near East very rapidly. Transjordan became independent in 1946. After persuading the United Nations to sanction a partition plan dividing Palestine between Jews and Arabs, the British pulled out precipitately in 1948. The British withdrawal was followed by almost a year of fighting, during which the Jews succeeded in gaining the independence of their new state of Israel against the opposition of the Palestinian Arabs and several neighboring Arab states. The British withdrew with similar haste from India in 1947, leaving Hindus and Moslems to fight among themselves. As a result, in the division of the subcontinent into the states of India and Pakistan, over a million civilians were killed. The withdrawal from Ceylon in 1947 and from Burma in 1948 was more peaceful; and after the defeat of Communist insurgents in Malaya, independence was given to most of Britain's colonies in Southeast Asia in the 1950s and 1960s. The British also took the lead in giving independence to their African possessions, beginning with the conversion of the Gold Coast into the state of Ghana in 1956. Within ten years, all British colonies in Africa were independent, including Southern Rhodesia, where the white settlers had declared themselves independent unilaterally.

Indonesian Struggle for Independence. The Dutch and the French were determined not to be ousted from Asia, and fought long, bloody, and futile wars to keep control of their possessions. The Dutch had invested over a quarter of their national capital in the Dutch East Indies, or In-

Dien Bien Phu, North Vietnam. French troops prepare the inner bastion, which was to be captured by the Viet Minh on May 6, 1954. (U.S. Information Agency.)

donesia, and had sent out a quarter of a million settlers. Their economic exploitation of the country in the prewar years had made them extremely unpopular, and the Nationalists under Sukarno who took control of Indonesia as the Japanese withdrew were widely supported. Refusing to recognize the impossibility of retaking the islands by force, the Dutch carried out a series of so-called police actions, in which they used paratroops and land forces to win control of the main cities. In reply, Sukarno's supporters organized guerrilla attacks on the Dutch, who found themselves simultaneously under international criticism not only from the Communist and neutralist countries but even from the United States and Australia too. After four years of fighting, they reluctantly recognized the independence of Indonesia; much of their investment was expropriated, and most Dutchmen were forced to return to Holland.

End of the French Colonial Empire. French opposition to granting independence to Indochina was even more stubborn and costly. They owned most of the industry and banking in Indochina and a large number of the plantations; and to protect this economic stake, they moved large forces into the south of Vietnam in 1945. After first compromising with the Communist leader, Ho Chi Minh, who held most of the north of Vietnam, they embarked on full-scale war in 1946. Ho Chi Minh's forces, led by the brilliant general Vo Nguyen Giap, embarked on revolutionary war against them—using terrorism, propaganda, and political indoctrination to win control of the peasantry. Receiving help from both the Soviet Union and Communist China, Minh's forces were able to set up their campaigns to make French losses intolerable. By 1954, the French had lost 91,000 men, and government in Paris was paralyzed by the inability of the parties to find a leader who would have the courage to declare that they had lost the war. Finally, when Giap's forces overwhelmed the French garrison of the important border fortress of Dien Bien Phu, the French parties in desperation named Pierre Mendès-France as premier, giving him the task of making immediate peace in Indochina. He did so with great skill, leaving North Vietnam in Ho Chi Minh's hands and giving independence at the same time to the states of Laos and Cambodia. He even avoided the outbreak of wars for independence in the French possessions of Tunisia and Morocco in North Africa, by promising them independence. Such firm action provoked fury at Mendès-France in the French Parliament, and he was overthrown as premier on the motion of members of his own party.

Thus, when a determined independence movement in Algeria struck savagely at French settlers and army forces, the government in Paris was headed by politicians who had neither the foresight to negotiate Algerian independence nor the ability to defeat the National Liberation Front. In 1956, the French joined with the British and the Israelis in an attack on the Suez Canal, ostensibly to prevent its nationalization by Egypt but primarily to overthrow the Egyptian government, which had been sending aid to the

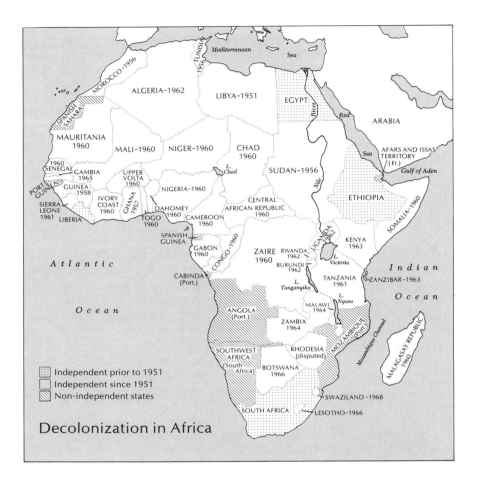

Decolonization in Africa

Independent prior to 1951
Independent since 1951
Non-independent states

Algerian rebels. The Anglo-French aggression was denounced by both the United States and the Soviet Union; the forces were withdrawn without achieving any political advantage. The Algerian war poisoned the political atmosphere in France. The army reached a state of rebellion against the civilian government; and in May 1958 it supported French settlers who seized control of Algeria, and even began to prepare a paratroop invasion of France itself. Chaos in France was averted only by the appointment of General de Gaulle as premier and after December 1958 as president, under a clear mandate to end the war in Algeria on his own terms. Even then it took de Gaulle four years of negotiation and fighting before a cease-fire was reached and Algerian independence finally recognized. But by then de Gaulle had already given independence to the rest of France's colonial possessions in Africa; and from 1962, free of most of their colonial problems, the French were able at last to begin a reassessment of their new role in world politics.

The Belgians hung on to their huge colony of the Congo until 1960, making no effort to prepare it, or Belgian public opinion, for independence. When internal unrest flared up in 1958, however, they made only a few ineffectual efforts to suppress it, and then pulled out rapidly, leaving the country in civil war that was ended, after United Nations intervention, by seizure of power by the army. The Portuguese refused to consider giving independence to their colonies of Angola and Mozambique, and at the beginning of the 1970s were maintaining large and expensive armies there in order to hold down an insurgent guerrilla movement.

Thus lack of effective political leadership in Europe unnecessarily prolonged and embittered the process of decolonization, inflicting vast human and economic losses on the colonial powers and on the liberated peoples. But once the fact of independence had been accepted, the European powers, far from suffering from the predicted depression due to loss of captive markets, sources of raw materials, and opportunities for high-return investments, found decolonization a stimulus. In most cases, economic relationships were maintained with the former colonial territories. The cost of colonial administration and of colonial military forces was ended; and the British were able even to abolish military conscription. Perhaps the greatest benefit was to force the European powers to turn back to Europe as the main sphere of their activity—a concentration that produced closer military collaboration, great advances toward economic integration, and even the beginnings of political unity.

Throughout Europe, the first months after the end of the fighting were spent in tackling the most immediate tasks of economic reconstruction. The transportation network had to be repaired—new railroad track laid, canals and rivers cleared, road surfaces restored. Electrical and telegraph wires had to be restrung. Reservoirs, water pipes and sewer mains had to be brought into working order. Flooded mines had to be pumped clear. War-damaged factories had to be reconstructed, housing repaired, and fuel provided for power and for heating. Seed and fertilizer had to be provided to enable the farmers to bring their land back into cultivation, and a start had to be made in rebuilding the decimated herds of animals. Over eleven million prisoners of war, forced laborers, and deportees had to be returned to their homes, or to new countries willing to receive them. Value had to be restored to the vastly inflated currencies. With considerable help from the United Nations Relief and Rehabilitation Agency (UNRRA), mostly funded by the United States, these jobs were carried out within two years by the individual national governments. Europe by the spring of 1947 was beginning to wear a deceptive air of successful convalescence.

ECONOMIC RESURGENCE AND SOCIAL CHANGE

The Marshall Plan. At that point, it became clear that the reconstruction program had met the most immediate problems but ignored the deeper economic problems that were preventing the European economy from embarking on a self-sustaining process of growth. The greatest difficulty of the preceding two years had been the lack of investment capital. Europeans had been compelled to spend whatever surplus their industry had produced on buying food. They had been unable to purchase necessary raw materials or machinery for rebuilding their factories and producing industrial goods for sale. The lack of consumer goods had been a significant inflationary pressure. And the national reconstruction programs had paid no attention to the need to create a viable economic structure for Europe as a whole. On June 5, 1947, the American secretary of state, George C. Marshall, offered large-scale American aid to all the countries of Europe on the condition that they draw up a joint plan to overcome the "dislocation of the entire fabric of the European economy." And he explained: "The truth of the matter is that Europe's requirements for the next three or four years of foreign food and other essential products—principally from America—are so much greater than her present ability to pay that she must have substantial additional help or face economic, social, and political deterioration of a very grave character."

The Russian government met immediately with the British and French to discuss the plan, but rejected the conditions for aid as unwarranted American interference in the internal affairs of other countries. It also compelled the other East European countries to refuse to participate, and hence the plan was restricted to sixteen non-Communist countries. By 1952, these countries had received over $13 billion, mostly in the form of grants rather than loans. Britain had received the most, $3.1 billion; Iceland the least, $29 million. Although very little coordination of national planning took place, in spite of Marshall's original conditions, the plan was enormously successful. During the four years of the plan's operation, the gross national product of the participating countries rose by one-quarter in real value; industrial production was 35 percent above prewar levels, agricultural production 10 percent higher. Even higher growth was achieved in certain industries, such as chemicals and steel, that were chosen for massive investment in the hope that their progress would drag up the other industries.

West European Economic Miracles. In the growing prosperity that followed Marshall aid, West Germany took the lead. Its currency had been stabilized by a harsh devaluation of 1948. Economics Minister Ludwig Erhard had allowed considerable freedom of planning and concentration to the major companies and banks, and they had engaged in vast programs of modernization. Workers had accepted long working hours and low wages in order to reconstruct the country; and there had been relatively few strikes. By 1953, production was 53 percent higher than before the war, and within three years, in spite of the annual flight to West Germany of over 200,000 East Germans, unemployment had been wiped out. By the middle of the 1950s it was clear that almost all of Western Europe was

enjoying a great economic boom; it was to continue with only minor set-
backs until the 1970s. France, for example, succeeded in striking a balance
between state planning and the freedom of the individual companies.
The state controlled directly several important sectors of the economy that
had been nationalized shortly before or immediately after the war, including the aircraft industry and the large Renault automobile company. The
rest of the economy was given planning goals by the Commissariat du Plan,
in collaboration with the Treasury, whose control over credit and interest
rates was used to compel the large companies to respect the Plan's advice.
Marshall aid was wisely used in several "propulsive" sectors of the economy, such as steel and agricultural machinery, which led the recovery.
Technological improvement was encouraged, new managerial techniques
imported from the United States, and the distribution system modernized.
For the first time in French history, the mass of the population began to
receive a more equitable share of the national wealth; by the 1960s, one-
half of French homes had a refrigerator and almost as many an automobile.
Italy, too, achieved a real growth rate of over five percent throughout the
1950s and 1960s, largely by concentrating on those areas of light industry
in which its shortage of natural resources could be compensated for by
skill in design and marketing. The Italian boom was centered on such
products as plastics, typewriters, washing machines and refrigerators, shoes
and textiles, in all of which it seized a large part of the European market.
Britain was the main exception to the pattern of generalized prosperity in
Western Europe. Many of its traditional markets overseas had been lost

**Krupp Factory, Rheinhausen,
West Germany.** By the
1950s, most of the vast
German companies of the
interwar years had been
reconstructed, and were
contributing to the German
"economic miracle." (German
Information Bureau photo.)

Pirelli Building, Milan. The Italian boom centered on Milan, where many companies built new headquarters, such as Pier Luigi Nervi's Centro Pirelli for Italy's leading tire manufacturer.

during the war. Its industrial plant was outdated, its natural resources depleted. Labor unions, still smarting with memories of the depression of 1929, permitted strikes to endanger productivity. Management lacked imagination, and failed to respond to the challenge of the reviving continental countries. The most costly examples of shortsightedness occurred in 1950 when the Labour government refused to join the European Coal and Steel Community, and in 1958 when the Conservative government refused membership in the Common Market; for economic integration was to prove an important stimulus to the progress of the continental countries.

Economic Integration in Western Europe. When in May 1950 French Foreign Minister Robert Schuman proposed the pooling of the coal and steel industries of France and Germany with those of any other European countries that would join them, he did so for political rather than economic reasons. He hoped to create a nucleus around which a genuine political union, a United States of Europe, would eventually be formed. His plan called for the free circulation within the European Coal and Steel Community (ECSC) of goods, workers, and capital in the coal and steel industries. The economic success of the plan, he believed, would be so great that it would lead the members of the Community to wish to create further ties that would eventually culminate in the creation of a European government. His proposal was accepted by Germany, Belgium, the Netherlands, Luxembourg, and Italy, and put into force in 1952. The economic results were even better than forecast. During the first five-year transitional period, trade among the Six in coal increased by 21 percent and in steel by 157 percent. Coal production reached a peak in 1956, after which the Community tried to phase out its production because of the competition with oil and natural gas. Steel production had doubled within ten years. Political results, however, had been disappointing. Even before the Community was in operation, the governments of the Six had attempted to create a similar organization called the European Defense Community (EDC) to run their armies on an integrated basis, and they had even drawn up plans for a European Political Community, which would act as a European government. The French parliament, however, had refused to ratify the EDC Treaty in 1954, and the two plans had died as a result of that vote. The most enthusiastic supporters of integration, especially the Belgians and the Dutch, reacted to this defeat by proposing more economic integration, and in 1955 the Six agreed to study plans for the integration of all sectors of their economy in a European Economic Community (EEC), or Common Market, and for the fusion of their atomic energy industries in a European Atomic Energy Community (Euratom). After two years of hard beginning, the completed treaties were signed in Michelangelo's palace on top of the Capitol Hill in Rome, a suitably symbolic setting for the re-creation of a Europe that had not been united since the Roman Empire.

**Atmospheric Refrigeration
Towers at Lacq, France.**
As part of its regional
development program, the
French government created
a large industrial complex
around the natural gas
deposits at Lacq in
southern France. (French
Embassy Press and Information Division photo.)

Euratom and the Common Market. Euratom was a failure almost from
the start, since all its members pressed on with their national atomic energy
programs. The Common Market, on the other hand, was an extraordinary
success. By 1968, all customs barriers among the six members had been
abolished. An extremely complicated system of commodity markets had
been created to integrate agricultural production at the same time as
industrial production; and through this rather controversial machinery
Community preference was extended to the farmers whose products received guaranteed prices or export subsidies. Favored treatment within
the Common Market was given to migrant laborers of the member countries.
An attempt was made to increase the free flow of capital in the Community; and in the 1970s a start was made on such delayed projects as
regional planning, a common currency, and creation of European-wide
companies. These measures opened to the industries and farms of the
Community a market of over 200 million consumers, and thus stimulated
specialization and encouraged the rapid expansion of the most efficient
companies. The Common Market played an important part in stimulating
the great economic boom that Europe enjoyed in the 1960s. The first
decade of the Common Market's operation was the most prosperous
Europe had ever known.

In 1961, the British recognized their mistake in not joining the Community, but their application for admission was vetoed two years later by
French President de Gaulle. De Gaulle thus destroyed the expansive
impetus of the Community at its most crucial point; and he continued to
attack the Community's potential for creating European political unity by
threatening vetoes to safeguard French interests, by boycotting the Com-

munity on one occasion for seven months, and by forcing from office the Community president who tried to give his office the status of an independent government. As a result, the Common Market did not become more than an economic union, and even the prospect of the entry in the 1970s of Britain, Denmark, and Ireland, offered little chance of stimulating future progress to political union. The Common Market was a great economic success but at least up to the early 1970's it had achieved few of the political goals of Robert Schuman's original proposal.

The Slow Economic Revival of Eastern Europe. The economic revival of Eastern Europe lagged far behind that of Western Europe. Wartime destruction of lives and property, especially in the Soviet Union, had been very heavy. In the immediate postwar years, the Soviet Union delayed the recovery of its satellites by taking reparations and dismantling East German industrial equipment, and through the operation of the joint-stock companies. The refusal of Marshall aid implied that the Communist countries would have to rebuild their economies through their own hard work and self-denial. In Russia, Stalin imposed very high goals of heavy industrialization in the Reconstruction Plan of 1946, which was largely successful. In the 1950s, greater flexibility was allowed to management, and greater incentives given to workers by provision of consumer goods. By 1960, industrial production had probably doubled. Agricultural production advanced much more slowly, in spite of various ambitious plans like the Virgin Lands scheme, for bringing large new areas under cultivation; and the Russian peasantry remained unenthusiastic participants in collectivized farming.

In East Europe, after a slow recovery up to 1950, large-scale plans of industrialization were undertaken, especially in East Germany and Czechoslovakia. Concentrating largely on markets in Eastern Europe and Russia, East Germany created a large iron and steel industry, and restored chemical production, and rebuilt its optical and machine tool industries. After the flight of refugees to the West had been halted by the construction of the Berlin Wall in 1961, its economy boomed, to make its industrial production the tenth in the world and the sixth in Europe. Rumania, too, determined to create a broad-based industrial economy, using its rich deposits of oil, natural gas, and metals; and during the 1960s, it quadrupled its industrial production. Agricultural collectivization, which was pushed with varying degrees throughout Eastern Europe, was not successful in creating large increases in production; and several countries, especially Poland and Hungary, allowed a considerable degree of private farming to continue to ensure a continuance for the cities of agricultural supplies.

By comparison with Western Europe, East European development was slow. Compared with their own achievements during the interwar years however, it was rapid, especially in the Balkan countries, which were converted from backward agricultural lands into modern industrialized states.

The Concorde. Ambitious projects of economic collaboration among West European governments included the joint Franco-British development of this supersonic airliner.

New Societies of Eastern and Western Europe. Social change was most dramatic in Eastern Europe, which underwent a social revolution similar to that of Russia after 1917. The old landed classes were rapidly dispossessed, and thus one of the most long-lived social aristocracies of Europe disappeared—the Junkers of East Germany, the aristocrats of Poland, the landed magnates of Hungary. But the peasantry too, who had hoped as the result of the annexation of the lands of the aristocracy and the church to become landholders themselves, were swept into the collective farms, and thus had to adapt to an entirely new way of life. The state took possession of the factories and housing of the old capitalist classes; and as a result, the class structure of Eastern Europe came to resemble that of the Soviet Union. Differences of salaries and of personal wealth were far less great than in the West, in part because of the lack of any investment opportunity. There was far less differentiation in living conditions, both in housing and consumption. The equalization was also furthered by state provision of most forms of recreation from vacations to inexpensive theater, by socialization of medical care, and by state provision of mass education. Yet in spite of these conditions, a new privileged class was created, consisting of party bureaucrats, military officers, and a technological, artistic, and managerial elite, who enjoyed higher salaries, better educational opportunities, and access to rare consumer goods.

In Western Europe, the affluence produced unexpected social tensions. The class structure changed remarkably little. An upper class of the extremely wealthy, merging with the older aristocracy of birth, succeeded, in spite of many attempts by the state to achieve a redistribution of wealth, in holding on to its high salaries and its accumulated capital. They also retained a disproportionate share of places in higher education, upper managerial positions, and diplomatic and high-level civil service appointments. In Britain, for example, one percent of the population owned two-fifths of the country's wealth. The middle classes were greatly benefited both by the economic boom and the welfare state. The boom created not only higher salaries but also more white-collar jobs in lower levels of industrial management and in the service sector. The welfare state removed the financial crisis of accident or sickness, and made available the best educational opportunities to the intelligent children of middle-class parents. Preserves of privilege, like Oxford and Cambridge universities in England, or the Ecole Nationale Supérieure in France, were thrown open; and many who profited from the educational openings were able to move without difficulties into the upper levels of business of government. Many, however, who lacked suitable family background ran into the invisible barriers to their upward mobility erected by the established upper class. In Britain, this exclusion produced the phenomenon of the ''angry young man,'' graphically portrayed in novels like Kingsley Amis's *Lucky Jim* and John Brain's *Room at the Top,* and in the plays of John Osborne. In France and Italy the protest often took political form, many highly educated young men joining the Communist party in protest against the petrified social structure of their country. The riots in 1968 were essentially a protest by students against a society from which they felt isolated.

The industrial working class enjoyed higher living standards and greater

New Town, Stevenage, England. To decentralize urban growth, the British government created a number of satellite towns, with a planned balance of industry, housing, and services. (British Tourist Authority photo.)

security from unemployment than ever before. Workers were able to engage in a spending spree on holidays, sports, household appliances, clothes, and even cars; but for many their affluence was insufficient compensation for the frustrations of their dull, repetitive work on the assembly line. Unable to change the nature of their work, they expressed their annoyance by frequent strikes for higher wages, regardless of increases in their own productivity. They wanted better educational opportunities for their children, to enable them to avoid the drudgery of the factory, but were rarely able to provide educational stimulus in their homes; and the children of workers rarely succeeded in gaining higher education and even more rarely high-ranking positions in business or government. In France, for example, only 12 percent of university students were children of workers, and even in Britain, the proportion was only 30 percent.

Perhaps the greatest social changes occurred in the countryside. Peasants were leaving the countryside in droves, in what was called the rural exodus, as mechanization of agriculture reduced the number of unskilled workers needed and as far greater opportunities for employment occurred in the cities. In Italy, for example, up to 300,000 were leaving agriculture each year; and the same phenomenon was observed in Eastern Europe and Russia and even, in the 1960s, in Spain and Portugal. The peasants who did remain on the land in Western Europe were compelled to change their way of life, consolidating their holdings, joining in cooperatives for marketing, and seeking greater technical education. Once the changes were accepted, the standard of life of the farmer rose rapidly, though not as rapidly as that of the industrial workers. Peasants were less isolated because they possessed a car or motorcycle, a radio and often a television set.

The flight from the land increased the urbanization of the European population. By 1970, 80 percent of Britain's population, 70 percent of West Germany's, and 54 percent of Russia's population lived in cities. In the Soviet Union and East Europe, further attempts were made to regulate this urbanization with the foundation of new cities, through either totally new foundations in undeveloped regions or satellite towns on the edge of older cities. In Western Europe, in spite of the foundation of a few new cities like the "new towns" around London, most of the population poured into the biggest cities. West Germany and Italy were fortunate that their delayed unification had left them with a large number of former capitals, like Stuttgart and Milan, where the urban amenities were still attractive to immigrants. But in most of the other countries, the choice of the migrants remained the capital city. Congestion of the European city was on a scale unknown even in the United States. Each of the European cities, as we have seen, possessed a small medieval heart of narrow, winding streets, in which most of the functions of government, economy, culture, and religion were centered. Around it had grown up in the nineteenth century a circle of residential and industrial suburbs. In the postwar period, spreading in a vast swathe around the cities, huge new housing settlements of un-

Freeway Building in Marseilles, France. The "Pénétrante-Nord" freeway linked the center of the Mediterranean port to the Paris-Nice freeways in the Rhône valley. (French Embassy Press and Information photo.)

paralleled dullness were built. The employment of the new suburban dwellers in the heart of the old city caused overcrowding on the railroads and buses and especially on the roads leading into the city. Thus, European cities came to know the problems that burdened New York City—pollution of the air and water, breakdown of municipal transportation systems, increased crime, overcrowded housing, and even occasionally racial, ethnic, or religious confrontations. In the renewed tension of the late 1960s, many Europeans asked whether they were still enduring that legacy of psychological unease bequeathed them by the totalitarianism of the interwar years and the inhumanity of the Second World War.

THE CULTURAL REVIVAL OF THE WEST

In the immediate aftermath of the Second World War, many writers tried to come to terms with the enormity of suffering that the war had inflicted and especially with the problem of human guilt and atonement. At first it was necessary to express what had been done, as when the Resistance writer Vercors showed, in *The Arms of Night* (1946), how the concentration camps in Germany had been used to destroy not only men's bodies but their ability to function as human beings. But it was also necessary to deal with the underlying causes of the inhumanity. For some, the corruption of society had to be blamed; coming back to East Berlin in 1945, Bertolt Brecht summed up his condemnation in his play *Mother Courage*. Jean Anouilh demonstrated the corruption of power at all times and in all places in his new version of *Antigone;* Carlo Levi, pondering on his experience of exile in a remote village of Southern Italy in *Christ Stopped at Eboli* (1947), found much human suffering in the sheer inertia of an underdeveloped society. But some of the most telling commentaries sought a moral or a religious judgment on the wartime experience. Albert Camus's *The Plague* (1947) presented a gruesome picture of the town of Oran in French Algeria during an outbreak of plague brought by infected rats. The town is isolated from the outer world, to live out, in a kind of allegory, the variegated human reactions to an intensity of suffering. At first, he describes the sense of exile of those imprisoned in the plague-ridden town, "that sensation of a void within which never left us, that irrational longing to hark back to the past or else to speed up the march of time, and those keen shafts of memory that stung like fire." Then followed a sense of panic as realization of the full danger and horror of the disease sank in; then an interlude of complete lethargy, followed by an attempt to fight back against the disease; and at last a feeling that all individual destinies had been replaced by a "collective destiny, made up of plague and the emotions shared by all." And, when the gates of the city were opened at the end of the plague, Camus saw in microcosm the experience of all Europe at war's end:

Among the heaps of corpses, the clanging bells of ambulances, the warnings of what goes by the name of fate, among unremitting waves of fear and agonized revolt, the horror that such things could be, always a great voice had been ringing in the ears of these forlorn, panicked people, a voice calling them back to the land of their desire, a homeland. It lay outside the walls of the stifled, strangled town, in the fragrant brushwood of the hills, in the waves of the sea, under free skies, and in the custody of love. And it was to this, their lost home, toward happiness, they longed to return, turning their backs disgustedly on all else. . . .

None the less, he knew that the tale he had to tell could not be one of final victory. It could be only the record of what had had to be done, and what assuredly would have to be done again in the never ending fight against terror and its relentless onslaught. [He knew] that the plague bacillus never dies or disappears for good; that it can lie dormant for years and years in furniture and linen-chests; that it bides its time in bedrooms, cellars, trunks, and bookshelves; and that perhaps the day would come when, for the bane and the enlightenment of men, it would rouse up its rats again and send them forth to die in a happy city.[4]

The most popular answer to the question of personal responsibility was given by the existentialist philosophers, of whom Jean Paul Sartre was the most influential. For several years, Sartre held court in the cafes of the Left Bank in Paris, teaching his large group of young disciples that

[4] Albert Camus, *The Plague*, trans. Stuart Gilbert (New York: Knopf, 1962), pp. 65, 270, 278.

Albert Camus (1913–1960). (French Embassy Press and Information Division photo.)

each man has complete freedom of choice in his actions and that by his actions a man not only gives value to his life but creates his own being. In a world that was absurd, meaningless, and incomprehensible, action in even the most baffling circumstances was essential. Sartre's ideas had a great vogue until the mid-1950s, when his retreat into dogmatic defense of Communism lost him many followers. His demand for choice even rings mutedly, with religious overtones, in T. S. Eliot's play, *The Cocktail Party,* in which the brittle chatter of an inconsequential party at the home of a couple whose marriage is breaking apart culminates in acceptance of hard personal choices by each of the guests. One of them goes off to Africa and is crucified, whereupon the psychiatrist, who in some curious way represents the Wisdom of God, remarks:

> *. . . it was obvious*
> *That here was a woman under sentence of death.*
> *That was her destiny. The only question*
> *Then was, what sort of death? I could not know;*
> *Because it was for her to choose the way of life*
> *To lead to death, and without knowing the end*
> *Yet choose the form of death. . . .*

Julia:

> *Everyone makes a choice, of one kind or another,*
> *And then must take the consequences. Celia chose*
> *A way of which the consequence was crucifixion;*
> *And now the consequence of the Chamberlaynes choice*
> *Is a cocktail party.*[5]

The very inconsequence of the Chamberlaynes choice gave it significance befitting their lives.

In the 1950s and 1960s the sense of disquiet remained, though its expression was directed against new targets. In England, for example, the protests of the ''Angry Young Men'' represented outrage at continuing social discrimination. In France, the rejection of the middle classes and especially of the wealthy upper crust, which had been stridently demanded by Sartre, took on forms of deliberately outrageous absurdity, in the plays of Jean Genêt or the semi-monologues of Samuel Becket. In Germany, with Günter Grass and Heinrich Böll, the criticism could often be brilliantly satirical. In the Soviet bloc, protest against the inhumanity of political intolerance could achieve great psychological insight, as in Alexander Solzhenitsyn's *Cancer Ward* or the Hungarian Tibor Dery's *Niki: The Portrait of a Dog.* In the United States, some of the finest writing expressed the suffering and the hopes of minority groups. The black search for identity, which had been cogently dramatized as early as 1940 in Richard Wright's *Native Son,* took on new dimensions, such as Ralph Ellison's *Invisible Man* (1952), which shows that even in personal contact the black remains invisible to the white, or James Baldwin's *Go Tell It on the Mountain* (1953) on his own upbringing in the black community. The problem of the Jew in America gave Saul Bellow the opportunity to create a low-key folk hero in *The Adventures of Augie March* (1953); the eternal and universal difficulty of survival for the Jew was the theme of Bernard Malamud's *The Fixer* (1966). And women's demand for their liberation produced not only a call to action in such books as Betty Friedan's *The Feminine Mystique* (1963) but novels like Sylvia Plath's *The Bell-Jar* (1965) or Sue Kaufmann's *Diary of a Mad Housewife* (1967).

In art, too, there was a prevailing mood of disquiet and revolt. At its most extreme, it rejected all the material achievements of twentieth-century civilization, as in the pop art of Andy Warhol and Claes Oldenbourg; and it saw a complete dehumanization of the individual, as in Richard Hunt's metal figures. But many artists set out, in subtler ways, to portray the uncertainty of the present—the uncertainty even of man's position in space, as in the hollowed-out figures of Henry Moore; the nightmare quality of his body reduced to its essential outlines, as in some of the sculptures of

Hero Construction, by Richard Hunt (1935–   ). (Courtesy of The Art Institute of Chicago.)

[5] From *The Cocktail Party,* copyright 1950, by T. S. Eliot. Reprinted by permission of Harcourt Brace Jovanovich, Inc. and Faber and Faber Ltd.

Alberto Giacometti; and the monstrous fear that informs William de Kooning's *Woman I.*

Thus, by the 1970s, it was clear that the postwar disquiet had not been mastered, but had even intensified. An age of tension had been reflected, as so often in the history of civilization, in its art and literature.

THE
HUMAN SCALE

Underlying much of this disquiet was a sense that the human being, the individual, had been lost sight of—by government, by industry, by educational institutions, by technology and science, by urban planners, by social morality, even by the individual himself. And here we return, at the very end of this long journey through the cities of our past, to a central concept that underlies this whole book—the civilized city. In the great cities of Western civilization, the individual was not forgotten. For the maximum number of human beings possible within the city's productive capacity, the truly civilized city enhanced the quality of life of the individual. It gave variety and meaning to his work, and enabled the efforts of individuals to be harmonized to produce a more productive economic system. By competition, by interaction, and by reward, it encouraged the creativity of mind; and the creativity of some enriched the lives of many others with an understanding of religion, of society, of science, and of beauty. The very urban setting was a source of individual satisfaction because it was on a human scale, in its buildings and in the daily contact of widely varied human beings. These benefits were not enjoyed by all the inhabitants of the cities we have studied, and indeed often only by a minority. But for sufficiently large numbers of people the city provided so great an enhancement of individual life that it was the stimulus behind the most worthwhile —and unfortunately the least worthwhile—features of our civilization. The present crisis of the city is one major facet of the crisis of civilization. "Can the needs and desires that have impelled men to live in cities recover, at a still higher level, all that Jerusalem, Athens, or Florence once seemed to promise?" Lewis Mumford asks:

The recovery of the essential activities and values that first were incorporated in the ancient cities, above all those of Greece, is accordingly a primary condition for the further development of the city in our time. Our elaborate rituals of mechanization cannot take the place of the human dialogue, the drama, the living circle of mates and associates, the society of friends. . . . Ours is an age in which the increasingly automatic processes of production and urban expansion have displaced the human goals they are supposed to serve. Quantitative production has become, for our mass-minded contemporaries, the only imperative: they value quantification without qualification. . . . When cities were first founded, an old Egyptian scribe tells us, the mission of the founder was to "put the gods in their shrines." The task of the coming city is not essentially different, its mission is to put the highest concerns of man at the center of all his activities: to unite the

The Human Scale: Amsterdam. (Netherlands Information Service photo.)

The Human Scale Forgotten: New York City. (TWA photo.)

scattered fragments of the human personality, turning artificially dismembered men—bureaucrats, specialists, "experts," depersonalized agents—into complete human beings.[6]

Mumford's conclusion is the theme of this book: "The best economy of cities is the care and culture of men."

SUGGESTED READING

All study of the postwar period becomes rapidly outdated, especially if the writer attempts to impose sweeping interpretations upon the overwhelming mass of his materials. One can choose therefore between unvarnished narrative, such as Wilfrid F. Knapp, *A History of War and Peace, 1939–1965* (1967), Peter Calvocoressi, *World Politics since 1945* (1968), and Walter Laquer, *Europe Since Hitler* (1970), or suggestive hypotheses, such as Raymond Aron, *The Century of Total War* (1954), J. Ellul, *The Technological Society* (1965), and C. P. Snow, *The Two Cultures and a Second Look* (1964).

The Cold War can be approached from several directions. The motives of the American government are appraised approvingly by John Lukacs, *A New History of the Cold War* (1966), and Louis J. Halle, *The Cold War as History* (1967). For a balanced, almost impartial European viewpoint, see André Fontaine, *A History of the Cold War* (1969). For biting, "revisionist" reappraisals of American responsibility for the confrontation with Russia, see William A. Williams, *The Tragedy of American Diplomacy* (1962), Gabriel Kolko, *The Politics of War* (1968) and Gar Alperovitz, *Atomic Diplomacy* (1965). Russian goals are analyzed in Adam B. Ulam, *Expansion and Coexistence* (1968) and Marshall D. Shulman, *Stalin's Foreign Policy Reappraised* (1963).

The most reliable account of the communization of Eastern Europe is Hugh Seton-Watson, *The East European Revolution* (1965), which should be supplemented with Zbigniew K. Brzezinski, *The Soviet Bloc: Unity and Conflict* (1961). For individual East European countries, see Richard Hiscock, *Poland: Bridge for the Abyss?* (1963); Ernst C. Helmreich, ed., *Hungary* (1957); Edward Taborsky, *Communism in Czechoslovakia, 1948–1960* (1961); and Stephen Fischer-Galati, ed., *Rumania* (1957). For East European events after the death of Stalin, see Paul E. Zinner, *Revolution in Hungary* (1962); R. R. James, ed., *The Czechoslovak Crisis, 1968* (1968); J. F. Brown, *The New Eastern Europe: The Khrushchev Era and After* (1966); David Childs, *East Germany* (1969); and William E. Griffith, ed., *Communism in Europe: Continuity, Change, and the Sino-Soviet Dispute* (1964–1966).

Russia since Stalin can be approached through the career of Khrushchev, in Edward Crankshaw's overly polemical *Khrushchev: A Career* (1964) or Konrad Kellen, *Khrushchev: A Political Portrait* (1961); but more institutional studies can

---

[6] Lewis Mumford, *The City in History* (New York: Harcourt, Brace and World, 1961), pp. 569–70, 573.

be revealing of the realities of Soviet life, as in Merle Fainsod, *How Russia Is Ruled* (1963); R. Kolkowicz, *The Soviet Military and the Communist Party* (1967); and David Granick, *The Red Executive* (1960). The origins of the dispute with China are surveyed in Klaus Mehnert, *Peking and Moscow* (1963), and Donald S. Zagoria, *The Sino-Soviet Conflict, 1956–1961* (1962).

General surveys of postwar Western Europe include Jacques Frémond, *Western Europe Since the War* (1964) and Stephen R. Graubard, *A New Europe?* (1968), a suggestive series of essays concentrating on European integration. The economic principles of European integration are boldly simplified in Dennis Swann, *The Economics of the Common Market* (1972), and the political attraction of the process subtly portrayed in Uwe Kitzinger, *The Politics and Economics of European Integration* (1964). F. Roy Willis discusses the troubled relationship of the two major Community partners in *France, Germany and the New Europe, 1945–1967* (1968), and shows the influence of integration on the social and economic structure of Italy in *Italy Chooses Europe* (1971). De Gaulle's attitude to the Common Market is sharply criticized in Nora Beloff, *The General Says No* (1963), and sympathetically presented in Charles de Gaulle, *Memoirs of Hope: Renewal and Endeavor* (1971). The success of the Common Market in creating a new form of state in Europe is assessed in Carl Friedrich, *Europe an Emergent Nation?* (1969).

Among the many excellent studies of individual European nations, one of the most suggestive is John Ardagh, *The New French Revolution: A Social and Economic Study of France, 1945–1968* (1968). Political developments in Italy are surveyed in Giuseppe Mammarella, *Italy After Fascism: A Political History, 1945–1963* (1964), and Norman Kogan, *A Political History of Postwar Italy* (1966). Social change in West Germany is analyzed in Ralf Dahrendorf, *Society and Democracy in Germany* (1968). British politics are soundly narrated in Francis Boyd, *British Politics in Transition, 1945–1963* (1964); British politicians are sharply criticized in Max Nicolson, *The System: The Misgovernment of Modern Britain* (1967), and viewed with bemused tolerance in Anthony Sampson, *Anatomy of Britain* (1962).

Andrew Shonfield, *Modern Capitalism* (1967) is an extremely optimistic view of Europe's supposed mastery of economic planning; M. M. Postan, *An Economic History of Western Europe, 1945–1964* (1967) explains the postwar economic miracles. On contemporary social change, see Gordon Wright, *Rural Revolution in France* (1964) and Laurence Wylie, *Village in the Vaucluse* (1957); David Granick, *The European Executive* (1962); F. Zweig, *The British Worker* (1952); and Anthony Sampson, *The New Europeans* (1968).

For reliable introductions to the literary and artistic movements of the postwar period, see Herbert Read, *A Concise History of Modern Painting* (1968) and his *Concise History of Modern Sculpture* (1964); Penelope Houston, *The Contemporary Cinema* (1963); Harry T. Moore, *Twentieth-Century German Literature* (1967); and C. Mauriac, *The New Literature* (1959), on new writers in France.

Finally, for informed views on the city of the future, see Le Corbusier, *Toward a New Architecture* (1970), a reprinting of his farsighted work of 1924; Richard Eells and Clarence Walton, eds., *Man in the City of the Future* (1968), a collection of predictions by architects and urban theorists; Peter Cook, *Architecture: Action and Place* (1967); and William H. Whyte, *The Last Landscape* (1968).

INDEX